THE PAGEANT
OF AMERICA

R.K.

Independence Edition

VOLUME X

THE PAGEANT OF AMERICA

A PICTORIAL HISTORY OF THE UNITED STATES

RALPH HENRY GABRIEL

EDITOR

PETER GUILDAY   JOHN CHESTER ADAMS

ASSOCIATE EDITORS

EDWIN MIMS, JR.

ASSISTANT EDITOR

CHARLES M. ANDREWS   ALLEN JOHNSON
HERBERT E. BOLTON   WILLIAM BENNETT MUNRO
IRVING N. COUNTRYMAN   VICTOR H. PALTSITS
WILLIAM E. DODD   ARTHUR M. SCHLESINGER
DIXON RYAN FOX   NATHANIEL WRIGHT STEPHENSON

ADVISORY EDITORS

DAVID M. MATTESON

INDEXER

Painted expressly for *The Pageant of America* by Charles Lennox Wright

THE VISION OF THE CIRCUIT RIDER

THE PAGEANT OF AMERICA

AMERICAN IDEALISM

BY

LUTHER A. WEIGLE

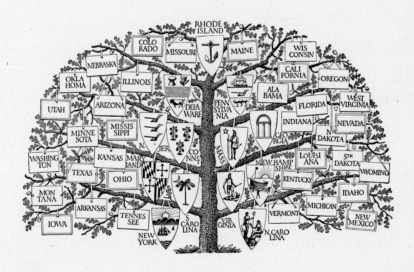

NEW HAVEN · YALE UNIVERSITY PRESS

TORONTO · GLASGOW, BROOK & CO.

LONDON · HUMPHREY MILFORD

OXFORD UNIVERSITY PRESS

TABLE OF CONTENTS

RELIGION IN AMERICAN LIFE

UNIVERSAL and perpetual is the necessity for men to adjust themselves to the conditions of life; to the natural environment as expressed in sea, land, or climate; to the social environment as expressed in the contact between nations or other groups of men; to the bisexuality of the race as expressed in the institutions of marriage and the family. These three, however, do not constitute all the life conditions requiring adjustment. Beyond the horizon of human knowledge stretches an infinite mystery which primitive men the world over have peopled with spirits and ghosts. To this unseen environment of mystery man from the beginning of his racial career has striven to adjust himself. In it uncivilized man has found the explanations for the summer rain and the winter cold, for sickness and accident, for the courage of the warrior and the wisdom of the chief. In it civilized man has found answers to those age-old questions: whence came he; why is he here; whither does he go. Looking back over the history of the race from the vantage point of the accumulated knowledge of the twentieth century we begin to understand more clearly the rôle of religion in the lives of men. It has held out hope to the despairing; it has brought comfort and inspiration to needy mortals; and it has disciplined mankind as has no other force in human life. The martyr is evidence of the fact that adjustment to the invisible environment becomes sometimes more important than life itself. The life of no people can be understood by examining merely their economic institutions, their political customs, or even their social and intellectual habits. Their adjustments to the invisible environment as expressed in their religion is vital to a true insight into their character.

The little *Mayflower* brought from Europe to the desolate coast of Massachusetts a sublime conception of the invisible environment. Far away, outside of the restless universe which He had created, was God, all-wise, almighty, eternal, directing with inexorable and inscrutable decrees every detail of that which he had called into being. All that was He had made; all that occurred He had ordained. He had made man who had become corrupt through Adam's sin. He had sent His Only Begotten Son into the world to atone for the corruption of humankind and to cleanse those who believed in His name. From the beginning the Almighty had willed that some men should be saved through this faith and that others should be damned eternally for His glory. In times past He had revealed a little of Himself to man in a divinely inspired Book. It was a guide pointing out the meaning and the way of life — even in the wilderness of America. When the humble folk of the *Mayflower* gathered on Sabbath days in the rude shelters which they had constructed, they prayed. In the language of Elizabethan England they told their God that they had come to this wild country at His behest in order to escape the cunning of the Devil and to worship Him according to His will. With implicit faith they committed themselves anew to His care. As the hard winter wore on and they looked again and again upon the lifeless clay that had been their brother or their sister, their thoughts turned not to the rigors and the dangers of their new environment, but to God who had called home these, His children, to rest awhile until the

1

Judgment Day when they should live eternally with Him. How fortunate, after all, were the departed. This was the sublime fatalism of Calvinism. Life demanded that these people adjust themselves to the hard conditions of their new habitat; their farming, fishing, and trading were the results. But for most of them the primary task was adjustment to the conditions of that eternal habitat whither, one after another, they set out alone in the darkness of death.

The religion which developed in the New World owed nothing to that of the Indians whom the white men found there. It had its origin entirely in that transfer of culture from the old communities of Europe to the raw wilderness of America. Long before the beginning of English settlements on the west coast of the Atlantic the Christian Church had begun to divide. Greek Catholics and Roman Catholics were going their separate ways and Martin Luther had appealed from the authority of the Pope to that of the Bible. In the seventeenth and eighteenth centuries Protestantism seemed to be the destiny of those English settlements which were ultimately to become the United States. To Virginia and the southern colonies was brought the organization and the worship of the conservative Church of England. To Maryland came English Catholics. New England became the refuge of those Puritan dissenters who sought to modify the practices of the Anglican church. To America also came many more radical sects both English and German; Brownists, Anabaptists, Quakers, Scotch Presbyterians, Lutherans, Moravians, Schwenckfelders, Salzburgers, and Mennonites. The conservatism of the established Catholic or Protestant Churches of Europe tended to drive the left wing of Protestantism to the empty continent across the Atlantic.

Here in the wilderness, little hindered by the hand of authority, discontented sects could undertake the task of building a society after their own models. So vast was the unoccupied area of the New World that sectarian collisions did not have the force which developed in Europe. Religious rivalry and persecution appeared in the New World but, as time passed, it resulted not in war, but merely in a more and more clearly marked geographical segregation of the sects. Quaker zealots interested in the upbuilding of Pennsylvania ceased disturbing the peace of Massachusetts. Certain colonies became refuges for people of different faiths. At the end of the seventeenth century, days of journeying through forest trails lay between different sectarian groups. In these communities, thus isolated from one another, religion played a part in shaping the development of the life of the group, more or less depending on the circumstances of the origin of the colony.

It would be easy, however, to exaggerate the differences between the sects. In forms of worship and in the character of church government they differed sharply from one another. But in underlying beliefs there was considerable similarity. Calvinism, that faith of the *Mayflower* folk, was the basis of the beliefs not only of the Puritans of New England, the Dutch of New York, the Moravians of Pennsylvania, and the Scotch-Irish Presbyterians who in the eighteenth century guarded the frontier from Pennsylvania to the Carolinas, but even the Anglican doctrines of the planters south of the Potomac were colored by it. Different from it was the faith of the handful of Catholics in Maryland and the peaceful Quakers.

Unlike the followers of Calvin, the Quakers sought God in the mysteries within the human heart. They were Friends who gathered on the Sabbath day in their meeting-houses, bare of decoration, where in silent meditation they sat together. Then it was that the divine spark hidden in the recesses of the soul grew, as a beacon grows in the darkness, until the whole being was filled with its radiance and, with vibrant voice and flashing eye, the man spoke not for himself but for God. The message ended, the radiance receded into the depths but left behind the warmth of the contact with the eternal Father. To one and another, aged patriarch and simple maid, came the same mystical experience. Seen across the intervening years, there is rare beauty in those rough old meetinghouses where folk thought they talked with God. "That which God hath given us the experience of, is the mystery, the hidden life, the inward spiritual appearance of our Lord." Among the Friends more than any other important early sect in America religious faith molded the social life. Dressed in their plain garb, speaking the hallowed language of the New Testament, raising their hand against no man, going their way in peace, they formed a group apart. But the conquest of the wild continent demanded struggle and war. Because they refused to enter into the full life of the New World they were left behind, an eddy beside the main stream.

Sectarian segregation in America accentuated the isolation of the frontier in America from the culture centers of the Old World. Life in the American wilderness inevitably brought intellectual retrogression. The settler's unremitting struggle with the forest and the rooty soil left little time for the life of the mind. When communities, like Massachusetts, sought to confine the life of this people within a restricted theological mold, the worst feature of frontier life was intensified. Puritanism, like Quakerism, fell behind the world advance. When the first generation had passed away and their wilderness-born children sat in the seats of power, the results of isolation became evident. The fire of religious fervor burned low. In Puritan New England the people bowed less readily to the theologians. Land hunger rather than religion had brought a majority, even of the Puritans, to the American wilderness. The ghost of liberty haunted the commonwealth of Massachusetts dominated still by the clergy. These called it "worldliness" and, as they felt power slipping from their hands, sought to discipline their folk with that dread sanction of their faith, the torment of the damned in Hell. Bending low over his pulpit a preacher hissed at his shrinking congregation, "When you shall have worn out the age of the sun, moon, and stars . . . without rest day or night, or one minute's ease, yet you shall have no hope, but shall know . . . that there still are the same groans, the same shrieks, the same doleful cries, incessantly to be made by you, and that the smoke of your torment shall still ascend for ever and ever: and that your souls which have been agitated with the wrath of God all this while, yet will still exist to bear more wrath." Yet the ghost was not laid. Calvinistic theology was losing touch with life as a "dead literalism" crept into the pulpits.

In the southern colonies the Church of England, though supported by the Government, had failed to grip the people. The ministers, sent from Britain, were sometimes men of character and ability but too often dissolute triflers. During the eighteenth century, moreover, the frontier pushed westward until it reached and entered the Appalachian mountains. In the scattered settlements of the back country the people were too poor to support adequate religious establishments and they received little help from the seaboard communities. As the first quarter of the eighteenth century passed, it seemed as though, in the matter of religion, over most of America the green of spring had been transformed into the dead stubble of autumn.

Suddenly, in the winter of 1734, a flame shot up in western Massachusetts and started a conflagration that for ten years swept the colonies north and south. The movement began with Jonathan Edwards in whom Calvinism, with all its terrors, found its most powerful defender. Yet Edwards put new life into that old system and adapted it to the changed needs of his day. In particular he brought nearer the far-away God of the Puritans. Edwards was a mystic. "My heart panted after this — to lie low before God, as in the dust; that I might be nothing and that God might be ALL." Up and down the Connecticut valley went the new prophet while the people flocked to hear him. Men craved a "vital" religion and Calvinism, revamped, met their needs. South of New England greater multitudes surged about a missionary from abroad, George White-field, a disciple of Wesley. By hundreds and thousands the lost sheep were gathered into the fold. Then, as suddenly as it came, the emotionalism passed and Whitefield, returning again, "found that the old magic had unaccountably lost its wonder-working power." During the Great Awakening and in the years that immediately followed, two new sects, the Methodists and the Baptists, both of European origin, gained a foot-hold in America. These organizations, together with the Presbyterians, built their churches from Georgia to New England. The day of the geographical segregation of the sects had passed and with it the attempt to confine the entire social development of a community within the limits of a particular theology. After all, the basic principle on which the religion of the seventeenth-century colonies had been founded was the liberty of the human soul to deal alone with the infinite God. This concept of liberty sent down deep roots in American character. It was in harmony with American conditions. The new thinking which came out of the Great Awakening was founded on it. Within a generation after the conclusion of the revival, American farmers and traders had defied the most powerful empire of the world in a hazardous war for political freedom. But before this war began, a movement for liberation from the old theology was under way.

Thinking men in America had followed with deep interest the work of Newton and Boyle and the other "natural philosophers" of the seventeenth and eighteenth centuries. In the person of Benjamin Franklin, famed for his experiments in electricity, provincial America had added one of the most important to their number. By the last decades of the eighteenth century enough progress had been made in the process of unraveling the tangle of natural law to warrant the conclusion that the world is governed by it. This came into collision with two basic principles of Calvinism: that God rules the universe by special decree and that His will can only be known through the revelations contained in the Scriptures. Out of the contradiction came an attitude known in the language of the day as "Deism." To the Deist God was the force that had called all things into being including natural law and now stood without the universe while His majestic creation ran on. The conclusions of the French thinkers who preceded the French Revolution had great influence in America. Thomas Jefferson took a leading part in bringing them to his countrymen. When the Bastille fell in 1789, sympathetic Americans drank deep of the doctrines of the great revolution in the Old World. They were in a rebellious mood. After a desperate and protracted struggle they had cast off the authority of England. Liberty, a concept in part born of the vastness of the new continent, was in the air and woe to the man or institution that opposed it. In such a time, when the established theocracies of the colonial settlements were tottering and when a new conception of the universe was competing with the old, religious liberty was established in the new Constitution of the United States. It was the inevitable result of the large number of denominations in America. Practically at the outset of its national history the American Republic, alone among the nations, undertook the experi-ment of allowing freedom of faith to its nationals. This is America's greatest contribution to the religious development of modern times. The results, however, were not always happy.

An established church, which conserves the experience of many generations and which views the problems of the present against the background of the past, acts as a check upon the development of hasty and ill-considered religious dogmas. As the nineteenth century opened in America there was no single religious organization with influence enough to prevent religious liberty degenerating at times to license. Perhaps no conceivable organization could have accomplished this; for America was confronted with a peculiar problem, a vast and swiftly moving frontier. In the first decades of the nineteenth century the people west of the Appalachian mountains presented, on a much larger scale than their predecessors on earlier frontiers had done, the problems which flow from isolation from the world of thought. In 1800 a revival broke out among them which surpassed anything of the character that America had ever seen. Forest camp meetings drew together huge crowds of simple frontier folk who had no defenses against the unchained emotions of the meetings and no knowledge with which to criticize the wonders which they beheld. As honest frontier preachers illumined the summer nights with the fires of Hell, men and women swooned or were thrown to the ground in paroxysms. To the backwoodsmen it seemed that God was thus cleansing the souls of sinners. Such revivals hastened a movement which was in progress before the American Revolution. Perhaps the most striking aspect of the development of religious institutions in the United States in the first half of the nineteenth century was the tendency to divide. New sects were formed and old ones were split again and again as persuasive leaders read new meanings into ancient Scriptural texts. More than once, men, reacting against creeds and sectarian rivalries and disputes, went apart by themselves to worship and to work for Christian unity only in the end to create new denominations. The army of Christian soldiers, marching to the conquest of the nation, was broken up into small bands, each skirmishing on its own account.

One result of the increased interest in religious matters which led to the multiplication of sects had, however, more than passing importance. Puritanism has had a far-reaching influence on American history. One of its important tenets was that education was an adjunct of the church. In the first half of the nineteenth century many denominations began the work of establishing academies and colleges where the rising generation might be trained in the things of both the mind and the spirit. The rapidly developing frontier West seemed the strategic place for the location of these institutions of learning for the propagating of the true faith. The result was the multitude of sectarian colleges and universities of the Mississippi valley. In the founding of these, genuine idealism, missionary zeal, and sectarian ambition were inextricably intermingled. They have served the nation well. But their service was most significant in those early days when they alone held the torch of learning aloft in the wilderness and brought the folk of the isolated frontier into touch with the thought life of the world. The time soon came, however, when the growing nation demanded that the larger part of its educational system be divorced from clerical control. Then it was that the state university rose to overshadow the sectarian college. Contemporaneous with the rise of the sectarian college the frontier witnessed one of the most interesting developments in American religious history.

The frontier community, like the embryo, tends to recapitulate the history of the race. No clearer example of reversion can be found than a religion which came out of western New York in the decade of the 'twenties. On the night of September 21, 1823, so the story is told, an angel, Moroni by name, stood beside the bed of an obscure young man living on the New York frontier and told him that God had chosen him to be His prophet. Five years to the day from that fateful interview the young man met Moroni at a hill, Cumorah, near the young man's home and, guided by the heavenly messenger, exhumed a stone box. Trembling, he peered within. There, glinting in ghostly radiance in the night, was a book whose leaves were of thin gold on which were characters in a strange tongue. Near by sparkled two crystals, the "Urim and Thummim." Early in 1830, five thousand copies of the Book of Mormon, translated by Joseph Smith, the young man, with the aid of the crystals, were printed in the office of the *Wayne Sentinel* at Palmyra, New York. Other books containing divine revelations through Joseph Smith appeared. Seventeen years passed. On a blazing day in mid-July, a little band of weary, travel-stained men looked out from the lofty highlands to which they had climbed over the valley of eastern Utah. They bared their heads, knelt, and gave thanks to God. Within a twelvemonth five thousand exiles, persecuted for conscience's sake, under a new prophet, Brigham Young, followed the long trail through the buffalo country to the haven in the mountains. There, under the shadow of the Rockies, they built a new holy commonwealth which, in the twentieth century, ministers to the needs of more than half a million souls.

The theology on which this commonwealth was founded had a quality to attract simple-hearted men and women, helpless in their restricted lives to cope with the intellectual problems of eternity. If religious liberty meant that every man was free to plumb for himself the infinite mysteries, there were many who shrank from that responsibility too great for their powers and sought the calm of a faith that spoke with authority. "Thus saith the Lord" permeated the Mormon creed. It built up an ecclesiastical hierarchy which in the early Utah days exercised a temporal and spiritual authority surpassing anything America has ever seen. In essence Mormonism was Christianity modified by what were for the most part reversions to more primitive beliefs. The God who revealed himself through the Mormon scriptures was one of many gods of varying ranks. He had a body like unto man's, infinitely powerful, infinitely beautiful. This approached the anthropomorphism of the old Greek and Roman gods. Through the universe drifted disembodied spirits, offspring of the deities, whose only hope of salvation and eternal happiness lay in their receiving bodies and being born on the earth where they might grow into the physical likeness of their beautiful god. The divinely imposed duty of bringing these spirits into the world is the theological foundation for that Mormon reversion to a practice that had long been discarded by men of European origin, polygamy. Mormonism was a product of the American frontier and also of American religious freedom. It is the most striking of the many strange cults which have sprung up and flourished from time to time in the United States. Mormonism has, however, no significance for the general religious development of the American people. The influence of a contemporary of Joseph Smith, however, is still widely felt within his native land.

Ralph Waldo Emerson broke away from Calvinism and became a Unitarian. His thinking was much like that of the eighteenth-century deists, but he breathed into their cold and lifeless system the warmth of transcendentalism. The poise and simplicity of the Sage of Concord, his fine face lighted at times as by an inner radiance, gave him an influence over Americans that few men have equaled. Year after year he went about among his fellow countrymen talking before learned societies, colleges, and rustic lyceums. He seemed to have caught the secret of the freer, deeper, more harmonious life, and men, particularly young men, were drawn to him as to the fountain head of truth. He looked into the vast sky through which this green earth swings and found God there. He looked at the wayside wild flower from which a noisy bee was gathering food and found God there. For him nature and the human soul were the only real Divine revelation. Man is part of nature and nature is part of the Deity. Mingling in the harmony of immutable law, the three are but phases of that one enshrouding, universal Spirit which touches infinity. So passed away among those to whom his influence spread the concept of the soul defiled by Adam's sin, the torments of eternal damnation, the rule of a far-off Deity by special providence and an inspired book. Yet, wide as was his power, these doctrines of an earlier day persisted. Not in one generation can the faith of centuries be shaken. Emerson died but the organized churches lived and with them the heritage of the past. Lowell, for the North, might say of his friend: "To him more than to all other causes did the young martyrs of our Civil War owe the sustaining strength of the thoughtful heroism that is so touching in every record of their lives." Yet Calvinism in the ardor of its first conquest of the South sent men to battle with the same spirit and the same fortitude.

This recrudescence of the Genevan doctrine in the Cotton Kingdom is one of the striking episodes of American religious history. The southern colonies had been, in the main, Anglican and, at the end of the eighteenth century, had come under the influence of Jefferson's deistic thinking. The Revival of 1800 had set up a current flowing in the opposite direction. Presbyterianism, growing more powerful with its success, gathered the planter aristocracy into its fold, while Methodists and Baptists gave life a new meaning for thousands of humbler folk. The Bible was read anew in the simple faith that its every word proceeded out of the mouth of God. Out of the Scriptures was built up an irrefutable justification for the South's "peculiar institution." God had created some men to rule and some to serve. Earnest men wrote and preached of the relations of Christian masters to their slaves. On the eve of the great struggle, when a breathless nation awaited the word from South Carolina, one of the saintliest and best beloved of the southern divines called his congregation to martyrdom. "The providential trust of the Southern people is to conserve and perpetuate the institution of domestic slavery as now existing. . . . If modern crusaders stand in serried ranks upon the plain of Esdraelon, there shall we be in defense of our trust. Not till the last man has fallen behind the last rampart, shall it drop from our hands; and then only in surrender to the God who gave it."

In the North the same churches preaching the same faith had, at first, opposed the abolition movement but, later, had swung into line behind it. As the sectional crisis developed, two of the greatest American sects, the Methodists and the Baptists, snapped asunder, followed by the Presbyterians and Lutherans after bloodshed had begun. There is a peculiar irony in the fact that the solitary figure who led the anti-slavery crusade to its triumph and who, at the same time, saved the Union was not allied to any of the sects. "When any church," said Lincoln, "will inscribe over its altar, as its sole qualification for membership, the Saviour's condensed statement of the substance of both Law and Gospel, 'Thou shalt love the Lord thy God, with all thy heart and with all thy soul, and with all thy mind, and thy neighbor as thyself,' that church will I join with all my heart and with all my soul." Through the great struggle the Catholics rose above the schism of the nation.

The organization, discipline, and faith of the Catholic Church is a part of the transfer of culture from the Old World to the New which has been in progress since the beginning of the history of the American people. The genius of this church is its ability to adapt itself to new environments and new conditions and at the same time to retain its hold on its ancient faith and traditions. The ideal of the seventeenth-century Puritan, though he would not have admitted it, was much like that of the Catholic. Both dreamed of a commonwealth in which there should be a division of duties between the state and the church, the one governing secular affairs, the other those of the spirit. Both believed that the duty of the church to pass on the religion which it taught required that it direct the education of the youth. Both had a social theory which held that the state was capable of sin and, like an individual, should confess and make amends for its faults. In the United States the Catholic Church never pressed its ancient theory of the unity of church and state, but rather accepted in good faith the religious liberty of the Constitution. In fact American Catholics could point to seventeenth-century Maryland when their record of toleration was in advance of the thought of the world of the day. The Catholics in the United States have increased mostly as a result of immigration until they are the largest single religious organization within the nation. While American Protestantism has been breaking away from the social and educational ideals of Puritanism the Catholics have gone quietly forward holding fast to their ancient principles. They have seen sectarian rivalry practically drive religion from the public schools and they have determined that their children shall be educated in the faith of their fathers. In a day when secular education has become almost a fetish in the United States the Roman Church has embarked upon a vast program of building Catholic schools and colleges. Catholics, beholding the Protestant ministry decline in power and authority because of an excess of democracy, of faulty ecclesiastical organization, or of shifting beliefs, have clung the more tenaciously to the power and authority of their ancient church, making adjustments to the scientific learning of the new day, and have preserved for the comfort and inspiration of men the faith which they have inherited from antiquity. Through the changing scenes of American religious history the Catholic Church has stood fast. It has been faithful to the heavenly vision which it received. It, too, has served the American people well and nowhere has its service been of more importance than in its ministry to the immigrant hordes that have sought America as a land of opportunity. In the twentieth century its leaders have watched the development of American Protestantism take a new turn.

In 1914 with appalling suddenness the forces of destruction which civilization has both begotten and chained were loosed, and the culture of Europe faced a danger greater than any since the barbarian invasions. The conflict showed how far Christianity is from realizing its great ideal of universal brotherhood. In the days when death was taking a terrible toll, the fundamental mysteries of life were brought home to people with unprecedented force. For a time the war caused men to think much on the problems of human duty and destiny. The spirit of a magnificent idealism was abroad, and there was a serious tone in human affairs. As the age-old mystery of death touched lives all over the western world, people flocked to the churches for explanation and comfort. Religious leaders leaped to the hasty conclusion that the fires of war were refining the dross from human nature and that Christianity was about to enter its day of greatness. They forgot that the war had also loosed passions which society only with the greatest of difficulty had brought under control.

America had been unified by the World War as never before in her history. While the glory of the great illusion shone in the land, her Protestant leaders thought the time propitious for the gathering of her religious forces into a common enterprise that would make American Christianity an example to the world. The Inter-Church World Movement was a splendid conception. Behind it lay the knowledge about organization and propaganda that the War had called into being. Within the hearts of its leaders burned the fires of a great purpose. The day of petty sectarianism seemed at an end. As the armies of the Allies had united to crush the monster, militarism, so the armies of Protestantism should be united to make war upon the powers of darkness. Yet the Inter-Church World Movement collapsed with a dismaying suddenness, probably the most spectacular failure of the Protestant churches in the New World. Within a decade after the tragedy American Protestantism found itself facing its most threatening schism. The new fight centered about the Bible.

The church of the twentieth century confronts a new set of conditions. Eighteenth- and nineteenth-century scholarship has borne fruit and the mass of knowledge which it has accumulated is a most important part of the foundation of modern civilization. The superstructure of our culture has been rebuilt in adjustment to the new learning. The church has been no exception; like every other human institution it has been compelled to adapt itself to the intellectual development of the last two centuries. Its first reactions of hostility to the findings of certain scientists and scholars resulted in defeat. Then Protestantism demonstrated its inherent strength. In a quiet way the results of the new scholarship were brought into religious thinking. More and more the method and the point of view of the investigator began to shape the work of the leaders in religious thought. The church itself applied the critical method to the investigation of that body of writings grouped together in the Bible. As a result the ancient doctrine of literal Biblical interpretation was sharply modified.

Because this development had gone on for practically half a century without arousing widespread opposition many people were surprised at the sudden reappearance of this old dogma in the Fundamentalist Movement which emerged soon after the World War. Not without significance is the fact that Fundamentalism has had its origin and greatest development in the United States. Certain characteristics of American Protestant churches help to explain the phenomenon. Protestantism, both in theory and in practice, is essentially democratic. Both its greatest strength and its greatest weakness come from this characteristic. Protestantism insists that every man, alone without the mediation of a priest, shall face the mysteries of life — shall be the captain of his own soul. Such a position breeds in some a rugged faith and is to others unendurable. There are many who shrink from the responsibility. To such folk the authority of supernatural revelation is indispensable.

Because church members govern the local organization, Protestant church leaders cannot in their preaching be very far in advance of the thinking of their parishioners. This makes for slow progress. Furthermore, parishioners, like voters, are susceptible to demagogic appeals and, when conditions are right, can be herded into great crusades. The Fundamentalist Movement is a crusade to save the Bible. Back of it is the havoc of the War — not only bringing mourning into the homes of the people, but making them ask how a good God could permit such a thing to come to pass. The question is not easy to answer and, very frequently, individual faith has been wrecked by storms of doubt. At such a time of crisis, it is inevitable that many people should seek the protection of authority. It is the easiest and most comforting way; and, it should be borne in mind, it is practically the only way for those less fortunate folk who have neither the training nor the capacity to wrestle with the intellectual problems of their generation. Protestants have no authority to which to turn except the Bible; so the old doctrine of literal interpretation has again raised its head.

But also behind the Fundamentalist Movement is the conservative traditionalism which has been the tendency of organized religion in all ages. Beliefs and rituals that have come down from the distant past acquire a sanctity that gives them a powerful grip on human life. They become the basis for elaborate ecclesiastical doctrines. If one of these foundation stones be struck from its place, there are many who believe the whole structure of faith must tumble in. So long as modern learning was confined to the colleges and universities and their relatively small number of graduates, its repudiation of many of the doctrines of antiquity was little noticed by the public. But when after the War the youth of the nation began flooding the institutions of higher learning and the popularization of knowledge through outlines of science, history, literature, and art became almost a fad, the religious conceptions of a host of workaday Americans came suddenly into collision with the new learning. To many people the Darwinian hypothesis seemed to drag men down to the level of the brute and the criticism of the Bible to profane the Lord's handiwork. The old beliefs they knew and loved; but the new ideas seemed to destroy the very foundations of religion and to leave men forsaken in a godless world. It was the instinct of self-preservation which raised from ocean to ocean a cry of fear from honest men and women who believed that all they held true and sacred was in jeopardy. Then a group of crusaders, both lay and ecclesiastical, dedicated their lives to the defense of Holy Writ.

Over against the halting and often perplexed modern seeker after truth they have put the Book of the Ages. With a splendid sincerity they have called to the minds of their countrymen the danger to their homes and institutions which, they fear, must grow out of the decay of the old religion. They have marshaled legislatures to their aid. Such is the development which threatens American Protestantism with schism. Yet the schism is of quite a different character from the influences which, a century earlier, caused the rapid splitting of American Protestantism into rival sects. Fundamentalism tends to unite as well as divide. It is a mode of thought and point of view which is held by large groups in many sects and tends to bind them together in mutual sympathy and a common purpose. In the same way it has tended to unite the non-Fundamentalist elements of the various sects and to bring the leaders of this group into closer harmony with that army of scholars who are seeking truth wherever it may be found. As the second quarter of the twentieth century opens the struggle is being waged hotly, albeit quietly. What the outcome will be no man can forsee.

No aspects of American life lie closer to the hearts of every-day folk, or are more intimately related to the diverse needs of local communities, than religion and education. It is obviously impossible, for lack of space, to record in this volume the history of each of the religious denominations, or to describe the development of schools and colleges in each of the forty-eight states. The author has undertaken, therefore, to present a panorama of the onward movement of American idealism, as expressed in churches and schools. Many individuals, episodes, and developments have perforce been omitted. Those selected have been either of outstanding importance or have been typical of particular movements.

RALPH H. GABRIEL

CHAPTER I

SPANISH AND FRENCH MISSIONARIES

WITH the Spanish and French explorers came to America the ministries of the Catholic Church. Christopher Columbus, religious zealot as well as daring adventurer, planted the cross of Christ where he landed and named the place San Salvador, in honor of the Savior. But neither his good will nor the scrupulous conscience of Queen Isabella could prevent the contact of Spanish colonists and natives from bringing about the practical enslavement of the Indians. Against the injustices and cruelties of the *encomienda* system Bartolomé de Las Casas protested vigorously, tirelessly, and in the end effectively. "Protector of the Indians," he devoted his life to their welfare. To similar humane and Christian service were devoted the lives of thousands of priests and friars, notably of the Franciscan and Dominican orders and of the Society of Jesus. Spain soon came to rely largely upon these missionaries for the civilizing of the frontier; and their courage, faith, and success in the face of difficulties and dangers that brought martyrdom to many, entered imperishably into the building of the Southwest.

Cartier, like Columbus, planted a cross on the St. Lawrence, and read from the Gospels to the wondering natives. Champlain brought Recollet friars, one of whom pushed as far westward as Georgian Bay. The Recollets were reinforced, and for a time replaced, by the better-equipped Jesuits. The French from the first made friends with the Indians. Here, too, there was conflict between the traders and the priests, but it was over the debauching of the Indians with liquor and robbing them in trade.

History knows no more stirring record of sustained, self-sacrificing devotion than that contained in the annual *Relations* by the Jesuits of their experience as missionaries to the Indians of New France. Misunderstandings of their teaching and of their intentions, and hostilities incident to the feud between the Hurons and the implacable Iroquois, caused some of them to be subjected to horrible torture and a martyr's death. Jean de Brébeuf and Isaac Jogues, to name only two of many, hold rightful place, not only in the annals of the church for whose Lord they gave their lives, and in the history of the two nations that now dwell in amity to the north and south of the Great Lakes and the St. Lawrence, but upon the list of those whose dauntless valor, exercised in the interest of peace and good will, reveals in undying glory the heroism of which the human race is capable.

From the St. Lawrence the Jesuits penetrated the forests about Lake Superior and Lake Michigan, and passed down the Mississippi valley, where centers of Catholic influence were established at Kaskaskia, St. Louis, and New Orleans. Claude Allouez, Jacques Marquette, and their fellow missionaries, prepared the way for Peter Gibault and other French priests who helped to win the Northwest Territory for the American Revolutionists, and to make the Louisiana Purchase a loyal part of the United States.

The early Catholic missions did not greatly influence the religious development of the colonies which, by the adoption of the Constitution, became the United States of America. This was due, not to lack of success, but to the changing international fortunes which made England, rather than Spain or France, the dominant power in North America. The permanent results of these missions are seen in the strength of the Catholic Church in the French-speaking areas of Canada, in the southwestern portions of the United States, in Mexico and the Spanish-American countries.

1 Columbus as Christ-bearer, inset on a facsimile of the La Cosa map of the world, 1500, from Jomard, *Les Monuments, de la Géographie*, in the New York Public Library, original in the Museo Naval, Madrid

CHRISTOPHER COLUMBUS, *ca.* 1446–1506, CHRIST–BEARER

ON the map drawn in 1500 by Juan de la Cosa, fellow voyager of Christopher Columbus, appears this representation of Columbus as the Christ-bearer. There was a "mystery," wrote Ferdinand Columbus, about his father's name and surname, for in them "is foretold and expressed the wonder he performed." "Christopher" means "Christ-bearer"; the legend was that St. Christopher won the name by carrying upon his shoulders across a turbulent river a child who revealed himself, finally, to be the Christ. So Christopher Columbus "went over safe himself, and his company, that those Indian nations might become citizens and inhabitants of the Church triumphant in heaven." "Columbus" means "dove"; we may say he was true *Columbus*, for as much as he conveyed the grace of the Holy Ghost into that new world which he discovered, showing those people who knew him not which was God's beloved Son, as the Holy Ghost did in the figure of a dove at St. John's baptism.

THE FRIENDLY INTEREST OF THE FRIARS

WHILE royal commissions of ecclesiastics, scientists and mariners judged his plan to be worthless, Columbus found counsel and aid in the friendship of three friars, Antonio de Marchena, a Franciscan versed in astronomy, Diego de Deza, prior of the Dominican convent at Salamanca and professor of theology in the University there, and Juan Perez, guardian of the Franciscans at Santa Maria de la Rabida near Palos. Deza was tutor to the young Prince Juan, and Perez had been father confessor to Queen Isabella. The influence of the former helped to induce the Spanish sovereigns to postpone decision, rather than to reject Columbus' proposal. It was Perez who captured the imagination of the Queen and gained her support for the enterprise. Fittingly, Palos was chosen as the port of departure; and Perez could thus hear the intrepid voyager's confession and invoke upon him the divine benediction, before he set sail at sunrise, August 3, 1492.

2 *Father Perez Blessing Columbus Before His Departure from Palos*, from the original painting by Luigi Gregori (1819–83), in the University of Notre Dame, Notre Dame, Indiana

A SIXTEENTH–CENTURY REPRESENTATION OF THE DIVINE GUIDANCE OF COLUMBUS

REFLECTION upon the career of Columbus has ever issued, except for those who have no god but luck, in the thought that it was providential. Changing in content and form have been the meanings attached to that term by the theologies of different groups and generations. Here is a pictorial representation from a book published in 1590. Columbus bears aloft the standard of the crucified Christ, while his ship is drawn forward by the favoring spirits of the deep and its monsters manifest welcome.

3   From an engraving *The Divine Guidance of Columbus*, in Theodore De Bry (1528–98), *Admiranda Narratio Fida Tamen, de Commodes et Incolarum*, Francoforti ad Moenum, 1590

Even pagan Neptune is in the picture, standing at attention while the new "High-Admiral of the Ocean-Sea" goes by. The inspiration and guidance of the Holy Spirit are symbolized by the dove upon the ship's bowsprit.

PLANTING THE CROSS IN THE WESTERN WORLD

THIS piece of twentieth-century sculpture represents a thought that was often in the mind of Columbus himself. Like most men concerned with great and far-reaching matters, he was a man of deep religious faith, keenly conscious of his dependence upon God. He believed himself, moreover, to be fulfilling a God-given

4   Group at the base of the Columbus statue, Buenos Aires, sculptured in Italy by Arnoldo Zocchi for the Argentine Government

mission. His expression of this faith recurs constantly in his *Journal* and letters. He rejoiced in the docility of the Indians, because he foresaw "coming to salvation so many souls of people hitherto lost." He dedicated the gold he was so sure he would find, to the conquest of Jerusalem and the recovery of the Holy Sepulchre. In the period of discouragement which followed his being sent back to Spain in chains by Bobadilla, he wrote in terms of fervid exaltation: "In the execution of my enterprise to India, human reason, mathematics and charts availed me nothing. The design was simply accomplished as the prophet Isaiah had predicted. Before the end of the world, all the prophecies must be fulfilled, the gospel be preached all over the earth, and the holy city restored to the Church. Our Lord wishes to do a miracle by my voyage to India. It was necessary to hasten his purpose, because, according to my calculations, there remain only one hundred and fifty years to the end of the world."

5   From an engraving *Columbus landing at Hispaniola*, from Theodore De Bry, *Collectiones Peregrinationum in Indiam Orientalem et Indiam Occidentalem*, 1590–1634, in the New York Public Library

COLUMBUS TAKES POSSESSION OF HISPANIOLA

It was Columbus' custom to erect a wooden cross in the New World "as an indication," he wrote, "that your Highnesses possess the country, and principally for a token of Jesus Christ our Lord, and the honour of Christianity." His *Journal* reveals a strange combination of motives: the desire to convert the natives to the Christian religion, willingness to exploit them in the pursuit of his own purposes, and the longing to find gold. "These people have no religion, neither are they idolators, but are a very gentle race, without the knowledge of any iniquity. . . . They have a knowledge that there is a God above, and are firmly persuaded that we come from heaven. They very quickly learn such prayers as we repeat to them, and also to make the sign of the cross. Your Highnesses should therefore adopt the resolution of converting them to Christianity, in which enterprise I am of opinion that a very short space of time would suffice to gain to our holy faith multitudes of people, and to Spain great riches and immense dominions, with all their inhabitants; there being, without doubt, in these countries vast quantities of gold."

THE RISEN CHRIST AND THE KING OF SPAIN

This curious woodcut is on the title-page of a pamphlet published in 1497, containing a German translation of Columbus' letter to the royal Treasurer, Luis de Santangel, announcing his discovery. It represents the risen Christ appearing to the King of Spain and his entourage. Christ is pointing to the wound in his hand; and the King also points toward it, to show that he comprehends the allusion and acknowledges its truth. The explanation of the picture is that the King, in his dealings with Columbus, had been a doubting Thomas, but is now convinced.

6   The Risen Christ Appearing to the King of Spain, from a wood engraving in a pamphlet, 1497, in the Royal Library, Munich, Germany

CHAMPLAIN'S SKETCH OF THE PUNISHMENT OF INDIANS

COLUMBUS greatly admired the Indians, whom he described as "a loving, uncovetous people, docile in all things: they love their neighbors as themselves, and they have the sweetest and gentlest way of talking in the world, and always with a smile." On the day that he first met them, October 12, 1492, he wrote in his *Journal* that he "perceived that they could be much more easily converted to our holy faith by love than by force." But force soon prevailed. In 1503, the Spanish sovereigns directed Nicholas de Ovando, then Governor, to compel the Indians to work, to attend and hear Mass, and to receive instruction in the faith; yet added that he was to compel them to do these things "as free persons, for so they are." Indians were gathered in villages and "put under protectors (*encomenderos*), who were obliged to teach and protect them, and were empowered to exact their labor, though for pay and as free men. This provision contained the essence of the *encomienda* system, which was designed to protect and civilize the native, as

7 Punishment of Indians, from the original drawing by Samuel de Champlain (1567–1635), in the John Carter Brown Library, Providence, R. I.

well as to exploit him. But there was always danger that the former aim would yield to the latter, and, contrary to royal will, the condition of the natives fast became one of practical slavery." — BOLTON AND MARSHALL, *The Colonization of North America 1492–1783*, p. 22. This drawing was made by Champlain, in 1599–1601, when he visited the West Indies and saw the Spanish system at work.

MESSENGERS FROM THE REALMS OF BLISS

THE Indians of Hispaniola (Hayti) were fast reduced in numbers because of the new diseases which the white man brought and the new mode of life which his coming forced upon them. Spanish masters were frequently cruel and enforced labor in the mines was crushing to an undeveloped people. Ovando asked authority to bring Indians from other islands "in order that they might enjoy the preaching and political customs" of Hispaniola. "Besides," he added, "they might assist in getting gold, and the King be much served." The King gave permission, and in 1509 ordered the Governor to "provide for the mines as many Indians as may be requisite." One of the first islands to suffer from this policy was San Salvador, the first land visited by Columbus, and by him named for the Savior. The Spaniards entrapped its inhabitants by announcing themselves as messengers from heaven, sent to convey them to the regions of eternal bliss, where their forefathers and beloved dead now dwelt and longed to welcome them. The Indians flocked eagerly upon the ships, which bore them, not to heaven, but to the hell of slavery. In five years, forty thousand deluded natives were carried from other islands to Hispaniola.

8 Indians Working in the Mines, from an engraving in the Latin edition of Bartolomé de las Casas, *Narratio Regionum Indicarum per Hispanos quosdam devastatarum verissima*, Frankfort, 1598

9 Indians seeking Death Rather than Slavery, from a wood engraving in Girolamo Benzoni, *Historia del Mondi Nuovo*, Venice, 1572

10   Father Bartolomé de las Casas, from the original painting by Felix Perra in the National Museum, City of Mexico

BARTOLOMÉ DE LAS CASAS, 1474–1566, "PROTECTOR OF THE INDIANS"

MANY Spaniards in the West Indies opposed the *encomienda* system on moral grounds. The most aggressive of these was Bartolomé de las Casas, who had been with Columbus on his third voyage and had settled in Hispaniola with Ovando in 1502. He became a priest in 1510, and in the next year he went to Cuba and was himself assigned an *encomienda* of Indians, by whose labor he began to grow rich. He became convinced that the whole system was iniquitous, and began to preach against it, having first renounced his own connection with it. With a Dominican, Father Antonio Montesino, Las Casas journeyed to Spain to lay the sufferings of the Indians before the King. By Cardinal Ximenes he was appointed "Protector of the Indians," and he devoted the remainder of his life to their service. He secured from Charles V laws to alleviate their condition, and providing that *encomiendas* should be abolished on the death of the present holders. These laws were strenuously opposed, until they were in part repealed. They were much evaded; in Peru the attempt to enforce them led to bloodshed. Las Casas continued his tireless efforts until his death at the age of ninety-two.

THE DESTRUCTION OF THE INDIES

LAS CASAS had the faults which are often characteristic of reformers. He was impatient, passionate in remonstrance, and inclined, for the sake of the good ends he sought, to overstate the abuses against which he protested. He thus aroused resentment, and some even who sympathized with his purposes deprecated his methods.

11   Title-page of Bartolomé de las Casas, *Breuissima relacion de la destruycion de las Indias*, Seville, 1552

In 1541 he wrote a bold, stirring account of what had happened in the West Indies, for presentation to Charles V and his ministers. Eleven years later it was published, all names of guilty "tyrants" being omitted. It was translated into several languages, and helped to make the name of Spain a byword for cruelty throughout Europe. In 1550 Las Casas met in public debate Dr. Juan Sepulveda, who had written an elaborate argument to prove the lawfulness of waging war against the natives of the New World. In a private letter, Sepulveda afterward described him as "most subtle, most vigilant, and most fluent, compared with whom the Ulysses of Homer was inert and stuttering."

12   Title-page of the Latin edition, Bartolomé de las Casas, *Narratio Regionum Indicarum per Hispanos quosdam devastatarum verissima*, Frankfort, 1598

HATHUEY'S DEFIANCE

A TYPICAL account by Las Casas is the story of Hathuey, Indian cacique of part of Cuba. He was informed by spies of the conduct of the Spaniards. Calling his people together, he displayed a basket of gold. "Here," he said, "is the god whom they serve, and after whom they go; wherefore let us make to him here a festival and dances, so that when they come, he may tell them to do us no harm." When the dances were done, Hathuey said that they should not keep the god of the Christians anywhere, "for even if it were in their entrails it would be torn out." So they threw the gold into the river. In 1511 the "population and pacification" of Cuba began in Hathuey's territory. He was captured and sentenced to be burned. At the

13 Hathuey Declines to Enter Heaven, from an engraving in the Latin edition of Bartolomé de las Casas, *Narratio Regionum Indicarum per Hispanos quosdam devastatarum verissima*, Frankfort, 1598

stake a friar exhorted him to be baptized and become a Christian, as he would then go to heaven. He inquired whether there would be any Spaniards in heaven, and when he was told that there would be some, he replied that he had no desire to go to that place.

14 Death of Father Juan de Segura, d. Feb. 8, 1571, from an engraving by Melch. Küsell after a drawing by Carl Screta (1604–74), in M. Tanner, *Societas Jesu Militans*, Prague, 1675

MARTYRS OF THE CROSS

IN 1536 Spanish colonists in Guatemala mockingly dared Las Casas to "try with words only to bring the Indians to the true faith." He agreed to convert the inhabitants of a yet unconquered province, known as the Land of War, if the Governor would forbid all other Spaniards to enter the territory for a period of five years, and would promise not to extend to it the *encomienda* system. Before the time had elapsed, he had succeeded; and the region bore a new name — Vera Paz, the Land of True Peace. Fray Luis Cancer, Las Casas' associate in this enterprise, believed that he could win the natives of Florida in the same way. But he landed where memories of De Soto still rankled, and the Indians slew him and his fellow friars without mercy. There were others who, like him, counted not their lives a great thing, and suffered martyrdom as missionaries of the cross — Father Juan de Padilla in New Mexico; Father Pedro Martinez in Florida; Father Louis de Quiros, Father Juan de Segura in Virginia; Fathers Pedro de Corpa, Blas Rodriguez, and Michael Auñon in Guale, which was later Georgia; Father Francisco Saeta in Sonora; Father Alonzo Terreros in Texas; Father Luis Jayme in California, and many more.

15   Francisco Pareja Teaching Christianity to the Indians, from a woodcut *Cathecismo, En Lengua Castellana, Y Timuquana*, Mexico, 1612, in the New York Historical Society

SUCCESS OF MISSIONS IN MEXICO

The largest share in the early work of Christian missions to the Indians was undertaken by the Franciscans. Of eighty-six priests, who here met martyrdom in the service of Christ, sixty-five were of this order. Three Franciscan friars from Belgium established the first mission in Mexico. In 1523 one of these, Pierre Van den Moere, better known as Fray Pedro de Gante, opened a school for Indian boys, which he conducted for nearly half a century. These first missionaries were soon reinforced by many of their own order; and other orders followed. The friars achieved substantial success in Mexico. The report of the miraculous appearance of the Virgin to an Indian near Mexico City resulted in the beginning of pilgrimages to the shrine of Our Lady of Guadalupe, who is represented as a gentle-faced Indian woman, and venerated as the patroness of the Indian. The missionaries learned hieroglyphic writing and used it for instruction in Christian doctrine;

and they taught trades and arts to the natives. They succeeded in making Christianity, the religion of an invader, appear to the natives to be not exotic, but in part at least indigenous, and in persuading them to accept it. Schools and colleges began to multiply. The University of Mexico was founded in 1551 and formally opened in 1553. The missionary orders advanced from Mexico City until they had brought the frontier of New Spain to California and Texas.

16   From the painting *Fray Pedro de Gante Teaching a Group of Indians*, reproduced in M. Cuevas, *Historia de la Iglesia en Mexico*, Mexico, 1921, original in the Museo Nacional, Mexico

17   From the original illustration, 1750(?), by Pablo de la Purisima Concepcion Beaumont, in the New York Public Library

18   From the original illustration, 1750(?), by Pablo de la Purisima Concepcion Beaumont, in the New York Public Library

FRIAR BEAUMONT'S PICTURES OF THE WORK OF THE MISSIONARIES

THESE contemporary sketches of the early work of the Franciscans in Mexico were made by Friar Pablo de la Purisima Concepcion Beaumont, in illustration of his manuscript *Cronica de la Provincia de los Santos Apostoles San Pedro y San Pablo de Michoacan*. One shows two missionaries meeting a native king and his three wives. Beneath the other group of sketches is a notation, which states that it portrays "the missionary fathers at work in the vineyard of the Lord" among the friendly Indians, preaching and baptizing. They were "fighting at the same time with the demons" for the souls of their hearers. They were helped in this good work by the "faithful and fervent" General Nañuma, who appears at the head of a band of converts.

MISSIONS IN FLORIDA AND GEORGIA

THE ill-fated attempt of the Dominican, Fray Luis Cancer, to convert the warlike Indians of Florida was followed, ten years later, by an effort of other Dominicans, associated with Tristan de Luna's unsuccessful expedition. In response to the appeal of Menendez de Aviles, founder of St. Augustine, who finally succeeded in establishing Spanish colonies in Florida, Jesuits came in 1566 and 1568. Some suffered martyrdom, and others were forced by the opposition of the Indians to abandon their missions in 1570. The Franciscans in 1573 began labors which, in spite of interruption by an Indian revolt in 1597 which cost the lives of a number of priests, resulted in the establishment of a chain of missions along the coasts which now belong to Florida, Georgia, and South Carolina, and later, groups of missions in various parts of the interior. The Bishop of Cuba, making in 1606 the first episcopal visitation on the soil of what was to become the United States, confirmed one thousand and seventy Indian neophytes at four missions in Guale, now Georgia. Father Francisco Pareja, missionary at San Juan, and afterward guardian of the Convent of the Immaculate Conception at St. Augustine, wrote three catechisms, a manual for confession, and other works, including a grammar, in the language of the Indians. The first of his Indian catechisms was printed in Mexico in 1612. In the second quarter of the seventeenth century from thirty to fifty Franciscan friars were serving the Florida missions, and the Christian Indians are said to have numbered thirty thousand. In 1655 the Governor urged that Florida be made an episcopal see. But this prosperity came to an end, and most of the missions were abandoned later.

19   Title-page of Francisco Pareja, *Cathecismo*, a catechism in the Spanish and Timuquana Indian languages, Mexico, 1612, from the original in the New York Historical Society

20   Fort Marcy and the *Parroquia*, from a drawing by Lieut. J. W. Abert, in Lieut. Col. W. H.
      Emory, *Notes of a Military Reconnaissance*, Washington, 1848

THE MEANING OF THE MISSIONS ON THE FRONTIER

THE missions throughout New Spain were more than an evangelizing agency. Conducted chiefly by Franciscans, Dominicans, and Jesuits, whose motive was definitely and consistently religious, they were yet agencies of the state as well as of the church. Realizing the failure of the *encomienda* system, which led to the exploitation of the Indians, Spain soon came to rely upon the missions for the civilizing of the frontier. The meager stipends of the missionaries were in many cases paid by the Government. They were not only to convert the Indians to the Christian faith, but to teach, train, and discipline them in the rudiments of civilization. The law was that in ten years the Indians of each new station were to be made self-supporting, the common mission lands distributed, the churches turned over to the secular clergy, and the missionaries were then to move on to another frontier post. This law was based, however, upon experience with the more highly developed native peoples of Mexico and Peru; and it was found that a longer period of tutelage was needed for the more barbarous tribes of the north.

MISSIONS IN NEW MEXICO

AN exploration of New Mexico in 1539 by a Franciscan friar, Fray Marcos of Nice, led to Coronado's expedition. Father Juan de Padilla, who remained thereafter to establish a mission, met death at the hands of hostile Indians in 1542. In 1581 another attempt was made by a Franciscan lay brother, Augustine Rodriguez; but he and the two friars accompanying him were killed. Oñate in 1598 succeeded in establishing the Spanish power in New Mexico, and missions were organized by the Franciscans in the principal pueblos. Father Gerónimo de Zárate Salmerón, in eight years service, 1618–26, at Jémez, baptized six thousand five hundred and fifty-six Indians, besides many more at three other pueblos which he served; and he wrote a catechism in their language. Fray Alonso de Benavides, custodian of the New Mexico missions, reported to the King of Spain in 1630 that eighty thousand Indians had been baptized, and that friars were at work in twenty-five missions, serving ninety pueblos. A revolt against Spanish rule took place fifty years later. Twenty-one missionaries were slain by the Indians, and three hundred and eighty others were killed, men, women and children. A determined effort was made to extirpate Christianity. But by the beginning of the eighteenth century the territory had been reconquered; and the missions were reëstablished.

21   Ruins of a Mission near Jémez, New Mexico, from a drawing by R. H. Kern in James H. Simpson,
      Journal of a Military Reconnaissance, Philadelphia, 1852

ANTONIO MARGIL, 1655–1726, FOUNDER OF MISSIONS IN TEXAS

AFTER earlier attempts of the Franciscans to establish missions in Texas had been balked by the failure of the Government to coöperate with them effectively, the decision, reached in 1715, that the territory must be occupied as a defense against French incursions from Louisiana, opened the way to the friars. The field was assigned to missionaries from the College of the Holy Cross at Queretaro, who were directed by Father Isidor Felis de Espinosa, and from the College of Our Lady of Guadalupe at Zacatecas, led by Father Antonio Margil. They were welcomed by the Asinai Indians. The missions grew slowly but substantially, in spite of interruptions and hardships at various times, due to lack of full coöperation on the part of the Government, or to wars with the French, or to raids by the Apaches and other hostile tribes. Father Margil was a man of unusual ability, who had rendered notable service for over thirty years in Mexico, Nicaragua, and Guatemala, and now, at an age when most men think of retiring from active service, gave six years to the arduous and dangerous work of organizing and upbuilding missions on the Texas frontier.

22 Father Antonio Margil, from an engraving in *Vida Portentosa del Americano Septentrional Apostol El V. P. Fr. Antonio Margil De Jesus*, Mexico, 1763

EUSEBIO FRANCISCO KINO, 1644–1711, MISSIONARY, RANCHMAN, AND EXPLORER

FATHER EUSEBIUS KUHN, Austrian Jesuit, refused a professorship of mathematics in the University of Ingolstadt to come to America to minister to the Indians. Taking the name of Francis in honor of St. Francis Xavier, he was known by the Spaniards as Eusebio Francisco Kino. In 1687 he founded, and for twenty-four years made his headquarters, the mission of Nuestra Señora de los Dolores in Pimeria Alta, now northern Sonora. From this base he made more than fifty journeys, some of a thousand miles, in exploration, settlement and administration of his territory. Not only a missionary and a church builder, he was a successful ranchman and an explorer and geographer. Tireless in the saddle, he pushed north to the Gila River and west to the Colorado. Fourteen of Kino's journeys were

23 *Mission Church of San Xavier del Bac* from *Reports of Explorations and Surveys for a Railroad*, Vol. VII, Washington, 1857

in exploration of what is now Arizona, where in 1700 he founded the mission of San Xavier del Bac, near the present site of Tucson. He did not fear to travel the Devil's Highway, where many less skilful pioneers have since perished of thirst. Beginning with a few cattle furnished him by older missions, he established at least nineteen stock ranches to provide for the material and economic needs of his people. These so prospered that he was able in one year to give seven hundred head of cattle to San Xavier del Bac, and to send a like number to Father Salvatierra at Loreto in Lower California.

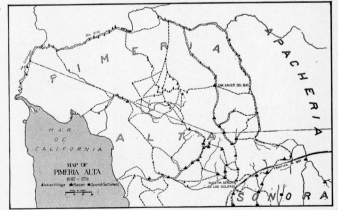

24 Map of Pimeria Alta showing Kino's journeys, simplified from the original *Kino's Historical Memoirs of Pimeria Alta*, edited by H. E. Bolton, A. H. Clark & Co., Cleveland, 1919

JUAN MARIA DE SALVATIERRA, 1644–1717

In 1683–85, Kino had endeavored to establish missions among the Indians of Lower California, but the enterprise was abandoned because of a prolonged drought, lack of supplies, and failure of Governmental support. In 1691, he proposed to Father Juan Maria de Salvatierra, then visiting him, that it be tried again; and promised coöperation from his own missions in Pimeria Alta, with their "lands so pleasant, so rich, so fertile, and able so easily to lend aid to the scanty lands of California." In 1697 Salvatierra began the work thus planned (see Vol. I, No. 735). Kino doubted the common belief that California was an island, and was eager to find a route for overland communication with Salvatierra. In 1701 they journeyed together to the head of the Gulf of California; and in the next year Kino explored the Colorado from the Gila to the Gulf, proving the falsity of the current notion. In 1767 King Charles III ordered all Jesuits to be expelled from the dominions of Spain. The missions in Lower California were placed in charge of the Dominicans, and the projected missions in Upper California were assigned to the Franciscans.

25   Juan Maria de Salvatierra, from E. P. Francisco Zavier Alegre, *Historia de la Compania de Jesu*, Mexico, 1842, in the Library of Congress, Washington

JUNIPERO SERRA, 1713–1784, FOUNDER OF CALIFORNIA MISSIONS

The hero of the settlement of "Upper" or "New" California was Junipero Serra, a Franciscan friar who had given up a professorship of philosophy in Europe to become a missionary. Though fifty-five years old, he journeyed overland with Governor Portola, and arrived in San Diego on June 30, 1769. Two weeks later he dedicated his first mission, San Diego de Alcalá. In the following year he built San Carlos mission near Monterey, which was his headquarters for the fourteen crowded years that remained to him. Nine of the twenty-one missions of the Franciscans in California were founded by Serra. He was greatly beloved by the Indians and by his associates, even by the soldiers of the Spanish presidios. "Love God," was his habitual greeting. Quite aside from the legends that have grown about his name, "the real Serra was indeed a remarkable man. . . . He possessed the traits which were most needed in the pioneer. He was an . . . unselfish, single-minded missionary. He subordinated everything, and himself most of all, to the demands of his evangelical task as he understood it. Withal, his administration as Father-President was so sound and his grasp of the needs of the province so clear that he was able to exercise a greater authority than would ordinarily have been permitted." — Charles E. Chapman, *A History of California: The Spanish Period*, p. 353.

26   Father Junipero Serra, from Palou, *Relacion de la vida y toreas del padre Junipero Serra*, Mexico, 1787

27   *Serra's First Mass at San Diego*, from the original painting by J. E. McBurney, in possession of Frank A. Miller, Master of The Mission Inn, Riverside, Calif.

28   Site of the Yuma Massacre, 1781, from John R. Bartlett, *Personal Narrative of Explorations*, Vol. I, New York, 1854

FRANCISCO GARCES, 1738–1781, EXPLORER, MISSIONARY, AND MARTYR

AN explorer whose achievements were of great importance for the advance of the frontier, and a missionary whose devotion met the supreme test, was Father Francisco Garces, who, when the missions of the Jesuits in the north were taken over by the Franciscans, was placed in charge of San Xavier del Bac, which had been founded by Kino. Entering upon his ministry there in June, 1768, he soon began a series of journeys much like those of the indefatigable earlier pioneer. The third of these, in 1771, carried him through the territory west of the Colorado River. In 1774 he accompanied de Anza on the memorable journey which established what Kino had so much desired to find, an overland route through desert and mountain from Sonora to Upper California. In 1775–76, with only three Indian companions, he traveled for nearly eleven months, exploring the interior of California as far north as the vicinity of Bakersfield and Tulare Lake. He carried a canvas containing on the one side a picture of the Virgin and the Child Jesus, and on the other side a portrayal of a condemned soul in hell. This he would unfold and explain wherever he stopped. His diary records that on this journey he visited nine nations of Indians, numbering in all twenty-four thousand five hundred people. In 1779 he settled among the Yuma Indians, at the junction of the Gila and Colorado rivers, where he attempted to establish missions. But his work was greatly hindered by the delay, lack of judgment, vacillation, and neglect of the Commandant-General, Teodoro de Croix. In 1781 the Indians, enraged by various acts of the Spanish soldiers and colonists, attacked the settlements. Father Garces and his fellow friars were martyred in the ensuing massacre.

29   Southeast View of Santa Barbara Convent, from a lithograph by Vischer, 1865, in the Collections of the University of California

FERMÍN FRANCISCO DE LASUÉN, *ca.* 1720–1803, PRESIDENT OF CALIFORNIA MISSIONS

THE brilliant success of Fermín Francisco de Lasuén during five years as sole missionary at Borja, the most difficult station in Lower California, led to his selection in 1773 for service in Upper California. Here he was placed in charge of San Diego mission. In 1785 he succeeded Serra as Father-President. He founded nine more missions, among these Santa Barbara, for which the site had been chosen by Father Serra shortly before his death. He strongly fostered the training of the Indians in the mechanical arts as well as in agriculture and stock-raising; and brought from New Spain carpenters, smiths, masons and other artisans to teach them.

30   Mission of San Antonio de Padua, near Jolon, Calif., from a photograph

THE SECULARIZATION OF THE MISSIONS

IN 1834, the twenty-one missions of California were directing the activities of fifteen thousand four hundred Indians, who herded one hundred and fifty-one thousand four hundred cattle, sixteen thousand horses and mules and one hundred and forty thousand sheep, hogs and goats, and harvested one hundred and twenty-three thousand bushels of grain, besides laboring in orchards and gardens and at wine press, loom, tannery, shop, and forge. In August of that year a decree of "secu-larization" was signed; and ten years later a proclamation authorized the rental or sale of the missions and such remaining lands as had not been distributed to the Indians or appropriated by land-grabbers and dishonest officials. The Government of the United States, which gained control of California in 1848, restored the mission buildings, with environing lands, to the church. There were about one hundred and thirty thousand Indians in California in the days of Serra; but there are not more than fifteen thousand now.

CHAMPLAIN BRINGS MISSIONARIES TO NEW FRANCE

IN 1534 Cartier, explorer of the St. Lawrence, erected a cross thirty feet high on the western shore of its gulf. At Hochelaga (Montreal) he read to the Indians, who welcomed him and his followers as gods, the opening verses of the Gospel of St. John and the account of the suffering and crucifixion of Christ. Champlain, colonizer and real founder of New France, took more effective measures for the conversion of the natives, who were living, he said, "like brute beasts, without faith, without law, without religion, without God." In 1615 he brought to Quebec four gray-clad friars of the Recollets, a branch of the Franciscans. One of these, Father Joseph Le Caron, pushed westward with the Huron Indians whom he met at Montreal, and preceded Champlain to their towns on Georgian Bay, where they built for the missionaries a chapel. Here Le Caron erected a simple altar, and on August 12, 1615, after Champlain had joined him, celebrated the first Mass in the country of the Hurons.

31   Title-page of the original in the New York Public Library

THE COMING OF THE JESUITS

In 1625 the Recollets welcomed reinforcement by the black-gowned Jesuits, who were not, like themselves, a mendicant order, dependent upon alms for support. The work of both groups was interrupted by the brief English occupation of 1629–32; and only the Jesuits returned. Under Father Paul Le Jeune, 1591–1664, their first Superior, and his successors, the number of missionaries steadily increased; and they were dispatched, singly or by twos, to the Indian settlements — to the Hurons around Georgian Bay, to the Algonquins north of the Ottawa, to the Abenakis in Maine and Acadia, to the Iroquois south of the St. Lawrence, and to the Chippewas, Ottawas, Illinois, and other tribes of the upper Lakes and the Mississippi valley. They were required to report annually a written journal of their doings; and each year, from 1632 to 1673, the Superior made up a narrative, or *Relation*, of the most important events which had occurred, sometimes quoting and sometimes summarizing the individual journals upon which it was based. The *Relations* were printed in Paris and awakened great interest in the missions.

TEACHING BY PICTURES

It was difficult to teach the Indians even the simplest articles of the Catholic faith. Their language contained no equivalents for the terms in which these were wont to be expressed; and now and

RELATION
DE CE QVI S'EST PASSE'
EN LA
NOVVELLE FRANCE
EN L'ANNE'E 1636.
Enuoyée au
R. PERE PROVINCIAL
de la Compagnie de IESVS
en la Prouince de France.
Par le P. Paul le Ieune de la mesme Compagnie,
Superieur de la Residence de Kébec.

A PARIS,
Chez SEBASTIEN CRAMOISY Imprimeur
ordinaire du Roy, ruë sainct Iacques,
aux Cicognes.
M. DC. XXXVII.
AVEC PRIVILEGE DV ROY.

32   Title-page of the original in the
New York Public Library

then some Indian of whom the priests inquired, would mislead the good fathers with scurrilous and obscene phrases. It was hard to make heaven appear attractive. "Do they hunt in heaven, or make war, or go to feasts?" asked one. "No," replied the missionary. "Then I will not go; it is not good to be lazy." "Heaven may be a good place for the French," said another; "but I want to be among Indians." It was natural, therefore, for the priests to dwell much upon the pains of hell, which their hearers could more readily understand. "You do good to your friends," said Father Le Jeune to an Algonquin chief, "and you burn your enemies. God does the same." Writing to his superior in Paris, Le Jeune asked for more and better pictures to be sent for use in the missions. "These holy representations are half the instruction that can be given to

33   Baron de La Hontan Showing a Painting of God to the Indians, from Baron de
La Hontan, *Nouveaux Voyages*, Vol. III, La Haye, 1703

the Indians. I wanted some pictures of hell and souls in perdition, and a few were sent us on paper; but they are too confused. The devils and the men are so mixed up, that one can make out nothing without particular attention. If three, four, or five devils were painted tormenting a soul with different punishments — one applying fire, another serpents, another tearing him with pincers, and another holding him fast with a chain — this would have a good effect, especially if everything were made distinct, and misery, rage and desperation appeared plainly in his face."

34   *Jean de Brébeuf before the Indian Council*, from the drawing by H. A. Ogden (1856–)

JEAN DE BRÉBEUF, 1593–1649, MISSIONARY TO THE HURONS

FATHER JEAN DE BRÉBEUF, scion of an ancient Norman family, tall and strong of body, keen-minded and great-hearted, was missionary to the Hurons from 1626 till his death. His work was interrupted for a time by the English occupation; but in 1634, at Ihontahira, near Thunder Bay, he organized the greatest of the Indian missions of New France. Drought and pestilence, after a year or two, awakened the apprehension of the Hurons, who attributed these to the magical powers of the black-robed visitors. The eagerness of the Jesuits to baptize dying children cast suspicion upon them. The report spread that they had concealed in their houses a corpse which was infecting the country — the result of some Indian's misunderstanding of what they sought to teach him concerning the body of Christ in the Eucharist. The pictures of the Last Judgment were regarded by some as portrayals of the intention of the missionaries to destroy the people. A great council of the Huron nations was held in August, 1637, at which only the courage and resourcefulness of Brébeuf and his companions sufficed to save their lives.

THE MARTYRDOM OF BRÉBEUF

IN 1640, while attempting to initiate a mission in the Neutral Nation, Father Brébeuf beheld in the sky a great cross that slowly approached over the forests toward the lands of the Iroquois. When his companions asked him how large it was, he answered, "Large enough to crucify us all." In 1649 his crucifixion came. Captured with Father Gabriel Lalemant, his associate, when the Iroquois sacked the Huron towns of St. Louis and St. Ignace, he was tortured by every method that savage minds could devise. Boiling water was poured over his naked body three times, in derision of baptism. A collar of hatchets, heated red-hot, was hung about his neck; a belt of bark, filled with pitch and resin, was fastened around his waist and set afire. Enraged because he did not cry out in pain, but continued to exhort his fellow captives, they cut off his lips and tongue and thrust a hot iron down his throat. They cut strips of flesh from his legs and arms, and devoured them before his eyes. Finally one cut out his heart and ate it, while others drank his blood, in the hope that it might make them as courageous as he.

35   Silver Bust of Jean de Brébeuf, containing
          his skull, in the Hôtel Dieu, Quebec

HOW THE INDIANS TORTURED THEIR CAPTIVES

THE *Journal* of David Pieterzoon de Vries, Dutch voyager and merchant, published in 1655, contains this picture and description: "The Indians put their enemies to death as horribly as this plate shows. . . . They place their foe against a tree or stake, and first tear all the nails from his fingers, and run them on a string, which they wear the same as we do gold chains. It is considered to the honor of any chief who has vanquished his enemies, if he bite off or cut off some of their members, as whole fingers. Afterwards, the prisoner is compelled to sing and dance, entirely naked, before them; and finally when they burn the captive, they

36 Indians Torturing a Captive, from David Pieterzoon De Vries, *Korte Historiael*, Hoorn, 1655

kill him with a slow fire, and then eat him up; the commoners eating the arms and thighs, and the chiefs eating the head. When these Indians fasten their enemy to the stake, he is compelled to sing, and accordingly begins to sing of his friends, who will avenge his death. . . . They prick his body with hot burning wood in different parts, till he is tormented to death. They then tear his heart out of his body, which every one eats a piece of, in order to embitter themselves against their enemies." The belief was widespread among the Indians that eating the flesh of an enemy would bring to the victor such desirable qualities as the vanquished possessed. Ceremonial cannibalism was found in many of the tribes with whom the French came into contact.

37 Father Isaac Jogues, from J. G. Shea, *History of the Catholic Missions Among the Indian Tribes of the United States*, New York. 1855

ISAAC JOGUES, 1607–1646, CAPTURED BY THE IROQUOIS

DE VRIES, who left New Amsterdam in October, 1643, recorded in his *Journal* a report from Fort Orange that the Iroquois had captured three Frenchmen, one of whom was a Jesuit, and that the Dutch were trying to secure their release. The Jesuit was Father Isaac Jogues, for six years one of Brébeuf's companions in the mission to the Hurons. In 1641, he and Father Charles Raymbault had journeyed for seventeen days until they reached the Sault de Sainte Marie and became the first missionaries to preach the gospel upon the shores of Lake Superior. In 1642, while returning from a journey to Quebec to secure supplies, his party was attacked by ambushed Iroquois. Jogues escaped them, but voluntarily surrendered when he saw that they had captured one of his lay companions, René Goupil, and some of his Huron converts. "'Could I indeed,' I said to myself, 'abandon [them] without giving them the help which the Church of my God has entrusted to me?' Flight seemed horrible to me. 'It must be,' I said in my heart, 'that my body suffer the fire of earth, in order to deliver these poor souls from the flames of hell; it must die a transient death, in order to procure for them an eternal life!'"

38 Torture of Father Jogues by the Indians, from an engraving by Melch. Küsell after a drawing by Carl Screta in M. Tanner, *Societas Jesu Militans,* Prague, 1675

JOGUES ESCAPES FROM THE INDIANS

WILLIAM COUTURE, who had also escaped, likewise returned to share the fate of his friends. The savages tore out the captives' nails with their teeth, gnawed their fingers, and cut off a thumb or forefinger of each. Couture eventually was adopted by an Indian family, and after three years was returned to the French. Jogues, treated as a slave, and tortured from time to time so cruelly that he longed to die, finally escaped at Fort Orange, with the help of Arendt Van Curler, manager of Rensselaerswyck, and Domine John Megapolensis, minister of the Dutch church. Governor Kieft gave him clothes and passage on a ship, and in January, 1644, he reached the Jesuit College at Rennes in France.

JOGUES RETURNS TO MEET DEATH

ALL France had been stirred by the report of Jogues' fate; and he was received with joy and reverence as one returned from the dead. The Queen desired to see him, and kissed his mangled hands. But he was eager to go back to his work. The Pope, by special dispensation, authorized him to celebrate the mass, notwithstanding his deformity, exclaiming, "It is not right that a martyr of Christ should not partake of his blood." Soon after Jogues returned to Montreal, the Iroquois made peace with the French; and it fell to him, because of his knowledge of their language and customs, to go among them, first as ambassador, and then to found a mission. "The Mission of the Martyrs," they planned to call it. Before he was chosen for this work, Jogues, knowing that his experience fitted him best for it, wrote to a friend: "My heart tells me that if I have the happiness of being employed in this mission, I will go and will not return; but I shall be happy if our Lord will complete the sacrifice where He has begun it, and make the little blood I have shed in that land the earnest of what I would give." His prophecy was true. The Indians respected him as an ambassador; but they slew him when he returned as missionary.

39 Father Jogues Memorial at Auriesville, N. Y., courtesy of Father Breen

40 Catherine Tekakwitha, 1656–80, from a portrait, 1681, by Father Claude Chauchetiere, in the Church of St. François Xavier du Sault, Caughnawaga, P. Q., Canada

MISSIONS TO THE IROQUOIS

THE Jesuits did not despair of converting even the Iroquois, and their persistent efforts met finally with some success. They often found it wise to encourage converts to leave the Iroquois villages, however, for the temptations to apostasy were strong. At La Prairie, opposite Montreal, a mission colony was begun in 1669, its first Indian dwellers being Catherine Ganneaktena and her husband, who had endured persecution among the Oneidas. The settlement grew, was organized as an Iroquois town, and was named St. François Xavier du Sault. No one was permitted to take up his residence who did not renounce three things: belief in dreams, the changing of wives, and drunkenness. Here, in 1677, came Catherine Tekakwitha, the "Lily of the Mohawks," whose virtues, as she sought to emulate her white sisters, the Ursulines and Hospitalieres, in wholehearted devotion to God, were such that Catholics of Canada and the United States have petitioned for her recognition as a saint.

41 François-Xavier de Laval de Montigny, 1622–1708, from a photogravure in possession of the publishers

THE LIQUOR TRAFFIC AMONG THE INDIANS

EVEN in this Christian Iroquois colony, the priests had to contend with the greed of traders and the Indian appetite for liquor. "We have here no other demon to contend against than liquor and drunkenness, which make a hell of all the Iroquois villages. . . . The French are the cause of its giving us much trouble here; for, in order to strip the savages to their very shirts, they follow them everywhere, to make them drink and become intoxicated." François-Xavier de Laval de Montigny, 1622–1708, the high-born, dauntless man who came to Quebec as Bishop and Vicar-Apostolic in 1659, fought the liquor traffic resolutely. Merchants and *coureurs de bois* argued that its prohibition would drive the trade of the Indians into the hands of the English. The priests insisted that its continuance not only involved the robbery of the Indians by unscrupulous traders, but was working their ruin, in body and soul.

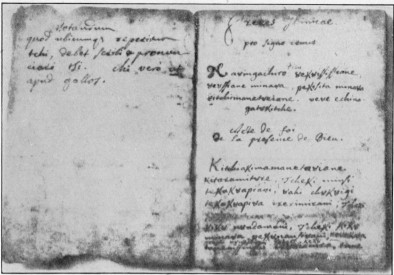

42 From the facsimile of the Prayer Book translated into Illinois by Claude Allouez, published by the Quebec Literary and Historical Society, Quebec, 1908, in the New York Public Library

CLAUDE ALLOUEZ, 1622–1689, "APOSTLE TO THE WEST"

NINETEEN years passed after the visit of Jogues and Raymbault before another missionary went to the Indians on Lake Superior. Then René Ménard, a veteran of twenty years service among the Hurons and Iroquois, was sent; but he perished in less than a year. In 1665 Claude Allouez was assigned the task, and was appointed Vicar General in the West by Bishop Laval. He gave the rest of his life — twenty-four years — to unwearied travel and service in the territory later covered by the states of Wisconsin and Illinois. The letter announcing his death spoke of him as "a second Xavier," and credited him with having instructed more than one hundred thousand Indians and baptized over ten thousand. Here are shown some pages from the prayer book, in the language of the Illinois, which he wrote for his colleague, Father Marquette.

JACQUES MARQUETTE, 1637–1675, EXPLORER OF THE MISSISSIPPI

SON of a wealthy and distinguished family in the ancient cathedral city of Laon, Jacques Marquette eagerly read the *Relations* of the Jesuit missionaries in America, and was fired with the ambition to become one of them. He joined the Society at seventeen, and twelve years later received the command he awaited — to embark for New France. His aptitude as a linguist led to his assignment, in 1668, to the western missions. He labored first at the Sault de Sainte Marie, then replaced Allouez at La Pointe du Saint Esprit, near the southwest corner of Lake Superior. Here traveling bands of Illinois told him of a great river which it henceforth became his ambition to explore. They invited him to come among them, promising to embrace Christianity if he would. But he cherished no illusions. "One must not hope that he can avoid Crosses in any of our Missions; and the best way to live there contentedly is not to fear them. . . . The Illinois wish for us in order that we may share their miseries with them, and suffer every imaginable hardship of barbarism. They are lost sheep, that must be sought for among the thickets and woods."

43 Jacques Marquette, from the original painting by J. Boyes, in the House of the Immaculate Conception, Montreal

44   The Marquette Party Entering the Wisconsin River at The Portage, from a bronze tablet by H. A.
MacNeil (1866–), in the Marquette Building, Chicago

JOLIET AND MARQUETTE AT THE PORTAGE ON THE WISCONSIN

A THREATENED attack by the Sioux terrified the Hurons and Ottawas at La Pointe du Saint Esprit. They decided to move eastward, and the mission had to be abandoned. The Hurons settled on Mackinac Island, and here, at the mission of St. Ignace, Marquette continued his work. He wrote to his Superior that at this mission he found "men's minds more gentle, more tractable, and better disposed to receive the instructions that are given them than in any other place. Meanwhile, I am preparing to leave it in the hands of another missionary, to go by Your Reverence's order and seek toward the south sea new nations that are unknown to us, to teach them to know our great God, of whom they have hitherto been ignorant." In December, 1672, the order came, borne by Sieur Louis Joliet, whom he was to accompany in an attempt "to discover the south sea and the great river Mississippi." In May they departed on their quest — down Green Bay and up the Fox River to the portage across to the waters of the Wisconsin, then down this river to the Mississippi.

MARQUETTE'S LAST JOURNEY

THE explorers floated down the Mississippi to the mouth of the Arkansas. They returned by way of the Illinois River, which gave access to Lake Michigan by several portages. Marquette promised the Illinois Indians at Kaskaskia that he would come back to them, and establish a mission. After a year, when he believed himself to have recovered from an ailment due to the hardships he had endured, he undertook the journey. His malady recurred, and he was forced to spend the winter in a rude hut upon the Chicago River. He pressed on in March, reached Kaskaskia, and preached to the people. But his strength was ebbing. He tried to return to St. Ignace, but died upon the eastern shores of Lake Michigan, near Ludington, May 18, 1675. Two years later, some of the Indians to whom he had preached at La Pointe du Saint Esprit, reverently uncovered his body, cleansed and dried his bones, and carried them, with a funeral procession of thirty canoes, to St. Ignace. Marquette was a man whose life in America was dominated by two motives. The explorer's desire for knowledge sent him down the Mississippi and took him, though weak from illness, along the shores of Lake Michigan. Yet he never lost sight of his primary calling which was to minister to the Indians.

45   Marquette Crossing the Site of Chicago in December 1674, from the bronze tablet by H. A.
MacNeil in the Marquette Building, Chicago

46   From the mural painting *Father Hennepin at the Falls of St. Anthony*, by Douglas Volk (1856–),
      in the State House, St. Paul, Minn. © Sweet Bros., Minneapolis

RECOLLET FRIARS WITH LA SALLE

Jean Baptiste Talon, first Intendant of New France, brought Recollet friars again to Quebec in 1670; and when Réné-Robert Cavelier, Sieur de La Salle, undertook his great enterprise of exploration and establishment of trading posts in the West, five Recollets were assigned to his expedition — Fathers Gabriel de la Ribourde, Zenobius Membré, Louis Hennepin, Luke Buisset, and Melithon Watteau.

Father Buisset remained at Fort Frontenac; Father Watteau was made chaplain of the post established at Niagara, to minister both to the French and to the neighboring Seneca Indians. The other three accompanied La Salle, and at Fort Crèvecœur, which he built near the site of Peoria, in Illinois, erected a chapel. From here Father Hennepin set out to explore the upper Mississippi; was captured by the Sioux Indians; saw and named the Falls of St. Anthony, where Minneapolis now stands; was rescued by the *coureur de bois* Dulhut; and in 1681 returned to Fort Frontenac, to Quebec, and to Europe. There he wrote his books, which, though braggart and not altogether trustworthy, were vastly popular in their day and record much that is of value concerning the geography and ethnography of those parts of North America which he had seen. Father de la Ribourde while at his devotions was slain by three wandering Kickapoo Indians. Father Membré accompanied La Salle to the mouth of the Mississippi, and returned with him to France. "All we have done," he wrote, "has been to see the state of these nations, and to open the way to the gospel and to missionaries, having baptized only two infants."

SEBASTIAN RALÉ, 1657–1724, MISSIONARY TO THE ABENAKIS

For thirty years Sebastian Ralé ministered with exceptional success to the Abenakis at Nanrantsouak, now Norridgewock, Maine. "I have built here a church which is suitable and very well appointed. I thought nothing ought to be spared either for its decoration or for the ornaments which are used in our holy ceremonies. Altarcloths, chasubles, copes, consecrated vessels — everything is appropriate, and would be so esteemed in our churches of Europe. I have formed a little brotherhood of about forty young Indians, who assist at divine service, in their cassocks and surplices. They have their assigned duties, to assist at the holy sacrifice of the mass, and to chant the divine office for the consecration of the holy sacrament, and for the processions which they make with a great concourse of natives, who often come from a long distance to attend them. You would be edified with the fine order which they maintain and the piety which they show."

47   From the original manuscript of Sebastian Ralé, *Abenaki Dictionary*,
      in the Harvard College Library, Cambridge, Mass.

THE DEATH OF FATHER RALÉ

THE Abenakis were devotedly attached to Father Ralé and to the faith he had taught them; and they indignantly rejected the proposal of the English to send them Bibles and a Puritan minister. Ralé's great influence is expressed in his own words: "If they hold a council, a frequent occurrence among the Indians, they send one of the principal men of the assembly to ask me to assist at the decision of their deliberations. I go as soon as possible to the place where the council is held; if I judge that they are taking a wise course, I approve it; if, on the contrary, I find anything to say against their decision,

48   Death of Father Ralé, from the engraving by D. L. Glover in Jared Sparks, *Library of American Biography*, Vol. 17, Boston, 1845

I declare to them my opinion, which I support by solid reasons, and they conform to it. My advice always shapes their resolutions." The English recognized this fact. They believed that Ralé did more than any other man to hold for France the territory in Maine which they claimed. They offered a reward for his capture. Finally, in a surprise attack upon Norridgewock in 1724, he was killed — a martyr to the jealousy and conflicting ambitions of France and England.

THE URSULINES IN NEW ORLEANS

DE BIENVILLE, who in 1718 founded New Orleans, brought Capuchin friars in 1722, and one of these opened a parish school for boys. In 1727 ten Ursuline Sisters, volunteers from various convents of that order in France, came to New Orleans and established a convent. They opened an academy for the daughters of well-to-do parents, and a free day school, beginning with twenty-four pupils in the former and forty in the latter. They also opened a hospital, and later an orphanage. Reading, writing, arithmetic, religion, and industrial training constituted the curriculum of their schools. The Ursulines in New Orleans have survived all vicissitudes and changes of Government. In 1824 they built a new convent in a location then removed from the city, but now well within its limits. Here their academy remains, a well-known center for the education of Catholic girls.

49   Landing of the Ursuline Nuns, Aug. 7, 1727, from a print in the Louisiana State Museum, New Orleans

CHAPTER II

PILGRIMS AND PURITANS

HENRY VIII, abjuring the authority of the Pope, made the Church of England an appendage of the Crown. From this subjection of church to state, of spiritual interests to civil authority, little groups of English citizens began to dissent. Through Luther, Tyndale, Calvin, and Knox they had learned to regard the Word of God contained in the Bible as their authority, and they began to think of a church as a voluntary association of believers in Christ who covenant together to walk in His ways.

Relentless persecution, even unto death, did not daunt them. In December, 1620, one of these groups after many vicissitudes landed on the west shore of Cape Cod Bay where they built a settlement which they named Plymouth. Nine years later these Pilgrims were followed by the first of many companies of Puritans who came to settle in neighboring regions. They, too, fled persecution. Intending at first not to separate themselves from the Church of England but simply to purify their worship from what they deemed to be its corruptions, they became in time convinced of the truth of the principles of the Pilgrims, and founded churches organized in "the congregational way."

The ideal of the Pilgrims and Puritans was a free church in a free state, both subject to the will of God as revealed in the Scriptures. They sought to establish a theocracy. One of the first ministers of the church at Hartford, Samuel Stone, commenting upon the regard which the people had for the competence of their ministers to interpret to them the will of God, said that a Congregational church was "a speaking aristocracy in the face of a silent democracy." But the seeds of democracy were there, and securely planted in fertile soil. The Puritans of New England first learned the principles of democracy in their church life, then in town meeting, and finally in the larger affairs of state and nation.

Though the Congregational churches were never "established" as state churches in the sense in which the Church of England was established, a curious interpenetration of church and state was characteristic of all the New England colonies except Rhode Island. Differing in details at various times, and in the several colonies, this general relation of church and state was due partly to their theocratic ideal, and partly to the difficulty of maintaining otherwise their precarious semi-independence of England, and conserving their hard-won freedom to worship God as conscience bade them. An easier age judges the Puritans intolerant because they would not grant to others the same freedom of worship which they came to America to enjoy. The epithet is hardly fair, for it connotes a certain perversity of temper of which they cannot justly be accused. Theirs was the intolerance bred of intense conviction and of fear lest their own freedom be taken from them.

Politically, the Puritan theocracy may be said to have ended with the annulment of the Massachusetts charter in 1684. Increase Mather, whose indefatigable labors secured for the colony an advantageous new charter, and his son, Cotton Mather, unwillingly witnessed the passing of the old ideal. Jonathan Edwards, mystic, theologian, and preacher of the Great Awakening, gave impetus to the growing idea of the complete separation of church and state by his insistence upon the need of conscious conversion and his exaltation of the church as a spiritual institution.

LUTHER APPEALS TO THE BIBLE

The Pilgrims and Puritans believed the Bible. The Word of God was their supreme authority. They shared in that far-reaching movement of the sixteenth century which, though it had manifold sources, found clear, ringing expression in Martin Luther's protest against certain abuses that had entrenched themselves in the life of the Catholic Church. Ordered to recant, he appealed above Pope and Councils to the Bible. Excommunicated by the church, and under

50   *Martin Luther Before the Diet of Worms, April 13, 1521*, from an engraving by F. Nargeot, London, 1862, after a painting, 1857, by Pierre Antoine Labouchère (1807–73)

the ban of the Empire, he used a period of enforced seclusion in his castle of the Wartburg to begin the translation of the Bible from the original Hebrew and Greek into German. He patiently sought for words that would make the meaning most clear to simple folk. He succeeded so well that his translation has never been superseded in common use.

WILLIAM TYNDALE TRANSLATES THE BIBLE INTO ENGLISH

William Tyndale, a young Cambridge scholar, undertook to do for England what Luther had done for Germany. "Because I had perceived by experience," he said, "how that it was impossible to establish the lay-people in any truth, except the Scripture was plainly laid before their eyes in their mother tongue, that they might see the process, order and meaning of the text." Other English translations of the Bible had been from the Latin Vulgate; his was the first from the original Hebrew and Greek. He was accused of wilfully perverting the meaning of the Scriptures; and his New Testaments were ordered to be burned as "untrue translations," intended "for the advancement and setting forth of Luther's abominable heresies." Tyndale was finally condemned and burned at the stake.

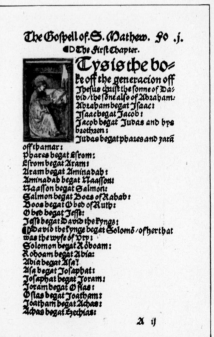

The Gospell of S. Mathew. 90 .j.
The first Chapter.

Tysis the boke off the generacion off Jhesus christ the sonne off Dauid/the sonne also of Abraham:
Abraham begat Isaac:
Isaac begat Jacob:
Jacob begat Judas and hys brethren:
Judas begat phares and zara off thamar:
Phares begat Esrom:
Esrom begat Aram:
Aram begat Aminadab:
Aminadab begat Naasson:
Naasson begat Salmon:
Salmon begat Boos off Rahab:
Boos begat Obed off Ruth:
Obed begat Jesse:
Jesse begat David the kynge:
David the kynge begat Solomō/of her that was the wyfe of Vry:
Solomon begat Roboam:
Roboam begat Abia:
Abia begat Asa:
Asa begat Josaphat:
Josaphat begat Joram:
Joram begat Onas:
Osias begat Joatham:
Joatham begat Achas:
Achas begat Ezechias:

A ij

52   From the facsimile edition, published by Francis Fry, Bristol, 1862, of the original William Tyndale, *New Testament*, 1525 or 1526, in the Library of the Baptist College, Bristol, England

GVILIELMVS TYNDALLVS MARTYR

To Ipeam docuit Crist̄i sapientia Legem
TINDALLE constate quæ tibi causa necis

51   William Tyndale, *ca.* 1492–1536, from Henry Holland, *Herwologia Anglica*, London, 1620

IOANNES. CALVINVS

53 John Calvin, 1509–64, from the original portrait, *ca.* 1550, in the Museum Boymans, Rotterdam, Netherlands

THE BEGINNINGS OF PURITANISM

HENRY VIII abjured the authority of the Pope and induced Parliament to declare himself and his successors to be "the only supreme head in earth of the Church of England." But it is hard to believe that this was because the Lord had opened his eyes. His revolt from papal authority was for political and personal reasons, rather than on grounds of conscience and religious conviction. He retained the doctrines and usages of the Roman Church with little change. The name Puritan came to be applied to an increasing group of folk who wished to purify or complete the reformation of the Church of England. Many of these were burned at the stake in the reign of Queen Mary, who undertook to restore Catholicism. Many others sought refuge on the Continent, where they came under the influence of John Calvin, whose system of church government became henceforth their model.

JOHN KNOX, *ca.* 1505–1572

THE greatest of the Puritan exiles who thus came under the influence of Calvin was John Knox, to whom, more than to any other man, Scotland owes its political and religious individuality. Inspired by his preaching, the Protestant barons of Scotland entered into a covenant to "establish the most blessed Word of God and His congregation." In 1560, a Confession of Faith which he had prepared was adopted by the Scottish parliament, and the first General Assembly of representatives of "particular kirks" was held. No more fearless or effective preacher ever lived. "Others sned (snipped) the branches; this man strikes at the root," said his hearers. "Think ye," said Mary Queen of Scots, smarting under his reproof, "that subjects, having power, may resist their princes?" "If their princes exceed their bounds, Madam, they may be resisted and even deposed."

54   *John Knox Preaching Before the Lords of the Congregation, June 10, 1559,* from an engraving by William Greatbach (b. 1802), after the original painting by Sir David Wilkie (1785–1841), in the Tate Gallery, London

QUEEN ELIZABETH, 1533–1603

QUEEN ELIZABETH became a Protestant, but a "pope in petticoats." The Act of Supremacy declared her to be the "Supreme Governor" of the Church of England, and placed in her hands the appointment of the members of the High Commission, its supreme judicatory. The Act of Uniformity ordered the use of the Anglican liturgy in public worship by every minister and in every religious assembly. The Puritans objected to certain features of this liturgy as savoring of Roman Catholicism; and, taught by Calvin, many of them believed that a congregation should have a voice in the selection of its minister. This was considered a challenge to Elizabeth's supremacy — a political offense as well as an expression of religious dissent.

55 Queen Elizabeth, from an engraving by Charles Turner (1773–1857), in the Emmet Collection, New York Public Library, after an engraving by Crispin de Passe from the drawing by Isaac Oliver (1556–1617) in Windsor Castle

56 Cells in the Old Court House, Guild Hall, Boston, England, photograph by G. E. Hackford

PERSECUTION OF THE SEPARATISTS

THE principles of democracy were nascent in the religious convictions of the more radical Puritans. They began to think of a church as a voluntary association of believers in Christ who covenant together to walk in His ways. Such a church will choose and ordain its own minister, rather than accept a priest assigned to them by a bishop who is an agent of the Crown, and it will undertake to conduct its worship and administer its affairs "according to the primitive pattern in the Word of God," rather than in conformity to the behests of political authority. So little groups began here and there to form their own congregations. Separatists, they were called. They were hunted out and punished. Five of their leaders, John Coppin, Elias Thacker, John Greenwood, Henry Barrowe, and John Penry, were hanged as heretics and inciters to sedition. When pressed to recant, Penry, still a young man in the early thirties, declared: "If my blood were an ocean sea, and every drop thereof were a life unto me, I would give them all for the maintenance of this my confession. Far be it from me that . . . the saving of an earthly life . . . or any other thing should enforce me, by denial of God's truth, to perjure my own soul." After his execution, Parliament passed a law making forfeiture of property and banishment from the realm the penalty for denial of the Queen's ecclesiastical supremacy or for attendance upon Separatist meetings.

57 The Old Court Room, Guild Hall, Boston, England, from a reconstructive view, 1907, by G. E. Hackford

58 Page containing the first reference to the settlers of New England as *Pilgrims*, from William Bradford, 1588–1657, *History of Plimoth Plantation*, facsimile edition, London, 1896, in the New York Public Library

THE SCROOBY SEPARATISTS BECOME PILGRIMS

AT Scrooby, in the north of England, a group of Separatists met in the manor house. "As the Lord's free people," wrote William Bradford, they "joined themselves by a covenant of the Lord into a church estate, in the fellowship of the Gospel, to walk in all his ways, made known, or to be made known unto them, according to their best endeavours, whatsoever it should cost them, the Lord assisting them." "And that it cost them something," he soberly adds, "this ensuing history will declare." To escape persecution, they fled to Holland; and after eleven years, fearing lest their English heritage be lost and their children fall into strange customs and untoward ways, resolved to remove to America. Edwin Sandys invited them to the Virginia colony. "These English," said the magistrates of Leyden, "have lived now amongst us ten years, and yet we never had any suit or accusation against them, or any of them."

JOHN ROBINSON'S FORWARD LOOK

IT was decided that a part of the church — "the youngest and strongest" — should go first. William Brewster, the elder, went with them; and John Robinson, the pastor, remained with those who were to follow later.

59 *Pilgrims About to Go on Board The Speedwell at Delft Haven*, from a photogravure after the original painting attributed to Albert Cuyp (1620–91), in John Fiske, *The Beginnings of New England*, Boston and New York, 1898. © 1898, Houghton Mifflin Co.

Robinson was a man of singular beauty of life, of sound judgment, and of great spiritual power. His parting counsel to those to embark is memorable: "He charged us . . . to follow him no further than he followed Christ; and if God should reveal anything to us by any other instrument of his, to be as ready to receive it as ever we were to receive any truth by his ministry; for he was very confident the Lord had more truth and light yet to break forth out of his holy Word." Robinson also said: "Men are often accounted heretics with greater sin through want of charity in the judges than in the judged through defect of faith."

60   *Sunday Services of Puritan Scouts*, Clark Island, from the original painting by George H. Boughton
(1836–1905), courtesy of Edwin Van Volkenburgh, New York

61   *The Pilgrims on the Mayflower Leaving Plymouth, England, Sept. 16,
1620*, from the original drawing by H. A. Ogden. © Chase &
Sanborn

THE FIRST SABBATH ON CLARK'S ISLAND

THE *Speedwell* carried the Pilgrims to England; but
it was the *Mayflower*, finally, which bore them from
Plymouth to America. They arrived at Cape Cod on
November 11, 1620, and spent a month in exploration.
On Saturday, December 9, an exploring party, after
many vicissitudes, landed on Clark's Island. They
"gave God thanks for his mercies, in their manifold
deliverances. And this being the last day of the week,
they prepared there to keep the Sabbath." On Monday they explored the neighboring mainland, found
it to be a "most hopeful place," and decided there to
build their homes. The new settlement was named
Plymouth, in remembrance of their port of departure.

> Ay, call it holy ground,
>   The soil where first they trod.
> They have left unstained what there they found —
>   Freedom to worship God.
>
> — FELICIA HEMANS, *The Pilgrim Fathers*.

62   Pulpit Rock, Clark Island, where the first sermon is said to have been preached

63 *Public Worship Led by Elder Brewster*, from the etching by J. Rennefeld after the painting, 1859, by Georg Johann Schwarze (1814–74), in Martinius Cohen Stuart, *The Pilgrim Fathers' First Meeting for Public Worship in North America*, Amsterdam, 1866

ELDER WILLIAM BREWSTER, *ca.* 1566–1644

THE Pilgrims at Plymouth were without a pastor for nine years. John Robinson died before he could join them. They were led in worship by William Brewster, the oldest of their company and ruling elder of the church. Robinson had advised him not to administer the sacraments; but "he taught twice every Sabbath, and that both powerfully and profitably. . . . In teaching, he was very moving and stirring of affections, also very plain and distinct in what he taught. . . . He had a singular good gift in prayer, both public and private. . . . He always thought it were better for ministers to pray oftener, and divide their prayers, than be long and tedious in the same."

PILGRIMS GOING TO CHURCH

A DUTCH merchant who visited Plymouth in 1627 thus described the meetinghouse and the congregation: "Upon the hill they have a large square house, with a flat roof, made of thick-sawn planks, stayed with oak beams, upon the top of which they have six cannons, which shoot iron balls of four and five pounds, and command the surrounding country. The lower part they use for their church, where they preach on Sundays and the usual holidays. They assemble by beat of drum, each with his musket or firelock, in front of the captain's [Myles Standish's] door; they have their cloaks on, and place themselves in order, three abreast, and are led by a sergeant without beat of drum. Behind comes the Governor [William Bradford], in a long robe; beside him, on the right hand, comes the preacher [Elder Brewster], with his cloak on, and on the left hand the captain, with his side-arms and cloak on, and with a small cane in his hand; and so they march in good order, and each sets his arms down near him."

64 The Pilgrim Meetinghouse, from a drawing in *The Pilgrim Almanac*, Boston, 1853

PURITANS SETTLE AROUND MASSACHUSETTS BAY

IN 1629, the *Mayflower* was one of six ships chartered by "The Governor and Company of the Massachusetts Bay in New England" to bring to Salem a body of settlers four times as large as the group of Pilgrims, and far better equipped. John Endicott had come with a vanguard in the previous autumn; John Winthrop brought the main company in 1630. By the end of that year, two thousand colonists had come to Massachusetts; and within a decade, more than twenty thousand. They were Puritans, who sought to escape the tyranny of Charles I and the zeal of Archbishop Laud.

Unlike the Pilgrims, the Puritans who settled Massachusetts Bay were not Separatists. They wished to purify and reform, not to forsake the Church of England. "We will not say, as the Separatists were wont to say at their leaving of England, 'Farewell, Babylon! Farewell, Rome!' but we will say 'Farewell, dear England, farewell, the Church of God in England and all the Christian friends there!' We do not go to New England as Separatists from the Church of England, though we cannot but separate from the corruptions in it; but we go to practice the positive part of church reformation, and propagate the gospel in America."

65 John Endicott, *ca.* 1588–1665, from the copy, 1737, by John Smibert (1684–1751), in the Massachusetts Historical Society, of the original portrait, painted, 1665, artist unknown, in the possession of William C. Endicott, Boston

---

76   *Governour Bradford's Letter Book.*

apart the same day, for the same ends, beseeching God as to withdraw his hand of correction, so to establish and direct them in his ways : and though the time be very short, yet since the causes are so urgent, we pray you be provoked to this godly work, wherein God will be honoured, and they and we undoubtedly have sweet comfort in so doing. Be you all kindly saluted in the Lord, together with the rest of our brethren : The Lord be with you and his spirit direct you, in this and all other actions that concern his glory and the good of his :

Your brethren in the faith of Christ,
And fellowship of the gospel,   SAMUEL FULLER,
Salem, July 26, Anno 1630.   EDWARD WINSLOW.

To his loving friend, Mr. WILLIAM BRADFORD, *Governour of Plymouth, these.*

SIR,

THERE is come hither a ship (with cattle, and more passengers) on Saturday last ; which brings this news out of England ; that the plague is sore, both in the city and country, and that the University of Cambridge is shut up by reason thereof ; also, that there is like to be a great dearth in the land by reason of a dry season. The Earl of Pembroke is dead, and Bishop Laud is Chancellor of Oxford ; and that five sundry ministers are to appear before the High Commission, amongst whom, Mr. Cotton, of Boston, is one. The sad news here is, that many are sick, and many are dead ; the Lord in mercy look upon them ! Some are here entered into a church covenant, the first was four, namely, the Governour, Mr. John Winthrop, Mr. Johnson, Mr. Dudley, and Mr. Willson ; since that, five more are joined unto them, and others it is like will add themselves to them daily. The Lord increase them, both in number and holiness, for his mercy's sake. I here but lose time and long to be at home : I can do them no good, for I want drugs, and things fitting to work with. I purpose to be at home this week (if God permit) and Mr. Johnson and captain Endicott will come with me ; and upon their offer, I requested the Governour to bear them company, who is desirous to come, but saith he cannot be absent two hours. Mrs. Cottington is dead. Here are divers honest christians that are desirous to see us ; some out of love, which they bear to us, and the good persuasion they have of us ; others to see whether we be so evil, as they have heard of us. We have a name of love and holiness to God and his saints ; the Lord make us answerable, and that it may be more than a name, or else it will do us no good. Be you lovingly saluted, and my sisters, with Mr. Brewster, and Mr. Smith, and all the rest of our friends. The Lord Jesus bless us and the whole Israel of God. Amen.

Your loving brother in law,
Charlestown, August 2, Anno 1630.   SAMUEL FULLER.

[But this worthy gentleman, Mr. Johnson, was prevented of his journey, for shortly after he fell sick and died, whose loss was great and much bewailed.]

66 From *Governour Bradford's Letter Book*, printed in the Massachusetts Historical Society *Collections*, Vol. III, Boston, 1794

DR. FULLER'S VISIT TO SALEM

BUT the Atlantic was wide; and the endeavor of these Puritans "to practice the positive part of church reformation" drew them nearer to the Pilgrims. John Robinson had predicted this, and had counseled his followers "rather to study union than division." Endicott was greatly pleased with the bearing and conversation of Dr. Samuel Fuller, deacon of the church at Plymouth, who was the only physician available when sore illness fell upon the vanguard at Salem. "I acknowledge myself much bound to you," he wrote to Governor Bradford, "for your kind love and care in sending Mr. Fuller among us, and rejoice much that I am by him satisfied touching your judgments of the outward form of God's worship. It is, as far as I can yet gather, no other than is warranted by the evidence of truth, and the same which I have professed and maintained ever since the Lord in mercy revealed himself unto me; being far from the common report that hath been spread of you touching that particular." There is no record of just what Endicott and Fuller talked about. It is safe to guess that they discussed such questions as the use of a distinct covenant as the basis of the organization of a local church; the right of a local congregation not only to elect, but to ordain its own ministers; the participation of the church as a whole in matters of discipline; the conduct of public worship; and the disadvantages of relationship to a national church three thousand miles across the sea. The Pilgrims were committed to "the congregational way." Eventually they won over the Puritans.

> *This second letter sheweth ther proceedings in their Church before at Salem, which was ye 2 church erected in these parts, and afterwards ye lord established many more in sundrie places*

[facsimile of handwritten letter]

Salem July 30. 1629　　　　At your service in what I may
　　　　　　　　　　　　　　Charles Gott.

67　From William Bradford, *History of Plimoth Plantation*, facsimile edition, London, 1896, in the New York Public Library

THE ORDINATION OF SKELTON AND HIGGINSON

A CHURCH was organized at Salem, upon the basis of a covenant similar to that of the Pilgrims. A day was appointed for the choice of a pastor and teacher, when Francis Higginson and Samuel Skelton were questioned as to what, in their view, constituted a call to the ministry. They stated that it was twofold: the inward call of God, evidenced by motive and endowment, and the outward call of choice by the free vote of a company of covenanted believers. A vote was taken; Mr. Skelton was elected pastor and Mr. Higginson teacher. Then followed an act of great significance. Both men were already ordained ministers of the Church of England; but this church proceeded to ordain them to its own service. "They accepting the choice, Mr. Higginson, with three or four of the gravest members of the church, laid their hands on Mr. Skelton, using prayers therewith. This being done, there was imposition of hands on Mr. Higginson."

THE ORGANIZATION OF A CHURCH IN BOSTON

DR. FULLER was kept busy in the following year, for there was much illness after the main company arrived and settled Dorchester, Watertown, Charlestown and Boston. Everywhere he spoke of the things of the spirit, as well as ministered to the needs of the body. He had many conferences with Governor Winthrop. "Opposers there is not wanting," he wrote to Bradford, "and Satan is busy, but if the Lord be on our side, who can be against us." Soon he was able to report the organization of a church, of which John Wilson was chosen and ordained teacher. "We used imposition of hands," Winthrop wrote in his *Journal*, "but with this protestation by all, that it was only as a sign of election and confirmation, not of any intent that Mr. Wilson should renounce his ministry he received in England." Though they organized Congregational churches, the Massachusetts Puritans continued for some time to regard themselves as members of the Church of England. This was one of the points on which Roger Williams berated them.

68　From a drawing *The Call to Church*, by Edwin A. Abbey (1852-1911), in *Harper's Weekly*, Feb. 7, 1880

CHURCH AND STATE IN MASSACHUSETTS

FOLLOWING the example of Salem and Boston, the other towns of Massachusetts organized churches according to "the congregational way." It has sometimes been said that early New England was "priest-ridden." The epithet is misleading. The ministers of these churches were pastors and teachers, not priests. They were called priests by the Quakers, who meant by that term to denote one who received pay for his ministry. But they exercised no priestly functions, for these churches acknowledged no hierarchy, rejected the Anglican liturgy, and denied all sacerdotal beliefs and practices. The organization of the New England churches was democratic; their ministers were elected by the free vote of the members and ordained by them. Each church, moreover, controlled its own affairs; and there was even question as to whether a minister could officiate in the ordinances to any other congregation than the one which he had been called to serve.

The churches were thus emancipated, in spiritual matters, from the control of the state. But Massachusetts came very near to making the state the servant of the churches. The sovereignty of God was the fundamental article of the Puritans' creed, and they sought to establish a theocracy. In the life of the state as well as in that of the church, they aimed at complete obedience to the will of God as revealed in the Scriptures. The statues of Governor Winthrop represent him holding the Bible in one hand and the Charter in the other.

69 Statue of John Winthrop by Richard Saltonstall Greenough (1819–1905), erected 1880, Boston, Mass.

From the standpoint of the State, the situation in Massachusetts was undemocratic. From 1631 to 1664 only church members were granted the right to vote as freemen; and such persons only were admitted to church membership as could give satisfactory evidence of regeneration. No other than Congregational churches were permitted, and the ministers of these churches were supported by public taxation. While not priest-ridden, seventeenth-century Massachusetts was church-dominated and clergy-led.

JOHN COTTON: "THE PATRIARCH OF NEW ENGLAND," 1585–1652

THE most influential of the ministers was John Cotton, who had been for twenty-one years vicar of St. Botolph's Church in Boston, Lincolnshire. Because he refused to observe certain ceremonies prescribed in the Anglican liturgy, the High Commission sought to arrest him; but he escaped to Massachusetts in 1633, and was elected teacher of the church in Boston, John Wilson having been made pastor. His catechism, entitled *Spiritual Milk for Boston Babes in either England,* was used for more than one hundred and fifty years and was incorporated, with various changes of title, in many editions of the *New England Primer.*

Spiritual·
MILK
FOR
BOSTON BABES
In either ENGLAND.

Drawn out of the
Breaſts of both TESTAMENTS
for their ſouls nouriſhment

But may be of like uſe to any
Children

By JOHN COTTON, B. D.
late Teacher to the Church of
Boſton in New-England.

CAMBRIDG
Printed by S. G. for Hezekiah Uſher
at Boſton in New-England
1 6 5 6

70 Title-page of the only known copy of the 1656 edition, in the New York Public Library

71 The Pulpit from St. Botolph's Church, Boston, England, in which John Cotton preached, now in the Massachusetts Historical Society

72 John Cotton; from an engraving by Hezekiah Wright Smith (1828–79), after the portrait, about 1735, by John Smibert, owned by John E. Thayer, Lancaster, Mass.

JOHN COTTON: THEOCRAT

COTTON was a clear expositor and energetic defender of "the way of Congregational churches," in answer to the queries and objections of Puritans in England, who felt that they were too separatistic. He was a profound believer in the principles of theocracy, and was the first in New England to use that term. "When a commonwealth hath liberty to mould his own frame, I conceive the Scripture hath given full direction for the right ordering of the same. Democracy I do not conceive that ever God did ordain as a fit government either for church or commonwealth. . . . As for monarchy and aristocracy, they are both of them clearly approved and directed in the Scripture, yet so as (God) referreth the sovereignty to himself and setteth up theocracy in both as the best form of government in the commonwealth as well as in the church."

THE LAWS OF MASSACHUSETTS

THE Massachusetts authorities were slow to devise a code of laws, partly because of their confidence in the sufficiency of Scripture; partly because of the feeling that the laws in this new country, as in England, "should arise *pro re nata* upon occasions," as an accumulating body of statutes and precedents; partly because certain of the Puritan customs could not be enacted into law without transgressing the Charter, which provided that there be "no laws repugnant to the laws of England." In 1636, at the request of the General Court, Cotton presented "a model of Moses his judicials, compiled in an exact method," which was subsequently published in England under the title *An Abstract of the Lawes of New England As they are now established*. The title is misleading, as this code was never accepted. The *Body of Liberties*, which was finally adopted in 1641, was drafted by Nathaniel Ward, of Ipswich, a minister who had formerly been a lawyer, assisted by Cotton. Both codes cite supporting texts of Scripture. While austere and harsh in the light of present-day standards, these codes were merciful as compared with other codes of their day. The first proposed death as the penalty for nineteen offences; the second reduced the number of capital offences to twelve;

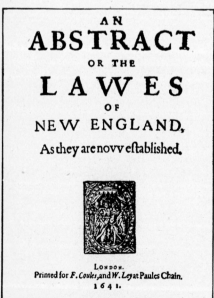

73 Title-page of John Cotton, *An Abstract of the Lawes of New England*, London, 1641, from the original in the New York Public Library

while in England, according to Blackstone, there were one hundred and sixty offences punishable by death. The most drastic feature of Cotton's code was that he suggested death as the penalty for various offences against theocracy, such as blasphemy, heresy, and profaning the Lord's day, those who reviled the chief magistrates, and even incorrigibly rebellious children.

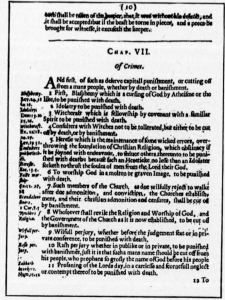

74 Text page from John Cotton, *An Abstract of the Lawes of New England*, London, 1641, from the original in the New York Public Library

ANNE HUTCHINSON, *ca.* 1600–1643

ANNE HUTCHINSON came to Massachusetts, bringing her husband and children, because she loved to hear John Cotton preach. She was a public-spirited woman, with a keen mind and a ready, sharp tongue, a born leader, a feminist, and a mystic. She began holding weekly meetings for women, at which she discussed the sermons of the previous Sabbath, expounded her own views and revelations, and criticized the ministers. John Cotton and her brother-in-law, John Wheelwright, whom she wished the Boston church to elect as Cotton's colleague, were the only ministers in the colony, she asserted, who had entered into the covenant of grace; John Wilson and the rest were in bondage to a covenant of works. She ridiculed the "black-coats" taught in the "ninnyversity," and would rise and leave the church when Wilson began to preach. The conflict thus engendered shook the colony to its foundations. Her teaching was a protest against the Old Testament legalism of Puritan ministers; but her doctrine that the Holy Ghost dwells in a true believer in a personal union so intimate as to become one being with him, with its corollaries of direct divine inspiration and of the relative unimportance of good works, seemed to them to lead to sheer spiritual anarchy. She and Wheelwright, who had proclaimed that those under the covenant of works were "Antichrists," were banished from the colony. Her husband, wrote Winthrop, was "a man of a very mild temper and weak parts, and wholly guided by his wife."

75 Statue of Anne Hutchinson and her daughter, Susanna, by Cyrus Dallin (1861–), in the State House, Boston

THOMAS HOOKER, 1586–1647, PROPHET OF DEMOCRACY

ON the same ship with John Cotton was another refugee no less eminent — Thomas Hooker, who had preached at Chelmsford in Essex with boldness and great power. He became pastor of a strong church at Newtown, now Cambridge. He opposed the restriction of the suffrage to church members and criticized the lack of a fundamental body of laws to safeguard the rights of the people. "After his coming," wrote an old historian, "it was observed that many of the freemen grew to be very jealous of their liberties." In 1636, he led his congregation to Connecticut, where they founded Hartford. In a sermon before the General Court which was to frame the Fundamental Orders of Connecticut, he expounded the principles that "the foundation of authority is laid in the free consent of the people"; that "the choice of public magistrates belongs unto the people by God's own allowance"; and that "they who have power to appoint officers and magistrates have the right also to set the bounds and limitations of the power and place unto which they call them." He added, what proponents of democracy sometimes forget, that the right of suffrage which belongs to the people ought not to be "exercised according to their humors, but according to the blessed will and law of God."

76 Thomas Hooker, from the design for the Hooker Memorial Window in Center Church, Hartford, Conn.
© Tiffany Studios, 1900

77 From the bronze tablet, *Departure for the Pequot War*, by J. Massey Rhind (1860–), for the Department of Public Parks, Hartford, Conn.

DEPARTURE FOR THE PEQUOT WAR

WITHIN a year, the Connecticut Colony had to fight for its life against the Pequot Indians, who had been roused to fury by a punitive expedition under John Endicott. The tablet represents Mr. Hooker invoking the blessing of God upon the little army of ninety-two men which set out to attack the Pequot village. Samuel Stone, Hooker's colleague, who went with them as chaplain, stands directly behind him. The Indian in the foreground is Uncas, sachem of the Mohegans, and ally of the English. The Old Testament principles of the Puritans are evidenced in Captain John Mason's account of Stone's services: "Mr. Stone was sent to preach and pray with those who went out in those Engagements against the Pequots. He lent his best Assistance and Counsel in the Management of those Designs, and the Night in which the Engagement was . . . he was with the Lord alone, wrestling with Him by Faith and Prayer, and surely his Prayers prevailed for a blessing; and in the very Time when our Israel was engaging with the blood-thirsty Pequots, he was in the Top of the Mount, and so held up his Hand, that Israel prevailed."

THE FOUNDING OF NEW HAVEN

WHEN Archbishop Laud learned that John Davenport, vicar of St. Stephen's Church, London, had escaped to New England, he was so incensed that he declared, "My arm shall reach him even there." With Theophilus Eaton, a wealthy parishioner who had been a boyhood friend, and a company of substantial London citizens, Davenport in 1638 established the colony of New Haven upon land purchased from the Quinnipiack Indians. Without charter or governmental constitution of any kind, they undertook to found a commonwealth "whose design is religion." "In the laying of the first foundations of this plantation and jurisdiction, upon a full debate with due and serious consideration it was agreed, concluded and settled as a fundamental law, not to be disputed or questioned hereafter, that the judicial laws of God, as they were delivered by Moses and expounded in other parts of Scripture, so far as they are a defence to the moral law, and neither typical nor ceremonial nor had reference to Canaan, shall be accounted of moral and binding equity and force, and as God shall help shall be a constant direction for all proceedings here, and a general rule in all courts of Justice." A year later they met to decide finally upon the form of their government. They unanimously reaffirmed their agreement to be directed in all matters by "those rules which the Scripture holds forth"; declared their intention, one and all, to seek admission to the fellowship of the church which they proposed to organize; and decided that only church members should exercise the full rights of citizenship. They chose twelve of their number as a committee, who then named seven men to constitute the church by "convenanting together and then receiving others into their fellowship." These seven men organized themselves, later, as a civil court, to membership in which they admitted others who had qualified as church members, and then proceeded to elect a Governor (Theophilus Eaton) and other civil officers. New Haven was the most theocratic of the colonies.

78 John Davenport Memorial Window, designed by Louis C. Tiffany (1848–), in Center Church, New Haven, Conn.

79   *The First Thanksgiving*, from the painting by W. L. Taylor (1854–1926), in *The Ladies' Home Journal*,
Nov. 1897. © The Curtis Publishing Co., Philadelphia

THANKSGIVING DAYS AND FAST DAYS

THE gathering of the first harvest at Plymouth in 1621 was celebrated by a week of joyous festivity. "Our harvest being gotten in, our Governor sent four men on fowling . . . they four in one day killed as much fowl, as with a little help beside, served the Company almost a week, at which time amongst other Recreations, we exercised our Arms, many of the Indians coming amongst us, and amongst the rest their greatest King Massasoit, with some ninety men, whom for three days we entertained and feasted, and they went out and killed five Deer, which they brought to the Plantation, and bestowed on our Governor, and upon the Captain, and others. And although it be not always so plentiful, as it was at this time with us, yet by the goodness of God, we are so far from want, that we often wish you partakers of our plenty." — *Mourt's Relation.*

In 1623 a prolonged drought threatened failure of the crops at Plymouth. This, with other sufferings, led the Pilgrims to appoint a day of fasting and prayer to God, beseeching his mercy. A refreshing series of showers, which began the next morning, seemed to be a direct answer to their petitions; and their immediate needs were relieved by the return of Captain Standish with a supply of provisions. "Having these many signs of God's favor and acceptation," wrote Edward Winslow, "we thought it would be great ingratitude, if secretly we should smother up the same, or content ourselves with private thanksgiving for that which by private prayer could not be obtained. And therefore another solemn day was set apart and appointed for that end; wherein we returned glory, honor, and praise, with all thankfulness, to our good God, which dealt so graciously with us . . ." It became the custom of the authorities in New England, to appoint occasional days of fasting or of thanksgiving for specific causes.

80 Earliest known Thanksgiving Proclamation, from the original in the Archives of the Commonwealth of Massachusetts, Boston

81 Proclamation for a Fast, New Haven, June 15, 1709, from the original in the Massachusetts Historical Society, Boston

82   A Thanksgiving Dinner Among the Puritans, from a drawing by J. W. Ehninger (1827–99),
in *Harper's Weekly*, Nov. 30, 1867

THE ANNUAL THANKSGIVING DAY

BECAUSE of the dependence of the colonists upon a propitious seedtime and an abundant harvest, it was natural to appoint a day of fasting and prayer in the spring, and a day of thanksgiving to God in the fall. So developed gradually the custom of appointing annual fast days and thanksgiving days. The latter day, especially, has become firmly established in the life of the American people. Thanksgiving Day, the last Thursday in November, early became a day, not only of religious devotion, but of family reunions, with rejoicing and festivity. It is thus related to the harvest festival as well as to the thanksgiving days of the Pilgrims and Puritans.

PREACHING TO THE INDIANS

SUCCESSIVE enactments of the General Court of Massachusetts in 1644, 1645, and 1646, urged the ministers of the colony to "make known the heavenly counsel of God among the Indians." An inspirer of these appeals and the first to respond to them was John Eliot, minister at Roxbury. After two years of study of the Indian language, he ventured to preach his first sermon to them in their own tongue on October 28, 1646. Five years later, at Natick, he organized the first Protestant Indian church. At the same time, Thomas Mayhew, 1621–57, son of Thomas Mayhew, 1592–1682, the grantee of Martha's Vineyard, was preaching with marked success to the Indians on that island. His work was continued, after his death at sea, first by his venerable father, then by his son John (d. 1689) and his grandson Experience, 1673–1758. By 1647 the "Praying Indians," as the converts were called, numbered about four thousand, and there were at least seven Indian churches, ministered to by native teachers as well as English missionaries. Though the outbreak of King Philip's War crippled his work, it was continued with patient persistence. Eliot, whose self-denying labors earned for him the title "Apostle to the Indians," protested vigorously against the decision of the Massachusetts authorities to sell some of the captives of war into slavery. "To sell souls for money seemeth to me a dangerous merchandise." His remonstrance was in vain. Among those sold were the wife and son of Philip.

83   John Eliot Preaching to the Indians, from an engraving, 1856, by John Chester Buttree (1821–93),
after a drawing by Johannes Adam Oretel (1823–1909), in possession of the publishers

THE COMPANY FOR THE PROPAGATION OF THE GOSPEL IN NEW ENGLAND

ELIOT sent to England a narrative of the beginning of his work, which was published in 1647 with the title *The Day-Breaking, if not the Sun-Rising of the Gospell with the Indians in New England.* In 1649, as a result of the interest which this and subsequent tracts aroused, Parliament chartered "A Corporation for the Promoting and Propagating the Gospel of Jesus Christ in New England," and twelve thousand pounds was soon raised to be invested as its endowment. When Charles II came to the throne, this body was reorganized and a new charter granted, with the name "The Company for Propagation of the Gospel in New England, and the parts adjacent in America." Unlike its later analogue, The Society for Propagating the Gospel in Foreign Parts (see cut 151), this Company consistently directed its attention to the support of missionary work among the Indians. After the Revolution, it transferred its interest to Canada; and citizens of Massachusetts, in 1787, organized the Society for Propagating the Gospel among the Indians and Others in North America, the first home missionary society in the new nation.

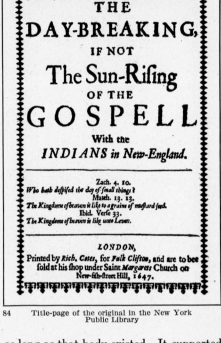

84 Title-page of the original in the New York Public Library

ELIOT'S *CATECHISM*

THE New England Company, as it was briefly called, administered its gifts through the Commissioners of the United Colonies, as long as that body existed. It supported the work of Eliot, the Mayhews, Richard Bourne, and others, by paying salaries, printing books, furnishing goods, tools and clothing to the natives, and helping to educate promising Indian youths. Eliot was indefatigable in his efforts to afford to the Indians printed materials for the understanding of the principles of the Christian religion, and the Company loyally paid the bills. Few missionary enterprises have been better supplied with resources for publication. Eliot's *Catechism*, printed in 1653, was the first book in the language of the Massachusetts Indians. It was followed by many other books intended for their religious education.

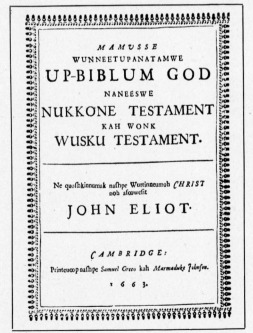

85 Title-page of the original in the New York Public Library

86 From John Eliot, *The Indian Primer*, Cambridge, 1669, original in the Edinburgh Museum

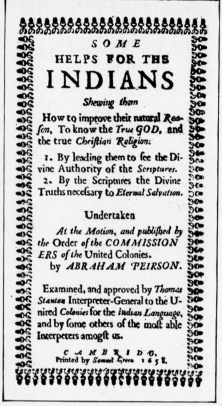

SOME
HELPS FOR THE
INDIANS

Shewing them

How to improve their natural Reason, To know the True GOD, and
the true Christian Religion:

1. By leading them to see the Divine Authority of the Scriptures.
2. By the Scriptures the Divine
Truths necessary to Eternal Salvation.

Undertaken

At the Motion, and published by
the Order of the COMMISSION
ERS of the United Colonies.
by ABRAHAM PEIRSON.

Examined, and approved by Thomas
Stanton Interpreter-General to the U-
nited Colonies for the indian Language,
and by some others of the most able
Interpreters amongst us.

C A M B R I D G.
Printed by Samuel Green 1658.

87 Title-page of Abraham Pierson, *Some Helps for the Indians*, Cambridge, Mass

SOME HELPS FOR THE INDIANS

IN 1661–63 Eliot's translation of the Bible was published — the first Bible to be printed in America. He translated a number of devotional books, such as Richard Baxter's *Call to the Unconverted*. He imported primers to teach the Indians to read English, moreover, and finally wrote one himself, from which the Lord's Prayer is here reproduced. Eliot was minister of the Roxbury church for fifty-eight years, and for

[4]

Some helps for
Poshshe Airenamáwetouwüngash wutshe
the Indians, shewing them
Eánsketámbawg, Okkekôodemúnganáuwaus
how to improve their natural Reason
ten auwárshan nejek arumbáuwe penauwuawunk
to know the only true
wauhshán webe waugh wauwérhummat Man-
God, and (the true Christian
do Iehovah, quah werramáuwe Christianáu-
religion First by lead-
we routásowank. Negónne spe summôoa-
ing them to see the divine Autho-
warránau nejek kenáwmen Mándowe tôuh-
rity of the Scriptures
kretássowunk wutshe God wuskwhégansh.
Secondly by the Scriptures the
Néesteetáuwe spe God wuskwhégansh mán-
divine Truths necessary
dowáious wérramauwüngansh queraúhikka-
to eternal Salvation.
muks re mishéme kejáhiitawunk.

NAT

88 From Abraham Pierson, *Some Helps for the Indians*, Cambridge, 1658

forty-three years it shared his labors with the surrounding Indian villages. Among books by other missionaries, printed at the cost of the Corporation, was this catechism by Abraham Pierson, minister of the Church at Branford, Connecticut, entitled *Some Helps for the Indians*. In the eighteenth century, as the frontier was pushed westward, the Indians were served by the devoted labors of missionaries who came to live among them. Notable in this service were David Brainerd, the two John Sergeants (father and son) Jonathan Edwards, Stephen West, Gideon Hawley, and Samuel Kirkland. The English colonists never equalled the Spaniards, however, in their zeal to convert the Indian.

The Lords Prayer.

OUr Father which art in Hea-
ven, Hallowed be thy Name :
Thy Kingdome come : Thy will be
done in Earth, as it is in Heaven.
Give us this day our daily bread.
And forgive us our trespasses, as
we forgive them that trespass a-
gainst us. And lead us not into
temptation, but deliver us from evil.
For thine is the Kingdome, the
Power, and the Glory, for ever.
Amen.

A 6   Nooshun

89 From John Eliot, *The Indian Primer*, Cambridge, 1669, original in the Edinburgh Museum

The Lords Prayer

NOOshun kesukqut, wunnee-
tupantamunach koowesu-
onk. Peyaumooutch kukkeitassoo-
tamoonk. Toh anantaman ne n-
naj okheit, neane kesukqur. Ase-
kesukokish petukqunnegash as-
saminnean yeu kesukok. Ahquon-
tamaiinnean nummatcheseongash,
neane matchenehikqueagig nut-
ahquontamauounonog. Abqne
sagkompaguninnean en qutchhu-
aonganit, webe pohquohwussin-
nan wutch matchitut ; newutche
keitassóotamoonk , kutahtauun ,
menuhkesuork, sohsumoonk mi-
ebeme kah micheme Amen.

Nae.

90 From John Eliot, *The Indian Primer*, Cambridge, 1669, original in the Edinburgh Museum

RICHARD MATHER, 1596–1669

LETTERS from Cotton and Hooker helped to persuade Richard Mather, suspended from a notable ministry at Liverpool because he would not wear a surplice, to come to Massachusetts in 1635. Refusing several other calls, he settled at Dorchester and organized a church. His preaching was direct, "aiming to shoot his Arrows not over his people's heads, but into their Hearts and Consciences." "The Lord gave him an excellent faculty in making abstruse things plain." Four of his six sons were ministers; and eighty clergymen were numbered among his descendants in a list made in 1890. The best known of these are Increase Mather, his son, and Cotton Mather, his grandson. The three men, father, son, and grandson, gave to Massachusetts nearly a century of devoted and distinguished service in places of leadership.

91 Richard Mather, from the original portrait, artist unknown, in the American Antiquarian Society, Worcester, Mass.

THE CONGREGATIONAL SYNODS

LIKE John Cotton, Richard Mather was a stanch defender of "the Congregational way," as opposed to the Presbyterian polity toward which Puritanism in old England was tending. He drafted the Cambridge Platform which was adopted in 1648 by a general council of ministers and lay "messengers" from the churches of New England. This was an ecclesiastical constitution defining the principles of Congregational polity and discipline, affirming the independence of the local church, yet declaring the fellowship of the churches. The Synod, as the council was somewhat improperly called, approved "for the substance thereof" the then newly published Westminster Confession. It was the only general council of the Congregational churches in America to be called until 1852.

Subsequent Synods, in 1662 and 1680, were attended by ministers and messengers from the Massachusetts churches only. The latter of these, known as the Reform Synod, was called in the time of discouragement succeeding King Philip's War, to inquire "What are the evils that have provoked the Lord to bring his judgments on New England?" and "What is to be done that so these evils may be reformed?" Among the evils enumerated were: pride and contentiousness, profanity, irreverence, Sabbath-breaking, neglect of the church, laxity in family discipline and irregularity in family worship, intemperance and the frequenting of taverns. The Synod also concerned itself with doctrine, and adopted a Congregational Confession of Faith, based upon a revision and adaptation of the Westminster Confession by Congregationalists in England.

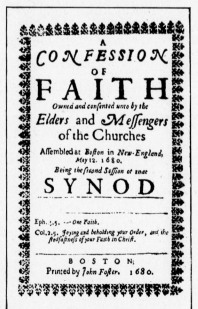

92 Title-page of the original in the New York Public Library

A Confession of Faith. 5

eties, which are to be ordered by the Light of Nature, and Christian Prudence, according to the general Rules of the Word, which are always to be observed.

VII.

All things in Scripture are not alike plain in themselves, nor alike clear unto all: yet those things which are necessary to be known, believed and observed for salvation, are so clearly propounded and opened in some place of Scripture or other, that not only the learned, but the unlearned, in a due use of the ordinary means, may attain unto a sufficient understanding of them.

VIII.

The Old Testament in Hebrew (which was the native Language of the People of God of old) and the New Testament in Greek (which at the time of writing of it was most generally known to the Nations) being immediately inspired by God, and by his singular care and providence kept pure in all Ages, are therefore Authentical; so as in all Controversies of Religion the Church is finally to appeal unto them. But because these Original Tongues are not known to all the people of God, who have right unto and interest in the Scriptures, and are com-

93 From *A Confession of Faith Owned and Consented Unto by the Elders and Messengers of the Churches*, Boston, 1680

94 Increase Mather, from the original portrait, artist unknown, in the American Antiquarian Society, Worcester,
Mass.

INCREASE MATHER, 1639–1723

INCREASE MATHER was for fifty-nine years minister of the Second (North) Church in Boston, then the largest and most influential of the Congregational churches; and he was for sixteen years President of Harvard College. His enemies called him "the Mahomet of New England." Sent to London as the agent of Massachusetts after its charter was annulled, he succeeded, after four years of labor, in obtaining a new charter which annexed Maine and Plymouth to Massachusetts and secured to its people a larger measure of legislative freedom and appointive power than was enjoyed by any other colony. He succeeded, besides, in conserving the prerogatives and protecting the endowments of Harvard College. He was opposed by extremists of quite different sorts — by royalists who regretted his success and by conservative Puritans who would be satisfied with nothing less than a renewal of the old charter, as well as by a group of younger men who were less strict than he in their views of the church. Their ingratitude has been reflected in the traditional estimate of him as narrow-minded and self-seeking, a misconception from which a truer reading of the facts is now emancipating historians.

COTTON MATHER, 1663–1728

SON of Increase Mather and grandson of John Cotton and Richard Mather, Cotton Mather was graduated from Harvard College at sixteen, and at eighteen was invited to become pastor of the First Church at New Haven. He chose rather to assist his father at the Second Church in Boston, and in 1685 he was ordained as its pastor and his father's colleague. Fearing that an impediment of speech unfitted him for the ministry, he had studied medicine; and throughout his life, his interests were as wide as the knowledge of his day. His advocacy of inoculation for smallpox aroused such opposition that an attempt was made to burn his home. He wrote voluminously on the history of New England, on witchcraft, and in favor of temperance, Indian missions, the education of negroes, public libraries, and the organization of philanthropic societies, as well as on the Bible and theological subjects. The most widely read and oftenest republished of his books was *Essays to do Good*, of which Benjamin Franklin wrote: "It gave me such a turn of thinking, as to have an influence on my conduct through life. . . . If I have been, as you seem to think, a useful citizen, the public owes all the advantage of it to that book." For all but five years of his ministry, Cotton Mather was colleague to his father, who remained in active service until his death at the age of eighty-five. Unwillingly, father and son witnessed the passing of the old theocratic order and the coming into vogue of new ideas and customs which they could not wholly approve.

95 Cotton Mather, from the original portrait by Peter
Pelham (1684–1751), in the American Antiquarian Society, Worcester, Mass.

BONIFACIUS.

AN ESSAY
Upon the GOOD, that is to be
Devifed and Defigned,
BY THOSE
Who Defire to Anfwer the Great END
of *Life*, and to DO GOOD
While they *Live*.

A BOOK Offered,
Firft, in General, unto all CHRISTIANS,
in a PERSONAL Capacity, or in
a RELATIVE.

Then more Particularly,
Unto MAGISTRATES, unto MINISTERS,
unto PHYSICIANS, unto LAWYERS,
unto SCHOLEMASTERS, unto Wealthy
GENTLEMEN, unto feveral Sorts of
OFFICERS, unto CHURCHES, and
unto all SOCIETIES of a Religious
Character and Intention. With Humble
PROPOSALS, of Unexceptionable
METHODS, to *Do Good* in the World.

Eph. VI. 18 *Knowing that whatfoever Good thing any
man does, the fame fhall he receive of the Lord.*

BOSTON in *N England*: Printed by B. *Green*, for
Samuel Gerrifb at his Shop in Corn Hill. 1 7 1 6

96   Title-page of the original in the New
York Public Library

97 *Torturing of a Knave and Two Witches at Cologne, 1589*, from a contemporary handbill published at Nürnberg, in the Kgl. Kupferstich-Kabinett, Berlin, Germany

THE WITCHCRAFT DELUSION IN EUROPE

FROM the fourteenth century to the eighteenth Europe was cursed with the witchcraft delusion. The theory, first definitely formulated by the University of Paris, was that the witch had renounced her baptism and taken Satan for her God, surrendering herself to him, body and soul, to be used as the instrument of his evil purposes. She had thus become the enemy of her fellow creatures, and should be hunted out and destroyed as one would destroy the seeds of a deadly pestilence. All over Europe the witch fires were fed. Folk who were queer or had incurred the enmity of their neighbors were condemned as witches and burned at the stake. The victims of this persecution numbered at least a half million. Trials and executions for witchcraft did not cease in continental Europe until the end of the eighteenth century.

THE PERSECUTION OF WITCHES IN ENGLAND

ENGLAND was the last of the European countries to succumb to the witchcraft delusion, and the first to awaken to its baseless horror. King James VI of Scotland, "the wisest fool in Christendom," had published a book on *Daemonologie* in 1597; and upon his accession to the throne of England in 1603 as James I secured the passage of a law condemning to death any one who "shall use, practise or exercise any Invocation or Conjuration of any evil and wicked Spirit, or shall consult, covenant with, entertain, employ, feed, or reward any evil and wicked Spirit to or for any intent or purpose." A technique of examination was developed, and "witch-finding" became a lucrative profession. The most notorious of the witch-finders, Matthew Hopkins, in 1645–47, sent nearly three hundred victims to the gallows. The tradition that he met a like fate is doubtless untrue, but is evidence of the detestation in which he came to be held.

98 From an engraving, 1792, of the frontispiece in Matthew Hopkins, *Discoverie of Witches*, London, 1647, reprinted in J. Caulfield, *Memoirs of Remarkable Persons*, Vol. II, London, 1813

ONE mark of a witch, it was assumed, was the presence upon her body of insensible spots, which could be located by pricking with a pin. In 1650 the common council of Newcastle brought from Scotland a noted witchpricker, contracting to pay his expenses and twenty shillings for every witch he found. The bellman was sent through the town, inviting all to make complaints. Thus

99   From Ralph Gardiner, *England's Grievance Discovered in relation to the Coal Trade*, London, 1655

thirty women were collected at the town hall, stripped and put to the pricking test. Fourteen women and one man were tried, found guilty, and, despite their protestations of innocence, were executed. Like epidemics of "witch alarm" were suffered by many other towns of England. At Bury St. Edmunds in Suffolk, sixteen women and two men were executed on August 27, 1645, and forty or fifty more a few weeks later.

A SEVENTEENTH–CENTURY "BEST SELLER"

A SEVENTEENTH-CENTURY "best seller" was Joseph Glanvil's *Some Philosophical Considerations touching Witches and Witchcraft*. First published in 1666, it passed through a number of editions, and finally appeared, revised and amplified, as *Saducismus Triumphatus*, which might be translated as "Unbelief Conquered." An Oxford M.A., Chaplain to King Charles II, and a philosophical reasoner of no mean ability, sceptically inclined, and versed in the new methods of Descartes, Glanvil was nevertheless woefully credulous of the "choice collection of modern relations" passed on to him by "honest and honourable friends."

100   Frontispiece and title-page from Joseph Glanvil, *Saducismus Triumphatus*, London, 1681   101

THE WITCHCRAFT EPIDEMIC AT SALEM VILLAGE

THE settlers in America shared the common belief in witchcraft, and King James' law was acknowledged in the colonies generally. In Virginia, as late as 1706, one Grace Sherwood was tried for witchcraft, and remanded to the common jail, to be kept in irons. In 1718, Pennsylvania specifically reënacted the statute of King James concerning witches, and this remained the law of the colony and the state until 1794. In view of the rigors of frontier life and the common belief that the Indians worshiped the devil, many cases of prosecution for witchcraft might have been expected. Yet the fact was just the opposite. They were surprisingly few. In over a century and a half, while victims in Europe were numbered in the hundred thousands, thirty-two persons were executed as witches in the English colonies, and two died in jail. None were burned.

Twenty-two of these thirty-four victims were at Salem Village in Massachusetts, where, from February, 1692 to January, 1693, there raged America's one epidemic of witch alarm. A special court of Oyer and Terminer, appointed by the royal Governor, tried the cases. Here are reproduced the death warrant of Bridget Bishop, a disreputable old woman, keeper of a drinking tavern, who was the first to be hanged; and a painting of the scene at the trial of George Jacobs, an aged farmer whose only crimes seem to have been that he had enemies, some property, and a wart that was interpreted as a witch mark.

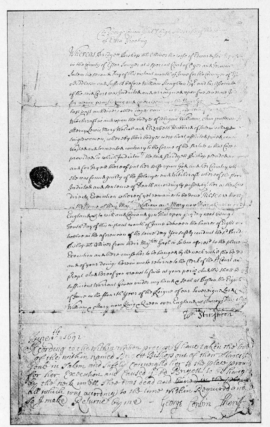

102   Warrant for the execution of Bridget Bishop, from the original in the Essex Institute, Salem, Mass.

103   *Trial of George Jacobs*, from the painting by T. H. Mattison (1868–), in the Essex Institute, Salem, Mass.

104   From the painting *Accused of Witchcraft*, by Douglas Volk (1856–), in the Corcoran Gallery, Washington

THE MINISTERS ADVISE AGAINST "SPECTRAL EVIDENCE"

THE trials at Salem hinged for the most part upon "spectral evidence." The claim of an afflicted person to have seen the specter of the accused, either in her own likeness or in that of an animal, was accepted as valid evidence of guilt, the presumption being that the devil could not thus simulate the likeness of an inno-

cent person. English courts accepted such "evidence"; Sir Matthew Hale, Chief Justice of England, and "allowed on all hands to be the most profound lawyer of his time," accepted it, and condemned "witches" to death because of it. The judges at Salem followed this precedent, against the advice of the foremost ministers of the colony, led by Increase Mather, who insisted that other evidence should be required, since "a Daemon may, by God's permission, appear even to ill purposes, in the Shape of an innocent, yea, and a virtuous Man." Believing in the reality of witchcraft, as did all but a very few men of their time, and anxious that it should not take root in New England, these ministers yet dissented strongly from the methods of the court. Their views prevailed with Governor Phips, who stopped its proceedings in October, 1692.

DISAPPROVAL OF COURT METHODS

THOMAS BRATTLE, in a letter written on the eighth of October, 1692, named Increase Mather and Samuel Willard as leaders in the group "that do utterly condemn the said proceedings, and do freely deliver their judgment in the case to be this, viz., that these methods will utterly ruin and undo poor N. E. . . . The Rev. Elders, almost throughout the whole country are very much dissatisfied. . . . Some of the Boston justices were resolved rather to throw up their commissions than be active in disturbing the liberty of their majestie's subjects, merely on the accusations of these afflicted, possessed children."

105   From Increase Mather, *Cases of Conscience Concerning Evil Spirits*, Boston, 1693, in the New York Public Library

74   *Mr. Brattle's Account of the Witchcraft,*

that there was as much ground, in the hour of it, to countenance the said Groton woman, and to apprehend and
imprison, on her accusations, as there is now to countenance these afflicted persons, and to apprehend and imprison on their accusations. But furthermore, it is worthy
of our deepest consideration, that in the conclusion, (after
multitudes have been imprisoned, and many have been put
to death,) these afflicted persons should own that all was a
mere fancy and delusion of the devil's, as the Groton woman did own and acknowledge with respect to herself; if,
I say, in after times, this be acknowledged by them, how
can the justices, judges, or any else concerned in these matters, look back upon these things without the greatest of
sorrow and grief imaginable? I confess to you, it makes me
tremble when I seriously consider of this thing. I have
heard that the chief judge* has expressed himself very
hardly of the accused woman at Groton, as though he believed her to be a witch to this day: but by such as knew
the said woman, this is judged a very uncharitable opinion
of the said judge, and I do not understand that any are
proselyted thereto.

Rev. Sir, these things I cannot but admire and wonder
at. Now, if so be it is the effect of my dulness that I thus
admire, I hope you will pity, not censure me: but if, on the
contrary, these things are just matter of admiration, I know
that you will join with me in expressing your admiration
hereat.

The chief judge is very zealous in these proceedings, and
says, he is very clear as to all that hath as yet been acted by
this court, and, as far as ever I could perceive, is very impatient in hearing any thing that looks another way. I
very highly honour and reverence the wisdom and integrity
of the said judge, and hope that this matter shall not diminish
my veneration for his honour; however, I cannot but say,
my great fear is, that wisdom and counsel are withheld from
his honour as to this matter, which yet I look upon not so
much as a judgment to his honour as to this poor land.

But although the chief judge, and some of the other
judges, be very zealous in these proceedings, yet this you
may take for a truth, that there are several about the Bay,
men for understanding, judgment, and piety, inferior to
                                                          few,

* William Stoughton, Lieutenant Governour.

in the county of Essex, 1692.   75

few, if any, in N. E. that do utterly condemn the said proceedings, and do freely deliver their judgment in the case
to be this, viz. that these methods will utterly ruin and undo
poor N. E. I shall nominate some of these to you, viz.
The Hon. Simon Bradstreet, Esq. [our late governor]; the
Hon. Thomas Danforth, Esq. [our late deputy governor];
the Rev. Mr. Increase Mather, and the Rev. Mr. Samuel
Willard. Major N. Saltonstall, Esq. who was one of the
judges, has left the court, and is very much dissatisfied with
the proceedings of it. Excepting Mr. Hale, Mr. Noyes,
and Mr. Parris, the Rev. Elders, almost throughout the
whole country are very much dissatisfied. Several of the
late justices, viz. Thomas Graves, Esq. N. Byfield, Esq.
Francis Foxcroft, Esq. are much dissatisfied; also several
of the present justices; and in particular, some of the Boston justices, were resolved rather to throw up their commissions than be active in disturbing the liberty of their
majesties' subjects, merely on the accusations of these afflicted, possessed children.

Finally; the principal gentlemen in Boston, and there-
about, are generally agreed that irregular and dangerous
methods have been taken as to these matters.

Sir, I would not willingly lead you into any error, and
therefore would desire you to note,

1. That when I call these afflicted *"the afflicted children,"*
I would not be understood as though I meant, that all that
are afflicted are *children*: there are several young men and
women that are afflicted, as well as children: but this term
has most prevailed among us, because of the younger sort
that were first afflicted, and therefore I make use of it.

2. That when I speak of the Salem gentlemen, I would
not be understood as though I meant every individual gentleman in Salem; nor yet as though I meant, that there
were no men but in Salem that run upon these notions:
some term they must have, and this seems not improper, because in Salem this sort of gentlemen does most abound.

3. That other justices in the country, besides the Salem
justices, have issued out their warrants, and imprisoned, on
the accusations of the afflicted as aforesaid; and therefore,
when I speak of the Salem justices, I do not mean them
exclusively.

4. That as to the above mentioned judges, that are
                                                commissioned

106   From a letter by Thomas Brattle, October 8, 1692, in the *Collections* of the Massachusetts
Historical Society, 1798

THE DECLINE OF WITCHCRAFT

The diary of Samuel Sewall, one of the justices, records the
opinion of his friend Thomas Danforth, late deputy-governor,
that the court cannot proceed "except there be some better
consent of Ministers and People." There was a sharp reaction on the part of the people generally when they began
to realize the absurdity, even measured by the beliefs of the
time, of so many witches in so small a community.

Cotton Mather, still a young man of twenty-nine, was
less judicial than his father; but the charge, first made by
a merchant named Robert Calef, that he, or the Puritan
clergy generally, fostered the witchcraft delusion and
furthered the excitement at Salem, for sake of their own
glory, is baseless. It is to Cotton Mather's credit that he
was the one man who sought to heal the afflicted persons
by rational methods of rest, ordered diet, kindly fellowship
and religious faith. He received several, at different times,
into his own home, and through such treatment effected
cures and restored them to society.

The Salem witchcraft episode, however, did not end the
belief in witches. Such a superstition was a logical outgrowth
of the theology of the day. Men had not yet arrived at
sufficient knowledge of nature to be able to explain puzzling
phenomena without reference to the supernatural. Gradually the growth of science purged religion of the old superstitions. The specter of the witch faded. The clergy taught less
about the wiles of the Devil and more about the love of God.

MORE
WONDERS
OF THE
INVISIBLE WORLD:
Or, The Wonders of the
Invisible World,
Display'd in Five Parts.

Part I. An Account of the Sufferings of *Margaret Rule*, Written by
the Reverend Mr. *C. M.*
P. II. Several Letters to the Author, *&c.* And his Reply relating
to Witchcraft.
P. III. The Differences between the Inhabitants of *Salem*-Village, and
Mr. *Parris* their Minister, in *New-England.*
P. IV. Letters of a Gentleman uninterested, Endeavouring to prove
the received Opinions about Witchcraft to be Orthodox. With short
Essays to their Answers.
P. V. A short Historical Accout of Matters of Fact in that Affair.

To which is added, A Postscript relating to a Book intitled, The
Life of Sir WILLIAM PHIPS.

Collected by *Robert Calef*, Merchant, of *Boston* in *New-England.*

Licensed and Entred according to Order.

LONDON:
Printed for *Nath. Hillar*, at the *Princes-Arms*, in *Leaden-Hall-street*,
over against St. *Mary-Ax*, and *Joseph Collyer*, at the *Golden-Bible*,
on *London-Bridge.* 1700.

107   Title-page of Robert Calef, *More Wonders of the Invisible
World*, from the original in the New York Public Library

108 Declaration of Sorrow of the Jurors, from Robert Calef, *More Wonders of the Invisible World*, London, 1700

THE PENITENCE OF MASSACHUSETTS

In one respect the episode at Salem was unique in the long annals of the witchcraft delusion. It was publicly repented. By vote of the General Court, January 14, 1697, was set apart as a day of prayer and fasting throughout Massachusetts, "That so all God's people may offer up Supplications unto him . . . that all Iniquity may be put away . . . that He would shew us what we know not, and help us, wherein we have done amiss, to do so no more;. and, especially, that whatever mistakes on either hand have been fallen into, either by the body of this People or any Orders of them, referring to the late Tragedy raised amongst us by Satan and his Instruments, through the awful Judgment of God, He would humble us therefor, and pardon all the Errors of His Servants and People that desire to love His Name; and be atoned to His Land." The twelve jurors published a declaration of sorrow that "for want of Knowledge" they had accepted "such evidence against the accused as, on further consideration and better information, we justly fear was insufficient," and humbly begged the forgiveness of God and of man. Samuel Sewall, one of the judges, rose in his pew at the South Church in Boston, and made public confession of a sense of guilt for his share in the tragedy, desiring "to take the Blame and shame of it, Asking pardon of men, And especially desiring prayers that God would pardon that sin and all other his sins." In 1711, damages were paid to the heirs of the Salem victims, and attainder was removed, restoring them to the full rights of citizenship. This public repentance of Massachusetts helped to awaken England to the folly and wrong of the witchcraft delusion.

JOHN WISE'S VINDICATION OF DEMOCRACY

In 1705, a series of Proposals was made by a committee of Massachusetts ministers providing for the organization of ministerial associations, to have charge of the licensure of ministers, and of permanent councils of "consociated churches," whose decisions should be binding under penalty of the withdrawal of fellowship.

These Proposals were strongly opposed as contrary to Congregational liberty, and were not adopted. They were attacked in two brilliant books, *The Churches Quarrel Espoused* and *A Vindication of the Government of New England Churches*, by John Wise (1652–1725), pastor at Ipswich. Under Governor Andros, Mr. Wise had suffered fine, suspension from the ministry, and imprisonment for leading his town in refusal to pay a tax not levied by a representative assembly. He had thus been the first conspicuous American opponent of taxation without representation. Now he asserted boldly that "Democracy is Christ's government in church and State"; that "Power is originally in the people"; and that "By a natural right all men are born free." He brought to clear expression the democratic tendencies of Congregationalism, and helped to determine its future course. In 1772, nearly fifty years after his death, his works were reprinted, and two editions were required to meet the demand of a people about to declare their political independence upon the basis of principles such as he had expounded.

109 From John Wise, *A Vindication of the Government of New England Churches*, Boston, 1772

110 Meetinghouse at Sandown, New Hampshire, courtesy of the Society
for the Preservation of New England Antiquities, Boston

111 Deerfield Meetinghouse, built 1696, from a print based on a contemporary drawing made in 1704, courtesy of Frances and Mary Allen

THE NEW ENGLAND MEETINGHOUSE

"MEETINGHOUSES," the Puritans called the buildings which they erected for the public worship of God. They applied the term "church" only to the organization of believers who met there to engage in worship. Cotton Mather wrote that he "found no just ground in Scripture to apply such a trope as church to a house for public assembly." The seventeenth-century meetinghouses were simple buildings — square wooden structures with hipped roof, surmounted, if the church could afford it, with a belfry containing a bell. In the eighteenth century these buildings began to be replaced by the rectangular type of meetinghouse, with a tall spire, which remains characteristic of New England. The Old South Meetinghouse in Boston (see No. 119, Vol. XIII), erected in 1729, is an example of those built by the larger churches; the meetinghouse at Sandown, New Hampshire, erected in 1773–74, is an example of those built by the small town churches.

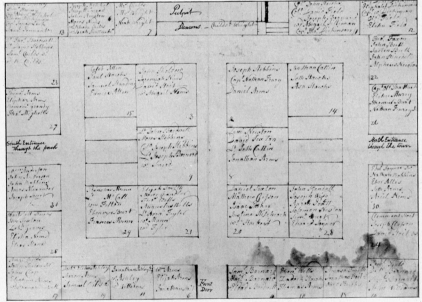

112   Plan of Seating, from the original plan in the Pocumtock Valley Memorial Association,
Deerfield, Mass.

SEATING THE MEETING

FOLK sat in assigned seats in these meetinghouses; and "seating the meeting" was an annual problem of grave importance and great delicacy, entrusted to a committee of the most influential men in the church. The "fore-seat," in front, on either side of the pulpit, was the place of highest dignity. The plan of seating here reproduced was for the meetinghouse at Deerfield. At the top of the sheet are the notations: "This plan reported March 7, 1783 was accepted in Town Meeting." "The numbers 1 to 31 indicate the rank and Dignity of each pew."

X—5

113   Sheep-Pen Pews in Old Ship Meetinghouse, Hingham, Mass., built 1681, courtesy of
the Hingham Historical Society

THE MEETINGHOUSE PEWS

Pews were square enclosures, with high walls, built by the holders at their own expense, with consequent diversity of pattern and material. They had narrow hinged seats which folded up against the sides of the pew when the occupants stood during the psalm-singing and the long prayers.

> And when at last the loud Amen
> Fell from aloft, how quickly then
> The seats came down with heavy rattle,
> Like musketry in fiercest battle.

Around the tops of the pews were usually little balustrades of wood. This corner in the Old Ship Meetinghouse at Hingham, Massachusetts, built in 1681, illustrates the type, though these pews are not as old as the building. On the floor of the meetinghouse at Sandown, New Hampshire, the pew tops have been cut down by removing the balustrades; but in the gallery the upper rail remains, though the spindles have disappeared. Tradition has it that the spindles were a great temptation to childish fingers, which would try them "to see which one would turn," for most of those that would turn would also squeak.

114   Interior of the Meetinghouse, Sandown, N. H., courtesy of the New
England Society for the Preservation of Antiquities, Boston

115   South Gallery, Meetinghouse, Sandown, N. H., courtesy of the
New England Society for the Preservation of Antiquities, Boston

LONG SERMONS AND PRAYERS

SERMONS and prayers were long. Nathaniel Ward, minister at Ipswich, confessed, "We have a strong weakness in New England that when we are speaking we know not how to conclude: we make many ends before we make an end." Cotton Mather's diary records that when he was ordained, a young man of twenty-two, he prayed about an hour and a quarter, and preached about an hour and three quarters. However long the prayer, the people stood; and this was said to be one of the reasons why the Congregationalists of Connecticut came to be known as the Standing Order. An hour glass was placed on a desk near the pulpit, and by it sat a sexton or clerk whose duty it was to turn it as often as the sands ran out. The ministers seem to have regarded this, not as a hint to stop preaching, but as encouragement to proceed. Sermons lasting two or three hours were common; some even ran through four turnings of the glass.

116 Hour glass, in the collections of the Pocumtock Valley Memorial Association, Deerfield, Mass.

117   Foot Stoves, in the collections of the Mattatuck Historical Society, Waterbury, Conn.

THE WINTER COLD

MEETINGHOUSES were unheated, and little foot stoves were carried to meeting for the comfort of women and children. In 1771, for fear of fire from forgotten foot stoves, the Old South Church voted "that the Sexton make diligent search on the Lord's Day evening and in the evening after a lecture, to see if any stoves are left in the house, and that if he find any there he take them to his own house; and it is expected that the owners of such stoves make reasonable satisfaction to the Sexton for his trouble before they take them away." Twelve years later, this church installed a large iron stove to heat the meetinghouse — a yielding to luxury which was sharply criticized in the *Evening Post* of January 25, 1783:

> Extinct our sacred fire of love,
>   Our zeal grown cold and dead,
> In the house of God we fix a stove
>   To warm us in their stead.

KEEPING THE LORD'S DAY

THE Puritans' favorite term for the first day of the week was the Lord's Day. By a Massachusetts law of 1646, attendance at public worship on the Lord's Day was required of everyone not incapacitated under penalty of a fine of five shillings for each absence. Constables were enjoined to "duly make search throughout the limits of their Towns" for absentees; and, during the time when the services were being held, "all Taverners, Victuallers, and Ordinaries, that are within one Mile of the Meetinghouse," were required to "Clear their houses of all persons able to go to meeting." Washington, traveling through Connecticut in 1789, rested on the Sabbath, and at "morning and evening service" at the meetinghouse, he "heard very lame discourses."

118   The Sabbath Inspection of Taverns, from an engraving by Hellaway, after the drawing by Kappes, in William Cullen Bryant and Sydney Gay, *Popular History of the United States*, Vol. II, New York, 1884

Boſton, On Tueſday the 23d Currant, Complaint being made to Edward Bromfield Eſqr. One of Her Majeſty's Council, and Juſtice of the Peace; of John Rogers & Son, of New London in Connecticut-Colony for Profanation of the Sabbath, in Driving of Cattle through the Town of Dedham to Boſton for a Market on the 21ſt Inſtant, being the Lords-Day; And opprobriouſly anſwering thoſe who diſſwaded him there-from; for which being brought before the ſaid Juſtice, and legally Convicted, he was Sentenced according to the Direction of the Law in that caſe, to pay the Fine of Twenty Shillings: He Appealed to the Quarter-Seſſions of the Peace, but obſtinately refuſed to give Security to proſecute his Appeal, and therefore is Committed to Priſon.

It was thought meet at the Deſire of ſeveral perſons to Publiſh this as a Caveat to others, to let People know, That Open Profanation of the LORDS-DAY, will not paſs Unpuniſhed. As alſo, Becauſe the man thus Fined, pretends himſelf to be a Sufferer for his Conſcience, and has therefore even courted the Inconveniencies that are come upon him. And whereas the Quakers have a while ſince endeavoured by their Falſe Addreſſes at home in England, to miſrepreſent the Government of this Province, for Making and Executing Several ſevere Laws, againſt their Friends, only for their Conſcientious Diſſent from the National Way; and not for any Evil Fact done by them: The Publick may be informed what kind of Severe Laws thoſe are, and what kind of Profanity may paſs for a Conſcientious Diſſent, among thoſe that Clamour againſt the Country for Perſecution, in Executing the Laws of God and man, of our Nation of England and this Province.

119   A Case of Sabbath Breaking, from the *Boston News Letter*, Oct. 29, 1705

THE TITHINGMAN

The pressure for seats of dignity in the meetinghouse was such that seating committees were usually betrayed into the unwisdom of seating all the boys together, either on the steps of the pulpit or in some of the lightly esteemed gallery pews. Tithingmen, armed with a staff, were charged with the task, seemingly hopeless under such conditions, of keeping them quiet and attentive to the sermon. It was also the duty of the tithingmen to rouse sleeping older people. Men and boys were rapped or prodded with

A SABBATH BREAKER'S EXCUSE

No "servile" work was permitted on the Lord's Day, and "uncivilly walking in the streets and fields, traveling from town to town, going on Ship-board, frequenting common houses and other places to drink, sport, or otherwise to misspend that precious time," were forbidden. There were of course objectors and evaders. This item from the *Boston News Letter* of October 29, 1705, records the case of a stock drover from Connecticut, who persisted in driving cattle through the streets of Dedham on the Lord's Day, and argued when arrested that he was being persecuted for conscience' sake.

120   Duties of a Tithingman, from the original in the Massachusetts Bay Colony Court Records, Vol. V, p. 233, Boston, Oct. 15, 1679

DUTIES OF TYTHINGMAN

" Also, the tythingmen are required diligently to inspect the manners of all disorderly persons, and whereby more private admonitions they will not be reclaymed, they are, frome time to time, to present their names to the next magistrate or commissioner invested wth magistratticall power, who shall proceed against them as the law directs; as also they are, in like manner, to present the names of all single persons that liue from vnder family government, stubborne and disorderly children & servants, night walkers, typlers, Saboath breakers, by night or by day, & such as absent themselves from the publicke worship of God on the Lords dayes, or whatever the course or practise of any person or persons whatsoever tending to debauchery, irreligion, prophaness, & atheisme among us, wherein by omission of family gouernment, nurture, & religious duties, & instrucçon of children & servants, or illeness, profligat, vnciviel, or rude practises of any sort, the names of all which persons, wth the fact whereof they are accused, & wittnesses thereof, they shall present to the next magistrate or comissioner, where any are in the sajd toune invested wth magistratticall power, who shall proceed against and punish all such misdemeanors by fine, imprisonment, or binding ouer to the County Court, as the law directs."

the heavy knob on one end of the official staff; matrons and girls were admonished by being tickled with a fox's tail or a hare's foot which adorned the other end. In many towns the tithingmen had various other duties which made them in effect general assistants to the constable, particularly with respect to breaches of the laws respecting observance of the Lord's Day.

121   Oath of Office for a Tythingman, from the original in the Massachusetts Bay Colony Court Records, Vol. V, p. 233, Boston, Oct. 15, 1679

" Whereas yow, A B, are chosen a tythingman wthin the toune of D for one yeare, & vntill others be chosen & sworne in your roome & stead, yow doe here sweare by the living God that yow will diligently endeavour, and to the vtmost of yor ability performe and intend, the duty of yor place according to the particulars specified in the lawes peculiar to yor office. So help yow God."

"A WANTON GOSPELLER"

MORE serious disturbances of public worship were by no means unknown. A Massachusetts law of 1646 provided that anyone who behaved himself contemptuously toward the "Word preached" or toward the preacher, interrupting, disputing or denying, thus "making God's ways contemptible or ridiculous," should for the first offence be rebuked by a magistrate and bound to good behavior, "and if a second time they break forth into the like contemptuous carriages, either to pay five pounds to the public treasury, or to stand two hours openly upon a block four feet high, on a lecture day, with a paper fixed on his breast, with this, A WANTON GOSPELLER, written in capital letters." But this

122 A Wanton Gospeller, from an engraving by Bobbett, after the drawing by Fredericks, in William Cullen Bryant and Sydney Gay, *A Popular History of the United States*, Vol. II, New York, 1884

law availed little to stop Baptists or Quakers from interrupting the service wherever they pleased; indeed it seemed rather to provoke them to outspoken expression of their contempt for certain aspects of the Puritan worship, and especially for the Puritan policy of compelling all citizens to attend their services in the meetinghouse on the Lord's Day.

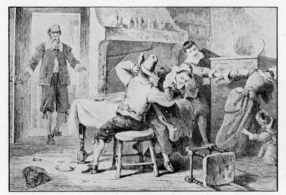

123 Stolen Frolic in a Puritan Farmhouse, from the drawing by F. O. C Darley (1822–88), in William A. Crafts, *Pioneers in the Settlement of America*, Vol. I, Boston, 1876

SUNDAY EVENING COURTSHIPS

THE Puritan Sabbath began at sunset on Saturday evening, for the Bible said "The evening and the morning were the first day." It lasted therefore until sunset on Sunday evening. It was inevitable, despite strenuous efforts to prolong the quiet of the Lord's Day to include its evening, that this should become a time of general good cheer. It was inevitable, too, that Sunday evening should be courting-time for Puritan youths and maidens. Many ministers found it necessary to preach against "Sabbath evening dissipations and mirth-making." "Street-

124 Courtship in Colonial Days, from the drawing by Juanita Smith, in *Harper's Weekly*, October 27, 1900

walking" was one of the sins condemned in young women; it meant nothing more serious than taking a walk with a lover on Sunday evening. No wonder that many took such walks, when most homes had no place to sit except by the fireplace where the whole family were gathered, so that the only chance for private conversation was through a "courting-stick" such as is here pictured. Sometimes, doubtless, young people stole away from supervising eyes, and kitchens witnessed less decorous scenes.

125   Statue of Deacon Chapin, Springfield, Mass., by Augustus
Saint-Gaudens (1848-1907).   From a photograph. © The
Detroit Publishing Co.

THE HALF-WAY COVENANT

THE closing years of the seventeenth century and the first third of the eighteenth were marked by moral deterioration and a decline in spiritual fervor. "It is the judgment of very learned men," said President Mather in a sermon at Harvard College in 1696, "that, in the glorious times promised to the church on earth, America will be Hell." How much of this gloomy view was due to disappointment that the Puritan hope of a theocratic commonwealth was now seen to be unrealizable, and how much was justified by actual moral conditions, we do not know. It is clear that the churches had lost much of their earlier spiritual power. One reason for this lay in the "Half-way Covenant" plan which had been adopted in 1662. It provided that those who had been baptized and desired to "own the covenant" but could render no such evidences of regeneration as were required to constitute one a member of the church in "full communion," should be granted a sort of half-membership and allowed to offer their children in baptism. The result was that most people were content to stop there. Infant baptism and the Half-Way Covenant became mere forms, as folk relied upon them to be substitutes for the vows of church membership and the moral evidences of a godly life. The Half-Way Covenant was an undesirable by-product of the connection of church and state.

JONATHAN EDWARDS, 1703-1758, PREACHER OF THE GREAT AWAKENING

AGAINST this decadence of morals and religion, Jonathan Edwards, pastor at Northampton from 1727 to 1750, set all the powers of a marvellous intellect, rare strength of personality, and a life wholly dedicated to God. As a theologian, he is to be classed with St. Augustine and Calvin; as a preacher, he had the effectiveness, if not the eloquence, of John Knox. The burden of his preaching was the absolute sovereignty and holiness of God, the sinfulness and complete dependence of man, the necessity of a changed heart and life, and the power of God's grace to bestow this gift. In six months of 1734–35 more than three hundred persons, half of whom were men, professed conversion and were admitted to full membership in the Northampton church. So began the "Great Awakening" in New England, which put an end to the Half-Way Covenant. Like stirrings of religious emotion were felt in nearly all the colonies, profoundly affecting the life of the churches; and the Great Awakening became a watershed redirecting — and dividing — the streams of spiritual energy. Edwards was dismissed as pastor by vote of the Northampton church in 1750, because most of its members resented his refusal to recognize the Half-Way Covenant as sufficient qualification for admission to the communion of the Lord's Supper. He served for seven years as missionary to the Indians at Stockbridge, then became president of the college at Princeton.

126   Jonathan Edwards Memorial Tablet in the First
Church, Northampton, Mass., courtesy of the sculptor,
Herbert Adams (1856–)

JONATHAN EDWARDS: THEOLOGIAN

EDWARDS preached the gospel of divine immanence and divine initiative. He saw that all things have their being in God; and that a god who is less than the source and power of all being, is but a half-god. Unfortunately, this greatest of all the truths of religion was bound up, for him, with two other ideas: the denial of the freedom of the human will; and the doctrine of particular election, that God has arbitrarily and irrevocably chosen some for salvation and some for damnation. Edwards himself did not distinguish between these transient elements of extreme Calvinism and the central truth which was inevitably distorted by them; and it is but natural that he should be remembered as a preacher of hell-fire. Yet the imprecatory sermons, upon which this reputation depends, are only eight in number; and the one most often quoted, preached at Enfield, seems to have been addressed to a community which stood in need of a message of that sort. "How many it is likely will remember this discourse in hell! And it would be a wonder if some that are now present should not be in hell in a very short time, before this year is out. And it would be no wonder if some persons that now sit here in some seats of this meeting-house, in health and quiet and secure, *should be there before tomorrow morning.*" Edwards was a preacher of powerful force. He was able to dominate his congregations and to shape the development of their faith. In the day of his greatest power he shook New England.

A careful and strict

ENQUIRY

INTO

The *modern* prevailing Notions

OF THAT

FREEDOM of WILL,

Which is supposed to be essential

TO

Moral Agency, Vertue and *Vice, Reward* and *Punishment, Praise* and *Blame.*

By JONATHAN EDWARDS, A.M.

Pastor of the Church in *Stockbridge.*

Rom. ix. 16. *It is not of him that willeth——*

BOSTON, N. E.

Printed and Sold by S. KNEELAND, in Queen-street, MDCCLIV.

127 Title-page of the original in the New York Public Library

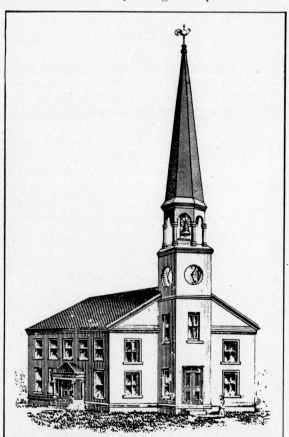

128 Third Meetinghouse, Northampton, erected 1737, from Solomon Clark, *Historical Catalogue of the Northampton First Church*, Northampton, 1891

JONATHAN EDWARDS: PHILOSOPHER

THOUGH he forsook philosophy to devote himself to theology, Edwards remains one of the greatest philosophers America has produced. To the solution of the difficult problems of theology he brought one of the most powerful minds that America has brought forth. His theology has philosophical grounding, depth, and poise; and his treatise on *The Freedom of the Will* has been said to be "the one large contribution which America has made to the deeper philosophic thought of the world." As a boy of fourteen, in his second year at Yale College, he read Locke's *Essay on the Human Understanding*, and was moved by it, in the next two years, to write *Notes on the Mind*, in which he set down the fundamental principles of a system of philosophy which is remarkably like that of Berkeley, though it is almost certain that he had never seen the latter's works. Unlike Increase Mather, Edwards did not concern himself with political issues and was not a man of affairs. Yet his influence upon these was far-reaching. His insistence upon religious conversion, and his exaltation of the church as a spiritual institution, emphasized the difference between church and state, and contributed mightily, though indirectly, to the movements which led to their eventual separation. Jonathan Edwards was one of the founders of religious freedom in America.

129 Jonathan Edwards, from the portrait, 1860, by Henry A. Loop (1831–95), in Princeton University, after the original portrait, 1740, by John Smibert, in the possession of Eugene B. Edwards, Stonington, Conn.

JONATHAN EDWARDS: MYSTIC

GREATER than all that he said or wrote, was the man himself. He walked with God. "On January 12, 1723, I made a solemn dedication of myself to God and wrote it down; giving up myself and all that I had to God, to be for the future in no respect my own; to act as one that had no right to himself in any respect; and solemnly vowed to take God for my whole portion and felicity, looking on nothing else as any part of my happiness, nor acting as if it were; and his law for the constant rule of my obedience, engaging to fight with all my might against the world, the flesh, and the devil, to the end of my life." If it be thought that this was the immature resolution of a youth of twenty, it must be remembered that he had graduated from college at sixteen, had completed his theological training, had been preaching for a year, and was about to begin teaching as a member of the faculty of Yale College. This resolution, moreover, was kept. No cloistered monk ever fulfilled his vow more perfectly than did this man for whom every common duty shone with heavenly light, and all nature sang of God.

THE FAMILY LIFE OF JONATHAN EDWARDS

IDYLLIC in beauty, epic in constancy, was the love story of Jonathan Edwards and Sarah Pierrepont. His description, written when he was twenty and she was thirteen, of the "young lady in New Haven who is beloved of that great Being who made and rules the world," is classic. Shortly after his ordination, when she was seventeen, they were married. "Patience," he had written her, "is commonly esteemed a virtue, but in this case I may almost regard it as a vice." George Whitefield, when he visited their home, was charmed with its spirit. "A sweeter couple I have not seen. Their children were dressed, not in silks and satins, but plain, as becomes the children of those who in all things ought to be examples of Christian simplicity. She is a woman adorned with a meek and quiet spirit, and talked so feelingly and so solidly of the things of God, and seemed to be such an helpmeet to her husband, that she caused me to renew those prayers which for some months I have put up to God, that He would send me a daughter of Abraham to be my wife." After a month of service as President of Princeton College, before Mrs. Edwards and the younger children could join him in their new home, Jonathan Edwards lay dying. "Tell her," he said, "that the uncommon union which has so long subsisted between us has been of such a nature as I trust is spiritual, and therefore will continue forever." The message was characteristic of the life and character of the man.

Jonathan Edwards was the greatest of American Puritans. If there be faults in his thought or his life, they are such as were inherent in Puritanism, for he revealed it at its best.

130   Home of Jonathan Edwards, Northampton, Mass., from Jonathan Edwards, *The Life of David Brainerd*, Evangelical Family Library, Vol. VII, New York, 1833(?)

CHAPTER III

THE CHURCH OF ENGLAND IN THE COLONIES

THE home of the Church of England in America was in Virginia, where it was from the beginning established, first by charter, then by legislation, as the state-supported church of the colony. In time, it was likewise established in the other southern colonies — Maryland, the Carolinas, and Georgia. In two other colonies, New York and New Jersey, the royal Governors attempted to make it the established church, but did not fully succeed.

In Pennsylvania, Delaware, and Rhode Island, which from the first avowed the principle of religious freedom, the Church of England had room to develop naturally, as did other churches and religious groups. In the New England colonies, except Rhode Island, it was an alien. When it finally succeeded in gaining a foothold in the Puritan strongholds, which it did in Massachusetts by force, and in Connecticut by peaceful penetration, it found itself in a position just the reverse of that which it held in England. There it was the religion of the state, and other groups were dissenters; in New England the Congregational churches had the support of the state, and the Church of England was a dissenting organization, commanding the adherence of only a small minority of the people.

In the southern colonies, especially in Virginia where the Church of England possessed the advantages of state establishment and support, it developed along democratic, "low-church" lines. In the northern colonies, especially in Massachusetts and Connecticut where it had to struggle to maintain its ground, the Church of England naturally emphasized the differences between itself and other religious societies, with the result that it tended to develop along more "high-church" lines. So began differences of emphasis which have ever since been present in the Protestant Episcopal Church which succeeded the Church of England after the American Revolution, though these differences are now quite independent of geography and politics.

The history of the Church of England in the American colonies illustrates "the crass folly of trying to propagate a system by mutilating it." The colonial churches had no bishop. No diocese was organized and no bishop even visited America. Clergy could be ordained and members of the church could receive the rite of confirmation only by taking the long sea voyage to England. That explains why many citizens of colonial Virginia, for example, were never confirmed, and some had scruples about partaking of the communion. At this distance in time, the failure of the English ecclesiastical authorities to send a bishop to America seems incredible stupidity. A more effective barrier to the growth and prosperity of the Church of England in this country could hardly have been devised.

Within the limits of their powers, however, the "commissaries" who were appointed by the Bishop of London to act as his representatives in America, rendered excellent service. The most notable were James Blair, Commissary of Virginia, founder of William and Mary College, and Thomas Bray, Commissary of Maryland, founder of the Society for the Promotion of Christian Knowledge and of the Society for Propagating the Gospel in Foreign Parts. The latter of these societies, commonly referred to as the "Venerable Society" or, more familiarly, as the "S. P. G.," labored for the spread of the Anglican faith, and was chiefly responsible for the growth of the Church of England in the colonies.

131   The Robert Hunt Memorial Tablet, Jamestown, Virginia, from a photograph by H. P. Cook, Richmond, Va.

THE FIRST CHURCH IN VIRGINIA

THE best loved member of the turbulent crew that settled Jamestown was, according to Captain John Smith, their minister, Robert Hunt, who during the voyage had "with the water of patience and his godly exhortations, but chiefly by his true devoted example, quenched the flames of envy and dissension." On June 21, 1607, he celebrated the first communion of Englishmen in America. The Epistle for the day fitted the occasion: "All of you be subject one to another, and be clothed with humility." "We did hang an old sail to three or four trees to shade us from the sun, our walls were rails of wood, our seats unhewed trees, our pulpit a bar of wood nailed to two neighboring trees. This was our church till we built a homely thing like a barn. . . . Yet we had daily Common Prayer morning and evening, every Sunday two sermons, and every three months the Holy Communion, till our minister died. . . . He was an honest, religious and courageous divine, during whose life our factions were oft qualified, our wants and greatest extremities so comforted, that they seemed easy in comparison of what we endured after his memorable death."

DALE'S LAWS

STERN measures seemed to be needed if the colony was to be saved from factiousness and idleness; and in 1611 the Virginia Company sent as Governor Sir Thomas Dale, a soldier who had served in the Netherlands. He promulgated a code of laws notable not only for its severity in dealing with crimes, but for its application of like measures to the neglect of religious duties. Impious speech against the Trinity, blasphemy, and words or acts derisive of God's Word were punishable by death. All were required to attend divine worship twice in each day, morning and evening, under penalty of being whipped and for the third offence condemned to the galleys for six months. A third wilful absence from the Sabbath services was punishable by death. The minister could require those insufficiently instructed in the principles of religion to present themselves for further instruction, under penalty of being whipped every day until they should prove docile. These laws concerning the observance of religious duties were never rigidly enforced, as the Governor and Council had power to remit penalties. They were meant to inspire wholesome fear in the minds of the lawless, wilfully disobedient and rebellious.

(3)

herein, encouraging others thereunto, and that such, who shall often and wilfully absent themselues, be duly punished according to the martiall law in that case prouided.

2   That no man speake impiously or maliciously, against the holy and blessed Trinitie, or any of the three persons, that is to say, against God the Father, God the Son, and God the holy Ghost, or against the knowne Articles of the Christian faith, vpon paine of death,

3   That no man blaspheme Gods holy name vpon paine of death, or vse vnlawfull oathes, taking the name of God in vaine, curse, or banne, vpon paine of seuere punishment for the first offence so committed, and for the second, to haue a bodkin thrust through his tongue, and if he so continue the blaspheming of Gods holy name, for the third time so offending, he shall be brought to a martiall court, and there receiue censure of death for his offence.

4   No man shall vse any traiterous words against his Maiesties Person, or royall authority vpon paine of death.

5   No man shall speake any word, or do any act, which may tend to the derision, or despight of Gods holy word vpon paine of death: Nor shall any man vnworthily demeane himselfe vnto any Preacher, or Minister of the same, but generally hold them in all reuerent regard, and dutifull intreatie, otherwise he the offender shall openly be whipt three times, and aske publike forgiuenesse in the assembly of the congregation three seuerall Saboth daies.

6   Euerie man and woman duly twice a day vpon

B 2   the

132   From William Strachey, For the Colony in Virginia Britannia, Laws Divine, Morall, and Martiall, London, 1612, in the John Carter Brown Library, Providence, R. I.

133 The Ducking Stool, from a contemporary woodcut in the British Museum, reproduced in Sir Walter Besant, *London in the Time of the Tudors*, London, 1904

134 The Stocks, from a contemporary woodcut reproduced in *The Art Journal*, Vol. II, New York, 1876

135 Whipping at the Cart's Tail, from a contemporary woodcut reproduced in *The Art Journal*, Vol. II, New York, 1876

136 Beheading and Quartering, from a contemporary woodcut reproduced in *The Art Journal*, Vol. II, New York, 1876

SEVENTEENTH– AND EIGHTEENTH– CENTURY PUNISHMENTS

PUNISHMENTS were drastic in all of the colonies. The settlers brought from Europe their ideas of penal justice, and Europe had not outgrown the cruel laws of the Middle Ages. Here are shown old contemporary prints of punishments in England — a ducking stool, whipping at the cart's tail, a pillory, a gallows, and the body of a traitor beheaded and quartered, feasted upon by carrion crows. A sentence to stand in the pillory was often accompanied by the cropping of one or both ears. Branding with a red-hot iron was a common punishment. SL was the mark standing for seditious libel; M for manslaughter; T for thief; R for rogue, and so on. The ducking stool was much used for the cure of scolds in the middle and southern colonies, but not in New England. The northern colonies chose to gag the culprit instead, usually by placing the tongue in a cleft stick. Public whipping was practiced everywhere, in Rhode Island and Pennsylvania as well as in Massachusetts and Virginia. Punishments in the seventeenth and eighteenth centuries were made as terrible and as public as possible; for they were intended, not so much to reform the criminal as to bring retribution upon him and, by his horrible example, to deter others from like offenses.

137 The Pillory, from a contemporary woodcut reproduced in *The Art Journal*, Vol. II, New York, 1876

138 Ancient Gallows, from a contemporary woodcut reproduced in *The Art Journal*, Vol. II, New York, 1876

139 From the engraving, *A Man and His Brother*, by R. Taylor
after a drawing by R. Caton Woodville (1820–55), in *Harper's
Weekly*, Dec. 11, 1886

"A MAN AND HIS BROTHER"

IN 1619 the first negro servants appeared in Virginia.
Thereby began a complication of the problems of just and
humane living which eventually helped to plunge America
into fratricidal war. The situation seemed simple enough
at first. Defiant black and bibulous, good-for-nothing white
sit side by side in the same stocks.

THE FIRST LEGISLATURE

DALE's code was abrogated in 1619, when the colonists
were granted a measure of self-government. The first
representative body of legislators constituted in this
country met in the church at Jamestown on July 30 in
that year. Among the enactments of this assembly were
laws establishing the authority of the Church of England
in the colony and providing for its support. The minister
in each borough was to have a glebe of one hundred acres,
and should receive from the parish a salary of at least
two hundred pounds. As it was most convenient to pay
the minister in tobacco, the legislature of 1621–22 fixed
the amount at fifteen hundred pounds of tobacco and sixteen barrels of corn. Every male inhabitant who had
reached the age of sixteen was taxed for this purpose, but
no individual was to be compelled to pay more than ten
pounds of tobacco and one barrel of corn. If the proceeds
of this tax should prove less in value than two hundred pounds, the law declared that "the minister is to be
content with less." The custom of paying ministers in tobacco led, nearly a century and a half later, to the
famous "Parsons' Case," and to Patrick Henry's fiery attack upon the Virginia clergy (see No. 269).

---

122   LAWS OF VIRGINIA,

No. of the
Acts.

1. TH\T there shall be in every plantation, where
the people use to meete for the worship of God,
a house or roome sequestred for that purpose, and

And, according to *Smith*, they debated all matters, thought expedient for
the good of the colony—See also *Burk's Hist. Virg.* vol. 1, pa. 203, and
notes.

This summer, 1619, were laid off four more corporations, which encrea-
sed the number of boroughs having a right to representation to *eleven* in
all : *Stith*, 161.

The acts passed at the general assembly in 1619, were probably a crude,
indigested mass, which never received the sanction of the treasurer and
company for Virginia, in England ; without whose approbation, *in a great
and general court*, they could not have the force of laws.

After a careful examination of the ancient records relating to Virginia,
the following is the only notice which I have been able to find of these
acts. –

At "An extraordinary court held the 20th of March, 1620," Ancient
Records, vol. 1, pa. 117, towards the close of the proceedings there is
this entry : * The acts of the general assembly in Virginia being yet
to read, together with a letter which Mr. Yeardley desireth should be
read for the cleering of his brother Sir George Yeardly, because it was
held inconvenient to spend an ordinary court therewith, it was agreed
that Monday next in the afternoon should be appointed for that purpose.

" At an imperfect court held for Virginia at Sir Edwin Sandys' house,
8th of April, 1620," ancient records, vol. 1, pa. 118, " Mr. Treasurer,"
(Sir Edwin Sandys,) " signified that having perused the acts of the general assembly, he found them in their greatest part to be very well and ju-
diciously carried and performed, but because they are to be ratified by a
great and *general court*, therefore he hath writ unto them that till then they
cannot be confirmed ; but in the mean time he moved that a select committee of choice men might be appointed to draw them into head, and to
ripen the business that it might be in readiness against the said court."

A committee was thereupon appointed, consisting of eight members,
four of the council, and four of the general *ly*, as they were termed, to
meet at a future day then assigned, with power to adjourn from day to
day.

At a subsequent meeting, another member was added to the committee,
and the proceedings of the " imperfect court," were confirmed. Ancient
Records, vol. 1, pa 132.

And " At a preparative court, held May 15th, 1620," Ancient Records,
vol. 1, pa. 135, there is the following entry.

* For the committee chosen for the acts of the General Assembly,
Mr. Treasurer signified that they had taken extraordinary pains therein,
but forasmuch as they were exceeding intricate and full of labour, he in
their behalf desired the court to dispense with them till the quarter court
in midsummer term, which will be about six weeks hence, which the court
with many thanks unto the committee for their great pains willingly assented unto."

No mention is made of these acts, at the next quarter court, or in any
subsequent part of the proceedings.

* The acts of this session are numbered, in the margin, as they are
here printed I have observed the same form, not only because I
think the original should be imitated as nearly as possible, but because,
in all the subsequent acts, for a series of years, the former laws are referred to by the *number* of the act and not by the *chapter*. In the infancy of our legislation, there was no such thing as a division of the several
acts by chapters.

It may not be improper to remark, that in the course of this work, I
shall preserve both the *arrangement* and *orthography* of the originals as
far as practicable. I cannot well conceive any thing more improper
than to give an *ancient* paper in a *modern* dress. Besides the suspicions,
which are naturally excited, that the paper is spurious, we are deprived
of an opportunity of tracing those gradual changes in language, from
rudeness to refinement, which are observable in the progress of civilization in all nations. If it were possible I would give a *fac simile* of the
hand writing. But this cannot be done. The most remarkable devia-
tion from the modern characters, in the acts of this session, are, that the

MARCH, 1623-4—21st JAMES 1st.   123

not to be for any temporal use whatsoever, and a
place empaled in, sequestered only to the burial of
the dead.

   House of
   worship.

That whosoever shall absent himselfe from divine
service any Sunday without an allowable excuse
shall forfeite a pound of tobacco, and he that absent-
eth himselfe a month shall forfeit 50lb. of tobacco.

   Penalty
   for being
   absent
   from
   church on
   Sunday

That there be an uniformity in our church as neere
as may be to the canons in England ; both in substance and circumstance, and that all persons yeild
readie obedience unto them under paine of censure.

   To be an
   uniformity
   in the doc
   trine and
   discipline
   of the
   church.

That the 22d of March* be yeerly solemnized as
holliday, and all other hollidays (except when they
fall two together) betwixt the feast of the annuntia-
tion of the blessed virgin and St. Michael the arch-
angell, then only the first to be observed by reason
of our necessities.

   The 22d
   of March
   to be ob-
   served as
   a holliday.

That no minister be absent from his church above
two months in all the yeare upon penalty of forfeit-
ing halfe his means, and whosoever shall absent
above towre months in the year shall forfeit his whole
means and cure.

   Penalty on
   ministers
   absenting
   them-
   selves
   from their
   church.

That whosoever shall disparage a minister without
bringing sufficient proofe to justify his reports whereby the number of his parishioners may be alienated
from him, and his ministry prove the less effectual by
their prejudication, shall not only pay 500lb. waight
of tobacco but also aske the minister so wronged
forgivenes publickly in the congregation.

   Penalty
   on disp a
   raging a
   minister

That no man dispose of any of his tobacco before
the minister be satisfied, upon pain of forfeiture double his part of the minister's means, and one man of
every plantation to collect his means out of the first
and best tobacco and corn.

   Ministers
   to be satis-
   fied before
   any tobac-
   co dispos-
   ed of.

small " e" nearly resembles the letter "o" with a horizontal cross near the
top,—the small " r" is exactly like the small round Greek *sigma*, with a
circumflex proceeding from the top.

* This was in commemoration of the escape of the colony from entire
extirpation by the Indians on the 22d of March,
1622. See Burk's Hist. Virg. vol 1, p 240

140   From William Waller Hening, *The Statutes at Large of Virginia*, New York, 1823

141 From the painting *Baptism of Pocahontas*, d. 1617, by John G. Chapman (1808–89), in the Capitol Rotunda, Washington

ALEXANDER WHITAKER, 1585–1617(?): "THE APOSTLE TO VIRGINIA"

WITH Governor Dale came the Reverend Alexander Whitaker, son of Dr. William Whitaker, Master of St. John's College, Cambridge University. His friends wondered at his decision. "I hereby let all men know," wrote one, "that a scholar, a graduate, a preacher, well born and friended in England; not in debt nor disgrace, but competently provided for, and liked and beloved where he lived; not in want, but (for a scholar, and as these days be) rich in possession, and more in possibility; of himself, without any persuasion but God's and his own heart, did voluntarily leave his warm nest; and to the wonder of his kindred and amazement of them that knew him, undertook this hard, but heroical resolution to go to Virginia, and help to bear the name of God unto the gentiles." Whitaker found great happiness in his work. His character and influence were such that he was called "The Apostle to Virginia." The picture is a highly imaginative portrayal of his baptism of Pocahontas.

THE UNIVERSITY AT HENRICO

IN 1618, the Virginia Company ordered that ten thousand acres of land be set aside for the endowment of a university to be built at Henrico, where Alexander Whitaker was minister. One of the colleges of the university was to be for the Indians, "for the training up of the children of those infidels in true religion, moral virtue, and civility." A general contribution was made in England, and large individual gifts were received, the whole amounting to more than four thousand pounds. George Thorpe, a member of the King's Council for Virginia, sailed for America to take charge of the university lands and supervise the erection of buildings. The Reverend Patrick Copland was chosen rector of the college for the Indians. Before he could leave England, however, news came of the massacre of the colonists by the Indians on March 22, 1622. The settlement at Henrico was one of those wiped out; Thorpe was killed; and the plans for a university were abandoned. A proposal by Edward Palmer, "an English scholar of wealth," to found an "Academia Virginiensis et Oxoniensis" came to naught. In 1662, the legislature provided for the establishing of "a college and free school," but this law was "permitted to slumber on the statute books."

142 Henrico Medallion, commemorating the destruction of the university at Henrico, courtesy of the Colonial Dames of America, Chapter I, Baltimore, Md.

143 Sir William Berkeley, *ca.* 1610–d. 1677, from the original portrait by Sir Peter Lely (1618–80), in possession of Lee, Buffalo, N. Y.

AWAY FROM PURITANISM

MANY of the Virginia Company sympathized with Puritan views. Sir Edwin Sandys, its treasurer and leading spirit, did not hesitate to subscribe himself as the "very loving friend" of John Robinson and William Brewster. "Choose the devil if you will," angrily exclaimed King James, demanding that a new treasurer be chosen, "but not Sir Edwin Sandys." The ministers in early Virginia wore no surplice, and modified the liturgy "to avoid giving offence." "I marvel much," wrote Alexander Whitaker, "that so few of our English ministers, that were so hot against the surplice and subscription, come hither, where neither are spoken of." But in 1624 the charter of the Company was abrogated, and Virginia passed into the direct control of the King. Under the royal Governors, the penalties for nonconformity were enforced with a severity pleasing to Archbishop Laud; and laws were enacted against the Puritans, "to prevent the infection from reaching this country." In response to a request signed by seventy-one citizens of Virginia, the General Court of Massachusetts sent three Congregational ministers; but they were quickly silenced and returned. Virginia yielded grudging submission to the Commonwealth. It restored the doughty royalist, Sir William Berkeley, to the Governorship sixteen months before the restoration of Charles II to the throne.

"NO FREE SCHOOLS, NOR PRINTING"

IT was difficult to secure ministers. Salaries were low, and often paid in poor tobacco, or not at all. Many parishes had no glebes. The churches were governed by vestries, composed of twelve "of the most able men of each parish." As these vestries were constituted self-perpetuating bodies which could be dissolved only by a special act of the General Assembly, they tended to become local aristocracies. Election to the office of vestryman was determined in part by social, political and economic considerations, as well as by moral character and spiritual devotion. The vestries fell into the habit of contracting with a minister for but a single year; and would not renew the contract if he did anything to displease them. Under these circumstances, according to a contemporary account, "very few of good conversation would adventure thither, yet many came such as wore black coats and could babble in a pulpit, roar in a tavern, exact from the parishioners, and rather by their dissoluteness destroy than feed their flocks. . . . Endeavors were made for better in their places, which were obtained, and these wolves in sheep's clothing were questioned, silenced, and some were forced to depart the country." In 1661, the author of *Virginia's Cure* wrote that not more than one fifth of the parishes were supplied with ministers. In 1671, Governor Berkeley reported a population of forty thousand, and added: "There are forty-eight parishes, and the ministers well-paid. The clergy by my consent would be better if they would pray oftener and preach less. But as of all other commodities, so of this, — the worst are sent us. . . . But I thank God there are no free schools, nor printing, and I hope we shall not have these hundred years; for learning has brought disobedience into the world, and printing has divulged them and libels against the best governments."

144 Plate from Communion Service used in Jamestown Church in 1694, courtesy of St. John's Church, Richmond, Va., from a photograph by H. P. Cook, Richmond

3

Virginia's Cure:

OR,

An Advisive NARRATIVE

CONCERNING

VIRGINIA.

TO shew the unhappy State of the Church in *Virginia*, and the true Remedy of it, I shall first give a brief Description of the Manner of our Peoples scatter'd Habitations there; next shew the sad unhappy consequents of such their scatter'd Living both in reference to themselves and the poor Heathen that are about them, and by the way briefly set down the cause of scattering their Habitations, then proceed to propound the Remedy, and means of procuring it; next assert the Benefits of it in reference both to themselves, and the Heathen; set down the cause why this Remedy hath not been hitherto compass'd: and lastly, till it can be procured, give directions for the present supply of their Churches.

That part of *Virginia* which hath at present craved your Lordships Assistance to preserve the Christian Religion, and to promote the Building Gods Church among them, by supplying them with sufficient Ministers of the Gospel, is bounded on the North by the great River *Patomek*, on the South by the River *Chawan*, including also the Land inhabited on the East side of *Chesipiack Bay*, called *Accomack*, and contains above half as much Land

145 Page from *Virginia's Cure*, from the original in the New York Public Library

THE CHURCH OF ENGLAND IN THE COLONIES

JAMES BLAIR, 1656–1743, COMMISSARY OF VIRGINIA

VIRGINIA needed a bishop. But, with strange shortsightedness, none was sent. In fact, none ever was sent; and the Church of England in America remained a missionary enterprise, under the direction of the Bishop of London, until the colonies became independent. In 1689, Bishop Compton did the next best thing. He appointed the Reverend James Blair, who had gone to Virginia as a missionary four years before, to be his representative or commissary. He was authorized to visit and inspect the churches, and to administer some measures of discipline. But he could not admit to the rite of confirmation, ordain ministers, or — what was sadly needed here and there — depose them. In this post, Blair rendered long and distinguished service. His work was surprisingly effective in view of the limitations under which he labored. When he died, at the age of eighty-seven, he had been for sixty-four years a minister of the Gospel; for fifty-three years Commissary of Virginia; for fifty years a member of the King's Council; and for forty-nine years President of William and Mary College.

146 James Blair, from the original portrait, about 1700, possibly by Henrietta Johnson (d. 1728–29), in the College of William and Mary, Williamsburg, Va.

147 "The College Standing in Williamsburg in which the Governor Has His Residence, 1702," from *Report of the Journey of Francois Louis Michel from Berne, Switzerland, to Virginia, Oct. 2 (1), 1701–December 1, 1702,* translated and edited by Prof. William J. Hinke, Ph.D., in the *Virginia Magazine of History*, Richmond, April 1916

THE FOUNDING OF WILLIAM AND MARY COLLEGE, 1693

BLAIR's first concern was for the founding of a college, in which the youth of Virginia should be "piously educated in good letters and manners," and which should also be "a Seminary for the breeding of good Ministers." With the sanction of the Governor and Assembly, he went to England to secure a charter and funds. When he urged Seymour, the lord treasurer, to consider that the people in Virginia had souls to be saved as well as the people in England, the answer was "Souls! Damn your souls! Make tobacco!" The college, named "William and Mary," was begun in 1693. The picture is a sketch, made by a Swiss traveler in 1702, of the first building, which was designed by Sir Christopher Wren. It was burned to the ground in 1705 but by "patience and good husbandry" it was replaced. Blair met other discouragements. He found it hard to collect subscriptions — "men being easily persuaded," he writes, "to keep their money" — and the Governors did not always agree with him. But he outlasted many Governors; was afraid of none; and procured the recall of three.

[*.*]

A GENERAL VIEW
OF THE
English Colonies in America,
With Respect to
RELIGION,
In order to shew what Provision is wanting for
the Propagation of Christianity in Those Parts.

Colonies.	Parishes & Churches	Ministers	Libraries
I. *New found land* Hath 3 or 4 English settlements, scattered one near 100 Families conveniently upon the shoars, besides the great Numbers of Ships that frequent those parts for the Fishing seasons.			
II. *New-England.*	Well provided for the Propagation of Religion in the Independent Way, having 110 Churches, together with an University; as also a Fund for the Propagation of the Faith amongst the Native *Indians.* There is also 1 Church at *Boston* after the Church of England Form.	1 Minister. 1 Assistant.	1 Library. Colonies.

148   From Thomas Bray, *Apostolick Charity*,
London, 1698

DR. BRAY'S PAROCHIAL LIBRARIES

Bray was a firm believer in libraries. Missionaries must have books, and could not afford to buy them for themselves. Princess Anne gave him four hundred pounds to purchase books for a library at Annapolis; and he founded libraries in thirty-eight other colonial parishes. He often met a rebuff that is as ancient and as modern as human selfishness: "We have poor parsons enough in England, and charity should begin at home." "Now he thought it not amiss to strike the nail that would drive," wrote one of his friends; so he began to collect funds to establish "lending libraries" for the clergy of rural England. Observing that his missionaries were often detained for some weeks at their port of departure, he established

THOMAS BRAY, 1656–1730, COMMISSARY OF MARYLAND

In contrast to Blair's long life in Virginia, the Reverend Thomas Bray spent only a few months in America. The Church of England was legally established in Maryland in 1692; and thirty-one parishes were organized, though there were but few ministers in the colony. Bray was made Commissary and conceived his work broadly as a missionary enterprise. He labored indefatigably, first to secure libraries for the ministers he desired to send to America, and then to find ministers of the right sort. He took measures, also, to keep out ministers of the wrong sort. When he visited Maryland in 1700, the clergy numbered seventeen. He recommended that "immediately upon the arrival of any ship, the nearest clergyman should make inquiry whether any minister was on board, and if so, what his demeanour had been upon the voyage . . . with a view of excluding him from a settlement in any parish if he were of evil report." In a Memorial requesting that forty missionaries be sent from England, he asked for men possessed of *a true missionary spirit*, having an ardent zeal for God's glory and the salvation of men's souls."

[*.*]

Colonies.	Parishes & Churches	Ministers	Libraries
III. *New-York.*	1 Church in the Fort. 1 Church in the City. 2 Dutch Churches. 1 French Church.	1 Minister in the Fort. 1 Minister in the City. 2 Dutch Ministers. 1 French Minister.	1 Library.
I. *Long-Island* A great and populous Colony on the Continent of *New-York*, wherein are 8 small Towns, not well supplied with Ministers; the number of Families being about 100, besides 200 Dutch Families.	13 Churches.	Not 1 church of England within it; tho' much desir'd in the English part. 1 Dutch Minister in the West-part.	
2. *Albany,* A large City, consisting of 400 Families, bordering upon the *Indians,* and belonging to the Government of *New-York.*	1 Church in the Fort for the Garrison, consisting of 2 Foot-Companies, and the English Inhabitants of the Town. 1 Dutch Church. 1 French Church. 1 Swedish Church.	1 Dutch Minister. 1 French Minister. 1 Swedish Minister.	
IV. *East New-Jersey.* V. *West New-Jersey.*	In *East-Jersey* there are 8 Towns, no Church. In this Province there are also several Towns.	1 Minister going over	A Library begun.
VI. *Pensylvania.*	1 Church at *Philadelphia,* having a considerable Number of Church of England Protestants.	1 Minister. 1 School-Master.	1 Library. Colonies.

Colonies.	Parishes & Churches	Ministers	Libraries
VII. *Mary-Land.*	30 Parishes, but meanly Endow'd, the Country being but lately divided into Parishes, and the Churches but lately built, to the great Charge of the present Governour Colonel *Nicholson,* and the Country.	16 Ministers.	16 Libraries.
VIII. *Virginia.*	50 Parishes, with 100 Churches & Chapels. There is also a Noble College now Erected and Endow'd by His present Majesty and the late Queen; and carry'd on from the first Foundation with the great Charge, Application, and Management of Colonel *Nicholson,* and the other Trustees and Governours thereof.	30 Ministers.	
IX. *North Carolina.* X. *South Carolina.* XI. *Bermudas.*	1 Church lately built at *Charles-Town.* 8 Tribes or Parishes, where in are 9 Churches, and near 1000 Families.	1 Minister going over 3 Ministers	1 Library. 3 Libraries
XII. *Bahama* Islands, viz. 1. *Providence.* 2. *Eleutheria.*	Has 80 Families with 1 Church lately built; Has about 20 Families. A	1 Minister.	Colo-

149   From Thomas Bray, *Apostolick Charity*, London, 1698

[12]

The exactest ACCOUNT that can at present be met with of the several LIBRARIES founded by Dr. BRAY, both at Home and Abroad.

I. Of LIBRARIES sent into *America*, and other Parts Abroad.

J. Into MARYLAND.

			N° of books.
1	To *Annapolis*	—	1095
2	To *St. Mary's*	—	314
3	To *Herring Creek*	—	150
4	To *South River*	—	109
5	To *North Sassafras*	—	42
6	To *King and Queen's Parish*	—	196
7	To *Christ-Church, Calvert County*	—	42
8	To *All Saints*	—	49
9	To *St. Paul's, Calvert County*	—	106
10	To *Great Choptank, Dorchester County*	—	76
11	To *St. Paul's, Baltimore County*	—	42
12	To *Stepney, Somerset County*	—	60
13	To *Porto Batto, Charles County*	—	30
14	To *St. Peter's, Talbot County*	—	15
15	To *St. Michael's, Talbot County*	—	13
16	To *All Filth's, Calvert County*	—	11
17	To *Nanjomi, Charles County*	—	10
18	To *Piskatoway, Charles County*	—	10
19	To *Broadneck alias Arundel*	—	10
20	To *St. John's, Baltimore*	—	10
21	To *St. George's, Baltimore*	—	10
22	To *Dorchester, Dorchester County*	—	10
23	To *Snowhill, Somerset County*	—	10
24	To *South Sassafras, Somerset*	—	10
25	To *St. Paul's, Kent County*	—	30
26	To *William and Mary, Charles County*	—	26
27	To *Somerset, Somerset County*	—	20
28	To *St. Paul's, Talbot County*	—	25
29	To *Coventry, Somerset County*	—	25

II. Into

[13]

BOOKS.

II. Into VIRGINIA.

1	To the College in *Virginia,* Books to the Value of 50l.	
2	To the several Parishes of the Province, to lay the Foundation of the Libraries	100
3	*Manicanton* on *James* River	38

III. Into the Government of NEW-YORK.

1	To *Boston* in *New-England*	221
2	To *New-York*	221
3	To *Amboy* in *New-Jersey*	39
4	To *Albany*	10

IV. Into PENNSYLVANIA.

	To *Philadelphia*	327

V. Into BERMUDAS.

1	To *St. George* Tribe	138
2	To *Devonshire* Tribe	115
3	To *Southampton* Tribe	34

VI. Into CAROLINA.

	To *Charles-Town*	225

VII. Into JAMAICA.

1	To *Port-Royal*	29
2	To *St. Andrew's*	27

VIII. Into BARBADOES.

To lay the Foundation of Parochial Libraries in the several Parishes, to the Value of 5l. 10s.

IX. Into ST. CHRISTOPHER'S.

X. Into ANTIGUA, Books to the Value of 110l.

XI. Into NEVIS, Books to the Value of 9l.

XII. Into MONTSERRAT   } 30

XIII. To Cape *Corso Castle,* in *Africa,* Books to the Value of 33l.

XIV. To BENGAL, in the *East-Indies,* Books to the Value of 50l.

XV. BONA VISTA, in *Newfoundland*   50

PAROCHIAL

150   From *An Account of the Designs of the Associates of the Late Dr. Bray; with an Abstract of Their Proceedings,* London, 1785

libraries in the chief seaports, "not only that they might lose no time toward their better improvement, but to prevent also the expense and scandal to which they might be exposed by sauntering away whole hours together in coffee-houses, or perhaps less sober places." In 1698 he organized The Society for the Promotion of Christian Knowledge, an agency for the publication and distribution of books which is still in active operation. This society is the oldest of its kind. In all parts of the world it assists Church of England missions, principally by providing them with books of devotion or theology, but also by supplying works of a more general nature. It has published books in ninety-nine different languages.

THE SOCIETY FOR PROPAGATING THE GOSPEL IN FOREIGN PARTS

BRAY'S crowning achievement was the organization of The Society for Propagating the Gospel in Foreign Parts, for which he secured a charter in 1701. The seal of the Society represents a ship approaching the land, its sails bellied by favoring winds, in its prow a minister bearing the open Scriptures, while on shore groups of naked natives hail its coming with gestures of joy. The greatest work of the Society, however, was not among the

Printed by Order of the Society.

John Chamberlayne,
SECRETARY

AN
ACCOUNT
OF THE
SOCIETY
FOR
PROPAGATING the GOSPEL In FOREIGN PARTS,
Established by the Royal Charter of
King WILLIAM III.
With their Proceedings and Success,
And Hopes of continual Progress under the HappyReign of Her most Excellent Majesty
QUEEN ANNE.

LONDON,
Printed by Joseph Downing, in Bartholomew-Close near West-Smithfield, 1706.

151   Frontispiece and title-page, from the original in the New York Public Library

Indians, but in supplying ministers and schoolmasters and affording "nursing care and protection" to the English churches among the colonists. When it was organized, there were only fifty ministers of the Church of England in the colonies, nearly all of whom were in Virginia and Maryland. Seventy-five years later, when the colonies declared their independence, there were about two hundred and fifty ministers and three hundred churches. This growth was due chiefly to the efforts of the S. P. G., as the Society was commonly called, which was able to report that it had in these years maintained three hundred and ten ordained missionaries, assisted two hundred and two central stations, and expended two hundred and twenty-seven thousand, four hundred and fifty-four pounds.

TRINITY CHURCH, NEW YORK

FOR more than thirty years after they had captured New Amsterdam, the English had no church in New York. Services were held according to the liturgy of the Church of England in the little Dutch chapel in the fort, conducted by the chaplain, after the Reformed service was over. In 1693, Governor Fletcher secured the passage of an act providing for support by public taxation of "a good sufficient Protestant minister," all freeholders having the right to vote for the vestrymen who should elect him. The building of Trinity Church was begun in 1695. The vestry chose to call William Vesey, a Congregational minister, but the Governor insisted upon an episcopally ordained clergyman. The issue was settled by Vesey consenting, upon a second call, to go to England for ordination. He served as rector for forty-nine years. The endowment of Trinity Church was begun by Lord Cornbury, who deeded to it a large tract of land in down-town New York.

152   Trinity Church, from an engraving by Tiebout after a drawing by I. Anderson, in the *New York Magazine*, Jan. 1790

153   William Vesey, 1674–1746, from a portrait by an unknown artist, courtesy of Trinity Parish, New York

X—6

RELIGIOUS INSTRUCTION OF THE SLAVES

THE importation of negro slaves increased as the decades passed. At the beginning of the eighteenth century, when New York's population was six thousand, one thousand of these were slaves. Elias Neau understood what slavery meant. A French Huguenot, he had suffered seven years' imprisonment at hard labor because he would not abjure his Protestant faith. He had found refuge in New York, and joined Trinity Church. In 1703 he called the attention of the Society for Propagating the Gospel to the slaves, "who were without God in the world, and of whose souls there was no manner of care taken." The officers of the Society prevailed upon him to accept appointment as a Catechist, and to devote himself to their education and religious instruction. In spite of many difficulties, not the least of which was the unwillingness of many masters to have their slaves taught, his efforts met with a good measure of success. In 1712 an outbreak on the part of a few negroes was quelled with savage severity. "Twenty-one were executed," reported Governor Hunter; "some were burnt, others hanged, one broke on the wheel, and one hung alive in chains in the town, so that there has been the most exemplary punishment inflicted that could be thought of." Neau was blamed for the trouble by some; but it was found that but one of the malcontent slaves had been under his instruction. The Governor exonerated him, and in a proclamation urged the promotion of his work.

154   License of Elias Neau as Catechist, as recorded in the *Book of Deeds*, Vol. 10, in the office of the Secretary of State, Albany

the Negroe Slaves.   243

mended it to the Clergy of the Country, to exhort their Congregations from the Pulpit, to promote the Inſtruction of the Negroes. *The School is again encouraged.*

THIS gave new Life again to the Work, and the *Negroes* frequented Mr. *Neau's* School, ſeveral were inſtructed, afterwards examined publickly in the Church, before the Congregation, by the Reverend Mr. *Veſey*, gave a very ſatisfactory Account of their Faith, and received Baptiſm. The Society had Accounts from Time to Time, of Mr. *Neau's* Diligence and good Succeſs; particularly one very ample Teſtimonial ſigned by the Governor of the Country (*Robert Hunter* Eſq;) the Council, the Mayor, and Recorder of *New-York*, and the two Chief Juſtices; ſetting forth, "That Mr. *Neau* had demeaned himſelf "in all Things, as a good Chriſtian and "a good Subject; that in his Station of "Catechiſt, he had, to the great Advance- "ment of Religion in general, and the "particular Benefit of the free *Indians*, "*Negroe* Slaves, and other Heathens in "thoſe Parts, with indefatigable Zeal and "Application, performed that Service "three Times a Week; and that they did "ſincerely believe, that as Catechiſt, he
R 2   "did

Mr. Neau is commended.

244   Endeavours to inſtruct

" did in a very eminent Degree, deſerve " the Countenance, Favour, and Protection " of the Society.

THE Society were fully ſatisfied with Mr. *Neau's* Behaviour, and continued to ſend him Numbers of Catechiſms, and of ſmall Tracts of Devotion and Inſtruction, to give among the Slaves and Servants at his Diſcretion. Mr. *Neau* perſevered with the ſame Diligence, till the Year 1722, in which he died, much regretted by all who knew his Labours. Mr. *Huddleſtone*, then Schoolmaſter in *New-York*, did for ſome Time ſupply his Place, and uſed to teach the *Negroes*, in the Church Steeple, every Sunday before Sermon, and at his own Houſe after Sermon. In a little Time the Society ſent the Reverend Mr. *Wetmore* to be Catechiſt there, and received Accounts of his diſcharging his Duty diligently. That he attended Catechiſing every Wedneſday and Friday, and Sunday Evening, at his own Houſe; and in the Church, every Sunday before Evening Service, where he had ſometimes near 200 Children, Servants and *Negroes*. He afterwards deſired to be appointed Miſſionary at *Rye* in that Government, and the Society complyed with his Requeſt. Soon after his Removal, the Rector, Church-Wardens,

Mr. Neau dies.

The Society ſend another Catechiſt.

155   Testimonial of Governor Robert Hunter, d. 1734, from David Humphrey, D.D., *Historical Account of Incorporated Society for the Propagation of the Gospel in Foreign Parts*, London, 1730

THE SUPPOSED "NEGRO PLOT" IN NEW YORK

IN 1741, from March to October, New York was swept by insensate panic and plunged into a tragedy more extensive and more horrible than the witchcraft delusion at Salem. Rumors spread that the negroes were plotting to burn the city, murder the white men, and make one Hughson, a low dram-shop keeper, king, and Caesar, a negro slave, governor. Without proper evidence, and without benefit of counsel, thirteen negroes were burned alive at the stake, eighteen were hanged, and seventy-one transported to be sold into slavery elsewhere. Four white persons were hanged, including a clergyman now believed to have belonged to the Church of England. September 24, 1741, was set apart as a day of public thanksgiving to God for His deliverance from "this horrible and execrable conspiracy." Hughson's body, hanging in chains, was said to have turned black, and Caesar's to have turned white: this was construed as a miraculous sign of their guilt and of Divine vengeance. Yet there is little doubt that there was no conspiracy at all, and that the whole of the evidence was manufactured, most of it by a lying fifteen-year-old servant girl. The persons executed were victims of public hysteria.

THE

New-York Weekly JOURNAL.

Containing the freshest Advices, foreign and Domestick.

MUNDAY September 14th 1741.

By the HONOURABLE.

George Clarke Esq; His Majesty's Lieutenant Governour and Commander in Chief in and over the Province of *New-York*, and the Territories thereon depending in *America*, &c.

A PROCLAMATION.

WHEREAS it hath pleased Almighty GOD, of his infinite Goodness and Mercy to Save and Defend the People of this Province from the late horrid and dangerous Conspiracy formed, set on Foot, and in Part Perpetrated, as well by several White People as a great Number of Negro Slaves, and others for the Ruin and Destruction of this City and Province, and to preserve us from eminent Danger hereof, when for our manifold Iniquities he might in Justice have given us over to their Cruel and Bloody Hands, and have suffer'd us to Perish by their Barbarous and Wicked Machinations which only his Divine Providence hath Prevented.

IT is Our Duty therefore to Return him Our Humble and Hearty Praises and Thanksgivings, as for all Things, so in particular Gracious and most Signal Instance of his Infinite Mercy to us. And that such our Praises and Thanksgivings may be rendered in the most Publick and Solemn manner.

I Do, by and with the Advice of His Majesty's Council for this Province issue this Proclamation, hereby Commanding and directing, that *Thursday* the Twenty fourth Day of *September* Instant, be set a-part and Observed as a Day of Publick and General THANKS - GIVING to Almighty GOD for his late Mercies vouchsafed unto Us, in delivering His Majesty's Subjects of this Province from the Destruction with which they were so generally Threatned by the said Horrid and Execrable Conspiracy. And all His Majesty's Subjects within this Province, as they tender the Favour of Almighty God, and have a due Gratitude for, and Sense of His great Mercies confered upon Us, and would avoid his Wrath and Indignation for Neglecting so Necessary and Religious a Duty, are hereby strictly Charged and Commanded to Observe the said Day so set a-part for the Service aforesaid, with decency and Reverence.

AND I do hereby Order and direct, That no Servile Labour be done on the said Day, hereby likewise enjoyning and directing, That Divine Service be Performed on the said Day in all the Churches, Chappels and other Places of Divine Worship, within the said Province. And all Rectors, Pastors, Vicars, Curates, and all other Ministers of the Gospel within the same, are hereby directed and Required to govern themselves accordingly, and to give Notice hereof, by Reading this Proclamation in their respective Churches, Chappels, and other

No. 406

156   From the original in the New York Public Library

MISSIONARIES AMONG THE INDIANS

MISSIONARY work among the Indians was discouraging. "The natives of the country are a decaying people," a missionary at Rye reported to the Society for Propagating the Gospel in 1708. "I have taken some pains to teach some of them but to no purpose, for they seem regardless of instruction; and when I have told them of the evil consequences of their hard drinking &c, they replied that Englishmen do the same: and that it is not so great a sin in an Indian as in an Englishman, because the Englishman's Religion forbids it, but an Indian's does not. They further say they will not be Christians nor do they see the necessity for so being, because we do not live according to the precepts of our religion. . . . I am heartily sorry that we should give them such a bad example and fill their mouths with such Objections against our blessed Religion."

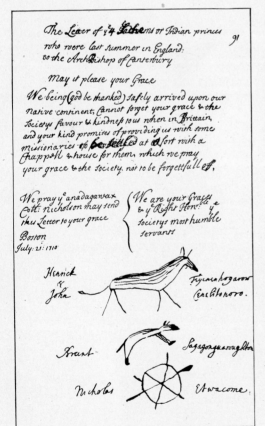

157   Letter of Four Iroquois Chiefs Who Visited England; from the original in the Library of Congress, Washington

The answer of the most
Reverend father in god
Thomas Ld ArchBishop of Canterbury
to the Letter of ye 4 sachems
or Indian princes

My most worthy Lord

I had the honour of your Letter Dated from Boston July
the 21. 1710 I have not been forgetfull of your Business which
is of such moment, & such I have at my heart but it pleased
god to visit me with a Long & severe sickness wch has
Disabled me from doing what I should have sooner accomplished
If god had given me health...as soon as we understand by
Coll Nicholson or by any other wayes you shall think
proper that the fort and Chappell & missionary house are
fitt to receive 2 missionary our society for propagating the
in faith among you, will take care you shall not want
2 good men & in order to Enabling you to build the fort
Chappell & house there is already Deposited in Coll
Perrys hand 136 wch Coll nicholson may draw for your
use, as soon as he pleases, he may also draw upon me
2 by more to make it up 400 as soon as you & he think fitt
I heartily commend you to the protection of god & pray
daily for yr good success of this mighty affair I am

yr affectionate Lord
Canterbury

158   Reply of the Archbishop of Canterbury, from the original in the Library of Congress, Washington

BARCLAY PREACHING TO THE MOHAWKS

THE most successful of the missionaries sent to the Indians by the Society for Propagating the Gospel was Henry Barclay, 1714–64, whose father, Thomas Barclay, was chaplain and rector at Albany from 1708 to 1728, and had organized the mission to the Iroquois. Born and reared in Albany, and educated at Yale, Henry Barclay was admirably fitted by experience as well as by temperament to take charge of the work among the Mohawks, which he did in 1735. He went to England for ordination two years

THE IROQUOIS ASK FOR MISSIONARIES

THE Iroquois, to whom both French priests and Dutch dominies had already carried Christian teaching, were the first to welcome the Society's missionaries. In 1709–10 four Iroquois sachems made the journey to England, where they were presented to the Queen and ratified the covenant between the Six Nations and the English. They asked that missionaries be sent them, and promised "that they would not admit any Jesuits or other French priests among them." Here are reproduced a letter (No. 157) which they addressed to the Archbishop of Canterbury immediately after their return to America, reminding him of their request, and the letter which he sent them in reply. The chapel among the Mohawks was dedicated, and the missionary began his labors in 1712.

159   Barclay Preaching to the Indians, 1738, from the bronze panel by Charles H. Niehaus (1855–), in Trinity Church, New York, courtesy of the Corporation of Trinity Church

later, and on his return, when many of the Indians, the record states, "shed tears for joy," he assumed also the rectorship of the Albany church. His work was interrupted in 1745 by the outbreak of hostilities with the French and their Indian allies; and he accepted a call to succeed William Vesey as rector of Trinity Church in New York. The mission continued under other men, and the Mohawks remained faithful to the English throughout the French and Indian wars.

CHRIST CHURCH, PHILADELPHIA

CHRIST CHURCH in Philadelphia was founded in 1695, and prospered from the start. Queen Anne presented to it a set of communion plate, as well as a library. The building, which is still in use, was begun in 1727. Benjamin Franklin for sixty years held a pew in this church. The Continental Congress came here in a body to attend divine services on July 20, 1775, which they had appointed as a day of fasting and prayer. President Washington and his family worshiped here for six years while Philadelphia was the National Capitol. The General Conventions of 1785, 1786 and 1789, which organized the Protestant Episcopal Church, met here. Dr. William White, the leader in that movement and first Bishop of Pennsylvania, was baptized in Christ Church, and served it, as assistant and rector, for sixty-four years.

160   Christ Church, Philadelphia, from a wooden model of the exterior constructed in 1866

THE FOUNDING OF KING'S CHAPEL, BOSTON

THE Puritans kept the Church of England out of New England as long as they had the power. After the Charter of Massachusetts was revoked, however, James II instructed Governor Andros "that liberty of conscience be allowed to all persons, and that such especially as shall be conformable to the rites of the Church of England be particularly countenanced and encouraged." Andros demanded that the Anglican minister be accorded the use of one of the meetinghouses. This was refused,

161 From an engraving *A South East View of ye great Town of Boston in New England in America*, 1743, published by William Price after a drawing by William Burgis in 1723, in the Massachusetts Historical Society

162 The Pulpit in Kings Chapel, from Rev. Henry W. Foote, *Annals of King's Chapel*, Boston, 1882

but he was granted the use of the Town-house, where Anglican services were held until Andros, on Good Friday and on Easter Sunday, 1687, took forcible possession of the Old South meetinghouse, which he thereafter shared with its proprietors. King's Chapel, the first Anglican church in New England, was completed in 1689. Edward Randolph had coolly proposed "that the three meeting-houses in Boston might pay twenty shillings a week a piece, out of their contributions, towards defraying our Church charges"; but this plan to support the Anglican church out of the voluntary contributions of the Congregational churches was too much for even an Archbishop of Canterbury's sense of humor, and it was not attempted.

THE BRATTLE ORGAN

IN their revolt from the ceremonies of the Church of England, the Puritans had denounced liturgical responses and the use of musical instruments in public worship. "We allow of the people joining with one voice in a plain tune, but not in tossing the psalms from one side to the other with mingling of organs." In 1713, Thomas Brattle, a wealthy Boston merchant, bequeathed to the Brattle Square Church, of which he had been the principal founder, an organ which he had imported from England, "if they shall accept thereof, and within a year after my decease procure a Sober person that can play skilfully thereon with a loud noise." The Church voted, "with all possible respect to the memory of our deceased Friend and Benefactor, that they did not think it proper to use the same in the public worship of God." Mr. Brattle had provided that, in this contingency, it should be offered to the Church of England worshiping in King's Chapel, which promptly accepted the gift. This organ was the first in New England, probably in all the colonies. It was replaced by a better instrument in 1756, and sold to St. Paul's Church, Newburyport. After eighty years of service there, it was bought by St. John's Church, Portsmouth, given a new case, and placed in the chapel, where it now is. "Singing by rule" eventually won its way, against much opposition, in the Congregational churches; and first pitch pipes and tuning forks, then bass viols, were introduced. Not until the nineteenth century did the use of church organs become general.

163 The Brattle Organ, now in St. John's Church, Portsmouth, N. H., from a photograph by J. W. Newell

This Evening,

The Tenth of *December*, at Six o'Clock, the

NEW

ORGAN,

At KING'S CHURCH, will be

play'd on by Mr. FLAGG.

A Number of Gentlemen belonging to the Town will affist on the Occafion, and perform the vocal Parts. A SERMON, on the Lawfulnefs, Excellency and Advantage of INSTRUMENTAL MUSIC in public Worfhip, will be preached by the Reverend JOHN GRAVES, after which a Collection will be made to defray the Expence of bringing the ORGAN from *Bofton*, and fixing it in the Church.

" *Praife him with ORGANS.*"---Pfalm cl. 4.

" *Praife him with danceing and the Stringed Instruments Pfm 150. 4th.*"

164   From the original announcement in the John Carter Brown Library, Providence

"PRAISE HIM WITH ORGANS"

THIS broadside announced the installation of an organ in King's Church, Providence, Rhode Island, which became St. John's Church after the Revolution. The writer of the additional text — "Praise him with dancing and the stringed instruments" — doubtless meant it in derision. It was a common Puritan argument that the use of instrumental music in worship belonged, with dancing, to the Jewish dispensation recorded in the Old Testament, but had no place in the Gospel proclaimed in the New Testament. "If we admit instrumental music in the worship of God," asked Cotton Mather, "how can we resist the imposition of all the Instruments used among the ancient Jews? Yea, Dancing as well as Playing, and several other Judaic actions."

RECTOR CUTLER, OF YALE, JOINS THE CHURCH OF ENGLAND

THE Anglican Church had forced its way into Massachusetts; its growth in Connecticut was by peaceful penetration. George Pigot, sent by the Society for Propagating the Gospel as missionary to Stratford, succeeded in persuading Samuel Johnson, pastor of the church at West Haven, and the entire faculty of Yale College, consisting of Timothy Cutler, Rector, and Daniel Brown, Tutor, that their "Presbyterian ordination" was invalid. The Trustees of the College were astonished when, after the Commencement exercises in 1722, Cutler and Brown presented a statement signed by themselves and five other Congregational ministers, concerning "the difficulties which we labor under in relation to our continuance out of the visible communion of an Episcopal Church, and a state of seeming opposition thereto." At a public discussion a month later, Cutler and Johnson upheld the principles of Episcopacy and Governor Saltonstall was the chief speaker in behalf of Congregationalism. The result was that three of the seven signers remained Congregationalists; but Cutler was not among these, and the Trustees voted to "excuse" him "from all further service as Rector of Yale College." Brown was likewise dismissed, and it was voted that thereafter those elected to the faculty should, before induction into office, declare assent to the Saybrook Confession of Faith and give assurance of their "opposition to Arminian and prelatical corruptions." Cutler, Johnson and Brown started at once for England to be ordained.

Rector Cutler and the Trustees

165   From the drawing by Theodore Diedrichsen, Jr., in Edwin Oviatt, *The Beginnings of Yale (1701–26)*, New Haven, 1916

CUTLER BECOMES RECTOR OF CHRIST CHURCH, BOSTON

CUTLER returned in 1723 as a missionary of the Society for Propagating the Gospel to become rector of the newly organized Christ Church in Boston. His friends in Connecticut greatly mourned his loss. To a passage extolling his scholarship, one of his successors adds, "He was of a high, lofty, and despotic mien, and made a grand figure as the Head of a College." The building of Christ Church remains to this day, the oldest house of worship in Boston. The interior has been restored as nearly as possible to its original condition. In the original steeple of this church were hung the lanterns that served as signal for Paul Revere's ride to arouse the militia against the British.

166 Interior of Christ Church (Old North), Boston, from a photograph by The Maynard Workshop, Waban, Mass.

167 Timothy Cutler, 1683-1765, from a copy of a mezzotint, 1750, by Peter Pelham, in the Collections of the Bostonian Society

SAMUEL JOHNSON, 1696-1772, FIRST PRESIDENT OF KING'S COLLEGE

JOHNSON returned with Cutler, and succeeded Pigot as missionary of the Society for Propagating the Gospel at Stratford. He had such power as a propagandist that he must be accounted the founder of the Episcopal Church in Connecticut. He was a man of unusual gifts — a scholar and administrator as well as a preacher, and possessed of such liberality of mind and sincerity of character as to retain the friendship of the Congregational authorities, in spite of his dissent from their system of belief and his success as an Episcopal missionary. He wrote textbooks on philosophy and ethics which were published in Philadelphia by Benjamin Franklin; and at Franklin's nomination he was invited to become the first president of the College and Academy of Philadelphia, now the University of Pennsylvania. He declined this invitation, but in 1754 accepted a call to become the first president of King's College in New York, now Columbia University. He resigned and returned to his parish at Stratford in 1763. His son, William Samuel Johnson, 1727-1819, judge of the Superior Court of Connecticut and one of its first United States Senators, became the first president of Columbia College under its new name and charter in 1787.

168 Christ Church, Stratford, 1743-1858, from E. Edwards Beardsley, History of the Episcopal Church in Connecticut, Vol. I, New York, 1865

169 Samuel Johnson, from the original portrait, attributed to Laurence Kilburn (d. 1775), in Columbia University, New York

DEAN BERKELEY VISITS AMERICA

FROM January, 1729 to October, 1731, George Berkeley, then Dean of Londonderry, world-famous philosopher of idealism, resided in America. He had planned to establish a university in Bermuda, but the promises made to him by the English authorities were never fulfilled, and he got no further than Rhode Island, where he spent nearly three years in study and writing. Samuel Johnson called upon him soon after his arrival, and the two men became fast friends. Johnson interested Berkeley in "the college at New Haven," and when the latter returned to London, he conveyed to Yale College, through Mr. Johnson, the title to his Rhode Island estate of ninety-six acres. Later, he sent to the college library a gift of nearly one thousand volumes — "the finest collection of books," said President Clap, "which had then ever been brought to America."

170 George Berkeley, 1684–1753, from the portrait, 1728, by John Smibert, in the Massachusetts Historical Society, Boston

CHRIST CHURCH, LANCASTER COUNTY, VIRGINIA

No less interesting than the Puritan meetinghouses of colonial New England are the Episcopal churches of eighteenth-century Virginia. Christ Church in Lancaster County is the only one which has never been altered. It was built in 1732 at the sole expense of Robert Carter of Corotoman — "King Carter," folk called him —

171   Christ Church, Lancaster County, Virginia, from a photograph by H. P. Cook, Richmond, Va.

lord of an estate of eight thousand acres. It is in the form of a Greek cross, measuring sixty-eight feet each way. The ceiling forms a groined arch over the intersection of the aisles, thirty-three feet from the floor.

172   Interior of Christ Church, Lancaster County, Virginia, courtesy of Robert A. Lancaster, Jr., Richmond

There are twenty-five pews of solid black walnut, of a soundness unimpaired by age. Twenty-two of these seat twelve persons each, and three will contain twenty persons each. As beautiful as the church itself was its setting. A straight road traversed the three miles of distance from the house of worship to Corotoman on the Rappahannock. On either side of this stood a close-set hedge of cedar trees. The stately Carter coach passed through this aisle of trees on a Sabbath morning while the congregation, according to tradition, waited outside the church until the great man had entered the portal.

173   Interior of Aquia Church, courtesy of Robert A. Lancaster, Jr., Richmond, Va.

AQUIA CHURCH, OVERWHARTON PARISH

AQUIA CHURCH in Overwharton Parish, Stafford County, was built in 1757. Like many of the Virginia churches, it is of brick and in the form of a cross. Unlike most of them, it has a bell and clock tower. The aisles are of stone, with a cross of marble at the intersection. The pulpit is what was called a "three-decker." The chancel contains a handsome reredos, with four panels, on which are the Ten Commandments, the Apostles' Creed, and the Lord's Prayer. The church also contains a gallery which is supported by pillars.

THE CHURCH GEORGE WASHINGTON BUILT

POHICK CHURCH, Truro Parish, Fairfax County, was the home church of George Mason, author of the Virginia Bill of Rights, and of George Washington. Washington was a vestryman of Truro Parish from 1762 to 1782. He chose the location for the new Pohick Church to be built in 1769, drew the plans, was chairman of the building committee which supervised its erection, and bore a large share of the expense. The interior of this church suffered damage during the Civil War, and was repaired in 1874. Restoration was made in 1906, the pews and other furnishings here shown being reproductions of the originals.

174   Pohick Church, from a photograph, courtesy of
Rau Studios, Inc., Philadelphia

175   Interior of Pohick Church, courtesy of Robert A. Lancaster, Jr., Richmond, Va.

CHAPTER IV

THE GROWTH OF RELIGIOUS FREEDOM

CUIUS REGIO EIUS RELIGIO was the Old World principle which underlay the establishment of state-supported churches. The terse Latin eludes translation by any phrase equally brief. "The lord of a land determines its religion" is the idea. The struggle for religious liberty has not been waged by one group alone, but by all groups when they found themselves in the minority or under restraint. In England the battle of conscience was fought by Catholics against Protestant oppression under Henry VIII, and by Protestants against Catholic oppression under Mary; by Catholics and Separatists against Elizabeth; by Puritans against Charles I; and, after his execution, by Independents against Presbyterians.

The first American colonies established upon a basis of religious freedom were Maryland, founded by the Catholic Lord Baltimore, and Rhode Island, founded by Roger Williams, Separatist, Baptist, and Seeker. The clearest early statement of the principles upon which such freedom should rest was made by John Clarke, Baptist physician and pastor, who as agent in London for the Rhode Island colony secured for it a charter so well conceived that it for many years served the State of Rhode Island as a constitution.

The Quakers made great contributions to the cause of religious freedom, not so much through their fiery denunciations of the "steeple-houses" and "priests" and "vain traditions" of other groups, or even through their sufferings, as through the positive, constructive examples of the working of the principle of religious freedom which they furnished to the world in the colonies where they had political power, especially in Pennsylvania.

The Great Awakening of the second decade of the eighteenth century, which stirred to a greater or less degree all Protestant groups in America except the Church of England, helped to overturn old conceptions and customs, and prepared men's minds for the general acceptance of the idea of religious freedom. We may now, as did many of their contemporaries, criticize certain methods of the revivalists and dissent from some of their theological ideas. The facts remain that they insisted that religion is an experience of the individual soul brought face to face with God, rather than mere creedal assent or liturgical conformity, and that this emphasis upon experience, with the individualism which it fostered, led to a conception of the church as a spiritual society quite independent of the state and not to be subjected to its patronage.

Of the thirteen colonies brought together by the Constitution of the United States, five had supported the Church of England as an established state church, three had supported the Congregational churches, three had declared for religious freedom, and two had been claimed by their Governors for the Church of England, over the dissent of the people. In view of this diversity of principle and practice, it was but fair that a guarantee of complete religious freedom should be made a part of the Constitution. That decision was rendered easier, moreover, by the fact that a strenuous battle for religious freedom had just been fought and won in Virginia by the Presbyterians and Baptists, with the powerful help of three of Virginia's greatest statesmen — Patrick Henry, Thomas Jefferson, and James Madison. To Madison we owe the elimination of the misleading word "toleration" and the substitution therefor of the unequivocal phrase: "all men are equally entitled to the free exercise of religion according to the dictates of conscience."

RELIGIOUS LIBERTY IN UTOPIA

SIR THOMAS MORE, who had been Lord Chancellor of England, was beheaded July 7, 1535, because he would not acknowledge King Henry VIII to be "the only supreme head on earth of the Church of England." Himself a Catholic so devoted that he has been given the title "Blessed" by his Church, More proposed religious liberty as one of the characteristics of the ideal state described in his *Utopia* (published in Latin, 1516, first English translation, 1551): "King Utopus made a decree that it should be lawful for every man to favor and follow what religion he would, and that he might do the best that he could to bring others to his opinion, so that he did it peaceably, gently, quietly and soberly, without hasty and contentious rebuking and inveighing against others. . . . Though there be one religion which alone is true and all other vain and superstitious, yet did he well foresee, if the matter were handled with reason and sober modesty, that the truth of its own power would at last issue out and come to light. But if contention and debate in that behalf should continually be used, as the worst men be most obstinate and stubborn and in their evil

176 Sir Thomas More, 1478–1535, from the portrait by Hans Holbein the younger (1497–1543), courtesy of the Frick Art Reference Library, New York

opinion most contrary, he perceived that then the best and holiest religion would be destroyed by vain superstitions, even as good corn is by thorns and weeds overgrown and choked. Therefore he gave to every man free liberty and choice to believe what he would. If he could not by fair and gentle speech induce them unto his opinion yet he should use no kind of violence, and refrain from displeasant and seditious words. . . . This law did King Utopus make not only for the maintenance of peace, but also because he thought the decree should make for the furtherance of religion. . . ."

THE FOUNDING OF MARYLAND

MORE did not put his ideal into practice. "Many things there be in the Utopian weal public which in our cities I may rather wish for than hope after." As Lord Chancellor of England he sanctioned the persecution of Protestants, and in an attack upon Tyndale he defended the practice of burning heretics. A century later George Calvert, Lord Baltimore, projected a colony in America based upon the Utopian principle of religious liberty. It fell to his son, Cecil Calvert, the second Lord Baltimore, to carry out his father's purpose. In his first proclamation, inviting adventurers to share in the settlement of Maryland, he promised freedom of religion to all Christians. The Calverts, father and son, were Catholics. Their motive was not material gain merely, as is sometimes asserted, nor even the founding of an asylum for persecuted Catholics; the truth seems rather to be that in the face of the growing encroachments of the Stuarts upon the liberties of English citizens, they sought to establish a state where these liberties should be forever secured. The feudal grant which the Calverts received became the abode of that handful of Englishmen who established the Catholic faith in the Colonies.

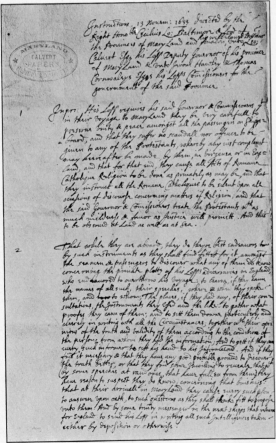

177 First page of Lord Baltimore's Instructions to the First Colonists, November 13, 1633, from the original in the *Calvert Papers*, Maryland Historical Society, Baltimore

178 Father Richard Blount, 1565–1638, from *Historia Provinciae Anglicanae Societatis Jesu*, etc., Andomari, 1660, in the Library of Stonyhurst College, England

THE ADVICE OF FATHER BLOUNT

LORD BALTIMORE saw that underlying all liberty is freedom of conscience. Among his close advisers was Father Richard Blount, Provincial of the Society of Jesus. In a paper considering the objections urged against the "license" which Baltimore's policy would grant to Catholics, as to others, to "have free liberty of their religion," Father Blount wrote these words, remarkable in an age that demanded religious conformity: "Conversion in matters of religion, if it be forced, should give little satisfaction to a wise state . . . for those who for worldly respects will break their faith with God, doubtless will do it, upon a fit occasion, much sooner with men."

PLANTING THE CROSS IN MARYLAND

BALTIMORE was compelled to remain in England to protect his enterprise against anti-Catholic agitation. He sent his two brothers "with very near twenty other gentlemen of very good fashion, and three hundred laboring men well provided in all things," to establish the colony. Baltimore's statement is not complete. At least one hundred and twenty-eight, and probably the majority, of the members of the expedition were Protestants; the gentlemen were Catholics, among them Father Andrew White and Father John Altham, Jesuit missionaries. They landed at an island in the Potomac which they named St. Clement's. "On the day of the Annunciation of the Blessed Virgin Mary in the year 1634, we celebrated the first Mass on that island; never before had it been offered in that region. After the holy sacrifice, bearing on our shoulders a huge cross, which we had hewn from a tree, we moved in procession to a spot selected, the Governor, Commissioners and other Catholics putting their hands unto it, and erected it as a trophy to Christ our Saviour; then, humbly kneeling, we recited with deep emotion the Litany of the Holy Cross."

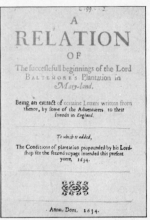

179 Title-page of the first publication relating to Maryland, from the original in the British Museum, London

180 *Landing of the Expedition under Leonard Calvert on St. Clement's Island, March 25, 1634*, from the original painting by Emanuel Leutze (1816–68), in the Maryland Historical Society, by permission of the owner, J. J. Mack, San Francisco

FATHER ANDREW WHITE, 1579–1656

FEARING lest it should lay him open to the charge of establishing Catholicism as the religion of the colony, Lord Baltimore gave the Jesuits no subsidy; but granted them land on the same conditions as other gentleman adventurers. Reinforced by others of their Society, they had great success in the conversion of the Indians. Father White wrote an Indian catechism and constructed a grammar and dictionary of the language of the Maryland natives. Some of the Indian chiefs ceded to the Jesuits large areas of land. This fact, together with the Jesuits' claim that they were subject to the Canon Law rather than to the laws of the state, aroused Baltimore's opposition; and he allowed them to remain only on condition that they surrender these lands and submit to the common law. "Baltimore was a good Catholic, but he was also a sturdy Englishman. We see in these conditions the fear lest the church should acquire too much real estate, lest the clergy should claim exemptions and immunities of a past age and assert independence of the common law and the constituted authorities." — THOMAS O'GORMAN, *A History of the Roman Catholic Church in the United States*, p. 224.

P. Andreas Vitus, S.J. Angl, in Anglia et Marilandia Americæ Provincia Apostolicis laboribus clarus. Obiit in Anglia prope octogenarius, A° 1655.

181 Father Andrew White Converting Indians, from an engraving by J. Kilian after a drawing by Johann Georg Heinsch (d. 1713), in M. Tanner, *Societas Jesu Apostolorum Imitatrix*, Prague, 1694

AN ACT CONCERNING RELIGION, 1649

UNDER the rule of Parliament, Lord Baltimore appointed a Protestant Governor, with a majority of Protestant councillors, and submitted to the Assembly for their enactment a carefully drafted body of laws. The first of these, An Act concerning Religion, which the Assembly passed in 1649, ordained death as the penalty of blasphemy or denial of the Trinity; and the use of "reproachful words" concerning the Virgin Mary, the Apostles, or Evangelists was to be punished by fine or whipping and, upon the third offence, by banishment and confiscation of goods. A fine of ten pounds, or whipping and imprisonment until public apology be tendered, was to be inflicted upon any one who calls another "Heretic, Schismatic, Idolator, Puritan, Presbyterian, Independent, Popish Priest, Jesuit, Jesuited Papist, Lutheran, Calvinist, Anabaptist, Brownist, Antinomian, Barrowist, Roundhead, Separatist, or other name or term in a reproachful manner, relating to a matter of religion." Fines, or imprisonment and whipping, are provided for profanation of the Lord's Day. Then is stated the principle of toleration: "Whereas the enforcing of the conscience in matters of religion hath frequently fallen out to be of dangerous consequence in those commonwealths where it hath been practised, and for the more quiet and peaceable government of this province, and the better to preserve mutual love and unity amongst the inhabitants here, be it . . . ordained and enacted . . . that no person or persons whatsoever . . . professing to believe in Jesus Christ, shall from henceforth be any ways troubled, molested, or discountenanced, for or in his or her religion, nor in the free exercise thereof . . . nor any way compelled to belief or exercise of any other religion against his or her consent."

244 *Assembly Proceedings, April 2–21, 1649.*

Liber A
p. 268
Acts of Assembly of the 21ᵗʰ of Aprill 1649.
Confirmed by the Lord Proprietary by an instrument under his hand & seale 26ᵗʰ of August 1650 Phillip Calvert.

Acts and Orders of Assembly assented vnto
Enacted and made at a Genall Sessions of the said Assembly held at Sᵗ Maries on the one and twentieth day of Aprill Anno Dm̄ 1649 as followeth viz.:

An Act concerning Religion

p. 269 fforasmuch as in a well governed and Xpian Com̄on Weath matters concerning Religion and the honor of God ought in the first place to bee taken, into serious consideracōn and endeavoured to bee settled. Be it therefore ordered and enacted by the Right Hoᵇˡᵉ Cecilius Lord Baron of Baltemore absolute Lord and Proprietary of this Province with the advise and consent of this Generall Assembly. That whatsoever pson or psons within this Province and the Islands thereunto belonging shall from henceforth blaspheme God, that is Curse him, or deny our Saviour Jesus Christ to bee the sonne of God, or shall deny the holy Trinity the ffather sonne and holy Ghost, or the Godhead of any of the said Three psons of the Trinity or the Vnity of the Godhead, or shall use or utter any reproachfull Speeches, words or language concerning the said Holy Trinity, or any of the said three psons thereof, shalbe punished with death and confiscatōn or forfeiture of all his or her lands and goods to the Lord Proprietary and his heires, And bee it also Enacted by the Authority and with the advise and assent aforesaid. That whatsoever pson or psons shall from henceforth use or utter any reproachfull words or Speeches concerning the blessed Virgin Mary the Mother of our Saviour or the holy Apostles or Evangelists or any of them shall in such case for the first offence forfeit to the said Lord Proprietary and his heirs Lords and Proprietaries of this Province the sume of ffive pound Sterling or the value thereof to be Levyed on the goods and chattells of every such pson soe offending, but in case such Offender or Offenders, shall not then have goods and chattells sufficient for the satisfyeing of such forfeiture, or that the same bee not otherwise speedily satisfyed that then such Offender or Offenders shalbe publiquely whipt and bee ymprisoned during the pleasure of the Lord Proprietary or the Leiveᵗ or cheife Governor of this Province for the time being. And that every such Offender or Offenders for every second offence shall forfeit tenne pound sterling or the value thereof to bee levyed as aforesaid, or in case such offender or Offenders shall not then haue goods and chattells within this Province sufficient for that purpose then to bee publiquely and severely whipt and

182 An Act Concerning Religion, from the *Archives of Maryland, 1637–64*, edited by William H. Brown, Baltimore, 1883, in the Library of Congress, Washington

183 Charles Carroll, 1737–1832, from the original portrait, 1836, by Thomas Sully (1783–1872), in the Historical Society of Pennsylvania, Philadelphia

THE CATHOLICS OF MARYLAND

Lord Baltimore's ideal of "mutual love and unity" was not realized. Maryland suffered many vicissitudes. The Puritan party sought to repeal the Act of 1649, and to persecute the Catholics; but Cromwell prevented them. In 1692 the Charter was revoked, and the Church of England made the established church of the colony. In 1704, An Act to Prevent the Growth of Popery forbade public worship to the Catholics, restricting them to worship within the limits of "a private family of the Romish communion." In 1716, Catholics were disqualified from public office unless they would abjure their faith; and in 1718, they were denied the ballot. Yet the liberty-loving Catholics of Maryland grew in number, and did much to determine the character of Catholic citizenship in this country. Charles Carroll of Carrollton, patriot and signer of the Declaration of Independence, was a worthy inheritor of the spirit of George and Cecil Calvert, first and second Lords Baltimore. From the Maryland group came also Father John Carroll, first bishop of the Catholic Church in the United States.

ENDICOTT CUTS THE CROSS FROM THE KING'S ENSIGN

On May 6, 1635, John Endicott, who had been and was again to be Governor of Massachusetts, was censured by the General Court, and disqualified for public office for one year. It was because, at a muster of the Salem militia, he had drawn his sword and cut from the flag the cross of St. George, which he denounced as a "relic of Antichrist." The time was especially critical, for Sir Ferdinando Gorges was in London, in favor with Archbishop Laud, and had begun suit to obtain the revocation of the Massachusetts Charter. It was

one of the occasions when sermons bear too much fruit, for Endicott had been roused to this action by the fiery preaching of Roger Williams, his pastor and intimate friend. However doubtful his fellow magistrates might be as to the propriety of using the Cross, which they regarded as a symbol of Catholicism, on the national ensign, there was no doubt in their minds as to the impropriety of mutilating the flag which was the symbol of the Government to which they owed allegiance.

184 Endicott Cutting the Cross from the King's Ensign, from an engraving by J. G. Smithwick after the drawing by Edwin A. Abbey (1852–1911), in William Cullen Bryant and Sydney Gay, A Popular History of the United States, Vol. I, New York, 1883

They were aghast at the foolhardiness of the act, and they were prompt to punish Endicott and to send letters to England disavowing what he had done.

185 Sword said to be that with which John Endicott cut the Cross from the King's Ensign, courtesy of William C. Endicott, Esq., Danvers, Mass.

186   Sentence to Banishment, Sept. 2, 1635, from the original in the Archives of the Commonwealth of Massachusetts, Boston

ROGER WILLIAMS IS BANISHED FROM MASSACHUSETTS

WILLIAMS had come to Massachusetts in 1631 and plunged at once into dispute. No more ardent and uncompromising Separatist ever lived; and few men have so combined great intellectual power with occasional lack of perspective, tolerance with exclusiveness, and patience with disputatiousness. Invited to become teacher of the Boston church (the office afterward filled by John Cotton) he refused to minister to "an unseparated people," and unsparingly denounced them "because they would not make a public declaration of their repentance for having communion with the churches of England while they lived there," and because they did not forbid their members, when visiting in England, to attend services and hear sermons in the English churches. He preached for two years at Plymouth, then became pastor at Salem, where Endicott became his enthusiastic friend and follower. Williams maintained that the civil court had no right to punish infractions of the first table of the Decalogue, such as blasphemy and breach of the Sabbath; that the use of the term "goodman" as a mode of address, was blasphemous, since God only is good; that women must wear veils over their faces in church; that it was wrong to require an oath of fidelity to the Government, for an oath is an act of worship in which unregenerate men may not engage, and no godly man may without sin have fellowship, either in prayer or in an oath, with one who is unregenerate. He affirmed that the charters granted by the King were worthless, since the land belonged to the Indians alone, and that to live under the terms of such a charter was sin; he charged the King with being a liar and blasphemer; and he wrote a letter to the King (which fortunately he did not send) apprising him of these views. He sent letters to the churches of the colony asking them to discipline the magistrates because they had denied a petition in which he was interested; and when this strange request was refused, announced to his church that it must break fellowship with the other churches "as full of anti-christian pollution." His church being unwilling to take this action, he broke fellowship with it; and refused even to hold family prayers or to say grace at table in the presence of his wife because she continued to attend public worship. He was sentenced to banishment in the fall of 1635, but was allowed to remain throughout the winter, on condition that he attempt to make no proselytes. He broke this condition. "To publish these ideas was ... with him a matter of conscience ... for he continued to do so. ... It soon became known that he was accustomed to gather together congregations ... to whom he continued to inveigh against the King's charter." The court was preparing, therefore, to ship him to England when he fled. His banishment was ordered not as an act of religious persecution, but as an act of political self-protection.

187   Temporary Suspension of Banishment, May 15, 1656, from the original in the Archives of the Commonwealth of Massachusetts, Boston

188 Conditional Suspension of Banishment, Mar. 31, 1676, from the original in the Archives of the Commonwealth of Massachusetts, Boston

ROGER WILLIAMS FOUNDS RHODE ISLAND

YET Roger Williams was one of the really great men to whom the world owes an imperishable debt. His sufferings chastened his spirit and clarified his vision. He became a pioneer in America of the principle of the complete freedom of the individual in matters of religion. Purchasing land from the Indians, he founded a settlement which, "in a sense of God's merciful providence unto me in my distress," he called Providence. "I desired it might be for a shelter for persons distressed in conscience." In time this was united with other settlements as the colony of Rhode Island, the first to be organized upon the basis of complete religious liberty and complete civic democracy. Williams never set foot in Massachusetts again. He conducted a long controversy with John Cotton which caused him to think through the full implications of the principles he had espoused. With forgiving spirit, he helped the authorities of Massachusetts to deal with the Narraganset Indians. Winslow and Winthrop and others of the Massachusetts leaders, remained his devoted personal friends. "We have often tried your patience," wrote Winthrop in one of his many letters to Williams, "but could never conquer it." "He was in his earlier years, as saith Governor Bradford, 'very unsettled in judgment.' He was as a man groping in darkness, and yet sure that somewhere beyond him lay the light, such as no man yet had seen. In the Bay Colony he was trammeled and confined, as one ever seeking for some great truth, which as often ever eluded him. In the Plantations at Providence, with no one about him with whom he essentially differed, and no conditions present which could provoke controversy, his mind was set free from its confinings and liberated into the light of a great human truth. . . . Under his fostering, the tender plant of religious liberty pushed its tiny rootlets far down into the barren soil of New England, until they reached for their nourishment the living stream of truth." — EDMUND J. CARPENTER, *Roger Williams*. The quality of Williams' mind is manifest in a letter he wrote as an old man to his "honoured deare and antient friend," Major Mason. "I have offered and doe by these presents to discusse by disputation writing or printing, among other points of differences these three positions; first that forced worship stincks in Gods nostrils. 2d that it denies Jesus Christ yet to be come, and makes the church yet national, figurative and ceremonial. 3d That in these flames about religion, as his Majestie his father and grandfather have yielded, there is no other prudent, christian way of preserving peace in the world but by permission of differing consciences."

Chriftenings
make not
CHRISTIANS,
OR

A Briefe Difcourfe concerning that name *Heathen*, commonly given to the INDIANS.

As alfo concerning that great point of their CONVERSION

Publifhed according to Order.

London, Printed by *Iane Coe*, for I. H. 1645.

189 From the facsimile reprint, *Rhode Island Historical Tracts*, 1st series, no. 14, edited by Henry Martyn Dexter, Providence, 1881

RELIGIOUS LIBERTY ON THE SHIP OF STATE

It is easy to claim license in the name of religious liberty, and Rhode Island naturally attracted individualists and agitators of various sorts, whose principles would have subverted the basis of liberty upon which the community was founded. In dealing with these, Williams expressed the relations of religious liberty to civic order and welfare in a clear, concrete figure: "There goes many a ship to sea, with many hundred souls in one ship, whose weal and woe is common, and is a true picture of a commonwealth. . . . It hath fallen out sometimes, that both papists and protestants, Jews and Turks, may be embarked in one ship; upon which supposal I affirm, that all the liberty of conscience, that ever I pleaded for, turns upon these two hinges — that none of the papists, protestants, Jews, or Turks, be forced to come to the ship's prayers or worship, nor compelled from their own particular prayers or worship, if they practice any. Notwithstanding this liberty, the commander of this ship ought to command the ship's course, yea, and also command that justice, peace and sobriety, be kept and practised, both among the seamen and all the passengers. If any of the seamen refuse to perform their services, or passengers to pay their freight;

First, That the blood of so many hundred thousand souls of *Protestants* and *Papists*, spilt in the *Wars* of present and former *Ages*, for their respective *Consciences*, is not *required* nor *accepted* by *Iesus Christ* the *Prince* of *Peace*.

Secondly, Pregnant *Scriptures* and *Arguments* are throughout the Worke proposed against the *Doctrine* of *Persecution* for for cause of *Conscience*.

Thirdly, Satisfactorie Answers are given to *Scriptures*, and *objections* produced by Mr. *Calvin*, *Beza*, Mr. *Cotton*, and the Ministers of the New English Churches, and others former and later, tending to prove the *Doctrine* of *Persecution* for cause of *Conscience*.

Fourthly, The *Doctrine* of *Persecution* for cause of *Conscience*, is proved guilty of all the *blood* of the *Soules* crying for *vengeance* under the *Altar*.

a 2   Fifth-

190   From Roger Williams, *The Bloudy Tenent of Persecution, for Cause of Conscience*, 1644

if any refuse to help, in person or purse, toward the common charges of defense; if any refuse to obey the common laws and orders of the ship, concerning their common peace or preservation; if any shall mutiny and rise up against their commanders and officers, if any should preach or write that there ought to be no commanders or officers, because all are equal in Christ, therefore no masters nor officers, nor corrections nor punishments; — in such cases, whatever is pretended, the commander or commanders may judge, resist, compel and punish such transgressors, according to their deserts and merits."

Fifthly, All *Civill States* with their Officers of justice in their respective constitutions and *administrations* are proved *essentially Civill*. and therefore not *Iudges*, *Governours* or *Defenaours* of the *Spirituall* or *Christian* state and *Worship*.

Sixtly, It is the will and command of *God*, that since the comming of his Sonne the *Lord Iesus*) a *permission* of the most *Paganish*, *Iewish*, *Turkish* or *Antichristian consciences* and *worships*, bee granted to *all* men in all *Nations* and *Countries*: and they are onely to bee *fought* against with that *Sword* which is only (in *Soule matters*) *able* to *conquer*, to wit, the *Sword* of *Gods Spirit*, the *Word* of *God*.

Seventhly, The *state* of the Land of *Israel* the *Kings* and *people* thereof in *Peace* & *War*, is proved *figurative* and *ceremoniall*, and no *patterne* nor *president* for any *Kingdom* or *civill state* in the *world* to follow.

Eightly, *God* requireth not an *uniformity* of

191 From Roger Williams, *The Bloudy Tenent of Persecution for Cause of Conscience*, 1644

of *Religion* to be *inacted* and *inforced* in any *civill state*; which inforced *uniformity* (sooner or later) is the greatest occasion of *civill Warre*, *ravishing* of *conscience*, *persecution* of *Christ Iesus* in his *servants*, and of the *hypocrisie* and *destruction* of *millions* of *souls*.

Ninthly, In holding an inforced *uniformity* of *Religion* in a *civill state*, we must necessarily *disclaime* our desires and hopes of the *Iewes conversion* to *Christ*.

Tenthly, An inforced *uniformity* of *Religion* throughout a *Nation* or *civill state*, confounds the *Civill* and *Religious*, denies the principles of Christianity and civility, and that *Iesu Christ* is come in the Flesh.

Eleventhly, The permission of other *consciences* and *worships* then a *state* professeth, only can (according to *God*) procure a firme and lasting *peace*, (good *assurance* being taken according to the *wisdome* of the *civill state* for *uniformity* of *civill obedience* from all sorts.)

a 3   Twelfth.

192 From Roger Williams, *The Bloudy Tenent of Persecution, for Cause of Conscience*, 1644

193   Interior view of First Baptist Church, built 1775, Providence, from a photograph
by S. T. Jordan

THE FIRST BAPTIST CHURCH IN AMERICA

THE Baptists, who have always stood for liberty of conscience and the separation of church and state, rightly claim Roger Williams as one of their leaders. In March, 1639, he repudiated the baptism he had received in infancy, was immersed by Ezekiel Holliman, and then immersed Holliman and eleven others. So was founded at Providence the first Baptist Church in America. Williams' actual connection with the Baptists was limited to three or four months, however, for he was seized with scruples as to the validity of what he had done, and decided finally that only a miraculous interposition of divine authority could restore the lost apostolic succession of true baptism. He withdrew from the church, and remained a "seeker," hoping for the miracle, throughout the rest of his life. He seems never to have realized that in this demand for apostolic succession he had swung the circle and returned to a position substantially like that of the Church of England.

JOHN CLARKE, 1609–1676, PHYSICIAN AND PREACHER

THE leader of the early Baptists in America was John Clarke, a physician who helped plant the settlements at Portsmouth and Newport and organized the church at Newport, of which he became the first pastor. He was for twelve years the agent of the colony in England, and succeeded in awakening the curiosity of Charles II to try the "lively experiment" whether or not civil government could exist with a full liberty of conscience. In 1663 he secured from Charles a new Charter, which declared "that no person within the said colony shall be in any wise molested, punished, disquieted, or called in question for any differences in opinions in matters of religion which do not actually disturb the civil peace of our said colony; but that all and every person and persons may from time to time, and at all times hereafter, freely and fully have and enjoy his and their own judgments and consciences in matters of religious concernments . . . they behaving themselves peaceably and quietly, and not using this liberty to licentiousness and profaneness, nor to the civil injury or outward disturbance of others." This Charter was so comprehensive in its provision for civil as well as religious liberty that it served Rhode Island as a constitution until 1843. Clarke was the principal author of the Code of Laws of 1647, with its memorable closing words: "These are the laws that concern all men, and these are the penalties for the transgression thereof, which by common consent are ratified and established throughout this whole colony; and otherwise than what is herein forbidden all men may walk as their consciences persuade them, every one in the name of his God."

194   King Charles Charter, 1663, from a manuscript facsimile in the Rhode Island Historical Society, Providence, of the original in the State House

ILL
NEWES
FROM
NEW·ENGLAND:
OR
A Narative of *New-Englands*
PERSECUTION.
WHERIN IS DECLARED
That while old *England* is becoming new,
New-England is become Old.

Alfo four Propofals to the Honoured Parliament and Councel of State.
touching the way to *Propagate the Gofpel of Chrift* (with fmall
charge and great fafety) both in Old *England* and New.

Alfo four conclufions touching the faith and order of the Gofpel of
Chrift out of his laft Will and Teftament, confirmed and juftified

By JOHN CLARK Phyfician of Rode Ifland in *America.*

Revel. 2. 25. *Hold faft till I come.*
3. 11. *Behol I come quickly.*
22. 20. *Amen, even fo come Lord Jefus.*

LONDON,
Printed by *Henry Hills* living in *Fleet-Yard* next door to the *Rofe*
and *Crown*, in the year 1 6 5 2.

195   Title-page of the original in the New York
Public Library

ILL NEWES FROM NEW-ENGLAND

WHEN Clarke went to England in 1651 as the agent of Rhode Island, he was afire with indignation at the authorities of Massachusetts. He, with John Crandall and Obadiah Holmes, had journeyed to Lynn to visit William Witter, an aged, blind man of Baptist conviction, who had requested them to come. While holding

A Faithfull and True Relation of the Profecution of Obe-
diah Holmes, John Crandall, *and* John Clarke, *meer-*
ly for Confcience towards God, by the principall Members of
the Church, or Common-wealth of the Matbatufets in
New-England, which rules over that part of the World;
whereby is fhewn their difcourteous Entertainment of Strangers, & how that Spirit by which they are led would order the
whole World, if either brought under them, or fhould come
in unto them : Drawn forth by the aforefaid John Clarke,
not fo much to anfwer the Importunity of Friends, as to flop
the mouthes, and flanderous reports of fuch as are Enemies
to the Crofs of Chrift. Let him that readeth it confider,
which Church is moft like the Church of Chrift (that Prince
of Peace, that meek and gentle Lamb, that came into this
World to fave Mens lives, not to deftroy them,) the Perfecu-
ted, or Perfecuting.

T came to pafs that we three, by the good hand of
our God, came into the *Matbatufets* Bay upon
the 16 day of the 5th Moneth, 51; and upon the
19th of the fame, upon occafion of bufineffe. we
came unto a Town in the fame Bay called *Lin*,
where we lodged at a Blind-mans houfe neer two
miles out of the Town, by name *William Witter*,
who being baptized into Chrift waits, as we alfo doe, for the Kingdom of God, and the full confolation of the Ifrael of God : Vpon
the 20th day, being the firft day of the week, not having freedom in
our Spirits for want of a clear Call from God to goe unto the Publike Affemblie to declare there what was the mind, and counfell of
C   God

196   From John Clarke, *Ill Newes from New-England,*
London, 1652

services on Sunday in Witter's house, they had been apprehended, imprisoned, and sentenced to pay a fine or be whipped. Friends paid the fines of Clarke and Crandall; but Holmes would not permit this, and was whipped with thirty strokes upon his bare back. Clarke published these facts to the world in a powerful arraignment of the Massachusetts authorities entitled *Ill Newes from New-England.*

SIR RICHARD SALTONSTALL'S PROTEST

THIS publication aroused feeling in England. Sir Richard Saltonstall, one of the original settlers and magistrates, who was then in the mother country, wrote to the ministers of the First Church in Boston a letter which states the issues clearly: "Reverend and dear friends, whom I unfeignedly love and respect: It doth not a little grieve my spirit to hear what sad things are reported daily of your tyranny and persecutions in New England, as that you fine, whip and imprison men for their consciences. First, you compel such to come into your assemblies as you know will not join with you in your worship, and when they show their dislike thereof or witness against it, then you stir up your magistrates to punish them for such (as you conceive) their public affronts. Truly, friends, this your practice of compelling any in matters of worship to do that whereof they are not fully persuaded, is to make them sin, for so the apostle tells us, and many are made hypocrites thereby, conforming in their outward man for fear of punishment. We pray for you and wish you prosperity every way, hoped the Lord would have given you so much light and love there, that you might have been eyes to God's people here, and not to practice those courses in a wilderness, which you went so far to prevent. These rigid ways have laid you very low in the hearts of the saints. I do assure you I have heard them pray in the public assemblies that the Lord would give you meek and humble spirits, not to strive so much for uniformity as to keep the unity of the spirit in the bond of peace."

197   Sir Richard Saltonstall, 1586–1658, from an engraving
after the portrait by Rembrandt (1606–69), in Samuel A.
Drake, *Old Landmarks of Boston*, Boston, 1900

198 The Meeting at Witter's House, from an engraving by Bobbett after a drawing by Alfred Fredericks, in William Cullen Bryant and Sydney Gay, *A Popular History of the United States*, New York, 1881

"BETTER BE HYPOCRITES THAN PROFANE"

JOHN COTTON'S answer to this letter is doubtless the least worthy screed that he ever penned. Besides protestations of injured innocence and sneers at Holmes, it contains sentences which bring out clearly the false principle which had begun to actuate his group: "You think to compel men in matter of worship is to make them sin. If the worship be lawful in itself, the magistrate compelling him to come to it, compelleth him not to sin, but the sin is in his will that needs to be compelled to a Christian duty. If it do make men hypocrites, yet better be hypocrites than profane persons. Hypocrites give God part of his due, the outward man, but the profane person giveth God neither outward nor inward man."

THE PURITAN FEAR OF BAPTIST PRINCIPLES

FROM the beginning there were folk of Baptist convictions in Massachusetts, even among the members of the churches. They remained unmolested; but banishment was decreed for such as undertook Baptist propaganda or publicly attacked the baptism of infants. William Witter had said that those who remained in the church while a child was baptized "do worship the devil." The attack upon infant baptism was felt to be an attack upon the established order of all Christendom; and Anabaptists were feared everywhere as anarchists and "incendiaries of the commonwealth." Certain of the Anabaptist groups, particularly that at Münster in Germany, had given reason for this fear. In Massachusetts, where church membership was a qualification for voting, "their very principle of making infant baptism a nullity, . . . doth make at once all our churches, and our religious civil state and polity, and all the officers and members thereof to be unbaptized and to be no Christians and so our churches to be no churches; and so we have no regular power to choose deputies for any General Court, nor to choose any magistrates." The Massachusetts Puritan had the Englishman's dislike of any radical movement which threatened the subversion of government. In an age when the relations between religion and the state were very close the teachings of the Baptists could not fail to have political significance.

199 The Whipping of Obadiah Holmes, from an engraving by Bobbett after a drawing by C. S. Reinhart (1844–96), in William Cullen Bryant and Sydney Gay, *A Popular History of the United States*, New York, 1881

200 Charles Chauncy, 1592–1672, from the original portrait, artist unknown, in the Widener Library, Harvard University, Cambridge, Mass.

PRESIDENT DUNSTER, OF HARVARD, DECLARES HIMSELF A BAPTIST

THE prosecution of Clarke, Crandall and Holmes was wrong. Roger Williams had been a political menace, and Anne Hutchinson a religious troublemaker; but these men were simply dissenters.

201 From the original manuscript of Henry Dunster, *Believers Visibly Only Are To Be Baptized*, Feb. 1654, in the Massachusetts Historical Society, Boston

One result was the awakening of the conscience of Henry Dunster, President of Harvard College since 1640, who had been one of the silent believers in Baptist principles. He now not only refused to present his child for baptism, but rose in church to protest the baptism of other children and to confute the sermon which had just been preached. After repeated conferences, and with a great deal of reluctance, his resignation was accepted. Charles Chauncy, who was elected to succeed him, was an immersionist also, but succeeded in working with those who differed from him.

THE FIRST BAPTIST CHURCH AT BOSTON

IN 1665 the First Baptist Church of Boston was organized. Its members were repeatedly fined and imprisoned, until vigorous protests were made by leading Congregational ministers in England. When King Philip's War began, William Turner, who had been several times imprisoned, gathered a company of volunteers; but their services were refused because most of them were Baptists. Later, when fortune was turning against the colonists, the magistrates asked him to accept a commission and raise a company, which he did. At the point on the Connecticut River now known as Turner's Falls, he surprised the Indians and achieved one of the crucial victories of the war, though with the loss of his own life. In 1679 the Baptists erected a meetinghouse in Boston; but it was closed by order of the Court. Soon, however, the Baptists shared in the general toleration secured by the new Charter. In 1718, Increase Mather extended the right hand of fellowship, and Cotton Mather preached the sermon, at the ordination of Elisha Callender as pastor of the Baptist Church.

[1678] IN NEW-ENGLAND. 481

court charges, and others only admonished and to pay court charges, which had not then been paid, and the constables were backward to make distress upon them if they could shift it off. Feb. 9, the church met, and purchased their meetinghouse with the land it was built upon, of Philip Squire, and Ellis Callender, for 60l. ; and they met in it for worship the 15th. They had built with so much caution as not openly to call it by that name till it was done. They had been often censured and reproached for meeting in *private houses*, but now say, " since we have for our convenience obtained a *public house* on purpose for that use we are become more offensive than before."* The leaders of the society were convented before the general court of May 10, who not finding any old law to suit their turn then made a new one, in these words.

" IT is ordered by the court and the authority thereof, that no person whatever, without the consent of the freemen of the town where they live, first orderly had, and obtained, at a public meeting assembled for that end, and licence of the county court, or in defeat of such consent, a licence by the special order of the general court, shall erect or *make use* of any house as aforesaid ; and in case any person or persons shall be convicted of transgressing this law, every such house or houses wherein such persons shall so meet more than three times, with the land whereon such house or houses stand, and all private ways leading thereto, shall be forfeited to the use of the county, and disposed of by the county treasurer, by sale or demolishing, as the court that gives judgment in the case shall order."†   P p p   How

* Russell, p. 10.
† Mass. Records.

202 Order Closing the First Baptist Church, Boston, 1679, from Isaac Backus, *A History of New England*, Vol. I, Boston, 1777

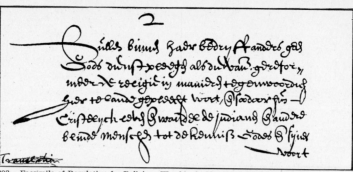

203 Facsimile of Regulation for Religious Worship in New Netherland, 1624, from the Van Rappord MSS in the Henry E. Huntington Library, San Marino, Cal.

THE STATE CHURCH IN NEW NETHERLAND

The Dutch West India Company decreed that "No other religion shall be publicly admitted in New Netherlands except the Reformed, as it is at present preached and practiced by public authority in the United Netherlands: and for this purpose the Company shall provide and maintain good and suitable preachers, school-masters and comforters of the sick." Privately, one might follow his own conscience, "provided he avoid frequenting any forbidden assemblies or conventicles, much less collect or get up any such." When the colony was surrendered to the English in 1664 it had eleven Reformed churches and six ministers. Chief among these were John Megapolensis, who had rescued Father Isaac Jogues from the Mohawks; and Samuel Drisius, who was called because he preached in several languages.

204 Quaker Woman Preaching in New Amsterdam, from an engraving by Schoonmaker after the drawing by Alfred R. Waud, in William Cullen Bryant and Sydney Gay, *A Popular History of the United States*, Vol. II, New York, 1881

STUYVESANT REPRESSES DISSENT

Director General Peter Stuyvesant was as strenuous in matters of morals and religion as in everything else. He sought to compel better observance of the Sabbath, to regulate marriage and divorce, and to remedy "the unreasonable and intemperate drinking" which was sapping the energy of the people. He opposed the immigration of Jews. He refused to let the Lutherans organize a church, and expelled their minister. He forbade all religious meetings, public or private, except those of the authorized Reformed Church. He banished Baptists who led a meeting at Flushing. The Quakers called forth the full fury of his temper; and for six years he did his utmost, by force of fines, imprisonment, and banishment, to extirpate them from the towns of Long Island. One, Robert Hodgson, was scourged with rods until he was near death.

205 Hodgson "retired to the Lord," from an engraving by McCracken after the drawing by Walter Shirlaw (1838–1910), in William Cullen Bryant and Sydney Gay, *A Popular History of the United States*, Vol. II, New York, 1881

JOHN BOWNE'S RESISTANCE OF STUYVESANT

STUYVESANT met his match in John Bowne, who had built a new home in Flushing, in which he and his wife invited their fellow members of the Society of Friends to meet for worship. He refused to pay a fine, and when banished went to Amsterdam, where he bore himself so sturdily before the Directors of the West India Company that they began to rue their policy. They wrote a letter

206   The John Bowne House at Flushing, built in 1661. © Keystone View Co., Inc.

to Stuyvesant counseling him to wink at religious dissent, if not too blatant. No level of moral and religious principle is reached in their advice, which is based simply upon the prudential consideration that a commercial company ought to encourage, rather than check, the growth of population. "Wherefore it is our opinion that some connivance would be useful; and that the consciences of men, at least, ought to remain free and unshackled. Let every one be unmolested as long as he is modest, moderate, his political conduct irreproachable, and as long as he does not offend others or oppose the government. This maxim of moderation has always been the guide of our magistrates in this city, and the consequence has been that people have flocked from every land to this asylum. Tread thus in their steps, and we doubt not you will be blessed."

THE JEWISH SYNAGOGUE AT NEWPORT

JEWS came to New Amsterdam in 1654. Stuyvesant's persistent hostility to them was rebuked by the West India Company; but a considerable group decided to remove to Newport, where they would have freedom of worship. Others came directly from Europe, and the Jewish group at Newport grew and prospered, particularly after 1750. On December 2, 1763, Ezra Stiles, then pastor of the Second Congregational Church, was present at the dedication of their synagogue, and wrote in his diary: "It began by a handsome procession, in which were carried the Books of the Law, to be deposited in the ark. Several portions of Scripture and of their service, with a prayer for the Royal family were read and finely sung by the priest and people. . . .

The order and decorum, the harmony and solemnity of the music, together with a handsome assembly of people, in an edifice the most perfect of the temple kind, perhaps, in America, and splendidly illuminated, could not but raise in the mind a faint idea of the majesty and grandeur of the ancient Jewish worship mentioned in Scripture. Dr. Isaac de Abraham Touro performed the service." The Jews of Newport gave liberally of their means to the support of the Colonies in the Revolution, and some served in the Continental Army.

207   Jewish Synagogue, Newport, Rhode Island, built 1763, Peter Harrison (1716-75), architect

RELIGIOUS DIFFERENCES IN NEW YORK

THE Duke of York was a Catholic; and when New Amsterdam, passing into his hands, became New York, he promulgated laws concerning religion which were stated in such general terms as to protect all Christians. In a report to the Committee of Trade, dated February 22, 1687, Governor Thomas Dongan, also a Catholic, described the diverse religious opinions then found in the town of New York: "Every town ought to have a minister. New York has first a chaplain, belonging to the fort, of the Church of England; secondly, a Dutch Calvinist; thirdly, a French Calvinist; fourthly, a Dutch Lutheran. Here be not many of the Church of England; a few Roman Catholics; abundance of Quaker preachers; men and women; especially Singing Quakers, Ranting Quakers; Sabbatarians; Antisabbatarians; some Anabaptists; some Independents; some Jews; in short, of all sorts of opinions there are some, and the most part of none at all. . . . The most prevailing opinion is that of the Dutch Calvinists. It is the endeavor of all persons here to bring up their children and servants in that opinion which themselves profess, but this I observe that they take no care of the conversion of their slaves. . . . As for the King's natural-born subjects that live on Long Island and other parts of the government, I find it a hard task to make them pay their ministers."

208 Letter of Governor Dongan to Governor Penn, from a facsimile in the Emmet Collection, New York Public Library

NEW YORK'S *CHARTER OF LIBERTIES*

A JUST and liberal man, Governor Dongan began his administration by calling a General Assembly of representatives of the people, elected by vote of the freeholders. It convened on October 17, 1683. *The Charter of Liberties and Privileges*, passed by this Assembly and assented to by Governor Dongan, contained a comprehensive bill of rights, providing for legislative liberty, for religious freedom, and for taxation only by consent. It declared that "no person or persons which profess faith in God by Jesus Christ shall at any time be anyways molested, punished, disquieted, or called in question for any difference of opinion or matter of religious concernment, who do not actually disturb the civil peace of the province; but that all and every such person or persons may, from time to time and at all times, freely have and fully enjoy his or their judgments or consciences in matters of religion throughout all the province; they behaving themselves peaceably and quietly, and not using this liberty to licentiousness nor to the civil injury or outward disturbance of others." When the Duke of York became King James II, in 1685, he refused to abide by the terms of this Charter, overriding the protests of Dongan, who was replaced by Andros in 1688. It is an example of the injustice of "the mind of the crowd" that, in the anti-Catholic feeling associated with the Revolution which resulted in the abdication of James II and the accession of William and Mary, the fair-minded Dongan, then living on his farm on Long Island, should have become an object of suspicion. He withdrew to Boston, and thence sailed to England.

THE ATTEMPT TO ESTABLISH THE CHURCH OF ENGLAND

UNDER William and Mary, the situation lost its humor. Governor Benjamin Fletcher, who took office in 1691, was bent upon securing the establishment of the Church of England as the state church of New York; and the Dutch had to fight against being placed in the position of dissenters. Fletcher could get from the Assembly nothing more than the passage of an Act for the maintenance of a "good sufficient Protestant minister" in certain specified parishes. The Church of England was never established in New York, though Fletcher and his successors took care always to speak and act as though it were. Dominie Henry Selyns felt that his church was endangered, and secured for it a charter in 1696, incorporating it as The Reformed Protestant Dutch Church of the City of New York. Trinity Church was incorporated a year later.

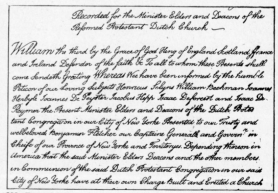

209 From the Charter of the Reformed Protestant Dutch Church, New York city, May 11, 1696, as recorded in the *Book of Patents*, 7, pp. 27-28, office of the Secretary of State, Albany

FRANCIS MAKEMIE'S DEFENSE OF RELIGIOUS LIBERTY

LORD CORNBURY was the most insistent of the royal Governors upon the pleasant fiction that the Church of England had been established in New York. He expelled from his church, parsonage, and glebe the minister of the Presbyterians at Jamaica, for no other reason than that he was a Presbyterian; and inducted an Episcopal missionary who gratefully reported to the Society for Propagating

210 From the painting *Francis Makemie before the Governor of New York, 1707*, by Harry A. Ogden (1856–)

the Gospel that the Governor was a "true nursing father to our infancy here." He arrested Francis Makemie and John Hampton, Presbyterian ministers from Virginia, for preaching in New York without first securing his permission.

Makemie knew the law better than he, and bested him in argument. They were imprisoned for several months, however, awaiting trial; and, though finally acquitted by the jury, were compelled to pay costs of over one hundred pounds.

A

NARRATIVE

Of a New and Unufual

AMERICAN

Imprifonment

Of Two

PRESBYTERIAN MINISTERS :

And Profecution of

Mr. Francis Makemie

One of them, for Preaching one SERMON at the City of *NEW-YORK.*

By a Learner of Law, and Lover of Liberty.

Printed for the Publifher. 1707.

211 Title-page of the original in the New York Public Library

FRANCIS MAKEMIE, *ca.* 1658–1708, FOUNDER OF AMERICAN PRESBYTERIANISM

WITH the restoration of the Stuarts had begun the emigration to America of the Scotch-Irish Presbyterians. Francis Makemie, a native of Donegal, was licensed by the Presbytery of Laggan in 1681, and came to America in 1683. A merchant as well as a minister, and possessed of considerable wealth, he lived with his family on a plantation in Virginia,

212 Rehoboth Presbyterian Church, built 1706, Francis Makemie, Pastor, 1683–86

213 Francis Makemie Statue, Holden's Creek, Accomack County, Virginia, courtesy of The Presbyterian Historical Society, Philadelphia

on the eastern shore of Chesapeake Bay. He traveled throughout the colonies and in Barbados, preaching and establishing churches. He and Jonas Mackie were the first dissenters to secure a certificate from the courts of Virginia, authorizing them to preach. Feeling the need of assistance, he corresponded with ministers in London and in Boston; and he crossed the ocean in 1703–04 to secure fellow laborers. He visited New England to consult with Increase Mather. In 1705 he helped to organize the Presbytery of Philadelphia, the first presbytery in America, and was elected its moderator. In 1717 a Synod was organized, with four constituent presbyteries, one each in New York, Pennsylvania, Delaware, and Maryland.

214 George Fox, from the portrait by Sir Peter Lely (1618–80), in the Friends' Historical Library, Swarthmore College, Swathmore, Pa.

GEORGE FOX, 1624–1691, THE FIRST OF THE QUAKERS

GEORGE FOX, a shoemaker's apprentice of Drayton in Leicestershire, after much travail of soul and vain search for help among those accounted priests and ministers, heard a voice which said, "There is one, even Christ Jesus, that can speak to thy condition." He lived thereafter in the inward light of "the immediate opening of the invisible Spirit," and believed himself to be "sent to turn people from darkness to light." "With and by this divine power and Spirit of God, and the light of Jesus, I was to bring people off from all their own ways, to Christ, the new and living way; and from their churches, which men had made and gathered, to the Church in God . . . which Christ is the head of; and off from the world's teachers, made by men, to learn of Christ . . . and off from all the world's worships, to know the Spirit of Truth in the inward parts, and to be led thereby; that in it they might worship the Father of spirits. . . . I was to bring people off from all the world's religions, which are vain . . . and from all the world's fellowships, and prayings, and singings, which stood in forms without power. . . . I was to bring people off from Jewish ceremonies, and from heathenish fables, and from men's inventions and windy doctrines . . . with their schools and colleges for making ministers, who are indeed ministers of their own making but not of Christ's; and from all their images and crosses, and sprinkling of infants, with all their holy days (so called) and all their vain traditions . . . which the Lord's power was against: in the dread and authority of which I was moved to declare against them all, and against all that preached and not freely, as being such as had not received freely from Christ."

A QUAKER EXHORTER IN NEW ENGLAND

Fox's followers called themselves Friends; the world called them Quakers. He inspired them with an intense, fiery missionary zeal. From prison, in 1656, he exhorted them by letter: "Let all nations hear the sound by word or writing. Spare no place, spare no tongue nor pen, but be obedient to the Lord God; go through the work; be valiant for the truth upon earth; and tread and trample upon all that is contrary." A minute of a General Meeting in 1660 records "We have received information of the great work and service of the Lord beyond the seas, in several parts and regions, as Germany, America, Virginia, and many other places, as Florence, Mantua, Palatine, Tuscany, Italy, Rome, Turkey, Jerusalem, France, Geneva, Norway, Barbados, Bermuda, Antigua, Jamaica, Surinam, Newfoundland, through all which Friends have passed in the service of the Lord." They let no ignorance of geography, conditions, or language, deter them. Mary Fisher, in 1660, carried her message to the Sultan of Turkey, who treated her kindly.

215 A Quaker Exhorter in New England, from a drawing by Howard Pyle (1853–1911), in Thomas Wentworth Higginson, *A Larger History of the United States of America*, New York, 1885

A SEASONABLE CAVEAT AGAINST THE GROWTH OF QUAKERISM

THE messages of these early Quaker missionaries were so largely negative and denunciatory that folk feared them as upsetters of established order and prophets of anarchy. Catholic, Anglican, Presbyterian, Congregationalist, Baptist, Quaker, Ranter — was the seventeenth-century scale whereon each group regarded those preceding itself as in bondage to superstition, and those following as on the road to ruin. At Nottingham, Fox heard a minister preach from the text: "We have also a more sure word of prophecy," expounding the Puritan doctrine of the supreme

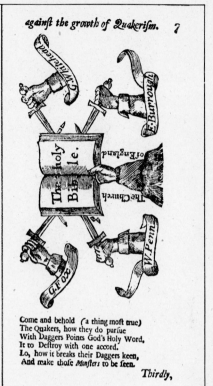

6 A Seasonable Coveat

Death, &c. And many other places could I Quote to fhew their Contempt of the Scriptures; but having been large on that Subject in my other Books, I chufe rather to Refer my Reader to Mr. *Mather's* Broad-fheet, Printed 1700. Wherein there is Forty Proofs out of the Quakers printed Books, fetting forth their Contempt of the Scriptures, as a Demonftration of their Defign to overturn Chriftianity ; and as an Emblem of their Malice, fee the Figure following thefe Verfes,

*F*OR unto me it plainly doth appear,
 They wound God's Word, as you both fee and hear :
Scarce fuch Elders are now to be found
At other Meetings now above the ground ;
Who by their Books, and by their Practice too,
God's Holy Word by fuch Contempt o'erthrow ;
Alfo his Supper founded thereupon,
Baptifm alfo recorded in St. John :
Confeffing Sin, practic'd by St. Paul,
Rejected are, as nothing worth at all.
Oh then, my Friends, here's Lamentation,
And the worft News in our Chriftian Nation !
What fhall we do ? What fhall we think or fay ?
What fhall we write ? Or how fhall we difplay
Their Errors great, their Teachers to make known,
To lay 'em open, their Witnefs fhall be fhown ?
I'll make them fpeak, I'll bring them forth to view
They fhall not fculk, but Witnefs what is * true.
    * A Miracle beyond G. Fox's.

against the growth of Quakerifm. 7

Come and behold (a thing moft true)
The Quakers, how they do purfue
With Daggers Points God's Holy Word,
It to Deftroy with one accord.
Lo, how it breaks their Daggers keen,
And make thofe *Monfters* to be feen.
    Thirdly,

216 From Francis Bugg, *A Seasonable Caveat Against the Growth of Quakerism*, London, 1701, in the Library of Congress, Washington

authority of Scripture. "I could not hold, but was made to cry out and say, 'Oh, no, it is not the Scriptures.' But I told them what it was, namely, the Holy Spirit." The Quakers were regarded generally, in these early years of their activity, as attacking the authority of the Bible. A book similar to the *Seasonable Caveat against the Growth of Quakerism*, but with a more pungent title, was *The Snake in the Grass; or Satan Transform'd into an Angel of Light, discovering the Deep and Unsuspected Subtility which is couched under the Pretended Simplicity of many of the Principal Leaders of those People call'd Quakers*, London, 1698. Its author was Charles Leslie, who also published a *Short and Easie Method with the Deists*, which was very popular.

217 A Quaker Trial, from an engraving by J. S. King after the drawing by C. S. Reinhart in William Cullen Bryant and Sydney Gay, *A Popular History of the United States*, Vol. II, New York, 1881

A QUAKER TRIAL

THE Quakers did not believe in consecrated churches, which Fox called "steeple-houses," or in holy days, or in ordained ministers, for they deemed all places, times, and persons, sacred. They denounced paid ministers, of whatever sect or polity, as "priests." They rejected set forms of worship, and met in silence, broken only as some were moved by the Spirit. They recognized no sacraments, since every act may be a means of grace, if done in the right spirit. They refused to take oaths, since in all his words man is under obligation to tell the truth. They devised a marriage ceremony of their own, without a minister. They would use no titles in speech or address; and would take off their hats to no one, since worship is due only to God. The trial of a Quaker generally began with an argument about his keeping his hat on his head, which usually culminated in the enraged magistrate ordering it to be knocked off.

218 Whipping a Quaker, from Samuel Adams Drake, *A Book of New England Legends and Folk Lore*, Boston, 1884

THE SCOURGING OF QUAKERS

THE first Quaker missionaries came to America in 1656. News of their doctrines had preceded them; and they were received with an almost panicky harshness in every colony except Rhode Island. Fines, imprisonment, scourging, confiscation of property and banishment were the common penalties. In Virginia, Mary Tomkins and Alice Ambrose were pilloried, given thirty-two lashes apiece from a nine-corded whip, deprived of all their goods, and expelled from the colony. Maryland decreed that Quaker emissaries should be whipped from constable to constable until they were out of the province. George Wilson suffered such cruelty that he died in the prison at Jamestown, Virginia; and his comrade, William Cole, never recovered from the effects of his experience. Humphrey Norton was flogged in New Haven, and the letter H, for Heretic, was burned with a red-hot iron deep into his right hand. These zealous missionaries met the usual fate of political and religious radicals.

THE EXPULSION OF NICHOLAS UPSHALL

THE conflict between the Quakers and the public authorities was sharpest in New England. The reason is obvious. Because of its peculiar relation to the state, religion meant more to the Puritans than to the people of New York, Maryland and Virginia. The Quakers' denunciations struck at the very foundations of the Puritan commonwealth. Even Roger Williams deemed them "insufferably proud and contemptuous" and held that "a due and moderate restraint and punishment of these incivilities, though pretending conscience, is so far from persecution, properly so called, that it is a duty and command of God." The authorities of Rhode Island stated their belief that "their doctrines tend to very absolute cutting down and overturning relations and civil government among men." Rhode Island reported to Massachusetts, however, that "we have no law among us whereby to punish any for only declaring by words their minds and understandings concerning the things and ways of God. . . . And we, moreover, find that in those places where these people . . . are most of all suffered to declare themselves freely . . . there they least of all desire to come; and we are informed that they begin to loathe this place, for that they are not opposed." That was sound advice, but the Massachusetts authorities did not realize it. They resolved to keep the Quakers out of the colony. Because Nicholas Upshall protested, he also was banished.

219   Expulsion of Quakers from Massachusetts, from a drawing by Edwin A. Abbey in the *London Graphic*, London, 1884

THE EXECUTION OF MARY DYER

WHIPPING, ear-cropping, even the threat of boring the tongue through with a hot iron, did not deter the Quakers, who persisted in returning to Massachusetts as fast as they were deported. Finally, a law was passed condemning to death any who, after banishment, should return. It was carried by only one vote. Deacon Wiswall, one of the deputies, who was ill, protested that he would have crept to the session on his hands and knees to prevent it. The first seven Quakers who fell subject to this law "felt liberty" to accept the opportunity given them to depart; but others found in the existence of the law a call of God to them to bear witness against its injustice. Four were hanged. Mary Dyer returned three times, and was thrice in jeopardy of death. The first time, she "felt liberty" to depart; the second time, she was reprieved, in the shadow of the gallows, at the petition of her son; the third time, in response to the plea of her husband, she was offered her life, if she would return home. "Nay, I cannot," was her answer. "In obedience to the will of the Lord God I came and in His will I abide faithful to death."

220 Drawn expressly for *The Pageant of America* by C. W. Jefferys

THE CART AND WHIP ACT

HANGINGS ceased because of a revulsion of public feeling, and because the Quakers declared their willingness "to go for England" and were released. A new law provided that Quakers "be stripped naked from the middle upwards, and be tied to a cart's tail, and whipped through the town," then conveyed to the next town and again whipped, and so on until out of the jurisdiction. Against this law Lydia Wardel protested by appearing in church entirely unclothed, and Deborah Wilson felt constrained in like fashion to walk the streets of Salem as "a naked sign." In 1677, Margaret Brewster came from Barbados, and on Sunday entered the South Church, "in sackcloth, with ashes upon her head, and barefoot, and her face blacked," and denounced the wickedness of Massachusetts. The whippings that followed her outbreak were the last to be inflicted here.

221   Whipping of Quakers at the Cart's Tail in Boston, from a drawing by W. L. Shepherd in
William A. Crafts, *Pioneers in the Settlement of America*, Boston, 1877

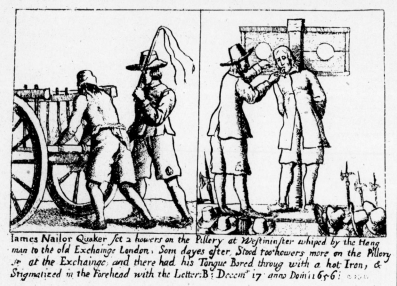

Iames Nailor Quaker *fet 2 howers on the Pillory at Weftminfter whiped by the Hang man to the old Exchainge London, Som dayes after, Stood too howers more on the Pillory .r at the Exchainge, and there had his Tongue Bored throug with a hot Iron, & Stigmatized in the Forehead with the Letter:B: Decem r 17 anno Dom 1656:*

222   From an engraving in H. D. Traill, *Social England*, G. P. Putnam's Sons, New York, 1909

THE PERSECUTION OF QUAKERS IN ENGLAND

EXCEPT for the hangings, the Quakers endured as bitter persecution in England. At one time, Charles II was prevailed upon to dispatch a letter to Massachusetts requiring that Quaker prisoners be sent to England for judgment, and to choose as his messenger Samuel Shattuck, a Quaker who had been banished from Salem on pain of death. The dramatic situation when he confronted Governor Endicott has been embellished by the imagination of Whittier in his poem *The King's Missive*. But the King's missive availed little; and in a later letter Charles stated that he had found it necessary to make sharp laws against the Quakers in England, and was "well contented that you do the like there." More than three hundred Quakers died under their sufferings in England from April, 1659 to May, 1660. Over four thousand were imprisoned in the early months of 1661. Of one hundred and fifty-three who were banished in 1665, only twenty-seven survived the hardships of the voyage upon a plague-stricken ship. Among those who were repeatedly imprisoned was William Penn, son of Admiral Penn, and friend of the Duke of York.

JOHN ARCHDALE UPHOLDS RELIGIOUS FREEDOM IN THE CAROLINAS

LIBERTY of conscience was a phrase of advertising value in the competition for settlers; and the Proprietors of Carolina published the promise, "to be kept inviolably," to grant religious freedom "in as ample a manner as the undertakers shall desire." What they granted was not of the amplest, however. The abortive *Fundamental Constitutions*, for which John Locke was responsible, not only excluded atheists from political and property rights, but declared that "No person above seventeen years of age shall have any benefit or protection of the law . . . who is not a member of some church." It provided for the establishment and exclusive support by public funds of the Church of England; but authorized the formation of dissenting churches by any group of seven or more persons, and forbade the molestation of any on account of his religious opinions or mode of worship. Baptists, Presbyterians, Huguenots, and Dutch Reformed were attracted by the advertisements, and settled here. The Quakers were the first to hold religious services in the colony, and grew strong, politically as well as in numbers. John Archdale, one of the proprietors and the best of the early Governors, was a Quaker. He thwarted a determined effort of an oligarchy of adherents of the Church of England, who, after the colony had been left without an Episcopal minister for more than twenty years, suddenly undertook to disfranchise everyone except members of their own church.

A NEW
DESCRIPTION
OF THAT
Fertile and Pleasant - Province
OF
CAROLINA:
WITH A
BRIEF ACCOUNT
OF ITS
Difcovery, Settling,
AND THE
GOVERNMENT
Thereof to this Time.

With feveral Remarkable Paffages of *Divine Providence* during my Time.

By *JOHN ARCHDALE*: Late *Governour of the fame.*

LONDON:
Printed for *John Wyat*, at the *Rofe* in St. *Paul's Church-Yard.* 1707.

223   Title-page of the original in the New York Public Library

A FOUNDATION FOR LIBERTY IN THE JERSEYS

IN 1672–73 George Fox visited America, and traveled throughout the colonies. He gained a wide hearing and shaped the permanent organization of the Friends. His visit led them to lay less stress upon denunciation of others, and more upon the showing in their own lives of the love, joy, and peace which are the fruits of the Spirit. With his counsel and that of William Penn, English Quakers purchased West Jersey in 1674 and East Jersey in 1681. They devised a body of "Concessions and Agreements of the Proprietors, Freeholders, and Inhabitants of West Jersey, in America" of which Penn wrote: "We have made concessions such as Friends will approve of. . . . There we lay a foundation for after ages to understand their liberty as men and Christians, that they may not be brought in bondage but by their own consent, for we put the power in the people."

WILLIAM PENN'S "HOLY EXPERIMENT"

WILLIAM PENN'S experience with the Jersey enterprise quickened a half-formed purpose of his student days at Oxford; and he suggested to the King, in 1681, that a debt of sixteen thousand pounds, due him as part of his father's estate, be paid by a grant of territory in America. This was named Pennsylvania, in honor of his father. "My country," Penn calls it in letters to his friends. "My God that has given it me through many difficulties, will, I believe, bless and make it the seed of a nation. . . . I have so obtained it and desire to keep it, that I may not be unworthy of His Love; but do that which may answer His kind providence and serve His Truth and people; that an example may be set up to the nations. There may be room there, though not here, for such an holy experiment." Penn proved himself to be one of the ablest Englishmen actively interested in colonization in America.

224 Statue of William Penn, 1644–1718, after the model by Sylvanus Bevan, a contemporary, in the Pennsylvania Hospital Grounds, Philadelphia

225   From a Copley print of the mural *Spirit of Religious Liberty*, by Edwin A. Abbey, in the Capitol Building, Harrisburg, Pa.
© Curtis & Cameron, Boston

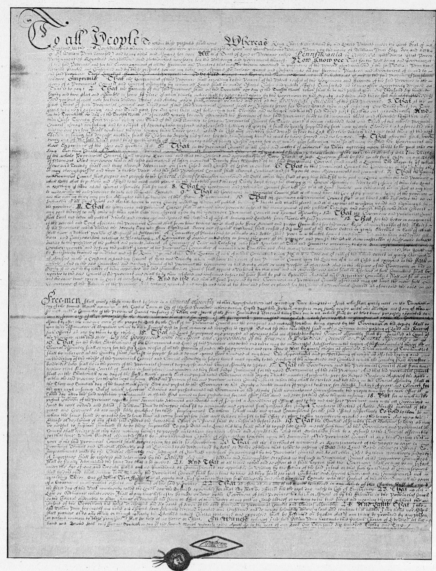

226   Facsimile of the original of William Penn's First Charter to the People of Pennsylvania, April 25, 1682, in the State House, Harrisburg, Pa.

CHRISTIAN DEMOCRACY IN PENNSYLVANIA

PENN had as definitely religious a purpose in the founding of Pennsylvania as had the Puritans in Massachusetts. Their Government was framed as a theocracy, however; his as a democracy. They sought to establish a righteous state by excluding all who would not conform to their understanding of God's will; he proposed to include men who differed, with liberty of conscience for all. "We must give the liberty we ask," he said. "We cannot be false to our principles. We would have none to suffer for dissent on any hand. . . . I abhor two principles in religion and pity them that own them; the first is obedience to authority without conviction; and the other is destroying them that differ from me for God's sake." Penn and Algernon Sidney, who advised him, were familiar with Plato's *Republic*, More's *Utopia*, and Locke's *Fundamental Constitutions;* and they devised a *Frame of Government* which is superior to any of these, in that it succeeded in actual practice. In one respect, the religious liberty which it embodied was less complete than that in Rhode Island: the right to vote and to hold public office in Pennsylvania was limited to "such as profess faith in Jesus Christ." There is profound truth in Penn's observation that "governments rather depend upon men than men upon governments. Let men be good, and the government cannot be bad. . . . But if men be bad, let the government be ever so good, they will endeavor to warp and spoil it to their turn."

THE PRINCIPLE OF BROTHERLY LOVE

PHILADELPHIA, the City of Brotherly Love, was laid out in 1682, with spacious streets, and public squares reserved "for the comfort and recreation of posterity." The laws of the first Assembly provided for freedom from oaths; for the observance of Sunday as a day of rest, "for the ease of the creation" and of opportunity for worship; that prisons should be workshops and places of reformation rather than mere dungeons of re-

227   From the original painting *Penn's Treaty*, by Benjamin West (1738–1820), in Independence Hall, Philadelphia

straint; that children were to be taught a useful trade; and that the penalty of death was to be inflicted only for willful murder or treason. Under a great elm on the banks of the Delaware, Penn met the Indians and concluded the agreement with them which, Voltaire said, was "the only Treaty between these people and the Christians never confirmed by an oath and never broken."

"A FREE COLONY FOR ALL MANKIND"

"I WOULD found a free colony for all mankind that shall come hither," Penn declared. His initial account of Pennsylvania, with proposals for its colonization, was widely distributed to stimulate emigration. To translations of this account into other languages than English there was appended a like translation of his *Liberty of Conscience*, to emphasize the religious freedom promised there. No colony grew and prospered more rapidly; and no other attracted as many racial and religious groups. Dutch, Swedes, Germans, Irish, Welsh, and Scotch-Irish, as well as English, settled in Pennsylvania.

SOME
ACCOUNT
OF THE
PROVINCE
OF
PENNSILVANIA
IN
AMERICA;
Lately Granted under the Great Seal
OF
ENGLAND
TO
William Penn, &c.
Together with Priviledges and Powers neces-
sary to the well-governing thereof.

Made publick for the Information of such as are or may be
disposed to Transport themselves or Servants
into those Parts.

LONDON: Printed, and Sold by *Benjamin Clark*
Bookseller in *George-Yard Lombard-street*, 1681.

228   Title-page of the original in the
New York Public Library

Eine
Nachricht
wegen der Landschaft
PENNSILVANIA
in
AMERICA.
Welche
Jüngstens unter dem Grossen Siegel
in
ENGELLAND
an
William Penn, &c.
Sambt den Freyheiten und der Macht / so zu behöriger
guten Regierung derselben nötig/
übergeben worden/
und

Zum Unterricht derer / so etwan bereits bewogen/ oder noch
inskünftig bewegen werden/ umb sich selbsten dahin
zu begeben/ oder einige Bediente und Gesinde
an diesen Ort zu senden/ hiermit
kund gethan wird.

Aus dem in London gedrucktem und albar bey Benjamin Clarck,
Buchhändlern in George-Yard Lombard-street befindlichem
Englischen übersetzet.

Nebenst beygefügtem ehemaligem im 1675. Jahr gedrucktem
Schreiben des obernehmten Will. Penns.

In Amsterdam/ gedruckt bey Christoff Cunraden,
Im Jahr 1681.

229   Title-page of the original German Edition
in the John Carter Brown Library, Providence

Een kort Bericht
Van de Provintie ofte Landschap
PENN-SYLVANIA
genaemt, leggende in
AMERICA;
Nu onlangs onder het groote Zegel van Engeland
gegeven aan
WILLIAM PENN, &c.
MITSGADERS
Van de Privilegien, ende Macht om
het selve wel te Regeeren.
Uyt het Engels overgeset na de Copye tot Londen gedrukt by *Benja-
min Clark*, Boekverkooper in George Yard Lombardstreet, 1681.
Waer by nu gevoegt is de Notificatie van s' Konings Placcaet/
in date van den 2. April 1681. waer inne de tegenwoordige
Inwoonders van PENN-SYLVANIA, belast word
WILLEM PENN en zijn Erfgenamen, als volkomene
Eygenaars en Gouverneurs, te gehoorsamen.
Als mede,
De Copye van een Brief by den selven W.P. geschreven aan
zekere Regeeringe Anno 1675. tegens de Vervolginge
en voor de Vryheyt van Conscientie, aan alle &c.

Tot ROTTERDAM,
Gedrukt by PIETER VAN WYNBRUGGE, Boek-Drukker in de
Leeuwestraat, in de Wereld Vol-Druk. Anno 1681.

230   Title-page of the original Dutch Edition in the John Carter Brown Library,
Providence

231 Southeast View of Wicaco Church (Gloria Dei), Southwark, Philadelphia, from John Curtis Clay, *Annals of the Swedes on the Delaware*, Philadelphia, 1836

232 Old Swede's Church, Wilmington, Del., from an engraving by J. Sartain (1808–97), after the drawing, 1845, by Benjamin Ferris, in Elizabeth Montgomery, *Reminiscences of Wilmington in Familiar Village Tales, Ancient and New*, Philadelphia, 1851

233 Title-page from John Companius, *Lutheri Catechismus, Öfwersatt på American—Virginite Språket*, Stockholm, 1696

SWEDISH LUTHERANS ON THE DELAWARE

BESIDES Quakers there came to Penn's colony Presbyterians, Episcopalians, Catholics, Lutherans, Reformed, Mennonites, Baptists, Dunkards, Schwenkfelders, and Moravians. The Pennsylvania Assembly finally yielded to pressure from England compelling the use of the "Test Oath" which excluded Catholics from public office; but St. Joseph's Church in Philadelphia was the only place in the thirteen colonies where the regular public celebration of the Mass was allowed prior to the Declaration of Independence. Penn found Swedish Lutherans already living in his domain. They had first come in 1637. Their first public worship was at Fort Christina, where Wilmington now stands. Two of their church buildings remain; the Old Swedes' Church at Wilmington, dedicated in 1699; and Gloria Dei Church in Philadelphia, built in 1700 upon a site then known as Wicaco, where a converted blockhouse had been used as a church since 1677. Pastors were sent from Sweden until the days of the Revolutionary War, when these churches declared that they wanted "preachers of their own choice, and native Americans." Being accustomed to be governed by bishops, the Swedish churches cultivated relations with the Church of England; and most of them in time became Episcopal churches. John Campanius, pastor under the Swedish Governor Printz in 1643–48, translated Luther's *Smaller Catechism* into the language of the Delaware Indians.

THE BEGINNINGS OF GERMAN IMMIGRATION

PENN was responsible for the beginning of German immigration. He had traveled in Germany as a Quaker missionary; and his advertisement of Pennsylvania was answered at once by a Frankfort company which purchased twenty-five thousand acres, where they founded Germantown. Twenty-five years later, inhabitants of the valley of the Rhine, especially in the Palatinate, which had been ravaged by Louis XIV of France, began to come in large numbers, settling in New York, Pennsylvania, and the Carolinas. Queen Anne, whose husband was a Lutheran, and the first two Georges, who were more German than English, favored German immigration, and held the Lutheran churches in sympathetic regard. A German Lutheran chapel was maintained at the English Court. Frederick M. Ziegenhagen, its pastor from 1722 to 1766, was indefatigable in his efforts in behalf of the spiritual interests of Germans in America.

234 Frederick Michael Ziegenhagen, 1694–1776, from Pennsylvania German Society *Proceedings*, Vol. XI, Lancaster, Pa., 1902

THE PERSECUTION OF THE SALZBURG LUTHERANS

THE Archbishop of Salzburg was its temporal lord as well as its spiritual head. For two hundred years successive archbishops strove vainly to suppress the Lutheran faith. Banishment, confiscation of property, and deprivation of their children, whom they were forced to surrender to the care of the state, did not daunt the Protestants of the little Alpine province.

THE EXPULSION OF THE SALZBURGERS

An exile poor, and nothing more,
    This is my sole profession;
Banished from home, of God's pure Word
    To make a clear confession.

Though all that I have be torn away,
    I still possess this treasure:
God dwells with me, and His pure faith
    Is wealth above all measure.

God, as Thou wilt, then; here am I,
    With Thee to stay forever.
Thy will is mine, and I am Thine;
    Nothing from Thee shall sever.

IN 1728 Leopold Anton von Firmian became Archbishop of Salzburg. He is said to have declared: "I will drive the heretics out of the country, even though thorns and thistles should grow upon the fields." On October 31, 1731, he issued an edict which allowed some but three days, and none more than three months, to depart. Over thirty thousand left their homes, and marched, singing as they went, on the way to Prussia, whose King promised to receive them.

Und Ich habe noch andere Schaaffe die sind nicht aus diesem Stall und dieselben muss Ich herführen u. sie werden meine Stimme hören, u. wird ein Heerde u. ein Hirt werden.

Die Unterweisung der Eltern an ihre Kinder zu der Evangl. Religion

Die Verbrennug der Evangl. Bücher.

Die um der Evangl. Religion bekennent gefangene Saltzburger.

235   From *Besonders Gespräche in dem Reiche der Lebendigen, zwischen einem Pömisch-Katholischen und Evangelisch-Lutherischen*, Frankfurt am Main, 1732

236   The Expulsion of the Salzburgers, from the original lithograph by Adolf von Menzel (1815–1905), in the New York Public Library

237   From a rare print by David Ulirch Bocklin (1686–1748), in the *Saltzburger Collection of Tracts*, New York Public Library

A FAMILY OF SALZBURG EXILES

This rare contemporary print shows the costumes of the Salzburg exiles. "I set my staff forward in God's name," the man is saying; "and wander cheerfully in a strange land. Though I must forsake house and home, the Lord is with us on our way." The verse at the bottom refers to the long road the exiles must tread to appease their hunger after God.

238   Jerusalem Church, Ebenezer, Ga., erected 1767, from the lithograph by T. Sinclair in Rev. P. A. Strobel, *The Salzburgers and their Descendants*, Baltimore, 1855

THE SALZBURGERS IN GEORGIA

Through Dr. Samuel Urlsperger, pastor at Augsburg, and Dr. Ziegenhagen, the Society for the Promotion of Christian Knowledge became interested in the Salzburgers and arranged for some of them to settle in Georgia, where General Oglethorpe was founding a colony, dedicated to the relief of human distress. Pastors were found for them, Bolzius and Gronau, teachers in the Latin school at Halle. The King of England sent with them a special envoy, Baron von Reck, who saw them safely established twenty-five miles up the Savannah River. They called their new home Ebenezer — "Hitherto hath the Lord helped us."

239   Johann Martin Bolzius, b. 1703, from Samuel Urlsperger, *Americanisches Ackerwerk Gottes*, Halle, 1754

240   Emigration from Salzburg, from *Die Göttliche Allmacht* . . . Frankfurt und Leipzig, 1732

JOHN WESLEY IN GEORGIA

WITH Oglethorpe, in 1736, came John and Charles Wesley, who, as students and fellows at Oxford University, had organized a group so scrupulous in conduct and religious observance, and so frank in rebuking sin, as to be called the "Holy Club." "Here is a new set of methodists sprung up," contemptuously exclaimed one student; and by that name the movement thus begun has come to be known. Charles Wesley, falling ill, soon returned to England; John Wesley remained for two years as missionary of the Society for Propagating the Gospel. His work was not successful. His undue severity and extreme high churchmanship aroused resentment. He declined to admit the godly Bolzius, pastor of the Salzburgers, to the communion because he had not been baptized by a clergyman episcopally ordained. When he denied the sacrament to a young woman who had refused to marry him and became the wife of another, her husband brought suit, and a majority of the grand jury found a true bill against him on ten counts, as having exceeded his ecclesiastical authority. On the home voyage he wrote: "What have I learned? Why (what I the least of all suspected), that I who went to America to convert others was never myself converted to God." He had "the faith of a servant though not that of a son."

241 John Wesley, 1703–91, from the original portrait, 1741, probably by John Michael Williams (d. 1780), in Didsbury College, Didsbury, Lancaster, England

JOHN WESLEY'S CONVERSION

YET Wesley's visit to America was providential, for it brought him into contact with the Moravians. A group of them were fellow passengers on the way to Georgia, and their calm faith in a time of threatened shipwreck and death convinced him that they knew God as he did not. Spangenberg, the leader of their settlement at Savannah, asked him: "Do you know Jesus Christ?" "I know that He is the Saviour of the world," was Wesley's somewhat embarrassed reply. "True," answered Spangenberg, "but do you know He has saved you?" When Wesley returned to England, he attended Moravian meetings; and conferred with Peter Böhler, a Moravian minister who was in London on his way to America. At a meeting of a society in Aldersgate Street, on May 24, 1738, hearing read Martin Luther's description of "the change which God works in the heart through faith in Christ," he experienced what he ever afterward felt to be his conversion. "I felt my heart strangely warmed. I felt I did trust in Christ, Christ alone, for salvation; and an assurance was given me that he had taken away *my* sins, even *mine*, and saved *me* from the law of sin and death." He devoted the summer to visiting the Moravians in Germany, with much benefit, though his visit brought out certain clear differences between their leader, Count von Zinzendorf, and himself which prevented their full coöperation. He returned to England in the fall to begin with power his life work, the organization of societies of Methodists.

242 August Gottlieb Spangenberg, 1704–92, from the contemporary portrait by Anton Graff (1736–1813), in the Session Hall of the Board of Directors of the Evang. Brüder-Unität in Deutschland, Herrnhut, Sachsen, Germany

243   Count Nicholaus Ludwig von Zinzendorf,
         from an engraving by Niederbühl

COUNT NICHOLAUS LUDWIG VON ZINZENDORF,
1700–1760

THE Moravian Brethren, or Unitas Fratrum, were the spiritual descendants of John Huss, who was burned at the stake by order of the Council of Constance in 1415. After three centuries of persecution, they found a refuge, which they named Herrnhut, on the estates of a Saxon nobleman, Count von Zinzendorf. A Lutheran, educated under pietistic influences at Halle, Zinzendorf became interested in the beliefs and practices of his protegees, and eventually was ordained a Moravian bishop and became their spiritual leader. He was banished from Saxony in 1736, as Frederick William I of Prussia aptly said, "because he wished to live piously though a count." In 1747 the Saxon Government rescinded the order of banishment, and besought him to establish more settlements like Herrnhut.

MORAVIAN CUSTOMS AND CEREMONIES

ZINZENDORF'S was a heart-religion which centered in personal fellowship with Christ. "I have one passion. It is Christ." He welded the Unitas Fratrum into a sort of Protestant monasticism, without vows of celibacy, its members bound to their Lord by a daily regimen of prayer and worship, counting their relation to Him above all other ties, and ready to go in His service to the ends of the world. The pictures, taken from a French account of Moravian usages, dated 1758, represent: prostration in prayer to Christ; the holy kiss of peace; the rite of foot-washing; and the baptism of Indians in America.

244   Prostration in Prayer, from *Briere et fidele Exposition de
            l'Origine de la doctrine des constitutions, etc.*, 1758

245   Holy Kiss of Peace, from *Briere et fidele Exposition de l'Origine
            de la doctrine des constitutions, etc.*, 1758

246   The Rite of Foot-Washing, from *Briere et fidele Exposition de
         l'Origine de la doctrine des constitutions, etc.*, 1758

247   Baptism of Indians in America, from *Briere et fidele Exposition
            de l'Orgine de la doctrine des constitutions, etc.*, 1758

248   View of Bethlehem, Pa., about 1770, from an engraving by Paul Sandy after the original sketch, drawn on the spot, by Governor Thomas Pownall, in the New York Public Library

THE SETTLEMENT OF BETHLEHEM, PENNSYLVANIA

UNDER the leadership of August Gottlieb Spangenberg, 1704–92, Moravians settled in Georgia in 1735 and in Pennsylvania in 1736. The Georgia group, experiencing trouble because of their refusal to bear arms, soon joined those in Pennsylvania, who steadily prospered. Zinzendorf, meeting with them in December, 1741, called the place Bethlehem. Their life, directed by Spangenberg's genius as an organizer, was semi-communistic, entailing a community of time and labor, but not of personal property. All work was carried on for the benefit of the church, under responsible committees. It is reported that besides the farms, thirty-two different industries were in operation by 1747; and that no other town in the interior of Pennsylvania could so well supply all wants. In 1762, however, Spangenberg was needed at Herrnhut, where he became Zinzendorf's successor as leader of the whole brotherhood; and it was deemed best that the communistic organization of industry be replaced by individual enterprises.

ZINZENDORF SEEKS TO EFFECT CHURCH UNITY

GERMANS had settled in Pennsylvania in great numbers. Zinzendorf estimated that there were one hundred thousand at the time of his visit in 1741–42. A little later Governor Thomas reported that they constituted about three fifths of the population, adding that they "imported with them all the religious whimsies of their country, and I believe have subdivided since their arrival here." They lacked ministers and schools; and there was grave danger of a lapse of religion among them. "It had become proverbial," Zinzendorf said, "respecting any one who cared not for God and His Word, that 'he is of the Pennsylvania religion.'" Zinzendorf's ambition was to unite these Germans into one evangelical church. With this in view he resigned his Moravian bishopric and came to America incognito, traveling as plain Ludwig Turnstein. He held

seven "Synods" or conferences in the early months of 1742, but they came to naught. He became pastor of the Lutheran church in Philadelphia; but factions arose, and he built a new stone church, out of his private funds, for those who held to him. This eventually became a Moravian church. Zinzendorf returned to Europe, and withdrew from further effort to influence the Pennsylvania Lutherans when young Pastor Muhlenberg, sent from Halle in tardy answer to a call nine years old, arrived upon the scene.

249   The First Moravian Church in Pennsylvania, 1742, from Abraham Ritter,
History of the Moravian Church in Philadelphia, Philadelphia, 1857

251   Muhlenberg Preaching in the Barn at Trappe, from *The Old Trappe Church*, edited by Rev. Ernest T. Kretschman, Philadelphia, 1893

250   Gotthilf Henry Ernest Muhlenberg, 1753–1815, from the portrait in Independence Hall, Philadelphia

HENRY M. MUHLENBERG, 1711–1787, PATRIARCH OF AMERICAN LUTHERANISM

MUHLENBERG was thirty-one years old when he arrived in Philadelphia and he gave forty-five years of unstinted service to the upbuilding of Lutheran churches. His motto was *Ecclesia plantanda* — "The Church must be planted." Though his office was that of pastor, first of the three churches at Philadelphia, Providence and New Hanover, then of the Philadelphia church only, the demands upon him were such that he was practically overseer of all the Lutheran churches in the colonies. Extracts from his regular, detailed reports to Halle were published from time to time as the *Hallesche Nachrichten*, and helped to bring both men and money to his aid. In 1748 he organized the first Lutheran Synod. He handled the difficult language problem with rare wisdom, preaching and catechising in English as well as in German whenever there was need or opportunity. His three sons, educated in Germany, returned to labor with him in the Lutheran ministry; and two of them, General Peter Muhlenberg and Frederick A. Muhlenberg, have names that live in American history for the distinguished military and political services which they rendered to their country. The pictures represent Muhlenberg's first sermon at Providence, now Trappe, and the church, still standing, which he built to replace the barn in which it was delivered.

252   Old Lutheran Church at Trappe, from Sherman Day, *Historical Collections of Pennsylvania*, Philadelphia, 1843

MICHAEL SCHLATTER, 1716–1790, FOUNDER OF REFORMED CHURCHES

IN 1748 the Dutch churches of Holland sent Michael Schlatter, a young Swiss minister, as a missionary to the German and Swiss immigrants in America who were of the Reformed faith. He traveled widely throughout the colonies, establishing churches; and in 1747 organized a Coetus, or Synod. He and Muhlenberg were close friends, and their work was unmarred by jealousy. In many places the Lutheran and Reformed congregations built union churches and it was a common saying, which is yet current among the Pennsylvania Germans, that the only difference between the two groups was that the Lutherans began the Lord's Prayer with *Vater unser*, and the Reformed with *Unser Vater*.

253   First Reformed Church, Philadelphia, 1747, from Rev. David Van Horne, *History of The Reformed Church in Philadelphia*, Philadelphia, 1876

SOCIETY FOR THE PROMOTION OF THE KNOWLEDGE OF GOD

In one respect, Schlatter's work was too successful. Going to Europe, he published an *Appeal* which quickly brought the sum of twelve thousand pounds. This was invested as an endowment for the Reformed churches of Pennsylvania. A well-meaning Englishman became interested in this *Appeal* and translated it, with the result that a Society for the Promotion of the Knowledge of God among the Germans was organized in England and soon gath-

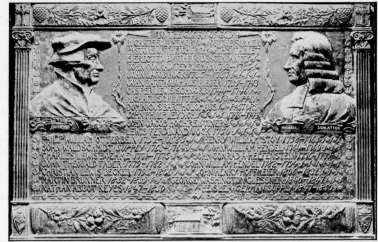

254　Memorial Tablet to Zwingli, Schlatter, and the early pastors of the Congregation, 1732–1850, in the First Reformed Church, Lancaster, Pa.

ered the sum of twenty thousand pounds, which it planned to use in the maintenance of charity schools in Pennsylvania. The German settlers would have none of the "foreign charity"; and Schlatter, who had let himself be persuaded to accept the superintendency of the proposed schools, lost his influence.

Drie Predicatien
De Eerste, Over
Jeſai 66. *v.* 2.
De Twede, Van de
Geregtigden, tot het
Heylige
Avontmael
Oover den 30 *Sondagh van den* Heydelbergſchen Catechiſmus.
De, Derde van het Gebruyck der
Sleutelen
Oover den 31 *Sondagh van den Heydel-* bergſchen Catechiſmus.
Gepredickt Door
Theodorus Jacobus Frilinghuiſen. Predicant van de Gereformeerde Nederduytſce *Kercke* op de *Rariuans.*————
Vit gegeven door eenige van ſyn Vrienden
Gedruckt tot *Niew-York* by William Bradford in den Jaere 1721

255　Title-page of the original in the New York Public Library

THE LOG COLLEGE

GILBERT TENNENT had been educated for the ministry by his father, William Tennent, an Irish minister who had come to America in 1716 and had become a Presbyterian. He had three sons younger than Gilbert, and in 1736 erected, opposite his manse in Neshaminy, Pennsylvania, a building in which he undertook to train them and other young men for the ministry. The "Log College," it was called in derision. Whitefield said that it was "the meanest building ever erected for such a purpose," and that "it reminded me of what might have been the schools of the prophets hinted at in the Old Testament."

THE GREAT AWAKENING

FROM 1720 to 1744, in all the colonies and among all groups of Protestants, were manifested those movements toward a more vital, conscious religious experience which are collectively known as the Great Awakening. It was America's share in the general reaction against the relatively dead, formal orthodoxy of state churches, which in Germany appeared as Pietism and in England as Methodism. Like all such movements, it can be attributed to no one source. Bolzius, Spangenberg, Wesley, and Whitefield brought its spirit to Georgia; Jonathan Edwards, quite independently, was responsible for its beginning in New England. But before any of these, revivals of religion had begun in New Jersey under the strongly evangelical preaching of Dominie Jacob Frelinghuysen, pastor of the Dutch church at Raritan from 1719 to 1746. He insisted upon the need of conscious conversion and the renewal of heart and life; and he profoundly influenced Gilbert Tennent, the young minister of the Presbyterian church at New Brunswick.

256　William Tennent, 1673–1746, from the *General Assembly's Missionary Magazine*, Philadelphia, March 1806

257   The Log College, Nishaminy, Pa., from a copy of an old print in the Presbyterian Historical Society, Philadelphia

THE LOG COLLEGE BECOMES THE CENTER FOR THE "NEW SIDE"

THE Log College became a center and source of the "New Side" or "New Light" party which rapidly formed in the Presbyterian Church, favoring revival methods and insisting upon conscious conversion and evidences of regeneration in both ministers and people. This party was opposed by the "Old Side," who believed that the question as to one's regeneration lay between him and God; that all baptized persons not heretical or immoral should be admitted to communion; and that no one should be licensed to preach who had not an adequate education, evidenced by a diploma from a European university or one of the New England colleges, or by examination by a committee of Synod.

GEORGE WHITEFIELD, 1714–1770, FIELD PREACHER

IN 1738, at the suggestion of John Wesley, with whom he had been associated in the "Holy Club" at Oxford, George Whitefield came to Georgia as a missionary. He became interested in the founding of an orphanage; and his travels to collect funds for that enterprise carried him to and fro throughout England and the colonies, and everywhere afforded him opportunity to preach. Because churches were denied him, he began to preach in the fields at Bristol, and soon commanded an audience of twenty thousand colliers, whose emotions were revealed by "the white gutters made by their tears, which plentifully fell down their black cheeks." A different evidence of his eloquence was recorded by Benjamin Franklin, who had determined that he would give him no contribution: "I had in my pocket a handful of copper money, three or four silver dollars, and five pistoles in gold. As he proceeded, I began to soften and concluded to give him the copper. Another stroke of his oratory made me ashamed of that, and determined me to give him the silver; and he finished so admirably, that I emptied my pocket wholly into the collector's dish, gold and all."

258   George Whitefield, from an engraving by Frederick Halpin (b. 1805–)

259   The Old Academy, Philadelphia, from E. R. Beadle, The Old and the New, The Second Presbyterian Church of Philadelphia, 1876

THE "OLD ACADEMY" AT PHILADELPHIA

WHITEFIELD's powerful evangelistic preaching, especially on his journey throughout the colonies in 1739–41, spread and integrated the Great Awakening. He preached on Boston Common, it is said, to nearly thirty thousand people. Franklin, who was curious, tested how far his voice could be heard in Philadelphia, and concluded that it would carry to that many. His friends in Philadelphia erected for him the first building in this country especially intended for an itinerant evangelist. Franklin was one of its trustees; and the subscriptions were made on condition that it should be for the "free use of itinerant preachers forever, as well as for the promulgation of the peculiar tenets and religious views called 'New Light.'" For nine years the Second (New Light) Presbyterian Church, of which Gilbert Tennent became pastor, worshiped there. In 1753, it became the first building of the College and Academy which grew into the University of Pennsylvania.

THE DANGER OF AN UNCONVERTED MINISTRY

THE besetting sin of itinerant evangelists is to belittle the work, and even attack the character, of resident ministers. Whitefield was not wholly exempt from this, and aroused some criticism, even on his first visit to New England, by remarks that he made about "unconverted ministers." Gilbert Tennent and his friends were restive under an action of the Presbyterian Synod, prohibiting ministers from preaching, without invitation from the incumbent, in any parishes but their own. They felt that this was a protective device on the part of "unconverted" pastors for keeping their flocks undisturbed by "gracious" ministers. In 1740 Tennent preached a fiery sermon on *The Danger of an Unconverted Ministry*, one result of which was to split the Presbyterian Church into two organizations, which remained apart for seventeen years. Whitefield said, "He is a son of thunder, whose preaching must either convert or enrage hypocrites." It had the latter effect on a considerable number of folk, when he visited Boston after Whitefield's departure.

260 Gilbert Tennent, 1703–64, from the *General Assembly's Missionary Magazine*, Philadelphia, May 1805

EXTRAVAGANCES OF SOME REVIVALISTS AND EXHORTERS

SOME imitators of Whitefield fell into questionable extravagances. A letter written home to England from Boston gives an account of what was going on, which is obviously unsympathetic, but doubtless not much exaggerated: "There is a Creature here which you perhaps never heard of before. It is called *an Exhorter*. It is of both Sexes, but generally of the Male, and young. Its distinguishing qualities, are *Ignorance, Impudence, Zeal*. . . . Such of them as have good Voices do *great Execution;* they move their hearers, make them cry, faint, swoon, fall into Convulsions. . . . The Ministers have generally endeavoured to preserve some kind of Order, and been satisfied with the crying out of a Number at the hearing of their Sermons (the Minister that never made Somebody or other cry, is unconverted); but the Exhorters tarry in the Meeting-house with the People after the Minister is gone, and sometimes several of them exhort at once in different parts of the House, and then there is terrible Doings. You may hear screaming, singing, laughing, praying, all at once; and, in other parts, they fall into Visions, Trances, Convulsions. When they come out of their Trances, they commonly tell a senseless Story of Heaven and Hell, and whom and what they saw there." The worst extravagances were those of the Rev. James Davenport, who received "impressions" that as Jonathan and his armor-bearer were called of God to attack the Philistines, he and a friend, whom he called his armor-bearer, were called to go into the parishes of other ministers, to convert the people. "Good Lord, I will not mince the matter any longer with thee," he addressed the Deity at a meeting in Boston; "for thou knowest that I know that most of the ministers of the town of Boston and of the country are unconverted, and are leading their people blindfold to hell." At New London, he persuaded people to burn such of their clothes as he deemed to be "idolatrous," together with the books of ministers whom he declared unsound. He was adjudged *non compos mentis;* and a year later, published a humble series of *Retractions*.

261 The Rev. James Davenport's *Retractions*, from *The Christian History*, Boston, September 22, 1744

THE

Chriſtian Hiſtory,

Saturday MARCH 5. 1743.   No I.

To be publiſh'd *Weekly* ;

Containing Accounts of the Propagation and Revival
of Religion ; more particularly

I. Authentick Accounts from Miniſters and other creditable
Perſons of the Revival of Religion in the ſeveral Parts of
NEW ENGLAND.

II. Extracts of the moſt remarkable Pieces in the *weekly Hiſto-
ries* of Religion, and *other Accounts*, PRINTED both in
England and *Scotland*.

III. Extracts of WRITTEN LETTERS both from *England,
Scotland, New-York, New-Jerſey, Penſylvania, South-Ca-
rolina,* and *Georgia* of a religious Nature, as they ſhall be
ſent hither from creditable Perſons and communicated to us.

IV. In Intervals of freſh Occurences, and on other Occaſions,
it is propoſed to give the Reader the *moſt remarkable Paſſages
Hiſtorical* and *Doctrinal*, out of the moſt famous OLD
WRITERS both of the Church of *England* and *Scotland*
from the Reformation, as alſo the *firſt Settlers of New-
England* and *their Children* · that we may ſee how far their
pious *Principles* and *Spirit* are at this Day revived : and
may alſo guard againſt all Extreams.

Pſal. 26. 7. *That I may* PUBLISH with the Voice of THANKS-
GIVING, *and tell of all* THY WONDROUS WORKS.

BOSTON,N.E. Printed by KNEELAND&GREEN,1743.
for THOMAS PRINCE, Junr. A. B.

262   Title-page of the first number, in the
New York Public Library

DEBATE ON THE VALUE OF REVIVALS

THERE was much debate, especially in New England, as to the
value of the revivals. The outstanding work, on the one side,
was Jonathan Edwards' *Thoughts on the Revival of Religion in
New England;* and on the other side, *Seasonable Thoughts on
the State of Religion in New England*, by Charles Chauncy, the
able, unemotional pastor of the First Church in Boston. The
two men agreed in condemning the censoriousness of the itinerant preachers, and in regarding with some misgiving the "bodily
effects" of religious emotion. Admitting the evils that were
attending the movement, Edwards nevertheless felt that much
good was being accomplished, and prayed that it might continue;
while Chauncy, granting that good had been done, believed
that the evil results outweighed it, and hoped the "commotion"
might stop. Edwards suggested, as a means of wise promotion,
the publication of a periodical to contain accounts of the progress of the movement in all sections; and this was undertaken
by Thomas Prince, who issued the first number of *The Christian
History* on March 5, 1743. The Great Awakening, in spite of the
excesses which characterized some of the revival meetings, had a
profound influence upon contemporary thought. It quickened,
as nothing else could have done, New England Puritanism,
steadily losing the influence over the people which it had wielded
in the seventeenth century. It helped to strengthen in an Ameri-
can-born generation the ideals and moral purpose which in 1776
made men willing to pledge to each other "our Lives, our Fortunes, and our sacred Honor" in the great cause of freedom.

OPPOSITION TO WHITEFIELD

WHEN Whitefield made a second visit to New England in 1744,
his welcome was not as warm as before. Various ministerial
associations took action cautioning their constituency concerning
him. The faculty of Harvard College published a *Testimony*
against his "enthusiasm" and his "conduct"; and the faculty
of Yale, a *Declaration* against his "principles and designs."
The word "enthusiast" stood for "one that acts either according
to dreams, or some sudden impulses and impressions upon his
mind, which he fondly imagines to be from the Spirit of God."
Yale suspended two students for attending a meeting of Separatists, or "Come-outers," as those were called who, following the
"New Light," withdrew from the existing Congregational
churches to form organizations of their own. Whitefield is reported to have said of the colleges that their light had become
darkness, "darkness that may be felt"; but he answered the
attacks upon him with moderation and good judgment. He was
heard by large audiences then and on subsequent visits, but the
Great Awakening was over. The Great Awakening had far-
reaching permanent results. It converted many, and multiplied
the churches. In New England, the number of converts to join
the churches was variously estimated at from twenty-five thousand to fifty thousand; and in the twenty years between 1740
and 1760, in spite of war, one hundred and fifty new churches
were organized, exclusive of those formed by separation.

THE

DECLARATION

OF THE

Rector and *Tutors* of *Yale-College* in
New-Haven,

Againſt the Reverend

Mr. *George Whitefield,*

His PRINCIPLES and DESIGNS.

In a LETTER to him

BOSTON:
Printed and ſold by *T. Fleet*, at the Heart and
Crown in Cornhill, 1745.

263   Title-page of the original in the New
York Public Library

THE RESULTS OF THE GREAT AWAKENING

THE number of Presbyterian ministers doubled in the seventeen years during which Old Side and New Side were divided; and the number of churches increased yet more. Princeton and Dartmouth Colleges were founded as direct results of the revival. But more important than these and other immediate results were two general trends of effect that have profoundly influenced American life. The first is the emphasis upon religion as an experience of the human soul, verifiable in life and inward assurance, rather than as mere creedal assent or liturgical conformity. The second is the emphasis upon the spiritual character of the church as an institution, which rendered impossible the old idea that the church is the creature of the state. When the church is thus spiritually conceived, it claims, and is willing to grant, liberty. The Great Awakening prepared the way for the principle of religious freedom which was soon to be achieved and written into the National Constitution.

264 Charles Chauncy, 1705–87, from the original portrait, artist unknown, in the Widener Library, Harvard University, Cambridge, Mass.

265 Baptist Church, Providence, R. I., begun 1775, from an engraving by Fenner and Sears in *The History and Topography of the United States*, edited by John Howard Hinton, London, 1832

CHURCH AND STATE IN 1776

THAT church and state are naturally related and that religious duties are properly to be enforced by civil authority was the universal assumption, as old as civilization, from which America was destined to emancipate mankind. When the Revolution began, the colonies differed greatly in the degree to which they had progressed toward religious freedom. Four degrees or types of relation between church and state may be distinguished:

(1) The state may support an established church by public taxation, compel attendance at its services, and forbid the worship of dissenting groups. None of the colonies, since the English Toleration Act of 1689, had done this.

(2) The state may by taxation compel all citizens to contribute to the support of an established church, though granting, under specified conditions, privileges of organization and freedom of worship to dissenting groups. In Virginia, Maryland, North Carolina, South Carolina and Georgia, the Church of England was thus established and supported.

(3) The state may levy general taxes for the support of religion, leaving it to the individual taxpayer to designate the religious body with which he is affiliated, and to which he wishes his contribution to go. This was the situation in Massachusetts, Connecticut and New Hampshire. The Congregational churches in these colonies were not established churches, in the proper sense of the term. They were independent churches, which enjoyed the avails of all taxes for the support of religion except those designated, under specified conditions, for some other religious body.

(4) State and church may be completely separate, in support as well as in control. This was the status in Rhode Island, Pennsylvania and Delaware.

The situation in New York and New Jersey was anomalous. The Church of England was not legally established in either colony; but the royal Governors, whenever they could, and as far as they dared, acted as though it were.

266   St. Paul's Church, Norfolk, Va., built 1739, from William Meade, *Old Churches and Families of Virginia*, Philadelphia, 1859

XXXIV. That all **Treaſurers**, Judges, Maſters of the Rolls, Sheriffs, Juſtices of the Peace, and other Officers or Perſons whatſoever, relating to Courts or Tryals of Cauſes, or any other Service in the Government, and all Members elected to ſerve in **Provincial Council** and **General Aſſembly**; and all that have Right to elect ſuch Members, ſhall be ſuch as profeſs **Faith in Jeſus Chriſt**, and that are not convicted of Ill Fame, or unſober and diſhoneſt Converſation, and that are of One and Twenty Years of Age at leaſt: and that all ſuch ſo qualified, ſhall be capable of the ſaid ſeveral Employments and Priviledges, as aforeſaid.

XXXV. That all Perſons living in this Province, who confeſs and acknowledge the One Almighty and Eternal God, to be the Creator, Upholder and Ruler of the World, and that hold themſelves obliged in Conſcience to live peaceably and juſtly in *Civil Society*, ſhall in no wayes be moleſted or prejudiced for their Religious Perſwaſion or Practice in matters of *Faith* and *Worſhip*, nor ſhall they be compelled at any time to frequent or maintain any Religious **Worſhip**, Place or **Miniſtry** whatever.

267   From William Penn, *The Frame of the Government of the Province of Pennsylvania in America*, London, 1682

RELIGIOUS TESTS IN 1776

RELIGIOUS tests of different sorts had abounded in colonial days, and had sometimes changed kaleidoscopically, reflecting changes in England. They varied from the original insistence of Massachusetts and New Haven upon church membership as a qualification for citizenship, to the general disqualification of Catholics for public office by requiring of them the Test Oath. Most of the colonies adopted state constitutions soon after 1776. Virginia was the only state which completely eliminated religious tests; Maryland and Massachusetts made belief in the Christian religion a condition of holding public office; New Jersey, Georgia and the Carolinas required profession of the Protestant religion. Pennsylvania restricted civil rights to persons "who acknowledge the being of a God," and demanded that officeholders affirm belief not only in God but in the inspiration of the Old and New Testaments. Delaware went yet further, and required a declaration of belief in the doctrine of the Trinity. New York retained an oath of abjuration of foreign allegiance in all matters, "ecclesiastical as well as civil," a phrase directed against Catholics; and it excluded clergymen from public office, on the ground that they "ought not to be diverted from their great duties of the service of God and the care of souls."

CHURCHES AND MINISTERS IN 1776

DENOMINATION	MINISTERS	CHURCHES
Congregational	575	700
Baptist	350	380
Church of England	250	300
Presbyterian	153	320
Dutch Reformed	25	60
Lutheran	25	60
German Reformed	25	60
Roman Catholic	26	52
Moravian	12	8
	1441	1940

CHURCHES AND MINISTERS IN 1776

AT the time of the signing of the Declaration of Independence, the population of the thirteen colonies was about three million, of whom nearly one sixth were slaves. There were about two thousand churches and fifteen hundred ministers — one minister for every two thousand souls. The estimate here given does not include the Quakers, of whom there were probably fifty thousand in the colonies at this time, a number exceeded only by the Congregationalists, Baptists, Anglicans, and Presbyterians. The Methodists are not named, as they then had no existence separate from the Church of England. Other relatively small groups were the Mennonites, Dunkards and other German sects, and the Jews.

SAMUEL DAVIES, 1723–1761, FOUNDER OF HANOVER PRESBYTERY

THE main battle for religious freedom was waged in Virginia, and the victory is to the credit of the Presbyterians, with the help, latterly, of the Baptists. The Scotch-Irish, who pushed westward in Pennsylvania and south along the mountains, were welcomed by the Governor of Virginia as a frontier line of defense against the Indians. Trouble arose when they began to spread in the eastern counties, and when some of their itinerant preachers violently attacked the clergy of the established church. Samuel Davies, pastor in Hanover County from 1747 to 1759, and first moderator of Hanover Presbytery, followed a constructive policy of scrupulous adherence to the law requiring the licensing of dissenters' meetinghouses as well as dissenting ministers. He did not hesitate to meet the formidable Peyton Randolph in legal combat, or to carry his case to the Bishop of London; and he secured the right, at first refused him, to register seven preaching appointments for his own service. With Gilbert Tennent, he spent a year in Britain in the interest of the newly founded College of New Jersey, now Princeton, and secured funds sufficient to assure its permanence. In 1759 he became its president, following Jonathan Edwards.

268   Samuel Davies, from the original portrait by James Massalon, at Princeton University, Princeton, New Jersey

PATRICK HENRY ATTACKS THE VIRGINIA CLERGY

269 Obverse of the seal of the Acts of 1720–22 of the Colony of Virginia, from the original in the Public Record Office, Richmond, Va.

270 Reverse of the seal of the Acts of 1720–22 of the Colony of Virginia, from the original in the Public Record Office, Richmond, Va.

BUT fighting parsons, though as sensible and fearless as Davies, could not have won the battle alone. They had the powerful help of three of Virginia's greatest statesmen, Patrick Henry, James Madison, and Thomas Jefferson. Patrick Henry's unusual ability as an orator and advocate first attracted public notice when he espoused the cause of the people against the clergy of the established church, who were demanding that their salaries be paid in tobacco, in a time of tobacco shortage, when a general law had been passed authorizing the payment of all debts in money, at a fixed rate of equivalence which the clergy were unwilling to accept.

His attack upon the King, who had vetoed the law, brought for the first time the cry of "Treason" which he was destined to hear again upon a memorable occasion; and his scathing portrayal of the lives of the Virginia clergy, whom he denounced as "rapacious harpies," was a blow to the prestige of the establishment and increased public sympathy with the dissenters.

PATRICK HENRY DEFENDS THE BAPTISTS

IN 1768, the local authorities in several Virginia counties began to persecute the Baptists, jailing their preachers as disturbers of the peace. Patrick Henry came to their defense, and in a number of cases appeared as their counsel, volunteering his services without charge, and at least once paying out of his own pocket the costs assessed against them. His unexpected appearance and stirring address upon the first of these occasions have been described in terms that embody the traditions associated with his name. "'May it please the Court, what did I hear read? Did I hear it distinctly, — or was it a mistake of my own? Did I hear an expression, as of a crime, that these men whom your worships are about to try for misdemeanor, are charged with — with — what?' Then in a low, solemn, heavy tone he continued — 'preaching the gospel of the Son of God?' Pausing amid profound silence, he waved the paper three times about his head, then raising his eyes and hands to heaven, with peculiar and impressive energy, he exclaimed — 'Great God!'" Thrice, in the course of a brief plea reminding the Court of the love of liberty then so deeply astir in the American colonies, he reached a like climax. Finally, "looking at the Court, he exclaimed with the full power of his strong voice — 'What laws have they violated?' ... The audience were excited; the bench and bar were moved; and the presiding magistrate ordered, 'Sheriff, discharge those men.'"

271 Bronze tablet at Bowling Green, Virginia

272 From the original Court Order, June 1771, in the Caroline County Courthouse, Bowling Green, Va.

JAMES MADISON REJECTS THE PRINCIPLE OF CHURCH ESTABLISHMENT

LIKE Patrick Henry and George Washington, James Madison was a devout Christian and a member of the established Church in Virginia. His education at Princeton brought him into sympathetic contact with the Presbyterians, and his own study of the Scriptures and of "divinity" was so thorough that, in later years, Jefferson turned to him for a list of theological books to be purchased for the library of the University of Virginia. This list is extant, and is evidence that he knew more of theology than most ministers. In a letter to a friend in Pennsylvania, January 24, 1774, he expressed his indignation at the persecution of Baptists and his distrust of the principle of church establishment. "I want again to breathe your free air. . . . That diabolical, hell-conceived principle of persecution rages among some; and, to their eternal infamy, the clergy can furnish their quota of imps for such purposes. There are, at this time, in the adjacent country, not less than five or six well-meaning men in close jail for publishing their religious sentiments. . . . If the Church of England had been the established and general religion in all the Northern colonies, as it has been among us here, and uninterrupted harmony had prevailed throughout the continent, it is clear to me that slavery and subjection might and would have been gradually insinuated among us. Union of religious sentiment begets a surprising confidence, and ecclesiastical establishments tend to great ignorance and corruption, all of which facilitate the execution of mischievous projects."

273 James Madison, 1751–1836, from a miniature, artist unknown, in the New York Historical Society

THE VIRGINIA BILL OF RIGHTS GUARANTEES RELIGIOUS FREEDOM

THE battle for the principle of religious freedom was won when the Bill of Rights, adopted by the Virginia Convention, June 12, 1776, included as its last article: "That religion, or the duty which we owe to our Creator and the manner of discharging it, can be directed only by reason and conviction, not by force or violence; and therefore all men are equally entitled to the free exercise of religion, according to the dictates of conscience; and that it is the mutual duty of all to practise Christian forbearance, love, and charity towards each other." The original draft of the Bill of Rights was by George Mason; but this article was proposed and drafted by Patrick Henry. As presented by him, the second clause read: "that all men should enjoy the fullest toleration in the exercise of religion, according. . . ." The clause finally adopted was proposed by James Madison, who wished to get rid of the term "toleration." That is a word which properly applies to a political system which maintains an established church and permits or tolerates dissent; it does not properly characterize what was from henceforth the American principle, that all men are entitled to equal religious freedom, that all religions stand without prejudice before the law of the state, and that liberty is not license.

274 Page from a copy of the first draft of the Bill of Rights, from the original in the Virginia State Library, Richmond

"A BILL FOR ESTABLISHING RELIGIOUS FREEDOM"

THE principle of religious freedom was won; but its full embodiment in legislation was not accomplished for nine years. The established Church was loath to surrender its privileges and fought every step. One proposition was that there be a general assessment for the support of the Christian religion, to be applied without preference to whatever church or form of worship each taxpayer should choose — a plan like the one then in vogue in Massachusetts, but without the preferred position which it gave to a particular group of churches. George Washington, Richard Henry Lee, and Patrick Henry favored this. The Presbyterians and Baptists opposed it, however; and Madison presented a "Memorial and Remonstrance" against it which was unanswerable. Finally, in 1785, the Bill for Establishing Religious Freedom, which had been drafted by Thomas Jefferson and presented six years before, was passed. It provided: "That no man shall be compelled to frequent or support any religious worship, place, or ministry whatsoever, nor shall be enforced, restrained, molested, or burdened in his body or goods, nor shall otherwise suffer, on account of his religious opinions or belief; but that all men shall be free to profess, and by argument to maintain, their opinions in matters of religion, and that the same shall in no wise diminish, enlarge, or affect their civil capacities." Jefferson so prided himself upon the authorship of this statute that he included it in his epitaph: "Here was buried Thomas Jefferson,

275 Jefferson Statue by Edward V. Valentine (1838–) in the Hotel Jefferson, Richmond, Va.

author of the Declaration of American Independence, the statute of Virginia for religious freedom, and father of the University of Virginia." Posterity has usually accepted his appraisal of himself on this point; and accounts abound of how he, against tremendous odds, led and won the battle for religious freedom. The fact is that we owe that victory to many men. Madison bore the brunt of the contest, and did most to determine its final outcome. The successive memorials of the Hanover Presbytery, moreover, which were presented before Jefferson drafted his Bill, had stated with remarkable precision and force the principles of religious freedom upon which it was based.

BAPTISTS PROTEST AGAINST MINISTERIAL RATES IN MASSACHUSETTS

MEANWHILE the Baptists in Massachusetts were making strenuous efforts to gain complete exemption from taxes for the support of religion. True, the "ministerial rates" paid by Baptists were used to pay their own ministers. But they complained that in many communities the law was not fairly administered, and they were forced to contribute to the support of the Congregational churches; that the required certificates of membership in a Baptist church were unduly difficult to obtain, and could be recorded only upon payment of a tax of fourpence which was as iniquitous as the tax of fourpence upon a pound of tea; that these certificates still left to the civil authorities the determination as to whether or not the persons certified were "conscientiously" Baptists; and that the whole principle of the exercise of civil authority in matters of religion was wrong. They sent Isaac Backus to present their grievances to the First Continental Congress — an inopportune procedure which naturally met with little success, and exposed them to the charge of trying to block the union of the colonies. The Massachusetts delegates promised to do for them what they could; but Samuel Adams intimated that "the complaint came from enthusiasts who made it a merit to suffer persecution," and John Adams commented that "they might as well turn the heavenly bodies out of their annual and diurnal courses, as the people of Massachusetts of the present day from their meeting-houses and Sunday laws." Certain measures of relief were granted;

276 Isaac Backus, 1724–1806, from Isaac Backus, A History of New England, Boston, 1839, in the John Carter Brown Library, Providence

but the support of religion by taxation continued until 1833.

X—9

277 Jacob Duché, 1737–98, from the original portrait by his son, Thomas Spence Duché (1763–90), in the Hopkinson Collection, Historical Society of Pennsylvania, Philadelphia

RELIGIOUS TOLERATION AND FELLOWSHIP IN THE CONTINENTAL CONGRESS

WHEN it was proposed to open the daily sessions of the Continental Congress with prayer, objection was made that this was impractical on account of the differing religious views and practices of its members. Samuel Adams met the issue squarely: "I am no bigot. I can hear a prayer from a man of piety and virtue, who is at the same time a friend of his country. I am a stranger in Philadelphia, but I have heard that Mr. Duché deserves that character; and therefore I move that Mr. Duché be desired to read prayers to the Congress tomorrow morning." Mr. Duché, who was rector of Christ Church, had the grace not only to "read prayers," but, John Adams wrote, "unexpectedly to everybody, struck out into an extemporary prayer, which filled the bosom of every man present. I must confess, I never heard a better prayer, or one so well pronounced." Duché was chaplain of the Congress for two years and was succeeded by other Episcopal and Presbyterian ministers. The religious spirit of Congress was marked, and its judgment, when religious issues were involved, was sound. It appointed July 20, 1775, "as a day of public humiliation, fasting and prayer"; and attended divine services in a body, at the Episcopal church in the morning and at the Presbyterian church in the afternoon. It continued, from time to time, to appoint days of public prayer. It proposed full freedom of conscience to the Catholics of Canada, appointed a Catholic chaplain for a regiment of Canadian volunteers, and attended the requiem mass in St. Joseph's Church at the death of the Spanish envoy. Benedict Arnold, traitor, was able to say that he had lately seen "your mean and profligate Congress at Mass for the soul of a Roman Catholic in purgatory, and participating in the rites of a Church against whose anti-Christian corruptions your pious ancestors would have witnessed with their blood."

RELIGIOUS FREEDOM IS GUARANTEED BY THE CONSTITUTION OF THE UNITED STATES

THE Constitution of the United States of America, as framed by the Convention, contained but one reference to religion, in Article VI, Section 3: "No religious test shall ever be required as a qualification to any office or public trust under the United States." This was generally approved; but six states suggested the need of a more comprehensive guarantee of religious freedom. The first of the Amendments proposed by Madison and adopted in 1789, to meet the popular demand for a Bill of Rights, affords this guarantee: "Congress shall make no law respecting an establishment of religion, or prohibiting the free exercise thereof." The constitutions of the several states differ; but all now embody the principle of religious freedom, in most cases to the full extent of the Federal Constitution. Justice Cooley enumerates five things which are not within the power of legislatures or public authorities, under any of the constitutions of this country: (1) "Any law respecting an establishment of religion"; (2) "Compulsory support, by taxation or otherwise, of religion"; (3) "Compulsory attendance upon religious worship"; (4) "Restraints upon the free exercise of religion according to the dictates of conscience"; (5) "Restraints upon the expression of religious belief."

278 From the statue sculptured in Rome by Moses Ezekiel (1844–1917), in Fairmount Park, Philadelphia

279   Benjamin Franklin's Motion for Prayers in Convention, from the original manuscript in the Library of Congress, Washington   280

FRANKLIN'S MOTION FOR PRAYERS IN THE CONSTITUTIONAL CONVENTION

THE Federal Convention of 1787 was animated by no such sense of devotion to a common cause as had earlier welded into fellowship the members of the Continental Congress. The Articles of Confederation had done their imperfect work, and the claims and interests of the several states were in conflict. Under these circumstances, no one seems to have thought of fellowship in prayer. The nearest utterance to prayer was Washington's solemn rebuke to those who proposed merely temporizing measures for fear that an adequate Constitution would not be approved by the people: "It is too probable that no plan we propose will be adopted. Perhaps another dreadful conflict is to be sustained. If, to please the people, we offer what we ourselves disapprove, how can we afterward defend our work? Let us raise a standard to which the wise and honest can repair; the event is in the hand of God." After a month of seemingly fruitless discussion, Benjamin Franklin called attention to the omission: "In this situation of the convention, groping, as it were, in the dark to find political truth, and scarce able to distinguish it when presented to us, how has it happened that we have not hitherto once thought of humbly applying to the Father of lights to illuminate our understanding? In the beginning of the contest with Great Britain, when we were sensible of danger, we had daily prayers in this hall for divine protection. Our prayers were heard, and they were graciously answered. . . . Have we now forgotten that powerful Friend? Or do we imagine that we no longer need His assistance? I have lived, sir, a long time; and the longer I live, the more convincing proofs I see of this truth, — that God governs in the affairs of men. And, if a sparrow cannot fall to the ground without His notice, is it probable that an empire can rise without His aid? We have been assured, sir, in the sacred writings, that 'except the Lord build the house, they labor in vain that build it.' I firmly believe this; and I also believe that, without His concurring aid, we shall succeed in this political building no better than the builders of Babel." He then moved that thereafter prayers be offered daily at the beginning of the sessions, by one or more of the clergy of the city. It was objected that to take such action at this point would be misunderstood and increase the anxiety which the public was beginning to feel concerning the outcome of the deliberations of the convention, and the session adjourned without voting on the motion.

CHAPTER V

THE CHURCHES AND THE REVOLUTION

THE American Revolution was a democratic movement. There was no central authority to command the several colonies to participate, no ruling class to throw its vassals into the struggle. It was necessary that public opinion be aroused and informed, and the people stirred to united action. Propaganda, therefore, which has come to play so large a part in modern warfare, was extensively used upon the American side in the Revolution. Of the various agencies for the dissemination of news and the influencing of public opinion, none was more active and effective than the churches, most of which deemed this to be a righteous war which they were bound in conscience to support.

One of the factors contributing to the general unrest and apprehension preceding the outbreak of hostilities was an ill-advised, untimely movement to secure a bishop for the Church of England in America. All other groups, and even most members of the Anglican Church in the southern colonies, feared the political power of a bishop and regarded the movement as another link in the chain of bondage which the King and Parliament were charged with forging for America.

The Congregational and Presbyterian churches and ministers were most active in the cause of the colonists. With them were associated in general the Baptists, Catholics, and members of the Lutheran and Reformed churches. The Methodists were very few and as yet unseparated from the Church of England.

The two religious groups that suffered most from the Revolution were the Quakers and members of the Church of England. Each faced a problem of conscience — the Quakers because of their opposition to all war; and the clergy, particularly, of the Church of England because King George was not only their political sovereign but their spiritual superior, "the only supreme head in earth" of their Church.

These problems were settled, as such problems usually are, by individuals doing what their own consciences approved. Many Quakers supported the War financially, and many of the younger Friends even fought in the Continental Army; but the Quakers as a group lost the political power they had previously exercised in Pennsylvania. In Virginia and the other southern colonies the state establishment of the Church of England did not deter the great majority of its lay members and most of its clergy from espousing the cause of Independence. It was only in the northern colonies that the ministers and people of the Church of England were predominantly loyalist or "Tory" in sympathy and behavior. Yet even here many took the side of the colonies. If Jacob Duché, rector of Christ Church, Philadelphia, and first chaplain of the Continental Congress, turned Tory, William White, his assistant, remained true to the American cause, and became one of the founders of the Protestant Episcopal Church in the United States.

Typical of the religious faith as well as of the loyalty and practical judgment of the citizens of the United States, was George Washington, commander in chief of the Continental Army and first President of the new republic. In his efforts to check the rising vices of army life, in his private habits of devotion, and in his public utterances of dependence upon the will of God, and in the picture of his fellowship at the holy communion with a Presbyterian congregation, though he was a member of the Church of England, are symbolized the common faith and aspiration of the country which he served.

THE MOVEMENT TO SECURE AN ANGLICAN BISHOP FOR AMERICA

THE Church of England was not established as a state church north of Maryland; in New England its adherents were in the position of dissenters; and in New York and New Jersey its clergy were regarded as usurpers. In 1766, a singularly inopportune time, the Anglican clergy of the northern colonies began a determined effort to secure the appointment of a bishop for their church in America. They met annually for this purpose, addressed petitions to England, and published appeals to the public. The movement awakened wide-spread apprehension. From 1766 to 1775 the Congregational and Presbyterian churches combined in "a plan of union . . . for preserving their religious liberty," in the face of the threatened danger. The Episcopal laymen in the southern colonies themselves opposed the movement; and only twelve out of a hundred Anglican clergy appeared at a Virginia convention called in its interest. Four of these did all they could against it; and were publicly thanked by a vote of the Virginia legislature for their "wise and well-timed opposition to the pernicious project."

AN
APPEAL to the PUBLIC,
IN
BEHALF
OF THE
CHURCH OF ENGLAND
IN
AMERICA.

By THOMAS BRADBURY CHANDLER, D.D.
Rector of St. John's Church, in Elizabeth-Town, New-Jersey,
and Missionary from the Society for the Propagation of
the Gospel, &c

" We desire a fair Trial—if we are guilty, punish us ; if
" we are innocent, protect us." JUSTIN MARTYR.

NEW-YORK:
Printed by JAMES PARKER, at the New-Print-
ing-Office, in Beaver-Street.
M,DCC,LXVII.

281   Title-page of the original in the
New York Public Library

POLITICAL OBJECTIONS TO THE APPOINTMENT OF AN ANGLICAN BISHOP

THE American people, with good reason, feared the political power of an Anglican bishop. John Adams wrote: "Fear of the Church of England contributed as much as any other cause to arrest the attention not only of the inquiring mind, but of the common people and urge them to close thinking on the constitutional authority of Parliament over the colonies. . . . The objection was not only to the office of a bishop, though that was dreaded, but to the authority of Parliament on which it must be founded. The reasoning was this: There is no power less than Parliament which can create bishops in America. But if Parliament can erect dioceses and appoint bishops, they may introduce the whole hierarchy, establish tithes, establish religion, forbid dissenters, make schism heresy, impose penalties extending to life and limb as well as to liberty and property."

THE
APPEAL
TO THE
PUBLIC ANSWERED,
In Behalf of the NON-EPISCOPAL
CHURCHES in AMERICA ;
CONTAINING
REMARKS on what Dr. THOMAS BRAD-
BURY CHANDLER has advanced, on the
four following Points.
The Original and Nature of the EPISCOPAL OFFICE,
Reasons for sending BISHOPS to AMERICA.
The PLAN on which it is proposed to send them.
And the OBJECTIONS against sending them obviated
and refuted.
WHEREIN THE
REASONS for an AMERICAN EPISCOPATE
are shewn to be insufficient, and the OB-
JECTIONS against it in full Force.
By CHARLES CHAUNCY, D.D
And Pastor of the first Church of Christ in Boston.

BOSTON: N.E.
Printed by KNEELAND and ADAMS, in Milk-Street, for
THOMAS LEVERETT, in Corn-Hill. 1768,

282   Title-page of the original in the
New York Public Library

"NO LORDS SPIRITUAL OR TEMPORAL"

THE tension of the situation is revealed by this cartoon from the *Political Register*, 1769. The bishop has attempted to land, but is greeted by cries of "No lords spiritual or temporal in New England!" "Shall they be obliged to maintain bishops who cannot maintain themselves!" He is bundled back on the ship, the wheels of his carriage dismantled, and his mitre and crosier thrown after him. A banner, surmounted by a liberty-cap, reads "Liberty and Freedom of Conscience." Copies are brandished of *Locke* and *Sydney on Government*; someone has hurled *Calvin's Works* at his head; and a Quaker stands by pointing to *Barclay's Apology*. With his gown floating in the breeze, the bishop is climbing the rigging, while he ejaculates: "Lord, now lettest thou thy servant depart in peace."

283   From a cartoon *An Attempt to land a Bishop in America*, in the *Political Register*, London, 1769

284 Jonathan Mayhew, 1720–66, from the mezzotint by Richard Jennys, Jr., in the American Antiquarian Society, Worcester, Mass.

THE PULPIT IN THE AMERICAN REVOLUTION

PROPAGANDA played a larger part in the American Revolution than in any previous war. In this effort to inform and influence public opinion, the ministers of the churches rendered inestimable service. J. W. Thornton's *The Pulpit of the American Revolution* has preserved in convenient form a few sermons characteristic of many. The first of these, entitled *A Discourse concerning Unlimited Submission and Non-resistance to the Higher Powers*, was delivered by Dr. Jonathan Mayhew, pastor of the West Church in Boston, on January 30, 1750, the anniversary of the execution of Charles I. It is a powerful argument against submission to royal power when arbitrarily exerted. In a striking peroration Mayhew concluded: "Let us all learn to be free and to be loyal; let us not profess ourselves vassals to the lawless pleasure of any man on earth; but let us remember, at the same time, government is sacred and not to be trifled with." Mayhew, in 1766, urged upon James Otis the desirability of a closer union of the colonies as "perhaps the only means of perpetuating their liberties." In 1774, the Governor of Massachusetts refused the request of the Assembly to appoint a public fast day, saying that it was "simply to give an opportunity for sedition to flow from the pulpit."

THE MINUTE MEN AND THE MINISTERS OF LEXINGTON

WITH the memory of the minute men of Lexington live the names of their ministers. For fifty-five years, 1697–1752, John Hancock, grandfather of a boy given his name, who was to be President of the Continental Congress, first signer of the Declaration of Independence, and Governor of Massachusetts, was pastor of the church at Lexington; and for fifty years, 1755–1805, the same pulpit was occupied by Jonas Clark. Clark's ministry, in the stirring days that preceded the Revolution, was such as to prepare his parishioners for their resistance on the momentous morning of April 19, 1775. His leadership in

285 Rev. John Hancock, 1671–1752, from the original portrait by John Smibert, in the Lexington Historical Society, Lexington, Mass.

286 Rev. Jonas Clark, 1730–1805, from a silhouette in the Lexington Historical Society, Lexington, Mass.

the affairs of the town was marked; and for fifteen years he had drawn up the papers of instruction, adopted by the town meeting, for their representatives in the Massachusetts Assembly. Samuel Adams and John Hancock were guests in his home on the fateful night when they were warned by Paul Revere of the approach of the British troops.

JOHN WITHERSPOON, 1722–1794, SIGNER OF THE DECLARATION OF INDEPENDENCE

A SECOND invitation, in 1768, induced John Witherspoon, widely-known and influential Scotch preacher, to accept the presidency of the College of New Jersey at Princeton. He soon won general recognition, not only as an educator and leader in the work of the Presbyterian churches, but as a man of wisdom and resource in the consideration of public affairs. His sermon on the Fast Day appointed by Congress, May 17, 1776, had much influence on this side of the Atlantic, but caused him to be called "traitor" and "rebel" on the other. He was elected a member of Congress in June and served for six years, holding many important committee assignments. He

288 Statue of John Witherspoon, in Fairmount Park, Philadelphia. © Rau Studios, Inc.

287 John Witherspoon, from the original portrait by C. W. Peale, in Independence Hall, Philadelphia

was the only clergyman among the signers of the Declaration of Independence. President Stiles of Yale in his election sermon of 1783 expressed the emotion of a contemporary as he read the list of the "signers." "All the ages of man will not obliterate . . . the meritorious names of that illustrious band of heroes and compatriots, those sensible and intrepid worthies who . . . resolutely and nobly dared, in the face of every danger, to sign the glorious act of Independence." In 1778 the question was raised whether ministers should not be excluded from civil offices in the United States but the proposition found little support.

"A TIME TO PREACH AND A TIME TO FIGHT"

IN January, 1776, the German Lutheran church at Woodstock, Virginia, was crowded with a congregation that had gathered to hear its pastor, Peter Muhlenberg, preach his farewell sermon. He had accepted a commission as colonel of the Eighth Regiment of Virginia militia, recently authorized by the colonial Assembly. In his sermon he described in plain, straight-forward terms the situation into which the colonies had been forced; then, in a ringing voice, he concluded: "In the language of Holy Writ, there is a time for all things. There is a time to preach and a time to fight; and now is the time to fight." He pronounced the benediction, then stripped from his shoulders the gown of the minister, and stood before the congregation in the uniform of a colonel of volunteers. Descending from the pulpit, he ordered the drums to beat at the church door for recruits. Three hundred of his frontier parishioners enlisted that day.

289   Bas relief on the General Peter Muhlenberg Statue, Philadelphia. © Rau Studios, Inc.

GENERAL PETER MUHLENBERG, 1746–1807, MINISTER AND SOLDIER

MUHLENBERG was the son of Henry Muhlenberg, the "patriarch" of American Lutheranism. In order that it might have full standing under the Virginia laws, the German Lutheran church of which he was pastor had affiliated with the Swedish churches, which were episcopally governed; and Muhlenberg himself had gone to London to secure episcopal ordination. He was the friend of Washington and Patrick Henry. He was chairman of the County Committee of Safety and Correspondence, and represented his county at the Virginia Conventions of 1774 and 1775. He did more than any other to enlist the whole-hearted support of the Germans for the American cause. The regiment which he raised, known as the "German regiment," served with distinction to the close of the war; and Muhlenberg rose to the rank of major-general.

JAMES CALDWELL, 1734–1781, CHAPLAIN AND COMMISSARY GENERAL

You've heard
Of Caldwell, the parson, who once preached the word
Down at Springfield? What, no? Come, that's bad! Why, he had
All the Jerseys aflame. And they gave him the name
Of the "rebel high priest." He stuck in their gorge,
For he loved the Lord God, and he hated King George
. . . . Think of him as you stand
By the old church today; think of him and that band
Of militant ploughboys. See the smoke and the heat
Of that reckless advance, of that straggling retreat!
. . . . They were left in the lurch
For the want of more wadding. He ran to the church,
Broke the door, stripped the pews, and dashed out in the road
With his arms full of hymn-books, and threw down his load
At their feet. Then above all the shouting and shots
Rang his voice: "Put Watts into 'em! Boys, give 'em Watts!"
                                    — BRET HARTE

290   From the statue of General Peter Muhlenberg by Blanch Nevin (1841–1925), in City Hall Square, Philadelphia

JAMES CALDWELL, pastor of the Presbyterian Church at Elizabethtown, and chaplain of a New Jersey regiment, had so marked an influence that the British offered a reward for his capture. In the darker days of the Revolutionary cause, when pay was lacking and provisions were low, he was appointed Assistant Commissary General and rendered services of great value. His church was burned by a Tory refugee, and his wife was killed by a shot through the window. He was murdered by a sentry, who was either drunk or had been bribed to do this deed. During the battle at Springfield, when wadding for the muskets of the patriots was running low, Caldwell had rushed to the Presbyterian Church and returned with his arms and pockets filled with copies of the psalm book by Isaac Watts. He scattered these among the soldiers, exclaiming, "Now, boys, give them Watts!"

291   *The Battle of Springfield, N. J.*, 1780, from the copyright painting by John Ward Dunsmore (1856–), in his possession

PSALM lxxv.   155
PSALM LXXV.

Power and Government from God alone.

Applied to the glorious Revolution of King WILLIAM, or the happy accession of King GEORGE to the Throne.

1. TO thee, moft holy, and moft high,
    To thee we bring our thankful praife;
    Thy works declare thy name is nigh,
    Thy works of wonder and of grace.

2. *Britain* was doom'd to be a flave,
    Her frame diffolv'd, her fears were great;
    When God a new fupporter gave,
    To bear the pillars of the ftate.

3. He from thy hand receiv'd his crown
    And fwear to rule by wholefome laws;
    His foot fhall tread th' oppreffor down,
    His arm defend the righteous caufe.

4. Let haughty finners fink their pride,
    Nor lift fo high their fcornful head;
    But lay their foolifh thoughts afide,
    And own the King that God hath made.

5. Such honours never come by chance,
    Nor do the winds promotion blow
    'Tis God the judge doth one advance,
    'Tis God that lays another low.

6. No vain pretence to royal birth,
    Shall fix a tyrant on the throne:
    God, the great fov'reign of the earth,
    Will rife and make his juftice known.

7. [His hand holds out the dreadful cup
    Of vengeance mix'd with various plagues,
    To make the wicked drink them up,
    Wring out and tafte the bitter dregs.

8. Now fhall the Lord exalt the juft,
    And while he tramples on the proud,

292 From Isaac Watts, *The Psalms of David*, Boston, 1774, in the New York Public Library

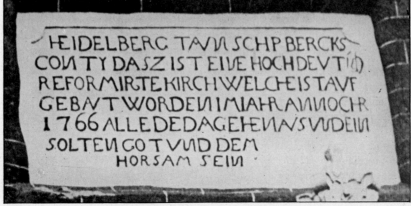

THE
PSALMS
OF
DAVID,
IMITATED IN THE
LANGUAGE OF THE
New Teftament,
AND APPLIED TO THE
CHRISTIAN STATE AND WORSHIP.

By I. WATTS, D. D.

THE FORTIETH EDITION, CORRECTED,
AND ACCOMMODATED TO THE USE OF
THE CHURCH OF CHRIST IN AMERICA.

LUKE xxiv. 44. *All things muft be fulfilled which were written ——— the PSALMS concerning me.*

HEB. xi. 31. *David, Samuel, and the prophets.* VER. 40. *That they without us fhould not be made perfect.*

NEWBURY-PORT:
Printed and Sold by JOHN MYCALL.
MDCCLXXXI.

293 Title-page of the original in the New York Public Library

WATTS "APPLIED TO THE GLORIOUS REVOLUTION IN AMERICA"

ONE reason, perhaps, why Mr. Caldwell was so ready to use Isaac Watts' *Psalms of David* for gun wadding was because these

158   PSALM LXXV.

PSALM LXXV.

Power and government from God alone.

Applied to the glorious revolution in *America*, *July 4th. 1776.*

1 TO thee, moft holy, and moft high,
   To thee we bring our thankful praife;
   Thy works declare thy hand is nigh,
   Thy works of wonder and of grace.

2 *America* was doom'd a flave,
   Her frame diffolv'd, her fears were great;
   When God a right'ous council gave,
   To bear the pillars of the ftate.

3 They from thy pow'r receiv'd their own,
   And fware to rule by wholefome laws;
   Thy foot fhall tread oppreffors down,
   Thy arm defend the right'ous caufe.

4 Let haughty finners fink their pride,
   Nor lift fo high their fcornful head:
   But lay their foolifh thoughts afide,
   And own the pow'rs which God hath made.

5 Such honors never come by chance,
   Nor do the winds promotion blow;
   'Tis God the Judge doth one advance,
   'Tis God who lays another low.

6 No vain pretence to royal birth
   Shall chain us to a tyrant's throne;
   God, the great Sov'reign of the earth,
   Shall crufh ufurpers with his frown.

[7 His hand holds out the dreadful cup
   Of veng'ance, mix'd with var'ous plagues,
   And makes the wicked drink them up,
   Wring out, and tafte the bitter dregs.

8 Now fhall the Lord exalt the juft,
   And while he tramples on the proud,
   And lays their glory in the duft,
   Our lips fhall fing his praife aloud.]

294 From Isaac Watts, *The Psalms of David*, Newburyport, 1781, in the New York Public Library

copies were of the old edition.   A new edition, "corrected and accommodated," was published in 1781.   Compare the two versions of Psalm LXXV.   According to the title-page, this was the fortieth edition of this book, which had been first published in 1719.   Watts wrote free poetic paraphrases, rather than the traditional crabbed metrical versions, of the Psalms; and some of these are really great hymns.   *O God, Our Help in Ages Past* is an example.

ELIMINATING THE KING

ANOTHER example of how the King was eliminated from things American is afforded by this inscription from Heidelburg Church, Berks County, Pennsylvania.   It reads: "Heidelburg Township, Berks County.   This is a High German Reformed Church, which was built in the year 1766.   All who go in and go out here shall be obedient to God and the. . . ."   The word "King," there originally, was cut out during the Revolution.

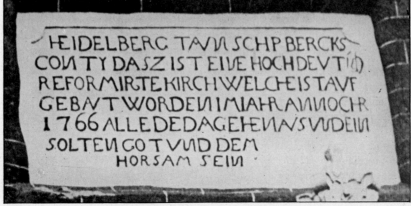

295   Inscription on Heidelburg Church, courtesy of Prof. William J. Hinke, Auburn, N. Y.

296   From the painting *Prayer Before Battle*, by Alfred Wordsworth Thompson (1840–96), showing the Old Dutch Church at Tarrytown, N. Y.

PRAYER BEFORE BATTLE

ON the day after assuming command of the Continental Army, George Washington issued the following order: "The General requires and expects of all officers and soldiers, not engaged on actual duty, a punctual attendance on divine service, to implore the blessing of Heaven upon the means used for our safety and defence." When the situation of the army did not permit the regular holding of Sunday services, he required the chaplains to hold services at other times, and to make report to him. He forbade profanity, drunkenness, and gambling, though his efforts to check these vices did not meet with full success. "While we are duly performing the duty of good soldiers we certainly ought not to be inattentive to the higher duties of religion," he declared. "To the distinguished character of a Patriot it should be our highest glory to add the more distinguished character of a Christian.

WASHINGTON PRAYING AT VALLEY FORGE

BEFORE the war, Washington had accepted religion in the easy-going, matter-of-course fashion of a Virginia gentleman of that day, punctual in the payment of its dues, concerned as vestryman with the affairs of the parish, and attending church services when he found this convenient. Public responsibility deepened his sense of its meaning. As Commander and President, he was faithful in attendance at public worship and regular in his habits of private devotion. It is probable that the pictures of him upon his knees in prayer at Valley Forge express a truth. It has been objected that there is not the testimony of enough accredited witnesses; but Washington was not the sort of man who would pray to be seen of men. Little minds have from time to time sought to show that in his constant references to God and His providence, and in his regular observance of religious duties, Washington was a hypocrite making concessions to public opinion, and asserting, for reasons of state, a reverence he did not feel. But the world refuses them credence, and continues to believe in Washington's sincerity and to have faith in his God.

297   Washington Praying at Valley Forge, from the bronze tablet by James E. Kelly (1855–), for the Washington Statue in Wall Street, New York

298 Washington Taking Communion with the Presbyterians at Morristown, from the original painting by Harry A. Ogden

WASHINGTON TAKES COMMUNION WITH THE PRESBYTERIANS AT MORRISTOWN

A TRADITION cherished by the First Presbyterian Church at Morristown, New Jersey, is that Washington, while the Continental Army was there encamped in the winter of 1776–77, participated in the semi-annual celebration of the Lord's Supper by the members of that church. He had come to know Dr. Timothy Johnes, pastor of the church, as they sat together in the meetings of the New Jersey Council of Safety. In answer to his inquiry whether "it accords with the canon of your church to admit communicants of another denomination," Dr. Johnes had replied, "Most certainly; ours is not the Presbyterian Table, but the Lord's Table; and we hence give the Lord's invitation to all his followers, of whatever name." The communion service was held in the apple orchard in the rear of the manse, the church building being occupied as a hospital for the troops.

PETER GIBAULT, 1737–1804, PATRIOT PRIEST OF THE NORTHWEST TERRITORY

WHEN Colonel George Rogers Clark, sent by Virginia to win from England the territory northwest of the Ohio River, surprised and captured Kaskaskia, he found there Father Peter Gibault, who had labored for ten years among the French Catholics and Indians of the Illinois country. In answer to the inquiry of a deputation headed by Gibault, "I told them," wrote Clark, "that the King of France had espoused the American cause, and that as regards their Church, all religions would be tolerated in America; that I had nothing to do with churches but to protect them from insult." Joyfully, they took the oath of allegiance. After taking Kaskaskia Clark marched to Vincennes which was won without a shot, for Gibault convinced its people that the colonists were their friends. He was Clark's counsellor and aid in a series of councils that established cordial relations with the Indians. He helped to maintain the Virginia troops by inducing his people to accept their paper money, and devoted "all his cattle and the tithes of his parishioners" to the same cause.

299 Peter Gibault, from the original drawing, artist unknown, in possession of The Filson Club, Louisville, Ky.

300   Charles Carroll, 1737–1832, from the portrait by Charles
Willson Peale in Independence Hall, Philadelphia

THE QUEBEC ACT

THE proposal to appoint a Roman Catholic bishop or vicar-apostolic for the American colonies was opposed by a *Laity Remonstrance*, dated July 16, 1765, signed by Charles Carroll of Annapolis and two hundred and fifty-eight other leading Catholic laymen of Maryland. This protest, which effectually blocked the proposal, emphasized the imprudence of such a step in view of conditions in America and the state of the public mind. The Quebec Act of 1774 awakened wide-spread indignation and apprehension, based not only upon its assignment to Quebec of all the land north of the Ohio River which subsequently came to be known as the Northwest Territory, but upon the fact that its provisions for the toleration and support of the Roman Catholic religion in Quebec were, naturally though wrongly, interpreted as the establishment of Catholicism as the state religion of that province. A temperate comment is that of President Samuel Langdon of Harvard College, in a sermon before the Massachusetts Provincial Congress, May 31, 1775: "When we consider the late Canada Bill, which implies not merely a toleration of the Roman Catholic religion (which would be just and liberal), but a firm establishment of it through that extensive province, now greatly enlarged to serve political purposes . . . have we not great reason to suspect that all the late measures respecting the colonies have originated from popish schemes of men who would gladly restore the race of Stuart, and who look on Popery as a religion most favorable to arbitrary power?" More direct and pungent was Alexander Hamilton, in his *Full Vindication of the Measures of Congress:* "Does not your blood run cold to think an English Parliament should pass an act for the establishment of arbitrary power and Popery in such an extensive land? . . . Beware of trusting yourselves to men who are capable of such an action. They may as well establish Popery in New York and the other colonies as they did in Canada. They had no more right to do it there than here. Your lives, your property, your religion, are all at stake."

CATHOLICS IN THE REVOLUTION

IN the common cause of American independence, Catholic and Protestant soon lost distrust of one another. The Catholics, like other groups, were divided. Some were Tories, but by far the greater number, following the lead of Charles Carroll of Carrollton (No. 183), espoused the cause of the colonies. Carroll and his cousin, Father John Carroll (No. 357) who later became the first bishop of the Catholic Church in the United States, accompanied Benjamin Franklin and Samuel Chase, at the request of the Continental Congress, on their fruitless mission in 1776 to secure the friendship and support of Canada. The alliance with France, the active coöperation of the French army, and the gift of six million dollars by the Catholic clergy of France in 1780, contributed to the wane of anti-Catholicism among the patriots of the Revolution. At the invitation of the French Minister, Gérard, the Continental Congress attended a Te Deum service at St. Mary's Church, Philadelphia, in recognition of the third anniversary of the signing of the Declaration of Independence. A similar service of thanksgiving, attended by the Congress, was held after the victory over Cornwallis at Yorktown. On both occasions the sermon was preached by Father Seraphim Bandol, chaplain of the French legation.

PHILADELPHIA.

ON Sunday laſt, the 4th of July, being the Anniverſary of the day which gave Freedom to the vaſt Republic of America, the Congreſs, the Preſident and Council of the State, with other the civil and miliary officers, and a number of principal gentlemen and ladies, at twelve o'clock attenſed at the Roman Chapel, agreeable to invitation received from the Miniſter Plenipotentiary of his Moſt Chriſtian Majeſty. A Te Deum was performed on the occaſion, to the great ſatisfaſtion of all preſent. And his Excellency's Chaplain delivered a ſhort and elegant addreſs to his audience, of which we have been favoured with the following copy.

301   From the *Pennsylvania Packet*, July 10, 1779

PRAYERS FOR THE KING

The Revolution confronted the clergy of the Church of England with a problem of conscience. They were officers of the crown, bound by the oath of ordination to render loyal obedience to the King not only as their sovereign but as supreme head of their church. To omit prayers for the King would be treasonable mutilation of the liturgy; yet, after the Declaration of Independence, to offer prayers for the King was treasonable in the eyes of their fellow citizens. Mr. Graves, of Norwich, who persisted in praying for the King, was "brought expeditiously to the level of the floor." The mark of the bullet is still to be seen on the sounding-board where Mr. Beach, of Redding, was fired upon. Jonathan Boucher, of Maryland, deploring the day when that dominion became "the ape of New England," was expelled from his pulpit, and sailed for England. Jacob Duché, rector of Christ Church, Philadelphia, and first chaplain of the Continental Congress, remained in the city when the British occupied it, restored to the service those portions of the Prayer Book which he had been omitting, and addressed a letter to Washington, urging him to persuade Congress to re-

302 Jonathan Boucher, 1738–1804, from an engraving by P. Condé after the portrait by William John Thompson (1771–1845), in possession of the publishers

scind "the hasty and ill-advised Declaration of Independence," or, failing in that, himself to negotiate for peace. Washington referred the letter to Congress, and Duché fled to England.

TORY REFUGEES IN NOVA SCOTIA

Canada became the principal refuge of more than thirty thousand dwellers in the colonies who chose to remain loyal to the King, and who were forced to quit their homes and refused citizenship in the independent states. The emigration of the Tories, as they were called, began when the British evacuated Boston in 1776. The greatest number went in 1783, when the issue of the war was finally settled. Between thirty and forty ministers of the Church of England were among them, the most notable being Mather Byles, Jr., of Christ Church, Boston; Jonathan Odell, of Burlington, New Jersey; Roger Viets, of Simsbury, Connecticut; and Charles Inglis, rector of Trinity Church, New York. The first edition of Inglis' pamphlet in answer to Paine's *Common Sense* had been seized and burned by the Sons of Liberty; but he had defied Washington himself by insisting upon praying for the King in his presence. He became the first Bishop of Nova Scotia.

303 The Rt. Rev. Charles Inglis, D.D., 1734–1816, courtesy of Trinity Church Corporation, New York

REVEREND SAMUEL PETERS

A figure befitting opera bouffe is the Reverend Samuel Peters, who took revenge for his expulsion from Hebron, Connecticut, by writing a *General History of Connecticut* which is a lively mixture of truth, gossip, satire and unbridled imagination. He professes for Connecticut the highest admiration, could it "once be freed of the skunk, the moping-owl, rattle-snake, and fanatic christian."

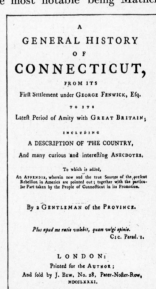

A
GENERAL HISTORY
OF
CONNECTICUT,
FROM ITS
First Settlement under George Fenwick, Esq.
TO ITS
Lateſt Period of Amity with Great Britain;
INCLUDING
A DESCRIPTION OF THE COUNTRY,
And many curious and intereſting Anecdotes.

To which is added,
An Appendix, wherein new and the true Sources of the preſent Rebellion in America are pointed out; together with the particular Part taken by the People of Connecticut in its Promotion.

By a Gentleman of the Province.

Plus apud me ratio valebit, quam vulgi opinie.
Cic. Parad. 1.

LONDON;
Printed for the Author;
And ſold by J. Bew, No. 28, Pater-Noſter-Row,
MDCCLXXXI.

304 From *A General History of Connecticut*, by a Gentleman of the Province [Rev. Samuel Peters], London, 1781

64   HISTORY OF

be difmiffed by the Governor, but fhall difmifs itfelf.

Confpiracy againft this Dominion fhall be punifhed with death.

Whoever fays there is a power and jurifdiction above and over this Dominion, fhall fuffer death and lofs of property.

Whoever attempts to change or over-turn this Dominion fhall fuffer death.

The judges fhall determine controver-fies without a jury.

No one fhall be a freeman, or give a vote, unlefs he be converted, and a mem-ber in full communion of one of the Churches allowed in this Dominion.

No man fhall hold any office, who is not found in the faith, and faithful to this Dominion; and whoever gives a vote to fuch a perfon, fhall pay a fine of 1l. for a fecond offence, he fhall be disfran-chifed.

Each freeman fhall fwear by the bleff-ed God to bear true allegiance to this Dominion,

CONNECTICUT.   65

Dominion, and that Jefus is the only King.

No quaker or diffenter from the eftablifhed worfhip of this Dominion fhall be allowed to give a vote for the election of Magiftrates, or any officer.

No food or lodging fhall be afforded to a Quaker, Adamite, or other Heretic.

If any perfon turns Quaker, he fhall be banifhed, and not fuffered to return but upon pain of death.

No Prieft fhall abide in the Dominion: he fhall be banifhed, and fuffer death on his return. Priefts may be feized by any one without a warrant.

No one to crofs a river, but with an authorized ferryman.

No one fhall run on the Sabbath-day, or walk in his garden or elfewhere, except reverently to and from meeting.

No one fhall travel, cook victuals, make beds, fweep houfe, cut hair, or fhave, on the Sabbath-day.

F   No

66   HISTORY OF

No woman fhall kifs her child on the Sabbath or fafting-day.

The Sabbath fhall begin at funfet on Saturday.

To pick an ear of corn growing in a neighbour's garden, fhall be deemed theft.

A perfon accufed of trefpafs in the night fhall be judged guilty, unlefs he clear himfelf by his oath.

When it appears that an accufed has confederates, and he refufes to difcover them, he may be racked.

No one fhall buy or fell lands without permiffion of the felectmen.

A drunkard fhall have a mafter ap-pointed by the felectmen, who are to debar him from the liberty of buying and felling.

Whoever publifhes a lye to the pre-judice of his neighbour, fhall fit in the ftocks, or be whipped fifteen ftripes.

No Minifter fhall keep a fchool.

Every

305   Pages from *A General History of Connecticut*, by a Gentleman of the Province [Rev. Samuel Peters], London, 1781

THE "BLUE-LAWS OF NEWHAVEN"

The "Blue-Laws of Newhaven," with which he embellished this work, are in part based upon actual laws, inexactly and vindictively stated, and in part the creation of what his strongest defender calls "the slovenly habits of a mind unmethodical in the extreme. When in his careless notes he came upon any excerpt embody-ing an unusually severe law, or when he conjured such a one up from his own memory, the ruling passion . . . would incline him to assign it to the dead limbo of New Haven." Peters went to England, where he lived for thirty years upon the bounty of the Government without exercising his ministry. In 1794 a handful of Epis-copalians living in Vermont, led by a minister temporarily among them, elected him Bishop of Vermont, an office which he accepted in a grandiloquent *Apostolical Epistle;* but neither the English nor the American bishops would consecrate him. When, in 1804, William Pitt struck his name from the pension rolls, he returned to America and gained a precarious livelihood, till he reached the age of ninety, by selling lands which he claimed were his on the eastern shore of the Mississippi, in what is now Minnesota.

WHY NEW ENGLANDERS WERE CALLED PUMPKIN-HEADS

"Newhaven is celebrated for having given the name of 'pump-kin-heads' to all the New-Englanders. It originated from the 'Blue Laws,' which enjoined every male to have his hair cut round by a cap. When caps were not to be had, they substituted the hard shell of a pumpkin, which being put on the head every Saturday, the hair is cut by the shell all round the head. What-ever religious virtue is supposed to be derived from this custom, I know not; but there is much prudence in it: first, it prevents the hair from snarling; secondly, it saves the use of combs, bags, and ribbons; thirdly, the hair cannot incommode the eyes by falling over them; and fourthly, such persons as have lost their ears for heresy, and other wickedness, cannot conceal their mis-fortune and disgrace." — SAMUEL PETERS, *General History of Connecticut,* pp. 153-54.

306   Method of Trimming Hair, In accordance with the Blue Laws of Connecticut, from *A General History of Connecticut,* by a Gentleman of the Province [Rev. Samuel Peters], London, 1781

PATRIOT CLERGY IN VIRGINIA

In Virginia, where it had been strongest, the Church of England suffered most. Its ministers were deprived of the salaries and glebes which had been theirs while it was the established church of the colony; and many of the church buildings fell into ruin, being used as barracks or stables by the soldiers of either side. Yet, contrary to the general impression, the majority of its clergy espoused the cause of the colonists; and many of them served upon the Committees of Safety of their respective counties. Of deep and widespread influence was the work of Devereux Jarratt, minister from 1763 to 1801 of Bath Parish in Dinwiddie County, who labored steadfastly for the moral good of his people, and preached with an evangelical earnestness and power that converted many from nominal to real religion. In ten years the number of communicants in his parish increased from eight to more than a thousand. At first in sympathy with the Methodists, he refused to follow them into their own organization; and devoted himself with energy to the spiritual renewal of what was henceforth to be the Protestant Episcopal Church in Virginia.

THE UNITED STATES ELEVATED TO GLORY AND HONOR

A

SERMON

PREACHED BEFORE THE

CONVENTION

OF THE PROTESTANT EPISCOPAL CHURCH,

IN VIRGINIA.

AT RICHMOND, MAY 3, 1792.

By DEVEREUX JARRATT,
Rector of BATH Parish, *Dinwiddie* County.

RICHMOND: (VIRGINIA) Printed.
New-London : Reprinted by T. GREEN and SON.

M,DCC,XCII.

307   Title-page of the original in the New
York Public Library

INTERESTING side lights on the times are to be found in the diaries and correspondence of Ezra Stiles, pastor of the Second Congregational Church at Newport from 1755 until the British occupied the city in 1776, then president of Yale College from 1778 till his death in 1795. When the minister of the Church of England at Newport preached in commemoration of the "martyrdom" of Charles I, Stiles said that the day, "if observed at all, should be celebrated as an anniversary of Thanksgiving . . . that one nation had so much fortitude and public justice as to make a royal tyrant bow to the sovereignty of the people." Later, the Anglican retaliated, on the day set apart by the colony of Rhode Island for public fasting and prayer in view of the threatening situation, by preaching on the text: "Fast not as the hypocrites." On May 2, 1783, the war over and independence won, President Stiles preached a triumphant Election Sermon before the Governor and Assembly of Connecticut, on the subject *The United States Elevated to Glory and Honor*, which is remarkable for its breadth and perspicacity. He set forth in detail the reasons which led him to expect that the states will be drawn into closer union, and will "prosper and flourish into a great American Republic . . . in high and distinguished honor among the nations of the earth." He foretold the dominance of the new nation by English traditions rather than by the traditions of other elements of her mixed people; and predicted a population of fifty millions by the close of the first century of national existence, and three hundred millions by the close of the third. "And now, my fellow citizens of this independent republic, . . . hear me this day, give audience. The Most High planted our fathers, a small handful, in this Jeshimon, and lo! we, their posterity, have arisen up to three millions of people. Our ears have heard, and our fathers have told us, the marvelous things God did for them; but our eyes have seen far more marvelous things done for us, whereof we are glad and rejoice this day. . . . Having fought the good fight, our warfare ended, let us not fail to look through providence up to the God of providence, and give glory to God the Lord of Hosts."

308   Ezra Stiles, 1727–95, from the original portrait by
Reuben Moulthrop, (1763–1814), in the School of Fine
Arts, Yale University, New Haven

CHAPTER VI

THE DEVELOPMENT OF FREE CHURCHES

FROM the standpoint of the churches the experiment of America in freeing the exercise of religion from all constraint and making its support voluntary was successful. It resulted not only in the multiplying of religious denominations, but in a growth of church membership which has considerably outrun the growth of the population. If it be granted that the first of these results is not wholly good, the second cannot be disputed, and constitutes an ample refutation of the doleful prophecies of those who thought religion could not flourish without the support of state establishment.

The years immediately succeeding the Revolutionary War were marked by a vogue of atheism and infidelity, due partly to the excesses of war, partly to the influence of the French Revolutionists, and partly to the Deism and the empty formalism into which many of the churches had fallen. A powerful counteragent to this lapse in faith and morals appeared in the rise of Methodism, which, under the leadership of Francis Asbury, severed connection with the Church of England and began to send its circuit riders, like shuttles weaving some vast web, throughout all parts of the country.

In the opening years of the nineteenth century, the "Second Awakening" in the eastern states and the "Great Revival" in the territory to the west of the Alleghenies brought fresh life to the churches and checked the current infidelity. These movements, in spite of the extravagances sometimes associated with them, exerted a powerful and lasting influence upon the development of the United States, especially on the frontier. The "Second Awakening" and the "Great Revival" turned the minds of men toward their ideals. These movements led to the organization of philanthropic societies, stimulated home-missionary effort, and initiated the foreign-missionary enterprise which has played so large a part in America's contact with non-Christian peoples. In education, likewise, these movements were profoundly influential. They led to the founding of Christian academies and colleges, and to the establishment of theological seminaries for the training of ministers.

The Great Immigration, which began in the 'thirties, added large numbers of at least nominal members to the churches, especially to the Catholic and the Lutheran. The effects were in some respects opposite in the case of these two largest beneficiaries of the influx from Europe. It caused the Catholics to enter more aggressively into the general life of the nation; while it brought about a conservative reaction among the Lutherans which set them further apart from their neighbors.

At the close of the colonial period, the drinking of liquor was common among all classes; and there are even records which show that rum was bought as one of the necessary supplies for the festivities attendant upon the ordination of a New England minister. A tide of temperance sentiment began to rise soon after the Revolution, and slowly gathered strength. The churches joined in the movement, first against the use of distilled liquors, then for the adoption of the principle of total abstinence. In the 'fifties, a number of states passed laws prohibiting the liquor traffic; but this movement was checked by various conditions prior to and associated with the Civil War.

With respect to slavery the record of the churches was less consistent. Even the Quakers divided, at least once, on that issue. In the end, it split the larger Protestant churches into northern and southern bodies.

138

309   The Contrast, after sketches in an old pamphlet published in Philadelphia, reproduced in Charle Careton Coffin,   310
Building the Nation, Harper & Brothers, New York, 1882

THE SPREAD OF INFIDELITY

In the closing years of the eighteenth century, the moral and religious life of America touched its lowest ebb. Infidelity and atheism became fashionable. A number of causes conspired to this result. The Revolutionary War, because of its long duration and because it was a civil war between Whigs and Tories dividing communities and even households, had fostered the growth of crime and immorality; and had plunged the country into debt and into the excesses that attend an inflation of currency. The well-meant but shallow Deism of English philosophy cast ridicule upon Christianity's claim to embody a revelation of God; and the scepticism of Hume seemed to emancipate humanity from any standards other than momentary desire. "Natural right" and "State of nature," moreover, had been potent phrases in the struggle for independence; it was an easy step to exalt natural impulses and to decry the scruples of piety as unwarranted limitations upon personal liberty. Then there was France! France had been our friend and helper. France, too, was now in revolution. With some difficulty, Washington succeeded in restraining the over-enthusiasm of his country-men; and he was obliged to demand the recall of Genêt, the presumptuous envoy of the French Revolutionists. Jacobin clubs and societies of "Illuminism" were founded in various sections of the country, devoted to the destruction of Christianity and the general revolutionizing of government and society. Many people did not see the differences between the liberty of atheism and the liberty which America had sought and won.

POPULAR DEISM

The popular books which expressed and stimulated the trend toward infidelity were not atheistic, but deistic. They asserted belief in the God of nature; but denounced all Bibles, Testaments, and institutions of so-called revelation, whether Christian or non-Christian, as the products of conscious or unconscious falsehood. Thomas Paine claimed that he caused his *Age of Reason* to be translated into French in order to stop the people of France in their headlong rush into atheism. Yet the positive affirmations of this and other books of its type were grounded in an optimism so shallow, so nearly blind to the problem of evil, as to carry little conviction; and these affirmations were quite overshadowed by the predominant effect of the virulent, mocking negations of Christian doctrines and institutions which accompanied them.

311   Thomas Paine, 1737–1809, from the marble bust by Sydney Morse in Independence Hall, Philadelphia

X—10

PROSPECT;
OR
VIEW OF THE MORAL WORLD.
BY ELIHU PALMER.

VOL. I. SATURDAY, June 2d, 1804. No. 26.

Comments upon the Sacred Writings of the Jews and Christians. Exodus Chapter 5th.

THIS chapter is as strange a piece of revelation as ever was seen; the greater part of it is taken up with a trifling and contemptible altercation between Pharaoh and the Children of Israel about making brick. The latter makes most grievous complaints for want of straw, and what the straw had to do with the making of bricks it is hard to say. If they made use of it for fuel to burn the bricks, they might almost as well have been without it; if they incorporated it with the bricks, it was a strange method of doing the business, and quite different from that of modern times. But all such enquiries and objections aside, the question naturally arises in every enquiring mind, where is the religion or revelation of this part of the book? This long conversation between Pharaoh and those he held in bondage about the manner and the materials of their work is wholly uninteresting to us, and Moses and whoever wrote the book of Exodus could surely tell such a story as this without being inspired. It is ignorance or something worse that induces the christian world to call such stuff the word of God. But there is another reflection arises upon reading this chapter, of a more serious and impressive nature. The God of Moses, it seems, was not very popular either with the Egyptians or his chosen people. Pharaoh rejects the idea of any acquaintance with him—he does not know him at all, for he says in verse 2d, of this chapter, "who is the Lord, that I should obey his voice to

312 From the original in the Library of Congress, Washington

"THE AGE OF REASON"

A HOME-MADE and homely, yet fairly original product was *Reason, the Only Oracle of Man; or, A Compendious System of Natural Religion. Alternately adorned with Confutations of a Variety of Doctrines incompatible with it*, 1784, by General Ethan Allen, the captor of Ticonderoga, and the blustering protagonist of home rule in Vermont. A foreign importation was Count de Volney's *Ruins, or Meditations on the Revolutions of Empires*, 1793, which was translated by Joel Barlow. The most widely read and influential of these books was Thomas Paine's *The Age of Reason*, the first English edition of which, printed in France in 1794, was spread broadcast through America, sold for a few pennies a copy or given away gratis, by the Jacobin clubs and societies of Illuminati. Paine's foremost American disciple was Elihu Palmer, who founded, in 1804, a short-lived journal named *The Prospect, or View of the Moral World*, the frontispiece to which showed the Book of Saints and the Ten Commandments dashed to the ground from the Altar of Truth and Justice, to be supplanted by *The Age of Reason* and *The Rights of Man*. The following sentences from Paine's first contribution to this journal exhibit his characteristic pungency and lack of taste: "Why do not the Christians, to be consistent, make Saints of Judas and Pontius Pilate, for they were the persons who accomplished the act of salvation. The merit of a sacrifice was never in the thing sacrificed, but in the persons offering up the sacrifice — and therefore Judas and Pontius Pilate ought to stand first in the calendar of Saints."

313 Thomas Cooper, from an engraving, 1829, by Asher Brown Durand (1796–1886), after the drawing by Charles Cromwell Ingham (d. 1863), in Thomas Cooper, *Lectures on the Elements of Political Economy*, London, 1831

THOMAS COOPER, 1759–1839, MILITANT MATERIALIST

EXCEPT for the philosophical works of Cadwallader Colden, 1688–1776, at the time without influence and now forgotten, materialism came to America with Joseph Priestley, who spent the closing years of his life, from 1794 to 1804, in Northumberland, Pennsylvania. His doctrines were spread assiduously by his friend and disciple, Thomas Cooper. A born agitator and a fervent advocate of the principles of the French Revolution, Cooper was continually in trouble, political or religious. Imprisoned for libel of President Adams, removed for arbitrary conduct from a judgeship in Pennsylvania, forced to resign from professorships in Dickinson College and the University of Virginia, he became in 1819 a member of the faculty of the College of South Carolina, and was for twelve years its president. Charged with unnecessary interference with the religious beliefs of the students, his conduct was formally investigated by the legislature in 1832, and he was exonerated. But people began to boycott the college; the number of students fell to twenty; and he resigned the presidency and later withdrew from the faculty. Says the historian of the college, writing of his ministrations as president in its chapel: "He read from the Bible whose authority he openly denied, and prayed to a God in whom he did not believe, with less of reverence than he would discuss the theory of phlogiston."

STUDENT SCEPTICISM

In the years following the Revolution, students needed no Cooper to teach them infidelity; they caught it as they would any other fashion. At Princeton, in 1782, there were but two students who professed to be Christians. Later, there was but one at Bowdoin. Bishop Meade wrote that the College of William and Mary was regarded as a hot bed of French politics and religion, and that in every educated young man in Virginia he expected to find a sceptic, if not an avowed unbeliever. In 1783, a revival at Yale had swelled the membership of the college church; but seventeen years later there were but five student members. "That was the day," wrote Lyman Beecher, "of the infidelity of the Tom Paine school. Boys that dressed flax in the barn, as I used to, read Tom Paine and believed him; I read, and fought him all the way. Never had a propensity to infidelity. But most of the class before me were infidels, and called each other Voltaire, Rousseau, D'Alembert, etc., etc. They thought the Faculty were afraid of free discussion. But when they handed Dr. Dwight a list of subjects for class disputation, to their surprise he selected this: 'Is the Bible the word of God?' and told them to do their best." Student scepticism was in a sense a part of the readjustments which necessarily followed the close of the Revolutionary War. That conflict, running through many weary years, had brought moral as well as material desolation to the American people.

Strain every nerve, our sinking cause to save —
Then shall no God alarm, no law endure —
O'er these dread foes, our flag shall fly, unfurl'd,
And we, my sons, victorious, rule the world.

314   From J. S. J. Gardiner, *Remarks on the Jacobiniad,* Boston, 1795

TIMOTHY DWIGHT, 1752–1817, PRESIDENT OF YALE COLLEGE

Timothy Dwight became president of Yale in 1795. He was a grandson of Jonathan Edwards, and a resolute opponent of deism and infidelity. He met the situation with good humor, sound judgment, human sympathy,

315   Timothy Dwight, from a miniature, 1804–05, by John Trumbull (1756–1843), in the School of Fine Arts, Yale University, New Haven

and the intellectual resources of a rare teacher. In the weekly disputations of the senior class, when he was accustomed, after free discussion, to render judgment and to defend his own view, he won the unstinted admiration of his students. He preached each Sunday in the college chapel upon the great themes of theology, the sermons forming in effect a four-years' course in that subject for every student. His baccalaureate address in 1797 was on *The Nature and Danger of Infidel Philosophy.* He wasted no time on Paine, but went back of him to grapple with the philosophical principles of deism and materialism. He put an end to fagging, abolished the old system of fines for misconduct, and made the discipline of the college morally educative by dealing with the students as friends. By wise management and educational leadership he made Yale in every respect a greater and more effective institution than he found it. And he won his battle against infidelity. In 1802, the college experienced a revival of religion, in which one third of the student body professed conversion; half of these became ministers. Three times more before his death, in 1808, 1812, and 1815, like movements of religious quickening were experienced among the students.

THE SECOND AWAKENING

IN Dartmouth, Amherst, Williams and other colleges similar revivals of religious interest were experienced. These revivals among students, like the scepticism before them, reflected the life of the world without the college halls. From 1797 on, New England experienced what has been called its "Second Awakening." This movement, with like movements in the Presbyterian churches elsewhere, differed markedly from the Great Awakening in its relative quietness and lack of extravagances (see Vol. XI), and in the fact that it was not attributable to a few outstanding leaders such as Edwards and Whitefield had been. It is to be known by its fruits rather than by any inexplicability or dramatic quality of the experiences associated with it and its direct fruits were greater and more permanent than those of the earlier movement. It checked the spread of infidelity, and resulted in a remarkable increase in the membership of the churches. It was responsible for the beginnings of home-missionary effort and of the foreign-missionary enterprise. It led to the founding of Christian colleges and academies and to the establishment of theological seminaries for the training of ministers. It stimulated the organization of philanthropic societies and gave impulse to the beginnings of religious journalism. It did not cease, moreover, but was reproduced in successive waves of revival that swept through the land at intervals until the Civil War — the last of these being in 1857–58.

THE

GENERAL ASSEMBLY'S

MISSIONARY MAGAZINE;

OR

EVANGELICAL INTELLIGENCER:

FOR 1805.

WILLIAM P. FARRAND, EDITOR.

VOL. I.

PHILADELPHIA:
PRINTED FOR, AND PUBLISHED BY, WILLIAM P. FARRAND AND CO.
No. 170, MARKET STREET.

1806.

316   Title-page of the original in the
New York Public Library

UNCONDITIONAL SUBMISSION TO THE WILL OF GOD

GREAT stress was laid, in the Second Awakening, upon the duty of unconditional submission to the will of God. A question commonly put to candidates for the Congregational ministry was: "Are you willing to be damned for the glory of God?" Easy-minded folk now laugh at this query, but there was more in it than appears on the surface. It expressed what Dr. Samuel Hopkins called "disinterested benevolence," the willingness to live and labor for the love of God and fellowmen with no thought of ulterior reward, no anxiety concerning what selfish happiness one's conduct will bring in this life or the life to come. This is how one young man put it: "The benevolent mind must consent to the misery of a part, that the whole may be perfect. The suffering part must be fixed, bearing a certain proportion to the whole. It must likewise be composed of a definite number of individuals. . . .
Now if the benevolent mind sees, that this suffering part cannot be secured to its exact proportion without its including himself, must he not acquiesce? And if he is unwilling to be included in this part, does he not place himself in opposition to the perfection of the system?" Let it be granted that there is a faulty premise here: that it is impossible for us to think that the perfection of the whole can include, much less demand, the misery of a part. But we must assent to the man's logic and stand in reverence before the life that was animated by it. For this was Gordon Hall, 1784–1826, first missionary of the American Board to India, who greatly served God and his fellowmen, and died at forty-two, stricken in a cholera epidemic, a martyr to his own "disinterested benevolence." The philosophy and the life of Hall were the antithesis of the student scepticism which marked years immediately following the Revolution. Thomas Paine could never have understood such a spirit.

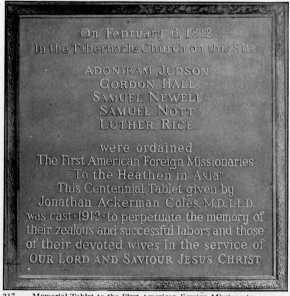

317   Memorial Tablet to the First American Foreign Missionaries
to Asia, on the Tabernacle Church, Salem, Mass.

THE HAYSTACK PRAYER MEETING

HALL had experienced conversion in a revival at Williams College, where he had become the close friend of Samuel J. Mills, 1783–1818, a fellow student who was aflame with zeal for the preaching of the Gospel to the non-Christian nations. On a hot, sultry afternoon in July or August, 1806, a group of five students, headed by Mills, were driven by a thunderstorm to seek shelter under a haystack, where they talked and prayed together concerning "the moral darkness of Asia" and the possibility of their going as missionaries to the peoples of that continent. In 1808 Mills and some of his friends organized a secret society, The Brethren, the members of which pledged themselves to devote their lives to missionary service. Most of the society entered Andover Theological Seminary, where they initiated into their fellowship Adoniram Judson, a recent graduate of Brown, Samuel Newell, of Harvard, and Samuel Nott, Jr., of Union College.

318 Haystack Monument, Williamstown, Mass., from a photograph by Kinsman

319 Ordination Scene, Feb. 6, 1812, from an engraving in possession of the American Board of Commissioners for Foreign Missions, Boston, Mass.

THE ORGANIZATION OF THE AMERICAN BOARD OF COMMISSIONERS FOR FOREIGN MISSIONS

THE Brethren had no means of going to Asia, and there was no organized missionary society or Board in America to which to appeal. Four of them therefore addressed a memorial, on June 27, 1810, to the General Association of Massachusetts, a newly formed body of evangelically minded Congregational ministers, asking "their advice, direction and prayers." The answer was the organization, within a few weeks, of the American Board of Commissioners for Foreign Missions. On February 6, 1812, in the Tabernacle Church at Salem, Gordon Hall, Adoniram Judson, Samuel Newell, Samuel Nott, and Luther Rice were ordained as

missionaries, and shortly thereafter set sail for India. Mills was not sent abroad, because it was deemed better by the rest of The Brethren that he remain in America to arouse and sustain the interest of the churches in foreign missions. This handful of young men were directing the pioneering spirit which permeated early nineteenth-century America to new fields of action. They were also evidence that, provincial as the mass of Americans might be, there were some sons of the young republic who thought in terms of broad world relationships and of a hoped for universal brotherhood of man. They initiated a movement in which America was destined to play a leading rôle. The American Board maintains missions in Africa, Turkey, India, China, Japan, and the Islands of the Pacific. Its work is educational and medical as well as evangelistic. It has sent into this service over four thousand three hundred missionaries and has collected and expended in one hundred and sixteen years gifts totaling more than thirty-six million dollars. At first intended to serve the churches generally, it is now recognized as the agency of the Congregational churches, for in time each of the denominations has organized its own board of foreign missions.

320 Tabernacle Church, Salem, Mass. (1777–1854), from a lithograph in possession of John Albree, Esq., Salem, Mass.

321 Adoniram Judson, from a lithograph after the original
portrait by Chester Harding (1792–1866), in the Essex
Institute, Salem, Mass.

ADONIRAM JUDSON, 1788–1850, BECOMES A BAPTIST

ADONIRAM JUDSON, the son of a Congregational minister, had been valedictorian of his class at Brown, and refused a call to become associate minister of the largest church in Boston, in order that he might go as a foreign missionary. Knowing that he would meet in India the great English Baptist missionary, William Carey, and his colleagues, Judson gave much time, during the four months' voyage, to thought and study concerning the differences between the Congregational and the Baptist positions. The result was that he became convinced that the Baptists were right. Luther Rice, 1783–1836, who came later on another ship, arrived at a similar conclusion. They were baptized in Calcutta by one of the English missionaries. Judson wrote to the American Board, resigning from its service, and addressed letters to the pastors of Baptist churches in Boston and Salem. "Should there be formed a Baptist Society for the support of a mission in these parts," he wrote, "I should be ready to consider myself their missionary."

THE ORGANIZATION OF THE GENERAL MISSIONARY CONVENTION OF THE BAPTIST DENOMINATION

THE news came like a bugle call to the Baptists of America. The society at Salem, which had been aiding Carey, voted at once to contribute to the support of Judson also. A Boston Society was organized a few days later. In September, 1813, Luther Rice returned to undertake a campaign for the organization of similar societies in all of the chief Baptist centers. At Philadelphia, on May 18, 1814, representatives from eleven of the eighteen states then in the Union met and organized the General Missionary Convention of the Baptist Denomination of the United States of America for Foreign Missions. Dr. Richard Furman, 1754–1826, of Charleston, the leading Baptist preacher of the South, was elected president. This was the first general organization of the Baptists, who are even more individualistic than the Congregationalists. Judson's conversion to Baptist principles not only resulted in the formation of a second nation-wide society for the support of missions; he brought the scattered Baptist churches together into a denominational organization.

322   Departure of the Missionaries, Feb. 19, 1812, from an engraving by W. S. Lawrence, in John Dowling, *The Judson Offering*, New York, 1847

OBOOKIAH AND THE BEGINNING OF MISSIONS IN HAWAII

WHILE a graduate student at Yale, where he went in 1809 to secure recruits for The Brethren, Mills met Henry Obookiah, 1792–1818, a young native of the Sandwich Islands, as the Hawaiian group was then called, whose family had been killed in a tribal war. A kindly sea captain had brought him to New Haven, and there he was found one day on the steps of one of the college buildings, weeping for loneliness and with hunger for education. Mills began to teach him, and soon placed him in Bradford Academy. A Foreign Mission School was organized, under the patronage of the American Board, at Cornwall, Connecticut, for the instruction of such youth. In 1823 it had

323 Departure of the Missionaries for the Sandwich Islands, from J. W. Barber, *New England Scenes*, New Haven, 1833

thirty-six students — "three Anglo-Saxons, nine Sandwich Islanders, one Malay, one Maori, three Chinese, one Portuguese, two Greeks, one Jew, and fifteen American Indians of nine different tribes." A visit to this school led Hiram Bingham, 1789–1869, a student at Andover Seminary, to volunteer for missionary service in the Sandwich Islands; and his classmate, Asa Thurston, 1787–1868, an athletic young graduate of Yale, agreed to go with him. At the head of a party of twenty-one, including three Hawaiians who had been trained at Cornwall, they set sail on October 23, 1819.

324 Henry Obookiah, from Edwin W. Dwight, *Memoirs of Henry Obookiah*, New Haven, 1818

KAMEHAMEHA II ACCEPTS CHRISTIANITY

WHEN the missionaries reached Hawaii on March 31, 1820, they were astonished to learn that the newly crowned king, Kamehameha II, with the advice and consent of many of the priests, had overthrown the traditional religion, denied its gods, and abolished its system of taboos. Soon he declared himself in favor of Christianity, and in 1825 the Ten Commandments were made the basis for the laws of the country. In 1838–39 Hawaii experienced a "Great Awakening," under the leadership, especially, of Titus Coan, 1801–82. On the first Sunday in July, 1838, he baptized one thousand seven hundred and five converts. In five years he received seven thousand five hundred and fifty-seven new members into his church at Hilo.

325 Titus Coan, from Mrs. Lydia Bingham Coan, *Titus Coan, A Memorial*, Chicago, 1884

326 Preaching in a Grove of Tu Tui Trees, from the engraving by J. A. Rolph
after a drawing by A. T. Agate (1816–46), in Charles Wilkes, *Narrative of the
United States Exploring Expedition*, Vol. IV, Philadelphia, 1845

THE SUCCESS OF THE HAWAIIAN MISSION

HISTORY records no more conspicuous example of successful missionary effort than this in Hawaii. In 1846 a new code of laws confirmed the abolition of idolatry, granted full religious toleration, and declared that "The Religion of the Lord Jesus Christ shall continue to be the established national religion of the Hawaiian Islands." Richard Henry Dana, making a tour of the world, wrote to the *New York Tribune* in 1860: "It is no small thing to say of the missionaries of the American Board, that in less than forty years they have taught this whole people to read and to write, to cipher and to sew. They have given them an alphabet, grammar, and dictionary; preserved their language from extinction; given it a literature, and translated into it the Bible and works of devotion, science and entertainment, etc., etc. They have established schools, reared up native teachers, and so pressed their work that now the proportion of inhabitants who can read and write is greater than in New England." The Christian churches of Hawaii early began to be self-supporting, and in 1870, fifty years after the mission began, the American Board formally announced complete withdrawal from the field, as the work it had undertaken was now accomplished. The early years of the mission had been marred by conflicts between the Americans and the French. The latter sent Catholic missionaries. These were expelled from the country and some of their converts persecuted for their faith.

327 Central Union Church, Honolulu, Hawaii,
dedicated May 18, 1924

KAPIOLANI DEFIES PÉLE

A DRAMATIC and heroic act was that of Kapiolani, queen of a tribe in southern Hawaii, which dwelt in the awe-inspiring play of shadow and glare from Kilauea, the largest active volcanic crater in the world. Her people lived in such abject terror of Péle, the fire-goddess whom they believed to dwell in its seething depths, that no mere proclamation could break its spell. Kapiolani determined therefore to prove the baselessness of their fear. To their protests she answered: "If I am destroyed you may all believe in Péle; but if I am not, then you must all turn to the true God." Disregarding alike the warnings of a prophetess and the real dangers of that hell-like place, she marched up the mountain to the brink of

328 View of Crater Kilauea, from an engraving by Jordan and Halpin after the drawing
by J. Drayton, in Charles Wilkes, *Narrative of the United States Exploring Expedition*,
Philadelphia, 1845

the crater, eating as she went of the berries sacred to Péle; then hurled stones into the great lake of fire, with cries of mockery and defiance. Returning to those who had timorously followed her over the lava crusts, she challenged them, as did Elijah at Mount Carmel, to acknowledge Jehovah as their God; and with hymn and prayer they worshiped Him on the slope of Péle's mountain. Thomas Carlyle told the story of Kapiolani. "Honor to the Brave who deliver us from Phantom-dynasties."

FRANCIS ASBURY, 1745–1816, "THE PROPHET OF THE LONG ROAD"

MEANTIME there had been riding up and down the country, from New Hampshire to Georgia, and from the Atlantic to Kentucky and Tennessee, a man to whom Paul's words concerning himself might be applied: "in journeyings often . . . in perils in the wilderness . . . in weariness and painfulness . . . that which cometh upon me daily, the care of all the churches." It was Francis Asbury, bishop of the Methodists. He never married. His salary was but eighty dollars a year. He had no home, not even hired lodgings; though he was a welcome guest and led family prayers in thousands of American homes, rich and poor. "The Rev^d. Bishop Asbury, North America," was the way Bishop Coke once addressed a letter to him from England. For forty-five years he was almost continually on the road. He organized and directed the circuit riders of Methodism; and he did it by himself tirelessly riding a circuit that embraced them all. The shrewd wisdom and the dauntless spirit which his contemporary, John Jacob Astor, brought to the fur trade, Asbury applied to religion. Astor won wealth; Asbury the satisfaction of a great work well done.

329   Statue of Francis Asbury by Henry Augustus Lukeman (1872–), Washington

THE FIRST METHODIST SOCIETY IN AMERICA

JOHN WESLEY intended Methodism to be a movement, not a church. He remained in full communion with the Church of England until his death. His organizations were societies for fellowship and development in the Christian life; and his preachers were itinerant because they could thus best minister to these rapidly multiplying groups. They did not seek ordination, or presume to offer the sacraments, or assume settled pastorates. The first Methodist society in America was organized in New York in October, 1766, by Philip Embury, a carpenter and schoolmaster who had been a class-leader and local preacher in Ireland. He had arrived in America, with a group of fellow Methodists, in 1760; but had not undertaken to preach until urged to do so by Barbara Heck, one of the group who, tradition says, was horrified to find some of her friends playing cards. In a few months Embury was reinforced by Captain Thomas Webb, barrack-master at Albany, who preached in his uniform. "The novelty of a man preaching in a scarlet coat soon brought great numbers to hear, more than the room could contain." They rented a rigging loft in William Street; but the society soon outgrew that, and a stone meetinghouse was built in John Street. In the meantime, Robert Strawbridge, another Irish carpenter, had settled in Frederick County, Maryland, built a log chapel, and begun to organize Methodist societies.

330   The Old Methodist Church in John Street, New York, from *A Short Historical Account of the early Society of Methodists, established in the City of New York, in the Year 1763*, New York, 1824

331 Francis Asbury, 1745–1816, from the original portrait,
1808, by Bruff in Drew Theological Seminary, Madison,
N. J.

ASBURY CHOOSES TO REMAIN IN AMERICA

IN response to the request of the New York society, Wesley began to send missionaries across the Atlantic in 1769. One of these was Asbury, who arrived in 1771. In the early years of the Revolutionary War the Methodists were under suspicion. Wesley made the mistake of issuing a *Calm Address to the American Colonies*, counseling submission to the King, which had quite other than a calming effect. All of Asbury's fellow missionaries went home; but he remained. "I can by no means agree to leave such a field for gathering souls to Christ as we have in America," he wrote in his Journal. "It would be an eternal dishonor to the Methodists that we should all leave the three thousand souls who desire to commit themselves to our care; neither is it the part of the Good Shepherd to leave his flock in time of danger. Therefore I am determined, by the grace of God, not to leave them, let the consequence be what it may." Some of the native-born Methodist preachers were whipped and imprisoned, and Asbury himself had to stay in retirement in Delaware for two years. But a letter of his, expressing his belief that the Americans would become a free and independent nation, and declaring his affection for them and his conviction that he had a great work to do here, fell into the hands of the authorities and convinced them of his sincerity. He was henceforth as free as any other citizen, and the persecution of the Methodists ceased.

THE ORGANIZATION OF THE METHODIST EPISCOPAL CHURCH

THE day before Christmas, 1784, was the birthday of the Methodist Episcopal Church. In spite of the Revolution, the number of Methodists had steadily increased. Thirteen years before, when Asbury arrived, there were about five hundred members in their societies; now there were fifteen thousand, with eighty-three preachers. Wesley saw the impossibility, now that the American states were independent, of maintaining the movement in dependence upon the Church of England; and he took a bold step. He ordained Thomas Coke to be "superintendent" of brethren in America, and sent with him a letter appointing Asbury likewise a superintendent, and authorizing them to organize a church. "As our American brethren are now totally disentangled, both from the state and the English hierarchy, we dare not entangle them again, either with the one or the other. They are now at full liberty, simply to follow the Scriptures and the primitive church. And we judge it best that they should stand fast in that liberty wherewith God has so strangely made them free." The wisdom of Wesley has been demonstrated by the growth of the church which he founded.

332   John Wesley, 1703–91, from the original portrait by Nathaniel
Hone (1717–84), in the National Portrait Gallery, London

ASBURY BECOMES BISHOP OF THE METHODIST EPISCOPAL CHURCH

ASBURY knew the spirit of America; and he knew that "superintendent" meant in fact "bishop." He would not accept his office by the appointment of Wesley merely, therefore; but insisted that a Conference be called, which met on the day before Christmas, 1784. Wesley's plan of organization was approved, the name "Methodist Episcopal" adopted, and Asbury elected to the superintendency, all by unanimous vote and with great joy. On successive days Asbury was ordained deacon, elder and superintendent. At the Conference of 1787 the title was changed to

333 *Consecration of Francis Asbury,* from an engraving by A. Gilchrist after the painting by Thomas Coke Ruckle, courtesy of the Methodist Book Concern, New York

bishop. When Asbury died in 1816, his Church had over two hundred thousand members, seven hundred itinerant preachers and two thousand local preachers. To-day, the bodies that constitute American Methodism have more than nine million communicant members, a number nearly five times as large as the total membership of Methodist churches in all the rest of the world.

THE SPIRIT OF METHODISM

THE remarkable growth of Methodism was due, it has well been said, to its preaching, its singing, and its organization. It was Wesley's policy "not to maintain its spiritual life by its doctrinal orthodoxy, but to maintain its orthodoxy by its spiritual life." The Methodists emphasized the Fatherhood of God and the loving reasonableness of His purposes rather than the inscrutability of His decrees; and they appealed to the freedom of the human will instead of proclaiming its impotence. There was a personal, experiential note in it all that was infectious; an evangelical fervor that made out of even the denunciation of sin an invitation to fellowship in the happiness of right living by the grace of God. And they not only preached and lived this gospel; they sang it. Charles Wesley's hymns had tremendous power because they had depth and meaning; they expressed true and personal religious experiences. It was James Martineau, a Unitarian, who said: "After the Scriptures, the Wesley hymn book appears to me the grandest instrument of popular religious culture that Christendom has ever produced."

PENITENTIAL.   39

Justice pursue, and mercy love,
    And humbly walk by faith with God.

5 But though my life henceforth be thine,
    Present for past can ne'er atone:
  Though I to thee the whole resign,
    I only give thee back thine own.

6 What have I then wherein to trust;
    I nothing have, I nothing am ;
  Excluded is my every boast:
    My glory swallow'd up in shame.

7 Guilty I stand before thy face;
    On me I feel thy wrath abide;
  'Tis just the sentence should take place,
    'Tis just,—but, O, thy Son hath died!

8 Jesus, the Lamb of God, hath bled,
    He bore our sins upon the tree;
  Beneath our curse he bow'd his head;
    'Tis finish'd! he hath died for me!

9 See, where before thy throne he stands,
    And pours the all-prevailing prayer!
  Points to his side, and lifts his hands,
    And shows that I am graven there!

10 He ever lives for me to pray;
    He prays that I with him may reign:
  Amen, to what my Lord doth say!
    Jesus, thou canst not pray in vain.

Hotham.]   HYMN 35.   8 *lines* 7's.

1 JESUS, lover of my soul,
    Let me to thy bosom fly,
  While the nearer waters roll,
    While the tempest still is high;
  Hide me, O my Saviour, hide,
    Till the storm of life is past,

334 From *A Collection of Hymns for the Use of the Methodist Episcopal Church,* New York, 1822

---

10   PENITENTIAL.

Safe into the haven guide,
    O receive my soul at last.

2 Other refuge have I none,
    Hangs my helpless soul on thee;
  Leave, Ah! leave me not alone,
    Still support and comfort me!
  All my trust on thee is stay'd,
    All my help from thee I bring,
  Cover my defenceless head
    With the shadow of thy wing.

3 Thou, O Christ, art all I want;
    More than all in thee I find,
  Raise the fall'n, cheer the faint,
    Heal the sick, and lead the blind.
  Just and holy is thy name;
    I am all unrighteousness;
  False, and full of sin I am,
    Thou art full of truth and grace.

4 Plenteous grace with thee is found,
    Grace to cover all my sin:
  Let the healing streams abound,
    Make and keep me pure within;
  Thou of life the fountain art;
    Freely let me take of thee:
  Spring thou up within my heart,
    Rise to all eternity!

Mount Zion.] HYMN 36. 4 8's & 2 6's.

1 O LOVE divine, how sweet thou art
    When shall I find my willing heart
  All taken up by thee?
  I thirst, I faint, I die to prove
  The greatness of redeeming love,
    The love of Christ to me.

2 Stronger his love than death or hell,
  Its riches are unsearchable;

335 From *A Collection of Hymns for the Use of the Methodist Episcopal Church,* New York, 1822

336   The Circuit Preacher, from the drawing by A. R. Waud in *Harper's Weekly*, Oct. 12, 1867

THE CIRCUIT PREACHER

THE Methodist organization of itinerant preachers, under the direction of bishops and presiding elders, was admirably suited to the work of propaganda and to the needs of a rapidly developing country with a shifting frontier. So faithful were the circuit riders that it became a proverbial saying, on a bitterly cold winter day: "There is nothing out today but crows and Methodist preachers." President Roosevelt once said that Methodism is "indissolubly interwoven with the history of our country. . . . Its essential democracy, its fiery and restless energy of spirit, and the wide play it gave to individual initiative, all tended to make it peculiarly congenial to a hardy and virile folk, democratic to the core, prizing individual independence above all earthly possessions, and engaged in the rough and stern work of conquering a continent. . . . The whole country is under a debt of gratitude to the Methodist circuit riders, the Methodist pioneer preachers, whose movement westward kept pace with the movement of the frontier, who shared all the hardships in the life of the frontiersman, while at the same time ministering to that frontiersman's spiritual needs and seeing that his pressing material cares and the hard and grinding poverty of his life did not wholly extinguish the divine fire within his soul."

PETER CARTWRIGHT, 1785–1872, "THE BACKWOODS PREACHER"

THE autobiography of Peter Cartwright is the classic portrayal of the life of a circuit rider on the western frontier. Born in Virginia, he was brought up in Logan County, Kentucky, which in the 1790's was called "Rogue's Harbor" because of the number of refugees from justice, from different parts of the Union, who had gathered there. Cartwright was converted and began to preach in 1802, and was ordained six years later. He was a muscular Christian, with a keen sense of humor, and a shrewd, homely resourcefulness that won his way in the face of every difficulty. To the end of his life, he held in disdain the "educated preachers" who reminded him of "lettuce growing under the shade of a peach-tree." "It is true that we could not, many of us, conjugate a verb or parse a sentence, and murdered the king's English almost every lick. But there was a Divine unction attended the word preached, and thousands fell under the mighty power of God, and thus the Methodist Episcopal Church was planted firmly in this western wilderness." Cartwright, who looked upon the world with the eyes of a frontiersman, did a work which doubtless no other could have accomplished. He was perfectly fitted for his peculiar task.

337   Peter Cartwright, from a daguerreotype in possession of the McLean County Historical Society, Bloomington, Ill.

THE GREAT REVIVAL IN KENTUCKY

PRESBYTERIANS and Baptists, as well as Methodists, crossed the mountains into Kentucky and Tennessee, to preach and establish churches. But there were not nearly enough ministers, and the ordinances of the church could not be administered regularly. Folk would come for many miles, therefore, to a "sacramental meeting"; and frequently the three denominations would unite in such occas-

338   Sacramental Scene in a Western Forest, from Joseph Smith, D.D., *Old Redstone*, Philadelphia, 1854

ions, ministers of each order being engaged in preaching, and the Methodists and Presbyterians partaking of the communion together. Under the preaching of James McGready and William McGee, Presbyterian, and John McGee, Methodist, there began in 1799 the remarkable awakening of religious interest known as the Great Revival of 1800–01. Particularly notable meetings were those at Red River, Gaspar River and Muddy River in 1800, and at Concord and Cane Ridge in 1801. The movement spread throughout the southern states. Because of the great crowds and the long distances that many came, the practice grew of camping over the week-end, from Thursday or Friday to Tuesday, with preaching every day and the administration of the sacrament on Sunday. These frontier people, unaccustomed to crowds, had few defenses against crowd psychology.

BODILY PHENOMENA OF THE GREAT REVIVAL

339   The Jerking Exercise, from Samuel G. Goodrich, *Recollections of a Lifetime*, New York, 1856

THE Great Revival, to a larger extent than any other such movement, was accompanied by bodily exercises, such as weeping, falling to the ground, loss of consciousness, muscular jerking, shouting, barking, singing, leaping, and dancing. There was much difference of opinion as to the value of these exercises. A great deal depended upon the preachers. Some helped folk to control themselves; others sought to rouse such convulsions. Cartwright, who did not think much of these commotions, vividly described the "jerks." "They would be taken under a warm song or sermon, and seized with a convulsive jerking all over, which they could not by any possibility avoid, and the more they resisted, the more they jerked. . . . Most usually persons taken with the jerks, to obtain relief, as they said, would rise up and dance. Some would run, but could not get away. . . . To see these proud young gentlemen and young ladies, dressed in their silks, jewelry and prunella, from top to toe, take the jerks, would often excite my risibilities. The first jerk or so, you would see their fine bonnets, caps and combs fly. . . . It was, on all occasions, my practice to recommend fervent prayer as a remedy, and it almost universally proved an effectual antidote." To great numbers of frontier folk these involuntary bodily exercises seemed to be manifestations of the Spirit of God working in men. As a consequence, excitement at times reached a pitch beyond the ability even of the most sophisticated to endure. Such emotional surgings, however, could not last. They quickly subsided.

340   The Camp Ground, from an engraving by Charles A. Jewett (1816–78), after the drawing by James
Smilie (1807–85), in possession of the publishers

341 Camp Meeting, from Jean Baptiste Gaspard Roux de Rochelle, *États-Unis
d'Ameriques*, Paris, 1837

THE CAMP MEETING AT CANE RIDGE

THE climax of the Revival was reached in the sacramental meeting at Cane Ridge, Kentucky, in August, 1801. It was estimated that twenty-five thousand people were in attendance. Presbyterian, Methodist, and Baptist preachers joined in the work, and the Governor of the state was present. Stands were erected in different sections of the wood, so that seven preachers could speak at the same time. "They were of one mind and soul," wrote Barton W. Stone, Presbyterian minister at Cane Ridge; "the salvation of sinners was the one object. We all engaged in singing the same songs, all united in prayer, all preached the same things. . . . The numbers converted will be known only in eternity. . . . This meeting continued six or seven days and nights, and would have continued longer, but food for the sustenance of such a multitude failed." A contemporary observer "noted a remarkable instance of a little girl, by the name of Barbara, about seven years old, who was set upon a man's shoulder, agreeably to her desire to speak to the multitude, which she did until she appeared almost exhausted, and leaned back her head upon her bearer." Cameras were not yet invented, and there seem to have been no artists on the ground. The illustrations present pictures of camp meetings as conceived by American, French and English artists — all bearing marks of having been drawn from imaginations fed on descriptions, rather than from actual observation.

342   Camp Meeting, from Mrs. Trollope, *Domestic Manners of the
Americans*, London, 1832

DARLEY'S CARICATURE OF A CAMP-MEETING SCENE

"When a person is struck down," reported an eye-witness of the Cane Ridge meeting, "he is carried by others out of the congregation, when some minister converses with, and prays for him; afterwards a few gather around and sing a hymn suitable to his case." This caricature by Darley of a camp-meeting scene belongs to a later date, having been drawn in 1870. Here is the imagination of a really great illustrator, evidently stimulated by observation. The pioneer

343   From the drawing by F. O. C. Darley (1822–88), in *Every Saturday*, Sept. 24, 1870

preachers of Kentucky were rougher and more virile figures than the unctuous Brother Stiggins in the foreground.

EFFECTS OF THE GREAT REVIVAL

The movement did not cease with the Cane Ridge meeting; it became diffused. Revivals of religion were experienced in all parts of the country in the first decade of the nineteenth century. It is easy for a more sophisticated age to find fault with the extravagances of the early camp meetings. But they were needed, and they wrought much good. A staid Presbyterian minister of Virginia, constitutionally indisposed to such wild doings as he heard were taking place in Kentucky in the name of religion, determined to investigate, and reported that the people there were now as remarkable for sobriety as they had formerly been for dissoluteness and immorality. "All things considered, the revival was peculiarly adapted to the circumstances of the country into which it came. Infidelity was triumphant and religion was on the point of expiring. Something extraordinary seemed necessary to arrest the attention of a giddy people. . . . This revival has done it." There were other effects of longer range. The Second Awakening and the Great Revival began in many of the churches of America a more or less conscious policy of revivalism — an expectation of the recurrence of seasons of especial awakening, and a disposition to stress such occasions to the relative undervaluation of the more quiet and constant processes of everyday life and service in the presence and power of God. These movements divided the churches, too. In New England, the Unitarians separated from the Congregationalists; among the Germans of Pennsylvania, the United Brethren and the Evangelical Association were organized; in the West and the South, the Cumberland Presbyterians, the Christians, and the Disciples of Christ originated in withdrawals from the Presbyterian Church. The upheavals of the revival period tended to increase denominational rivalry and disputation between members of different sects. One of the interesting manifestations of this was the founding of what amounted to a new religion, Mormonism, by Joseph Smith in the opening years of the second quarter of the nineteenth century.

THE
KENTUCKY REVIVAL,
OR,
A SHORT HISTORY
Of the late extraordinary out-pouring of the Spirit of God, in the western States of America, agreeably to Scripture-promises, and Prophecies concerning the Latter Day:

WITH A BRIEF ACCOUNT
OF THE ENTRANCE AND PROGRESS OF WHAT THE
WORLD CALL

SHAKERISM,

AMONG THE SUBJECTS OF THE LATE REVIVAL
IN OHIO AND KENTUCKY.

PRESENTED TO THE
TRUE ZION-TRAVELLER,
AS A MEMORIAL OF THE WILDERNESS JOURNEY.

By Richard M'Nemar.

*" When ye see a cloud rise out of the west, straightway ye say, there
cometh a shower ; and so it is : And when ye feel the south wind
blow, ye say, there will be heat ; and it cometh to pass——Can ye
not discern the signs of the times.*
CHRIST.

CINCINNATI:
FROM THE PRESS OF JOHN W. BROWNE,
OFFICE OF LIBERTY HALL.
1807.

344   Title-page of the original in the
New York Public Library

345   Barton W. Stone, from James R. Rogers, *The Cane Ridge Meeting-House*, Cincinnati

BARTON W. STONE, 1772–1844, REPUDIATES SECTARIAN NAMES AND CREEDS

WHEN Barton W. Stone, applying for ordination by the Presbytery of Transylvania, was asked whether he accepted the Westminster Confession, he answered: "As far as I see it consistent with the Word of God." As pastor of the church at Cane Ridge during the Great Revival, he was profoundly impressed with the Christian fellowship it fostered, and with the fundamental agreement of those who bore different sectarian names. With five other ministers, he withdrew from the Presbyterian Church in 1804, being determined to be known by no other name than Christian, and to acknowledge no creed but the Bible. His followers in time became associated with groups led by James O'Kelly, formerly a Methodist minister, in Virginia and the Carolinas, and by Abner Jones and Elias Smith, formerly Baptist ministers, in New England, to form the American Christian Convention. Their weekly newspaper, *The Herald of Gospel Liberty*, was founded by Elias Smith in 1808, and has been issued continuously since that time.

ALEXANDER CAMPBELL, 1788–1866

IN 1809, Thomas Campbell was tried by his fellow ministers of the Presbytery of Chartiers in Western Pennsylvania, for admitting folk to the Lord's Supper who were not Presbyterians of their particular stripe. He was released from censure, but withdrew from the Presbyterian ministry and organized The Christian Association of Washington, Pa., to labor for the union of all Christians. He declared that "nothing ought to be inculcated upon Christians as articles of faith, nor required of them as terms of communion, but what is expressly taught and enjoined upon them in the Word of God." "Where the Scriptures speak we speak, and where the Scriptures are silent we are silent," was his rule. His

HERALD F GOSPEL LIBERTY
ELIAS SMITH.

NO. 1.]   THURSDAY EVENING, SEPTEMBER 1, 1808.   [VOL. I.

346   From a facsimile of the first edition, courtesy of the Christian Publishing Association, Dayton, Ohio

347   From an original portrait by Roberts, at Bethany College, Bethany, W. Va.

son, Alexander Campbell, brought to the leadership of the movement an acute mind and a powerful, aggressive personality. Having become convinced that immersion was the Scriptural mode of baptism, the Campbells and their followers were for a time affiliated with the Baptists. The elder Campbell and Stone were the inevitable products of a time in which very great emphasis was placed upon denominational differences. They hoped to lead their fellow countrymen away from sectarian disputes and toward a spirit more nearly in harmony with that of the disciples whom Jesus gathered about him. Campbell was a resourceful debater, and relied much upon public debates with outstanding advocates of the views he criticized. Wide publicity was given to his debates with the Catholic Bishop Purcell and with N. L. Rice, Presbyterian.

DISCIPLES OF CHRIST

IN 1832 Barton W. Stone reached an agreement with Alexander Campbell, whereby their movements should be united; but many of Stone's group refused to follow him in this. Under the name of Disciples of Christ the followers of Campbell are now the fifth Protestant body in the United States, numbering nearly one million eight hundred thousand communicants, and being exceeded only by the Methodists, Baptists, Presbyterians, and Lutherans. There is tragic irony in the fact that Stone and

348   Alexander Campbell Study, Bethany College, Bethany, W. Va.

Campbell, seeking to rid Christendom of sects and divisive creeds, should have succeeded only in establishing additional denominations. In 1841 Campbell became President of Bethany College, which had been chartered by the legislature of Virginia in the previous year. From this post, which he occupied until his death, and through the pages of the *Millennial Harbinger*, a journal which he had founded in 1830, Campbell exercised a remarkable influence upon his generation, especially throughout the Middle West. Bethany College has grown and its curriculum has broadened in scope. Several men prominent in the national public life of their day have been numbered among its graduates.

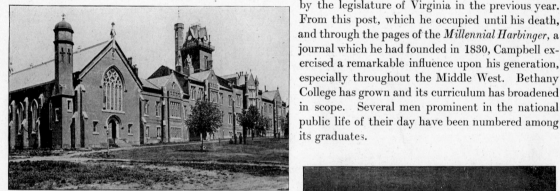

349   Bethany College, Bethany, W. Va., about 1872

THE PLIGHT OF THE EPISCOPAL CHURCHES

THE colonial churches of the Anglican order were hard hit by the Revolution. The political independence of the states sundered these churches from the English episcopate; and they had no bishop of their own, and no means of ordaining one. The financial support formerly afforded by the Society for the Propagation of the Gospel ceased; and disestablishment in the southern states deprived them of property and accustomed revenues. The flight of the Tories and the separation of the Methodists lost to them many thousands of members. There were wide differences between the rigid high churchmanship of the Episcopal churches in the northern states, which had been obliged to fight for their existence against the "Standing Order" of Congregationalism, and the laxer ways of the churches which had enjoyed the privileges of state establishment in the South. It was a difficult and delicate task to bring these shattered remnants together into a united, living American Episcopal Church. But there was a man equal to the task. It was William White, American patriot, rector of Christ Church, Philadelphia.

350 Bishop William White, 1748–1836, from the original portrait by Gilbert Stuart (1755–1828), in the Pennsylvania Academy of Fine Arts, Philadelphia

X—11

351 William White, from William H. Brown, *Portrait Gallery of Distinguished American Citizens*, Hartford, Conn., 1846

WILLIAM WHITE, PATRIARCH OF THE PROTESTANT EPISCOPAL CHURCH

A STURDY patriot, White had prayed for Congress instead of for the King as soon as the Declaration of Independence was passed; and had accepted its chaplaincy in the time of greatest danger, when the British occupied Philadelphia. As soon as hostilities ceased, he published a pamphlet proposing a plan for the organization of the Episcopal churches by means of a Convention which should include lay as well as clerical representatives. With tact, consecration, and tireless patience, he toiled through a long series of negotiations and preliminary conferences and conventions, until all parties united in the General Convention of 1789 which organized the Protestant Episcopal Church. A petition was addressed to the English bishops in 1785, asking that they ordain bishops elected by conventions in the several American states; and John Adams in person presented it to the Archbishop of Canterbury and urged that it be granted. An Act of Parliament author-

352 Bishop Samuel Seabury, 1729–96, from the original portrait by Thomas Spence Duché, in Trinity College, Hartford, Conn.

ized the consecration of three American bishops; and Bishop White of Pennsylvania and Bishop Provoost of New York were ordained in London in 1787. Bishop Madison of Virginia was similarly ordained in 1790; and the three joined with Bishop Seabury of Connecticut, who had independently secured consecration by the Scottish bishops, to establish the succession of Episcopal ordination in this country. The quiet establishment of the Episcopal Church in America on an independent footing was an event of considerable importance in the religious history of the New World. It showed, moreover, that war had not destroyed in the hearts of Englishmen the spirit of conciliation.

353 From the memorial in Trinity Church, New York

JOHN HENRY HOBART, 1775–1830, BISHOP OF NEW YORK

BISHOP WHITE was of evangelical temper. He loved to worship God according to the stately liturgy of his church, and he believed in Christian nurture rather than in the emotional, sometimes explosive experiences that were coming to be associated with revivalism; but he strongly opposed the type of theology and of church polity "comprised in the words *Priest, Altar, Sacrifice.*" His pupil, John Henry Hobart, who became Bishop of New York, was, on the contrary, an uncompromising high churchman. His intellectual gifts, his ability as an administrator, his decisiveness and energy, his zeal in philanthropic, educational and missionary enterprises, and his single-minded, mystic devotion lifted his church to a new level of aggressive effort and conscious power. He died at fifty-five, having burned himself out with work. "Give me a little zealous imprudence," was one of his favorite phrases. When his wife cautioned him, as he started upon the visitation of the churches which ended in his death, saying, "You are undertaking too much," he answered, "How can I do too much for Him who has done everything for me."

THE LANGUAGE CONTROVERSY IN THE LUTHERAN CHURCHES

THE Episcopal churches received a considerable influx from the English-speaking element among the Lutherans. The Lutheran patriarch, Muhlenberg, had encouraged the churches in his care to cultivate the English language; but a party in the next generation sought jealously to maintain the German, and preferred to lose their young people rather than to admit preaching in English. In 1797, when a newly organized English Lutheran Church in New York sought recognition by the Lutheran Ministerium, it was denied and its members were bluntly told that they might join the Episcopalians — which they naturally did, pastor, officers, and the entire congregation. In Philadelphia the language controversy was bitter and prolonged; and the party which advocated the use of English, led by General Peter Muhlenberg, won the victory. Some of the arguments put forth by the German party are amazing: "What would Philadelphia be in forty years if the Germans there were to remain German, and retain their language and customs? It would not be forty years until Philadelphia would be a German city. . . . The English would be driven to the bushes. . . . What would be the result throughout Pennsylvania and northern Maryland in forty or fifty years? An entirely German State, where, as formerly in Germantown, the beautiful German language would be used in the legislative halls and the courts of justice."

TRIAL

OF

FREDERICK EBERLE AND OTHERS,

At a Nisi Prius Court, held at Philadelphia, July 1816

BEFORE THE

HONORABLE JASPER YEATES, JUSTICE.

FOR ILLEGALLY CONSPIRING TOGETHER BY ALL MEANS LAW-
FUL AND UNLAWFUL, " WITH THEIR BODIES AND LIVES "
TO PREVENT THE INTRODUCTION OF THE ENG-
LISH LANGUAGE INTO THE
SERVICE OF

ST. MICHAEL'S AND ZION'S CHURCHES,

Belonging to the German Lutheran Congregation, in the City of Philadelphia.

TAKEN IN SHORT HAND

BY JAMES CARSON,

ATTORNEY AT LAW

PHILADELPHIA.

PUBLISHED FOR THE REPORTER.

1847

354   Title-page of the original in the New York Public Library

355   Lutheran Theological Seminary, Gettysburg, Pa., from a lithograph in possession of the publishers

356   Samuel S. Schmucker, from the engraving by John Sartain (1808–97), courtesy of the Lutheran Historical Society, Gettysburg, Pa.

THE ORGANIZATION OF THE LUTHERAN GENERAL SYNOD

THE celebration in 1817 of the three-hundredth anniversary of the Protestant Reformation stimulated the Lutheran churches; and in 1820 a General Synod was organized. Its growing strength was due largely to the leadership of Samuel S. Schmucker, 1799–1873, a young minister who had been trained at Princeton. He founded a Lutheran Theological Seminary in 1826 and Pennsylvania College in 1832, at Gettysburg, where he spent the remainder of his life as a teacher of theology. The General Synod soon came to use the English language chiefly. It declared adherence to the Augsburg Confession as "a correct exhibition of the fundamental doctrines of the Word of God" — a statement which obviously permits freedom of interpretation. Schmucker earnestly sought to adapt Lutheranism to the needs of America as he saw them; he published plans and proposals looking toward the ultimate unity of the Protestant churches; and he was one of the first advocates of the movement which culminated in the formation in 1846 of the Evangelical Alliance. With the great influx of German immigration in the middle of the century, however, a reaction set in toward a more strict, conservative adherence to the traditional positions of the Lutheran Church.

357 John Carroll, from an engraving by William Satchwell Leney (1769–1831), and Benjamin Tanner (1775–1848), after the portrait by Jeremiah Paul (d. 1820), in the New York Public Library

JOHN CARROLL, 1735–1815, FIRST BISHOP OF THE CATHOLIC CHURCH IN THE UNITED STATES

FOR some years before the Revolution the Catholics in the English colonies had been under the direction of the Vicar Apostolic at London; but intercourse with him ceased during the war. In 1783 the priests in Maryland and Pennsylvania addressed a petition to the Pope, calling his attention to the religious freedom now established in the United States; declaring it to be impossible for them to be dependent upon a foreign jurisdiction, "more than that which is essential to our religion, an acknowledgment of the Pope's spiritual supremacy over the whole Christian world"; and asking him to place the episcopal powers "in the hands of one amongst us, whose virtue, knowledge, and integrity of faith, shall be certified by ourselves." A determined effort was made by the French hierarchy to gain control of the American churches, seeking to subject them to a French bishop who was to reside in France and there establish a seminary to train priests for service in America. But the scheme failed, and in 1784 John Carroll, native American, was appointed Prefect Apostolic of the Catholic Church in the United States. He was made bishop in 1790, having been elected by his fellows; and Archbishop in 1808. The appointment marks an epoch in the history of Catholicism in the United States.

BISHOP CARROLL'S ADMINISTRATION

BISHOP CARROLL was an able administrator. He set himself resolutely against "trusteeism," a term applied to the insistence of the trustees of certain churches that they had a right to choose their own priests without interference by the bishop. "If ever such principles should become predominant," he wrote, "the unity and catholicity of our church would be at an end; and it would be formed into distinct and independent societies, nearly in the same manner as the Congregational Presbyterians." He successfully opposed "nationalism,"

the attempt to divide the Church into independent groups based upon language and previous nationality, especially insisted upon by Germans in Philadelphia and Baltimore. He established a seminary for the training of priests, and founded Georgetown College in 1789. He labored zealously for the erection of the Cathedral in Baltimore, though he did not live to see it completed. He had "a rare goodness of heart," said a contemporary. "His patriotism was as decided as his piety." He accomplished much for the church to whose service he devoted his life.

358 Baltimore Cathedral, Baltimore, Md. © Detroit Publishing Co.

MOTHER ELIZABETH ANN SETON, 1774–1821, FOUNDER OF THE SISTERS OF CHARITY

IN 1805, Elizabeth Ann Seton, daughter of Dr. Richard Bayley, first professor of anatomy in what is now Columbia University, widow of William M. Seton, a merchant of New York, and mother of five young children, was received into the Catholic Church. She had been converted to its doctrines at the home of friends in Italy, who cared for her during a long illness following her husband's death. With the encouragement of Bishop Carroll, she established in 1809 a religious community at Emmitsburg, Maryland, of women who took the name of Sisters of Charity. Her primary interest was in the care and education of children. The devoted service of the order she founded, and of similar teaching orders, both of men and of women, has made possible the establishment and maintenance of the Catholic parochial schools.

359 Mother Elizabeth Ann Seton, from the miniature, 1796, by Charles B. J. F. de St. Memin (1770–1852), in the possession of T. Seton Jevons, Esq., New York city

TRINITARIAN AND ANTI–TRINITARIAN IN MASSACHUSETTS

IN the Massachusetts churches there was a growing rift between folk of orthodox, evangelical conviction and those who denied the distinctive doctrines of Calvinism and even questioned the deity of Christ. The differences had begun back in the days of the Great Awakening, were fostered by the vogue of Deism, and were intensified by the Second Awakening. King's Chapel, the oldest Episcopal church in New England, became avowedly Unitarian in 1782. The Congregational churches remained ostensibly in fellowship, but ministers and people were fast becoming aligned in two groups. The first church to be divided over the issue

was, strangely enough, the old church of the Pilgrims at Plymouth. In 1800 this church voted by a small majority to call a "liberal" pastor; and almost exactly one half of the members withdrew and formed a new church upon the basis of the faith of the fathers, leaving the ancient church in the hands of the party soon to be known as Unitarian. The tenseness of the times is hardly reflected in the peaceful, partly somnolent air of this picture of a church service in winter. The Congregational churches of eastern Massachusetts in the Dedham case soon reaped the bitter harvest of their early connection with the state. The church in a Massachusetts community was composed, like churches elsewhere, of those who had been admitted to full spiritual fellowship; but the financial support of the church was in hands of the town or parish, which included all voters and taxpayers. Naturally, the parish was usually more "liberal" than the church, and the parish held the purse-strings. Trouble was brewing in such a situation.

360 From the painting *A Winter Service At Church*, by W. L. Taylor (1854–1926), in *The Ladies' Home Journal*, Jan. 1901. © The Curtis Publishing Co.

361　From *Catalogue of the Theological Seminary, Andover, Mass.,*
Andover, 1849

THE FOUNDING OF ANDOVER THEOLOGICAL SEMINARY

In 1805, an anti-trinitarian was elected to the Hollis Professorship in Harvard College. This event roused the evangelical group to defend itself by the founding of Andover Theological Seminary in 1808. The new institution not only proved effective as a barrier to the spread of Unitarianism, but became notable for the spirit of devotion to home and foreign missions which developed among its students. For a half century prior to this time, it had been the custom of young men looking forward to the ministry to study in the home of some prominent divine — Joseph Bellamy, of Bethlehem, Connecticut, is said to have trained sixty such candidates, and Nathaniel Emmons, of Franklin, Massachusetts, at least one hundred. The success of Andover put an end to this practice, and inaugurated a new era in the professional education of ministers. Within twenty years seventeen theological seminaries were established and there are now one hundred and seventy-two.

WILLIAM ELLERY CHANNING, 1780–1842, PROPHET OF UNITARIANISM

William Ellery Channing, minister of the Federal Street Church in Boston, preached a sermon in 1819 at the ordination of Jared Sparks in Baltimore, which, with his subsequent articles, constituted a platform of the Unitarian movement. He accepted the term "Unitarian," because it seemed to him presumptuous to use the word "Liberal" as the designation of a party, since it is an adjective that may be applied to men of all opinions. But he gave to the term, which had hitherto been used to designate the materialistic views of men like Priestley, a new meaning, defining it simply as anti-trinitarianism: "The word Unitarian, taken in . . . its true sense, . . . includes all who believe that there is no distinction of persons in God." The American Unitarian Association was organized in 1825; and a new religious denomination had come into being.

362　From a photograph in the Athenaeum, Boston, of the original portrait, 1839, by S. Gambardella in possession of W. E. C. Eustis, Milton, Mass.

363　The Unitarian and Orthodox Churches, Dedham, Mass., from J. W. Barber, *Historical Collections of Massachusetts*, Worcester, 1839

THE DEDHAM CASE

At Dedham, in 1818, the voters of the parish, who were predominantly Unitarian in sentiment, forced the settlement of a minister of Unitarian views, over the protest of the church, which was predominantly evangelical. A majority of the members of the church thereupon withdrew; and, claiming that they, rather than the minority that remained, constituted the First Church of Dedham, demanded the meetinghouse and property. The case was carried to the Supreme Court of the state, which decided against them. "When the majority of the members of a Congregational Church separate from the majority of the parish, the members who remain, although a minority, constitute the church in such parish, and retain the rights and property thereto." This was a tremendous reversal! In ancient Massachusetts only church members could vote in town meeting; now the churches themselves were at the mercy of the voters. And the voters were not slow to assert their power. A report made in 1836 enumerates eighty-one churches from which three thousand nine hundred evangelical members withdrew because of actions similar to that of the parish at Dedham, leaving property worth more than six hundred thousand dollars for the use of one thousand two hundred and eighty-two Unitarian members who remained. It was a time of bitter strife. Both parties were glad to unite in the action of 1833 whereby taxes for the support of religion were abolished and the maintenance of the churches became entirely voluntary.

HORACE BUSHNELL, 1802–1876, PREACHER AND THEOLOGIAN

UNITARIANISM made no headway in Connecticut, largely because the influence of Yale College and Divinity School was consistently evangelical, and because, under the leadership of President Dwight and Professor Nathaniel W. Taylor, modifications were made in the traditionally Calvinistic theology which forestalled the more radical criticism. The greatest of the Connecticut ministers was Horace Bushnell. Converted in the revival at Yale College in 1831, he forsook the study of law to enter the Divinity School, and became pastor of the North Church in Hartford. His work, in the pulpit and with his pen, marks the passing of extreme Calvinism in the New England churches. He helped to emancipate them, Dr. Theodore T. Munger, his biographer, has said, at four points: "first, from a revivalism that ignored the law of Christian growth; second, from a conception of the Trinity bordering on tritheism; third, from a view of miracles that implied a suspension of natural law; and fourth, from a theory of the atonement that . . . failed to declare the law of human life."

364 Horace Bushnell, from a daguerreotype, 1848, courtesy of Charles Scribner's Sons, New York

DISCOURSES

ON

CHRISTIAN NURTURE.

BY HORACE BUSHNELL.
PASTOR OF THE NORTH CHURCH, HARTFORD.

Approved by the Committee of Publication.

BOSTON:
MASSACHUSETTS SABBATH SCHOOL SOCIETY,
Depository, No. 13 Cornhill.
1847.

365 Title-page of the original edition in the Yale University Library, New Haven

CHRISTIAN NURTURE

BUSHNELL wrote on high themes — the divinity of Christ, the principles of atonement, the relation of nature and the supernatural. But the most far-reaching in influence of all his works was a little book, first published in 1846, subsequently expanded, on *Christian Nurture*. In this he sharply criticized the prevalent individualism of the non-liturgical churches, their reliance upon revivals, and their insistence upon a conscious, dated, emotional experience of conversion. The true principle of Christian education, he maintained, is "That the child is to grow up a Christian, and never know himself as being otherwise." This is possible, he believed, if the life of the family in the home is truly Christian, and if children are afforded their proper place in the life of the church. The book remarkably anticipates present-day convictions concerning the nature of childhood and the possibility of moral and religious education and it is yet widely read. Its principles are timely, because eternally true.

"OLD SCHOOL" AND "NEW SCHOOL" PRESBYTERIANS

IN 1837 the conservatives, or "old school" men in the Presbyterian Church gained a majority in the General Assembly, and proceeded to purge it of everything that savored of the "new school." They abrogated the "Plan of Union" in accordance with which they had been co-operating with the Congregational Churches since 1801, withdrew from the missionary and educational societies in which they had been associated with the Congregationalists, and exscinded four Synods which had been formed under the Plan of Union. They felt that their

366 High Street, with the First Presbyterian Church, Philadelphia, from an engraving, 1800, by William Birch (1755–1834)

church was being infected by the "New Haven theology" and undermined by Congregational principles. The issue had been joined in the trial for "errors" of Albert Barnes, pastor of the First Presbyterian Church, Philadelphia, who was accused of expressing views in substantial agreement with Professor Taylor and out of harmony with the Westminster Confession. The excinded Synods refused to accept excision; and for thirty-three years "Old School" and "New School" Assemblies divided the Presbyterian Church.

367   From an engraving *American Friends going to meeting in a settled frost,* 1804–06,
            in Robert Sutcliffe, *Travels in Some Parts of North America,* York, 1815

SEPARATIONS AMONG
THE FRIENDS

EVEN the peaceful Quakers split during these controversial years. They had suffered during the Revolution, especially in Pennsylvania, for their "testimony against war"; and had disowned many of their members for engaging in it. Religiously, they had lost the flaming evangelistic zeal that had characterized them in the early days, and had adopted a defensive policy. They had devised rigid rules with respect to dress and language, and expelled members who married outside of their fellowship. They admitted children to membership as a matter of birthright; and often failed to instruct them in the truths of religion, or even to practice with them the regular reading of the Bible, "from the fear of interfering with the work of the Spirit in the hearts of the children." In 1827–28 a considerable group separated from the Yearly Meetings of the Friends, following the leadership of Elias Hicks, 1748–1830, who so exclusively exalted the "Light within" as to pass to negations concerning the person and work of Christ and the inspiration of the Scriptures, which were akin to the views of the Unitarians. Another group, following John Wilbur, separated later. Orthodox, Hicksite and Wilburite Friends are still divided.

368   From an engraving *American Friends going to meeting in summer,* 1804–06, in
            Robert Sutcliffe, *Travels in Some Parts of North America,* York, 1815

THE FRIENDS' TESTIMONY
AGAINST SLAVERY

THE evil of slavery had early been a matter of concern to the Quakers. The first public protest against slavery in America was by a group of German Friends in Philadelphia in 1688. Five years later the Philadelphia Yearly Meeting took action recommending to all Friends to buy no slaves "except to set free," and to set their present slaves at liberty, "after a reasonable time of service . . . and during the time they have them, to teach them to read, and give them a Christian Education." In 1758 the same body directed John Woolman and others "to visit and treat with all Friends who have any slaves"; and in 1776 it was decided that slaveholders should be "disowned," that is, expelled from membership, if they persisted in refusing to emancipate their slaves. Other Yearly Meetings took similar action. By the year 1787 there was not a slave remaining in the possession of an acknowledged Quaker. This was largely the result of the self-denying labors of John Woolman, 1720–72, who traveled throughout the colonies, preaching everywhere the gospel of freedom for the slave. Woolman, one of the most remarkable religious figures of his day, stands out as a pioneer in the long crusade which finally resulted in the abolition of the institution of human slavery in the United States.

369   *Monday Morning View of Friends Meeting House and Academy, Philadelphia, Forty Years Ago,* from the lithograph by W. L. Breton, 1829, reproduced
in *The Friends Meeting House,* Centennial Edition, Philadelphia, 1904

370   From the repainting and enlargement, 1885, of the original drawing, 1844, *Indiana Yearly Meeting of Friends*, by Marcus Mote

THE ABOLITION MOVEMENT DIVIDES THE FRIENDS IN INDIANA

NOT all Quakers, however, favored the anti-slavery movement. In Indiana advocates of a "let-it-alone" policy gained control of the Yearly Meeting, and adopted a minute advising Friends not to join anti-slavery societies or to become associated with groups pledging themselves to buy only goods produced by free labor. In 1842, the Yearly Meeting disqualified eight prominent members of its most important committee for disregarding this advice. It took the unprecedented step, moreover, of giving to Henry Clay a prominent seat in its First-day meeting, and greeting him at its close with what was, for Quakers, an ovation. Clay was not a Friend, was at the time a candidate for the Presidential nomination, and had just answered a petition requesting him to free his own slaves with the statement: "I consider them as property. I have an idea that whatever the law secures as property, is property." The advocates of abolition withdrew, and organized the Indiana Yearly Meeting of Anti-slavery Friends, which continued its separate existence for fourteen years.

371   From the mural painting *Moved by the Spirit*, by C. Y. Turner (1850–1918), in the Friends' Meetinghouse, Park Street, Baltimore. © by the artist

MOVED BY THE SPIRIT

WOMEN have always had equal place with men in the fellowship of the Friends; and have had equal right, when moved by the Spirit, to break the silence of their worship. No more effective advocates of the immediate emancipation of the slaves appeared before the public than the Quaker women, Lucretia Mott and Sarah and Angelina Grimké, who had been trained to frank, natural expression of their deepest convictions in meetings such as that which is here depicted.

A
DIALOGUE,
CONCERNING THE
S L A V E R Y
OF THE
A F R I C A N S ;
Shewing it to be the *Duty* and *Interest* of
the *American* Colonies to emancipate
all their *African* Slaves :
WITH AN
ADDRESS to the Owners of such Slaves.
DEDICATED TO THE HONORABLE THE
Continental Congress.

*Open thy mouth, judge righteously, and plead the cause of
this poor and needy*   PROV. XXXI. 9.
*And as ye would that men should do to you, do ye also to
them likewise.*   LUKE VI 31.

NORWICH:
Printed and sold by JUDAH P. SPOONER. 1776.

372   Title-page of the original in the Library of
              Congress, Washington

THE CHURCHES DECLARE SLAVERY TO BE WRONG

PRIOR to 1830, the churches had moved steadily, though more slowly than the Quakers, in the direction of the abolition of slavery. Before the Revolution, Ezra Stiles and Samuel Hopkins, pastors of Congregational churches at Newport, Rhode Island, then the chief center of the slave trade, had preached boldly against the business which was enriching their parishioners. The Baptists of Virginia, in 1789, resolved: "That slavery is a violent deprivation of the rights of nature, and inconsistent with a republican government, and we therefore recommend . . . every legal measure to extirpate this horrid evil from the land." The Presbyterian General Assembly in 1818 declared: "We consider the . . . enslaving of one part of the human race by another as a gross violation of the . . . sacred rights of human nature; as utterly inconsistent with the law of God, which requires us to love our neighbor as ourselves; and as totally irreconcilable with . . . the gospel of Christ, which enjoin that 'all things whatsoever ye would that men should do to you, do ye even so to them.'" The Methodists had determined in 1784 "to extirpate this abomination from among us," but later authorized an edition of their *Discipline* for use in southern states "with the section and rule on slavery left out."

SLAVERY, BY WILLIAM E. CHANNING

No wiser discussion of the slavery question was published, in the hectic years after 1830, than William E. Channing's *Slavery*. "Not what is profitable, but what is Right." "Man cannot justly be held and used as property. . . . He is a Person, not a Thing." "Slavery ought to be discussed . . . with a deep feeling of responsibility, and so done as not to put in jeopardy the peace of the slave-holding States." "In ranking slavery among the greatest wrongs, I speak of the injury endured by the slave, and not of the character of the master. These are distinct points." "To the slave-holder belongs the duty of settling and employing the best methods of liberation, and to no other. . . . It is of the highest importance that slavery should be succeeded by a friendly relation between master and slave; and to produce this, the latter must see in the former his benefactor and deliverer." "The great step toward the removal of slavery is to prepare the slaves for self-support." After 1830, when Garrison first began to publish the *Liberator*, the abolition movement in the North veered sharply toward radicalism. So extreme were the demands of many abolitionists that their favorite reform should be immediately effected that large numbers of conservative folk were antagonized. The southerners naturally resented the unbridled attacks of the northern radicals.

373   William Ellery Channing, 1780–1842, from a gravure after a portrait by
              Gilbert Stuart in the possession of Mrs. John A. Jeffries, Boston

SHALL SLAVEHOLDERS BE EXCOMMUNICATED?

THE more radical Abolitionists insisted that all slaveholders be excommunicated. "No fellowship with slave-holders"; "Slave-holding is always and everywhere a sin," were their war cries. But this demand ignored the undeniable facts that not all slaveholders were such by choice; and that the laws of some of the states forbade emancipation. The churches refused to be stampeded, and thereby incurred the bitter enmity of William Lloyd Garrison and his radical group. The New School Assembly of the Presbyterian Church pressed the principles of the Declaration of 1818 consistently and with increasing acumen upon the consciences of its constituent Presbyteries, churches and individual members. In 1850, finally, it declared that the holding of slaves is an offense to be dealt with by the discipline of the church, "except in those cases where it is unavoidable, by the laws of the State, the obligations of guardianship, or the demands of humanity." In 1853, it asked the Presbyteries in the slave-holding states for information as to (1) the number of slaveholders connected with their churches and the number of slaves held by them; (2) the extent to which these slaves are held by an unavoidable necessity; and (3) what provision is made for their religious well-being. Leaders of the church were striving earnestly to prevent a break over the question which was dividing the North and South into two hostile camps about to abandon peaceful discussion for the sword.

56   THE CHURCH AND SLAVERY.

and as speedily as possible to efface this blot on our holy religion, and to obtain the complete abolition of slavery throughout Christendom, and if possible throughout the world.

"We rejoice that the church to which we belong commenced, as early as any other in this country, the good work of endeavouring to put an end to slavery, and that in the same work many of its members have ever since been, and now are, among the most active, vigorous, and efficient labourers. We do, indeed, tenderly sympathize with those portions of our church and our country where the evil of slavery has been entailed upon them; where a *great*, and *the most virtuous*, part of *the community* abhor slavery, and wish its extermination as sincerely as any others; but where the number of slaves, their ignorance, and their vicious habits generally, render an immediate and universal emancipation inconsistent alike with the safety and happiness of the master and the slave. With those who are thus circumstanced, we repeat that we tenderly sympathize. At the same time, we earnestly exhort them to continue, and, if possible, to increase, their exertions TO EFFECT A TOTAL ABOLITION OF SLAVERY. We exhort them to suffer no greater delay to take place in this most interesting concern than a regard to the public welfare *truly* and *indispensably* demands.

"*The manifest violation or disregard of the injunction here given, in its true spirit and intention, ought to be considered as just ground for the discipline and censures of the church. And if it shall ever happen that a Christian professor, in our communion, shall sell a slave who is also in communion and good standing with our church, contrary to his or her will and inclination, it ought immediately to claim the particular attention of the proper church judicature; and, unless there be such peculiar circumstances attending the case as can but seldom happen, it ought to be followed, without delay, by a suspension of the offender from all the privileges of the church till he repent and make all the reparation in his power to the injured party.*"

374   From Albert Barnes, *The Church and Slavery,*
Philadelphia, 1857

REVIEW

OF A LETTER,

FROM THE

PRESBYTERY OF CHILLICOTHE,

TO THE

PRESBYTERY OF MISSISSIPPI,

ON THE SUBJECT OF SLAVERY

BY REV. JAMES SMYLIE, A. M.

A Member of the Amite Presbytery.

QUEM DEUS VULT PERDERE, PRIUS DEMENTAT.

WOODVILLE, MI:

PRINTED BY WM. A. NORRIS AND CO

1836.

375   Title-page of the original in the New York
Public Library

THE CHANGE OF SENTIMENT IN THE SOUTH

MOST of the southern Presbyteries refused to answer the inquiry. The Presbytery of Lexington responded that ministers and members of its churches were slaveholders by choice and on principle. A great change of sentiment had taken place in the South. As late as 1831–32, it was generally acknowledged that the institution of slavery was wrong in principle and ought to be abolished when a practicable way could be found. The majority of the speakers in the famous debate in the Virginia legislature of that winter, condemned the system in the most outspoken terms — "a great and appalling evil, a blighting and withering curse upon this land." But this was mere debate; it came to nothing. Then the publicists, professors and preachers of the South began to find reasons to justify the perpetuation of slavery. Professor Dew, of William and Mary College, elaborated a philosophical argument to show that emancipation was undesirable or impossible. The Governor of South Carolina, in 1835, said that "Domestic slavery is the corner-stone of our republican edifice." Dr. John Bachman, Lutheran pastor in Charleston, declared that "Our defense of slavery is contained in the Holy Scriptures." An article in the *Church Review* (Episcopal) in 1854 described slavery as "a wise and benevolent institution," with "the undoubted sanction of Holy-writ"; and said that all the people of the South are "united in one sentiment, to sustain the institution at all hazards."

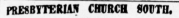

THE

CHRISTIAN DOCTRINE

OF

SLAVERY.

BY

GEO. D. ARMSTRONG, D.D.,

PASTOR OF THE PRESBYTERIAN CHURCH OF NORFOLK, VA.

"Wholesome words, even the words of our Lord Jesus Christ, and the doctrine
which is according to godliness."—1 TIM. VI. 8.

NEW YORK:

CHARLES SCRIBNER, 377 & 379 BROADWAY.

LOUISVILLE, KY.:—A. DAVIDSON.

1857.

376 Title-page of the original in the New
York Public Library

THE CHRISTIAN DOCTRINE OF SLAVERY

THE "discovery" that the Bible sanctions and inculcates slavery was made by James Smylie, a Presbyterian minister of Mississippi, who investigated the subject in 1833 and reached results that "surprised himself." A clear exposition of *The Christian Doctrine of Slavery* was made in 1857 by George D. Armstrong, Old-School Presbyterian pastor at Norfolk, Virginia, in answer to the book by Albert Barnes, New-School Presbyterian, on *The Church and Slavery.* He found in the Scriptures "apostolic example," "apostolic precept," and "apostolic injunction" for slavery; and declared it to be "God's appointment" for the punishment and recovery of a people when they sink so low in sin "as to become incapable of safe and righteous self-government." It is the function of the church not to intrude upon the province of the state, but to labor to secure in the slaves a "Christian life on earth and meetness for the heavenly kingdom."

THE DIVISION OF THE CHURCHES

IT was inevitable, in view of this conviction that slavery was a God-appointed institution, to be sustained as a part of what a later generation called "the white man's burden," that the southern churches should secede. The Baptists did this in 1845, organizing the Southern Baptist Convention. In the same year the Methodists withdrew from the jurisdiction of their General Conference and organized the Methodist Episcopal Church, South. Henry Clay sought to prevent this action: "Scarcely any public occurrence has happened for a long time that gave me so much real concern and pain as the menaced separation of the church by a line throwing all the free States on one side and all the slave States on the other. I will not say that such a separation would necessarily produce a dissolution of the political union of these States; but the example would be fraught with imminent danger." The Southern Presbyterians withdrew from the New School Assembly in 1858, and from the Old School after the political secession in 1861; the Southern Lutherans withdrew in 1863.

GERMAN LUTHERAN IMMIGRATION

IN the 'thirties the Great Immigration began. In the years before the Civil War, it was chiefly from the North and West of Europe, especially from Germany and Ireland. The Lutheran Church, which had just kept pace with the growth of the country, increased three times as rapidly as the general population from 1830 to 1870. German immigration was largely responsible for the conservative reaction which put an end to the "American Lutheranism" advocated by Dr. Samuel S. Schmucker, hitherto leader of the General Synod. A group from Saxony, which settled in and about St. Louis in 1839, became, under the leadership of Carl F. W. Walther, 1811–87, the nucleus for the religious organization of the German immigrants in the Mississippi valley.

PRESBYTERIAN CHURCH SOUTH.

Concluding Proceedings—A Midnight Session.

A Southern Presbyterian Church to be Organized.

Special Correspondence of the N. Y. Daily Times.

RICHMOND, VA., Tuesday, Sept. 1, 1857.

The Presbyterian Convention, which has been in session since Thursday last, has this moment adjourned—so nearly at the hour of midnight that your correspondent hardly knows whether to say "Sept. 1," or "Sept. 2." The meeting of this evening was not prolonged by reason of any excitement of debate, but from a general desire to conclude the business without taxing the Convention with another day's time. The meeting was well attended even to the close; and the results of the five days' deliberations, as embodied in the final resolution, seems to be generally satisfactory to the house.

The final action of the Convention, taken a few moments ago, is as was predicted by your correspondent in a former letter. A *New Southern Church is to be organized.* The object for which the Convention was originally called was to recommend this plan to the Presbyteries and Churches; and this object has now been carried out, in the adoption of a series of resolutions, which, after expressing the views of this Convention on the subject of slavery, appoint another Convention to be held at Knoxville, Tenn., on the first Thursday of April next, for the purpose of organizing a General Synod, under the name of "The United Synod of the Presbyterian Church of the United States of America." Thus, the late secession from the New-School General Assembly, has become a permanent schism. There is but little expectation or desire, that the two disagreeing bodies, now separated, will ever again be united; at least, so long as the question on which they split continues to agitate the Church and the State.

FOURTH DAY'S PROCEEDINGS.

Dr. BOYD, the Chairman of the Committee on Business, and the drafter of the resolutions which, after some amendments, were finally passed, made an able speech in defence of his report. His ground was one of strong opposition to a union with the Old School General Assembly. His remarks took the same ...

377 From the *New York Times,*
September 5, 1857

378 Carl F. W. Walther, courtesy of the
Lutheran Historical Society, Gettysburg, Pa.

379　　　　　　　　*Concordia Seminary*, St. Louis, Mo.

THE MISSOURI LUTHERANS

WALTHER succeeded in doing what Muhlenberg had not tried to do — in maintaining the German language and requiring strict adherence not only to the Augsburg Confession but to the whole body of symbolical books associated with it as "the pure and uncorrupted explanation and statement of the Divine Word." He founded a weekly, *Der Lutheraner*, and a monthly, *Lehre und Wehre*, for the dissemination of the "pure doctrine." He urged all congregations to maintain parochial schools for the education of their children. He established a seminary for the training of ministers, which now sends out as large a number of graduates each year as any other Protestant seminary in America. Until the formation of the United Lutheran Church in 1918, the Missouri Synod was the largest and most vigorous body of Lutherans in this country.

380　　　　　　　St. Olaf Choir, St. Olaf College, Northfield, Minn.

NORWEGIANS IN THE NORTHWEST PRAIRIES

IMMIGRATION from the Scandinavian countries was attracted to the fertile prairies of the northern Mississippi valley; and in the 'eighties this constituted one of the largest, as it was one of the most desirable, elements in the influx of population. Discontent with the state churches of their native land is assigned as the reason why many of them — perhaps two thirds — did not ally themselves with the Lutheran Church here; yet they have made this the largest Protestant denomination in Minnesota, Wisconsin and the Dakotas. The Norwegians first came in the 'thirties and organized a Synod in 1853. Other bodies were organized later, and divisions took place; but they celebrated the four hundredth anniversary of the Protestant Reformation in 1917 by unification into the Norwegian Lutheran Church of America. The choir of their largest college, St. Olaf, is famous for its *a capella* singing.

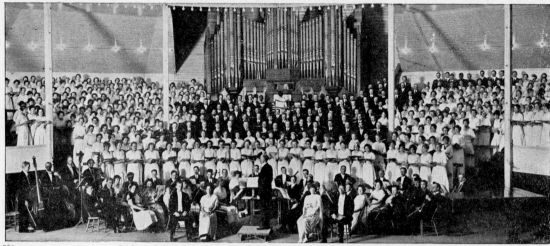

381   Bethany College Oratorio Society, Lindsborg, Kansas, courtesy of President Pihlblad

THE SWEDISH AUGUSTANA SYNOD

The Swedes began to come in the 'forties, and owe their early churches to the indefatigable labors of Lars P. Esbjorn, 1808–70, who enlisted, for his pioneer work in Illinois, the support of the American Home Missionary Society as well as of the Lutheran churches in the eastern states. The Augustana Synod was organized in 1860, and Augustana College, now at Rock Island, Illinois, was founded in that same year. The annual music festival at Bethany College, Lindsborg, Kansas, culminating in the rendition of Handel's *Messiah*, is characteristic of the genius of this music-loving people.

HAS THE CATHOLIC IMMIGRANT KEPT THE FAITH?

Much greater than the Lutheran, has been the Catholic immigration, which came from both Germany and Ireland in the early years, and latterly has been swelled by tremendous numbers from the South and East of Europe. It has been a common supposition, traceable to a hasty and inaccurate computation made by Bishop John England, that the Catholic Church in this country has suffered great losses through failing to hold the immigrant. Recent studies show the falsity of this idea. The fact is that the immigrant has kept the faith. The Catholic Church has grown from about thirty thousand in 1789, to about twenty million now, an increase from approximately one per cent to almost twenty per cent of the population of the United States. The study by a Catholic historian, upon which the following graph (No. 382) is based, computes that eighty-five per cent of the present Catholic population is due to immigration since 1820.

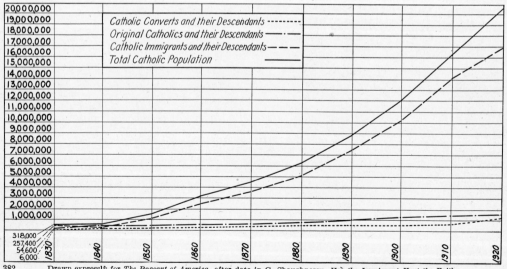

382   Drawn expressly for *The Pageant of America*, after data in G. Shaughnessy, *Has the Immigrant Kept the Faith,*
The MacMillan Company, New York, 1925

THE NATIVE AMERICAN PARTY

THE growing strength of the Catholic Church awakened apprehensions in the minds of some. The Native American party began in 1837 as a crusade against unlimited immigration and lax naturalization laws; it demanded that twenty-one years of residence be made a condition of admission to citizenship. Soon it became frankly anti-Catholic. Its national platform in 1855 contained a plank advocating: "Resistance to the aggressive policy and corrupting tendencies of the Roman Catholic Church in our country by the advancement to all political stations . . . of those only who do not hold civil allegiance, directly or indirectly, to any foreign power, whether civil or ecclesiastical." In May and July, 1844, there were anti-Catholic riots in Philadelphia, in which some of the rioters were killed, and some Catholic churches and residences burned.

BISHOP HUGHES FORESTALLS RIOTS IN NEW YORK

NEW YORK had a Catholic bishop, John Hughes, who did not hesitate to make warlike preparations to meet the exigency. "He caused each church in the city to be occupied," says his biographer, "by an armed force of one or two thousand men, resolved, after taking as many lives as they could in defense of their property, to give up, if necessary, their own lives for the same cause." — J. R. G. HASSARD, *Life of the Most Reverend John Hughes*, p. 276. His bold stand, and the decisive measures taken by the Mayor of the city, caused the sponsors of a demonstration planned in the interest of the Native American party to revoke it, and the anticipated riots did not take place.

"New York escaped a terrible danger, for a large Irish society, with divisions throughout the city, had resolved that in case a single church was attacked, buildings should be fired in all quarters and the great city should be involved in a general conflagration." — T. O'GORMAN, *History of the Roman Catholic Church in the United States*, p. 375. In the summer of 1854 anti-Catholic sentiment in New England broke into open violence. Some churches in Massachusetts and New Hampshire were destroyed and a member of the Jesuit order was tarred and feathered at Ellsworth, Maine. As a result of widely circulated sensational charges the Massachusetts Legislature ordered an investigation of convents. The Civil War brought the excitement to an end.

"YOUNG SAM"

OR,

NATIVE AMERICANS' OWN BOOK!

CONTAINING THE

PRINCIPLES AND PLATFORM

ON WHICH

THE ORDER STANDS;

ACCOMPANIED BY

AN ARRAY OF SOME OF THE MOST THRILLING FACTS EVER PUBLISHED.

Shall Foreign Influence Rule? Never!!!

BY A NATIVE AMERICAN

NEW YORK:
AMERICAN FAMILY PUBLICATION ESTABLISHMENT,
128 NASSAU STREET.
1855

383 Title-page of the original in the New York Public Library

384   From the *New York Freeman's Journal*, May 11, 1844, in the New York Historical Society

JOHN HUGHES, 1797–1864, ARCHBISHOP OF NEW YORK

ARCHBISHOP HUGHES was himself an immigrant. Coming to America when a young man of twenty, to escape the penal laws which oppressed Catholics in Ireland, he worked as a day laborer in Pennsylvania, and gained admission to Mount St. Mary's College, to prepare for the priesthood, only by accepting employment as college gardener. He became an incisive and aggressive defender of the doctrines and institutions of his Church in public debate and in the public press. At the suggestion of President Lincoln, Secretary Seward requested him to undertake a special mission to Europe in 1861–62. He traveled for almost a year in France, Italy and Ireland, seeking to counteract the efforts of the Confederacy to win European support. After his return, he advocated conscription to recruit the Union Army; and he used his influence to help quell the Anti-draft Riots of July, 1863. "He had the faith, the valour, the irrepressibility, and the piety of the old Irish race."

385 From the original portrait by George Peter Alexander Healy (1813–94), in the Cardinal's Residence, New York

ST. PATRICK'S CATHEDRAL, NEW YORK

IN the twenty-five years of his service as bishop and archbishop of New York, Dr. Hughes organized and built more than one hundred churches, and won the final victory over "trusteeism." He founded St. John's College and St. Joseph's Seminary at Fordham in 1841. He began the erection of St. Patrick's Cathedral in 1858. The work being interrupted by the financial stress incident to the Civil War, the building was not completed until twenty-one years later, when it was dedicated by his successor, Cardinal McCloskey.

WILLIAM MILLER, 1782–1849, PROPHESIES THE END OF THE WORLD

WILLIAM MILLER, a New England farmer and veteran of the War of 1812, in which he had been a captain, was converted from Deism in 1816, and joined a Baptist church. Assid-

386 St. Patrick's Cathedral, from *The Art Journal*, New York, 1876

uously studying the Bible, which he treated with absolute literalism, he became interested in calculations based upon figures given in the books of Daniel and Revelation, and arrived at the conclusion that the end of the world was near at hand. He began to lecture on the subject in 1831, his message being "that Christ would appear a second time in the clouds of heaven some time between 1843 and 1844; that He would then raise the righteous dead and judge them together with the righteous living, who would be caught up to meet Him in the air; that He would purify the earth by fire causing the wicked and all their works to be consumed in the general conflagration, and would shut up their souls in the place prepared for the Devil and his angels; that the saints would live and reign with Christ on the new earth a thousand years; that then Satan and the wicked dead would be raised, this being the second resurrection, and being judged, would make war upon the saints, be defeated and cast down to hell forever."

387 William Miller, from a lithograph by B. W. Thayer after the painting by W. M. Prior in Joshua V. Hines, *Views of the Prophecies and Prophetic Chronology, Selected from Manuscripts of William Miller*, Boston, 1841

MILLER'S CONVERTS DISILLUSIONED

Two unusual occurrences aided Miller to make converts to his belief. On the evening of November 13, 1833, a meteoric shower was witnessed in all parts of the United States, which, Professor Olmsted, of Yale College, described as "probably the greatest display of celestial fireworks that has ever been seen within the annals covered by the pages of history." This terrified many beholders, who thought it portended the ending of the starry universe. One said that he kept his eye upon the morning star, feeling that if that fell, he would give up all hope. In March and April, 1843, a great comet appeared, so bright as to be

388   End of the World, Oct. 22, 1844, from a broadside in the New York Public Library

visible even at mid-day. It was regarded by many as the beginning of the judgment Miller predicted. But the date passed without the coming of the Lord; then he chose another day, and that passed; another finally, but still the hopes and fears of the credulous were disappointed. Most of his converts, who had numbered perhaps fifty thousand, fell away. The movement survives in various bodies of Adventists; but few of them attempt any longer to predict the date of the Second Coming of Christ.

389   Father Miller's Tent and Camp Ground at Newark, N. J., from a sketch
in the *New York Herald*, Nov. 14, 1842

THE SEER OF POUGHKEEPSIE

PHRENOLOGY was popular in the late 'thirties. Educators like Horace Mann, Samuel G. Howe, and Cyrus Pierce believed it to be a science and to afford a basis for the better education of the human race. George Combe, the Scotch phrenologist, who visited America in 1838–40, lectured to eager audiences, and Mann became his life-long friend. With phrenology was associated mesmerism. Leroy Sunderland, 1802–85, a revival preacher and abolitionist, becoming interested in these fields, maintained an essentially scientific attitude, and in time emancipated himself from early extravagances and mistakes. Andrew Jackson Davis, 1826–1910, on the contrary, who loved to be known as the "Poughkeepsie Seer," became a professional clairvoyant.

390   Andrew Jackson Davis, from an engraving by Samuel Sartain (1830–1906), after an ambrotype by I. Rehn in Emma Hardinge, *Modern American Spiritualism*, New York, 1869

X —12

No. 1.	No. 2.	No. 3.	No. 4.
The Ordinary State.	**The Psychological State.**	**The Somnambulic State.**	**The Superior Condition.**
SEPARATE PERSONAL SPHERES.	PARTIAL BLENDING OF SPHERES.	COMPLETE BLENDING OF SPHERES.	MENTAL SPHERES SEPARATED.
The above represents the operator and subject beginning the magnetic process.	The above condition is favorable to sympathetic and transitional phenomena.	The above state brings out excursional, examining, and medical clairvoyance.	The above state leads to independent clairvoyance and intuitional wisdom.

391   From Andrew Jackson Davis, *The Magic Staff, An Autobiography*, New York, 1858

DAVIS SETS UP BUSINESS AS A HEALER

DAVIS set up business as a healer; then began, while in a trance, to receive messages from the spirit world, which he dictated to a scribe. For sheer amount, his messages from what he called "Summer Land" doubtless surpass those received by any other individual, for they fill more than thirty volumes. Ponderous and encyclopedic, too, they claim to present a general philosophy of the universe and of life. An enthusiastic devotee of spiritualism, writing in 1869, called Davis' work the "John Baptist which inaugurated that sunlit day when faith became knowledge, hope of immortality a glorious realization, and the dark, spectral shadow of death became transfigured into the radiant form of a ministering spirit, in the bright illuminating beams of modern Spiritualism."

THE FOX SISTERS

MODERN spiritualism, in the sense meant by this writer, a religion based upon the belief in communication through certain mediums with the spirits of those who have departed from the present life, began in a small house in Hydesville, Wayne County, New York, on March 31, 1848. Its occupants, a farmer named Fox, his wife, and their daughters Margaretta fifteen and Kate twelve, had been disturbed by rapping noises, and on that night discovered that the raps were directed by an intelligence willing to answer questions. The Fox sisters traveled to New York and other large cities to give demonstrations of their powers; and Horace Greeley, in August, 1850, professed himself to be satisfied that they did not themselves produce the raps. Later a committee of physicians claimed to have proved that the raps were caused by the girls "cracking the joints" of the knees or toes. Kate is said to have confessed this to be true in 1851; and both sisters confessed it in 1888. Physicians' reports and girls' con-

392   The Fox Sisters, The Original Spirit Rappers, from *Ballou's Pictorial*, June 14, 1856

fessions were of no avail, however. Spiritualism was started. Rapping, table-tiltings, automatic writing, and other phenomena occurred over too wide an area, and to too many people, to be accounted for by fraud. In 1855, a writer in the *North American Review* refused to dispute the claim of the New England Spiritualists Association that there were nearly two million believers in Spiritualism in this country. In Baltimore in 1852, a speaker in discussing problems of Christianity was reported to have estimated that Spiritualism had claimed eleven million adherents — one third of the population of the country! These were wild guesses.

393   The House at Hydesville, from Leah Underhill, *The Missing Link in Modern Spiritualism*, New York, 1885

THE RISE OF SPIRITUALISM

A. J. Davis, in 1873, claimed two million adherents, but admitted that there were in the United States but one hundred and fifty public mediums and one hundred lecturers on Spiritualism. Figures for 1926 credit the Spiritualistic bodies with a membership of one hundred and twenty-six thousand. As a religion, Spiritualism has nothing distinctive except the belief in communication with the spirits of deceased men and women. No spirit messages have yet brought any information concerning life beyond death which is really new or different from the possible products of lively mundane imaginations. Charles Beecher, 1815–82, in 1853 judged spiritualism to be non-Christian because it rejected the authority of the Bible, denied the reality of sin, and issued in a sort of "polytheistic

394   A Spiritual Seance — a materialization at the residence of Mr. H. Eddy, Chittenden, Vt., from a drawing by Kappes in the *Daily Graphic*, Aug. 29, 1874

pantheism, disguising under the name of spirit a subtle but genuine materialism." Henry James the elder, 1811–82, himself a Swedenborgian clergyman, wrote "On the whole I am inclined to regard the so-called spirits rather as so many vermin revealing themselves in the tumble-down walls of our old theological hostelry, than as any very saintly or sweet persons, whose acquaintance it were edifying or even comfortable to make."

THE PROGRESS OF PSYCHICAL RESEARCH

It is as a field of scientific investigation, rather than as a religion, that Spiritualism challenges attention to-day. Its phenomena are closely related to those of physics on the one hand, and of psychology on the other, particularly to those involved in the various forms of suggestion, dissociation and secondary personality, as well as in what is called telepathy. The Society for Psychical Research, founded in England in 1882, with an American branch organized in 1884, has made real progress in the scientific study of this baffling field; but no proof of communication with the spirits of the deceased has yet been found which commands general assent. The first American scientist to undertake an experimental investigation of spiritistic phenomena was Dr. Robert Hare, 1781–1858, Emeritus Professor of Chemistry in the University of Pennsylvania. He was seventy-two years old, however, when he began the study in 1853, and he became convinced of the truth of Spiritualism so quickly, and exhibited such

395   Robert Hare, from an engraving in Emma Hardinge, *Modern American Spiritualism*, New York, 1869

trustful credulity, that he failed to convince any of his scientific colleagues. The Seybert Commission, appointed in 1884 by the same University, reported in 1887 the unmasking of a great deal of fraud, and complete failure to discover any positive evidence of the truth of the spiritualistic hypothesis. The World War, bringing the people of the western world face to face with loss of life on an unprecedented scale, caused for a time an increase in popular interest in the claims of Spiritualism. This interest was sufficient to cause commissions of qualified scientists again to investigate the reported psychical phenomena. None of these commissions has yet agreed that the members of the spiritualistic cult have established a scientific basis for their claims.

396 Apparatus for detecting trickery on the part of the Medium, from Emma Hardinge, *Modern American Spiritualism*, New York, 1869

397 Charles G. Finney, courtesy of Oberlin College, Oberlin, Ohio

CHARLES G. FINNEY, 1792–1875, REVIVALIST

THE most effective revivalist of the period before the Civil War was Charles G. Finney. His own study of the Bible, while a young lawyer, led him to experience a remarkable conversion; and, at the age of thirty-two, he was licensed to preach. Beginning in the smaller towns of Western New York, he gave for some years the whole, and later a part, of his time to the conducting of revival meetings. He became the first pastor of Broadway Tabernacle in New York, and the first professor of theology in Oberlin College, later its president. Twice he conducted extensive revivals in England and Scotland. His *Lectures on Revivals of Religion*, published in 1834, passed through many editions and was translated into several languages. One of two rival houses which published it in England reported a sale of eighty thousand copies previous to 1850.

THE FIRST YOUNG MEN'S CHRISTIAN ASSOCIATION

398 Sir George Williams, 1821–1905, from the original portrait by the Hon. John Collier, in the London Central Young Men's Christian Association, London, England

THE reading of Finney's *Lectures* helped to inspire a little group of drapers' employees in London, headed by George Williams, who on June 6, 1844, organized the first Young Men's Christian Association. Its object was stated to be "the improvement of the spiritual condition of young men engaged in the drapery and other trades." This purpose was soon widened to include young men generally, and to recognize the fact that spiritual improvement involves provision for mental, social and physical development as well. Rooms were secured "to present some counter-attraction to the places of social and convivial resort." Employers and public became interested in the movement; and it was one of the chief factors in shortening the hours of labor for young men in commercial houses. By 1851, there were eight such societies in London, and sixteen elsewhere in Great Britain.

THE BEGINNINGS OF THE Y.M.C.A. IN THE UNITED STATES

IN December, 1851, led by Thomas V. Sullivan, a converted sea captain, thirty-two young men, representing twenty churches of Boston, organized the first Young Men's Christian Association in the United States. Like the

399 Young Men's Christian Association Building, Boston, reproduced by courtesy of the Association

Associations in England, it admitted to associate membership any young man "of good moral character"; but unlike their requirement that active members "give evidence of conversion," no test was required of active members except that they be "members in regular standing of an evangelical church." Thus was begun the intimate connection with the churches which has been an outstanding characteristic of the Y.M.C.A. movement in this country, and one of the sources of its strength. Before the opening of the Civil War two hundred Associations had been organized. The first International Convention of Young Men's Christian Associations was held in Buffalo in 1854.

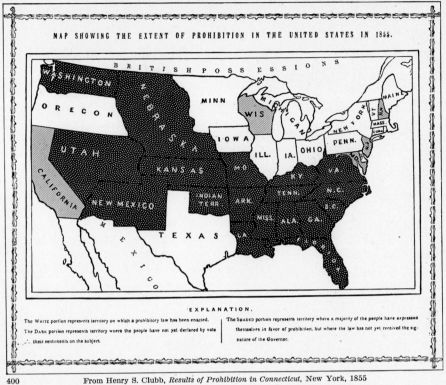

MAP SHOWING THE EXTENT OF PROHIBITION IN THE UNITED STATES IN 1855.

EXPLANATION.

The WHITE portion represents territory on which a prohibitory law has been enacted. The DARK portion represents territory where the people have not yet declared by vote their sentiments on the subject.

The SHADED portion represents territory where a majority of the people have expressed themselves in favor of prohibition, but where the law has not yet received the signature of the Governor.

400   From Henry S. Clubb, *Results of Prohibition in Connecticut*, New York, 1855

THE PROHIBITION OF THE LIQUOR TRAFFIC

In 1851 the Legislature of Maine enacted a law prohibiting the manufacture, sale and keeping for sale of intoxicating liquors. Twelve states, in the next four years, followed Maine's example; and in other states license laws were repealed and anti-saloon legislation enacted. This movement toward the prohibition of the liquor traffic was the result of a growing tide of temperance sentiment which began to rise soon after the Revolution, and gathered strength in the 'thirties and 'forties.

DR. BENJAMIN RUSH, 1745–1813, DESCRIBES THE EFFECTS OF ARDENT SPIRITS

The beginnings of intelligent and effective public opinion in favor of temperance are to be credited to Dr. Benjamin Rush, of Philadelphia, who in 1785 published *An Inquiry into the Effects of Ardent Spirits on the Human Body and Mind*. Dr. Rush was one of the signers of the Declaration of Independence, a member of the Constitutional Convention of 1787, and a man foremost in public service. Among American physicians he occupied a position of undisputed preëminence, and was Professor of the Theory and Practice of Medicine in the University of Pennsylvania. His essay describing the physical and mental effects of the use of distilled liquors was frequently republished and widely distributed. He asserted that these liquors, "where used habitually, moderately, or in excessive quantities, always diminish the strength of the body, and render man more susceptible of disease, and unfit for any service in which vigor or activity is required." Less scientific than the essay, but useful in stirring public discussion was the *Moral Thermometer* devised by Dr. Rush, which is here reproduced.

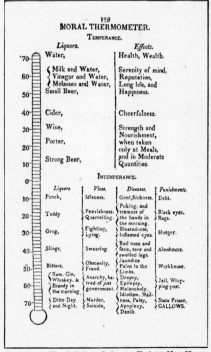

128
MORAL THERMOMETER.
TEMPERANCE.

Liquors.	Effects.
'70 Water,	Health, Wealth.
60 Milk and Water, Vinegar and Water, Molasses and Water, Small Beer,	Serenity of mind, Reputation, Long life, and Happiness.
50	
40 Cider,	Cheerfulness.
30 Wine,	Strength and Nourishment,
20 Porter,	when taken only at Meals, and in Moderate
10 Strong Beer,	Quantities.

INTEMPERANCE.

Liquors.	Vices.	Diseases.	Punishments.
10 Punch,	Idleness.	Gout, Sickness.	Debt.
20 Toddy	Peevishness, Quarrelling.	Puking, and tremors of the hands in the morning.	Black eyes, Rags.
30 Grog,	Fighting, Lying.	Bloatedness, Inflamed eyes.	Hunger.
40 Slings,	Swearing.	Red nose and face, sore and swelled legs.	Almshouse.
50 Bitters,	Obscenity, Fraud.	Jaundice Pains in the Limbs,	Workhouse.
60 Rum, Gin, Whiskey, & Brandy in the morning.	Anarchy, hatred of just government.	Dropsy, Epilepsy, Melancholy.	Jail, Whipping-post.
70 Ditto Day and Night.	Murder, Suicide,	Idiotism. Madness, Palsy, Apoplexy, Death.	State Prison, GALLOWS.

401   From *The Religious Informer*, Enfield, New Hampshire, August, 1825, in the John Carter Brown Library, Providence

The DRUNKARD'S PROGRESS,

(OR THE DIRECT ROAD TO POVERTY, WRETCHEDNESS & RUIN.)

The MORNING DRAM.   The CONFIRMED DRUNKARD.   CONCLUDING SCENE

402   From the broadside *The Drunkard's Progress*, 1826, designed and published by
J. W. Barber (1798–1885), in the New York Historical Society

THE CHURCHES ESPOUSE THE CAUSE OF TEMPERANCE

IN 1808 Dr. Rush's essay fell into the hands of a young Congregational minister, Lyman Beecher, then in his first pastorate at East Hampton, Long Island. He was so profoundly impressed by it that he preached a sermon on temperance and "blocked out" a fuller discussion which eventually took the form of his famous six sermons "on the Nature, Occasion, Signs, Evils, and Remedy of Intemperance," first preached at Litchfield, Connecticut, in 1825, published in Boston in 1826, many times reprinted, translated into several languages, and circulated throughout Christendom. In 1811 Dr. Rush presented one thousand copies of his essay to the General Assembly of the Presbyterian Church, and urged it to take action to check the prevailing intemperance. A committee presented a comprehensive report in the following year, the adoption of which placed the Assembly unequivocally on record as favoring the temperance movement. The Methodist General Conference and the Congregational Associations of Massachusetts and Connecticut took similar action — in the latter case only after Lyman Beecher moved that a hesitant committee be discharged and another appointed, of which he was himself made chairman. The first temperance society was organized in the town of Moreau, Saratoga County, New York. With the endorsement of the churches the organization of local temperance societies proceeded rapidly, and in 1826 the American Temperance Society was organized at Boston. College presidents, as well as ministers, were prominent in the more aggressive campaign for temperance thereby instituted. Among them were Francis Wayland, of Brown; Eliphalet Nott, of Union; Heman Humphrey, of Amherst; Wilbur Fisk, of Wesleyan; Mark Hopkins, of Williams; Jesse Appleton, of Bowdoin; Nathan Lord, of Dartmouth; and Jeremiah Day, of Yale.

DEACON GILES' DISTILLERY

GEORGE B. CHEEVER, classmate at Bowdoin of Longfellow and Hawthorne, was minister at Salem, where his soul was moved with indignation at the business done by four distilleries. One of these was owned by a deacon in one of the churches, who was also treasurer of a Bible Society and kept Bibles for sale in one corner of his distillery. One night Cheever had a dream "which was not all a dream." It was published in the Salem *Landmark*, in February, 1825. It was about one Deacon Giles, who owned a distillery where he sold Bibles as well as liquor, and unwittingly hired as workmen a crew of demons who played a trick on him.

They wrote inscriptions upon the casks, which remained invisible until liquor was drawn from them for sale, then blazed out in letters of red fire: "Insanity and Murder. Inquire at Deacon Giles' Distillery." "Delirium Tremens. Inquire at Deacon Giles' Distillery." "Distilled Death and Liquid Damnation." "The Elixir of Hell." The real deacon recognized himself at once, and brought suit for libel. Mr. Cheever was fined and imprisoned for thirty days; but his "Dream" spread over the country like wildfire.

403   From George Barrell Cheever, *The Dream or The True History of Deacon Giles's
Distillery and Deacon Jones's Brewery*, New York and Boston, 1830

THE PRINCIPLE OF TOTAL ABSTINENCE

THE early temperance movement was directed against the use of "ardent spirits," as distilled liquors were then called. Here are reproduced a panegyric, published in 1788, "in honour of American Beer and Cyder," which extols these beverages as "Federal liquors" and in contrast brands "Spirituous Liquors" as "Anti-federal" and vicious; and an elaborately engrossed certificate, signed in October, 1834, by the President of the United States and the two surviving ex-Presidents, urging abstinence from ardent spirits. Distilleries decreased from eleven hundred and forty-nine in 1829 to three hundred and thirty-seven in 1835. But breweries multiplied, cider drinking became more general, and the importation of wines almost doubled from 1826 to 1836. "It was soon discovered," said the President of the Congressional Total Abstinence Society at a meeting held in the Hall of the House of Representatives in 1842, "that the exclusion of ardent spirits, whilst all the lighter intoxicating drinks were freely indulged in, did not extinguish the fire which was burning through the land. Multitudes of intemperate men, who pledged themselves to abstain from ardent spirits, and who believed they had re-established their self-control, were turned back to ruin by the use of wine and other fermented liquors." In 1836 a number of societies were merged into the American Temperance Union, which adopted the principle of total abstinence from all intoxicating liquors.

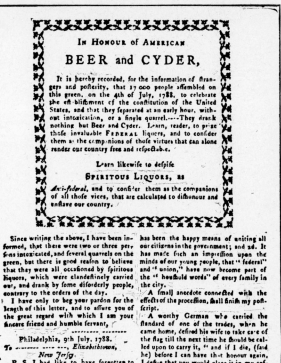

404   From the *American Museum*, Philadelphia, July 1788

405   From the original certificate, in the possession of Victor H. Paltsits, New York

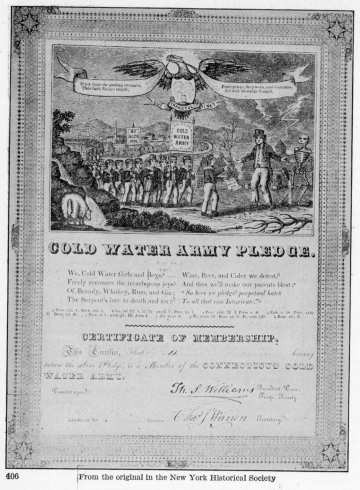

COLD WATER ARMY PLEDGE.

We, Cold Water Girls and Boys,
Freely renounce the treacherous joys
Of Brandy, Whiskey, Rum, and Gin;
The Serpent's lure to death and sin;

Wine, Beer, and Cider we detest,
And thus we'll make our parents blest;
"So here we pledge perpetual hate
To all that can Intoxicate."

CERTIFICATE OF MEMBERSHIP.

This Certifies, That _____ having taken the above Pledge, is a Member of the CONNECTICUT COLD WATER ARMY.

(Countersigned)

Th. S. Williams, President Conn. Temp. Society.

Leader of the _____ Division.

Cha's J. Warren, Secretary.

406   From the original in the New York Historical Society

"THE COLD WATER ARMY"

THE total abstinence pledge was often called "The Cold Water Pledge," and the name "Cold Water Army" was applied to temperance societies of children which were organized in large numbers in the 'thirties and 'forties. These societies usually held celebrations, with songs and exercises by the children, addresses by older persons, and parades, on Washington's Birthday and the Fourth of July. The movement centered too exclusively upon these celebrations and upon inducing children to sign the pledge, without teaching them enough about the principles of temperance. In time it gave place, therefore, to other organizations for children whose plans were more definitely educational, such as the Junior Templars, Bands of Hope, Cadets of Temperance, and Loyal Temperance Legion. Meanwhile was preparing one of the most dramatic phases of the temperance movement of the first half of the nineteenth century. Most reformers had ignored the drunkard on the theory that he was incapable of regeneration. He was now about to play his part in the crusade.

THE WASHINGTONIANS

ON one evening in April, 1840, when a temperance lecturer spoke in one of the churches of Baltimore, a club of half a dozen hard drinkers, gathered as was their nightly custom at Chase's Tavern, sent two of their number to hear him. When they returned with a favorable report, the tavern keeper broke into a tirade of abuse, denouncing all advocates of temperance as hypocrites and fools. "It is to your interest to cry them down," retorted one of the topers; and a hot discussion ensued, which resulted in the six men forming themselves into a club which they called The Washingtonian Total Abstinence Society, and adopting a pledge requiring total abstinence from the use of all intoxicating liquors. They promised to meet the next night, and each to bring in a new recruit. The movement spread with contagious enthusiasm. Washingtonian Societies were organized throughout the country, and over six hundred thousand drunkards are said to have professed reformation. The movement proved that more than enthusiasm or even determination is needed, however, for it spent its force by 1843, and the majority of the "reformed" drunkards went back to their cups. The most effective leaders which it won for the cause of temperance were John H. W. Hawkins, 1797–1858, and John B. Gough, 1817–86, both reclaimed drunkards who became powerful and convincing public speakers.

407   John B. Gough, from a carte de visite by Warren, Boston

408   Abraham Lincoln, 1809–65, from the earliest known portrait, about 1846,
in Frank E. Stevens, *The Black Hawk War*, 1903

ABRAHAM LINCOLN ADVOCATES TOTAL ABSTINENCE

At the invitation of the Washingtonian Society of Springfield, Illinois, Abraham Lincoln delivered an address on Washington's Birthday, 1842, in the course of which he said: "Whether or not the world would be vastly benefited by a total and final banishment from it of all intoxicating drinks, seems to me not now an open question. Three-fourths of mankind confess the affirmative with their tongues; and, I believe, all the rest acknowledge it in their hearts. . . . If the relative grandeur of revolutions shall be estimated by the great amount of human misery they alleviate and the small amount they inflict, then, indeed, will this be the grandest the world shall ever have seen. Of our political revolution of '76, we all are justly proud. It has given us a degree of political freedom, far exceeding that of any other of the nations of the earth. In it the world has found a solution of that long mooted problem, as to the capability of man to govern himself. In it was the germ which has vegetated, and still is to grow and expand into the universal liberty of mankind. . . . Turn now to the temperance revolution, in *it*, we shall find a stronger bondage broken; a viler slavery manumitted; a greater tyrant deposed. . . . And what a noble ally this, to the cause of political freedom. With such an aid, its march cannot fail to be on and on, till every son of earth shall drink in rich fruition, the sorrow quenching draughts of perfect liberty. Happy day, when, all appetites controlled, all passions subdued, all matters subjected, *mind*, all conquering *mind*, shall live and move the monarch of the world. . . . And when the victory shall be complete, when there shall be neither a slave nor a drunkard on earth, how proud the title of that *Land*, which may truly claim to be the birthplace and the cradle of both those revolutions that shall have ended in that victory! How nobly distinguished that People, who shall have planted, and nurtured to maturity both the political and moral freedom of their species." In 1855 Lincoln drafted a law prohibiting the liquor traffic which was passed by both houses of the Illinois Legislature, but was rejected by a referendum vote. Lincoln campaigned in its behalf, and the law was defeated largely because Stephen A. Douglas, his constant, and as yet successful political rival, called upon the people to "bury Maine-Lawism and Abolitionism in the same grave."

FRATERNAL TEMPERANCE ORDERS

One of the results of the Washingtonian movement was the institution of fraternal temperance orders. The Order of the Sons of Temperance was founded in New York on September 29, 1842. Its objects were declared to be: "To shield its members from the evils of intemperance; to afford mutual assistance in case of sickness; and to elevate their characters as men." The Independent Order of Rechabites, a British organization, established a "tent" in Boston a few months earlier. The Independent Order of Good Templars originated in Oneida County, New York, in 1851. Without the beneficiary features of other societies, it became the largest of the fraternal temperance orders. Other organizations are The Daughters of Temperance, the Templars of Honor and Temperance, the Independent Order of Good Samaritans, and the United Friends of Temperance. The picture shows General Samuel F. Cary, 1814–1900, in his regalia as Most Worthy Patriarch of the Sons of Temperance.

409 Samuel F. Cary, from an engraving by T. Doney after the daguerreotype by Root

THE VISIT OF FATHER MATHEW

On July 2, 1849, an Irish priest who was accorded a formal public welcome by the authorities of New York city, and an ovation by its populace, landed at Castle Garden. He was Father Theobald Mathew, 1790–1856, of Cork, the apostle of temperance who waged a campaign so remarkable that over two million of his countrymen had been brought, through him, to sign the pledge of total abstinence. He was accorded similar welcomes in the other great cities of the Union. Remaining in America for two years, he visited twenty-five states and administered the pledge to some six hundred thousand persons, most of whom, of his own faith and race, were being reached by no other agencies. His work was followed later by the devoted labor of parish priests and Jesuit and Paulist missioners; and in 1872, a national organization, the Catholic Total Abstinence Union, was formed.

410 Father Theobald Mathew, from a photograph by Landy, Cincinnati

NEAL DOW, 1804–1897, AND THE MAINE LAW

The father of the Maine Law was Neal Dow, a Portland business man of Quaker upbringing. He secured a position for a friend, a college graduate whom liquor had brought low, with the understanding that his tenure of the job depended upon his keeping strictly sober. Dow asked the neighboring saloon keeper, under

the circumstances, not to sell liquor to his friend, but was met with a brusque refusal. "My business is to sell liquor; I have paid my money for this privilege. That money helps to pay your taxes, and it is small business for a man to come around here trying to prevent me from doing what business I can, and have a right to under the law. If this man comes in here in a sober condition and asks for liquor, I have a right to sell it to him, and shall do so. And I don't want you to come around whining about it, either." Dow, indignant, decided that the license system makes the state in fact a partner in the liquor business, and he determined not to rest until the law should prohibit rather than protect the liquor traffic. In 1846, after years of persistent campaigning, he secured the passage of the first state prohibitory law, and in 1851, the enactment of the more effective measure which came to be known as the Maine Law. The passage of the Maine Law was a heavy blow to a considerable element in the ranks of the temperance reformers who considered that the appeal to legislation was an admission of defeat and who were opposed to the putting of the great moral crusade into politics.

411 Neal Dow, courtesy of Fred N. Dow, Portland, Me.

THE WOMEN'S TEMPERANCE PETITION

FROM *The Illustrated News* for February 12, 1853, is taken the following account of how women were received when they began to express themselves politically, even though it was by the relatively harmless method of presenting a petition: "An interesting, and we believe unprecedented scene occurred in the New York Legislature, on the 21st of January. During the period for presenting petitions, Mr. Burroughs announced that there was a delegation in the house from the Women's State Temperance Society, who asked permission to present in person the memorial of twenty-eight

412　Ladies Presenting the Great Temperance Petition at Albany, from an illustration by Dallas in *The Illustrated News*, New York, Feb. 12, 1853

thousand women for the Maine Law. He therefore moved to suspend the rules, and that they be permitted, through one of their number, to present their petition to the house. Upon this Mr. O'Keefe rather ungallantly remarked, that as the permission appeared to be a foregone conclusion, he would suggest that the imposition be submitted to as gracefully as possible, and proceeded as follows: 'Sir, as this is a most extraordinary application, so let it meet with a most extraordinary reception. When ladies are solicitous of leaving the holy sphere in which Nature and Nature's God has beneficently placed them, and when they are desirous of emulating the sterner sex in the race for fame and glory, by mingling in the world as lawyers, statesmen and generals, they should be gently taken by the hand, and encouraged in their manly, and it may be unfeminine aspirations. Let these high-minded, high-strung and spirited women — discard as worthless the antique dress of the Elizabethan age, and glory in the more modern habiliments of jackets and pants — let them walk down the middle aisle of the chamber, and with a masculine stride, which so admirably becomes such feminine delicacy as theirs, present their petitions . . . I shall reserve my opinion upon the main subject till the proper time arrive.'"

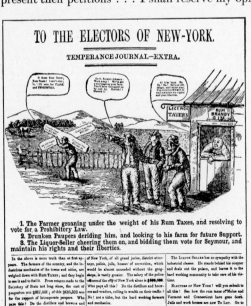

413　From the original in the New York Public Library

THE WANING OF THE PROHIBITION MOVEMENT

THIS cartoon was published during the New York campaign in 1854, when Myron H. Clark, advocate of prohibition, defeated Governor Seymour, who had vetoed a prohibitory bill passed by the Legislature. This was typical of a country-wide movement in the early 'fifties. After 1855, however, the enactment of prohibition laws ceased, and the states began to return to the license system. In 1875 but three states, Maine, Vermont and New Hampshire, retained their prohibitory legislation. Among the reasons assigned for this reversal of public policy are the emergence of the slavery issue to a place of preponderant, absorbing interest and unique urgency; the adoption by the Federal Government in 1862 of an Internal Revenue Act which entrenched the liquor business by relying upon it, in part, for financial support; the organization of the United States Brewers' Association and other bodies devoted to the perpetuation of the liquor traffic; and the disposition of well-meaning people to rest content with the securing of prohibitory legislation, and to neglect both effective measures of enforcement and the constant need for the education of public opinion.

414   A German Beer Garden in New York on Sunday Evening, from
Harper's Weekly, October 8, 1859, after a drawing by A. Fredericks

415   A Broadway Sunday Sacred Concert in New York, from *Harper's
Weekly*, October 15, 1859, after a drawing by A. Fredericks

IMMIGRATION, TEMPERANCE AND SUNDAY LAWS

IMMIGRATION has been a factor in determining the play of public opinion with respect to the sale and consumption of liquor. Just what and how great its influence has been, no one knows precisely, and opinions are largely swayed by prejudice. These cartoons reproduced above illustrated a series of articles, published in *Harper's Weekly* in 1859, entitled *Sketches of the People who Oppose our Sunday Laws*. One depicts "A Broadway Sunday sacred concert in New York"; and the other "A German beer garden in New York city on Sunday evening." At the Congress of the United States Brewers' Association in 1873, the editor of the brewers' journal, analyzing the vote in recent elections in the North and West said: "It will be seen that the foreign-born citizens and their children are strong enough in every one of those states to turn the scale in favor of either one or the other of the contending parties. In most of those states it can be done by the German vote alone. It is, therefore, for the liberal people but necessary to be united and in earnest to give the death-blow to puritanical tyranny. The future is ours! The enormous influx of immigration will in a few years overreach the puritanical element in every state in the Union." Immigration, however, was but one of many factors behind the changing customs and attitudes of the day.

THE PRAYER–MEETING REVIVAL OF 1857–1858

IN September, 1857, the North Dutch Church of New York opened a Wednesday noon prayer meeting for business men, which, after two weeks, was held daily. The interest grew and the plan spread, until twenty such informal noon meetings were being held in New York, with over one hundred additional meetings at other hours in the day; and like meetings were established in most of the larger cities and towns, attended by great numbers of people. The financial panic of that fall had doubtless something to do with the readiness of some folk to turn to God; but the movement cannot be accounted for as a mere result of business depression. It was distinguished from other notable religious awakenings by its emphasis upon prayer rather than upon preaching, by the entire absence of excitement and physical agitations, by the leadership of laymen, and by the effective service of the public press in affording it publicity. It resulted in large additions to the membership of the churches, in the promotion of interdenominational fellowship, and in the training of laymen to more energetic and responsible participation in the activities of organized religion. It has been described as "a providential preparation for the Civil War," which was soon to make tremendous demands upon the spiritual resources engendered by it.

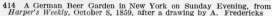

THE RELIGIOUS AWAKENING.

Origin and Progress of the Work.

THE DAILY PRAYER MEETINGS

It can hardly have escaped general observation that there is now being manifested, in this city, an unusual and increasing attention to religion. A remarkably earnest state of feeling on this subject has been developing itself for some time past among all classes of the community here—from the highest to the lowest—including those out of the church as well as those in it. Nor has this quickened interest in religion, and this increased attendance on religious meetings, been in anywise confined or peculiar to this city; for it extends in an equal and, in many instances, in a still greater degree to all parts of the country. The exchange newspapers, both religious and secular, that come to us from all quarters, speak of an unwonted revival of religious feeling in their vicinity, and in the country far and near around them. In fact, a sudden fervor seems to have seized the public mind. Everywhere men are crowding to religious meetings, and the spirit

416   From the *New York Daily Tribune*, March 1, 1858

CITY AFFAIRS.

SCENES AT JAYNE'S HALL.—A very large audience again assembled for religious exercises yesterday, at the above place. The interest of the services was, if anything, rather increased than diminished. The meeting was led by Paul T. Jones, Esq., a merchant of this city, and in a very capable and acceptable manner.

After prayer and singing, some very interesting remarks were made by Rev. Dr. Goddard. Dr. G. said: "It was my privilege, dear friends, to be with our late beloved brother in Christ, Dudley A. Tyng, during his last hours, and I am happy in being here to witness to you that his death was in keeping with his life. There are none of us here, who knew him, who could for a moment have entertained any apprehension as to his fitness for Heaven, had he been removed from us without an opportunity of testifying to the all-sufficiency of the Saviour's blood. But on his dying bed his faith was declared, and I was with him and can bear testimony to the sufficiency of God's grace to sustain the Christian in the dying hour. For him the blessed promises of Scripture were all-consoling. Never, perhaps, has a more perfect illustration been afforded of the serenity with which the Christian sinks into the embrace of Death. He was not only peaceful himself, but even endeavored to soothe and comfort those around him. He was sustained by the power of the Gospel, and was happy in the sweet assurance of the heavenly home upon whose portals his feet were just treading. It was my privilege to be then present with him. As I entered his room he smiled—that sweet, peculiar smile of his that I can see now—extended his only remaining hand, and said, 'Brother, I am so glad to see you.' He then spoke of this dispensation of God. He thought it was sent in order to instil into him new energy, to bring him closer to the cross, to make him more diligent and single in his Master's service. He said that when he recovered—for he did not expect to die—he should serve God better than he had ever done before—that he should preach as he had never yet preached. Up to within an hour of his death he did not expect his injury to terminate fatally. By his family his demise was fully expected, but he himself still believed his work unfinished. He longed still for his labor in the ministry, and to participate in scenes like this, and still believed that God would raise him up. His expectations of recovery were not abandoned until about an hour previous to his death. At that time the Doctor entered. The dying saint then said, "Doctor, my family consider my case hopeless. Is this so?" The Doctor tearfully replied, "It is even true." "It is all right," said Mr. Tyng, with a sweet smile upon his countenance; "It is all right—I have not a word to say." He then called his agonized wife to his bedside, and calmly gave to her his dying charge. His children—six little orphaned babes—were brought to his bedside and received his dying blessing. He then committed them to the care of his wife as their protector, and charged her that his sons —God helping her—should be brought up to the ministry. His next words were to his physician, a worthy man, but one not professing to be a disciple of Jesus. "My dear sir," said he, "in taking leave of you, after thanking you for your great kindness to me, let me—oh, let me counsel you to take my Savior for your friend; seek to become a follower of Jesus, and when you come to die He will be with you, as He now is with me." Then, last of all, turning to his father he said to him, "My father, stand up for Jesus!" To us, he said, "tell all my ministering brethren to stand up for Jesus; tell the Young Men's Christian Association, and tell the people everywhere to stand up for Jesus." I told his story to two young men of my congregation who were inquiring after the way of life, and it determined them to come out from the world and enroll themselves as followers of Christ. "After this beloved man had bade adieu to all, he asked us to sing "Rock of ages cleft for me," and desired his wife to join. And broken as was her heart at the afflicting dispensation, she was buoyed up by the divine Spirit, and she sung with us the beautiful hymn. As we were singing the last verse—

"When I draw this fleeting breath;
When my soul is lost in death, etc."

—the spirit of our brother sweetly passed from the clay, and the soul ascended upward to the realms of bliss. Think then, my dear friends, of the glorious

417   Account of the Death of Dudley A. Tyng, from the *North American and United States Gazette*, April 22, 1858

STAND UP, STAND UP FOR JESUS!

THE Episcopal ministers of the evangelical party joined heartily in the meetings of this Revival; and Bishop McIlvaine, of Ohio, was one of its prominent leaders. Dudley A. Tyng, the young rector of the Church of the Covenant, at Philadelphia, preached one Sunday in Jaynes Hall, the largest auditorium in the city, to an audience of five thousand men, from the text: "Go now, ye that are men and serve the Lord." On the following Wednesday he was so injured in an accident that he died a few hours later. Being asked if he had any message for his friends, he said: "Tell them to stand up for Jesus." George Duffield, pastor of one of the Presbyterian churches, wrote for a memorial service the hymn that is now sung throughout all Christendom:

Stand up, stand up for Jesus!
　Ye soldiers of the cross;
Lift high His royal banner,
　It must not suffer loss.

Ye that are men now serve Him
　Against unnumbered foes;
Let courage rise with danger,
　And strength to strength oppose.

WILLIAM A. MUHLENBERG, 1796–1879, "EVANGELICAL CATHOLIC"

THE 'forties had been years of rivalry and debate within the Protestant Episcopal Church. The Oxford Movement in England led John Henry Newman and some of his friends into the Roman Catholic Church, and increased the aggressiveness of the high-church party in this country. It was opposed by the Evangelical party, which inherited the spirit of Bishop White. The conflict culminated at the General Convention of 1853, when Bishop Ives, of North Carolina, was deposed, having submitted to the Roman Catholic Church, and a Memorial was presented by a group of ministers headed by William A. Muhlenberg. This urged that "a broader and more comprehensive ecclesiastical system," with more "freedom in opinion, discipline, and worship," was needed for the sake of larger and more effective service. Muhlenberg called

418   William A. Muhlenberg, from the original portrait by Daniel A. Huntington (1816–1906), in St. Luke's Hospital, New York city

himself an "Evangelical Catholic." He felt that "high and low parties were wasting their strength in quarrel over rubrics," and that "the best way for reconciliation was larger room for real work." The Memorialists did not secure all that they sought; but the strife was resolved. The Protestant Episcopal Church embraces in one communion men of divergent liturgical views, and is deeply interested in the ideal of Christian unity. This victory for reconciliation was a noteworthy event suggesting that the time was passing in the United States when denominations could be divided and re-divided on account of minor differences in belief or polity.

419   St. Luke's Hospital, Cathedral Heights, New York city, courtesy of
W. M. Williams, Supt.

ST. LUKE'S HOSPITAL

MUHLENBERG exercised leadership through the clarity of his prophetic vision and the measureless devotion of his life, rather than by authority of official station. His school for boys at Flushing became the model for the private secondary schools which constitute the chief contribution of the Episcopal Church to American education. He established the principle of free churches, open to all without renting of pews, in his pastorate of the Church of the Holy Communion. He developed the first order of Protestant deaconesses in this country, and founded the first church hospital, St. Luke's in New York city, to which he devoted his fortune and the personal service of the last twenty years of his life. Muhlenberg was a religious statesman of broad vision and rare ability. He greatly served his church and his generation.

METHODIST CAMP MEETINGS

THE holding of camp meetings in the summer had become an established custom of the Methodists. The pictures represent scenes at meetings held in 1858–59 on Cape Cod and at Sing Sing, New York, which were typical of those held in all parts of the country. These camp meet-

420   Meeting at Millenial Grove, Mass., August 4–10, 1858, from *Ballou's Pictorial*, Aug. 21, 1858

ings were reminiscent of the gatherings of excited souls in the frontier revivals which marked the opening of the nineteenth century. The physical exercises of the former day, however, rarely appeared.

421   Camp Meeting at Sing Sing, New York, August 1859, from *Harper's Weekly*, Sept. 10, 1859

LYMAN BEECHER, 1775–1863

No life, perhaps, touched the development of religion in the United States before the Civil War at more points than that of Lyman Beecher. Born in the year before the Declaration of Independence, he lived until after the Proclamation of Emancipation. Educated at Yale, he studied theology under President Dwight. He exemplified the Plan of Union between Congregationalists and Presbyterians, serving two churches of each order. He built up a strong evangelical church, which became a center of revivals of religion, against the tide of Unitarianism in Boston. He was the first president of Lane Theological Seminary in Cincinnati. He was prosecuted for "heresy, slander and hypocrisy," but acquitted by his Synod, in spite of its "Old School" temper. His sermon on *Duelling* (1806) roused public opinion against that evil; and his *Six Sermons on Temperance* (1825) ran through many editions and was translated into a number of languages. All of his seven sons became ministers; and his two daughters were well-known

422   Reverend Lyman Beecher, from *Harper's Weekly*, January 31, 1863

authors. The Lyman Beecher Lectures on Preaching, delivered annually at Yale University since 1871, are his perpetual memorial.

HENRY WARD BEECHER, 1813–1887

HENRY WARD BEECHER, for forty years pastor of Plymouth Church, Brooklyn, was the acknowledged leader of American preachers in his day. A vigorous, keen, versatile mind, a fertile and vivid imagination, wide interests, swift intuitions, broad human sympathies, and an instinctively dramatic power of impersonation, here lent themselves to the service of a heart aflame with the gospel of God's love. "It pleased God to reveal to my wandering soul the idea that it was His nature to love a man in his sins for the sake of helping them out of them; . . . that He was not furious with wrath toward the sinner, but pitied him — in short that He felt towards me as my mother felt towards me, to whose eyes my wrong-doing brought tears, who never pressed me so close to her as when I had done wrong, and who would fain with her yearning love lift me out of trouble. And when I found that it was Christ's nature to lift men out of weakness to strength, out of impurity to goodness, out of everything low and debasing, I felt that I had found a God."

423   Henry Ward Beecher, from a carte de visite by Sarony, New York city

BEECHER'S DEFENSE OF THE UNION

BEECHER was intensely opposed to slavery, though not an Abolitionist of the more radical sort. He sold slaves from Plymouth pulpit, on several occasions, and remitted the price to their masters. When the struggle for Kansas was at its height, he declared at a meeting held to enlist and equip a party of emigrants that a Sharpe's rifle was better than a Bible to convert a border ruffian — an epigram that caused these rifles to be known as "Beecher's Bibles." His remarkable power to appeal to the understanding and enlist the sympathy of audiences was exhibited, in the face of determined heckling, in a series of addresses in England in 1863, which helped to change public sentiment in that country toward the United States and to prevent recognition of the Confederacy by the British Government.

THE WAR CHRISTIANS!
THEIR DOCTRINES.

At a Jubilee Demonstration in NEW YORK, in January last,

REV. JOHN J. RAYMOND,

The Appointed Chaplain of the Meeting, in his Opening Prayer, said,

We thank Thee, O God, that Thou hast seen fit to raise up one, ABRAHAM, surnamed LINCOLN. . . He is a man whom God SHOULD bless, and the People delight to honour.'

UNITED STATES SENATOR LANE,

In his Address to the Great Union Meeting at Washington, said,

.I would like to live long enough to see every white man now in South Carolina in Hell.'

REV. H. WARD BEECHER,

In his Address in Glasgow, last Monday, said,

.They,' alluding to the NORTH, . rose like ONE MAN, and with a voice that reverberated throughout the whole WORLD, cried— LET FLY,' alluding to the SOUTH, 'with all its attendant horrors, GO TO HELL.'

From the 'Manchester Guardian's' Correspondence :

' Is this the same Reverend Mr. Beecher who, at a Meeting in America during the discussion of the "Trent" affair, said, "That the best blood of England must flow as an atonement for the outrage England had committed on America"'

424   From an original placard in the Long Island Historical Society, Brooklyn, N. Y.

425 First Presbyterian Church, Springfield, Illinois,
         where Lincoln rented a pew

THE FAITH OF ABRAHAM LINCOLN

ABRAHAM LINCOLN was reared in the country of the Great Revival. His parents were Predestinarian Baptists. As a young man he read Volney and Paine; but their gibes at Christianity did not shatter the fundamental faith in the providence of God, amounting almost to fatalism, which was his by temperament and early Calvinistic training. This faith grew more profound as his burdens increased and he was driven to more conscious dependence upon God in prayer. "The will of God prevails." "Being a humble instrument in the hands of our Heavenly Father, as I am, and as we all are, to work out His great purposes, I have desired that all my works and acts may be according to His will; and that it might be so, I have sought His aid." "Let us renew our trust in God and go forward without fear and with manly hearts." One of the best statements of Lincoln's religion is to be found in a proclamation dated August 12, 1861. ". . . it is fit and becoming in all people at all times to acknowledge and revere the supreme government of God, to bow in humble submission to his chastisements, to confess and deplore their sins and transgressions in the full conviction that the fear of the Lord is the beginning of wisdom, and to pray with all fervency and contrition for the pardon of their past offenses and for a blessing upon their present and prospective action. . . ."

LINCOLN AND THE CHURCHES

ONE of the most interesting documents formerly in possession of the Methodist Episcopal Church is a sheet of paper containing President Lincoln's response to an address presented to him by delegates from the General Conference of 1864. This is here reproduced and can easily be read in Lincoln's bold, plain handwriting. It concludes: "God bless the Methodist Church — bless all the churches — and blessed be God, Who, in this our great trial, giveth us the churches." Though he attended the public worship of God regularly, Lincoln never joined a church. "I have never united myself to any church, because I have found difficulty in giving my assent, without mental reservation, to the long, complicated statements of Christian doctrine which characterize their articles of belief and confessions of faith. When any church will inscribe over its altars, as its sole qualification of membership, the Saviour's condensed statement of both law and gospel, 'Thou shalt love the Lord thy God with all thy heart, and with all thy soul, and with all thy mind, and thy neighbor as thyself,' that church will I join with all my heart and all my soul." The soul of Lincoln was deeply stirred by the calamity of war. Again and again the thoughts of the harrassed President turned to religion. He welcomed the help of all religious bodies.

Gentlemen.

In response to your address, allow me to attest the accuracy of its historical statements, indorse the sentiments it expresses; and thank you, in the nation's name, for the sure promise it gives.

Nobly sustained as the government has been by all the churches, I would utter nothing which might, in the least, appear invidious against any. Yet, without this, it may fairly be said that the Methodist Episcopal Church, not less devoted than the best, is, by its greater numbers, the most important of all. It is no fault in others that the Methodist Church sends more soldiers to the field, more nurses to the hospital, and more prayers to Heaven than any. God bless the Methodist Church — bless all the churches — and blessed be God, Who, in this our great trial, giveth us the churches.

A. Lincoln

May 18. 1864.

426 From the original Lincoln letter in the Library of Congress, Washington

CHAPTER VII

THE MATURITY OF THE CHURCHES

THE organization and growth of the Young Men's Christian Associations, the Prayer-meeting Revival of 1857–58, the work of the United States Christian Commission, and the Moody and Sankey revivals, were characteristic of a new emphasis which began to be placed upon the active participation of laymen in the services and ministries of organized religion. The Sunday-School movement greatly increased in extent and influence after the adoption in 1872 of the International Uniform Sunday School Lessons. Women as well as men came into more responsible and active relation to the interests of the churches. In various quarters, moreover, new organizations of the young people of the churches began to be formed, the most widely spread of which was the Young People's Society of Christian Endeavour. Analogous movements of laymen, women, and young people, were organized among Catholics and Jews — for example, the Knights of Columbus and the Young Men's Hebrew Association.

The transformation of industry by machines and systems of mass production, the rapid growth of the cities and consequent changes in home life, the organization of "big business" and new possibilities of corruption in politics gave the churches new and difficult problems. How apply to these new conditions the eternal gospel of the Fatherhood of God and the Brotherhood of Man? Representatives of all groups, Catholic, Protestant, and Jewish, have shared in the social emphasis and interpretation given to the principles of religion under stress of the conditions of modern life. Among Christians, new phrases became current: "the social gospel," "the institutional church."

A primary interest of most of the churches has been the temperance movement, which quickly rallied in the face of the growth of the liquor traffic after the Civil War. Working chiefly through independent organizations, especially the Women's Christian Temperance Union and the Anti-saloon League, a persistent and strenuous campaign was waged in the interest of total abstinence for the individual and prohibition of the liquor traffic by the state, which issued in the adoption of a prohibitory amendment to the Constitution of the United States.

The revision of the English Bible brought to the common run of folk concrete evidence of the development of Biblical scholarship. The better resources for the understanding of the Bible which this scholarship has made available, together with the remarkable progress of science, have thrown into question certain older, more mechanical ways of conceiving divine revelation. Strife has centered particularly about the concept of organic evolution. Within some churches a party of "Fundamentalists" vigorously opposes what they term "Modernism." Outside the churches both parties find themselves confronted by a recrudescence of irreligion, largely mere passive indifference, but in a few quarters active and blatant.

In spite of these disquieting features of the religious situation, there has been a steady growth of the churches and synagogues, which now have a responsible membership, not counting dependent children, of over forty-seven million people. There has been a well-marked trend, moreover, toward coöperation between the various religious bodies, evidenced particularly within the bounds of Protestantism, but effective also in many local situations and in the interest of specific causes between Catholics, Protestants, and Jews.

427　　Field Headquarters of the United States Christian Commission, from a photograph by Gardner, Washington

THE UNITED STATES CHRISTIAN COMMISSION

THE Young Men's Christian Associations in many communities were for a time broken up by the Civil War, for practically all of their members enlisted. In 1862 it was reported that only twenty of the two hundred Associations were active and prosperous. The National Committee of the Y.M.C.A. had been responsible,

however, for the organization of the United States Christian Commission, a voluntary agency which, together with the Sanitary Commission, carried the ministrations of the folk at home to the boys at the front. Its object was stated to be to promote the "spiritual good, intellectual improvement, and social and physical comfort" of the soldiers. In the four years of its service the Commission distributed nearly three million dollars' worth of goods, and over four million library books, Bibles, hymn books and magazines. It commanded the voluntary service, for periods of six weeks or more, of four thousand eight hundred and fifty-nine men whom it commissioned as "delegates"; and it received and expended two million five hundred and thirteen thousand seven hundred and forty-one dollars. Practically all of this money represented the free-will offerings of the people, for the Commission did not encourage the use of fairs and similar expedients for raising money. "There is one association," President Lincoln said, "whose objects and motives I have never heard in any degree impugned or questioned; and that is the Christian Commission."

428　　Commission of a delegate to the United States Christian Commission, from the original in the Yale University Library

A SONG THAT LINCOLN LIKED

If you cannot on the ocean
　　Sail among the swiftest fleet, . . .

was a song that became associated with the
work of the Christian Commission, and
widely popular because Lincoln liked it
so well, as sung by Philip Phillips. Its
title was *Your Mission*, and it had been
written by Mrs. Ellen Huntington Gates,
a sister of Collis P. Huntington. The
closing stanzas appealed strongly to the
feelings of folk who must stay at home,
while sons and husbands, brothers and
sweethearts were at the front:

If you cannot in the conflict
　Prove yourself a soldier true —
If, where fire and smoke are thickest,
　There's no work for you to do;
When the battle-field is silent,
　You can go with careful tread,
You can bear away the wounded,
　You can cover up the dead.

Do not, then, stand idly waiting,
　For some greater work to do;
Fortune is a lazy goddess —
　She will never come to you.
Go and toil in any vineyard,
　Do not fear to do or dare;
If you want a field of labor,
　You can find it anywhere.

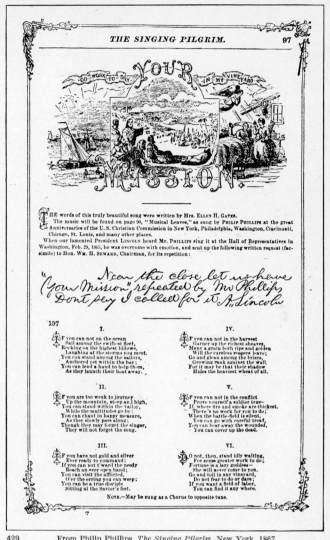

From Philip Phillips, *The Singing Pilgrim*, New York, 1867

430 Archbishop M. J. Spalding, 1810–72, from an
engraving after a photograph published by Moore
and Goodspeed, New York

THE SECOND PLENARY COUNCIL
OF BALTIMORE

THE Episcopal dioceses in the seceding South had organized the
"Protestant Episcopal Church in the Confederate States";
but they returned to the fellowship of the General Convention
when the war was over, and were heartily welcomed. The
Catholic Church, with an organization quite independent of
political boundaries, suffered no division; and in 1866 Archbishop Spalding convened at Baltimore its Second Plenary
Council. "The principal motives for holding a council were,
first, that at the close of the national crisis, which had acted as
a dissolvent upon all sectarian ecclesiastical organizations, the
Catholic Church might present to the country and the world
a striking proof of the strong bond of unity with which her members are knit together. Secondly, that the collective wisdom
of the church in this country might determine what measures should be adopted in order to meet the new
phase of national life which the result of the war had just inaugurated." It was attended by seven archbishops, thirty-eight bishops, three mitred abbots, and more than one hundred and twenty theologians.

431 Henry B. Smith, 1815–77, from a photograph, courtesy of Henry Goodwin Smith

THE REUNION OF "OLD-SCHOOL" AND "NEW-SCHOOL" PRESBYTERIANS

THE northern and southern organizations of the Baptists, Methodists, Presbyterians and Lutherans remained apart. On each side of Mason and Dixon's Line, however, Old-School and New-School groups of Presbyterians were reconciled. The union of the two northern Assemblies was finally consummated in 1870, at a meeting appropriately held in the First Church in Philadelphia, of which Albert Barnes was pastor. The "hero of Reunion," among the ministers, was Henry Boynton Smith, professor of theology in Union Theological Seminary. With mediating, irenic spirit he had for twenty years prepared the way by teaching a theology which so exalted the person and work of Christ as to transcend the old disputes. As moderator of the New-School Assembly in 1864, he preached a remarkable sermon on "Christian Union and Ecclesiastical Reunion"; as chairman of its committee on church polity, he labored indefatigably to find a formula upon which the two groups would unite; and by trenchant articles in various reviews he cleared the ground of objections.

GEORGE H. STUART, 1816–1890, PRESIDENT OF THE CHRISTIAN COMMISSION

THE hero of reunion among the laymen was George H. Stuart, who was the prime mover and chairman of a convention of representatives from all Presbyterian bodies which met in Philadelphia in 1867 to consider the possibility of a general reunion of Presbyterians. He was a Reformed Presbyterian, or Covenanter, and in 1868 was suspended from membership by the General Synod of his church on the ground that he "had sung hymns of human composition and communed with other than Reformed Presbyterians." The congregation to which he belonged then joined the main body of Presbyterians constituting the General Assembly. Stuart was born in Ireland and in 1831 came to Philadelphia where he became a merchant. He devoted much of his own time and energy as well as his wealth to the public good. His greatest service was rendered as president of the United States Christian Commission, the work of which he directed throughout the whole period of its existence.

432 George H. Stuart, from an engraving in *The Life of George H. Stuart*, Philadelphia, 1890

WILLIAM E. DODGE, 1805–1883, CHRISTIAN MERCHANT

ASSOCIATED with Mr. Stuart in the work of the Christian Commission and prominent in the reunion of the Presbyterians was William E. Dodge, of whom it was said that he was the best example in his generation of the business man in religion and the religious man in business. His children and children's children have maintained his ideals of Christian service and philanthropy. His son, William E. Dodge, Jr., was for many years national president of the Y.M.C.A. Another son, D. Stuart Dodge, founded the Syrian Protestant College at Beirut, of which a great-grandson, Bayard Dodge, is now president. A grandson, Cleveland H. Dodge, was president of the trustees of Robert College, Constantinople; he initiated and served as treasurer of the Near East Relief, and in 1917 directed the United War Work campaign which raised more than one hundred and seventy million dollars for the welfare of the soldiers. A granddaughter, Grace H. Dodge, was a pioneer organizer of working girls' clubs, a member of the New York City Board of Education, one of the founders and for many years treasurer of Teachers' College, and president of the National Board of the Y.W.C.A.

433 William E. Dodge, from a painting by Daniel Huntington in the New York Chamber of Commerce

THE NATIONAL COUNCIL OF CONGREGATIONAL CHURCHES

THE Congregational churches had been strongly anti-slavery in sentiment and were faced by no problems of reunion. Yet the ending of the Civil War marked a new beginning in their life. In June, 1865, they met in a National Council, only the second to be called since 1648, and adopted a Declaration of Faith which was in two respects noteworthy: in the breadth of its fellowship, marked by the omission of all party names, notably that of Calvin; and in the strongly social note which characterized its expression of faith in the redemptive power of the gospel. In 1871 a permanent National Council of Congregational Churches was organized. Major General O. O. Howard, Christian soldier and devoted friend of both negroes and "poor whites," was a member of the committee which devised its constitution, and was elected one of its moderators.

434 General Oliver Otis Howard, 1830–1909, from a photograph in Howard University, Washington

435 Parade of the Brooklyn Sunday-School Children, from a sketch by Theodore R. Davis in *Harper's Weekly*, June 13, 1868

"THE CITY OF CHURCHES"

THE church-going habit which is characteristic of the American people was especially marked in the 'sixties and 'seventies. These were the years when Brooklyn came to be called the "City of Churches." There were no motion-picture cameras then, but the artists of *Harper's Weekly* and other illustrated periodicals sketched scenes which were judged worthy of representation and preservation. The sketches here reproduced portray a meeting in the Brooklyn Tabernacle erected in 1873 for T. Dewitt Talmage, fluent and sensational pulpit orator; and a parade on May 26, 1868, of the Sunday-school children of the city. The records show that there were more boys in that procession than are to be seen in the picture.

436 Plymouth Church, Brooklyn, from a sketch in *Leslie's Illustrated Weekly*, Aug. 8, 1874

437 Interior of the Brooklyn Tabernacle, from a sketch in *Harper's Weekly*, Jan. 11, 1873

438   The Country Church — Before Service in the Morning, from a sketch by W. H. Davenport in
Harper's Weekly, Oct. 17, 1868

THE COUNTRY CHURCH — BEFORE THE MORNING SERVICE

IN the days of the horse and buggy the weekly or semi-weekly preaching service at the country church was a social occasion as well as a religious observance. Dressed in their Sunday best, village folk and farmers with their families came early and lingered in the churchyard to greet and converse with one another, to exchange news and retail gossip — but never, unless one were inclined to be ungodly, to drive a bargain or make a trade.

439   The Long Sermon and the Waiting Christmas Dinner, from a sketch by Mary McDonald in
Frank Leslie's Illustrated Newspaper, Dec. 3, 1887

WATCHING THE CLOCK

A COLLEGE president, asked by a visiting minister how long he should preach at a Sunday service in the college chapel, is said to have replied, "Preach as long as you want to, but no souls are saved after the first twenty minutes." Folk in the 'eighties when this picture was drawn had quite outgrown the disposition of their Puritan forefathers to delight in two- or three-hour sermons. The agony of this occasion is intensified by the fact that it is Christmas day, and at home are Christmas dinners waiting to be eaten.

A LOVE FEAST AMONG THE DUNKERS

SOME of the fairest sections of rural Pennsylvania, Ohio, Indiana and other agricultural states are cultivated by Dunkers, descendants of German Baptists who, to escape persecution, began to come to this country in 1719. The name refers to their mode of baptism, being derived from the German *tunken*, to dip; but they call themselves Brethren. They endeavor to shape their lives in strict and literal accord-

440   A Love Feast Among the Dunkers, from a drawing by Howard Pyle in *Harper's Weekly*, March 17, 1883

ance with the content of the New Testament; and emphasize non-conformity to the world by extreme plainness of dress and language, as well as by refusal to engage in war or litigation. They observe certain primitive rites, such as foot-washing, the kiss of charity, and the *agape*, or love-feast preceding the communion of the Lord's Supper. In 1880, when this sketch was made, they numbered about seventy thousand, though statistics were difficult to secure because many of them, on Scriptural grounds, opposed numbering the people; now they have over one hundred and fifty thousand communicants.

A NEGRO CAMP MEETING IN THE SOUTH

W. E. BURGHARDT DUBOIS, born in Massachusetts of negro ancestry, educated at Harvard, and long a professor in Atlanta University, has thus described his first experience of a negro camp meeting in the South, "A sort of suppressed terror hung in the air and seemed to seize us, — a Pythian madness, a demoniac possession, that lent terrible reality to song and word. The black and massive form of the preacher swayed and quivered as the words crowded to his lips and flew at us in singular eloquence. The people moaned and fluttered, and then the gaunt-cheeked brown woman beside me suddenly leaped straight into the air and shrieked

441   A Negro Camp Meeting in the South, from a drawing by Sol Eytinge, Jr., in *Harper's Weekly*, Aug. 10, 1872

like a lost soul, while round about came wail and groan and outcry, and a scene of human passion such as I had never conceived before. Those who have not thus witnessed the frenzy of a negro revival in the untouched backwoods of the South can but dimly realize the religious feeling of the slave; as described, such scenes appear grotesque and funny, but as seen they are awful." — *The Souls of Black Folk*, p. 190. These outbursts of religious emotion differed little, however, from like scenes in the camp meetings of "white folks."

442   Negro Baptism in the United States, from a drawing by Felix Regamy (1844–1907)
in the *Illustrated London News*, May 21, 1887

THE GROWTH OF THE NEGRO CHURCHES

THE negro slaves' association with the church was surer and more free than their contact with the school or their possession of a home. It was one of the bitter paradoxes of the institution of slavery that masters shared their religion with their slaves at the same time that they withheld education and made difficult, often impossible, the maintenance of monogamic family life. Accurate figures concerning the slave membership of the churches are not to be found except in the case of the Methodist Episcopal Church, South, which had two hundred and seven thousand seven hundred and forty-two negro members in 1860. There were more negro Baptists, doubtless two hundred and fifty thousand. The emancipation of the slaves and the ending of the war were followed by a tremendous growth of negro churches and their organization into separate state and national bodies. In 1890 there were two million six hundred and seventy-four thousand communicant members of negro churches; in 1927 there were five million. More than one half of these are Baptists, and over nine tenths of the remainder are Methodists. The negro "loves these denominations, and seems to find in them an atmosphere more congenial to his warm, sunny nature, and fuller scope for his religious activity, than in other communions."

THE NEGRO CHURCH AS A SOCIAL CENTER

"THE Negro church of today is the social centre of Negro life in the United States, and the most characteristic expression of African character. Take a typical church in a small Virginian town: it is the "First Baptist" — a roomy brick edifice seating five hundred or more persons, tastefully finished in Georgia pine, with a carpet, a small organ, and stained-glass windows. Underneath is a large assembly room with benches. This building is the central club-house of a community of a thousand or more Negroes. Various organizations meet here — the church proper, the Sunday school, two or three insurance societies, women's societies, secret societies, and mass meetings of various kinds. Entertainments, suppers, and lectures are held beside the five or six regular weekly religious services. Considerable sums of money are collected and expended here, employment is found for the idle, strangers are introduced, news is disseminated and charity distributed. At the same time this social, intellectual, and economic centre is a religious centre of great power. Depravity, Sin, Redemption, Heaven, Hell, and Damnation are preached twice a Sunday with much fervor, and revivals take place every year after the crops are laid by." — W. E. B. DuBois, *The Souls of Black Folk*, p. 193.

443   St. John's Church, Nashville, Tennessee, from a photograph
by Calvert Brothers, Nashville

"A PASTORAL VISIT"

THE negro preacher occupies a place of unique influence comparable to that of the Puritan minister in early New England. It was inevitable in view of the background of slavery and the rapid expansion of the negro churches that the great majority of the negro preachers should be uneducated men. It was perhaps inevitable, also, that some of them should be self-seeking and even immoral men. But the standard of ministerial education has been steadily rising, and the negro churches have done much to purge themselves of unworthy as-

444   *A Pastoral Visit*, from the painting by Richard N. Brooke (1847–1920), in the Corcoran Art Gallery, Washington

pirants to positions of clerical influence. As the foundation of all, American negroes have made tremendous progress in the upbuilding of wholesome family life and the establishment and maintenance of homes. The spirit of the scene here depicted is by no means exceptional.

BISHOP DANIEL A. PAYNE, 1811–1893

NEGRO Methodists had their own associations of churches long before the Civil War. The African Methodist Episcopal Church was organized in 1816, and the African Methodist Episcopal Zion Church in 1820. Bishop Daniel A. Payne of the former body was a pioneer among the group of negro ministers who led the way toward higher standards. Born in Charleston, South Carolina, in 1811, he attended a school established by free colored people of that city for the education of their children, and became himself a school-teacher. Coming north he was graduated from the Lutheran Theological Seminary at Gettysburg, Pennsylvania, in 1837, and was ordained and served as a Lutheran minister. After a few years he transferred to the African Methodist Episcopal Church of which he was elected bishop in 1852. In 1863 in the name of his Church he purchased the building of Wilberforce University near Xenia, Ohio, and devoted himself to the upbuilding there of an institution of higher education for his race. Besides a college and theological seminary Wilberforce University

includes a normal and industrial school, maintained in part by the state of Ohio. The choice of Bishop Payne to preside over one of the sessions of the World's Parliament of Religions at Chicago in 1893 was a deserved recognition of a long life of distinguished service. In the same year the good bishop passed from the scene of his earthly labors, mourned by Christians of both races.

445   Wilberforce University in 1876, from a lithograph in *Laws and Historical Sketch of Wilberforce University*, Cincinnati, 1876

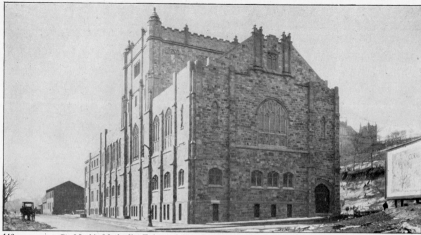

446   St. Mark's Methodist Episcopal Church, Harlem, from a photograph by Richards-
Ward Studio, New York

NEGRO THRIFT AND SUPPORT OF RELIGION

In 1890, less than thirty years after emancipation from slavery, the negroes of this country had made such substantial economic progress and had so expressed it in the support of religion, that Dr. H. K. Carroll, commenting upon the facts revealed by the census of that year, wrote: "The negro, considering the little wealth he had when slavery ceased, has achieved wonders in the accumulation of church property. The value of the churches he owns is twenty-six million six hundred and twenty-six thousand dollars, the number of edifices being twenty-three thousand seven hundred and seventy. Making due allowance for the generous help which the whites have given, it still appears that the negro has not been unwilling to make large sacrifices for the sake of religion, and that his industry, thrift, and business capacity have been made to contribute to his successful endeavors to provide himself with suitable accommodations and to encourage men of his own race to fit themselves to serve him as ministers in the expectation of a reasonable support." — H. K. Carroll, *The Religious Forces of the United States*, p. li.

The negro *Yearbook* for the year 1925–26 estimates the number of negro churches in this country as forty-seven thousand five hundred and fifteen, and the value of the church property owned by negroes as ninety-eight million seventy-five thousand seven hundred and eighty dollars. The Publishing House of the National Baptist Convention, at Nashville, is a headquarters and business plant of which that denomination is justly proud. The new building of the St. Mark's Methodist Episcopal Church in the Harlem section of New York city is equipped to minister to the social, recreational, and educational needs of its constituency, as well as for worship and evangelistic effort. The swift and steady development of the negro is one of the outstanding phenomena of twentieth-century America. He has made extraordinary economic and cultural progress. With every passing year the colored man increases the contribution by which he is enriching American life. In many cities, especially in the South, groups of the more influential citizens, white and black, have constituted inter-racial commissions in the interest of mutual understanding and coöperation.

447   Publishing House of the National Baptist Convention, Nashville, Tenn.

DWIGHT L. MOODY, 1837–1899, VOLUNTEER EVANGELIST

IN 1856 a young man joined Plymouth Church in Chicago. He began to invite other young men to share his pew, and soon was renting four pews, which he filled each Sunday with guests. But when he undertook to speak in prayer meeting he was advised to keep still. "You make too many mistakes in grammar," said his critic. "I know I make mistakes," he answered, "and I lack a great many things, but I am doing the best I can with what I've got." He paused and looked at the man searchingly, then added in his characteristic, irresistible way, "Look here, friend, you've got

448   Moody's Bodyguard, from W. R. Moody, *Life of Dwight L. Moody*, Fleming Revell Co., New York, 1900

grammar enough — what are you doing with it for the Master?" The young man was Dwight L. Moody. He went out into the streets and gathered a Sunday-school class of young hoodlums who came to be known as "Moody's bodyguard." He organized a Sunday school in one of the most needy districts of the city, succeeded in getting John V. Farwell, great Christian merchant, to become its superintendent, and soon had an attendance of six hundred pupils. Abraham Lincoln visited this school when on his way to Washington to enter upon his first term as President, and a few months later more than fifty of its boys enlisted in answer to his first call for volunteers.

MOODY DEVOTES FULL TIME TO CHRISTIAN SERVICE

IN 1860 Moody gave up his work as a traveling salesman, though in the previous year it had paid him five thousand dollars in commissions above his salary, in order to devote himself entirely to Christian service. With Mr. Farwell and B. F. Jacobs he headed the Chicago Auxiliary of the United States Christian Comsion. He organized and erected the Illinois Street Church, growing out of his Sunday school; he strengthened and developed the work of the Chicago Y.M.C.A.; and secured funds for the erection of Farwell Hall, the first Y.M.C.A. building in this country. The constitution of the Association was amended to state as its object, "the spiritual, intellectual and social improvement of all within its reach, irrespective of age, sex or condition." In 1871 he induced Ira D. Sankey, gifted singer, to join him in the evangelistic work which under this charter he was doing in Chicago. In the great fire that devastated Chicago in 1871 the church of which Moody was the unordained pastor was burned to the ground together with his house and furniture. Undaunted by this blow his followers proceeded to erect a much larger church to replace it.

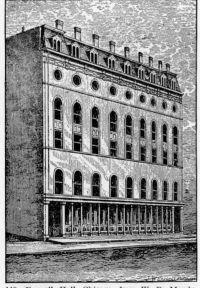

449   Farwell Hall, Chicago, from W. R. Moody, *Life of Dwight L. Moody*, Fleming Revell Co., New York, 1900

450   Certificate of membership in the Y.M.C.A., from W. R. Moody, *Life of Dwight L. Moody*, Fleming Revell Co., New York, 1900

451 Dwight L. Moody, from a photograph by
Shorey, Brattleboro, Vt.

MOODY AND SANKEY IN GREAT BRITAIN

FOR two years, 1873–75, Moody and Sankey conducted evangelistic meetings in the cities of England, Scotland and Ireland, with results so amazing as to be comparable only to the work of Whitefield and Wesley. Their visit closed with a four-months' mission in London, in the course of which two hundred and eighty-five meetings were held, attended by two million five hundred and thirty thousand people. Ministers and laymen of all denominations joined in the services. When requested to print his creed, Moody replied,

452   Ira D. Sankey, from a photograph
in the Albert Davis Collection

"My creed is in print." "Where?" he was asked. "In the fifty-third chapter of Isaiah," he answered. The leading Catholic paper in Dublin expressed its friendly interest in his work as a defense against popular agnosticism and materialism. Early opposition melted away, and the worst that scoffers could find to say was that they were confident that P. T. Barnum was back of it all. Moody and Sankey devoted four years more, 1881–84 and 1891–92, to evangelistic work in Great Britain.

MOODY AND SANKEY IN THE CITIES OF AMERICA

WHEN Moody and Sankey returned to America in 1875 they found themselves famous. They conducted meetings in Brooklyn, Philadelphia and New York during the following winter. It was the heydey of roller skating and the Brooklyn meetings were held in a large skating rink. In Philadelphia the old Pennsylvania Railroad freight house was used, and in New York the Hippodrome, on the site later occupied by Madison

453   Caricature of Moody, from *Vanity Fair*, New York, April 3, 1875

Square Garden. In 1876–77 the evangelists held meetings in Chicago and Boston. For more than twenty years, except for the time devoted to Great Britain, they worked with remarkable success in the leading cities of America, from Maine to California and Mexico. Moody differed from many revivalists in the emphasis which he placed upon individual, man-to-man evangelism; and in his lack of emphasis upon statistics, for which he cared little. When a minister once asked him how many souls had been saved under his preaching he answered, "I don't know anything about that. Thank God, I don't have to. I don't keep the Lamb's Book of Life." He was one of the greatest influences for righteousness in his day.

454 Moody preaching at the Hippodrome, from a sketch by C. S. Reinhart in *Harper's Weekly*, March 11, 1876

MOODY FOUNDS THE NORTHFIELD SCHOOLS

MOODY had been born and lived as a boy at Northfield, Massachusetts, and there he bought a home when he returned from his first extended campaign in Great Britain. In 1879 he founded the Northfield Seminary for Young Women, intended for

455   Northfield Seminary, from a gravure in the possession of the publishers

those "in the humbler walks of life, who never would get a Christian education but for a school like this." Two years later on the hills across the Connecticut River he founded the Mount Hermon School for Boys. The royalties from the various volumes of *Gospel Hymns* which the evangelists compiled for use in their meetings were large — more than three hundred and fifty thousand dollars up to September, 1885. Moody and Sankey refused to accept any of this money for personal use; and it was received by a board of well-known business men, who distributed it to various benevolent and educational institutions, and finally decided that the Northfield Schools should receive the income from this source.

456   The Auditorium at Northfield, from a photograph by E. H. Putnam and Son, Antrim, New Hampshire

THE NORTHFIELD CONFERENCES

IN 1880 Moody organized the first of the Northfield Summer Conferences of Christian Workers, which, with the exception of three years when he was in Great Britain, have been held annually since that time. These Conferences have been widely and deeply influential. It has been the policy to bring over each year one or more outstanding British leaders. Among those who have thus made contacts and friendships in America are F. B. Meyer, Andrew Murray, G. Campbell Morgan, John Hutton, Henry Drummond, and George Adam Smith. Moody was able to work happily and profitably with men who differed from him as widely in some respects as did the last two of these men. In 1886 the first Students' Conference was held, with an attendance of two hundred and fifty students from eighty colleges in twenty-five states; and in 1893 a similar series of Conferences for Woman Students was begun.

BENJAMIN FRANKLIN JACOBS, 1834–1902, PROTAGONIST OF UNIFORM SUNDAY SCHOOL LESSONS

ASSOCIATED with Dwight L. Moody and John V. Farwell in the Christian Commission and in the work of the Y.M.C.A. at Chicago was B. F. Jacobs, a young business man who had come to Chicago in 1854 and united with the First Baptist Church. For forty-five years, in five different schools, he served his community as a Sunday-school superintendent; and he became widely known as a leader of interdenominational and international coöperation in Sunday-school work. It was due to his "tireless persistency, vehement urging, unruffled and imperturbable good nature and general faculty for having his own way," one of his opponents said, that the Fifth National Sunday School Convention, held in Indianapolis in 1872, adopted the plan of Uniform Sunday School Lessons, and appointed the first International Sunday School Lesson Committee. The lessons were uniform in that all teachers and pupils, in all schools, were to study the same passage of Scripture at the same time. They were international in that Canada, by direct representation, and Great Britain, by a corresponding committee, coöperated in their selection.

457   Benjamin Franklin Jacobs, from a photograph

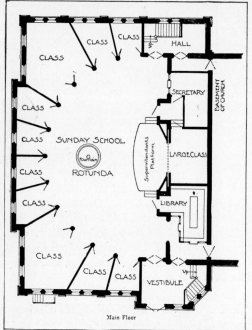

458   Plan of original Sunday School Building in connection with the First Methodist Episcopal Church of Akron, Ohio, from Marion Lawrance, *Housing the Sunday School*, The Westminster Press, Philadelphia, 1911

THE GROWTH OF THE SUNDAY SCHOOLS

THE Uniform Lessons and the evangelistic fervor of the time conspired to give a great impetus to Bible study, and the plan inspired the Sunday-school movement with the enthusiasm of conscious regimentation. Old and young went to Sunday school together, and studied the weekly lesson together. Hymns and prayers and superintendent's talk bore upon the one theme. At weekly meetings the pastor and the superintendent instructed the teachers on the lessons for the next Sunday. Saturday's newspaper contained a column or two of comment upon it. The coöperation of publishers afforded attractive and interesting aids to study and teaching. Churches began to erect substantial Sunday-school buildings modeled upon the plans devised in 1867 by Lewis Miller of Akron, with classrooms in a semicircle, so arranged that the classes were separate for the teaching of the lesson, yet could see and be seen from the superintendent's desk, and "with a minimum of movement" could be "brought together in a moment for simultaneous exercises."

459   Lewis Miller and John H. Vincent, from a photograph, courtesy of the Chautauqua Institution

JOHN H. VINCENT, 1832–1920, FIRST CHAIRMAN OF THE INTERNATIONAL SUNDAY SCHOOL LESSON COMMITTEE

THE man who did most to shape the International Uniform Sunday School Lesson system was John H. Vincent. As a young pastor in Chicago he began in 1865 to devise and publish schemes of lessons, and the favor with which these were received suggested to Mr. Jacobs the idea of general uniformity. From 1868 until his election as bishop in 1888, he was editor of the Sunday school publications of the Methodist Episcopal Church. He was the first chairman of the International Sunday School Lesson Committee, and held this post for twenty-four years. With Lewis Miller, in 1874 he founded a Summer Assembly on Chautauqua Lake, New York, for the broader and more effective training of Sunday-school teachers. The natural development of this original purpose has led to the broadly educational work of the present Chautauqua Institution.

460   A Chautauqua gathering, from a photograph, courtesy of the Chautauqua Institution

461 Hall of Philosophy, from a photograph, courtesy of
the Chautauqua Institution, Chautauqua, New York

462 Hall of Christ, Chautauqua Institution, from a photograph, courtesy
of the Chautauqua Institution, Chautauqua, New York

THE CHAUTAUQUA INSTITUTION

In 1878 the Chautauqua Literary and Scientific Circle was instituted, providing a system of popular education through home reading and study. In 1879 the first of the Summer Schools was organized, and these developed rapidly under the leadership of William R. Harper, then a teacher at Yale, but soon to become first president of the University of Chicago. The platform at Chautauqua in an auditorium seating nearly six thousand people has furnished a forum for a notable succession of statesmen, authors, ministers, and leaders of social reform. "Chautauqua," said Theodore Roosevelt on his last visit there, "is the most American thing in America." It has consistently and effectively preached the gospel of popular adult education; it has insisted that all education is at bottom self-education; that one is never too old to learn, and that for folk with any ambition education ends only with life.

463 Small town tent Chautauqua, from a photograph,
courtesy of the Swarthmore Chautauqua

THE CHAUTAUQUA IDEA

The Chautauqua idea has spread far beyond the Chautauqua Institution. It is to be seen in the summer schools of colleges and universities, and in the summer assemblies, conferences and training schools, maintained by various religious and secular organizations, which are much more numerous and ubiquitous than were the old-fashioned camp meetings, which they have almost entirely displaced. It is to be seen in the "Outlines" of this subject and that, which people are to-day so eager to buy and read, and in the widespread interest in adult education. The word "Chautauqua" has even come to be used as a common noun denoting a summer course of lectures and entertainments; and hundreds of smaller American communities, with the aid of various bureaus, have a "Chautauqua" of their own for a week or ten days each summer.

464 The Plaza at Chautauqua, from a photograph, courtesy of the Chautauqua Institution,
Chautauqua, New York

465   Young Women's Christian Association Building at Hartford, courtesy of the Young Women's Christian Association, Hartford, Conn.

THE FIRST YOUNG WOMEN'S CHRISTIAN ASSOCIATIONS

ONE result of the revival of 1857–58 was the organization in New York city of a Ladies' Christian Association which was especially interested in helping "young women of the operative class." The first Young Women's Christian Association was organized in Boston, March 3, 1866, under the leadership of Mrs. Henry F. Durant, founder, with her husband, of Wellesley College. Its object was "the temporal, moral and religious welfare of young women who are dependent upon their own exertions for support." A similar Association in Hartford, organized a year later, erected the first building designed for the use of a Y.W.C.A. The movement spread rapidly, especially during the 'eighties and in the growing cities of the Middle West, where the term "business women" began to be substituted for "working girls."

466   Sewing Class in New York City Y.W.C.A., 1889, from Elizabeth Wilson, *Fifty Years of Association Work*, New York, 1916, courtesy of the Woman's Press, New York

MEETING THE NEEDS OF WORKING GIRLS

THE Young Women's Christian Association movement found its distinctive field more quickly than had its prototype among young men. The Associations in general conceived their object in broad terms as the endeavor to meet the fundamental needs of working girls, "religious fellowship and instruction, individual needs of employment, protection, housing and food, acquaintance with the right kind of friends and books, study for culture and self-support, physical preparedness for life, and a chance to work together in being useful to the whole community." The picture, published in 1889, shows a class in dressmaking in the then newly-erected building of the New York City Y.W.C.A., three stories of which were devoted to classrooms for instruction in thirty or more trades. The Y.W.C.A. was, therefore, an adjustment to the new needs of women which arose out of the new conditions brought about by the vast industrial changes following the Civil War. The status of woman was rising swiftly toward equality with man. Under such circumstances the importance of the Y.W.C.A. can hardly be overemphasized.

467   National Training School of the Y.W.C.A., New York, from a photograph by Keystone View Co., New York

THE NATIONAL BOARD OF THE Y.W.C.A.

IN 1906 the Young Women's Christian Associations of the United States hitherto organized in two country-wide groups united to form one National Board. Miss Grace H. Dodge had led the movement toward consolidation, and was president of the Board until her death in 1914. A National Training School for Y.W.C.A. secretaries was opened in New York, and in 1912 an eleven-story building was erected for its use and for the administrative offices of the National Board.

THE HOUSING PROBLEM OF YOUNG WOMEN

An important part of the service which the Y.W.C.A. renders to the community is in helping young women, away from home and employed in various occupations, to solve the problem of finding comfortable and reasonably priced places of residence. Many Associations maintain buildings of their own for this purpose. One of the largest and most beautiful of these is the Mary A. Clark Memorial Home at Los Angeles, California. Not content with its great work in the United States the Association has turned its attention to foreign lands.

468   Mary A. Clark Memorial Home, Los Angeles, California, from a photograph by Pierce, Los Angeles

469   Gymnastic Drill in Shanghai, from Elizabeth Wilson, *Fifty Years of Association Work*, New York, 1916, courtesy of the Woman's Press, New York .

470   Morse Hall, Lahore, India, from Elizabeth Wilson, *Fifty Years of Association Work*, New York, 1916, courtesy of the Woman's Press, New York

X—14

THE WORLD'S Y.W.C.A.

The Y.W.C.A. movement has spread to many countries. In 1894 the World's Young Women's Christian Association was organized, with headquarters in London, and its first general secretary an American woman, Miss Anne Reynolds. The pictures show a gymnastic class of young Chinese women, directed by Miss Ying Mei Chun, who was trained for this work in America, and Morse Hall, the building of the Y.W.C.A. at Lahore, India.

471   Edward Everett Hale, from a gravure,
   after a photograph in the possession of
   the publishers

"LEND A HAND"

BEGINNING in 1856 a forty-three years pastorate of South Congregational (Unitarian) Church in Boston, Edward Everett Hale, 1822–1909, inspired his parishioners to conceive their church "not as a club of well-to-do Christians who have associated for their profit and pleasure, but as a working-place in the world, of men and women who want to bring in God's Kingdom." Next to *The Man without a Country* in its appeal to popular imagination and in its effect upon the lives of countless readers, was his story *Ten Times One is Ten*, depicting the character of Harry Wadsworth, and expressing the spirit of the religion of Faith, Hope and Love in the mottoes:

> Look up and not down
> Look forward and not back
> Look out and not in
> Lend a hand!

It not only led to the formation among young people of Lend a Hand Clubs, Wadsworth Clubs, Ten Times One Clubs, Look Up Legions, I. H. N. Clubs, King's Daughters, and like organizations; but contributed greatly to a new emphasis upon the principle of service as characteristic of all good living.

THE YOUNG PEOPLE'S SOCIETY OF CHRISTIAN ENDEAVOR

WEEKLY prayer meetings of young people in which both sexes joined were inaugurated in various churches during the revival of the late 'fifties. In 1867 Theodore L. Cuyler, pastor of the Lafayette Avenue Presbyterian Church in Brooklyn, organized the young people of his church, who had been maintaining such a meeting, into a Young People's Association, aiming at "the conversion of souls, the development of Christian character, and the training of new converts in religious work." The success of this and similar organizations encouraged Francis E. Clark, pastor of Williston Congregational Church in Portland, Maine, to organize on February 2, 1881, about the nucleus of a "Mizpah Circle" engaged in missionary study a "Young People's Society of Christian Endeavor." Using one of Moody's characteristic phrases, he des-

472   The Original Mizpah Circle, courtesy of the
   World's Christian Endeavor Union, Boston

cribed its purpose to be an "out-and-out" religious society. Its activities centered about the weekly prayer meeting, in which each member pledged himself to "take some part aside from singing."

"FATHER ENDEAVOR" CLARK, 1852–1927

THERE was nothing especially original about the plan except the particular wording of the pledge. Even the name "Christian Endeavor" had been used by Edward Eggleston, when pastor in Brookyn, as a translation better fitting the locality, of the Hoosier Schoolmaster's "Church of the Best Licks." But the time was ripe; the idea caught the imagination of young people everywhere; and Dr. Clark became to the youth movement within the churches, what Robert Raikes had been to the Sunday-school movement. He became more, in fact, for two years after the organization in 1885 of the United Society of Christian Endeavor, he resigned the pastorate and devoted his entire time to the Christian Endeavor movement. A kindly wag proclaimed that his initials "F. E." stood for "Father Endeavor," and he is better known by this soubriquet than by his real name.

473   Francis E. Clark, courtesy of the World's
   Christian Endeavor Union, Boston

THE YOUNG PEOPLE'S MOVE- MENT IN THE CHURCHES

CHRISTIAN ENDEAVOR societies multiplied surprisingly. By 1887 over seven thousand societies were reported, with nearly half a million members. In 1895, at the international convention held in Boston, fifty-six thousand four hundred and twenty-five delegates were registered. The idea spread over the world, and Christian En-

474   The Christian Endeavor Chorus at Washington, 1896, from a photograph, courtesy of the World's Christian Endeavor Union, Boston

deavor societies were organized in all lands where there were Christian churches. There are now eighty thousand societies with approximately four million members; of these forty-six thousand societies are in the United States. The success of the Christian Endeavor movement is not to be measured by the number of its avowed adherents, however; for it stimulated the organization, within the various denominations, of many like societies, such as the Epworth League of the Methodists, the Baptist Young People's Union, the Luther League, and the Young People's Christian Union of the United Presbyterians.

GROWTH OF THE LIQUOR TRAFFIC

ONE result of the Civil War was to strengthen the hold of the liquor traffic upon the American people. This was largely due to the fact that in 1862, under pressure of the need for money to carry on the war, Congress had passed an Internal Revenue Act which included the licensing of the liquor business. It was thus afforded the sanction of the Federal Government and began to be concentrated in the hands of men who made it their chief business. The saloon was developed as a specialized institution for the promotion of drink sales; and the liquor interests began to organize and enter politics. These results were foreseen by some members of Congress. Senator Henry Wilson of Massachusetts predicted them with fair accuracy, and protested: "I would as soon give my sanction to the traffic of the slave-trade as I would to the sale of liquors." But the need for revenue overruled his and other objections. Similar excise taxes had been laid upon liquor after the Revolution and during the War of 1812, but both had been removed as soon as possible. The excise had always been a most unpopular form of tax and had led in the Whiskey Rebellion to open outbreak. (See Volume VIII.) The excise taxes following the Civil War came to be looked upon as part of the permanent fiscal policy of the nation. The growth and development of the liquor business was the result not merely of Federal legislation but of the changed conditions brought about by the rapid industrialization of the United States following the Civil War. Conforming to the tendencies of the day the manufacture of spirituous liquor became a "big business." To meet the demands of a swiftly increasing urban population the "corner saloon" was developed, becoming not only a place for the retailing of alcoholic beverages but the "poor man's club."

475   The Poor Drunkard, from a drawing in *Harper's Weekly*, Apr. 18, 1874

476   The Black Valley Railroad, from a broadside in the possession of the American Antiquarian Society

THE RALLYING OF THE TEMPERANCE MOVEMENT

THE advocates of temperance were not slow to rally in the face of this situation. In 1865 a national temperance convention was held at Saratoga, which brought together existing organizations into a new body, The National Temperance Society and Publication House. William E. Dodge was its first president. Its basis was total abstinence for the individual and total prohibition for the state. An aggressive campaign of agitation and education was initiated. Here are reproduced typical cartoons of the period. "Black Valley Railroad" was published in 1863; "King Death's Distribution of Prizes" seven years later.

477   From a drawing by Thomas Nast in *Harper's Weekly*, May 28, 1870

THE WOMAN'S CRUSADE

THE most remarkable of the temperance movements was the Woman's Crusade, which began in Hillsboro, Ohio, on December 24, 1873. The idea was suggested by Dr. Dio Lewis, a traveling lecturer. Led by Mrs. Eliza J. Thompson, 1816–1905, daughter of a Governor and wife of a Judge, seventy-five women gathered at a church, read the 146th Psalm, sang and prayed, then marched two by two to the saloons of the town in each of which they appealed to the liquor seller to give up the business.

478   From a drawing *Here They Come*, by C. S. Reinhart in *Harper's Weekly*, Mar. 14, 1874

479   From a drawing *You Shust Get Out!*, by C. S. Reinhart in *Harper's Weekly*, Mar. 14, 1874

THE CRUSADE BURNS ITSELF OUT

IF a liquor dealer would not agree to give up his business, the crusading women would hold a prayer meeting right there, and then come back day after day until he capitulated. At Washington Court House, Ohio, a similar movement began a day later, and in eight days all of the eleven liquor dealers of the place surrendered their stock and quit the business. The Crusade spread throughout the country, and hundreds of liquor sellers yielded. The one dealer in Hillsboro who fought the ladies in the courts won a verdict of five dollars damages, but went into bankruptcy. After six months the Crusade burned itself out. Though it temporarily closed many saloons, there were always men who would open other saloons. Washington Court House, where all had been closed, had after fifteen months more saloons than before. The movement, however, was significant of a demand for the reform of a great national evil, that would not be silenced permanently.

480   From a drawing *The Sentinel*, by C. S. Reinhart in *Harper's Weekly*, Mar. 14, 1874

481   From a drawing *Pleading with a Saloon Keeper*, by C. S. Reinhart in *Harper's Weekly*, Mar. 14, 1874

482   From a cartoon *A Cold Reception Everywhere*, by Joseph Keppler in *Puck*, July 3, 1889

THE PROHIBITION PARTY

In 1869 a National Prohibition Party was organized, pledged to "the total prohibition of the manufacturing, importation and traffic of intoxicating beverages." Its first platform advocated also woman suffrage and the direct election of United States Senators, both of which, as well as prohibition, have since been adopted as amendments to the Constitution of the United States. Despair of securing an unequivocal stand on the part of either of the old parties prompted the organization of a separate party.

The cartoon from *Harper's Weekly* illustrates how the established parties played with the subject. Ohio since 1851 had an anti-license clause in its constitution. Sentiment for prohibition grew until the party in power agreed in 1883 to submit for vote by the people a prohibition amendment, provided a license amendment be submitted at the same time. Before the vote could be taken the party evaded the existing constitution and sought to confuse the issue, by passing the Scott Tax Law, which was simply a liquor license law under another name. The argument was that this secures revenue for the state, and "puts the burden" of maintaining poorhouses, jails and penitentiaries "where it belongs," on the saloon keeper. The license amendment lost overwhelmingly; and the prohibition amendment won by a majority of eighty-two thousand two hundred and fourteen. Yet the major parties gained their end, for this was not a majority of all the votes cast, and the amendment did not become part of the state constitution.

The cartoons from *Puck* portray on the one hand its sense of the power of the liquor business in politics, and on the other hand its dislike of the Prohibition movement. Many felt that prohibition was not the most effective method of bringing the American people to accept temperance.

483   From a cartoon *The Scott Liquor Law in Ohio — Putting the Burden Where it Belongs*, by W. A. Rogers in *Harper's Weekly*, Sept. 29, 1883

484   From a cartoon *Coming to the Wrong Shop*, by F. Opper in *Puck*, July 3, 1889

THE WOMEN'S CHRISTIAN TEMPERANCE UNION

THE Woman's Crusade had one permanent result of far-reaching significance. At Chautauqua, New York, in August, 1874, a group of women determined that something should be done to conserve and utilize the resources of sentiment and devotion it had called forth. In November at the call of this group a convention was held in Cleveland which organized the Women's Christian Temperance Union.

485 Frances Willard, from a photograph, courtesy of the Union Signal, Evanston, Ill.

Under the brilliant leadership of Frances E. Willard, 1839–98, corresponding secretary until 1879, and thereafter president, the W.C.T.U., as it was familiarly called, exerted a powerful influence in behalf of total abstinence and the prohibition of the liquor traffic. In 1883 Miss Willard visited every state and territory in the Union, and completed an organization in each. In 1887 a World's W.C.T.U. was organized, of which she became president.

486 Statue of Frances Willard in the Capitol, Washington, from a photograph by the Commercial Studio, Washington

Miss Willard had been a public-school teacher, a university professor, and president of a college for women; she was an educator as well as a capable administrator. In 1880 she secured Mrs. Mary H. Hunt as superintendent of a new department of scientific temperance instruction, which succeeded in introducing instruction concerning the effects of alcohol and narcotics upon the human body into the public schools of all the states, and induced the International Sunday School Lesson Committee to devote lessons to the subject of temperance. There is no exact way of measuring results, but it is significant that the wave of prohibitory legislation which began in 1907 coincided with the growth to maturity and the induction into major responsibilities of the children who had been taught about alcohol and temperance in the schools.

Miss Willard advocated political action, and supported the Prohibition party. She said that she was "profoundly interested in politics as the mightiest force on earth except Christianity." The state of Illinois placed a statue of Miss Willard in Statuary Hall in the Capitol at Washington — the only woman in American history who has been so honored by any state.

487   From a cartoon *Prohibition is Coming*, by Joseph Keppler in *Puck*, August 4, 1886

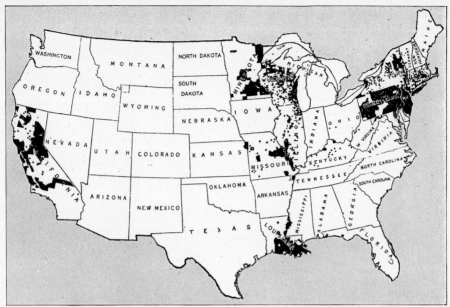

488   Map showing the extent of dry territory, by state and local enactment, in 1919, from *The Handbook of the World League against Alcoholism*, The Anti-Saloon League, New York, 1919

THE ANTI–SALOON LEAGUE AND THE EIGHTEENTH AMENDMENT

IN 1893 at Oberlin, Ohio, was organized the Anti-Saloon League, a self-perpetuating, voluntary organization, which described itself as omni-partisan and inter-denominational. It refused alliance with any political party, its method being to concentrate upon "candidates and the things they stand for . . . irrespective of party affiliations." Increasingly it got the confidence of the churches, and in time it described itself as

"the church in action against the saloon." It has had to meet much criticism; from "wets" because they believe it to be dia-bolically cunning and unprincipled; from old-line prohibitionists because they blame it for much that is weak and ineffective in the present situation. Let the blame or credit fall where it may, the facts remain that in 1907 a wave of prohibitory legislation began in this country; that by 1919 thirty-three states had by statute or Constitutional provision prohibited the liquor traffic; that the Eighteenth Amendment to the National Constitution, submitted by Congress to the states on December 22, 1917, was ratified by thirty-six states by January 16, 1919, and later by ten more. The problem of the enforcement of prohibition remains.

TEMPLE EMANU–EL, NEW YORK

ON September 11, 1868, the Jewish Congregation Temple Emanu-El dedicated a magnificent new synagogue at Fifth Avenue and Forty-third Street, New York. This congregation had been organized in 1845, and was one of the first two avowedly Reform Jewish congregations in this country, the other being Har Sinai Congregation in Baltimore, organized in 1842. In contrast to the poverty of its beginning when its total annual budget was but fifteen hundred dollars, the rapid growth and prosperity of Temple Emanu-El warranted an expenditure for the new building of over six hundred thousand dollars; and more than seven hundred thousand dollars was realized on the sale by auc-tion of two hundred thirty-one and a half pews.

489   Temple Emanu-El, New York, from an engraving after a photograph by Rockwood, in *Harper's Weekly*, Nov. 14, 1868

ISAAC M. WISE, 1819–1900, LEADER OF JEWISH UNION AND REFORM

THE Jewish Reform movement which began in Germany found its first American expression in a petition presented to their vestry in 1824 by forty-seven members of the Congregation Beth Elohim in Charleston, South Carolina, urging the use of English in prayers and sermon and the abridgment of the service. The Reform leader, who, "more than any other man, stamped his individuality upon the history and development of Jewish life in the United States," was Isaac M. Wise, rabbi for eleven years of congregations at Albany, then for forty-six years rabbi of Bene Yeshurun Congregation in Cincinnati. In 1848 he began agitation for a union of congregations, but it took twenty-five years of persistent effort before his plan was realized by the organization in 1873 of the Union of American Hebrew Congregations. He was founder and first president of the Hebrew Union College, a theological seminary for the training of rabbis established at Cincinnati in 1875. He was chiefly responsible for the organization of the Central Conference of American Rabbis in 1889.

490   Isaac M. Wise, from a photograph, courtesy of the Union of American Hebrew Congregations, Cincinnati, Ohio

THE PRINCIPLES OF REFORM JUDAISM

REFORM Judaism accepts as binding only the moral laws of the Mosaic code; it rejects such ceremonial and rabbinical laws as it deems not adapted to modern life. It recognizes the principle of development in all religion, and emphasizes the prophetic, universal aspects of the Jewish faith, in contrast to the nationalism involved in the expectation of a return to Palestine and the restoration of the Aaronic priesthood and the Jewish state. It conceives the Messianic hope in terms of the dawning of an era rather than the coming of a person. It seeks the upbuilding of society upon the basis of righteousness and justice.

Rabbi Wise in 1854 set forth five practical principles of reform which might well apply to religious systems generally: "(1) All forms to which no meaning is attached any longer are an impediment to our religion, and must be done away with. (2) Whatever makes us ridiculous before the world as it now is, may safely be and should be abolished. (3) Whatever tends to the elevation of the divine service, to inspire the heart of the worshipper and attract him, should be done without any unnecessary delay. (4) Whenever religious observances and the just demands of civilized society exclude each other, the former have lost their power. (5) Religion is intended to make man happy, good, just, active, charitable, and intelligent."

491   Hebrew Union College, Cincinnati, from a photograph, courtesy of Hebrew Union College, Cincinnati

492   Sinai Congregation, Chicago, from a photograph, courtesy of The Emil G. Hirsch Center, Chicago

OTHER REFORM JEWISH LEADERS

THE Congregation Temple Beth-El in New York, organized in 1874 by consolidation of two existing congregations, occupied an important place in the Reform movement through the fearless, constructive work of two of its rabbis, David Einhorn, 1809–79, and Kaufmann Kohler, 1843–1926. Einhorn, rabbi of Har Sinai Congregation in Baltimore in 1861, had been compelled to flee from that city because of his outspoken denunciations of slavery. Kohler was the first to introduce Sunday services among the Jewish congregations of New York. He was made president of the Hebrew Union College in 1903 and his work on *Jewish Theology*, 1918, is regarded as a standard exposition of the faith of the modern Jew. Sinai Congregation in Chicago, organized in 1860, dealt with the Sabbath question by introducing Sunday services in 1874, and for thirteen years held services on both Saturday and Sunday. In 1887 under the leadership of Rabbi Emil G. Hirsch, 1852–1923, the services on Saturday were discontinued.

ORTHODOX JUDAISM

THE great majority of the Jewish congregations in this country remain orthodox, and do not share in the Reform movement.

Immigration from Russia and Poland has increased the numbers of the more conservative congregations during the last half century. The illustration shows the traditional use of the phylactery for head and hand, containing designated scriptural passages. The Jewish Theological Seminary, established in New York in 1886, represents

493   A New York Rabbi, from a drawing by T. V. Chominski, in *Harper's Weekly*, Feb. 14, 1891

494   The Jewish Theological Seminary in New York from a photograph by Keystone View Co., New York

the orthodox tradition. In 1901 Dr. Solomon Schechter, 1847–1915, a noted rabbinical scholar who had long taught at Cambridge University in England, became its president.

THE SOCIETY FOR ETHICAL CULTURE

Son of Samuel Adler, 1809–1901, the scholarly rabbi of Congregation Emanu-El, New York, Felix Adler, 1851–, went to Germany to be trained for the Jewish ministry. But he reached an attitude toward the beliefs of Judaism which made this impossible; and in 1876 he founded in New York the Society for Ethical Culture, based upon the principle of right living without regard to religious sanctions. Its motto was "Deed not Creed." The moral law, it asserts, has an immediate authority not contingent upon the truth of religious beliefs or philosophical theories. Similar societies were formed in Chicago, Philadelphia and St. Louis, as well as in England, Germany and other countries. In 1906 an International Conference adopted a statement of aim, "To assert the supreme importance of the ethical factor in all the relations of life — personal, social, national, and international, apart from theological and metaphysical considerations."

The practical activities of the Ethical Societies are much like those of the churches. The *Yearbook* of the New York Society for 1904–05 said: "The Society fills more and more the place of a church in the lives of its members. The leaders act as ministers of religion: consecrating marriages; officiating at funerals; consoling the suffering; advising the troubled

495 Felix Adler, from a photograph, courtesy of The Society for Ethical Culture of New York

and confused; dedicating childhood to the higher ends of life in the 'name ceremony' (which takes the place of baptism); teaching and supervising the training of the young in Sunday school, and clubs and classes for young men and women; and seeking to create and maintain an atmosphere of reverent attention to the high mysteries of life and to the sacredness of the obligation, imposed by man's moral nature, to follow without swerving the dictates of duty according to the best light that is in each individual."

496 Phillips Brooks, from a photograph by Ramsstorff Brothers, Malden, Mass.

PHILLIPS BROOKS, 1835–1893

The successor of Henry Ward Beecher as the first among American preachers was Phillips Brooks, a descendant of John Cotton and of Samuel Phillips. The first ten years of his ministry were in Philadelphia, and from 1869 until his election in 1891 as Protestant Episcopal Bishop of Massachusetts he was rector of Trinity Church, Boston. A man of deep religious experience and of strongly evangelical temper, extraordinarily sensitive to human need as well as to moral and spiritual truth, he devoted his life and his great intellectual powers unreservedly to the work of preaching, which he described as "the bringing of truth through personality." When asked how Brooks compared with the great preachers of Scotland and England, Professor A. B. Bruce of Glasgow said, "Our great preachers take into the pulpit a bucket full or half full of the Word of God, and then, by the force of personal magnetism, they attempt to convey it to the congregation. But this man is just a great water main, attached to the everlasting reservoir of God's truth and grace and love, and streams of life, by a heavenly gravitation, pour through him to refresh every weary soul."

497 Statue of Phillips Brooks before Trinity Church, Boston, from a
photograph by the Halliday Historic Photograph Company, Boston

THE GENIUS OF PHILLIPS BROOKS

Bishop Clark called Phillips Brooks "the Shakespeare of the pulpit." The comparison, bold though it be, is not inappropriate. Brooks had preëminent genius as a preacher, and his message was singularly free from limitations of time, space and circumstance. He drew his materials "not from his religious autobiography, but from the spiritual biography of the race." More fully than any other American preacher, he rose above sectarian differences. A loyal member, minister and bishop of the Protestant Episcopal Church, he indignantly rejected the assertion on its behalf of authority derived from an apostolic succession not shared by other Protestant churches; and he was claimed by Christians generally, and listened to by all, without regard to differences of creed and polity. It was a Methodist who wrote: "All men, of all classes and conditions, claimed him, because in his magnificent heart and sympathy he seemed to be all men, and to enter into their disappointments and into their successes, and to make them his own."

THE EVANGELICAL ALLIANCE

In 1838, Dr. S. S. Schmucker had published a "Fraternal Appeal" to the evangelical churches of America, offering a "Plan for Protestant Union" which received wide endorsement. The movement thus begun was one of the factors contributing to the organization at London in 1846 of the Evangelical Alliance, which differed from Dr. Schmucker's proposal in that it was an association of individuals rather than a federation of denominations. The American Branch of the Evangelical Alliance was organized in 1867, and in 1873 was host to the General Conference of delegates from the various branches throughout the world. Other significant conferences were those at Washington in 1887 and at Boston in 1889. Under the leadership of its Secretary, Josiah Strong, the Alliance did much to awaken the churches to the new problems involved in the application of Christian principles to the increasingly complex social and industrial order. In the twentieth century it was practically replaced, and its work taken over, by the Federal Council of the Churches of Christ in America.

498   Meeting of the Evangelical Alliance, from a drawing in *Harper's Weekly*, Oct. 14, 1873

WASHINGTON GLADDEN, 1836–1918

A PIONEER in the preaching and practice of "Applied Christianity," as he called it, under the new conditions of modern urban and industrial life, was Washington Gladden, for thirty-six years pastor of the First Congregational Church in Columbus, Ohio. For one term he served as a member of the City Council of Columbus, where he advocated the municipal ownership of public-service industries. The principle of *laissez faire*, he said, usually means "Let ill enough alone." Yet he refused assent to Socialism, and based his social creed upon the principle of good will which he found to be Christ's law of life. As early as 1875, he began to apply this principle to the relations between employers and workingmen, and to the settlement of strikes. Far-sighted, broad-minded, and independent in judgment, he labored tirelessly for social righteousness and the common good; yet never seemed hurried or worried. He possessed the imperturbable calm of one who is a friend of his fellows, at peace with conscience, and at home with God.

499 Washington Gladden, from a photograph in the Baker Art Galleries, Columbus, Ohio

500 Charles H. Parkhurst from a photograph by Underwood & Underwood, New York

CHARLES H. PARKHURST, 1842–

FEARLESS in denunciation of wrong, and tireless in seeking its hidden sources was Charles H. Parkhurst, for thirty-eight years minister of the Madison Square Presbyterian Church in New York city. In 1891 he became president of the Society for the Prevention of Crime and found that the police of the city were protecting certain forms of vice in return for fixed revenues paid to them personally. In scathing sermons he attacked this system and the municipal authorities who were behind it, and personally secured evidence to sustain his charges. Investigations by the Grand Jury and by the Legislature of New York resulted in an exposure of corrupt practices in the municipal Government that shocked the country, and led to movements in many cities toward more honesty and effectiveness in the administration of their affairs.

"RAMPAGEOUS PREACHERS"

PARKHURST was neither a sensation-monger nor a seeker after notoriety. Such are at times to be found in the pulpit; and *Puck*, in the 'eighties, had mercilessly lampooned the "rampageous preachers" who, it said, should be put under the same restrictions as other Sabbath-breakers. When Parkhurst launched his attack upon the criminal alliance between the violators of law and the officers who were sworn to administer it, *Puck* ridiculed his efforts. Where political questions involve ethical issues, the preachers of America, from the earliest days, have not feared to discuss them.

THE SENSATION-SERMON MANIA

501 From a cartoon *The Sensation-sermon Mania*, by F. Opper in *Puck*, Oct. 3, 1883

502   William S. Rainsford, 1850–, from a photograph, courtesy of St. George's Church, New
   York

THE WORK OF AN INSTITUTIONAL CHURCH

In 1883 St. George's Church on the lower East Side of New York city which had begun in 1748 as the first offshoot of Trinity Church had dwindled to a membership of about twenty families. William S. Rainsford, called to be rector, accepted on condition that the old system of pew rent be abolished and the church be made free. Sixteen years later the roll of the church numbered more than seven thousand people, of whom five thousand lived in tenements and seventeen hundred in boarding houses and apartments, while the majority of the five hundred who lived in private homes were domestic servants. St. George's had become the outstanding example of what was coming to be called an "institutional church," undertaking to minister through its staff of curates, deaconesses and other workers, its Sunday school, its various clubs and societies, its gymnasium, trade-classes and social rooms to the manifold week-day needs of all ages and classes of folk whom it united in the worship of God. "He brought the church close to the busy, working life of a great city," wrote President Roosevelt in a congratulatory letter when Dr. Rainsford retired from active service in 1906.

WALTER RAUSCHENBUSCH, 1861–1918, PROPHET OF THE SOCIAL GOSPEL

The principles of the "social gospel" found clear and effective expression in the work of Walter Rauschenbusch, in whom was "the learning of the scholar, the vision of the poet, and the passion of the prophet." For eleven years minister of a small German Baptist church in New York city he gave himself without stint to the service of the poor. As professor in Rochester Theological Seminary he wrote in 1907 an arresting and inspiring book on *Christianity and the Social Crisis* which he followed by other works in the same general field, notably *The Social Principles of Jesus* and *A Theology for the Social Gospel*. With the courage of a Savonarola, he combined the gentleness and love of a St. Francis. He was "so humble that he knew not he was great, so truly a follower of the Master that he was all unconscious of his own leadership."

503   Walter Rauschenbusch, from a
   photograph

FOR THE COOPERATIVE COMMONWEALTH

O GOD, we praise thee for the dream of the golden city of peace and righteousness which has ever haunted the prophets of humanity, and we rejoice with joy unspeakable that at last the people have conquered the freedom and knowledge and power which may avail to turn into reality the vision that so long has beckoned in vain.

Speed now the day when the plains and the hills and the wealth thereof shall be the people's own, and thy freemen shall not live as tenants of men on the earth which thou hast given to all; when no babe shall be born without its equal birthright in the riches and knowledge wrought out by the labor of the ages; and when the mighty engines of industry shall throb with a gladder music because the men who ply these great tools shall be their owners and masters.

Bring to an end, O Lord, the inhumanity of the present, in which all men are ridden

[139]

504   Facsimile page from Walter Rauschenbusch,
   Prayers of the Social Awakening, Pilgrim Press,
   Boston, 1925

PRAYERS OF THE SOCIAL AWAKENING

In the castle of my soul
Is a little postern gate,
Whereat, when I enter,
I am in the presence of God.
In a moment, in the turning of a thought,
I am where God is.

So wrote Walter Rauschenbusch. He was more than a social reformer; he was a mystic of the simplest, highest type, who realized in his own life what Brother Lawrence called "the practice of the presence of God." His *Prayers of the Social Awakening* brought a new note into the language of worship, and remain a permanent enrichment of the liturgies of the churches. Where can be found a truer, more needful prayer than that on the page here reproduced?

THE RELIGION OF THEODORE ROOSEVELT

THE reorganization of the Police Department of New York city after the exposure of its corruption which Dr. Parkhurst initiated was entrusted to Theodore Roosevelt, who was destined six years later to become President of the United States. Roosevelt's progressive ideals in politics were matched by the vigor and sincerity of his thought and action in morals and religion. He stressed the active, constructive virtues; and his sympathies, religiously, were with such protagonists of the application of Christian principles to the life of this present world as Gladden, Parkhurst, Rainsford, and Rauschenbusch. "If, with the best of intentions, we can only manage to deserve the epithet of 'harmless,' it is hardly worth while to have lived in the world at all. . . . Alike for the nation and the individual, the one indispensable requisite is character — character that does and dares as well as endures, character that is active in the performance of virtue no less than firm in the refusal to do aught that is vicious or degraded."

505 Bust of Roosevelt, by James L. Fraser in the Senate Corridor, the Capitol, Washington, from a photograph by the Commercial Photo Company, Washington

WHAT ROOSEVELT THOUGHT OF RELIGION

ROOSEVELT'S favorite text was from Micah; "to do justly and to love mercy and to walk humbly with thy God." Like most men in places of high responsibility who come to know their fellowmen widely he had little regard for the refinements of creed and ritual that divide people into sects. But he had profound respect for the church. At sixteen he joined the Dutch Reformed Church of Saint Nicholas in New York city of which his father and grandfather were members, and he maintained this connection throughout his life. He was always a faithful attendant at public worship. "In this actual world a churchless community, a community in which men have abandoned or scoffed at or ignored their religious needs, is a community on the rapid down-grade. I advocate a man's joining in church work for the sake of showing his faith by his work. Church work and church attendance mean the cultivation of the habit of feeling some responsibility for others. Yes, I know all the excuses. I know that one can worship the Creator in a grove of trees or in his own house. But I also know as a matter of cold fact that the average man does not thus worship."

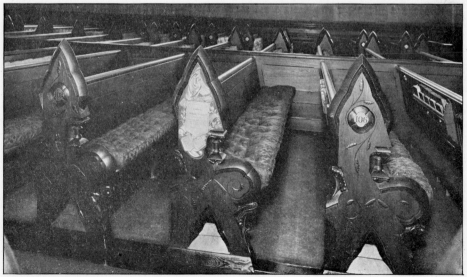

506   Theodore Roosevelt's Pew in the Church of St. Nicholas, New York, from a photograph by Bogart, New York

JAMES GIBBONS, 1834–1921, CATHOLIC CARDINAL AND AMERICAN CITIZEN

THE greatest leader of the Roman Catholic Church in America was Cardinal Gibbons. Ordained in 1861 he witnessed a tenfold increase in the membership of his church before his death sixty years later. Preaching at Rome in 1887, upon the occasion of his formal installation as a Cardinal, he boldly praised the American principle of the separation of church and state, and he had little difficulty in convincing Pope Leo XIII of the truth of his position. He strenuously fought and finally defeated the so-called "Cahensly movement," which sought to maintain distinct national groups among the foreign-born Catholics in this country — a movement which was particularly strong among the Germans, led by Peter Cahensly. At Milwaukee, one of its strongholds, Gibbons delivered an address which was both a rebuke and a challenge: "Let us glory in the title of American citizen. We owe our allegiance to one country, and that country is America. We must be in harmony with our political institutions. It matters not whether this is the land of our birth or the land of our adoption. It is the land of our destiny."

507   Cardinal Gibbons, from a photograph. © Bachrach, Baltimore, 1917

THE THIRD PLENARY COUNCIL OF BALTIMORE

As a young priest, secretary to Archbishop Spalding, Gibbons had been assistant chancellor of the Second Plenary Council of the Catholic Church in the United States, held at Baltimore in 1866. As Archbishop of Baltimore and Apostolic Delegate he organized and presided over the Third Plenary Council in 1884. The legislation of this Council was so comprehensive and wisely conceived, that it has ever since served to regulate the work of the Catholic Church in this country. A primary interest of the Council was in problems of educational policy. It devised plans for the more adequate training of candidates for the priesthood; it founded the Catholic University of America; and it made obligatory upon priests and people the establishment and maintenance of parochial schools for the education of Catholic children.

508   Members of the Third Plenary Council, from a drawing after a photograph by Bendann in *Harper's Weekly*, Nov. 29, 1884

LEGISLATION AGAINST SECRET SOCIETIES

A PAPAL encyclical of April 20, 1884 had condemned "the Masonic and kindred societies" as in many countries so hostile to the Catholic Church as to "virtually aim at substituting a world-wide fraternity of their own for the universal brotherhood of Jesus Christ." The Council decided that secrecy creates always a strong presumption against any society, and that membership in secret societies is forbidden to Catholics when the obligation is such as to bind them to blind obedience or to a secrecy that evades the rightful questions of competent authority. Various Protes-

509   Scottish Rite Temple, Washington, from a photograph by Underwood & Underwood, New York

tant churches hold analogous positions, notably certain bodies of Lutherans and Presbyterians. One of the "four points" which have kept the Lutherans in America from uniting is the insistence of more conservative groups that membership in secret societies involves denial of Christ, imposes oaths contrary to God's word, and interferes with supreme loyalty to the church.

510 The Anarchist Riot in Chicago — A Dynamite Bomb Exploding Among the Police, from a drawing by T. De Thulstrup, after sketches and photographs, in *Harper's Weekly*, May 19, 1886

CARDINAL GIBBONS AND THE KNIGHTS OF LABOR

IN the 'eighties the sudden growth and meteoric career of the Knights of Labor under the leadership of Terence V. Powderly awakened widespread apprehension. Anarchist riots in 1886 in Chicago had set the country on edge. The national leaders of the Knights of Labor charged that the men accused of being connected with the bomb outrage were being persecuted unfairly. The Catholic bishops of Canada condemned the Knights of Labor on the ground that it was a secret society, and their condemnation was approved by the Congregation of the Holy Office. Cardinal Gibbons after extended conferences with Master Workman Powderly decided that its pledge was not such as to come under the ban of the Church and that its aims were legitimate. He addressed a letter to Rome containing an argument so well-conceived and unanswerable that the decision of the Holy Office with respect to Canada was reversed, and the Church's recognition of the right of labor to organize for the protection of its interests was assured. *Puck*, as usual, bitterly caricatured Cardinal Gibbons, and associated with him Cardinal Manning of England who had shared in his stand. The Knights of Labor was, as he declared it would be, an "unstable and transient" organization. But as it dwindled the American Federation of Labor grew, with the result that the right to form lawful unions for the betterment of labor is **now** generally conceded.

> 28   KNIGHTS OF LABOR.
>
> *Unknown Knight*—Master Workman, our friend has satisfactorily answered all inquiries, and now desires to be covered with our shield, and admitted to fellowship in this Order.
>
> After a short pause, and amid perfect silence, the Master Workman will say:
>
> *Master Workman*—Place our friend at the centre, and administer the pledge of honor.
>
> The Unknown Knight places the candidate at the centre with directions to place the left hand on the heart, and raise the right hand.
> The Unknown Knight then administers the following pledge, which the candidate must repeat:
>
> OBLIGATION.
>
> I do truly promise, on my honor, that I will never reveal to any person or persons whatsoever, any of the signs, or secret workings of the Order that may be now or hereafter confided to me, any acts done or objects intended, except in a lawful and authorized manner, or by special permission of the Order granted to me.
>
> That I will not reveal to any employer or other person the name or person of any one a member of the Order without permission of the member.
>
> That I will strictly obey all laws and lawful summons that may be sent, said or handed to me, and that, during my connection with the Order, I will, to the best of my ability, defend the life, interest, reputation and family of all true members of this Order; help and assist all employed and unemployed, unfortunate or distressed members to procure employ, and secure just remuneration; relieve their distress, and counsel others to aid them, so that they and theirs may receive and enjoy the just fruits of their labor and exercise of their art.
>
> And I do further promise that I will, without reservation or evasion, consider the pledge of secrecy I have taken binding upon me until death.

511 Facsimile page of the Knights of Labor Ritual, from *The Knights of Labor Illustrated*, Chicago, 1886

512   Scene at one of the sessions of the World's Parliament of Religions, from the *Official Report of the World's Parliament of Religions*, New York, 1894

THE WORLD'S PARLIAMENT OF RELIGIONS

IN connection with the World's Columbian Exposition at Chicago in 1893, a series of more than two hundred congresses were held dealing with various fields of cultural achievement.   The most remarkable of these was the World's Parliament of Religions under the chairmanship of Dr. John Henry Barrows, which brought together for seventeen days leaders representing all of the great religious faiths of mankind.   The motto of the Parliament suggested by Dr. Adler, Chief Rabbi of the British Empire, was "Have we not all one Father? Hath not one God created us?" and its first act was to unite in the Lord's Prayer, led by Cardinal Gibbons. A characteristic moment was on the fourteenth day when H. Dharmapala, Buddhist delegate from Ceylon, rose to grasp the hand of George T. Candlin, Christian missionary in China, who was tendered a great ovation at the close of his address on *The Bearing of Religious Unity on the Work of Christian Missions*. Mr. Candlin clothed in Chinese costume had declared that "all religion whatever in any age or country is in its essential spring good and not evil," and affirmed the desire of himself and his fellow missionaries "to approach the non-Christian religions in a spirit of love and not of antagonism, to understand and justly rate their value as expressions of the religious principle in man, to replace indiscriminate condemnation by reverential study, and to obtain conquest, not by crushing resistance, but by winning allegiance."

MARY BAKER G. EDDY, 1821–1910, FOUNDER OF CHRISTIAN SCIENCE

THE youngest of the religious systems represented at the Parliament of Religions was Christian Science, founded by Mary Baker G. Eddy, who claimed to have discovered its principles, untaught by "human pen or tongue" in 1866. Its fundamental propositions which she held to be mathematically proved because equally true if reversed are, "1. God is All-in-all. 2. God is good. Good is mind. 3. God, Spirit, being all, nothing is matter. 4. Life, God, omnipotent good, deny death, evil, sin, disease." Christian Science affirms that God alone is real, and that God is "Principle, not person." Matter has no real existence; neither has evil, sin, sickness, and death. All these are illusions of "material sense" or "mortal mind," phrases which themselves stand for "something which has no real existence." Mrs. Eddy based upon these principles a system of mental healing through simple affirmation and realization of the teachings set forth in *Science and Health*, first published in 1875, and thereafter issued in many and frequently revised editions.

513   Mary Baker G. Eddy, from a photograph, courtesy of the Christian Science Committee on Publication

THE GROWTH OF CHRISTIAN SCIENCE

Mrs. Eddy organized a Christian Science Association in Lynn, Massachusetts, in 1876, and a church in 1879. In the latter year she began lecturing on Sunday afternoons in Boston, and she soon removed to that city. Here the "First Church of Christ, Scientist" was organized, henceforth to be known as "The Mother Church." The cult spread with fair rapidity. A thousand churches existed in the United States at the time of Mrs. Eddy's death in 1910, and there are two thousand now, with about three hundred more in other countries. Figures for membership are not given; an official says that "estimates vary from three hundred thousand to upwards of one million." Mrs. Eddy did not hesitate to claim divine origin for her doctrines, or to make allusions to analogies between herself and Jesus Christ. The illustration is from her book entitled *Christ and Christmas*, published in 1894. Opposite the picture stands the verse:

514   From a drawing in Mary Baker Eddy, *Christ and Christmas*, Boston, 1894

As in blessed Palestine's hour, so in our age
'Tis the same hand unfolds His power and writes the page.

515   Philip Schaff, from a photograph, courtesy of the Reverend David Schaff

PHILIP SCHAFF, 1819–1893, CHURCH HISTORIAN, TEACHER, AND LEADER OF MEN

Philip Schaff, Professor of Church History in Union Theological Seminary, braved the danger of a second stroke of paralysis to attend the World's Parliament of Religions, where he presented an address on *The Reunion of Christendom*, memorable for its knowledge of the facts, its tolerance, sympathy, and appreciation of the good in all communions, its optimistic faith, and its practical common sense. Dr. Schaff described himself as "a Swiss by birth, a German by education, an American by choice." He forsook a career of great promise in Germany where he had begun work as a teacher in the University of Berlin to come to America in 1844 as professor in the Mercersburg Theological Seminary of the Reformed Church. In 1870 he accepted a professorship in Union Seminary. The fiftieth anniversary of his entrance upon the work of a teacher found him still in active service, and was celebrated by tributes from both sides of the Atlantic. His practical leadership was as remarkable as his erudition, and the output of his labors was prodigious. It was said of him that he set more men at work in the projects of scholarship and accomplished more for Christian unity than any other man of his time.

516   Room in Westminster Abbey in which the work of revision was done, from a drawing in *Harper's Weekly*, June 4, 1881

THE REVISION OF THE ENGLISH BIBLE

DR. SCHAFF was president of the American Committee of thirty-four scholars which collaborated with an English Committee of sixty-seven to revise the translation of the Bible from the original Hebrew and Greek into English, made under the authority of King James I and published in 1611, which had become the generally accepted version among English-speaking Protestants. Catholics use the Douai version, translated from the Latin Vulgate by English refugees in France during the reign of Queen Elizabeth. The King James version is faithful to the original in so far as this was available to its translators, and the simplicity and purity of its diction cause it to be generally acknowledged as an English classic. The aim of the revisers was simply to "adapt King James' version to the present state of the English language without changing the idiom and vocabulary," and to avail themselves of the further knowledge of the original text and its meaning which the growth of Biblical scholarship throughout a period of nearly three hundred years had made possible. They sought to make only such changes as were necessary for "greater accuracy, clearness and consistency."

PUBLIC INTEREST IN THE REVISED VERSION OF THE ENGLISH BIBLE

THE revisers labored for ten and a half years upon the New Testament and fourteen upon the Old Testament, holding monthly sessions of from two to four days. The Revision of the New Testament was published on May 20, 1881, and two hundred thousand copies were sold in New York on that day. In their Sunday issues of May 22 the Chicago *Times* and the Chicago *Tribune* printed the entire text. The *Times* received the four Gospels, the Acts of the Apostles, and the Epistle to the Romans by telegraph from New York to make this publication possible; and it stated with pardonable pride that "this portion of the New Testament contains about one hundred and eighteen thousand words, and constitutes by manifold the largest despatch ever sent over the wires." The Revision of the Old Testament was issued four years later in May, 1885.

9 After this manner therefore pray ye: [b] Our Father which art in heaven, [c] Hallowed be thy name.
10 [e] Thy kingdom come. [f] Thy will be done in earth, [h] as *it is* in heaven.
11 Give us this day our [k] daily bread.
12 And forgive us our [m] debts, as we forgive our debtors.
13 [n] And lead us not into temptation, but deliver us [o] from evil: [q] For thine is the kingdom, and the power, and the glory, for ever. Amen.
14 [r] For if ye forgive men their trespasses, your heavenly Father will also forgive you:

517   The Lord's Prayer, from the King James Version of the New Testament

ye ask him. After this manner therefore pray 9 ye: Our Father which art in heaven, Hallowed be thy name. Thy kingdom come. Thy will 10 be done, as in heaven, so on earth. Give us 11 this day [2] our daily bread. And forgive us our 12 debts, as we also have forgiven our debtors. And bring us not into temptation, but deliver 13 us from [3] the evil *one*.[4] For if ye forgive men 14 their trespasses, your heavenly Father will also forgive you. But if ye forgive not men their 15 trespasses, neither will your Father forgive your trespasses.
Moreover when ye fast, be not, as the hypo- 16 crites, of a sad countenance: for they disfigure their faces, that they may be seen of men to fast. Verily I say unto you, They have received their reward. But thou, when thou 17 fastest, anoint thy head, and wash thy face; that thou be not seen of men to fast, but of 18 thy Father which is in secret: and thy Father,

518   The Lord's Prayer, from the Revised Version of the New Testament

THE AMERICAN STANDARD VERSION OF THE BIBLE

THE Revised Version was disappointing to many. Partisans found old proof-texts upset, conservatives thought that the revisers had made too many changes, and liberals that they had made too few. The great mass of common folk were disturbed by it, and preferred to keep on reading "the Old Version" in family worship and in private devotions. In 1901 an American Standard Edition of the Revised Version was published containing the readings preferred by the American Committee. This revision of the Revision is fast winning its way to general acceptance in this country in spite of one substitution — "Jehovah" for "LORD" and "GOD" — which is of doubtful value. Other English translations have appeared in the last twenty-five years. Some of these, based upon new knowledge of the differences between classical and Hellenistic Greek, are illuminating; others, which aim chiefly at up-to-date English, are naturally transient.

519 *The Old Version*, from an engraving after the painting by Thomas Hovenden (1840–95), in *Harper's Weekly*, April 1, 1882

CREED–REVISION AND HERESY–TRIALS IN THE PRESBYTERIAN CHURCH

IN 1889, suggested by similar actions taken by the Presbyterian Churches of Scotland and England, overtures were presented to the General Assembly of the Presbyterian Church for the revision of the Westminster Confession. The discussion thus precipitated was widespread and intense. Though it became clear that the opponents of revision as well as its advocates did not hold the view with respect to the damnation of infants which the authors of the Confession seem to have held, the movement failed to obtain the necessary two-thirds vote, and the subsequent proposal that a wholly new creedal statement be prepared was laid on the table. This result was in part due to a reaction toward conservatism aroused by the belligerently uncompromising attitudes of Professor Charles A. Briggs of Union Seminary, who was suspended from the Presbyterian ministry by the General Assembly of 1893 for his teachings concerning the composition and errancy of the Scriptures and concerning the sources of authority in religion. Professor Henry P. Smith of Lane Seminary who had been suspended by his Presbytery for similar teaching was denied an appeal by the same Assembly. The Briggs case was unfortunate. It helped to divide the church into conservative and liberal groups, and caused Union Seminary to withdraw from affiliation with the General Assembly. In two respects, moreover, the decision was complicated by novel ideas which a calmer judgment would have hesitated to fasten upon the church; Professor Briggs' offense of error in teaching was confused with personal sin, by describing it as a "violation" of his ordination vow which called for "repentance"; and the Assembly committed itself to the dogma of the inerrancy of the original texts of Scripture while admitting that these are now lost — a position quite different from that of the Westminster Confession.

520 Charles O. Briggs, 1841–1913, from a photograph, courtesy of Mrs. Charles O. Briggs

THE NAUGHTINESS OF THE NOISY NEWTON AND THE PERPLEXITY OF THE PEACEFUL POTTER.

521   From a cartoon by Joseph Keppler in *Puck*, Feb. 4, 1885

TWO WAYS OF DEALING WITH HERESY

PROFESSOR BRIGGS found fellowship in the Protestant Episcopal Church of which he was ordained priest in 1899. Since the days of the Muhlenberg Memorial this church had shown a remarkable power to hold in its communion men of diverse liturgical and doctrinal views. In 1884 and again in 1886 and 1891 Bishop Henry C. Potter had disposed of the case of Dr. R. Heber Newton who insisted on preaching the "higher criticism" by the simple expedient of asking him to preach only what in good conscience he believed to be helpful to his people, and then receiving and pigeon-holing without further action the protests against his "heresy." In 1906 however Dr. Algernon S. Crapsey, Rector of St. Andrews' Church in Rochester, was deposed from the ministry for his use of the pulpit of his church to deny certain articles of its Creed, particularly that concerning the virgin birth of Christ. The "myths" portrayed in the cartoon had nothing to do with the case, which turned entirely upon Dr. Crapsey's interpretation of the New Testament and the Apostles' Creed; but this was as close as *Puck* generally got to the real issue in such matters.

A MYTHICAL KICK COMING.

PRESIDENT ADAM.—Fellow Myths! We are gathered here to-day to protest against the heretical utterances of one Dr. Crapsey, who repeatedly asserts that we never existed.

ROBERT G. INGERSOLL, 1833–1899, AGNOSTIC

THE most eloquent "infidel" of the last quarter of the nineteenth century was Colonel Robert G. Ingersoll, a minister's son who revolted from the extreme Calvinistic orthodoxy in which he had been reared. Like Huxley he wished to be known as an agnostic: "I do not deny. I do not know — but I do not believe." He ridiculed the Bible, and traveled throughout the country lecturing on *Some Mistakes of Moses*. He caricatured theology, and regarded ministers as impostors, "The clergy know that I know that they know that they do not know." "I do not hate Presbyterians, I hate Presbyterianism. I hate with all my heart the creed of that church, and I most heartily despise the God described in the Confession of Faith. Some of the best friends I have in the world are afflicted with the mental malady known as Presbyterianism. They are the victims of the consolation growing out of the belief that a vast majority of their fellowmen are doomed to suffer eternal torment, to the end that their Creator may be eternally glorified. I do not despise a man because he has the rheumatism; I despise the rheumatism because it has a man." "Somebody ought to tell the truth about the Bible. The preachers dare not, because they would be driven from their pulpits. Professors

523   Robert G. Ingersoll, from a photograph by Rockwood, New York

in colleges dare not, because they would lose their salaries. Politicians dare not. They would be defeated. Editors dare not. They would lose subscribers. Merchants dare not, because they might lose customers. Men of fashion dare not, fearing that they would lose caste. Even clerks dare not, because they might be discharged. And so, I thought I would do it myself."

Ingersoll praised science for much that it does not pretend to do. "Science is the providence of man, the worker of true miracles. . . . Science is the great physician. . . . Science is the destroyer of disease, builder of happy homes, the preserver of life and love. Science is the teacher of every virtue, the enemy of every vice. Science has given the true basis of morals, the origin and office of conscience, revealed the nature of obligation, of duty, of virtue in its highest, noblest forms, and has demonstrated that true happiness is the only possible good. . . . Science is the only true religion. Science is the only Savior of the world. . . . To love justice, to long for the right, to love mercy, to pity the suffering, to assist the weak, to forget wrongs and remember benefits — to love the truth, to be sincere, to utter honest words, to love liberty, to wage relentless war against slavery in all its forms, to love wife and child and friend, to make a happy home, to love the beautiful in art, in nature, to cultivate the mind, to be familiar with the mighty thoughts that genius has expressed, the noble deeds of all the world, to cultivate courage and cheerfulness, to make others happy, to fill life with the splendor of generous acts, the warmth of loving words . . . to receive new truths with gladness, to cultivate hope, to see the calm before the storm, the dawn before the night, to do the best that can be done and then be resigned — this is the religion of reason, the creed of science."

524   From a cartoon *The Universal Church of the Future*, by Joseph Keppler in *Puck*, Jan. 10, 1883

525   Andrew D. White, from a photograph by Pack
Bros., New York

"THE WARFARE OF SCIENCE WITH THEOLOGY"

RELIGION is more than a way of living; it is a way of living undergirded and sustained by a belief concerning the character of the Universe. It holds that Nature is the expression of the creative purpose and immanent will of a God, whose power and love assure the conservation of all such values as are fit to be eternal. This belief is entirely independent of the particular form of the mechanisms, processes and laws which constitute the details of God's method in Nature. Atoms may or may not be divisible; creation may or may not be through natural selection; religious belief may be justified in either case. Yet because the beliefs of religion cannot be intelligibly expressed except in current concepts, there is always chance for confusion between the truth which is essential and the passing forms in which it is clothed. At times the protagonists of religion, falling into this confusion, have resisted the progress of scientific discovery because it seemed to them at some point to contradict and subvert religious faith. An interesting and useful, though somewhat one-sided account of the conflicts thus engendered, was written by Andrew D. White, 1832–1918, president of Cornell University, in his two-volume *History of the Warfare of Science with Theology in Christendom.*

DOES EVOLUTION DENY GOD?

THE principle of evolution enunciated by Charles Darwin awakened especial apprehension because it seemed to contradict the Biblical account of creation, and because in the person of Huxley it became associated with agnosticism, and was expanded by Herbert Spencer into a naturalistic philosophy. Many saw, however, that the laws of evolution are no more inconsistent with theism than are the laws of gravitation; and that acceptance of the principle of evolution is not subversive of religious faith unless it be made the basis of a naturalistic philosophy which goes quite beyond the deliverances of science. *Puck* ridiculed the efforts of Henry Ward Beecher, near the close of his life, to show this. But the defenders of a theistic interpretation of evolution, as opposed to naturalism, were too effective to be silenced by ridicule. Joseph Le Conte, 1823–1901, professor of geology in the University of California, wrote *Religion and Science* as early as 1874; and in 1888 published *Evolution; its History, its Evidences, and its Relation to Religious Thought.* Henry Drummond's *Natural Law in the Spiritual World* and *The Ascent of Man,* and E. Griffith-Jones' *The Ascent through Christ,* written in England, were widely read here. Other books of large influence in this field were John Fiske, 1842–1901, *The Idea of God, The Destiny of Man,* and *Through Nature to God;* Newman Smythe, 1843–1925, *Through Science to Faith;* George Harris, 1844–1922, *Moral Evolution;* and Lyman Abbott, *The Theology of an Evolutionist.*

THE OLD ATTEMPT.

526   From a cartoon *The Old Attempt,* in *Puck,* June 3, 1885

LYMAN ABBOTT, 1835–1922, PREACHER OF DIVINE IMMANENCE

"EVOLUTION," John Fiske said, "is God's way of doing things." Lyman Abbott, successor to Henry Ward Beecher as pastor of Plymouth Church, Brooklyn, held that Creation is "a process, not a product"; God is not merely a Great First Cause, but "the One Great Cause from whom all forms of nature and of life continuously proceed." Revelation must be progressive, for it is "God's education of man." He disposed of the traditional doctrine that

In Adam's fall
We sinned all

by quoting a bon mot attributed to Professor Roswell D. Hitchcock, of Union Theological Seminary, "Adam did not represent me, for I never voted for him." As an editor and public lecturer he became the counsellor of multitudes who were perplexed concerning the mutual relations of science and religion, and did much to direct the life and thought of his day toward modernism.

527 Lyman Abbott, from a photograph by Sherman McHugh, New York

ADONIRAM JUDSON GORDON, 1836–1895, PREACHER OF THE SECOND COMING OF CHRIST

ADONIRAM JUDSON GORDON, minister of the Clarendon Street Baptist Church in Boston, held a position opposed to that of Dr. Abbott. He asserted that the ministry of the churches was in peril of being "impoverished by excess of learning." "Reason and faith are like the two compartments of an hour-glass; when one is full the other is empty." He believed that this present world is inherently evil and will always remain evil; that redemption of the race through social evolution is hopeless; and that "progress" is an illusion. He looked with confident expectation for the "glorious appearing" of Christ, who is to come again with power, and will "smite the nations" and reign on earth for a thousand years, from the first to the second resurrection.

528 Adoniram Judson Gordon, from a photograph, courtesy of the Reverend A. H. Gordon

FUNDAMENTALISM

IN 1910 a paper-bound volume entitled *The Fundamentals: A Testimony to the Truth*, was sent gratuitously to ministers and other Christian leaders throughout the English-speaking world. Other volumes followed at intervals of a few months, until twelve had been distributed. The movement thus stimulated, known as Fundamentalism, has occasioned much controversy, particularly in the Baptist and Presbyterian churches, and among the Disciples of Christ. The five test-points of Fundamentalism are the Virgin Birth of Christ, the physical resurrection, the inerrancy of the Scriptures in matters of historical and scientific fact as well as in principles of religious faith, the substitutionary theory of the Atonement, and the imminent, physical Second Coming of Christ. To believe these doctrines is regarded as evidence of one's soundness in the faith; to falter or doubt on any of these points causes one to be denounced as "no Christian." The movement is fostered by the Moody Bible Institute at Chicago and a Bible Institute at Los Angeles, and spread by "prophetic conferences" which bring together large numbers of people without regard to their denominational affiliation.

The Fundamentals

A Testimony to the Truth

Volume V

Compliments of
Two Christian Laymen

TESTIMONY PUBLISHING COMPANY
(Not Inc.)
808 La Salle Ave., Chicago, Ill., U. S. A.

529 Facsimile of title-page of *The Fundamentals*, Chicago, 1910

530   Union Theological Seminary, from a photograph by Keystone
View Co., New York

MODERNISM

MODERNISM, the bogey of Fundamentalists, is more difficult to define, for it is unorganized and has no list of shibboleths. In general, a modernist accepts the methods and results of modern science, including the laws of biological evolution; he believes in the possible redemption of this present world by the social application of the principles of Jesus; and interprets the Bible using the historian's methods of criticism of documents. Extreme modernism goes so far as to reduce religion to ethics and deny the metaphysical reality of God. Most Christians are neither Fundamentalists nor extreme modernists.

They are evangelical. They believe in the gospel of God's redeeming love as revealed in Jesus Christ, and they find that this gospel is distorted and obscured by the legalism and pre-millenarianism of one party, while it is denied by the other.

HARRY EMERSON FOSDICK, 1878–, EVANGELICAL MODERNIST

As pastor of the First Baptist Church of Montclair, New Jersey, Harry Emerson Fosdick won high reputation as a preacher. He became professor of practical theology in Union Theological Seminary in 1915, and invited to serve also as permanent preacher for the First Presbyterian Church of New York, he accepted on condition that he be allowed to remain a Baptist. Aroused by his sermon entitled *Shall the Fundamentalists Win?* the Presbytery of Philadelphia charged him with heresy and urged inquiry into his ecclesiastical status. The General Assembly of 1924, without passing judgment upon his views, invited him to enter the ministry of the Presbyterian Church or to vacate his pulpit. He accepted the latter alternative, declaring that "Creedal subscription to ancient confessions of faith is a practice dangerous to the welfare of the Church and to the integrity of the individual conscience."

531   Harry Emerson Fosdick, from a photograph by Underwood & Underwood, New York

"ABIDING EXPERIENCES AND CHANGING CATEGORIES"

As preëminent in pulpit power as were Henry Ward Beecher and Phillips Brooks, Dr. Fosdick has also made effective use of the printed page; and his books, especially *The Manhood of the Master* and *The Meaning of Prayer*, have had large influence. His Lyman Beecher Lectures at Yale on *The Modern Use of the Bible*

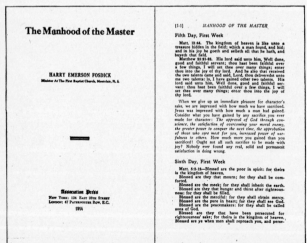

532   Facsimile of pages from Harry Emerson Fosdick, *The Manhood of the Master*, Association Press, New York, 1914

present a most effective exposition of evangelical modernism. "What is permanent in Christianity is not mental frameworks but abiding experiences that phrase and rephrase themselves in successive generations' ways of thinking and grow in assured certainty and in richness of content." "Jesus does not give us rules and regulations. . . . Instead, he has given us in timeless terms expressed in universally applicable life a form of conduct, a quality of spirit, which changing circumstances do not affect. . . . Preach him, therefore, not as those who timidly suspect that outgrown categories have lost their cause, but as those who know that all the categories ever used about him have been but partial appreciations of his divine reality." "It is not so much the humanity of Jesus that makes him imitable as it is his divinity."

THE TENNESSEE ANTI–EVOLUTION LAW

In 1925 the Legislature of Tennessee passed an act prohibiting teachers in any schools supported wholly or partly by public funds "to teach any theory which denies the story of the Divine creation of man as taught in the Bible, and to teach instead that man has descended from lower forms of animals." John T. Scopes, a young teacher of biology in Dayton, was arrested. His trial aroused world-wide interest. William Jennings Bryan, assisting the prosecution, sought to prove that the Biblical account of creation is in all details to be literally believed as a revelation inspired of God. Clarence Darrow, agnostic, denounced the law as "the most brazen and bold attempt to destroy liberty since the Middle Ages." Unfortunately, expert testimony, both of scientists and theologians, was excluded; and judgment was rendered against the defendant without facing the broad issues involved. One of the most striking aspects of the religious developments in twentieth-century

533 Judge Raulston charging the Jury at the Scopes Trial, from a photograph by the Pacific and Atlantic Photo Co., New York

America is the occasional tendency of state legislatures to undertake, by majority vote, to determine what is religious orthodoxy and what is scientific truth. The so-called anti-evolution laws apply only to public schools maintained at public expense.

DENY SCIENCE WARS AGAINST RELIGION

Forty Scientists, Clergymen and Prominent Educators Attack "Two Erroneous Views."

SEE DEITY TWICE REVEALED

Science Shows His Work in Nature, Religion Develops Spiritual Ideals, They Assert.

WASHINGTON, May 26.—A joint statement holding that there is no an-tagonism between science and religion was issued here tonight as representing the conclusions of a group of forty distinguished Americans on a subject which recently has aroused bitter and widespread controversy.

The names of two Cabinet officers, Secretaries Hoover and Davis; three Bishops and many others in positions of leadership in the political, business, scientific and religious world, are attached to the declaration, which was prepared by Dr. R. A. Millikan, director of the Norman Bridge Laboratory of Physics, at Pasadena, Cal.

"The purpose," said an accompanying explanation, "is to assist in correcting two erroneous impressions that seem to be current among certain groups of persons. The first is that religion today stands for medieval theology, the second that science is materialistic and irreligious."

The statement itself reads:

"We, the undersigned, deeply regret that in recent controversies there has been a tendency to present science and religion as irreconcilable and antagonistic domains of thought, for, in fact, they meet distinct human needs, and in the rounding out of human life they supplement rather than displace or oppose each other.

"The purpose of science is to develop, without prejudice or preconception of any kind, a knowledge of the facts, the laws and the processes of nature. The even more important task of religion, on the other hand, is to develop the consciences, the ideals and the aspirations of mankind. Each of these two activities represents a deep and vital function of the soul of man, and both are necessary for the life, the progress and the happiness of the human race.

"It is a sublime conception of God which is furnished by science, and one wholly consonant with the highest ideals of religion, when it represents Him as revealing Himself through countless ages in the development of the earth as an abode for man and in the age-long inbreathing of life into its constituent matter, culminating in man with his spiritual nature and all his Godlike powers."

Besides Secretaries Hoover and Davis, those whose names were attached to the statement included Bishops William Lawrence and William Thomas Manning of the Episcopal Church, and Bishop Francis J. McConnell of the Methodist Episcopal Church; Dr. Charles D. Walcott of the Smithsonian Institution, who is President of the National Academy of Sciences; President

534   From the *New York Times*, May 27, 1923

THE RELATIONS OF SCIENCE AND RELIGION

In June, 1923, a group of distinguished men issued *A Joint Statement upon the Relations of Science and Religion*, which asserted that they are complementary rather than antagonistic. "The purpose of science is to develop, without prejudice or preconception of any kind, a knowledge of the facts, the laws, and the processes of nature. The even more important task of religion, on the other hand, is to develop the consciences, the ideals, and the aspirations of mankind. Each of these two activities . . . is necessary for the life, the progress, and the happiness of the human race." The statement was proposed by Robert A. Millikan, world-famed physicist; and among the scientists who signed it were Charles D. Walcott, President of the American Association for the Advancement of Science and Head of the Smithsonian Institution; Henry Fairfield Osborn, president of the American Museum of Natural History; John C. Merriam, president of the Carnegie Institution; Gano Dunn, Chairman of the National Research Council; James R. Angell, psychologist and president of Yale University; William W. Campbell, astronomer, president of the University of California; Michael I. Pupin, physicist and engineer; Dr. William J. Mayo, surgeon; and Dr. William H. Welch, pathologist.

535

The Procession of the Blessed Eucharist, from a photograph by Kaufman and Fabry, Chicago

THE EUCHARISTIC CONGRESS AT CHICAGO

THE greatest religious gathering in point of attendance and splendor ever held in America was the Twenty-eighth International Eucharistic Congress of the Roman Catholic Church, which assembled in Chicago, June 20–24, 1926. Its purpose was not deliberative, but devotional. Thirteen cardinals, five hundred bishops, five thousand priests, and more than a million lay members of the Church gathered to pay homage to the Lord Jesus Christ, who is really present, according to their faith, in the Eucharist. As St. Thomas Aquinas expressed it, nearly seven centuries ago:

Taught by Christ the church maintaineth
That the bread its substance changeth
Into Flesh, the wine to Blood.
Doth it pass thy comprehending?
Faith, the law of sight transcending
Leaps to things not understood.

At the Mass of the Angels, on Soldiers Field, a choir of sixty thousand children sang. The climax of the Congress was the Procession of the Blessed Eucharist, on the beautiful grounds of St. Mary of the Lakes Seminary at Mundelein. A well-known Protestant minister of Chicago wrote: "The Roman Catholic Church has been for centuries the incomparable mistress of pageantry and ceremonial; and every resource was drawn upon to the full to make the Congress the most splendid event possible. . . . In color, in symbolism, in stately march, in the timing of events, in dramatic effect realized by great groups acting in concert, it dwarfed any civic ceremony that ever had been seen by the hundreds of thousands of spectators. One was swept off his feet by the overwhelming effect of procession, song, and stately ritual which was charged with the deepest and most sacred symbolism. The spectator might not assent at all to the dogmatic implications of the scenes; but he could not remain unmoved by the artistic beauty of the spectacle." — OZORA S. DAVIS, *The Outlook*, July 7, 1926.

536   Meeting of the Society of the Holy Name in Washington, Sept. 21, 1924, from a photograph by Cullen Saulbury De Souza, Washington

THE SOCIETY OF THE HOLY NAME

ON the evening of the third day of the Congress, one hundred and fifty thousand men, gathered in Soldiers Field, took the pledge of the Holy Name Society: "I pledge my loyalty to my flag and my country and to the God-given principles of freedom, justice, and happiness for which it stands. I pledge my support to all lawful authority, both civil and religious. I dedicate my manhood to the honor of the sacred name of Jesus Christ and beg that he will keep me faithful to these pledges until death." Then, the flame passing from rank to rank, there were lighted one hundred and fifty thousand candles, one borne by each member of the great throng. The Society of the Holy Name originated in the thirteenth century. Its work was encouraged by Pope Leo XIII in 1896, and it has had a steady growth since that time. There are now two million four hundred and twenty-nine thousand five hundred and fifty members in the United States.

BUILDING AMERICAN CATHEDRALS

A COMMUNITY enterprise to which Catholics, Jews, and members of all Protestant churches have contributed in the hope that it will be a "great, unifying, spiritual and civic force," is the Cathedral of St. John the Divine, on Morningside Heights, New York. The corner stone was laid by Bishop Henry C. Potter of the

537   The Washington Cathedral, from an architect's drawing, courtesy of the National Cathedral Association, Washington

Protestant Episcopal Church in 1892, and the choir, with seven encircling chapels, was built in the following years. Work was begun on the nave in 1925. When completed, it will be one of the three greatest cathedrals in the world, being exceeded in size only by St. Peter's in Rome and the Cathedral of Seville. A national Protestant Episcopal Cathedral, named for SS. Peter and Paul, is in process of erection at Washington. Such buildings express in enduring stone the eternal supremacy of the spirit which religion asserts. Their spaciousness forbids petty distinctions; their majesty and beauty impel to worship, and help men to realize the presence of God.

538 Federal Council Executive Committee Meeting in Minneapolis, Dec. 1912, from a photograph, courtesy of the Federal Council of Churches, New York

THE FEDERAL COUNCIL OF THE CHURCHES OF CHRIST IN AMERICA

THE first quarter of the twentieth century has been marked by growing coöperation of the Protestant churches in the various fields of their interest. Theodore Roosevelt, addressing a meeting in 1900 which organized the New York State Federation of Churches, said, "There are plenty of targets that we need to hit without firing into each other." The Federal Council of Churches of Christ in America was organized in 1908 by official action of twenty-nine national denominational bodies in order "more fully to manifest the essential oneness of the Christian Churches of America in Jesus Christ as their divine Lord and Saviour and to promote the spirit of fellowship, service, and coöperation among them. One of the particular aims included under this general statement of purpose is: "To secure a larger combined influence for the Churches of Christ in all matters affecting the moral and social condition of the people."

The effectiveness of the Federal Council in this respect has awakened the fears of many Christians who believe that this church organization is guilty of dangerous meddling and who have charged it with "mixing in politics" and "attempting to control the affairs of civil government." The Council has answered that it "does not consider any question involving principles of right and justice as being secular. . . . The people in the churches are rapidly coming to look at all public affairs as matters of Christian ethics. . . . The leaders of the church are tired of preaching justice in theory and closing their eyes to injustice in practice. . . . The churches should sedulously refrain from 'lobbying' or from any attempt to coerce legislators by organizing the voting strength of their districts for or against them. . . . But the church has not only the right, but the duty, to educate public opinion concerning the Christian principles that are at stake in legislative proposals. . . . Surely Christian ethics are not left entirely to be determined by Congress."

THE INTERNATIONAL COUNCIL OF RELIGIOUS EDUCATION

WITH the opening of the present century, the Protestant churches began to awake to the danger involved in the omission of religion from the program and curriculum of otherwise competent public schools, and the throwing of responsibility for the religious training of the young upon educationally incompetent Sunday schools. In 1903 the Religious Education Association was organized, with the declared purpose "to inspire the educational forces of our country with the religious ideal, to inspire the religious forces of our country with the educational ideal, and to keep before the public mind the ideal of religious education and the sense of its need and value." In 1922, by a merger of former organizations, was formed the International Council of Religious Education, an agency for the coöperative effort of the Protestant churches. Under its leadership new standards are set for the work of the Sunday schools; the training of teachers has been lifted to a higher level; problems of curriculum, method and educational administration are being studied in an experimental and scientific way; and progress has been made in the establishment of new types of week-day and vacation church schools for the teaching of religion.

539 Dedication of the Marion Lawrance Memorial at Lake Geneva, July 31, 1927, from a photograph in the possession of the International Council of Religious Education, Chicago

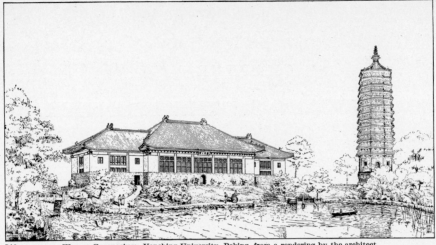

540   Warner Gymnasium, Yenching University, Peking, from a rendering by the architect,
Henry Killam Murphy

PROTESTANT COÖPERATION IN MISSIONARY WORK

IN 1893 was established the Foreign Missions Conference of North America, in which all of the Protestant foreign-missionary societies and boards of the United States and Canada are now associated. It meets once a year for the discussion of common problems, and its Committee on Reference and Counsel, with a permanent office and an employed staff, constitutes in effect a board of strategy with respect to missionary policies and measures which has done much to further coöperation between the various denominations in their work upon the foreign fields. The Home Missions Council, organized in 1908, undertakes similarly to serve the home-missionary organizations, thirty-six of which are represented in its membership. Home mission boards concern themselves with the underprivileged groups all over the nation, new immigrants, racial and lingual groups, migrant workers; with problems of social justice and industrial welfare; with the organization of rural churches into "larger parishes," coöperating in worship, religious education, social life, and community service, under leadership more competent than each could command alone; with the establishment of community houses and social settlements in the tenement district of great cities. The task of the home mission is "to mobilize all the resources of the Church for the Christianization of the country as a whole."

THE GROWTH OF THE PROTESTANT CHURCHES

IT is difficult to secure comparative statistics for the growth of the churches, on account of their varying practices with respect to the reception and retention of membership. Figures showing the remarkable growth of the Catholic Church in this country have been given on page 168. The Protestant churches, too, have grown at a rate far exceeding that of the general population. In 1800 seven out of every hundred citizens were members of Protestant churches; in 1850, fifteen; in 1900, twenty-four; in 1925, twenty-six out of every hundred. In the twenty years from 1906 to 1925 the population of the country increased thirty-six per cent, while the Protestant church membership increased forty-six per cent. The table gives the membership in 1925, based upon the returns of the various denominational bodies of the eleven Protestant groups which have a membership of two hundred thousand or more. The total membership of the Protestant churches, not counting dependent children or others attached by ties less responsible than full communicant fellowship, is nearly thirty million. Ninety-five per cent of this Protestant membership is in the eleven groups of churches here listed.

MEMBERSHIP OF PRINCIPAL PROTESTANT DENOMINATIONS, 1925

Methodists (15 bodies)	8,920,190
Baptists (14 bodies)	8,397,914
Presbyterians (9 bodies)	2,561,986
Lutherans (17 bodies)	2,546,127
Disciples (2 bodies)	1,759,399
Protestant Episcopal	1,164,911
Congregationalists	907,583
Latter Day Saints (2 bodies)	625,160
Reformed (3 bodies)	540,987
Evangelical (2 bodies)	508,612
United Brethren (2 bodies)	411,956

CHAPTER VIII

RELIGION ON THE FRONTIER

AMONG the evils enumerated by the "Reform Synod" of the Massachusetts churches in 1680 was the eagerness of many to push westward and to appropriate lands upon the frontier: "There hath been in many professors an insatiable desire after Land and worldly Accommodations, yea, so as to forsake Churches and Ordinances, and to live like Heathen, only so they might have Elbow-room enough in the world. . . . We cannot but solemnly bear witness against that practice of settling Plantations without any Ministry amongst them, which is to prefer the world before the Gospel."

It would have required far more than the vote of a few ministers meeting in Boston to stop the steady advance westward of the line of the frontier. Into western Massachusetts and northern New York, across the Alleghenies into Ohio, Tennessee, and the blue grass of Kentucky, into the woods of Michigan and over the rolling prairies of the Mississippi valley, across the Rockies to Oregon and California, north to Alaska, finally back to transform the Indian Territory into Oklahoma — for over two centuries longer the trek of pioneer settlers continued, until in the last decade of the nineteenth century there was no more land to be distributed freely to homesteaders.

The first home missionaries were to the Indians, but soon the spiritual needs of the white folk in the frontier settlements claimed the preponderant interest of the missionary societies that began to be formed. Groups of theological students in a number of cases formed associations or "bands," pledging themselves to go together to some chosen territory upon the frontier and there to devote their lives to the building up of churches, schools, and colleges. At first aided by the eastern societies, it was the ambition of every such man, as soon as possible, to make himself and his churches self-supporting.

The two Protestant groups which now exceed all others in membership — the Methodist and the Baptist — owe much of their growth to their adaptation to frontier conditions. The direct simplicity and infectious fervor of their appeal to the emotions well suited the mind of the pioneer. And this was coupled, in the case of the Methodists, with an almost military-like effectiveness of organization that was admirably adapted to spiritual campaigning under hard conditions, and, in the case of the Baptists, with an individualism that fitted the frontiersman's lonely independence.

The frontier was more than an outpost of a culture already achieved on the eastern seaboard and destined only to be extended. It had its own difficulties and problems. And the efforts of the nation to meet and solve these did much to determine the course of the history of the United States as a whole and to shape American institutions.

To tell the story of religion on the frontier would be to describe the rude beginnings of hundreds of local communities. Every county and town west of the Alleghenies has its stirring tale of the hardships and bravery of the pioneers, and of the devotion of good men and women who would let no difficulty keep them from God and who with their own hands built churches and schools. This chapter can present only a few of these stories, chosen from many of which they are types: the Illinois and Iowa Bands; Jason Lee, Marcus Whitman, Pierre de Smet, and the winning of the Northwest; William Taylor, Methodist street preacher, and Samuel Willey, Presbyterian pastor, both Forty-niners in California; and the remarkable career of Sheldon Jackson, home-missionary statesman.

JOHN SERGEANT, 1710–1749, MISSIONARY TO THE HOUSATONIC INDIANS

IN 1734 John Sergeant, a tutor in Yale College, accepted appointment by the Massachusetts Commissioners for Indian Affairs to teach and preach to the Housatonic Indians at Stockbridge, on the western frontier. In spite of the Dutch traders from the Hudson and the rum they peddled, he succeeded in converting most of the tribe, and in teaching many to read and to sing. He built a church and a schoolhouse, and devised a plan of education which divided the time of the Indian children and youth between study and manual labor, training the boys in agriculture and the girls in the duties of domestic life. His successor was Jonathan Edwards. In 1775 his son, John Sergeant, Jr., took charge of the work. He moved with his flock when they migrated to New Stockbridge, on the Oneida Reservation in New York, built a church large enough to seat five hundred people, and remained the Indians' minister until his death at the age of seventy-seven in 1824.

541 John Sergeant, from a lithograph by Childs and Inman in the possession of the publishers

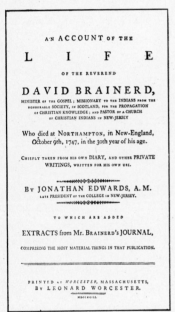

A·N ACCOUNT of THE

L I F E

OF THE REVEREND

DAVID BRAINERD,

MINISTER OF THE GOSPEL; MISSIONARY TO THE INDIANS FROM THE HONOURABLE SOCIETY, IN SCOTLAND, FOR THE PROPAGATION OF CHRISTIAN KNOWLEDGE; AND PASTOR OF A CHURCH OF CHRISTIAN INDIANS IN NEW-JERSEY.

Who died at NORTHAMPTON, in New-England, October 9th, 1747, in the 30th year of his age.

CHIEFLY TAKEN FROM HIS OWN DIARY, AND OTHER PRIVATE WRITINGS, WRITTEN FOR HIS OWN USE.

BY JONATHAN EDWARDS, A. M.
LATE PRESIDENT OF THE COLLEGE IN NEW-JERSEY.

TO WHICH ARE ADDED

EXTRACTS from Mr. BRAINERD's JOURNAL,

COMPRISING THE MOST MATERIAL THINGS IN THAT PUBLICATION.

PRINTED AT WORCESTER, MASSACHUSETTS,
BY LEONARD WORCESTER.

MDCCXCIII.

542 From the original in the New York Public Library

DAVID BRAINERD, 1718–1747, MISSIONARY TO THE DELAWARES

DAVID BRAINERD, most brilliant member of the class of 1743 at Yale College, was expelled in his Junior year for making a derogatory comment concerning the piety of a tutor and attending a Separatist meeting in defiance of the Rector's prohibition. First at Kaunaumeek, near Stockbridge, where he began work under the tutelage of John Sergeant, then among the Delawares in eastern Pennsylvania and New Jersey, he spent himself with ardent devotion as a missionary to the Indians, reckless of failing strength. After only four years of service, he died at the home of Jonathan Edwards, who wrote an *Account* of his life, based upon his diary, which has become a classic. This *Account*, together with his *Journal*, published by the Scotch Society which employed him, caused Brainerd's work to have an influence far exceeding its limited extent and duration. The modern missionary movement owes much to these records of his self-sacrificing zeal and consecration. To name only two men — William Carey and Henry Martyn, justly reckoned among the founders of that movement, were moved by reading about Brainerd to imitate his example.

DAVID ZEISBERGER, 1721–1808, "DESTINIRTER HEIDENBOTE"

DURING his visit to Pennsylvania in 1742 Count Ludwig Nicolaus von Zinzendorf, bishop of the Moravians, chancing to meet a group of Iroquois sachems at the home of Conrad Weiser, Indian agent and interpreter, won their consent to his establishing a mission among them. "Brother," they said, "you have journeyed a long way, from beyond the sea, to preach to the white people and the Indians. You did not know that we were here; we had no knowledge of your coming. The Great Spirit has brought us together. Come to our people. You shall be welcome. Take this fathom of wampum. It is a token that our words are true." So began a friendship which existed for many years between the Iroquois and the Moravians, and gave to the latter a standing among all other tribes. In December, 1744, David Zeisberger, whose name had been recorded as "destinirter Heidenbote" — destined to be a messenger to the heathen — set out upon his journey to Hendrick, Chief of the Mohawks.

543 David Zeisberger, from J. Taylor Hamilton, *History of the Moravian Church*, Times Publishing Co., Bethlehem, 1900

X —16

544 Gnadenhütten destroyed and the Missionaries massacred by the Indians, from Choules, *Origin and History of Missions*, Boston, 1837

HOSTILE INDIANS MASSACRE THE MISSIONARIES AT GNADENHÜTTEN

At Canajoharie Zeisberger and his companion were welcomed by Hendrick; but they were soon arrested by the authorities of New York, who suspected them of sympathy with the French. They were sent back to Pennsylvania after four months' detention in prison. Zeisberger's missionary career lasted sixty-four strenuous years. He was adopted into the tribe of Onondagas, and given the name of Ganousseracheri. Until the outbreak of the French and Indian War in 1755, he labored chiefly among the Iroquois, first at Shamokin, the principal Indian town of Pennsylvania, then at Onondaga, the capital of the Iroquois Confederacy. In 1746 he helped to found Gnadenhütten — "Tents of Grace" — on the Lehigh River as a permanent settlement for converted Indians who wished to forsake the customs of the pagan villages. On November 24, 1755, this settlement was captured and ten Moravians massacred by hostile Indians. Zeisberger, who was on the road hither, escaped only by a chance delay.

ZEISBERGER PREACHING TO THE INDIANS AT GOSCHGOSCHÜNK

During the French and Indian War Zeisberger, kept from access to the Iroquois, was busied with other duties, but found time to complete a grammar of the Onondaga language and a German-

546 The Monument at Gnadenhütten, from a photograph, courtesy of Mr. C. M. Hay, Coshocton, Ohio

545 Zeisberger preaching to the Indians at Goschgoschunk, from an engraving after a painting by Christian Schussele in the possession of the Moravian Missionary Society, Bethlehem, Pa.

Onondaga lexicon in seven manuscript volumes. In 1767 for some unknown reason, the Moravians decided to relinquish the work among the Iroquois for which Zeisberger's experience had so uniquely equipped him, and dispatched him into wholly new territory at Goschgoschünk, in northwestern Pennsylvania. Warned by a friendly chief that the Indians there were bad and would kill him, Zeisberger answered: "If they are very wicked, that is just the reason why I ought to go and preach to them." He preached with such eloquence and boldness that, in spite of the determined resistance of the medicine man, whom he finally denounced as "the servant of the devil and a preacher of lies," he obtained the consent of the Indians to establish a mission.

AMERICAN MILITIA MURDER THE CHRISTIAN INDIANS

Zeisberger pressed on into Ohio, and at the principal town of the Delawares, on March 14, 1771, preached the first Protestant sermon in that territory. His success here was so great that he advised the Christian Indians from Pennsylvania to come to Ohio, where he founded a new Gnadenhütten in 1772. The refusal of the Moravians and their Indian followers to engage in war, and their position between the settlements of the British and the colonists in revolt caused them during the Revolution to become objects of suspicion to both parties. The missionaries were taken to Detroit under arrest by the British. A company of colonial militia sent from Fort Pitt under the command of Colonel Williamson to punish hostile Indians captured the non-resisting Christian Indians of Gnadenhütten; and on the following day, March 8, 1782, murdered them — twenty-nine men, twenty-seven women, and thirty-four children — in cold blood.

THE ORDINANCE ESTABLISHING THE NORTHWEST TERRITORY, 1787

In 1788 the Ohio Company of Associates, principally veterans of the Revolutionary Army, led by General Rufus Putnam, 1738–1824, founded Marietta, the first permanent settlement in Ohio, on lands purchased from Congress. Manasseh Cutler, one of the five directors of the Company, conducted the negotiations with Congress. It is probable that he suggested the articles of the Ordinance of 1787 establishing the Northwest Territory, which forbid slavery and provide for religion and education. The third article reads: "Religion, morality and knowledge being necessary to good government and the happiness of mankind, schools and the means of education shall forever be encouraged." One section of six hundred and forty acres in each

547 First Congregational Church, Marietta, from a photograph in the Public Library, Marietta, Ohio

township of the Ohio Company's purchase was set aside for the support of religion and a like provision was made for the support of schools; while two townships were given as an endowment for the establishment of a university.

548 Manasseh Cutler, from a portrait by N. Lakeman in the Essex Institute, Salem, Mass.

MANASSEH CUTLER, 1742–1823, PREACHER, SCIENTIST, AND CITIZEN

Cutler was pastor of the Congregational Church at Hamilton, Massachusetts, from 1771 until his death. Astute in matters of business and resourceful in dealing with men, he conducted the difficult negotiations with Congress tactfully and with good judgment, but with firmness, and in the end secured not only the terms, but recognition of the principles which he and his associates had in mind. He made a number of journeys to Marietta, procured a minister for the newly organized church, and drafted a charter for the University, which was founded in 1804. Cutler was versed in law and medicine, as well as in theology. He made and recorded astronomical and meteorological observations, and was one of the first Americans to make researches of real scientific value in botany. He was a member of Congress from 1801 to 1805.

THE ORGANIZATION OF HOME MISSIONARY SOCIETIES

The ministers of Connecticut began to be exercised concerning "the state of settlements now forming to the Westward and Northwestward of us, who are destitute of the preached gospel, many of whom are our brethren emigrants from this colony." In June, 1798, the Missionary Society of Connecticut was organized, its object being "to Christianize the heathen of North America, and to support and promote Christian knowledge in the new settlements within the United States." Within less than a decade the Congregational churches of each of the other New England states organized for the same purpose. In 1802 the General Assembly of the Presbyterian Church appointed a Standing Committee of Missions; and in the same year the Massachusetts Domestic Missionary Society, the first such organization among American Baptists, was formed. Alone and afoot, with no outfit but what he could carry, David Bacon, 1771–1817, first missionary of the Connecticut Society, set out from Hartford on August 7, 1800, to go to the Indians "south and west of Lake Erie."

549 David Bacon, from an engraving in Leonard Bacon, *Sketch of Reverend David Bacon*, Boston, 1876

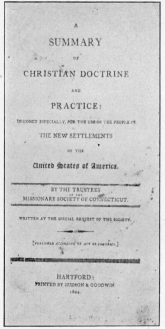

550   From the original in the New
       York Public Library

JOSEPH BADGER, 1757–1845, MISSIONARY TO THE WESTERN RESERVE

THE officers of the Connecticut Society had little understanding of conditions in the Western Reserve and adjacent territory, and they were of an exceedingly economical disposition. They paid Bacon four hundred dollars from August, 1800, to September, 1803; they reduced Joseph Badger's "compensation" after he had been in their service two years, from seven dollars to six dollars a week. Bacon's spirit was finally broken and his death hastened by financial difficulties; Badger, older, more experienced, and a veteran of the Revolution, did not hesitate to say what he thought of the matter, and to accept the support of the Western Missionary Society, a Presbyterian organization with headquarters at Pittsburgh. The "Plan of Union" upon which Congregationalists and Presbyterians had agreed in 1801, as a basis of coöperation on the home-missionary fields, made that a natural step. Itinerating as did the Methodist circuit riders, Badger helped to establish ninety churches in the Western Reserve.

WILLIAM McKENDREE, 1757–1835, METHODIST ORGANIZER AND ADMINISTRATOR

THE commander of the Methodist forces in the West was William McKendree. Son of a Virginia planter and himself a

551 Bishop McKendree, from an engraving after a painting, courtesy of The Christian Advocate, New York

veteran of the Revolution, he experienced conversion in 1787 and soon thereafter entered the itinerant ministry. Notable success as a presiding elder in Virginia led to his appointment in 1801 as general superintendent of the newly organized Western Conference, and presiding elder of the Kentucky District, which included Ohio, Western Virginia, Illinois, Tennessee and Mississippi as well. He directed the rapidly expanding work of the Methodist circuit riders throughout the Great Revival. In 1808 he was elected bishop, the first native American to be chosen to that office by the Methodists; and he became Asbury's successor as head of the movement. "McKendree was one of the greatest preachers Methodism has ever produced, yet it was not as a preacher that he made his abiding contribution. He was an administrator of the first order. . . . It became his task to turn Methodism away from the personal absolutism of Asbury to a settled, legal order, in which bishops, presiding elders, General, Annual, Quarterly, and local Conferences alike felt themselves bound to a line of action definitely laid out by rules in the making of which all had a part. McKendree knew how to blow the great revival of the camp-meeting period to a white-hot flame, and at the same time how to weld a new church, in the heat of this flame, into a firm and lasting order." — LUCCOCK AND HUTCHINSON, *The Story of Methodism*, p. 279.

552   McKendree Church, Nashville, in 1790 and in 1812, from drawings in the possession of *The Christian Advocate*, Nashville, Tenn.   553

A MISSIONARY SURVEY OF THE COUNTRY, 1812–1815

SAMUEL J. MILLS, 1783–1818, the leader of a group of students at Williams College and at Andover Theological Seminary who had dedicated themselves to foreign-missionary service, was not one of the five first chosen to be sent abroad, because it was thought that he would be of greater service by remaining at home to arouse the interest of the churches in missions. In 1812–13, with John F. Schermerhorn, and again in 1814–15, with David Smith, he traversed the country, going as far west as St. Louis and south to New Orleans. The two journeys covered about ten thousand miles, much of the travel being through wilderness. Everywhere he inquired into the moral conditions and spiritual needs of the people, distributed Bibles and organized Bible Societies. He found that the Illinois Territory, with a population of twelve thousand, had five Baptist churches with a total membership of one hundred and twenty, and six Methodist preachers with a following of six hundred members. In New Orleans he distributed three thousand copies of the New Testament in French.

THE AMERICAN BIBLE SOCIETY

THERE was a surprising lack of Bibles. Not far from New York, on the west shore of the Hudson, ninety-five out of one hundred and seventy-nine families had no copy of the Scriptures. At Kaskaskia, then the capital of Illinois Territory, in one hundred families Mills found five Bibles.

REPORT

OF A

MISSIONARY TOUR

THROUGH THAT PART OF THE UNITED STATES

WHICH LIES WEST OF

THE ALLEGANY MOUNTAINS;

PERFORMED UNDER THE DIRECTION

OF THE

MASSACHUSETTS MISSIONARY SOCIETY.

BY SAMUEL J. MILLS AND DANIEL SMITH.

ANDOVER:

PRINTED BY FLAGG AND GOULD.

1815.

554 From the original in the New York Public Library

555 Colporteur Entering a Village, from a drawing by W. H. Browne in *The American Protestant Magazine*, New York, 1846

Local Bible Societies multiplied after the organization of the first in Philadelphia in 1808, and in 1816 there were one hundred and thirty-two such societies in the land. Mills' report revealed the need for more coöperation, and on May 8, 1816, a representative assembly of ministers and laymen, meeting in New York, organized a national body, the American Bible Society. In 1829–30 this society made a systematic effort to supply every family in the United States, that lacked one, with a Bible. The American Tract Society, for the publication and distribution of religious literature, was organized in 1825. The drawing depicts a colporteur of these societies entering a settlement in the log-cabin country.

THE FIRST PROTESTANT CHURCH IN ST. LOUIS

THE report of Mills and Smith captured the imagination of Salmon Giddings, 1782–1828, a tutor in Williams College, and he obtained a commission from the Connecticut Missionary Society to labor in "the Western country." Starting on horseback in December, 1815, he arrived four months later in St. Louis, which he made

his headquarters. He exemplified the "Plan of Union" by organizing the First Presbyterian Church with nine members, of whom five were Massachusetts Congregationalists. He devoted half of his time to its pastorate, and half to missionary itinerancy and the organization of churches throughout the territory. "He valued the great common Christianity above anything that marked mere denominational differences," wrote John M. Peck. "He delighted to encourage every one's efforts in doing good. We coöperated in the formation and management of the first Bible, Sunday School, Tract, and Colonization Societies in St. Louis."

556 The First Presbyterian Church in St. Louis, from a photograph in the Missouri Historical Society

557   The Old Fee Fee Church House, from a drawing in the Missouri Historical
Society, St. Louis, Mo.

EARLY BAPTIST CHURCHES IN MISSOURI

BAPTIST families emigrated from the Carolinas and Kentucky into Upper Louisiana, now Missouri, as early as 1796 — among them children and relatives of Daniel Boone. Under both Spain and France the Catholic Church alone was recognized. When application was made to Commandant Trudeau at St. Louis for permission to have preaching, he rejected the petition in terms that showed friendly sympathy: "You must not put a bell on your house, and call it a church, nor suffer any person to christen your children but the parish priest. But if any of your friends choose to meet at your house, sing, pray, and talk about religion, you will not be molested, provided you continue, as I believe you are, good Christians." He knew, the chronicler comments, that they disbelieved in infant baptism, and that frontiersmen could find the way to meeting without the sound of the church bell. The first Baptist church was organized in 1804 in Cape Girardeau County, and others soon followed in various settlements. John M. Peck, sent as a missionary by the Baptist Board, organized a church in St. Louis in February, 1818.

JOHN M. PECK, 1789–1858, BAPTIST LEADER IN THE MIDDLE WEST

PECK was a vigorous, self-made man. The Foreign Mission Board had commissioned him, for there was then no home-missionary organization among the Baptists. In three years they felt compelled to withdraw support; but, undaunted, Peck remained. In 1827 he established a school which grew to be Shurtleff College, for the endowment of which he secured funds. In 1832 he helped to organize and set in operation the American Baptist Home Missionary Society. He founded, and for twelve years edited and published *The Pioneer*, the first religious newspaper in the western states. His *Emigrant's Guide* (1832) and *Gazetteer of Illinois* (1834) were widely circulated and much used. He was for two years Secretary of the American Baptist Publication Society. All the while he was helping in the organization of churches in Illinois and Missouri,

558   John M. Peck, from Rufus Babcock,
Memoir of John Mason Peck, Philadelphia, 1864

and in the furtherance there of temperance, anti-slavery, and other movements for moral betterment and social reform. Shurtleff College, while remaining small in size, has expanded the scope of its work. Its curriculum includes a preparatory department, an academic department and a conservatory of music. All departments are coeducational. Typical of the denominational college of the Middle West, it is a fitting memorial to the idealism of the men who shared in its founding.

559   Shurtleff College, from Rufus Babcock, *Memoir of John Mason Peck*,
Philadelphia, 1864

ANTI–MISSIONARY BAPTISTS

PECK was opposed by groups who came to be known as Anti-missionary or Primitive Baptists. These formed Associations which decline fellowship with any churches which support any "missionary, Bible, tract, or Sunday school society or advocate State conventions or theological schools." His most annoying opponent was Daniel Parker, founder of the Old Two-Seed-in-the-Spirit Predestinarian Baptists, a small body of folk who out-primitive the Primitives. "Mr. Parker," wrote Peck in 1841, "is one of those singular beings whom Divine providence permits to arise as a scourge to his church, and as a stumbling block in the way of religious effort. Raised on the frontiers of Georgia, without education, uncouth in manners, slovenly in dress, diminutive in person, unprepossessing in appearance, with shrivelled features and a small piercing eye, few men, for a series of years, have exerted a wider influence on the lower and less educated class of frontier people. With a zeal and enthusiasm bordering on insanity, firmness that amounted to obstinacy, and perseverance that would have done honor to a good cause, Daniel Parker exerted himself to the utmost to induce the churches within his range to declare non-fellowship with all Baptists who united with any missionary or other benevolent (or as he called them, newfangled) societies."

560   *The Mountain Preacher*, from the painting by
James R. Hopkins (1877–)

ELIJAH P. LOVEJOY, 1802–1837, DEFENDS WITH HIS LIFE THE FREEDOM OF THE PRESS

ELIJAH P. LOVEJOY, editor of the St. Louis *Times*, a Whig newspaper, was converted in 1832, and went to Princeton to study for the Presbyterian ministry. After being licensed to preach, he returned to St. Louis and was made editor of the St. Louis *Observer*, the religious organ of the Presbyterians and Congregationalists of Illinois and Missouri. His advocacy of the gradual emancipation of the slaves in editorials looking forward to the state constitutional convention called for December, 1835, awakened resentment, and the demand was made that he keep silent on the subject. He met this by a firm insistence upon the constitutional right of freedom of speech and of the press. "See the danger, and the natural and inevitable result, to which the first step here will lead. Today, a public meeting declares that you shall not discuss the subject of slavery. . . . Right or wrong, the press must be silent. . . . The next day, it is, in a similar manner, declared that not a word must be said against distilleries, dram-shops, or drunkenness. And so on. . . . The truth is, my fellow-citizens, if you give ground a single inch, there is no stopping place. I deem it, therefore, my duty to take my stand upon the Constitution. . . . I am a citizen of these United States, a citizen of Missouri, freeborn; and having never forfeited the inestimable privileges attached to such a condition, I cannot consent to surrender them. . . . I am ready, not to fight, but to suffer, and if need be, to die for them." Two years later, that is what he did. He was murdered by a pro-slavery mob at Alton, Illinois.

561   Mob attacking a warehouse on the night of Lovejoy's martyrdom, from a drawing in
Henry Tanner, *The Martyrdom of Lovejoy*, Chicago, 1881

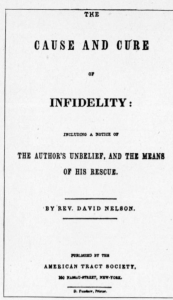

THE

CAUSE AND CURE

OF

INFIDELITY:

INCLUDING A NOTICE OF

THE AUTHOR'S UNBELIEF, AND THE MEANS
OF HIS RESCUE.

BY REV. DAVID NELSON.

PUBLISHED BY THE

AMERICAN TRACT SOCIETY,
150 NASSAU-STREET, NEW-YORK.

D. Fanshaw, Printer.

562   From the original in the New York
Public Library

DAVID NELSON, 1793–1844, OPPONENT OF INFIDELITY AND SLAVERY

DAVID NELSON, a Tennessee physician who had been a surgeon in Jackson's army, was converted from infidelity through his own thought and reading, coming to feel that writers like Thomas Paine misquoted and perverted the Scriptures and misrepresented the facts of history. He gave up a lucrative practice to enter the Presbyterian ministry, emancipated his slaves, and became pastor of churches, first in Kentucky, then in Missouri. Here he founded a college at Marion, and became its first president. His views with respect to slavery so enraged some of his neighbors that he was compelled to hide for three days in a thicket on the banks of the Mississippi. Rescued by friends from the Illinois shore, he remained for the rest of his life near Quincy. While in hiding he wrote on the backs of letters a hymn which has been much used:

> My days are gliding swiftly by,
> And I, a pilgrim stranger,
> Would not detain them as they fly,
> Those hours of toil and danger.

His greatest contribution to the life of his time was a powerful book on *The Cause and Cure of Infidelity*, first published in 1836, and reprinted in many editions.

THE ILLINOIS BAND

AT a meeting in December, 1828, of the Society of Inquiry at the Yale Divinity School, Theron Baldwin, 1801–70, read a stirring essay on *The Call of the West*. With eleven of his fellow-students he formed the Illinois Association, more familiarly known as the "Illinois Band"; and they pledged themselves to seek service in that state, as teachers and ministers. All but one went to Illinois directly from the seminary, commissioned by the American Home Missionary Society. Baldwin and Julian M. Sturtevant, 1805–86, went first, and founded Illinois College, of which Sturtevant became the first instructor. Baldwin settled as pastor at Vandalia, and labored to secure funds and a charter for the college. In 1843 he helped to organize the Society for the Promotion of Collegiate and Theological Education in the West, with headquarters in New York. As secretary of this Society, he devoted twenty-seven years to unremitting service in behalf of institutions of higher education in the frontier states, till he came to be known as "The Father of Western Colleges."

563   Theron Baldwin, from *The Congregational Quarterly*, 1875

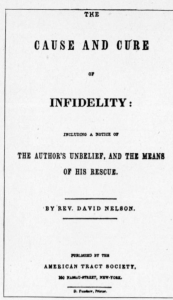

564   Asa Turner, from an engraving after a photograph in G. F. Magoun, *Asa Turner and His Times*, Boston and Chicago, 1889

THE IOWA BAND

ONE of the Illinois Band, Asa Turner (1799–1885), after eight years as pastor at Quincy, struck farther west into the "Black Hawk Purchase," which in 1838, with other lands, was organized as the Territory of Iowa. Here, at Denmark, he established a Congregational church. "As to the country," he wrote, "I see but one objection. It is so beautiful that there might be an unwillingness to exchange it for the paradise above." Next came Reuben Gaylord (1812–80), a Yale friend, who settled at Danville, and traveling from this place organized a number of churches. In the fall of 1843 came a great reinforcement, eleven young men who had just graduated from Andover Theological Seminary. They were ordained in the little church at Denmark, then scattered to various fields throughout the Territory. In 1848 the little group of home missionaries succeeded in opening Iowa College at Davenport. It was subsequently moved to Grinnell, and is now known as Grinnell College. In 1855 Gaylord moved on to Omaha, and became the organizer of Congregational missions in Nebraska.

565   Shakers at Lebanon, the Singing Meeting, from *Frank Leslie's Illustrated Newspaper*, January 11, 1873

THE SHAKERS

PROPHETS of communism naturally seek the frontier, where land can be had cheaply and larger freedom is afforded for deviations from established practices of society. America has therefore been the scene of more experiments in communistic living, until recently, than the older countries of Europe. Between 1840 and 1850, only two actual experiments based upon the theories of Fourier were made in France, but there were forty-one in the United States, the most famous being that at Brook Farm, West Roxbury, Massachusetts.

An early propagandist of religious communism was Ann Lee, 1736–84, a member of the Shaking Quakers in Manchester, England, who, believing herself to be led by a divine revelation, came to America in 1774 and became the founder of the Shakers. Her followers believe in strict celibacy, regarding marriage and reproduction as unchristian. "There never was, nor can be, a child conceived and born under Christian auspices." They practice the oral confession of sin, whether by thought, word or deed, in the presence of one another; the common possession of all goods, material and spiritual; and separation from the world, dwelling apart in "communities" or "families" with a distinctive organization. They believe that God is both male and female; that Christ first appeared in Jesus as a male, then in Ann Lee as a female; and that from this union of spiritual influences proceeds the new birth which empowers the children of God to live a sinless life. The second coming of Christ has therefore taken place, and we are living in the millenium, hence they call themselves the Millenial Church. The distinctive feature of their worship is marching and dancing, with songs and rhythmic, symbolic gestures. Nineteen Shaker Societies, each with two or more "families," have existed in the United States. There are now six Societies, with two hundred and fifty members.

566   Shakers Dancing, Enfield, from John W. Barber, *Connecticut Historical Collections*, Hartford, 1836

567   The Shaker Ironing Room, from *Frank Leslie's Illustrated Newspaper*, Sept. 13, 1873

568   The Harmony Community, from an old print

NEW HARMONY AND ECONOMY

In 1826 Robert Owen, the English social reformer, started a community at New Harmony, Indiana (Vol. V, p. 80), which broke up in less than two years. He had bought land and live stock from George Rapp, 1757–1847, a native of Wurtemburg, in Germany, who had led a group of people to America in 1803 in order that they might be free without molestation to live in communistic fellowship after what they conceived to be the practice of the primitive Christian Church. After selling their Indiana lands to Owen, Rapp and his followers founded the community of Economy, in Beaver County, Pennsylvania, where their patient, well-organized habits of industry met with considerable success. They had adopted the rule of celibacy, however, in 1807; and this, together with secessions, made their numbers diminish. In 1878 the Society had shrunk from a thousand to a hundred members; and an inquiry made in 1907 discovered none. Economy was sold to a land company in 1904.

THE ONEIDA COMMUNITY

The most successful of the communistic societies, from an economic point of view, was that founded in 1847 at Oneida, New York, by John Humphrey Noyes, 1811–86. He was a graduate of Dartmouth, studied theology at Andover and Yale, and was licensed to preach by the New Haven Association; but his license was revoked after a year on account of his peculiar doctrines. He believed in "Perfectionism" — that present salvation may be so complete as to render one absolutely sinless and incapable of sinning. He coupled with this the idea that the principle of communism involves not only property but all human relations. Within their community, therefore, his followers practiced what they called "complex marriage." In deference to aroused public sentiment this practice was given up in 1879. On January 1, 1881, the whole enterprise was transformed, and its distinctively communistic features abolished, by transferring the business and property of the community to an incorporated stock company, in which each person's interest was represented by the shares of stock standing in his name on the books.

569   Oneida Community, from a *Handbook of the Oneida Community*, 1874, in the New York Public Library

JOSEPH SMITH, 1805–1844, FOUNDER OF MORMONISM

In 1830 at Palmyra, New York, was printed *The Book of Mormon*, which Joseph Smith claimed to have translated from the "reformed Egyptian" "caractors" engraved upon a book of gold plates, which, at the behest of an angel, he had dug out of a hill near his home. The translation was made, he said, by the miraculous aid of a pair of crystals, "Urim and Thummim," found with the book, and then the plates were taken away by an angel.

570   Smith's "Caractors," from I. Woodbridge Riley, *The Founder of Mormonism*, Dodd, Mead & Company, New York, 1902

THE MORMON CHURCH ORGANIZED

UPON the basis of this book and of his claim to be a prophet receiving direct revelations from God, Smith organized a church and gained a following, aided by Sidney Rigdon, a practiced revivalistic preacher who had belonged to the Disciples of Christ. At Rigdon's suggestion the name "Church of Jesus Christ of Latter-Day Saints" was adopted, but Smith's followers are popularly known as Mormons. Seeking to establish themselves in a "New Jerusalem" promised in a "revelation" promulgated by Smith, they were driven by enraged neighbors from locations, first in Missouri, then in Illinois. Smith was killed by a mob at Carthage, Illinois, on June 27, 1844.

571 Joseph Smith, from a painting, courtesy of the Church of Jesus Christ of Latter-Day Saints, Salt Lake City

572 Brigham Young, from a photograph, courtesy of the Church of Jesus Christ of Latter-Day Saints, Salt Lake City

BRIGHAM YOUNG, 1801–1877, PRESIDENT OF THE MORMON CHURCH

UNDER Brigham Young, Smith's successor as President and Prophet, the Mormons migrated in 1847–48 to the valley of the Great Salt Lake in Utah. Young was a hard-headed, practical-minded, iron-willed man who did not hesitate to assume absolute dictatorship. Once when asked if he regarded himself as a prophet, he answered: "I am of profit to my people." Through measures of theocratic organization, social discipline, industrial coöperation, and commercial monopoly, aided by the fortunate circumstance of the discovery of gold in California, he built up a prosperous and compact body of believers. The Mormons now number well over a half million adherents; while the Reorganized Church, which refused to accept Young's leadership, has ninety thousand more.

THE BELIEFS OF MORMONISM

JOSEPH SMITH did not compare himself to Jesus Christ, as did Ann Lee and Mary Baker Eddy. He declared, however, that he would "become the second Mohammed of this generation." Mormonism is an errant form of Christianity. Accepting the Bible and many Christian beliefs and practices, it gives to these a peculiar perspective by its emphasis upon matter, bodies and sexual reproduction. Great stress is laid upon the thought that man is made in the image

573 The Tabernacle Square and Temple, from a photograph, courtesy of the Church of Jesus Christ of Latter-Day Saints, Salt Lake City

of God; but the principle is practically reversed, and the gods of Mormonism are made in the image of man. Mormons believe that there are many gods, with bodies of flesh and bone, who are polygamous human beings grown divine. Among the gods are grades of divinity, Adam being supreme and identified with God the Father of ordinary Christian belief. Christ is asserted to have been a polygamist, and himself the bridegroom at Cana of Galilee. The gods are busied in the begetting, through sexual procreation, of souls or spirits; it is the business of men and women in this world to beget bodies in which these spirits may become incarnate. Women reach heaven only through being "sealed" to man; and the glory of a saint in the hereafter depends upon the number of his wives and children.

574   Bringing Home Another Wife, from C. C. Coffin, *Building the Nation*, New York and London 1882

THE PRACTICE OF POLYGAMY

The "revelation" sanctioning polygamy is dated July 12, 1843, though it was not publicly promulgated until 1852. The Mormon Church strenuously resisted the enforcement of Federal laws against it, claiming that these laws interfered with their constitutional right of religious liberty. The Supreme Court in 1878 decided that the plea of religious belief cannot justify practices so contrary to the legally established organization of society. In a Manifesto issued September 25, 1890, W. W. Woodruff, then President of the Church, declared his intention to submit, and advised his people "to refrain from contracting any marriage forbidden by the law of the land." The practice of polygamy has now almost wholly ceased. The doctrine still remains in Mormon theology, however. On this and other points an inevitable conflict is being waged within Mormonism between old institutions and new ideas. In general, there is a noticeable "shift of Mormon emphasis from distinctively Mormon doctrines to those which are more Christian in their content." The book of Mormon, the first of the sacred writings of the church, contains an explicit command that no polygamy should be practiced. The theology which was developed in the formative years of the sect provided, however, the basis for the practice. Before Smith's death other sacred writings had come from his pen, his followers believing him to be the intermediary in a long series of divine revelations.

575   Brigham Young's wives in the great Mormon Tabernacle, from a sketch in *Harper's Weekly*, Sept. 26, 1874

576   Mormons at the Communion Table, from a sketch in *Harper's Weekly*, Sept. 26, 1874

INDIANS OF THE NORTHWEST SEEK THE BOOK

In the *Christian Advocate* of March 1, 1833, was published a letter that moved the hearts of the entire country. It told of the visit to General William Clark at St. Louis, in October, 1831, of a deputation of four Indian chiefs from the Northwest. Their tribe had heard "that the white people away toward the rising of the sun had been put in possession of the true mode of worshipping the Great Spirit. They had a book containing directions how to conduct themselves in order to enjoy his favor and hold converse with him; and with this guide no one need go astray but everyone that would follow the directions laid down there could enjoy, in this life, his favor, and after death would be received into the country where the Great Spirit resides, and live forever with him." The subject was considered at a tribal council, and the four chiefs were sent to ask General Clark to tell them the truth.

The Indians remained for several months. They were taken to the various churches and to theaters and other places of entertainment; and General Clark sought to answer their queries. Two of them became ill and died. The following address, the authenticity of which is not clear, is said to have been delivered by the spokesman when he bade General Clark farewell:

"I came to you over a trail of many moons from the setting sun. You were the friend of my fathers, who have all gone the long way. I came with one eye partly opened, for more light for my people who sit in darkness. I go back with both eyes closed. How can I go back blind to my blind people? I made my way to you with strong arms, through many enemies and strange lands, that I might carry back much to them. I go back with both arms broken and empty. The two fathers who came with me — the braves of many winters and wars — we leave asleep here by your great water. They were tired in many moons and their moccasins wore out.

"My people sent me to get the white man's Book from Heaven. You took me where you allow your women to dance, as we do not ours, and the Book was not there. You took me where they worship the Great Spirit with candles, and the Book was not there. You showed me the images of good spirits and pictures of the good land beyond, but the Book was not among them. I am going back the long, sad trail to my people of the dark land. You make my feet heavy with burdens of gifts, and my moccasins will grow old in carrying them, but the Book is not among them. When I tell my poor blind people, after one more snow, in the big council, that I did not bring the Book, no word will be spoken by our old men or by our young braves. One by one they will rise up and go out in silence. My people will die in darkness, and they will go on the long path to the other hunting grounds. No white man will go with them and no white man's Book, to make the way plain. I have no more words."

> They arrived at St. Louis, and presented themselves to Gen. C. The latter was somewhat puzzled being sensible of the responsibility that rested on him; he however proceeded by informing them that what they had been told by the white man in their own country, was true. Then went into a succinct history of man, from his creation down to the advent of the Saviour, explained to them all the moral precepts contained in the Bible, expounded to them the decalogue. Informed them of the advent of the Saviour, his life, precepts, his death, resurrection, ascension, and the relation he now stands to man as a mediator—that he will judge the world, &c.
>
> Poor fellows, they were not all permitted to return home to their people with the intelligence. Two died in St. Louis, and the remaining two, though somewhat indisposed, set out for their native land. Whether they reached home or not, is not known. The change of climate and diet operated very severely upon their health. Their diet when at home is chiefly vegetables and fish.
>
> If they died on their way home, peace be to their manes! They died inquirers after the truth. I was informed that the Flat-Heads, as a nation, have the fewest vices of any tribe of Indians on the continent of America.
>
> I had just concluded I would lay this rough and uncouth scroll aside and revise it before I would send it, but if I lay aside you will never receive it; so I will send it to you just as it is, "with all its imperfections," hoping that you may be able to decipher it. You are at liberty to make what use you please of it.   Yours in haste,
>
> **WM. WALKER.**
>
> **G. P. Disosway, Esq.**

577 Account of the Meeting of the Indians with Clark, from the *Christian Advocate and Journal*, March 1, 1832

578 Page of Jason Lee's diary, from the original in the Oregon Historical Society

JASON LEE, 1803–1845, PIONEER MISSIONARY TO OREGON

The *Christian Advocate* of March 22, 1833, contained a stirring letter from Wilbur Fisk, president of Wesleyan University, urging the establishment of a mission to the Indians of the Northwest. Jason Lee, one of his former pupils, was chosen to head it; and spent eight months touring the East, securing funds. With four associates he crossed the Rocky mountains in the company of trappers and traders led by Captain N. J. Wyeth. He preached his first sermons in the Oregon country at Fort Vancouver on September 28, 1834. A page from his diary is here reproduced.

579   Jason Lee, from a reproduction of a photograph in the Oregon Historical Society

LEE'S WORK AS A COLONIZER

LEE conceived his task in statesmanlike fashion. He was soon convinced that his work was not with Indians only, but with the white settlers of Oregon as well, and that more settlers must be brought from the United States to save the territory from becoming a British possession. Under his leadership three successive petitions were presented to Congress, requesting the establishment of a territorial Government. In 1838–39 he spent a year in the East, securing funds and organizing a company of forty-five, including ministers, physicians, teachers, carpenters, farmers, and a blacksmith, with their wives and children, who sailed from New York to Oregon, for the reinforcement of the Methodist missions. The expedition cost forty-two thousand dollars, of which the Federal Government appropriated five thousand dollars. In ten years the Methodist Missionary Society expended one hundred and seventy-three thousand three hundred and sixty-five dollars upon the Oregon Mission, much of which sum was secured by Jason Lee himself. He planted his mission stations at points of strategic importance: Salem, in the Willamette valley; the Dalles; Astoria; Oregon City and Nisqually, on Puget Sound.

LEE'S WORK WITH THE INDIANS

LEE emphasized education in his work with the Indians, and maintained a school for their youth from the first. In 1842 he erected an excellent building for the Indian manual-labor school. When the Mission terminated, two years later, this was bought for the use of Oregon Institute, a school for white children which was another of his enterprises and which afterward became Willamette University. In 1838–39, he took three young Indians upon his tour of the East. One of them, William Brooks, was something of a

580   Old Mission House, Oregon, from a drawing, courtesy of the
Oregon Historical Society

wit, and became able to speak effectively in English to large audiences. "The Indians of Oregon must have agreement in writing," he once said, "that white man do not sell whiskey to Indians; white man make it, and white man must drink it." Pausing, he added, quizzically, "O, these Yankees." On another occasion a lady questioned him about the process by which the Indians flattened the head, and criticized the custom

581   Statue of the Pioneer Preacher in the grounds
of the State House, Salem, Oregon

severely. He replied: "All people have fashions. Chinamen make little the foot, Indian make flat the head. You (looking at her waist and putting his hands on his own) make little here."

LEE'S REMOVAL AND DEATH

ON May 2, 1843, a meeting of settlers voted to establish a provisional Government in Oregon, the general understanding being that this action looked toward the early extension of the authority of the United States over the country. The narrowness of the margin, fifty-two to fifty, by which this proposal carried evidences the timeliness of Lee's colonizing activities. In 1844, without notice and without hearing, he was removed by the Methodist Board from the superintendency of the Oregon Mission. He had incurred the ill-will of some; he had labored and spent money for the Christian colonization of Oregon instead of confining his interest strictly to Indians; and he had not sufficiently restrained the land-greedy acts of some of his associates. The Mission was discontinued and the property sold.

Oregon had been saved for the Union, and Methodism securely planted; but the man who had labored to secure these results died broken-hearted at his old home in New England, March 12, 1845.

582   The Mission at Waiilatpu, from a drawing, courtesy of the Oregon Historical Society

THE MARTYRDOM OF MARCUS AND NARCISSA WHITMAN

YET more tragic was the fate of Dr. Marcus Whitman, missionary of the American Board to the Cayuse Indians at Waiilatpu, near the present site of Walla Walla, Washington. A preliminary exploration in 1835 convinced him of the need and the opportunity; and in 1836 he brought his bride, Narcissa Prentiss, to the Oregon country. She and Mrs. Spalding, the wife of his associate, were the first white women to cross the Rocky mountains. Dr. and Mrs. Whitman gave themselves unsparingly to the work among the Indians, teaching the children, showing the adults how to plant and reap wheat, grinding flour in a grist mill they erected, printing the Scriptures, hymns, and school lessons in the Indian language upon a small press given them by the native church at Honolulu, besides caring for their souls and healing their bodies. But on October 29, 1847, with twelve others, Dr. and Mrs. Whitman were brutally killed by the Indians they were seeking to serve.

MARCUS WHITMAN'S RIDE

ON October 2, 1842, Dr. Whitman, with one companion, left Waiilatpu to ride across the continent to Washington and Boston. It was a deed of splendid daring, to try to cross the Rockies in winter. He was compelled to circle southward by way of the Santa Fe trail, a thousand miles farther than the direct route, because of the snows and hostile Indians. Only considerations of the utmost urgency could justify the attempt.

Men have sharply differed as to Whitman's purpose in undertaking this journey. There is no objective contemporary evidence to prove that it was for anything more than to secure action by his Board rescinding an order to close the station at Waiilatpu. Yet his closest associates claimed, after the lapse of twenty years, that he had another reason for haste. He believed that there was danger that the United States Government would surrender to Great Britain that portion of Oregon lying north of the Columbia River; and he wished to urge upon the President and the Secretary of State the desirability of retaining this territory and the fact, of which no one else had fuller experience or more adequate knowledge than he, of its accessibility to emigrants by wagon. On his return, he joined a company of eight hundred emigrants at the Platte River, and was their sole guide after they passed Fort Hall. Their wagons were the first, except his own, to make the journey from Fort Hall to the Columbia River; and they were encouraged to attempt it by his insistence that he would lead them through. His station was of great service to emigrants during the four years that remained to him.

It now seems clear that Whitman's ride was not necessary to "save Oregon"; but it is probable that he undertook it for that purpose. It deepens the tragedy of his memory that so bitter a controversy should have been waged about the meaning and value of this heroic exploit, which, whatever form its purpose took in Whitman's mind, was undoubtedly an act of self-sacrificial devotion to what he believed to be the good of Oregon. A map of his route appears on the following page.

Said the Shoshonee to the Nez Percé,
  "Who rides with the storm, ho, ho!
With a robe of ice was covered his form,
  And covered his tracks the snow?"
Said the Nez Percé to the Shoshonee,
  "He came and went with the wind,
He followed the guide of his soul before,
  And left no trail behind.
The gods him beckoned; he went his way,"
  Said the Shoshonee and the Nez Percé.

. . . .

The winter deepened, sharper grew
  The hail and sleet, the frost and snow;
Not e'en the eagle o'er him flew,
  And scarce the partridge's wing below.
The land became a long white sea,
  And then a deep with scarce a coast,

The stars refused their light, till he
  Was in the wildering mazes lost.
He dropped the rein, his stiffened hand
  Was like a statue's hand of clay.
"My trusty beast, 't is the command,
  Go on, I leave to thee the way.
The open Bible 'neath the flag
  I set upon the mountain crag,
  While screamed the eagles in the sun;
  I must defend what I have won.
I must go on, I must go on,
  Whatever lot may fall to me;
On! 't is for others' sake I ride,
  For others I may never see,
And dare the clouds, O Great Divide,
  Not for myself, O Walla Walla,
  Not for myself, O Washington;
  But for thy future, Oregon."

— HEZEKIAH BUTTERWORTH, *Whitman's Ride for Oregon*

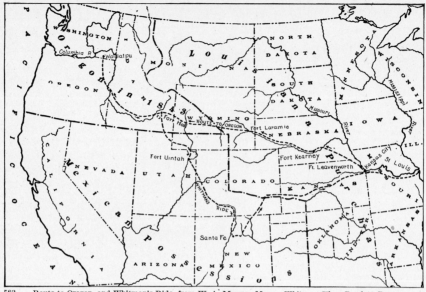

583   Route to Oregon, and Whitman's Ride, from W. A. Mowry, *Marcus Whitman*, Silver Burdett Co., New York, 1901

PIERRE JEAN DE SMET, 1801-1873, FOUNDER OF CATHOLIC MISSIONS IN THE NORTHWEST

IN response to the request of a group of French Canadians who had settled in the Willamette valley, the Archbishop of Quebec in 1838 sent two priests, one of whom, Francis N. Blanchet, was made Archbishop of Oregon in 1844. The Flathead Indians, meanwhile, had learned something of the Catholic religion from Old Ignace, leader of a little band of wandering Iroquois, whose name bears witness to the Jesuit associations of his early days. Disappointed when they met Parker and Whitman, the Protestant missionaries, in 1835, the Flatheads sent Old Ignace with a deputation to St. Louis to ask for priests. His son, Young Ignace, with another Iroquois, made the journey again in 1839. Father Pierre Jean De Smet was detailed to go and, guided by Young Ignace, reached the Bitter Root valley the next summer. In 1841 he returned to establish St. Mary's Mission.

584 Father De Smet, from an engraving, courtesy of the Century Company, New York

THE SUCCESS OF THE CATHOLIC MISSIONS

BOTH De Smet and Blanchet went to Europe to seek funds and reinforcements. De Smet returned in 1844, and Blanchet in 1847, each with priests, lay brothers, and sisters of Notre Dame de Namur, as well as with funds and supplies. De Smet founded missions among the Cœur d'Alenes, the Pend d'Oreilles, and the Kalispels, besides a central mission with schools in the Willamette valley, and a number of stations. It was claimed that in six years six thousand natives embraced the Catholic faith. In 1846 a brick church, one hundred feet by forty-five, was dedicated at St. Paul's. But in that same year De Smet returned to St. Louis, and was never permitted to resume service in this field. Like Jason Lee, he suffered from reports that he was planning on too large a scale. The success of the Catholic missions was not unalloyed. In 1851 the Flathead mission was closed, because of the hostility of the Indians. It was reopened in 1857.

585 The Pend d'Oreille Mission in the Rocky Mountains in 1862, from a drawing in Captain John Mullan, *Report of the Construction of a Military Road*, 1862

DE SMET AS PEACEMAKER

UNLIKE his French confreres, De Smet desired that Oregon should become a part of the United States rather than of Canada. He was friendly with Marcus Whitman, to whom he presented a Douay Bible. De Smet's books and voluminous letters are among the best of our sources for the understanding of the Indians of the Northwest. He was repeatedly asked by the Federal Government to assist in the difficult peace negotiations with the hostile Indians, and he rendered effective service of this sort in '51, '58, '64, '67, and '68. On the last occasion, leaving the Commissioners, Generals

586   De Smet's Meeting with the hostile Sioux, from a drawing in Chittenden and Richardson, *De Smet's Life and Travels*, F. P. Harper, New York, 1905

Sherman, Sheridan, Harney, and others, to meet him at Fort Rice, he penetrated the Bad Lands, with but one white interpreter and an escort of friendly Sioux, to the camp of Sitting Bull, and persuaded him to meet the Commissioners and to make peace. He left with the Indians the banner which he carried, "with the holy name of Jesus on one side and on the other the image of the Virgin Mary, surrounded with gilt stars."

587   George H. Atkinson, from a photograph, courtesy of Pacific University

THE SUCCESSORS OF MARCUS WHITMAN

MARCUS WHITMAN's work in Oregon was not wasted. His associates, H. H. Spalding, Elkanah Walker, and Cushing Eells, remained in the territory and devoted their lives to the planting and upbuilding of churches and schools. George H. Atkinson, 1819–89, a Dartmouth graduate, in 1847 surrendered appointment to the Zulu mission in South Africa to undertake home-missionary service in Oregon. He became the statesman of the movement, laboring for forty years, as pastor and superintendent of missions, for the welfare of churches, schools and colleges, and for the material development and prosperity of the state. In 1849, under his leadership, Tualatin Academy was founded at Forest Grove, which five years later became Pacific University.

In 1859, the country east of the Cascade mountains, which had been closed to settlers since the massacre at Waiilatpu, was opened; and Cushing Eells, 1810–93, who had been teaching in Tualatin Academy, returned to Walla Walla. In 1860 he founded Whitman Seminary, which became Whitman College in 1883. A group of six members of the Class of 1890 at the Yale Divinity School formed a Washington Band, and together went into home-missionary service in that field. One of them, Stephen B. L. Penrose, has been since 1894 the president of Whitman College.

588   Whitman College, from a photograph, courtesy of Whitman College

X—17

589 William Taylor, courtesy of the *Christian Advocate*, New York

WILLIAM TAYLOR, 1821–1902, "A SPIRITUAL FORTY-NINER"

WILLIAM TAYLOR, sent by the Methodists as a missionary to California, went around Cape Horn, a voyage of one hundred and fifty-five days, and landed in San Francisco in September, 1849. He began to preach in the streets, and with his own hands hewed logs to erect a house of worship. No difficulty daunted him, nothing distracted him, and competing noises were not strong enough to drown his powerful voice. For seven years he labored in San Francisco, establishing Methodist churches in this and other California communities, conducting a seaman's "Bethel," and preaching regularly in the open air on Portsmouth Square, familiarly known as the Plaza. Then he came East to solicit funds for his work; and he never returned to California. He became an evangelist and missionary, and the world was thenceforth his home. He labored from time to time in all of its continents; and in 1884 he was made Bishop of the Methodist Episcopal Church in Africa.

SAMUEL H. WILLEY, 1821–1914, A BUILDER OF CALIFORNIA

UNLIKE Taylor, Samuel H. Willey remained in California, and devoted his life to the upbuilding of that state. He and John W. Douglas were sent to California by the American Home Missionary Society. Passengers on the first steamship to take the route by the Isthmus of Panama, they landed at Monterey on February 23, 1849. At San Francisco they found T. Dwight Hunt, from Honolulu, whom the people had elected to be "chaplain of the town" for one year. The three constituted themselves a Presbytery. Willey was chaplain of the Constitutional Convention of 1849, alternating with Padre Antonio Ramirez. In 1850 he organized the Howard Street Presbyterian Church of San Francisco, of which he was pastor until 1862. As early as 1849, he headed an effort to found a college. In 1855 a charter was secured, the preparatory department opened, and Willey went East to secure funds. But he found that people would not give money to California: that seemed to them absurd. Secretary of the Board of Trustees, and president, he was a chief factor in

590 Samuel H. Willey, from Z. S. Eldredge, *History of California*, History Co., New York, 1915

the development of the College of California, and one of the leaders in the founding of the University of California.

SHELDON JACKSON, 1834–1909, "PATHFINDER AND PROSPECTOR OF THE MISSIONARY VANGUARD"

591 Sheldon Jackson, from a photograph, courtesy of Miss Lesley Jackson

WHAT Francis Asbury, Methodist, was to the country east of the Mississippi River, Sheldon Jackson, Presbyterian, was to the Rocky Mountain frontier. "Short, bewhiskered, spectacled. By inside measurement a giant," a local newspaper once described him. When a presiding officer, mistaking some one else for him, announced to an audience that they would now be addressed by "our stalwart friend from the Rocky Mountains," and a laugh arose at his little figure, Jackson began, with undisturbed good humor: "If I had been more stalwart in height, I could not have slept so many nights on the four-and-a-half-foot seat of a Rocky Mountain stage." Possessed of indomitable energy, tremendous faith, and exceptional ability as an organizer, he set the pace for the more aggressive activity of the Protestant boards in establishing churches throughout the West.

RIDING THE CIRCUIT IN MINNESOTA

JACKSON began his work in Minnesota where he labored from 1859 to 1869. Commissioned as pastor of the as yet unorganized churches of La Crescent, Hokah, and vicinity, he interpreted "vicinity" to mean every community he could reach; and he traveled a circuit which ranged from Chippewa Falls, a hundred and twenty miles north, to Jackson, two hundred miles west. Among the little group of home missionaries, he soon assumed the leadership in service, which his temperament made natural to him. By personal appeals to wealthy churches and individuals in the East, he supplemented the meager appropriations of the Board of Missions, and kept the missionaries alive and the churches advancing during the financially stringent 'sixties. The picture is from a home-missionary paper which he edited later.

592 From the *Rocky Mountain Presbyterian*, February 1880

JACKSON BECOMES SUPERINTENDENT OF MISSIONS

ON May 10, 1869, the Union Pacific Railroad was completed. The three Presbyteries of Iowa, when the Board refused their request for a superintendent of missions to organize churches in the vast region thus opened, asked Sheldon Jackson to undertake the work, with the understanding that he would secure the funds. Before the final vote, on April 29, 1869, with two other ministers, he climbed Prospect Hill, a high bluff overlooking the river at Sioux City, from which he could see four states; and there they knelt upon the ground in prayer for Divine guidance. He accepted the task, "independently of, but not in opposition to, the Board of Domestic Missions." Within a week he had placed three men at strategic points along the Union Pacific; within eight months he had ten new men at work. Money came, too, over ten thousand dollars in the first year and a half. Men had confidence in him. "I will give him double and ask no questions," said one business man.

593 Monument to Sheldon Jackson at Sioux City, from a photograph by Woodworth, Sioux City

FREE TRANSPORTATION

THE work of Sheldon Jackson symbolized the new day in the fast developing West. It was made possible only because lines of regular and rapid transportation were multiplying. The officials of these lines, both railroad and stagecoach, believed that he was contributing greatly to the civilization and development of the regions in which they were interested; and gave him free transportation, as well as reduced rates for his missionaries. The pass here shown was good over stage lines in fourteen states.

594 Obverse of stage-coach pass, from R. L. Stewart, *Sheldon Jackson*, Fleming Revell Co., New York and Chicago, 1908

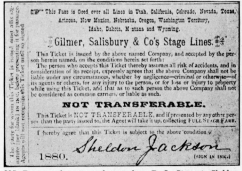

595 Reverse of stage-coach pass, from R. L. Stewart, *Sheldon Jackson*, Fleming Revell Co., New York and Chicago, 1908

596   Map showing frontier line of the Presbyterian Church in 1858, from R. L. Stewart, *Sheldon
Jackson*, Fleming Revell Co., New York and Chicago, 1908

PLANTING CHURCHES IN THE ROCKY MOUNTAIN STATES

From July 15 to August 17, 1869, Jackson traveled twenty-three hundred miles by rail and twelve hundred by stagecoach; and organized eight churches, at Cheyenne, Rawlins, and Laramie, in Wyoming; at Helena, Montana; and Grand Island, Columbus, Blair, and Fremont, Nebraska. That is a characteristic sample of his activity for the next ten years. Leaving the work in Western Iowa and Nebraska to others, he soon moved his headquarters to Denver. Traveling out from here, he was responsible for the planting and fostering of churches in Colorado, Wyoming, Montana, Utah, Arizona, and New Mexico; and he did some work in Nevada and Texas. The map shows the frontier line of the Presbyterian churches in 1858, when he began his ministry.

597   Mrs. McFarland's Missionary School at Wrangel Island, from
The Rocky Mountain Presbyterian, June 1879

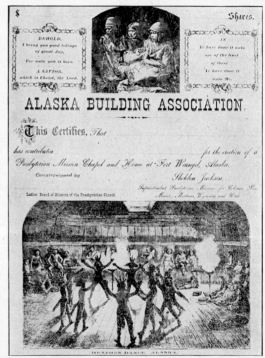

598   Certificate of Alaska Building Association, from *The
Rocky Mountain Presbyterian*, January 1879

MISSIONS IN ALASKA

In 1877 a soldier stationed at Fort Wrangell, himself not a church member, wrote a letter to General O. O. Howard, informing him of the pathetic efforts of the natives near that post to learn more about Christianity from some visiting Indians of British Columbia, and asking him to secure for them a Christian teacher. Sheldon Jackson journeyed to Alaska in reply, taking Mrs. A. R. McFarland who opened a school. Alaska became henceforth one of Jackson's primary interests. He awakened the churches and the school teachers of America to the need of its natives. In six years he delivered nine hundred addresses on the subject, besides writing a book, and from 1884 to his death he gave his whole time to this territory. In 1885 he added to his responsibilities as missionary those of General Agent of Education for Alaska, under the United States Bureau of Education. He held this post for twenty-three years, and built up in Alaska an effective public-school system, in spite of repeated opposition from inefficient or dishonest officials. In 1891, seeing that the sea animals and fish upon which the natives had relied for food were disappearing under the white man's wholesale methods of slaughter, he began to bring from Siberia herds of domesticated reindeer, to furnish a permanent food supply, and advance the Eskimos in the scale of civilization by changing them from hunters to herders.

CHAPTER IX

ELEMENTARY AND SECONDARY SCHOOLS

FAMILY, church and state are interested in the education of the young. In some of the American colonies, except where it was a matter of charity, education was left to parents, who employed tutors or paid for the tuition of their children in private schools. In other colonies, it was a primary concern of the churches, which maintained parochial schools for the education of the children of their adherents. In the New England colonies, a policy of direct public responsibility for education early began to be developed. Here originated "the little red schoolhouse."

In time the New England idea prevailed and became the policy of the country in general. State systems of public schools have largely displaced private and parochial schools in the elementary and secondary grades. These schools are maintained by general taxation, from which no one is excused on the plea of conscientious objection or dissent from public educational policy. They are open, free of tuition charges, to all the children of all the people. Compulsory education laws, moreover, require parents and guardians to see to it that their children are educated.

The principle of public responsibility for education did not prevail without a long and hard battle. No subject except slavery and perhaps the liquor traffic has been more bitterly and stubbornly contested than the establishment of free, tax-supported public schools. The victory was due chiefly to growing recognition of the function of such schools in educating for the duties of citizenship in a democracy, to changes in industrial organization and the demands of workingmen for equality of educational opportunity, and to the public-spirited labors of leaders in the various states, most of whom were men of New England stock or Scotch-Irish Presbyterian heritage.

Yet America's educational policy is one of freedom. There is no provision concerning education in the Constitution of the United States, and there is no nationally controlled system of schools. Private schools and parochial schools have full freedom to exist and carry on their work, and attendance at these schools is construed as a fulfillment of the compulsory education laws.

Catholics are committed to the maintenance of Catholic schools because of their conviction concerning the essential place of religion in education. Because religion has been so generally conceived in sectarian terms, the public schools have been obliged, not only to cease teaching it, but in some communities to ignore it entirely. Among citizens generally the conviction is growing that we still face unsolved problems with respect to the place of morals and religion in the life and work of the schools.

The traditional Latin School gave way in time to the academy, and the academy to the free public high school. In both elementary and secondary grades America has shared in the betterment of educational methods and the closer approach of the schools to real life which have been brought about under the leadership of teachers inspired by the great educational reformers. Distinctive contributions of the public schools are their service as assimilators of the widely different racial and lingual groups which immigration has brought to these shores, and the consistency with which as yet they have been able to avoid the early fixing of vocational grooves or social status and to maintain for all American youth "an open ladder from the primary school to the university."

(12)

NEW ENGLANDS FIRST FRUITS.

2. In refpect of the Colledge, and the proceedings of *Learning* therein.

Fter God had carried us fafe to *New England*, and wee had builded our houfes, provided neceffaries for our liveli-hood, rear'd convenient places for Gods worfhip, and fetled the Civill Government: One of the next things we longed for. and looked after was to advance *Learning* and perpetuate it to Pofterity; dreading to leave an illiterate Miniftery to the Churches, when our prefent Minifters fhall lie in the Duft. And as wee were thinking and confulting how to effect this great Work ;it pleafed God to ftir up the heart of one Mr. *Harvard* (a godly Gentleman and a lover of Learning, there living amongft us) to give the one halfe of his Eftate (it being in all about 1700 l.) towards the erecting of a Colledge. and all his Library. after him another gave 300. l. others after them caft in more. and the publique hand of the State added the reft : the Colledge was by common confent, appointed to be at *Cambridge*, (a place very pleafant and accommodate and is called (according to the name of the firft founder) *Harvard Colledge*.

The Edifice is very faire and comely within and without having in it a fpacious Hall ; (where they daily meet at Common Lectures) Exercifes, and a large Library with fome Bookes to it. the gifts of diverfe

599 The opening page of *New England's First Fruits*, London, 1643, from the original in the New York Public Library

NEW ENGLAND'S FIRST FRUITS

THE opening sentence of a pamphlet entitled *New England's First Fruits* which was printed in London in 1643 expresses the attitude of the Puritans who settled New England toward education: "After God had carried us safe to New England and we had builded our houses, provided necessaries for our livelihood, reared convenient places for God's worship, and settled the civil government, one of the next things we longed for and looked after was to advance learning and perpetuate it to posterity, dreading to leave an illiterate ministry to the churches when our present ministers shall lie in the dust."

THE BOSTON LATIN SCHOOL

JOHN ELIOT and John Cotton were chiefly responsible for the early establishment of schools in Massachusetts. There is record of one occasion, typical of many, when Eliot cast his exhortation of the people into the form of a prayer to God: "Lord for schools everywhere among us! O! that schools may flourish! That every member of this assembly may go home and provide a good school to be arranged in the town where he lives; that before we die we may see a good school arranged in every plantation in the country." In 1635 the town of Boston chose a schoolmaster who opened the school which soon became the Boston Latin Grammar School. The first building for this school was erected in 1645 on the north side of School street. A year later, a grammar school was established at Newtown (Cambridge); other towns also followed Boston's example. These schools were modeled after the Latin grammar schools of England. Latin was the language of learning. Mastery of it set a man off from his fellows. In school he learned little of numbers or of the accurate use of his native language. About the age of fifteen, however, when he had conquered Tully, he was ready to enter college.

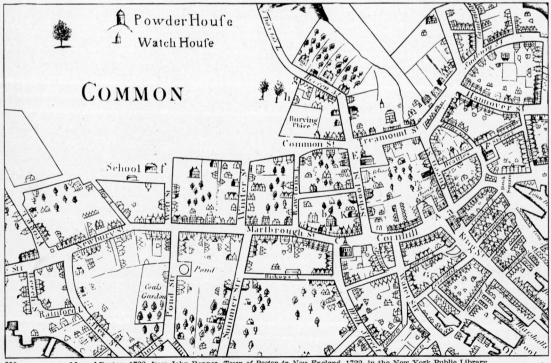

600   Map of Boston, 1722, from John Bonner, *Town of Boston in New England*, 1722, in the New York Public Library

DAME SCHOOLS

THE elementary education of children was largely cared for in the early period by dame schools, as was also the custom in England. A dame school consisted simply of a group of children gathered in the kitchen or living room of some housewife who taught them to read. The first teacher in Northfield, Massachusetts, cared for her household, with four children of her own, while teaching the children of the neighborhood for a term of twenty-two weeks, yet found time to make shirts at eight pence each. Such elementary teaching offered women of slender resources an opportunity to secure a small income. Such schools combined the functions of day nurseries and of the lowest elemen-

601 *A New England Dame School*, drawn expressly for *The Pageant of America* by H. A. Ogden (1856–)

tary grades. The more idealized of the pictures here given represents the teacher making letters and figures with a rod on the sanded floor of the kitchen, and the pupils copying them with bits of charcoal upon pieces of birch bark. The less attractive drawing of *The Young Rebel*, which is reproduced below, is in line with the description of a dame school by the English poet, George Crabbe:

602 *The Young Rebel*, from a drawing in *Parley's Magazine*, 1841, in the New York Public Library

" . . . a deaf, poor, patient widow sits
And awes some thirty infants as she knits;
Infants of humble, busy wives who pay
Some trifling price for freedom through the day.
At this good matron's hut the children meet,
Who thus becomes the mother of the street.
Her room is small, they cannot widely stray,
Her threshold high, they cannot run away.
With band of yarn she keeps offenders in,
And to her gown the sturdiest rogue can pin."

THE MASSACHUSETTS EDUCATION LAWS OF 1642 AND 1647

BECAUSE many parents neglected the education of their children, the Massachusetts Court in 1642 ordered the officers of each town to see to it that children were taught, especially "to read and understand the principles of religion and the capital laws of this country," and empowered them to fine parents who refused. In 1647, "it being one chief project of the old deluder, Satan, to keep men from the knowledge of the Scriptures," the Court ordered every town of fifty families or more to appoint a teacher of reading and writing, whose wages should be paid as the vote of the town might determine; and it further ordered that every town of one hundred families should provide a Latin grammar school, "to instruct youth so far as they shall be fitted for the university." With minor changes, these laws were embodied in the Connecticut Code of 1650. The Massachusetts laws were epoch-making. The principles involved in this legislation were new and far-reaching. The universal education of youth is essential to the welfare of the state. Though on the shoulders of the parent rests the obligation of education, the state may enforce the obligation. The state, moreover, may determine the amount and kind of education

It is therefore ord^red, y^t ev^ry towneship in this iurisdiction, aft^r ye Lord hath increased y^m to ye number of 50 household^rs, shall then forthw^th appoint one w^thin their towne to teach all such children as shall resort to him to write & reade, whose wages shall be paid eith^r by ye parents or mast^rs of such children, or by ye inhabitants in gen^rall, by way of supply, as ye maior p^t of those y^t ord^r ye prudentials of ye towne shall appoint.

603 From the Education Law of 1647 in the *Records of Massachusetts Bay*, vol. II, Boston, 1853

required. The expense may be met by a general tax even though many taxpayers may have no children to benefit by the schools the state supports. The proceeds of this tax may be applied to secondary as well as primary education. These institutions were the forerunners of the American public school.

604 The School at Dedham, from the *New England Magazine*, 1902

TAX–SUPPORTED SCHOOLS AT DORCHESTER AND DEDHAM

In 1639 the town of Dorchester provided for a school by means of a tax laid upon the holders of property upon Thompson's Island. Three "wardens or overseers" were chosen in 1645 to have "charge, oversight, and ordering" of all the affairs of this school: this is the first example of the control of public schools by officers elected by the people for that specific purpose. The first town to have a school supported by a general tax on all property holders was Dedham, which took this action in 1648, and built a schoolhouse eighteen by fifteen feet. It had a high lean-to back of the chimney, with windows on all sides, to serve as a watchtower for the town sentinel.

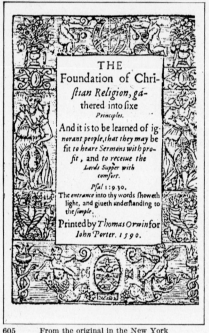

605   From the original in the New York
        Public Library

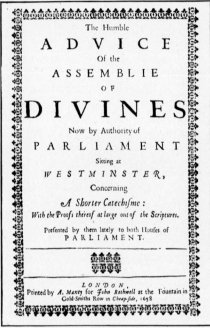

606   From the original in the Lenox Collection
        in the New York Public Library

THE RELIGIOUS CHARACTER OF THE EARLY PUBLIC SCHOOLS

In accordance with the religious motives which led to their establishment, the early public schools of New England gave large place to the teaching of religion. Learning to read, children followed what John Locke in 1690 reported to be "the ordinary road of Hornbook, Primer, Psalter, Testament and Bible." The New Haven Code of 1655 required that they be made "able duly to read the Scriptures . . . and in some competent measure to understand the main grounds and principles of Christian Religion necessary to salvation." The rules of the grammar school at Dorchester, adopted by town meeting in 1645, required the schoolmaster "to commend his scholars and his labors amongst them unto God by prayer morning and evening, taking care that his scholars do reverently attend during the same"; to examine them each Monday noon as to what they had learned from the Sabbath sermon; and at two o'clock each Friday afternoon to catechise them "in the principles of Christian religion." The sixteenth and seventeenth centuries were a catechism-writing and catechism-studying age; Increase Mather estimated that there were "no less than five hundred Catechisms extant." Many were written for local use in the towns of New England. New Haven used a catechism written by John Davenport and William Hooke; Hartford, one by Samuel Stone; and Cambridge, *The First Principles of the Oracles of God*, written by Thomas Shepard. The most widely used catechism was one which the Puritans brought from England, *The Foundation of Christian Religion gathered into six Principles*, by William Perkins. Later, the Westminster Catechism tended to displace all others.

SCHOOLS OF NEW NETHERLAND

In 1638 an elementary school was opened by the Dutch at New Amsterdam. It chanced that the first schoolmaster, Adam Roelantsen, was not of blameless character; but he did not hold the office long, and was succeeded by more worthy men. This school and other schools in the various villages of New Netherland were much like the New England schools in their religious motive, in their emphasis upon the Scriptures and the catechism, and in

607   A Dutch School for Children of the Burgher Class, from *Historic New York*, G. P. Putnam's Sons, New York, 1899

the joint responsibility of ecclesiastical and civil authorities for their supervision and control. When the English came into possession of the colony the support of this school devolved wholly upon the Dutch Reformed Church, and it became, in the usual sense of the term, a parochial school. It is still in existence, the oldest elementary school in the country.

608 German Schoolhouse on Cherry Street, Philadelphia, courtesy of The Historical Society of Pennsylvania

PAROCHIAL SCHOOLS IN THE MIDDLE COLONIES

The population of the middle colonies, New York, New Jersey, Pennsylvania and Delaware, was more heterogeneous than that of New England, with respect both to language and to religion. It was natural, therefore, and at the time in the interest of freedom, that these colonies should rely mainly upon parochial schools for the education of children. Lutherans, Reformed, Presbyterians, Baptists, Quakers, Moravians, Mennonites and Catholics — all maintained schools in connection with their churches. Some of these schools received moderate tuition fees from parents who could afford it; all taught the children of the poor gratuitously. The picture shows a schoolhouse built in 1760 by a large German Lutheran congregation in Philadelphia.

QUAKER AND BAPTIST CATECHISMS

Lutherans, Reformed, and Presbyterians are to be expected to teach religion by means of catechisms. Luther's *Smaller Catechism*, the *Heidelberg Catechism*, and the *Westminster Shorter Catechism* are classics that will not perish so long as evangelical Protestantism endures. But in the eighteenth century even Baptists and Quakers used the catechism as an instrument of teaching. Robert Barclay's *A Catechism and Confession of Faith, Approved of, and agreed unto, by the General Assembly of the Patriarchs, Prophets, and Apostles, Christ Himself chief Speaker in and among them* was very popular with the Quakers. The title-page and frontispiece of a widely used Baptist catechism are reproduced on this page.

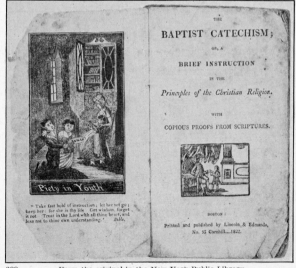

609   From the original in the New York Public Library

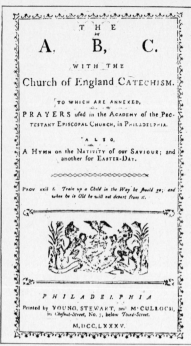

THE
A, B, C.
WITH THE
Church of England CATECHISM.
[TO WHICH ARE ANNEXED,]
PRAYERS used in the ACADEMY of the PROTESTANT EPISCOPAL CHURCH, in PHILADELPHIA.
ALSO,
A HYMN on the NATIVITY of our SAVIOUR; and another for EASTER-DAY.

PROV. xxii 6. Train up a Child in the Way he should go; and when he is Old he will not depart from it.

PHILADELPHIA
Printed by YOUNG, STEWART, and M'CULLOCH, in Chesnut-Street, No. 7, below Third-Street.
M.DCC.LXXXV.

610   From the original in the New York
Public Library

A PROTESTANT EPISCOPAL PRIMER

THIS Primer, with Prayers and the Church of England Catechism, was published in 1785, shortly after the Revolution. Note the explanation that blanks have been left where the word "King" was formerly used: "as that Form of Expression does not suit our Republican Governments, the Teacher will be pleased to fill up the Blanks with what Words he may deem Expedient." What useful purpose the learning of the sixty different syllables could have served remains a mystery.

The Roman Alphabets.

A a b c d e f g h i j k l m n o
p q r f s t u v w x y z &.

A B C D E F G H I J K L M N O P Q R
S T U V W X Y Z Æ Œ.

The Italic Alphabets.

*A B C D E F G H I J K L M N O P Q R
S T U V W X Y Z Æ.*

*A a b c d e f g h i j k l m n o p
q r f s t u v w x y z &.*

& ſh ſt ſſ ſſ fi fi fl ffi ffi ffl ſſ æ œ.

, ; : . ? ! - ( ) [ ] * † ‡ § ¶ ℣.

Ab	eb	ib	ob	ub	al	el	il	ol	ul
ac	ec	ic	oc	uc	an	en	in	on	un
ad	ed	id	od	ud	ap	ep	ip	op	up
af	ef	if	of	uf	ar	er	ir	or	ur
ag	eg	ig	og	ug	as	es	is	os	us
ak	ek	ik	ok	uk	at	et	it	ot	ut

☞ *The Blanks left in Page 6, were formerly filled up with the Words (King) and (him); but as that Form of Expression does not suit our Republican Governments, the Teacher will be pleased to fill up the Blanks with what Words he may deem Expedient.*

611   From *The A B C with the Church of England Catechism*, Philadelphia, 1785, in the New York Public Library

ST. MARY'S PARISH SCHOOL, PHILADELPHIA

IN 1782, upon a lot purchased from the Quakers, the Catholics of St. Mary's Church, Philadelphia, erected a new schoolhouse, two stories high, with plastered walls and painted interior woodwork. The records show that one item of expense was "308 panes of window glass," each eight by ten inches. The upper story was for the younger children, the lower for "such as shall be fit for Writing and Cyphering." This "may be said to have been the mother-school of all the parochial schools in the English-speaking States," writes the historian of Catholic education in this country. The success of this school, in what was then the largest city, and in the largest and richest Catholic parish in the United States, helped to fix "an educational ideal which has struck its roots deeper and more firmly into the Catholic American mind with every year that has since elapsed." — J. A. BURNS, *Principles, Origin, and Establishment of the Catholic School System in the United States*, pp. 141–42. Since the beginning made at Philadelphia the parochial school has undergone a vast development.

THE
CATHOLIC CHRISTIAN
INSTRUCTED,
IN THE
SACRAMENTS, SACRIFICE, CEREMONIES
AND
OBSERVANCES OF THE CHURCH.

By way of Question and Answer.

BY THE MOST REV. DR. CHALLONER.

NEW EDITION, CAREFULLY REVISED AND CORRECTED.

BALTIMORE:
PUBLISHED BY FIELDING LUCAS, JUN'R.
No. 138 Market street.

612   From the original in the New
York Public Library

THE
CATHOLIC CHRISTIAN
INSTRUCTED,
IN THE
SACRAMENTS, SACRIFICE, CEREMONIES.
AND
OBSERVANCES OF THE CHURCH.

CHAPTER I.
Of the Sign of the Cross.

Q. WHY do you treat of the sign of the cross, before you begin to speak of the sacraments?
A. Because this holy sign is made use of in all the sacraments, to give us to understand, that they all have their whole force and efficacy from the cross, that is, from the death and passion of Jesus Christ. What is the sign of Christ, says St. Augustine*, which all know, but the cross of Christ, which sign if it be not applied to the foreheads of the believers to the water with which they are baptized, to the chrism, with which they are anointed, to the sacrifice with which they are fed, none of these things is duly performed.
Q. But did the primitive Christians only make use of the sign of the cross in the administration of the sacraments?
A. Not only then, but also upon all other occasions at every step, says the ancient and learned Tertullian, at every coming in and going out, when we put on our clothes or shoes, when we wash, when we sit down to table, when we light a candle, when we go to bed—whatsoever conversation employs us we imprint on our foreheads, the sign of the cross.

Tract 119 in Joan.   † L. de Corona Milit. c. 3.

613   From Challoner, *The Catholic Christian Instructed*, Baltimore

PRIVATE EDUCATION IN THE SOUTH

THE population of the plantation colonies of the South was scattered over wide areas. The homes of neighbors were normally far apart. The compact village of New England type was virtually non-existent. The conditions of life upon large plantations, the traditions of the Cavaliers, and the customs of the Church of England, conspired to cause the southern colonists to view the education of children as the parent's private duty. All who aspired to any social standing employed private tutors in their homes, or paid for the tuition of their children in small, select, private schools; or if they could possibly afford it sent their boys to England to be educated. Only orphans and the children of the poor were taught in the pauper-schools or charity-schools which were maintained, sometimes by public authorities, sometimes by the gifts or endowment of generous individuals, generally by churches. Here are typical Virginia advertisements — two seeking private tutors, one seeking a teacher for an endowed charity-school, and one announcing the opening of a new private school.

ANY fingle Man, capable of teaching *Greek, Latin,* and the Mathematicks, who can be well recommended, may meet with good Encouragement, by applying to the Subscriber, in *Prince-George* County.

Theophilus Field.

614   Advertisement from the *Virginia Gazette,* Apr. 3, 1752, in the New York Public Library

A PERSON well recommended for teaching Reading, Writing and Arithmetick, may hear of handfome Encouragement, in Private Family on applying to the Printer.

615   Advertisement from the *Virginia Gazette,* Feb. 12, 1762, in the New York Public Library

NOTICE is hereby given, That *Symes's* Free School, in *Elizabeth-City* County, will be vacant on the 25th of *March* Inft. a Tutor of a good Character, and properly qualified, may meet with good Encouragement, by applying to the Truftees of the faid School.

N. B. The Land Rent of the faid School is 31 *l. per Ann.* befides Perquifites.

616   Advertisement from the *Williamsburg Gazette,* Mar. 12, 1752, in the New York Public Library

JOHN WALKER,

LATELY arriv'd in *Williamfburg* from *London,* and who for ten Years paft has been engag'd in the Education of Youth, undertakes to inftruct young Gentlemen in Reading, Writing, Arithmetick, the moft material Branches of Claffical Learning, and ancient and modern Geography and Hiftory; but, as the nobleft End of Erudition and Human Attainments, he will exert his principal Endeavours to improve their Morals, in Proportion to their Progrefs in Learning, that no Parent may repent his Choice in trufting him with the Education of his Children.

Mrs. *Walker,* likewife, teaches young Ladies all Kinds of Needle Work; makes Capuchins, Shades, Hats, and Bonnets; and will endeavour to give Satisfaction to thofe who fhall honour her with their Cuftom.

The above-mentioned *John Walker,* and his Wife, live at Mr. *Cobb's* new Houfe, next to Mr. *Coke's,* near the Road going down to the Capitol Landing; where there is alfo to be fold, Mens Shoes and Pumps, *Turkey* Coffee, Edging and Lace for Ladies Caps, and fome Gold Rings.

617   Advertisement from the *Virginia Gazette,* Nov. 17, 1752, in the New York Public Library

PRIVATE SCHOOLS IN THE NORTH

PRIVATE schools were not limited to the South. There were some in the northern colonies, even in New England. They especially advertised training in the mathematical subjects, which both parochial and public schools taught more sparingly than the languages, literature, and religion. These advertisements are from Philadelphia, Boston and New York. Note the elevated tone of Mr. Davis' announcement, and the miscellaneous character of the articles which Mr. Brownell sells on the side — from dry fish and cheese to kid gloves, Bibles, "classick authors," and a one-horse chaise.

EDUCATION.

Mr. D A V I S,

RETURNS his hearty and fincere thanks to his friends and the Public, for the great encouragement he has received, and the kind indulgence he has met with from them: The pleafure he now has in making this acknowledgment, emboldens him to affure them of the great delight he has in teaching, which he will always take, to the end that his Pupils might flourifh; for every motive that is dear, urges him to fuch an end: The good will of his friends, the ftability of his School; and the honour and importance of his calling: No ambition to him is greater than to merit the efteem and approbation of his friends and employers; therefore takes this liberty to inform them, that he has opened an

Evening School,

At his School-Houfe, No. 63, Maiden-lane, where are to be taught the Englifh Grammar, Writing, Arithmetic, Book-keeping, Geometry, Trigonometry, both plain and Spheric, Geography, Menfuration, Navigation, Surveying, and Algebra, &c.

Ye hopeful Youths, come learn what he has told,
Exalt your Minds and be what ye behold;
While Genius foaring, greater Heights explore,
And grace your Talents with true Beauties o'er,
Till ornamented with the Flowers of Truth,
Ye fhine bright Patterns for unlearned Youth.

619   From an advertisement in the *New York Gazette,* Oct. 21, 1782, in the New York Public Library

Advertifement.

READING, Writing, Arithmetick, Merchants Accompts, Geometry, Trigonometry, Plain and Sphærical Dyalling, Gauging, Aftronomy and Navigation are Taught: And Bonds, Bills, Indentures, Charter-parties, &c. are Drawn; and Youth Boarded, in *Crofs-ftreet, Bofton.* By *John Green.*

618   From an advertisement in the *American Weekly Mercury,* Nov. 27, 1735, in the New York Public Library

At the Houfe of *George Brownell,* *Late the Houfe of* John. Knight. *Deceafed, in* Second-ftreet,

IS TAUGHT,

READING, Writing, Cyphering, Dancing, Plain Work, Marking. with Variety of Needle Work. Boarding for Scholars.

☞ *N. B.* A new One Horfe Chaife, Alfo Dry Fifh, Mackerel, *Rhode-Ifland* Cheefe, Raifins, Currants, Hops, Iron Pots and Kettles, Falling Axes, Glue, cut Whale Bone, Cedar Buckets. Spanifh Soap for fine Linen, Sives, Fringes, Kid Gloves, Red Leather for Chairs and Shoes, &c. Primers, Pfalters, Teftaments, Bibles, the Claffick Authors *in ufum Delphini,* Writing Books, &c. To be SOLD.

620   From an advertisement in the *Boston News Letter,* Mar. 28, 1709, in the New York Public Library

Over againft the POST-OFFICE, In *Second-ftreet, PHILADELPHIA,* IS TAUGHT,

READING, Writing, Vulgar and Decimal Arithmetick, Merchants Accompts, Geometry, Menfuration, Surveying, Gauging, Algebra, Plain and Spherical Trigonometry, Navigation, the Projection of the Sphere, Dialling, and Aftronomy:

ALSO,

The Ufe of Globes, Maps, Planifpheres, Scales, Sliding Rules, and all forts of Mathematical Inftruments; very reafonably, after the beft Methods, by

THEOPHILUS GREW.

621   From an advertisement in the *American Weekly Mercury,* Dec. 30, 1735, in the New York Public Library

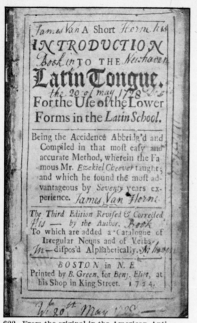

EZEKIEL CHEEVER, 1614–1708, BOSTON SCHOOLMASTER

THE best of the colonial teachers were the teachers in the Latin grammar schools of New England. The most famous of these were Ezekiel Cheever, headmaster of the Boston Latin School, and Elijah Corlett (1611–87), headmaster of the Cambridge Latin School. Cheever taught at New Haven, Ipswich and Charlestown before accepting the Boston post in 1670. He continued in active service until his death thirty-eight years later, at the age of ninety-four years. "He had been a skillful, painful schoolmaster for seventy years," wrote Cotton Mather; "and had the singular favor of Heaven, that though he had usefully spent his life among children, yet he had not become twice a child; but held his abilities, with his usefulness, in an unusual degree to the very last." His method of teaching Latin was published in 1709 by one of his assistants. It passed through at least twenty editions, and retained its popularity for more than a century, the last edition being published in 1838. It has the distinction of being the only school textbook of American origin prior to the Revolution.

THE VISIBLE WORLD

A BOOK long and widely popular in America, as throughout Europe, was the *Orbis Sensualium Pictus*, or *Visible World*, by John Amos Comenius, 1592–1670, Bishop of the Moravians, and one of the great educational reformers of all time. Things must be learned before words, Comenius insisted; and in this book things were represented by pictures. It was the first illustrated textbook for schools. Enough pages are here reproduced to enable the reader to see the method thus used in teaching Latin.

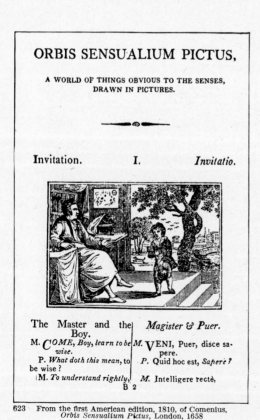

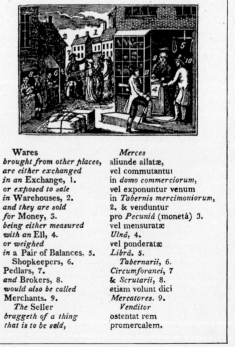

THE
SCHOOL
OF
GOOD MANNERS.

Composed for the Help of Parents in teaching their Children how to carry it in their Places during their Minority.

PRINTED by B. EDES & SON, in *Kilby-Street*, BOSTON. 1794.

20   The SCHOOL of

Of Children's Behaviour at the School.

BOW at coming in, pulling off thy hat ; especially if thy master or usher be in the school.

Loiter not, but immediately take thine own seat ; and move not from one place to another, till school-time be over.

If any stranger come into the school, rise up and bow, and set down in thy place again, keeping a profound silence.

If thy master be discoursing in the school with a stranger, stare not confidently on them, nor hearken to their talk.

Interrupt not thy master while a stranger or visitant is with him, with any question, request or complaint ; but refer any such matter until he be at leisure.

At no time quarrel or talk in the school

625 John Vinal, from the portrait by John Furnass in the Copley Gallery, Boston

626 From *The School of Good Manners*, Boston, 1794, in the New York Public Library

627 From *The School of Good Manners*, Boston, 1794, in the New York Public Library

A SCHOOLMASTER'S FACE

LESS famous than Cheever or Corlett, John Vinal, 1736–1823, one of Cheever's successors, is here pictured because of the schoolmasterish lines of his face. If one may judge by looks, he was less kindly, too, than his illustrious predecessor. He was not the author of *The School of Good Manners*, "compiled by a late famous School-Master in Boston," and published in 1794; but it is easy to imagine him enforcing its instructions concerning "Children's Behaviour at the School." Those were days when children were expected to be seen, not heard, except when spoken to. Punishments were harsh, and some schools had five-foot whipping posts erected either on the floor of the schoolroom itself or in the yard or street outside.

628 Margaret and Obed meet the Master in the Wood, from an engraving by Karl Huber, New York, after a drawing by Felix O. C. Darley, in Sylvester Judd, *Margaret*, New York, 1856

A COLONIAL SCHOOLMASTER

THE following description of a colonial schoolmaster's costume is from Sylvester Judd's *Margaret:* "He wore a three-cornered hat, with a very broad brim tied with a black ribbon over the top. His coat, of drab kerseymere, descended in long, broad, square skirts, quite to the calves of his legs. It had no buttons in front, but in lieu thereof, slashes, like long buttonholes, and laced with silk embroidery. He had on nankeen small-clothes, white ribbed silk stockings, paste knee and shoe buckles, and white silk knee-bands. His waistcoat, or vest, was of yellow embossed silk, with long skirts or lappels, rounded and open at the bottom, and bordered with white silk fringe. The sleeves and skirts of his coat were garnished with rows of silver buttons. He wore ruffle cuffs that turned back over his wrists and reached almost to his elbows; on his neck was a snow-white linen plaited stock, fastened behind with a large paste buckle, that glistened above the low collar of his coat. Under his hat appeared his grey wig, falling in rolls over his shoulders, and gathered behind with a black ribbon. From his side depended a large gold watch-seal and key, on a long gold chain. He had on a pair of tortoise-shell bridge spectacles. A golden-headed cane was thrust under his arm."

629 Instructions for Schoolmasters, from A Collection of Papers Printed by order of the Society for Propagating the Gospel in Foreign Parts, London, 1706

SCHOOLMASTERS OF THE S.P.G.

NEXT to the grammar-school teachers of New England in point of qual-ifications and efficiency, were the teachers of the parochial schools, most of whom came from Europe. They were carefully selected as a rule, and fairly well fitted to teach. This was especially true of the teachers and catechists of the Church of England who were commissioned and main-tained by the Society for Propagating the Gospel in Foreign Parts, usually referred to as the S.P.G. (see No. 151), from 1702 until the close of the Revolution. The Society's instructions to these schoolmasters were sensible and definite; they received fair salaries, and were furnished books as needed. They were required to teach "manners and morals" as well as the Catechism, and were expected to "rule by love rather than by fear," and in their own lives to be "an example of piety and virtue."

HORNBOOKS

THE teaching of children to read began with the hornbook, which was not a book, but a flat piece of wood with a handle. On the face was placed a piece of vellum or paper on which the lesson was inscribed, and this was covered by a thin sheet of transparent horn, held by narrow strips of brass. The covering protected the lesson from being soiled. The handle of the hornbook was usually pierced with a hole, through which a string was passed, to hang the hornbook around the child's neck or attach it to his girdle. The earliest evidence of the use of hornbooks in Europe is from a manuscript dated about 1400. They were in common use from the sixteenth century to the end of the eighteenth, and came to America with the colonists. The first of the hornbooks pictured is of an unusual type, being made of bone and containing only the alphabet and a decorative figure. The second is more characteristic. It contains the alphabet, the vowels, a list of syllables, the formula of invoca-tion of the Trinity used in exorcism and benediction, and the Lord's Prayer. All is preceded by the cross, and the first line of the alphabet was called the criss-cross (Christ's cross) row. The third is a mold for mak-ing gingerbread hornbooks, an inducement to learning which eighteenth-century boys and girls must have greatly prized.

To Master John the English Maid
A hornbook gives of gingerbread;
And that the child may learn the better,
As he can say he eats the letter.

630 From a photograph of a hornbook, in the Smithsonian Institution, Wash-ington

631 From a photograph of a hornbook, in the New York Public Library

632 From a photograph of a mold of a gingerbread hornbook, reproduced by courtesy of G. A. Plimpton, Norwood, Mass.

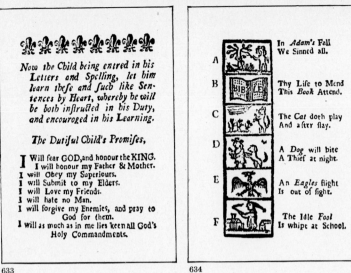

Now the Child being entred in his Letters and Spelling, let him learn thefe and fuch like Sentences by Heart, whereby he will be both inftructed in his Duty, and encouroged in his Learning.

The Dutiful Child's Promifes,

I Will fear GOD, and honour the KING.
I will honour my Father & Mother.
I will Obey my Superiours.
I will Submit to my Elders.
I will Love my Friends.
I will hate no Man.
I will forgive my Enemies, and pray to God for them.
I will as much as in me lies keen all God's Holy Commandments.

A In *Adam's* Fall We Sinned all.

B Thy Life to Mend This *Book* Attend.

C The *Cat* doth play And a ftrr flay.

D A *Dog* will bite A Thief at night.

E An *Eagles* flight Is out of fight.

F The Idle Fool Is whipt at School.

G As runs the *Glafs* Mans life doth pafs.

H My *Book* and *Heart* Shall never part.

J *Job* feels the Rod Yet bleffes GOD.

K Our *KING* the good No man of blood.

L The *Lion* bold The *Lamb* doth hold.

M The *Moon* gives light In time of night.

633   634   635

From *The New England Primer*, 1727, in the New York Public Library

THE NEW ENGLAND PRIMER

BETWEEN 1687 and 1690 Benjamin Harris, a London printer whose strenuous Protestantism made England an "uneasie Place" for him during the reign of the Catholic King James II, published in Boston the first edition of *The New England Primer*, which was "for one hundred years *the* schoolbook of the dissenters of America, and for another hundred was frequently reprinted." Between 1749 and 1766 Benjamin Franklin's firm in Philadelphia sold thirty-seven thousand one hundred copies; and the sales were yet greater in localities more largely Presbyterian and Congregational. It has been estimated that in one hundred and fifty years at least three million copies were sold. True to the Puritans' fear of idolatry, this *Primer* omitted the cross which preceded the alphabet in the hornbooks. Its most characteristic feature was the rhymed alphabet, which is here reproduced as it appeared in the earliest edition extant, printed in 1727. Many changes were made in these verses, as successive editions appeared. The first rhyme for the letter "K," for example, named "King Charles the Good"; later King William's name was inserted; then the general formula here given was used. As America became dissatisfied with the King, praise was turned into admonition: "Kings should be good, not men of blood." After the Revolution, the rhyme became "The British King lost States thirteen," or "Queens and Kings are gaudy things."

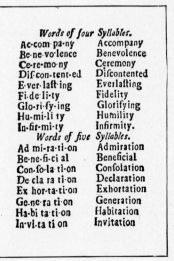

N Nightingales fing In Time of Spring.

O The *Royal Oak* it was the Tree That fav'd His Royal Majeftie.

P Peter denies His Lord and cries

Q Queen *Efther* comes in Royal State To Save the JEWS from difmal Fate

R Rachel doth mour. For her firft born.

S Samuel anoints Whom God appoints

T Time cuts down all Both great and fmall.

U *Uriah's* beauteous Wife Made *David* feek his Life.

W Whales in the Sea God's Voice obey.

X *Xerxes* the great did die, And fo muft you & I.

Y *Youth* forward flips Death fooneft nips.

Z Zacheus he Did climb the Tree His Lord to fee,

Words of four Syllables.

Ac·com·pa·ny	Accompany
Be·ne·vo·lence	Benevolence
Ce·re·mo·ny	Ceremony
Dif·con·tent·ed	Difcontented
E·ver·laft·ing	Everlafting
Fi·de·li·ty	Fidelity
Glo·ri·fy·ing	Glorifying
Hu·mi·li·ty	Humility
In·fir·mi·ty	Infirmity.

Words of five Syllables.

Ad·mi·ra·ti·on	Admiration
Be·ne·fi·ci·al	Beneficial
Con·fo·la·ti·on	Confolation
De·cla·ra·ti·on	Declaration
Ex·hor·ta·ti·on	Exhortation
Ge·ne·ra·ti·on	Generation
Ha·bi·ta·ti·on	Habitation
In·vi·ta·ti·on	Invitation

636   637   638

From *The New England Primer*, 1727, in the New York Public Library

at her Breaſt, following him to the Stake, with which ſorrowful fight he was not in the leaſt daunted, but with wonderful Patience died couragiouſly for the Goſpel of Jeſus Chriſt.

Some few Days before his Death, he writ the following Exhortation to his Children.

Give ear my Children to my words,
  whom God hath dearly bought,
Lay up his Laws within your heart,
  and print them in your thought.
I leave you here a little Book,
  for you to look upon :
That you may ſee your Fathers face,
  when he is dead and gone.
Who for the hope of heavenly things,
  while he did here remain,
Gave over all his golden Years
  to Priſon and to Pain.
Where I among my Iron Bands,
  incloſed in the dark,

MR. *John Rogers*, Miniſter of the Goſpel in *London*, was the firſt Martyr in Q. *Mary's* Reign, and was burnt at *Smithfield, February* the fourteenth. 1554. His Wife, with nine ſmall Children, and one at

639   John Rogers at the Stake, from *The New England Primer*, 1727, in the New York Public Library

THE BURNING OF JOHN ROGERS

ANOTHER characteristic feature of the *New England Primer* was a picture of the burning at the stake of John Rogers, the first Protestant to suffer martyrdom under Queen Mary, together with a poem which he was said to have written to be read to his children. Critics have made much of the facts that the poem was the work of another man, Robert Smith, who was burned at about the same time; that Rogers had really eleven children; and that it is not proved that his wife and children witnessed his burning. But these seem after all to be minor details. The major fact, which none can gainsay, was that John Rogers was burned at the stake for his refusal to recant the principles of Protestantism; that fact gave to picture and poem their permanent place in the *Primer*.

SECULARIZING THE *NEW ENGLAND PRIMER*

THE *Primer* also contained either the *Westminster Shorter Catechism* or John Cotton's *Milk for Babes*, or often both; and *A Dialogue between Christ, Youth and the Devil*. After the middle of the eighteenth century most editions contained Isaac Watts' *Cradle Hymn* and similar material. In 1781 first appeared the prayer which is still often taught to children:

> Now I lay me down to sleep
> I pray the Lord my soul to keep
> If I should die before I wake
> I pray the Lord my soul to take.

Many of the verses which had originally been of a mundane sort were changed or displaced in the period succeeding the Great Awakening, in the interest of more direct allusions to Scripture. The letter "O," for example, which had been associated with rhymes about Oaks and Owls, now stands opposite the sentiment: "Young Obadias, David, Josias, All were pious." The Dog is displaced by the Deluge, a Fool by Felix, the Lion by Lot, and Nightingales by Noah. Later, a secularizing tendency set in, and many of the Scriptural rhymes were removed. Among other innovations were the inane verses here standing above the picture alphabet.

He that ne'er learns his A, B, C,
For ever will a Blockhead be ;

Aſs	Bull	Cat
Dog	Eagle	Fox
Goat	Hog	Indian
King	Lion	Monkey

But he that learns theſe letters fair
Shall have a Coach to take the air.

NNag	OOwl	PPeacock
QQueen	RRobin	SSquirrel
TTop	VVine	WWhale
XXerxes	Yyoung Lamb	ZZania

640   Picture-alphabet from *The New England Primer*, Newport, 1800, in the New York Public Library

THE HON. SAMUEL ADAMS *Eſquire.*

641   Frontispiece from *The New England Primer*, Hartford, 1777

KINGS, PATRIOTS, AND SCHOOL–MAMS

THE frontispiece varied more than any other feature in the successive editions of the *New England Primer*. As long as the colonies were subject to England, the picture of the reigning King appeared. In 1776 the portrait of George III was relabelled "John Hancock"; and in 1777 a proper cut of Hancock appeared, and in another edition, one of Samuel Adams. After the Revolution, the likeness of Washington became the standard frontispiece, though one edition had a cut of Isaac Watts, and another the picture of a "School-Mam."

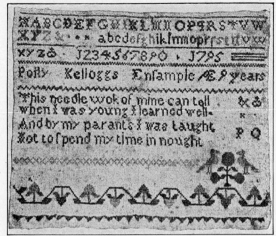

642 Polly Kellogg's sampler, from a photograph of the original in the Goodwin Historical Museum, Hadley, Mass.

643 Patty Coggeshall's sampler, from a photograph of the original in the Metropolitan Museum of Art, New York

SAMPLERS

THE hornbook doubtless set the model for the first samplers. There was little provision for the education of girls, as a rule, in colonial schools. In New England their attendance was usually limited to the summer, and they were entirely excluded from the Latin grammar schools. Sewing, spinning, weaving, embroidering, knitting, with the more prosaic duties of the household, were the staples of their education. Every girl worked at least one sampler in colored silks upon linen. These always contained the alphabet, both small letters and capitals, and the numerals; then generally the Lord's Prayer, a verse of Scripture, or a rhymed sentiment, in the composition of which the minister seems to have been consulted; below all, the name of the little worker, her age, and the date when her task was completed. Embellishments were added, as suited the ingenuity and industry of the child. The term "sampler" refers not simply to its presentation of an example of the young seamstress' proficiency, but to its use as preserving a pattern for the marking of household linen. Here are a simple and a more elaborate example of such work, both finished in 1795. Polly was then nine years of age, and Patty fifteen.

WHERE NATHAN HALE TAUGHT

A GOOD example of a country schoolhouse in colonial New England is this in East Haddam, Connecticut, where Nathan Hale, then eighteen years old, taught for four or five months immediately after his graduation from Yale College in the fall of 1773. He left this post to accept the mastership of the Union School at New London, a private school maintained by twenty-four of the more well-to-do citizens of that place, among whom was Governor Trumbull. "I love my employment," he wrote to friends in New Haven. In July, 1775, he resigned to accept a commission in the Revolutionary Army; and on September 22, 1776, he was executed as a spy by the British, who captured him within their lines, disguised as a Dutch schoolmaster. Hale is a fine example of an American type that has persisted from the eighteenth century to the present. He sensed the great importance of the calling of the schoolmaster. It was no accident that such a man should volunteer for a dangerous mission and should give his life for the ideals which he held dear.

644 Nathan Hale Schoolhouse, East Haddam, Conn., from a photograph by Hugh Spencer, Chester, Conn.

645   The schoolhouse in which Garfield taught, from a drawing in
Henry Howe, *Historical Collections of Ohio*, Cincinnati, 1850

LOG–CABIN SCHOOLHOUSES

SCHOOLHOUSES on the frontier were usually cabins of round logs. "For ceilings, poles were thrown across overhead, and brush placed on the poles and covered with earth. Above this was a clapboard roof held down by weight poles. Some of the better class of houses had puncheon floors; others had nothing but the naked earth. For light, a log was left out of the building, and newspapers greased and pasted over the opening. Seats were rude benches made of split logs, and desks were constructed by boring into the logs and placing a split piece of timber on pins driven into these holes. The fire-place included the entire end of the building, made of stone, mortar and sticks." —

J. P. WICKERSHAM, *A History of Education in Pennsylvania*, p. 189. At Blue Rock, Muskingum County, Ohio, James A. Garfield, afterward President of the United States, wrote in 1851, "I am teaching in a miserable old log school-house with a tall stove in it for burning stove coal and furnished with four-legged benches, and as smutty as a blacksmith's shop." He dug coal, when he needed it, from the hill behind the house.

"EIGHT–SQUARE SCHOOLHOUSES"

OCTAGONAL schoolhouses of stone, called "eight-square," were erected in Chester County, Pennsylvania, in the early nineteenth century. "The desks were placed round against the walls, and the pupils occupying them sat facing the windows. Benches without backs, for the smaller scholars, occupied the middle of the room. The windows were quite long, longitudinally, and from two to three panes wide, perpendicularly. A desk for the teacher, a huge stove in the middle of the room, a bucket, and what was called the 'Pass,' a small paddle, having the words 'in' and 'out' written on its opposite sides, constituted the furniture of the room." — WICKERSHAM, *op. cit.*, p. 188.

646   Old Eight-Square Schoolhouse, from James P. Wickersham, *A History of Education in Pennsylvania*, Lancaster, 1886

THE GROWTH OF ACADEMIES

FROM the middle of the eighteenth century the Latin grammar schools, which had been modeled after those of England, began to give way before the development of a more distinctively American institution — the academy. The first academy, probably, was that founded by Benjamin Franklin at Philadelphia in 1751,

647   The Mansion House, Dummer Academy, from a photograph reproduced by courtesy of Dummer Academy

which soon became the University of Pennsylvania. William Dummer, 1677–1761, by will set apart his mansion house and farm at South Byfield to establish a free academy which was opened in 1763 and still exists. Georgia in 1783 created a system of county academies. The movement spread rapidly in the nineteenth century. By 1850 there were over six thousand academies in the United States. Most of these schools aimed, not simply to prepare students for college, but to fit them for the duties of life.

648   Samuel Phillips, from a portrait, artist unknown, in the possession of Phillips Academy

THE PHILLIPS ACADEMIES AT ANDOVER AND EXETER

AFTER 1850 the academies in turn began to be replaced by the newly developing free public high schools. Most of the academies that now remain are endowed private schools, appealing to a wider than local constituency, and preparing students for the colleges and universities. An outstanding example of such institutions is Phillips Acad-

649   Eliphalet Pearson, from a portrait by Samuel F. B. Morse (1791–1872). in the possession of Phillips Academy

emy at Andover, founded in 1778 by Samuel Phillips, 1751–1802, a young graduate of Dummer Academy and Harvard College, who persuaded his father, Samuel Phillips, 1715–90, and his uncle, John Phillips, 1719–95, to give a large endowment of land and money for the purpose. His grandfather, Samuel Phillips, 1690–1771, had been for sixty-one years pastor of the South Church at Andover. The Constitution of Phillips Academy states the purpose of the founders "to lay the foundation of a public free School or Academy for the purpose of instructing Youth, not only in English and Latin Grammar, Writing, Arithmetic, and those Sciences wherein they are commonly taught; but more especially to learn them the GREAT END AND REAL BUSINESS OF LIVING." The first master was Eliphalet Pearson, a classmate of Phillips at Dummer and Harvard, whose name irreverent boys soon corrupted to "Elephant."

> . . . Great Eliphalet (I can see him now), —
> Big name, big frame, big voice, and beetling brow.

In 1781 Phillips Academy at Exeter was chartered, being founded and endowed by John Phillips. It was the first educational institution to be chartered by the New Hampshire legislature. In founding these two academies the Phillips family rendered a service of inestimable importance to the nation. To the present they have ranked among the first of privately endowed secondary schools.

650   Facsimile of letter from George Washington, Apr. 21, 1795, courtesy of Phillips Academy, Andover, Mass.

651   First home of Phillips Academy, Andover, from an engraving in John L. Taylor, *A Memoir of His Honor, Samuel Phillips*, Boston, 1856

MR. ALDEN'S ACADEMY

MANY academies were for both sexes. This broadside is the catalogue for the quarter ending October 13, 1807, of Timothy Alden's Academy at Portsmouth, New Hampshire. The paragraph below the list of pupils explains the various figures and letters appended to each name, and reveals the emphasis then placed upon memoriter methods of learning. Interpreted in its light, the list of names discloses individual differences of capacity or application, or both. Note how Elizabeth Goddard, Elizabeth Carter, Almira Porter, and Benjamin Franklin Salter excel in lessons memorized and certificates won. The preponderance of girls among the pupils may be due to the fact that this was the summer term, traditionally the time for girls to attend school and boys to labor upon the farm.

Timothy Alden, 1771–1839, was a descendant of John Alden, the young Pilgrim whose name Longfellow has made immortal. A graduate of Phillips Academy and of Harvard, and a Congregational minister, he was more interested in teaching than in preaching. In 1815 he founded Allegheny College at Meadville, Pennsylvania, and became its first president.

653   Certificate from Mr. Alden's Academy, in the New York Historical Society

REWARDS OF MERIT

GREAT reliance was placed upon certificates and rewards of merit by the schoolmasters of the early nineteenth century. They varied from the dignified, signed certificate awarded to Margaret Frost Mead in Mr. Alden's Academy, to the cheap card stating that "The Bearer" has received this "token of approbation." "Reward stimulates youth to exertion," says one. True, doubtless, as a general principle; but it may be questioned whether the teachers who used these cards had penetrated very deeply into the psychology of motivation.

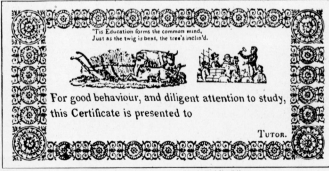

654   Reward of Merit, in the New York Public Library

655   Reward of Merit, in the New York Public Library

THE ACADEMY OF THE VISITATION AT GEORGETOWN

IN 1799, Alice Lalor, with two friends who like her were anxious to devote their lives to religion, opened a school in Georgetown, encouraged by her pastor, Leonard Neale, who in that year became president of Georgetown College. In 1816, Neale having become John Carroll's successor as Archbishop of Baltimore, they secured permission to take the vows and organize a convent of the Order of the Visitation. Henceforth the academy which

656   Convent of the Visitation, Georgetown, D. C., from a circular published
by the convent before 1826

was the outgrowth of their first school prospered and became a well-known school for girls. The picture is from its first published circular. "Although this institution is essentially Catholic," it said, "scholars of any other religious denomination are received, by complying with the exterior discipline of the house."

EMMA WILLARD, 1787–1870, PIONEER TEACHER OF WOMEN

EMMA WILLARD had begun teaching in a district school in Connecticut as a girl of sixteen. Her successful experience as teacher and principal in academies at Berlin, Westfield, and Middlebury encouraged her to present to Governor De Witt Clinton of New York "A Plan for Improving Female Education," in which she urged the establishment at public expense of an institution for the higher education of women. Clinton's repeated recommendations failed to secure favorable action by the Legislature; but with the help of the city of Troy and individual loans Mrs. Willard in 1821 founded the Troy Female Seminary. Here she did pioneer work in the collegiate education of women and in providing for the special training of women teachers. She did much to further the common school movement. Feeling that the country was "in need of educational missionary work," she devoted to such service a major part of her time after 1838. In 1846–47 she traveled over eight thousand miles through the South and West, speaking in behalf of public education, and conferring with leaders in the various states.

657 Emma Willard, from a photograph in the possession of the Emma Willard School, Troy, N. Y.

658   Recitation Room, Troy Female Seminary, as it was before 1840, from a photograph of
a restoration, in the possession of the Emma Willard School, Troy, N. Y.

659　Robert Raikes, 1735–1811, from a drawing in the
European Magazine and London Review, Nov. 1788

PHILANTHROPY IN EDUCATION

The Declaration of Independence and the Constitution of the United States were based upon principles of democracy which made inevitable the assumption by the states of responsibility for the education of their future citizens. Yet other states were slow to adopt the plan of publicly controlled, tax-supported schools which the New England colonies, except Rhode Island, had chosen to follow. For the first fifty years of national independence, the movement toward better and more general provisions for education depended largely upon voluntary, philanthropic associations. Among the earliest of these were various societies for the promotion of Sunday schools. Robert Raikes, a journalist of Gloucester, England, had in 1780 employed women on Sunday to teach reading, religion and morals to the neglected children who were employed throughout the week in the pin factories of that city. These Sunday schools marked the beginnings of popular education in England.

THE SUNDAY SCHOOL MOVEMENT

In 1790 a "First Day or Sunday School Society" was organized in Philadelphia, for the maintenance of schools according to Raikes' plan. The double title indicates the fact that it united men of different religious affiliations. Dr. Benjamin Rush, Universalist; Bishop William White, Episcopalian; Matthew Carey, Roman Catholic; and Joseph Sharpless, Quaker, were prominent directors. The Sunday-school movement spread rapidly. Sunday-school unions were organized in various cities after the close of the War of 1812–15; and in 1824 a national society, the American Sunday School Union, was founded. In two respects, the Sunday schools in this country soon began to depart from the type fostered by Raikes: they extended to all children and young people, well-to-do as well as poor; and they were adopted by the churches as an agency of religious education, and gradually ceased to teach reading and writing.

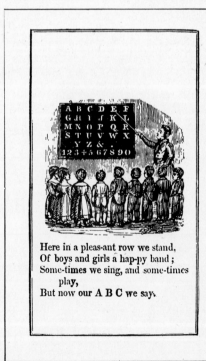

Here in a pleas-ant row we stand,
Of boys and girls a hap-py band;
Some-times we sing, and some-times play,
But now our A B C we say.

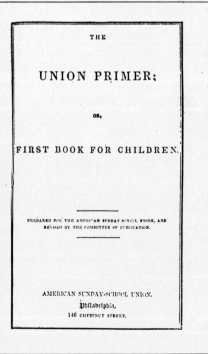

THE

UNION PRIMER;

OR,

FIRST BOOK FOR CHILDREN.

PREPARED FOR THE AMERICAN SUNDAY SCHOOL UNION, AND
REVISED BY THE COMMITTEE OF PUBLICATION.

AMERICAN SUNDAY-SCHOOL UNION.
Philadelphia,
146 CHESTNUT STREET.

660　　　　　　　　　From the original in the New York Public Library

BENJAMIN RUSH PROPOSES FREE SCHOOLS IN PENNSYLVANIA

THE First Day Society forwarded a petition to the Legislature of Pennsylvania, declaring that "the proper education of youth is an object of the first importance, particularly in free countries, as the surest preservation of the virtue, liberty, and happiness of the people," and urging the establishment of schools at public expense. This was doubtless the work of Dr. Benjamin Rush, professor of medicine in the University of Pennsylvania, and signer of the Declaration of Independence. In 1786 he had presented to the Legislature a comprehensive "Plan for Establishing Public Schools." To the objection of expense he answered that such schools would in the end lessen taxes. "But shall the estates of orphans, bachelors, and persons who have no children, be taxed to pay the support of schools from which they can derive no benefit? I answer in the affirmative, to the first part of the objection, and I deny the truth of the latter part of it. Every member of

661 Dr. Benjamin Rush, 1745–1813, from the painting by Thomas Sully in the possession of the Pennsylvania Hospital, Philadelphia

---

FREE SCHOOL.

THE trustees of the Society for establishing a Free School in the city of New York, for the education of such poor children as do not belong to, or are not provided for by any religious Society, having engaged a Teacher, and procured a School House for the accommodation of a School, have now the pleasure of announcing that it is proposed to receive scholars of the descriptions alluded to without delay; applications may be made to either of the subscribers, viz.

JOHN MURRAY, JUN.
HENRY TENBROOK
GARRIT H. VAN WAGENEN.

May 16   2w

662 From an advertisement of the New York Free School Society, in *The Evening Post*, New York, May 14, 1806

---

the community is interested in the propagation of virtue and knowledge in the State." "I conceive the education of our youth in this country to be peculiarly necessary in Pennsylvania, while our citizens are composed of the natives of so many different kingdoms in Europe. Our schools of learning, by producing one general and uniform system of education, will render the mass of the people more homogeneous, and thereby fit them more easily for a uniform and peaceable government."

SCHOOL SOCIETIES

AMONG school societies organized in Philadelphia were "The Society for the Free Instruction of Indigent Boys," 1800; "The Society for the Promotion of Public Schools in Pennsylvania," 1827. School societies were organized in most of the cities of the states which lacked public schools, as Providence, Albany, Baltimore, Washington, Savannah and Augusta. The most effective of these voluntary associations was the "New York Free School Society," organized in 1805, "for the education of such poor children as do not belong to, or are not provided for by any religious Society." In 1807 it began to receive grants from public funds, as did the churches, both Protestant and Catholic, which maintained schools. In 1825 it became the sole recipient of such funds in New York city, and public aid was no longer given to the church schools. It thereupon changed its name to "The Public School Society of New York"; and was soon permitted also to levy a local tax. In 1842 it ceased to receive public funds, and a City Board of Education was created, to which the Society turned over its buildings and property when, in 1853, it disbanded.

Public School No. 17, here shown, was erected by the Society in 1843, at a cost of seventeen thousand dollars, and was regarded as a model building. The Primary School was on the first floor, the Girls' School in a large room seating two hundred and fifty-two pupils on the second floor, and the Boys' School in a similar room on the third. The work in the Boys' School was minutely organized, if the *Manual* of the Society presents a fair sample of its method. The precise mathematical positions of thumb, fingers and body seem to have been computed for each of the seven stages in the process of receiving, opening, reading, closing, and returning a book.

663 Public School No. 17 — A model school, from *A Manual of The System of Discipline and Instruction for the Schools of the Public School Society of New York*, New York, 1845

664   Plate of School when in Draughts, from the *Manual of the Lancastrian System of Teaching Reading, Writing, Arithmetic and Needle Work, as practised in the Schools of the Free-school Society of New York*, New York, 1820

LANCASTRIAN SCHOOLS

ORGANIZATION was the keynote of the plan of instruction devised by Joseph Lancaster, 1778–1838, an English schoolmaster who came to America in 1818.   The school was divided into "drafts" of ten pupils, each of which was in charge of a moni-

665   From a woodcut, *Show States*, in *The British System for Education, being a complete epitome of the Improvements and Inventions practised by Joseph Lancaster, to which is added, A Report of the Trustees of the Lancaster School at Georgetown*, Washington, 1812

tor, who was himself a pupil chosen for this service because he was bright and alert.   The teacher taught the lesson to the monitors, and they in turn taught it to the members of their drafts.   By following the careful, detailed directions given in the *Manual* a teacher could easily handle in this way a school of as many pupils as could be gathered in one room, up to a thousand or more.   This monitorial system was enthusiastically received here.   The New York Free School Society employed it from 1817 to 1832, when it began to be dropped.   The public schools for the "indigent," maintained in Philadelphia from 1818 to 1836, were organized upon the Lancastrian plan.   The scheme spread to many cities, south and west;   Maryland and North Carolina flirted with the idea of state systems of Lancastrian schools;   one Governor of Connecticut proposed that these be substituted, where practicable, for the public schools which that state had long possessed.   From 1830 to 1840, however, the plan was gradually superseded.

In spite of its defects, which are obvious, the Lancastrian plan was of great service.   It made possible the transition to better plans.   Its cheapness enabled schools to be maintained in the period when they depended chiefly upon the slender resources of philanthropic benevolence.   It interested people in schools, and prepared their minds for the expense involved in the support by general taxation of better and consequently more costly schools.   It substituted the idea of class-teaching for the purely individual instruction, with intervening periods of idleness, which had hitherto been the rule.   "Let every child at every moment have something to do and a motive for doing it," was one of Lancaster's maxims.   It helped people to realize that organization, order, and group discipline may be of value in the processes of education;   and it stirred some to think and experiment on the technique of teaching. It showed that trained teachers are necessary, and it began the training of many, who passed from the status of monitor to that of teacher.   The abandonment of the Lancastrian plan was evidence, not so much of failure, as of its success in pointing beyond itself.

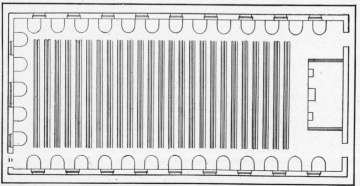

666   Plan of a Lancastrian Schoolroom, from the *Manual of the Lancastrian System, etc.*

INFANT SCHOOLS

THE younger children were the last to be provided for in the organization of public schools. They were supposed to learn reading and writing at home or in dame schools, and were not usually received into the public schools until about eight years of age. In 1818, stimulated by reports of Robert Owen's experiments with Infant Schools, Boston organized a system of Primary Schools, which remained

667   Infant School in New York in 1825, from a print in the New York Public Library

under separate management from the Grammar Schools until 1854. Infant School Societies were formed in various cities. The Public School Society of New York organized Primary Departments in its schools after 1830; and the movement became general. The illustrations are from its early stages, while these schools were yet too much influenced by the practices of the Lancastrian system. The children were mounted row above row upon a sort of wide stairs, and taught by word of mouth. They were drilled to march to and from their elevated seats with strict military precision. These methods were soon displaced by more natural ways of dealing with little children. It is interesting, however, to find old cuts and verses from the *New England Primer* still appearing in this *Infant School Alphabet*, published in 1832.

668   Children marching and keeping time, from Mrs. Howland,
The Infant School Manual, Worcester, 1830

6   THE INFANT SCHOOL ALPHABET.

Bee   Wren

Bat	bet	bit	bot	but
lad	led	lid	lod	lud
pan	pen	fin	lot	tun
rag	peg	pig	log	mug
tar	ten	tin	top	sum

Book.

Thy life to mend,
This Book attend,
In spirit and in truth.

THE INFANT SCHOOL ALPHABET.   7

Nest   Goose

Band	bend	dint	bond
land	rend	lint	fond
sand	tend	mint	pond
bang	belt	fist	dock
bent	rest	fork	song

Youth.

Youth forward slips,
Death soonest nips.

669   From *The Infant School Alphabet*, Philadelphia, 1832

670 Gideon Hawley, from a portrait in the possession of
the State Department of Education, Albany, New York

THE FIRST STATE SUPERINTENDENT
OF COMMON SCHOOLS

George Clinton, Governor of New York in 1777–95 and
1801–04, was untiring in his efforts to secure the establishment of
public schools. In response to his recommendations, the Legislature in 1784 created the Board of Regents of the University
of the State of New York, empowered to found and supervise
academies and colleges; and in 1795 it passed an "Act for the
Encouragement of Schools," providing appropriations for five
years in aid of common schools. In 1805 a permanent state
school fund was created. In 1812, finally, a state system of common schools was authorized, under the supervision of an officer
to be known as the Superintendent of Common Schools. Gideon
Hawley, 1785–1870, appointed to this office, was the first state
superintendent of schools in the country. His work was so
efficient and vigorous as to awaken the distrust of politicians,
and in 1821 he was removed, and his duties assigned to the Secretary of State, *ex officio*.

DE WITT CLINTON, 1769–1828, PROTAGONIST OF EDUCATION FOR CITIZENSHIP

To none of its citizens does New York owe more than to De Witt Clinton, Mayor of New York city for ten
years, and Governor of the state in 1817–23 and 1825–28. He was responsible for the building of the Erie
Canal, and was active in securing the abolition of slavery and of imprisonment for debt. He labored for
the removal of property limitations upon the exercise of the right of suffrage, and for the betterment of the
schools. He enunciated the intrinsic connection of democracy and education in clear, cogent terms. "Without the right of suffrage, liberty cannot exist. . . . But the right of suffrage cannot be exercised in a salu-
tary manner without intelligence. . . . Upon education we must
therefore rely for the purity, the preservation, and the perpetuation of republican government. . . . The first duty of
government and the surest evidence of good government is
the encouragement of education. . . . I consider the system
of our common schools as the palladium of our freedom, for
no reasonable apprehension
can be entertained of its
subversion, as long as the
great body of the people are
enlightened by education."

Clinton's interest in education was intimate and
personal. He was president
of the Free School Society
from its organization until
his death. He was president

672   From the original in the New York
Public Library

671   De Witt Clinton, from a portrait by Samuel
F. B. Morse, in the Metropolitan Museum of Art,
New York

also of the Literary and Philosophical Society, the New York Historical
Society, the American Academy of Arts and Sciences, the American
Bible Society, and the Presbyterian Education Society. He was far
ahead of his time in advocating an enrichment of the curriculum of the
common schools, which usually taught simply the "four R's," reading,
'riting, 'rithmetic, and religion. He held that the common schools should
be planned for ten years of the child's life, and that competent teachers
could in that time impart not only these fundamental subjects, but the
elements of "geography, algebra, mineralogy, agriculture, chemistry,
mechanical philosophy, surveying, geometry, astronomy, political economy, and ethics."

WORKINGMEN DEMAND FREE PUBLIC SCHOOLS

THE second quarter of the nineteenth century was a period of rapid industrial development. The era of machines and factories was well under way. Workingmen began to organize to protect and further their interests. One of the first of their demands was for adequate and equitable systems of schools. In Pennsylvania, for example, only the children of "the poor" were taught "gratis" in the schools provided by the public authorities. The workingmen of Philadelphia appointed a committee which in 1830 submitted a careful and detailed report on the educational situation in the state, and the demand was formulated for "an equal and a general system of education." The leading feature of the existing "school districts," the report asserted, is the "pauperism" which they imply and foster. "They are confined exclusively to the children of *the poor*, while there are, perhaps, thousands of children whose parents are unable to afford for them a good private education, yet whose standing, professions, or connexions in society effectually exclude them from taking the benefit of a *poor law*. There are great numbers, even of the poorest parents, who hold a dependence upon the public bounty to be incompatible with the rights and liberties of an American citizen and whose deep and cherished consciousness of *independence* determines them rather to starve the intellect of their offspring, than submit to become the objects of public charity." Public funds have been liberally granted to colleges and universities, but these appropriations are "exclusively for the benefit of the wealthy, who are thereby enabled to procure a liberal education for their children upon *lower terms* than it could otherwise be afforded them." Such policies "can never secure the common prosperity of a nation nor confer *intellectual* as well as political equality on a people."

From the (Alabama) Spirit of the Age.

SPIRIT OF IMPROVEMENT.

We have, on several occasions, called the attention of our readers to the efforts that are making, by the working classes, in the eastern cities, to advance the political interests of the great class of producers, of every name, whether farmers, mechanics, or other laborers. But our columns being very much engrossed, recently, with other matters, those efforts have not had as great a share of our attention, as in our opinion they merit.

The complaint is, that the poor are oppressed, and constrained to the performance of excessive labor; that their children are deprived of education, for want of suitable institutions—for want of pecuniary means, and for want of leisure. Legislators, it is said, are generally selected from the nonproductive classes; and the existing system of things is such, in its tendency, as to make the poor poorer, and the rich richer; to enable the few to live at ease on the labors of the many.

It is, therefore, contended that there is something radically wrong in the laws and institutions of the country; and that these existing evils ought to be remedied. The opinion also prevails that a remedy cannot reasonably be looked for, but by those who are most deeply interested taking their affairs into their own hands. Hence the origin of what has been sometimes called the working men's party.

The extent of this excitement may be inferred from the fact, that there are now in the city of New York two daily papers, the "Friend of Equal Rights," and the "New York Daily Sentinel," and one weekly paper, the "Working Man's Advocate," devoted to the interest of the working men.

673 From *The Working Man's Advocate*, New York, Mar. 6, 1830, in the New York Public Library

THE BATTLE FOR FREE PUBLIC SCHOOLS IN PENNSYLVANIA

THE well-planned campaign conducted by the Society for the Promotion of Public Schools, organized in 1827, and the persistent, effective efforts of George Wolf, Governor of Pennsylvania from 1829 to 1835, finally issued in the passage of "An Act to Establish a General System of Education by Common Schools" in 1834. Every ward, township and borough in the state was made a school district, and it was left to the vote of each district to accept the new plan of common schools, involving both local taxation and state aid, or to provide as before for the children of the poor only. There ensued the most memorable division of public opinion in the history of the state. Out of nine hundred and eighty-seven districts, five hundred and two accepted the plan, two hundred and sixty-four rejected it, and two hundred and twenty-one took no action. The northern counties, settled largely by folk from New England and New York,

favored the law, as did the Scotch-Irish on the western frontier. The Germans generally opposed it, fearing the loss of their parochial schools and the displacing of the German language. Some argued "that the education of the masses was dangerous, and would breed mischief of many kinds, idleness, vice, crime; that the taxes required to support free schools would greatly impoverish if not entirely bankrupt the people; that it was unjust to compel those who had no children to pay for the education of the children of others . . . that the schools ought to be called *Zwing Schulen*, forced schools, rather than free schools"; and so on. The question became the major issue of the political campaign in the autumn of 1834.

674 The Pennsylvania School Election of 1835, from Cubberley, *Public Education in the United States*, Houghton, Mifflin Co., Boston, 1919

Shading shows the percentage of school districts in each county organizing under and accepting the School Law of 1834. Percentage of district accepting is indicated in figures on the map for a few of the counties.

675   Thaddeus Stevens, from a photograph
              by Brady, Washington

THADDEUS STEVENS, 1792–1868, DEFENDS
THE COMMON SCHOOLS

THE Legislature of 1835 was bombarded with petitions urging the repeal of the School Law. A special committee appointed to consider them found that thirty-two thousand people had asked for the repeal, that sixty-six of these had signed by making their mark, that many names were illegibly written, and that "in most of the petitions not more than five names out of every hundred are written in English." The Senate voted to repeal the law; but the House, by a vote of fifty to thirty-eight, refused to

> If an elective Republic is to endure for any great length of time, every elector must have sufficient information, not only to accumulate wealth and take care of his pecuniary concerns, but to direct wisely the Legislature, the ambassadors, and the Executive of the Nation—for some part of all these things, some agency in approving or disapproving of them, falls to every freeman. If, then, the permanency of our Government depends upon such knowledge, it is the duty of Government to see that the means of information be diffused to every citizen. This is a sufficient answer to those who deem education a private and not a public duty—who argue that they are willing to educate their own children, but not their neighbors children.

676   Passage from a speech of Thaddeus Stevens, in
              the *Pennsylvania School Journal*, 1835

concur, and finally forced the Senate to accept a bill amending and strengthening it. The leader of the battle in the House was Thaddeus Stevens, a Vermont-born lawyer from Gettysburg, whose powerful speech in behalf of the schools and in derision of their opponents, lives in Pennsylvania tradition as an outstanding example of effective eloquence.

DISTRICT SCHOOLS IN MASSACHUSETTS

THE public schools in Massachusetts had not kept pace with the general development of the state. Privately supported academies had generally taken the place of the Latin grammar schools; and the Law of 1647 had been relaxed by successive exemptions until in 1824 only seven towns were legally required to furnish education higher than the rudiments. In place of the town, moreover, the school district had become the unit of public-school administration. Each school district was practically free to manage its own affairs. The year 1827, when the assignment of the educational responsibilities of the town to the districts reached its culmination, marked "the utmost limit to the subdivision of American sovereignty — the high-water mark of modern democracy, and the low-water mark of the Massachusetts school system." — G. H. MARTIN, *The Evolution of the Massachusetts Public School System*, p. 92. Under the district plan, wages were low, and the most important qualification of a candidate for a teaching "contract" was, for a woman, to be related to the school committeeman; for a man, to be able to whip the older pupils. The "little red schoolhouse," glorified by tradition, was usually a poor affair. In one town, the amount annually appropriated for repairs on eight district schoolhouses, for a series of years, was five dollars — an average of sixty-two and one half cents each. The period, however, was one in which reform was in the air. Movements for the betterment of society were manifold and particularly strong in New England. A reaction against the poor schools brought about by the legislation of 1827 was inevitable.

677   From a cartoon *School Meeting*, in the *Common School Assistant*, Oct. 1839

BEGINNINGS OF THE COMMON-SCHOOL REVIVAL IN MASSACHUSETTS

PUBLIC attention was called to the defects and dangers of the district system by James G. Carter, 1795–1849, a Harvard graduate still in his twenties, who taught a private school at Lancaster. He began writing to the newspapers in 1821, and three years later published *Letters . . . on the Free Schools of New England*, followed by a series of *Essays upon Popular Education*. Laws were passed in 1826–27 designed to put a check upon the vagaries of the districts. In 1834 a state school fund was created, and conditions imposed for sharing in its income. In 1835 Carter was elected to the Legislature. Here, as Chairman of the House Committee on Education, he was largely responsible for the enactment, in 1837, of a law creating a State Board of Education. At the first meeting of this Board, Horace Mann, a well-known lawyer, for ten years a member of the Legislature, and for the past two years President of the Senate, was elected its Secretary.

678 James G. Carter, from a photograph in the *American Journal of Education*, Vol. V

679 Horace Mann, from a photograph in the American Antiquarian Society, Worcester, Mass.

HORACE MANN, 1796–1859, SECRETARY OF THE MASSACHUSETTS BOARD OF EDUCATION

MANN took up his work with rare devotion, intelligence, and vigor. "So long as I hold this office," he wrote in his diary on the day that he accepted it, "I devote myself to the supremest welfare of mankind on earth." Closing his law office, he said, "The interests of a client are small compared with the interests of the next generation. Let the next generation be my client." The Legislature fixed his salary at but fifteen hundred dollars, with no allowance for expenses or even for office rent; but he kept cheerfully on, commenting, "I will be revenged on them; I will do them more than fifteen hundred dollars worth of good."

EDUCATING PUBLIC OPINION CONCERNING SCHOOLS

MANN amply fulfilled that promise. He began holding conventions on education in the various counties of the state, and addressing audiences wherever he deemed it to be for the good of the cause. He published a semi-monthly magazine, *The Common School Journal*. He held teachers' institutes, and organized the first three state normal schools in America. He wrote twelve annual *Reports* which commanded attention throughout the country, and are still regarded as "among the best expositions, if, indeed, they are not the very best ones, of the practical benefits of a common school education both to the individual and to the state." — B. A. HINSDALE, *Horace Mann and the Common School Revival*, p. 180. Never limited to routine matters, each of these was a campaign document, centering upon some phase of the educational situation which Mann made the objective of his

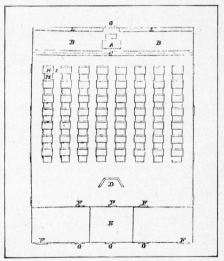

680 Plan of a model schoolhouse, from Horace Mann, *Report of the Secretary of the Board of Education*, Boston, 1836

LEGEND: *A.* Teacher's desk; *B.* Teacher's platform; *C.* Step for ascending the platform; *D.* Place for stove, if one be used; *E.* Room for recitation, for retiring in case of sudden indisposition, etc.; *F.* Doors into boys' and girls' entries; *G.* Windows; *H.* Pupils' desks; *I.* Aisles; *L.* Case for books, apparatus, etc.; *M.* Pupils' seats.

drive in that year. The *First*, for example, dealt with the construction and equipment of schoolhouses; the *Fourth* and *Tenth* exposed the defects of the district system; and the *Second* described better methods of teaching reading and composition.

PENITENTIAL TEARS:

..

A CRY FROM THE DUST,

BY

"THE THIRTY-ONE,"

PROSTRATED AND PULVERIZED BY THE HAND OF

HORACE MANN,

SECRETARY. &c.

Γουναύμαι σ', 'Αχιλευ· μι λι·

BOSTON:
C. STIMPSON, 106, WASHINGTON STREET.

MDCCCXLV

681   From the original in the New York
Public Library

MANN IS ATTACKED BY THE BOSTON SCHOOLMASTERS

THE *Seventh Report*, 1843, described the schools of Europe as Mann had observed them during a tour just ended. His praise of many of their methods touched the pride and aroused the resentment of the schoolmasters of Boston. Thirty-one of them bitterly attacked him in one hundred and forty-four pages of *Remarks*, mostly opprobrious. Mann struck back with a severe *Reply*, to which the schoolmasters made a *Rejoinder*, and this called from him an *Answer*. Other pamphlets were published, attacking or defending him. Nineteen in all were printed during the controversy. Here is the ironical title-page of one.

RELIGIOUS SECTARIANISM AND THE SCHOOLS

MANN was attacked by some in the name of religion. The Law of 1827 had forbidden the use in the common schools of any textbooks "calculated to favor the tenets of any particular sect of Christians." People of all parties and denominations had agreed on this principle ten years before Mann was chosen Secretary of the Board of Education. In accordance with this law, he refused to admit to the schools certain books published by the American Sunday School Union, and thereby incurred the enmity of the editor of its publications, who attacked him, first openly, and then anonymously, in various journals, to give the impression of a more general disaffection. Mann was a Unitarian, and this exposed him to the suspicion of others who assailed him. Some went so far as to assert that the people of each school district have a right to teach in the common schools the sectarian beliefs of the majority in the district, and that dissenters may withdraw, being granted their share of the public funds. This would have meant the destruction of the common school system, and Mann met the proposal with a careful and full reply. These attacks did not represent the great majority of the Orthodox people of the state, however. They sustained him on this as on other points. Mann did not "exclude the Bible from the schools," as is sometimes asserted; he believed that it should be read daily in the schools, without sectarian comment.

Mann is rightly regarded as the greatest of the builders of the American system of free public schools. "No one did more than he to establish in the minds of the American people the conception that education should be universal, non-sectarian, and free, and that its aim should be social efficiency, civic virtue, and character, rather than mere learning or the advancement of sectarian ends. Under his practical leadership an unorganized and heterogeneous series of community school systems was reduced to organization and welded together into a state school system and the people of Massachusetts were effectively recalled to their ancient belief in and duty toward the education of the people." — E. P. CUBBERLEY, *Public Education in the United States*, p. 167.

THE

COMMON SCHOOL

CONTROVERSY;

CONSISTING OF

THREE LETTERS OF THE SECRETARY

OF THE

BOARD OF EDUCATION,

OF THE

STATE OF MASSACHUSETTS,

IN REPLY TO

CHARGES PREFERRED AGAINST THE BOARD,

BY THE EDITOR OF THE CHRISTIAN WITNESS

AND BY

EDWARD A. NEWTON ESQ.

OF PITTSFIELD,

ONCE A MEMBER OF THE BOARD;

TO WHICH ARE ADDED

EXTRACTS FROM THE DAILY PRESS,

IN REGARD TO THE CONTROVERSY.

BOSTON:
PRINTED BY J. N. BRADLEY & CO.
1844.

682   From the original in the New York
Public Library

COUSIN'S "REPORT ON PUBLIC INSTRUCTION IN PRUSSIA"

MANN judged the schools of Prussia to be the best that he had visited, and those of England the poorest. After its humiliation at the hands of Napoleon, Prussia was rebuilding its national life, relying primarily upon a complete reorganization of its schools. They were now controlled by the state, and modeled upon the principles and methods of the great Swiss teacher, Pestalozzi. The success of the new system was so marked as to attract the attention of educators and publicists throughout Europe and America. In 1831 France sent Victor Cousin to study the schools of the German states, particularly of Prussia; and his *Report*, published in the following year, pronounced the School Law of Prussia to be "the most comprehensive and complete law concerning primary education" within his knowledge. A translation of the *Report* was printed in England in 1834; and part of this, explaining the Prussian system, was reprinted in New York in 1835. It helped to form the ideas of the men who, like Mann, were striving to establish strong systems of public schools in the various states. It is an interesting example of the continued influence of Europe upon American development.

RAPPORT

SUR L'ÉTAT

DE

L'INSTRUCTION PUBLIQUE

DANS

QUELQUES PAYS DE L'ALLEMAGNE,

ET PARTICULIÈREMENT EN PRUSSE.

PAR M. V. COUSIN,

CONSEILLER D'ÉTAT, PROFESSEUR DE PHILOSOPHIE, MEMBRE DE L'INSTITUT
ET DU CONSEIL ROYAL DE L'INSTRUCTION PUBLIQUE

Nouvelle édition.

PARIS,

Chez F. G. LEVRAULT, rue de la Harpe, n.° 81;
STRASBOURG, même maison, rue des Juifs, n.° 33

1833

683 From the original in the New York Public Library

684 Charles Brooks, from a photograph in the Hingham Historical Society

CHARLES BROOKS, 1795–1872, PROPAGANDIST FOR EDUCATION

IN 1834–35 Charles Brooks, minister of the Congregational Church at Hingham, Massachusetts, traveled in Europe, and made an extended study of the Prussian school system. He discussed its principles with Dr. H. Julius, of Hamburg, a Prussian commissioner who chanced to be a fellow voyager. He returned an enthusiastic propagandist of the educational ideas he had thus gained. At his own expense he traveled throughout the state in the years 1835–38, explaining to the people the better methods he had observed, gathering and leading groups for the discussion of educational problems, and urging the establishment of "seminaries" for the training of teachers. He did much to create the public opinion which sustained Horace Mann's work. Here is reproduced one of his broadsides calling a convention on education to meet at Plymouth on December 7, 1836, proposing topics for discussion, and suggesting to his fellow ministers that Cousin's *Report* contains good material for Thanksgiving Day sermons.

TO THE FRIENDS OF EDUCATION IN PLYMOUTH COUNTY.

[Broadside text addressed "Fellow Citizens," signed CHARLES BROOKS, dated Hingham, November 10th, 1836.]

685 From the original in the New York Public Library

686   The first State Normal School, Lexington, Mass., opened July 4, 1839, from a sketch in the Lexington Historical Society

THE FIRST STATE NORMAL SCHOOLS IN AMERICA

"The teacher makes the school" was one of Cousin's maxims. New York had been relying upon the academies to train teachers for its schools; but Carter, Mann, and Brooks were agreed that there should be distinct institutions for this purpose, like the "teachers' seminaries" of Prussia. In 1838 Edmund Dwight, a wealthy merchant of Boston, offered ten thousand dollars to the state for the promotion of the training of teachers, provided the legislature would appropriate an equal amount. With local coöperation, three normal schools were opened in 1839–40, at Lexington, Barre, and Bridgewater. In 1844 New York founded a normal school at Albany. By 1860 there were twelve such schools in the United States; and after the Civil War the number increased rapidly.

HENRY BARNARD, 1811–1900, "THE SCHOLAR OF THE PUBLIC SCHOOL AWAKENING"

Next to Horace Mann in the significance of his labors for the public schools of America stands Henry Barnard. Traveling in Europe in 1835–37, he became interested in the methods of Pestalozzi. As a member of the Legislature of Connecticut, he secured the passage in 1838 of a law creating a State Board of Commissioners for Common Schools. As its Secretary in 1838–42 and again in 1851–55, he put new life into the schools of Connecticut; and in the intervening years rendered a like service to Rhode Island. Connecticut was the first state to establish a permanent school fund, and its people had begun to think that this rendered local taxation unnecessary. This fact, together with the usual defects of the district system, had caused the schools to deteriorate. Barnard secured adequate legislation, organized institutes for the training of teachers, published a *Connecticut Common School Journal*, was President of the first Normal School, established libraries and organized lecture courses in the various towns, and even devised a traveling model school, with teacher and children in a wagon fitted out to demonstrate effective methods of teaching. He edited and published *The American Journal of Education*, 1855–81, "a vast encyclopedia of educational information" which did much to stimulate teachers everywhere to conceive their work in terms of high professional ideals. He served from 1867 to 1870 as the first United States Commissioner of Education. Barnard was a scholar whose dominant interest was education. He and Mann were the two great leaders of the public school awakening of the second quarter of the nineteenth century. Both men made great contributions to the development of the American people.

687   Henry Barnard, from a portrait, by Franklin Tuttle in the Connecticut Historical Society, Hartford, Conn.

JOHN D. PIERCE, 1797–1882, "FATHER OF THE MICHIGAN SCHOOL SYSTEM"

A COPY of Cousin's *Report* came into the hands of John D. Pierce, a Presbyterian home missionary at Marshall, Michigan. Deeply impressed by it, he passed it on to his friend and parishioner, Isaac E. Crary, who was made chairman of the Committee on Education at the convention in 1835 which framed the Constitution of the State of Michigan. The article on education, drafted by Crary, provided for the appointment of a State Superintendent of Public Instruction and the establishment of a permanent school fund, and enjoined upon the Legislature the creation of a state system of schools, including a University. Pierce was chosen the first Superintendent, and devised the laws whereby, in 1837, the system thus proposed was actually established. "The common schools," Pierce said, "are truly republican. . . . The object is universal education — the education of every individual. . . . In the public schools all classes are blended together; the rich mingle with the poor, and both are educated in company. . . . In these schools the poor are as likely to excel as the rich, for there is no monopoly of talent, of industry, or of acquirements. . . . Let free schools be established and

688 John D. Pierce, from a photograph in B. A. Hinsdale, *History of the University of Michigan*, Ann Arbor, 1906

maintained in perpetuity and there can be no such thing as a permanent aristocracy in our land; for the monopoly of wealth is powerless when mind is allowed freely to come in contact with mind."

STOWE'S *REPORT ON ELEMENTARY EDUCATION IN EUROPE*

IN 1829, the "Western Academic Institute and Board of Education" was organized in Cincinnati, a private, voluntary association for the purpose of securing better educational conditions in Ohio. One of its members, Calvin E. Stowe, 1802–86, professor in Lane Theological Seminary, and husband of Harriet Beecher Stowe, visited the schools of Europe in 1836, and on his return presented to the Legislature a *Report on Elementary Education in Europe* which attracted wide attention. It was reprinted and circulated by the legislatures of Pennsylvania, Massachusetts, Michigan, North Carolina, and Virginia, as well as Ohio. Stowe insisted that his recommendations were practical, because based upon actual experience. "If it can be done in Prussia, I know it can be done in Ohio. The people have but to say the word and provide the means . . . for the word of the people here is even more powerful than the word of the king there; and the means of the people here are altogether more abundant." In 1850

689 Calvin E. Stowe, from a photograph by Warner, Hartford, courtesy of Lyman B. Stowe

Stowe accepted a professorship at Bowdoin, and in 1852 he was appointed to fill the chair of sacred literature at Andover Seminary.

SAMUEL LEWIS, 1791–1854, SUPERINTENDENT OF COMMON SCHOOLS IN OHIO

SAMUEL LEWIS, lawyer and Methodist local preacher, was elected in 1837 as the first state Superintendent of Common Schools in Ohio, and succeeded in placing the school system of the state upon firm foundations before the politicians abolished his office in 1840. One legislator opposed the printing of his last report, "unless his constituents could have copies in German, because they could not read English; another member demanded copies in Welsh, because his constituents could not read either English or German; and another member said that a portion of his constituents could not read at all, therefore he was opposed to the printing, unless a committee was appointed to go around and read the report to them."

690 Samuel Lewis, from an engraving in the State Department of Education, Columbus, Ohio

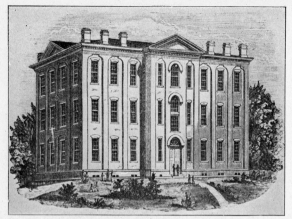

691 Frankfort High School, the first High School building in Kentucky,
from Richard H. Collins, *History of Kentucky*, Covington, 1874

ROBERT J. BRECKINRIDGE, 1800–1871, SAVES THE SCHOOL FUND OF KENTUCKY

ON January 1, 1837, after the distribution of a surplus which had accumulated in the United States Treasury (see Vol. VIII, p. 255), most of the states devoted their share of this money, wholly or in part, to education. But legislatures were slow to be converted to the need for better public schools, and there were always other wants that seemed more urgent, so that in many states the school fund suffered from poor management or was preyed upon by misappropriation. In Kentucky, where one half of the children had never attended school, and one third of the adult population could not read or write, the major part of this dividend of surplus revenue was made a state school fund, and invested in state internal improvement bonds. But the state began to default the interest on these bonds in 1840, and the legislature of 1845 ordered them to be destroyed and repudiated the debt to the school fund. Robert J. Breckinridge, Presbyterian minister, with Irish fire and Scotch persistence, accepted the state Superintendency of Common Schools in 1847, and led the fight to recover this money and to lay permanent financial foundations for a worthy school system. In 1848, he obtained from the legislature a new bond, restoring the confiscated funds with all unpaid interest. In 1849, he stumped the state, appealing to the people to vote for a two-mill state school tax, and secured the adoption of his proposal by a large majority. In 1850, he secured constitutional provisions for a state school system, which declared the state school fund to be inviolable. Finally, despite the opposition of the Governor, he induced the legislature to pass a law making interest due to the schools a first charge upon the state treasury.

CALEB MILLS, 1806–1879, "ONE OF THE PEOPLE"

THE name Hoosier was once a popular synonym for ignorance. In 1840 one seventh, and in 1850 one fifth, of the adult population of Indiana were illiterate. Indiana stood lowest in intelligence of all the free states, and below some of the slave states. Only one third of the children of school age attended any school. Then began a remarkable campaign. In 1846 there appeared "An Address to the Legislature of Indiana at the commencement of its session," with the superscription "Read, Circulate, Discuss," and the signature "One

of the People." Like messages were addressed to the legislatures of 1847, 1848, and 1849, to the Constitutional Convention of 1850, and to the legislature of 1852. Step by step these pamphlets outlined a program of educational reform which won general assent. After the second had appeared, the voters of Indiana declared themselves, by a substantial majority, in favor of free schools; and after the last, a state system was organized. "One of the People" was afterward revealed to be Caleb Mills, professor in Wabash College. His argument was courteous and good-humored, yet shrewd, adroit, and inexorable. "There is but one way to secure good schools, and that is to pay for them. There is but one method to induce the youth to frequent them, and that is to make them what they ought to be. . . . This can be effectually done only by drawing a large share of the funds for their support, directly from the pockets of the people, upon the ad valorem principle of taxation. . . . What costs nothing is worth nothing. . . . Public funds are desirable only to encourage effort, not to supersede the necessity of exertion. . . . It is the duty of the state to furnish the means of primary education to the entire youth within her bounds."

692   Caleb Mills, from the *American Journal
of Education*, Vol. XXXI

CALVIN H. WILEY, 1819-1887, AND THE PUBLIC SCHOOLS OF NORTH CAROLINA

THE Governors of North Carolina began urging the establishment of a public-school system as early as 1802; but an elaborate plan, presented to the legislature in 1817 failed to be passed. In 1825 a permanent "Literary Fund" was begun, which was greatly augmented in 1837 by the addition of a portion of North Carolina's share in the distribution of surplus revenue by the United States Treasury. In 1839 the first public-school law was passed, providing for school support by a combination of local taxation and appropriations from the Literary Fund. But there was lack of organization and "general listlessness" until Calvin H. Wiley, a brilliant young lawyer, became in 1853 the first state superintendent of public schools. A man of high educational ideals and of practical administrative ability, he rendered a service to North Carolina, in thirteen years of strenuous activity, comparable to the service of Horace Mann in Massachusetts and Henry Barnard in Connecticut. He managed to preserve the Literary Fund inviolate and to keep the public schools in service during the dark days of the War. But the collapse of the Confederacy left worthless most of the securities in which the Literary Fund had been invested, and a

693 Calvin H. Wiley, from a photograph in the possession of the State Department of Education, North Carolina

"Reconstruction" legislature abolished his office in 1866. New public-school laws were passed in 1868. The state rallied with determination from the devastating effects of the War and the Reconstruction period. From 1900 on it experienced an educational revival under the leadership of Governor Charles B. Aycock. "For the first time in the history of North Carolina politics yielded first place in public interest to education." Since then the story has been one of consistent and uninterrupted progress.

WILLIAM H. RUFFNER, 1824-1908, BUILDER OF THE VIRGINIA PUBLIC-SCHOOL SYSTEM

UNLIKE North Carolina, Virginia had developed no well administered public-school system before the Civil War. Its Literary Fund, begun in 1810, was distributed in part for the education of "indigent children" and in part for the support of institutions of higher education. A law of 1846 providing for primary schools was permissive merely, and was adopted by only nine counties. The Reconstruction Constitution of 1869 made the first effective provision for public schools. William H. Ruffner, a Presbyterian minister, was elected the first state superintendent of public instruction. He had to fight the persistent disposition of the legislature and the state treasurer to divert the public-school funds to other uses; and he was bitterly assailed by friends of the "old Virginia system," headed by Dr. Robert L. Dabney, of Hampden-Sidney College. Dabney insisted that universal education was not a proper function of the state, and that it would unfit the laboring classes for their lot in life. He especially opposed the education of negroes. In the face of these difficulties, Ruffner labored for twelve years with such energy, good sense and diplomacy that he placed the new system upon a permanent basis, and secured its general acceptance by public opinion.

694 William H. Ruffner, from a photograph in the possession of H. P. Cook, Richmond, Va.

695   The Social-Religious Building, Peabody College for Teachers, Nashville, Tenn., from a photograph,
                                   courtesy of Peabody College

THE PEABODY EDUCATION FUND

"Perhaps the most wholesome and beneficial influence affecting education in all the Southern States," says a southern historian, "came through the work of the Peabody Fund." This was the gift in 1867–69 of George Peabody, 1796–1869, merchant and banker, a native of Massachusetts then resident in London, who devoted his vast fortune almost wholly to philanthropic purposes. The Fund amounted to three million dollars; and was given for "the educational needs of those portions of our beloved and common country which have suffered from the destructive ravages and not less disastrous consequences of civil war." The Trustees of the Fund were fortunate in securing as its first general agent Barnas Sears, 1802–80, who had been Horace Mann's successor in Massachusetts and was at the time president of Brown University. Under his guidance, the income was distributed in such ways as best stimulated and encouraged local initiative and responsibility. It was used first to help southern cities and towns to develop systems of public schools; then to encourage the several states to establish state systems; later to aid the consolidation and supervision of rural schools. In 1875 a normal school was established at Nashville, and the trustees began to devote increasing attention to plans for aiding in the preparation and training of teachers, with the result that in time all of the southern states established their own training schools. In 1913 the Nashville institution became the George Peabody College for Teachers, to the endowment of which the Peabody Fund has now been turned over.

THE EDUCATION OF THE FREEDMEN

The education of the freed negroes involved grave and perplexing problems. In the fear of slave insurrections, for a generation preceding the War, many of the southern states had passed laws forbidding the instruction of the blacks in reading and writing. Now, in the fever of "Reconstruction," the more radical negroes demanded "mixed schools." Superintendent McIver, of the North Carolina schools, probably expressed the general sentiment of the white public when he said: "Opposition to mixed schools is so strong that if the people are free to choose between mixed schools and no schools, they will prefer the latter." The Freedmen's Bureau, established by Congress in 1865, and various charitable and religious organizations, notably the American Missionary Association, took the lead in establishing separate schools for negroes, without waiting for those which began to be set up as part of the public-school systems of the various southern states.

Most of their teachers were white, many were women, and practically all came from the North. These facts, together with their failure generally to enlist the sympathy and coöperation of the white people of the South, engendered misunderstandings which probably justified this statement by a Connecticut woman who taught in Hampton Institute: "When the combat was over, and the 'Yankee schoolma'ams' followed in the train of the Northern armies, the business of educating the negroes was a continuation of hostilities against the vanquished South, and was so regarded, to a considerable extent, on both sides." — Alice M. Bacon, *The Negro and the Atlanta Exposition*, p. 6, Baltimore, 1896.

696   Primary School for Freedmen in charge of Mrs. Green, at Vicksburg, Miss., from a drawing in *Harper's Weekly*, June 23, 1866

SAMUEL C. ARMSTRONG, 1839–1893, FOUNDER OF HAMPTON INSTITUTE

MOST successful in meeting this situation, with vision and accomplishment that give him place among America's really great educational leaders, was General Samuel C. Armstrong. Son of a missionary to Hawaii, pupil of Mark Hopkins at Williams College, he had commanded negro troops in the Union Army, and became convinced that the "excellent qualities and capacities" of the black folk entitled them to "as good a chance as any people." In 1866, the Freedmen's Bureau placed him in charge of the especially difficult and irritating situation in the ten counties of eastern Virginia, centering about the great camp of "contraband" negroes at Hampton. With the assistance of the American Missionary Association, he here opened, in 1868, the Hampton Normal and Agricultural Institute. His aim was, in his own words: "To train selected Negro youth who should go out and teach and lead their people, first by example by getting land and homes; to give them not a dollar that they could earn for themselves; to teach respect for labor; to replace stupid

697   Samuel C. Armstrong, from a photograph in the possession of Hampton Institute

drudgery with skilled hands; and, to these ends, to build up an industrial system, for the sake not only of self-support and intelligent labor, but also for the sake of character." To those who objected that the "manual-labor" plan of education had been tried before and would not pay, he answered: "Of course it cannot pay in a *money* way, but it will pay in a *moral* way. It will make men and women."

Armstrong's work met with extraordinary success. Hampton Institute has not only trained thousands of negroes to become responsible and useful citizens; it has pioneered and shown the way in industrial education. General Armstrong was a prophet of many characteristic features of modern educational theory. He said: "Didactic and dogmatic work has little to do with the formation of character, which is our point. This is done by making the school a little world in itself; mingling hard days' work in field or shop with social pleasures, making success depend on behavior rather than on study marks. School life should be like real life." — *Southern Workman*, November, 1880.

698   Hampton Institute, from a photograph, courtesy of Hampton Institute

699   Students' Dining Hall at Tuskegee Institute, from a photograph, courtesy of Tuskegee Institute

BOOKER T. WASHINGTON, *ca.* 1859–1915, LEADER OF THE NEGRO RACE

THE greatest of General Armstrong's pupils, and the outstanding leader of his race in America, was Booker Taliaferro Washington, whose autobiography *Up from Slavery* has become one of the classics of American literature. Graduating from Hampton Institute at the head of his class in 1875, he taught school for two years, then for eight months attended a seminary in Washington devoted wholly to "book education." The comparison convinced him more fully of the value of the industrial training given at Hampton; and when, in 1881, he was called to head a new school for negroes to be opened in Tuskegee, Alabama, he organized its work along the lines followed by Armstrong. By indefatigable industry, wise management, and exceptional aptitude for understanding and leading people, he built up an institution which stands a fit companion to that at Hampton.

Professor Paul Monroe, of Teachers' College, Columbia University, visiting Tuskegee in 1904, wrote: "Here I find illustrated the two most marked tendencies which are being formulated in the most advanced educational thought, but are being worked out slowly and with great difficulty. These tendencies are: first, the endeavor to draw the subject matter of education, or the 'stuff' of schoolroom work, directly from the life of the pupils; and second, to relate the outcome of education to life's activities, occupations and duties of the pupil in such a way that the connection is made directly and immediately between schoolroom work and the other activities of the person being educated. This is the ideal at Tuskegee, and, to a much greater extent than in any other institution I know of, the practice. . . . Tuskegee and Hampton are of quite as great interest to the student of education on account of the illumination they are giving to educational theory as they are to those interested practically in the elevation of the Negro people and in the solution of a serious social problem."

Dr. Washington was a most effective public speaker. At the opening of the Altanta Exposition in 1895, when he was invited to speak as the representative of his race, he made a memorable plea for friendship and coöperation between white and black. "In all things that are purely social," he said, "we can be as separate as the fingers, yet one as the hand in all things essential to mutual progress. There is no defence or security for any of us except in the highest intelligence and development of all." His address was characterized by the editor of the Atlanta Constitution as "a platform upon which blacks and whites can stand with full justice to each other." President Cleveland wrote that "the Exposition would be fully justified if it did not do more than furnish the opportunity for its delivery."

700   Booker T. Washington, from a photograph in
the possession of Tuskegee Institute

ATTICUS G. HAYGOOD, 1839–1896, AND THE SLATER FUND

IN the same year, 1881, that Booker T. Washington began his work at Tuskegee, Atticus Greene Haygood, white minister, one-time chaplain in the Army of Virginia, and then president of Emory College, published a remarkable book entitled *Our Brother in Black*. Its candor, courage, and good sense disarmed criticism and did much to promote mutual understanding between sections and between the races. Describing the work of various northern organizations for the education of negroes in the South, he expressed regret that the southern people had not coöperated more cordially, and announced his own conclusion that "it is God's work" and that "Southern white people must take part in the work of teaching negro schools." He was soon given opportunity to prove his creed, for the Trustees of the John F. Slater Fund for the Education of Freedmen, established in 1882 by John F. Slater, 1815–84, of Norwich, Connecticut, with an endowment of one million dollars, asked him to become its first General Agent. He accepted this responsibility, and administered the Fund in the interest of negro schools until he resigned in 1890 to become one of the bishops of the Methodist Episcopal Church, South. Other Funds devoted, as a whole or

701 Atticus G. Haygood, from an engraving after a photograph in *Harper's Weekly*, Oct. 11, 1886

702 School at Harper's Ferry, from a photograph by Clifton Johnson

in part, to negro education are the Anna T. Jeanes Fund (1908), the Phelps-Stokes Fund (1911), and the Julius Rosenwald Fund (1917).

THE DEVELOPMENT OF NEGRO SCHOOLS

THESE Funds have been and are now of large service in subsidizing normal schools for the training of negro teachers and in securing better supervision for negro schools. Beside the schools emphasizing industrial education, like Hampton and Tuskegee, and normal schools of the usual type, there are a number of colleges and universities for negroes, providing academic and professional courses. Many of these are largely engaged in the work of training teachers for the elementary and secondary public schools for negro children. Notable among them are Fisk University at Nashville, founded in 1866, famous for its Jubilee Singers; and Howard University at Washington, founded in 1867. The former of these is named after General Clinton B. Fisk, 1828–90, who helped to organize it; and the latter after General Oliver O. Howard, 1830–1909, head of the Freedmen's Bureau, its benefactor and first president.

703 High school for negro pupils in Richmond, Va., from a photograph by H. P. Cook, Richmond

704   From a drawing *The School Examination*, by C. E. Reinhart in C. C. Coffin, *Building the Nation*, New York and London, 1882

SCHOOL LIFE IN THE 'SEVENTIES

THE years following the Civil War were a period of slow development in public education, in the North as well as in the South. Expenses were kept down, and buildings and equipment remained practically unchanged. The district system of school administration was still almost universal, with all of the local prides, jealousies and inequalities which it fostered. The chief change brought about in these years was the great increase in the number of women teachers which was an indirect result of the War. The growing influence of the "school-ma'am" as contrasted with the lessening proportion of "school-masters" was hailed in the 'seventies as a great advance step in the humanizing of education. Folk did not foresee the cry that would in time be raised over the "feminization" of American schools. The cartoons, all drawn in the 'seventies, portray a school examination conducted by the members of the district school board; the board's consideration of applicants for the position of teacher; and a deserted schoolroom during the noon recess, with a "kept-in" pupil and a pensive teacher.

705   From a drawing *Before the School Board*, by Edwin A. Abbey in *Harper's Weekly*, Feb. 10, 1877

706   From a drawing *Noon Recess*, by Winslow Homer in *Harper's Weekly*, June 28, 1873

707   The school at work, from a photograph by Clifton Johnson

COUNTRY SCHOOLS

THE one-room, ungraded school which was typical of the district system has not yet disappeared, even in New England. These pictures of pupils at work in country schools of Maine and Massachusetts were taken in the early years of the present century. They could be duplicated to-day, in these and many other states, for almost half of the rural schools of America are still ungraded.

In the 'eighties many states began to abandon the district system, and a movement toward the consolidation of rural schools began. In most states this has taken place by the voluntary union of adjacent districts; in some the county has been made the unit of school administration, and consolidation of former districts has been involved in a general reorganization. In either case, the consolidation makes possible the erection of an adequate building in a central location, with sufficient classrooms to maintain a graded school, with an enriched curriculum and a competent corps of teachers. To and from this school pupils are transported by wagon or automobile each day. Such a school building may also serve as a community center, with an assembly hall, public library, and even indoor rooms for recreation and play.

708   A district schoolroom in Maine, from a photograph by Clifton Johnson

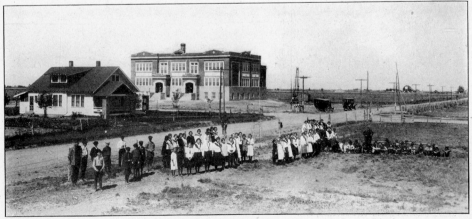

709   Sargent Consolidated School near Monte Vista, Colo., courtesy of the Sargent School

710 The first High School in the United States, Boston, from Cubberley, *Public Education in the United States*, Houghton, Mifflin Co., Boston, 1919

THE KALAMAZOO CASE AND THE GROWTH OF PUBLIC HIGH SCHOOLS

THE first public high school was established in Boston in 1821, to furnish boys who did not intend to go on to college "with the means of completing a good English education to fit them for active life or qualify them for eminence in private or public station." In 1827 Massachusetts passed a law requiring every town of five hundred families to maintain such a high school. The movement spread slowly, as the academies occupied the field, and the need was not felt in many communities. In certain states the legality of extending to secondary schools the principle of support by public taxation was attacked in the courts. The most widely influential case of this sort was in Kalamazoo, Michigan, in 1872, where a citizen sought to restrain the school board from collecting the additional taxes necessary to establish a high school and employ a superintendent of schools, on the ground that high schools were not included under the term "common schools" and that a supervisory officer was not needed. He doubtless did not know it, but Michigan, where John D. Pierce had laid broad foundations for a system of public education that included a university, was perhaps the least likely state in the Union in which to propound such an argument. The Supreme Court gave a ringing decision against the petitioner: "Neither in our state policy, in our constitution, nor in our laws, do we find the primary school districts restricted in the branches of knowledge which their officers may cause to be taught, or the grade of instruction that may be given, if their voters consent in regular form to bear the expense and raise the taxes for the purpose."

Since 1880, the public high schools have multiplied and developed amazingly. In 1889–90 there were two thousand two hundred and fifty-six public high schools in the country, with an enrollment of two hundred and two thousand nine hundred and sixty-eight students. This was sixty-eight per cent of the total number of pupils in secondary schools, the remaining thirty-two per cent being enrolled in private schools and academies.

In 1899–1900 there were six thousand and five public high schools, and in 1909–10 there were ten thousand two hundred and thirteen. In 1926 there were twenty-one thousand seven hundred public high schools, with three million seven hundred and fifty-seven thousand, four hundred and sixty-six students. This was over ninety-three per cent of the total number of pupils in secondary schools.

711 Manhattan Trade School, New York city, from a photograph, courtesy of the Board of Education, New York

712 The Edward Lee McClain High School, Greenfield, Ohio, from a photograph, courtesy of Edward Lee McClain

713   Chapel at Mercersburg Academy, Mercersburg, Pa., from a photograph,
courtesy of Mercersburg Academy

PRIVATE SECONDARY SCHOOLS

THE number of private secondary schools reported to the United States Bureau of Education in 1924 was somewhat less than in 1895 — two thousand one hundred and twenty-four as compared with two thousand one hundred and eighty.   When it is noted that these figures include an increase of Roman Catholic secondary schools from two hundred and eighty to one thousand and twenty-one, they bear evidence of the decrease of private academies among Protestants generally.   Most of those which remain are either missionary schools in the general sense of that term, adapted to the needs of some territory or group not adequately provided for by public schools; or boarding schools intended to provide a completeness of educational environment which the public schools do not undertake to furnish.   Many of these specialize in the preparation of boys for college. For such institutions there will always be room and need.   Especially desirable is the experimentation with new educational methods which private schools are often more free to undertake than schools controlled by public policy.   It is to the interest rather than to the detriment of public education, that there should exist, at every level of the educative process, privately controlled schools which are not cast in the same mold. Here are pictured the interior of the Chapel of Mercersburg Academy, a secondary school for boys founded in 1836, and the buildings of St. Paul's School, Concord, New Hampshire, founded in 1855.

714   St. Paul's School, Concord, N. H., from a photograph by Underwood & Underwood, New York

715 "The Gate of Opportunity," Berry School, from a photograph, courtesy of the Berry School

"THE GATE OF OPPORTUNITY"

BACK of "The Gate of Opportunity" at Mount Berry, Georgia, lie six thousand acres of pleasant land, on which is located the Berry School, founded in 1902 by Miss Martha Berry. It is an excellent example of the private schools intended for a particular group of otherwise underprivileged folk. This is for young people of the southern mountains, fifteen years of age or over, who are prevented by poverty from attending a more expensive school. Farming, dairying, cooking, laundering, even the erection of the buildings of the school, are done by the pupils themselves under expert supervision. Two consecutive days a week are given by each pupil to manual work, and four days to study. In addition to academic work the boys are required to take courses in agriculture and mechanics, and the girls take domestic science, gardening and dairying. "We do not provide them," said Miss Berry, "with equipment which they cannot afford in their own homes. It is not our object to cultivate in them tastes which they have not the means to gratify, but rather to inculcate in them a love of beauty and a sense of the fitness of things which will make their homes the dearer to them when they return."

THE BIBLE IN THE PUBLIC SCHOOLS

THE curricula of the early public schools gave large place to the teaching of religion. This was gradually lessened, partly because of the growth of secular knowledge, partly because of the necessity, in these schools, of avoiding all that could be construed as religious sectarianism. The disestablishment of Congregationalism in Connecticut in 1818 and the strife between Trinitarian and Unitarian in Massachusetts in the eighteen twenties, for example, contributed to the secularization of public education in these states. By the middle of the nineteenth century, throughout the country generally, the explicitly religious elements in the life of the public schools were reduced to the practice of reading a passage from the Bible, without note or comment, and the use of the Lord's Prayer, with sometimes the singing of a hymn, at the opening of each day's session. This, be it noted, was no new thing. It was not, as was sometimes asserted, the "introduction" of the Bible into the public schools. The Bible had always been read in these schools. This was simply the continuance of a custom that dated back to the beginning. In the early public schools, indeed, both the Bible and the catechisms had been used as textbooks. Now, the Bible was used simply as an act of the common worship of God.

716 From a drawing *Morning Prayer in the Primary Department*, by C. C. Pyne in the New York *Illustrated News*, Apr. 4, 1863

PROTESTS, DEBATES, AND COURT DECISIONS

AGAINST this practice of reading the Bible in the public schools Catholics have protested, especially since 1840, on the grounds that the Bible, as read by Protestants, is "a version made under sectarian bias"; that its reading in the schools encourages the idea of the right of private judgment and individual interpretation, in contrast to the authoritative judgment of the Church; that reading the Bible, together with the recital of the Lord's Prayer, constitutes a type of worship not in accord with their belief and practice, which their children ought not to be compelled to attend; and that the practice of granting relief of conscience by excusing their children while the rest of the school engages in such worship, places these children at a disadvantage, causes them inconvenience, and throws them open to the contempt of their fellows. The Pastoral Letters of the Catholic bishops in 1840 and 1843 dealt defin-

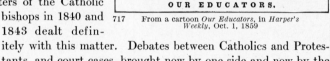

OUR EDUCATORS.

717   From a cartoon *Our Educators*, in *Harper's Weekly*, Oct. 1, 1859

itely with this matter. Debates between Catholics and Protestants, and court cases, brought now by one side and now by the other, have recurred from time to time. There are many cartoons on the subject, most of which are too virulent to have originated in religious motives only. Two of the milder are here reproduced. The first reflects the hot debates of the eighteen fifties; the second expresses the general tension after the Cincinnati Case in 1869–72, when, in answer to the Protestant contention that the local school board had exceeded its authority in forbidding the reading of the Bible in the schools, the Supreme Court of Ohio decided that the matter lay within its discretion. The present practice varies. Some states by law require the Bible to be read in the public schools, and since 1913 there has been a definite movement in this direction. Other states as expressly permit it. A few forbid it, though only indirectly, by interpretation of statutes forbidding sectarianism in the schools. In many of the states the policy is determined by local custom, without express legislation.

THE PUBLIC SCHOOLS.
MISTRESS. "Now, Bridget, take the children to School."
BRIDGET. "What, to thim Prodestan Publics? I wouldn't risk me sowl, Ma'am, wid the likes."

718   From a cartoon *The Public Schools*, in *Harper's Weekly*, Apr. 12, 1873

719 Cathedral High School, New York, from a photograph, courtesy of the architect, Robert Reiley

PAROCHIAL SCHOOLS

THE General Assembly of the Old School Presbyterian Church tried in the 'forties and 'fifties to commit its churches to a policy of maintaining parochial schools; but the movement met with no great measure of success, and was dropped. The Missouri Lutherans and a few other bodies have established such schools for the education of their children. The Catholic Church has followed the policy of church-controlled education most consistently; and the Third Plenary Council, in 1884, made mandatory the establishment by each church of a parochial school. The principles underlying this legislation are that religion is an essential part of education, that it must therefore have a vital place in the life of the school, and that to this end the school must be subject to the authority of the Church. Both elementary and secondary Catholic schools have multiplied and grown rapidly in the last forty years. They are staffed by brothers or sisters of the various teaching orders of the Church.

A MANUAL

OF

ELEMENTARY INSTRUCTION,

FOR THE

USE OF PUBLIC AND PRIVATE SCHOOLS AND
NORMAL CLASSES;

CONTAINING A GRADUATED COURSE OF

OBJECT LESSONS

FOR

TRAINING THE SENSES AND DEVELOPING THE FACULTIES OF
CHILDREN.

BY E. A. SHELDON,

SUPERINTENDENT OF SCHOOLS, OSWEGO, N. Y.;

ASSISTED BY

MISS M. E. M. JONES AND PROF. H. KRUSI.

SIXTH EDITION, REVISED AND ENLARGED.

NEW YORK:
SCRIBNER, ARMSTRONG & CO.,
1878.

720   From the original in the New York
       Public Library

THE OSWEGO MOVEMENT

In the early schools the learning of children was by words merely, memorized out of books, and the work of the teacher was usually confined to hearing them recite their lessons, and whipping them when they could not. The great Swiss reformer, Pestalozzi, had pointed the way to truer, more genuinely educative methods; but his ideas made no great impression upon America until they reached Edward A. Sheldon, 1823–97, superintendent of schools at Oswego, New York. In 1858 Sheldon saw at Toronto, Canada, a set of materials for object-teaching which had been prepared by an English society in accordance with their understanding of Pestalozzian principles. He secured the materials, and, because the school board of Oswego had no money to spend upon such innovations, he and his teachers gave half of their salaries for a year to bring to America an English teacher to show them how to use these. In 1861, the board established upon the basis of the new methods a city training-school for teachers, of which they made Sheldon principal. Soon he secured Herman Krüsi, Jr., 1817–1903, son of Pestalozzi's foremost associate. Krüsi taught at Oswego for twenty-five years. The school was made a state normal school in 1866, and became a center whence radiated a reform that emancipated teaching from the old bondage to the textbook and memoriter methods. It brought pupils into contact with things, and taught them to use their senses and to describe orally what they had themselves experienced.

WILLIAM T. HARRIS, 1835–1908, PHILOSOPHER AND ADMINISTRATOR

William T. Harris was what the common mind deems an impossible combination — both a philosopher and a practical administrator. He began to teach in St. Louis in 1857 and from 1867 to 1880 was superintendent of the schools of that city. The courses of study which he formulated, especially in the elementary teaching of the sciences, were widely copied, and the St. Louis school system came to hold a position of commanding influence. From 1889 to 1906 he was United States Commissioner of Education. Throughout his life he was an ardent student of philosophy, and he became one of the foremost American expositors of Hegel. He founded and edited, from 1867 to 1893, the *Journal of Speculative Philosophy;* and he was one of the founders of the Concord School of Philosophy (1879–88). All of his writings and his work manifest the thorough, sure grasp of a man who has thought his way through to ultimate principles. He viewed education as "a process of conscious evolution . . . the only rational, reliable agency by which man may work out his destiny in harmony with the will of the Divine Being." The United States Bureau of Education, which Harris headed for seventeen years, was initiated in 1867. The object of the Bureau was "to collect statistics and facts concerning the condition and progress of education in the several States and Territories, and to diffuse information respecting the organization and management of schools and school systems and methods of teaching." Within this limited field the Bureau has rendered excellent service. There are those who feel, however, that many of the educational problems of the country are national in their scope and that the solving of these problems should not be left entirely to the several states. Repeated efforts have been made to induce Congress to organize a Department of Education which would be responsible for the framing and conduct of national policies in this field. These efforts have not yet succeeded: some believe that more might be lost than gained if the control of education were to pass from the states into the hands of the Federal Government.

721   William T. Harris, from a photograph, courtesy
       of the Bureau of Education, Washington

THE KINDERGARTEN

The kindergarten, begun in Germany by Friedrich Froebel, who had been a pupil of Pestalozzi, was brought to America by German immigrants in 1855. The first was opened in Watertown, Wisconsin, by Mrs. Carl Schurz. The first English-speaking kindergarten was opened in Boston in 1860 by Elizabeth P. Peabody, 1804–94, sister of Mrs. Horace Mann. In 1873 William T. Harris secured Miss Susan E. Blow to open a kindergarten as part of the public-school system of St. Louis, and

722   Equipment of Kindergarten in New York, courtesy of the Department
of Education, New York

from this center the public kindergarten idea spread. The principles underlying the kindergarten have greatly influenced education throughout all the grades. The ideas of self-activity, of educative play, of appeal to the natural laws of child development, of teaching through social fellowship and coöperation, are now generally accepted. So true is this that the kindergarten itself is called upon to revise certain of its own procedures in the light of the more adequate knowledge of child-psychology which we now possess.

THE INFLUENCE OF HERBART

In the 'nineties, American education was profoundly influenced by the ideas of the German philosopher Herbart, who was the first to undertake a scientific study of the educative process itself. In 1892, a National Herbart Society was formed to study education along lines suggested by the Herbartian principles. Many of the ideas which have shaped modern school life are traceable to the work of the Herbartians, such as: the revolt against formal discipline, or the theory that the important thing in education is to exercise the mind, quite aside from the question of the value of the material upon which it is exercised; the emphasis upon interest and motivation; the study of the technique of instruction; the weighing of curriculum values; the idea of the essential relatedness of the various school subjects; the conception of the aim of education in terms of moral character and social efficiency; the new appreciation of the human values in the teaching of history, literature, and geography. We are not content, of course, with Herbart's own formulation of these ideas. The fact that the National Herbart Society in 1902 changed its name to the National Society for the Scientific Study of Education is evidence of the success, rather than the failure, of the movement. Like every true scientific procedure, Herbartianism led beyond itself. It was an instrument of discovery, rather than a goal.

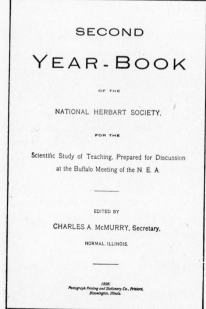

SECOND

YEAR-BOOK

OF THE

NATIONAL HERBART SOCIETY.

FOR THE

Scientific Study of Teaching, Prepared for Discussion
at the Buffalo Meeting of the N. E. A.

EDITED BY

CHARLES A. McMURRY, Secretary.

NORMAL, ILLINOIS.

1896.
Pantagraph Printing and Stationery Co., Printers,
Bloomington, Illinois.

723   From the original in the New York
Public Library

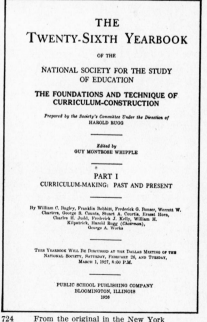

THE
Twenty-Sixth Yearbook
OF THE
NATIONAL SOCIETY FOR THE STUDY
OF EDUCATION

THE FOUNDATIONS AND TECHNIQUE OF
CURRICULUM-CONSTRUCTION

Prepared by the Society's Committee Under the Direction of
HAROLD RUGG

Edited by
GUY MONTROSE WHIPPLE

PART I
CURRICULUM-MAKING: PAST AND PRESENT

By William C. Bagley, Franklin Bobbitt, Frederick G. Bonser, Werrett W.
Charters, George S. Counts, Stuart A. Courtis, Ernest Horn,
Charles H. Judd, Frederick J. Kelly, William H.
Kilpatrick, Harold Rugg (Chairman),
George A. Works

This Yearbook Will Be Discussed at the Dallas Meeting of the
National Society, Saturday, February 26, and Tuesday,
March 1, 1927, 8:00 P.M.

PUBLIC SCHOOL PUBLISHING COMPANY
BLOOMINGTON, ILLINOIS
1926

724   From the original in the New York
Public Library

725 Francis W. Parker, from a photograph, courtesy of Doctor William B. Owen, Chicago, Ill.

FRANCIS W. PARKER, 1837–1902, REORGANIZER OF ELEMENTARY EDUCATION

AN outstanding constructive critic and reorganizer of elementary education, in the light of his own experience plus a thorough acquaintance with Pestalozzian, Froebelian and Herbartian principles, was Colonel Francis Wayland Parker, an officer in the Civil War who later studied for three years in Germany. As superintendent of the schools of Quincy, Massachusetts, he was "given a free hand" by a school committee of which Charles Francis Adams was the leading spirit; and he developed a remarkable *esprit de corps* among both teachers and pupils by the free, self-active, concrete methods which he encouraged them to use. From 1883 to 1899 he was principal of the Cook County (Chicago) Normal School, and he organized what is now the School of Education of the University of Chicago. He did much to modify and enrich the course of study in the elementary schools. "He was a lover of childhood, and he had the insight to see educational problems from the standpoint of the child."

JOHN DEWEY, 1859–, PHILOSOPHER OF DEMOCRACY AND EDUCATION

PARKER'S successor as Director of the School of Education at the University of Chicago was John Dewey, professor of philosophy in that institution. In 1904 Dewey accepted a call to Columbia University. No one has done more than he to interpret the educational significance of the changed social and industrial conditions of modern life, and to define the functions of the school in view of these conditions. For Dewey, education faces toward the future rather than toward the past. It is the process whereby society reproduces its own life, perpetuates and enriches its interests and ideals, shapes its future, and ensures its progress. The end of education is not knowledge merely, or power, but social efficiency, which includes, in a democratic society, the development of initiative, responsibility and good will. Such social efficiency can be acquired only by actual participation in the life and activities of a democratic society. It is the business of the school, therefore, to foster such a society, and to induce such participation on the part of children. The school should thus be a miniature world of real experiences, real opportunities, real interests, and real social relations. It must, of course, be a world simplified and suited to the understanding and active powers of children; it will be a world, moreover, widened, balanced, purified, and rightly proportioned as compared to the particular section of the great grown-up world that lies immediately about it; it is a world, again, which contains a teacher who is at once leader, inspirer, interpreter, and friend. But it is a real world with interests continuous with the fundamental, truer interests and values of the world without. In this school world children learn by working rather than by merely listening or reading; and they develop originality, initiative, responsibility, coöperation and self-control by engaging in projects which call forth these qualities.

726 John Dewey, from a photograph by Keystone View Co., New York

THE DEVELOPMENT OF EDUCATIONAL PSYCHOLOGY

IT is a far cry from the old school of whippings, artificial prizes, and individualistic competition, to the ideal school of Dewey's theory. Yet the schools of to-day are ever more fully basing their procedures upon principles such as he has expounded. The reason is, not simply that we are living in a more complicated world than our fathers, but that we understand children better. The psychologizing of education, basing its methods upon a clearer understanding of the natural laws of child-development, has been the vision of all educational reformers since Rousseau. That vision has in our day become the common aspiration of parents and teachers. The science of psychology, working by experimental and exact methods, has given a new comprehension of the laws of learning, and has revealed some of the undesirable by-products of the old methods within the child's mind and character, as well as the possibility of a more wholesome appeal to native interests and

727   Edward L. Thorndike, from a photograph by
                    Bachrach, New York

capacities. It has even made progress toward the measurement of children's abilities and achievements. Leaders in this application of scientific methods to the processes of education are Edward L. Thorndike, 1874–, of Columbia University, and Lewis M. Terman, 1877–, of Leland Stanford Junior University.

EDUCATION FOR HEALTH

NOT only psychology, but new knowledge in the fields of physiology, hygiene, public sanitation, and preventive medicine, is contributing to the transformation of the schools. The old idea that mental development and physical strength were somehow incompatible, and that bright children were necessarily "delicate," has been exploded. We now know that a sound body helps to make a sound mind, and that ill health is a drag upon mental efficiency. Through better-constructed schoolhouses and more wisely planned daily programs; through the employment of school physicians and nurses who make regular medical inspections, tests of eye and ear, and general physical examinations, through the teaching of hygiene, dietetics, and sanitation;

728   Child Welfare Work in Schools, from a photograph, courtesy of the Child Health
                             Organization, New York

and through supervised physical training and play, the better schools of to-day are undertaking a constructive program of education for health and physical welfare. They are providing for "the formation of health habits, the imparting of health information, and the development of a health conscience." The principles and methods of this program, moreover, are accessible to every teacher and parent; and through state and county units of school administration this work is carried even into rural communities.

729   Statue of Thomas Hopkins Gallaudet by Daniel Chester French, from a
            photograph, courtesy of Gallaudet College, Washington

THE EDUCATION OF DEFECTIVE AND EXCEPTIONAL CHILDREN

THE new emphasis upon health education does not mean that handicapped or defective children are neglected. On the contrary, more account is taken of individual differences to-day than ever before. Education of the deaf began in this country with the founding of a school in Hartford, in 1816, by Thomas Hopkins Gallaudet, 1787–1851. A school for the blind was opened in Boston in 1832 by Samuel G. Howe, 1801–76. In 1848 Dr. Howe started a class for feeble-minded children, and in that same year Dr. Edouard Seguin, 1812–80, transferred to America his remarkable pioneer work in this field. There are now institutions for all these groups in practically every state, and many cities maintain special classes or schools for one or more of them. Public school boards maintain many special classes or schools for crippled children, for those threatened with tuber, culosis, for stutterers and stammerers, and other exceptional children. The needs of the exceptionally gifted child are more generally recognized and provided for, also; and a definite attempt is made in many public-school systems to discover and adapt the teaching to individual differences of capacity and achievement.

SCHOOLS AND LIFE

THE schools of to-day are coming closer to life, not only in their spirit and method, but in the content of their curricula. In these schools children learn not only "the three R's" — reading, 'riting and 'rithmetic — the languages, and the older subjects of literature, history, and geography. They are taught also the physical and biological sciences and their applications; and they may elect from a wide range of vocational subjects — such as cooking, sewing, and domestic economy; carpentering and cabinet-making;

730   High School Girls Operating a Cafeteria at the Flower Technical High School,
            Chicago, from a photograph by Underwood & Underwood, Chicago

metal working, forging, and the use and care of machinery; gardening, agriculture, dairying, and stock raising; stenography, typewriting, and bookkeeping; journalism and printing; drawing, painting, music, dancing; dramatic expression and public speaking. The fact is that we are relying upon the schools very largely, not only to impart to children the new knowledge and power with which science, invention and discovery are so richly endowing our time, but to afford to them much of the vocational training and guidance, and much of the sense experience, motor training and moral discipline, which under simpler social conditions were afforded to children by the incidental activities and contacts of everyday life in the home and in the community. But we must not imagine that the school can do the whole work of education. There is still need — perhaps there never was more need — of whole-hearted coöperation between home and school and church and community life, if our children are to become all that we could wish them to be.

CHAPTER X

COLLEGES AND UNIVERSITIES

THE connection of religion with higher education in America has been especially intimate. The first college, Harvard, was founded to protect the churches from "an illiterate ministry." Each of the eleven colleges established in the colonial period avowed a distinct religious purpose; and but one lacked connection with the churches of a particular denomination.

The motives for higher education have widened, yet the churches have continued, throughout the nearly three centuries that have elapsed since the founding of Harvard, to render notable service by the establishment of colleges wherever the need was manifest. The contribution of the churches to higher education has been more effective and permanent than their service to elementary and secondary education. It is a contribution, moreover, which has often been sacrificial, for churches have given out of their poverty that colleges might be maintained in frontier communities; and it has usually been self-forgetting, for the churches have sought to minister, through these institutions, not merely to their own interests, but to the general welfare.

The founding of colleges was stimulated by the decision of the Supreme Court of the United States in 1819 which blocked the attempt of the state of New Hampshire to change Dartmouth College into a state institution. Affirming that the charter of a college is a contract, the obligation of which a legislature cannot impair, this decision guaranteed the inviolability of endowments, and gave confidence to the founders of colleges that the new institutions would not be at the mercy of changing political majorities.

Of two hundred and forty-six colleges founded by the close of the year 1860, only seventeen were state institutions. The Morrill Land-grant Act of 1862 stimulated the establishment by the states of colleges for instruction in agriculture and the mechanic arts; and the movement thus begun soon resulted in the rapid development and expansion of state universities. Of the colleges and universities now at work, roughly speaking, two thirds bear direct relation to the churches and are in varying measure under their control; one sixth are privately endowed and controlled, many of which have a religious origin and history and still maintain a sympathetic relationship with the churches; and one sixth are maintained by public funds and are state controlled. More than one third of the college and university students of the country are enrolled in the state institutions.

The traditional college curriculum was almost wholly literary and largely devoted to the classical languages. The introduction of the sciences, modern languages, and the social and economic subjects, with some freedom of choice afforded to the student, was sponsored by President Nott, of Union, and Wayland, of Brown. The merits of the "elective system" were much debated until the influence of President Eliot, of Harvard, helped to establish the principle of election as a feature of practically all college curricula.

Of outstanding significance has been the development since the Civil War of universities as distinguished from colleges — institutions devoted to research and to graduate study as well as to various types of professional training. They have been created in some cases by the expansion of existing colleges, as Harvard, Yale, and Columbia; in some cases by private benefaction, as Johns Hopkins, Chicago, and Leland Stanford; and in some cases by the resources of a state, as Michigan, Wisconsin, and California.

731   The John Harvard Statue, Harvard University, by Daniel
Chester French, from a photograph. © Detroit Photographic Co.

THE FOUNDING OF HARVARD COLLEGE

On October 28, 1636, the General Court of Massachusetts Bay Colony voted to grant four hundred pounds for the founding of a "Schoole or Colledge." This was the first time, it is said, that a free people, of their own will, through their representatives voted a sum of money to establish an institution of learning. Twelve of the principal men in the colony, headed by John Winthrop, were appointed its Governors. It was decided that the college should be at Newtown — "a place very pleasant and accommodate" — and the name of this place was changed to Cambridge, in memory of the English university at which many of the colonists had been educated. In 1638 John Harvard, 1607-38, a young Puritan minister whose brief life in Massachusetts had been so beset by illness as to prevent his acceptance of regular pastoral duties, died and left to the college one half of his estate — nearly eight hundred pounds — and all of his library. This gift made possible the immediate opening of the college and stimulated others to give. Besides money and books, goods and property of various kinds were given, including such items as "a number of sheep, a quantity of cotton cloth worth nine shillings, a pewter flagon worth ten shillings, a fruit dish, a sugar spoon, a silver-tipped jug, one great salt, and one small trencher-salt." In March, 1639, it was voted that the college should be called Harvard College.

HARVARD COMMENCEMENT
THESES, 1643

The first head of the school was a rascal whom the General Court was obliged to dismiss. The first president of the College, Henry Dunster, 1609-59, elected shortly after his arrival from England, took office August 27, 1640. The first class was graduated in 1642. Here is reproduced a copy of the program of the commencement exercises in 1643, listing the theses which the members of the graduating class — "Johannes Jonesius, Samuel Matherus, Samuel Danforthus, and Johannes Allinus" — were to discuss. They are stated in Latin, in which language all ordinary recitations and public disputations were conducted, except when they were in Greek or Hebrew. The list includes such propositions as: "Grammatic iii. The English language is second to none." "Rhetoric iii. To speak aptly is better than to speak ornately." "Logic vi. If one opposite be affirmed, the other is denied." "Ethic xii. There is no true friendship among the wicked." "Physic x. Imagination produces real effects." "Metaphysic v. Truth is the conformity of the intellect with the thing."

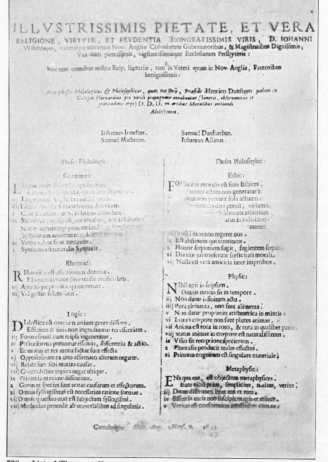

732   List of Theses at Harvard Commencement in 1643, from the original
in the Massachusetts Historical Society

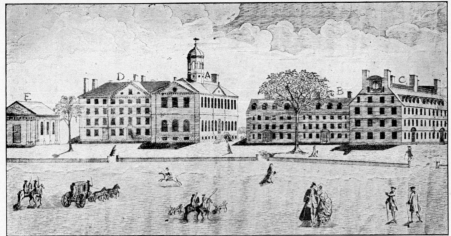

733   *A Westerly View of the Colledges in Cambridge, New England,* engraved by Paul Revere after a drawing
by Joshua Chadwick, in the Museum of the Essex Institute, Salem

HARVARD BUILDINGS IN REVOLUTIONARY DAYS

A CONTEMPORARY account of the infant college, contained in *New England's First Fruits,* is reproduced in
Chapter IX, No. 599. It describes the first edifice as "very fair and comely within and without, having in it
a spacious Hall, where they daily meet at Common Lectures, Exercises, and a large Library with some Books
to it, the gifts of divers of our friends, their Chambers and studies also fitted for and possessed by the Students,
and all other rooms of Office necessary and convenient." The only known picture of this first Harvard Hall
is reproduced in Vol. XIII, No. 596. Here is copied an engraving by Paul Revere of the Harvard College
buildings as they were during the Revolution. At the center is Harvard Hall, built in 1766 upon the site of
the original building, which had been destroyed by fire. Next on the right is Stoughton Hall, gift of William
Stoughton, presiding judge at the Salem witch trials, destined to be torn down and replaced in 1805. On the
extreme right is Massachusetts Hall (1720). On the left are Holden Chapel (1737) and Hollis Hall (1762).

WILLIAM AND MARY COLLEGE

THE second colonial college was the College of William and Mary at Williamsburg, Virginia. The story of
its founding in 1693 by James Blair has been told in Chapter III, No. 147. It is notable for the number of
its graduates who have assumed places of leadership in public service. They include the majority of the
members of the Committees of Correspondence and Safety for Virginia; four signers of the Declaration of
Independence, including its author, Thomas Jefferson; and fifteen members of the Continental Congress,
including its first president, Peyton Randolph, Benjamin Harrison, and Edmund Randolph; Chief Justice
John Marshall and three of his successors; and three Presidents of the United States, Jefferson, Monroe, and

734   The Main Building of William and Mary College, from a photograph,
courtesy of William and Mary College

Tyler. Here, under James Madison, 1749–1812, Bishop of Virginia and president of the college from 1777 to his death, were introduced what were at the time startling innovations — the elective system of studies, the honor system in examinations, and the first college courses in modern languages, law, political economy and history. Here, in 1776, was founded the first college fraternity, Phi Beta Kappa, which now, as an honorary society devoted to the furtherance of scholarship, has become an important factor in American student life.

735   Grave of Elihu Yale, from a photograph in the collection of Oliver McKee *

THE BEGINNINGS OF YALE COLLEGE

THE founding of a college in Connecticut in 1701 marked the readiness of the New World, after two generations, to undertake the education of its own leaders. All but one of the ten ministers associated in the enterprise which began, tradition says, in each bringing a gift of books, were American-trained men, graduates of
Harvard College. The purpose of the foundation, as stated in the first charter, was broad and democratic.
It was to establish a school "wherein youth may be instructed in the arts and sciences, who through the blessing of Almighty God may be fitted for public employment, both in church and civil state."

For some years the Collegiate School, as the institution was first called, was "ambulatory, like the tabernacle
in the wilderness," nominally located at Saybrook,
but with students in various places, at the homes of
the ministers who gave instruction. In 1716 it was
permanently settled at New Haven and two years later
it was named Yale College, in recognition of the gifts
of Elihu Yale, 1649–1721. Yale had been born in
Boston, son of one of the original settlers in New
Haven; he had amassed great wealth in India, where
for twenty-five years he was Governor of the East
India Company's settlement at Madras. He had become interested in the New Haven college through
Jeremiah Dummer, the agent of New Haven Colony
in England; and Cotton Mather (see No. 95) had
written him suggesting further gifts: "If what is
forming at New Haven might wear the name of Yale
College, it would be better than a name of sons and
daughters."

Elihu Yale's mildly bombastic epitaph in the church-
yard of St. Giles, Wrexham, Wales, is characteristic
of the retired seventeenth-century man of affairs:

> Born in America, in Europe bred,
> In Africa travell'd, and in Asia wed,
> Where long he liv'd and thriv'd; in London dead.
> Much good, some ill, he did; so hope all's even
> And that his soul thro' mercy's gone to Heaven.
> You that survive and read this tale, take care
> For this most certain exit to prepare:
> Where blest in peace, the actions of the just
> Smell sweet and blossom in the silent dust.

736   Elihu Yale, from the painting by Enoch Zeeman (1694–1744),
in the possession of Yale University

737   A View of the Buildings of Yale College at New Haven, 1807, drawn and engraved by
Amos Doolittle, New Haven

A STUDENT'S DIARY

THE diary of Ebenezer Baldwin, who was a Junior at Yale in 1762, gives a picture of college life which is almost photographic in its fidelity to detail. The following extracts are from entries for March and April:

"29. Attended Coll. Exs. Studied Homer almost ye whole day. Read a few pages in Tuscul. Disput. Had no recns to-day, our Tutor being out of town.

"30. Attended prayers. Studied Homer in forenoon. Writ argument on our forensick question, wh. was WHETHER ADAM KNEW YT ETERNAL DAMNATION WOULD BE HIS DOOM IF HE EAT THE FORBIDDEN FRUIT? Had no recitation. Afternoon worked out a question in Algebra and studied some in Septuagint.

"April 1. Studied Homer most of ye day. Some in Martin's Philosophy.

"Friday, 9. Attended Col. Exs. Studied Homer in the forenoon. In the afternoon read in Martin's Philosophy and in Whiston's Ast [Astronomical] Principles of Religion. At night Nichols, Halliock, and Brewster were publickly admonished for having a dance at Milford, and for their general conduct. Bull, for going to Milford without liberty and for his general conduct, was ordered to depart from College and to live under the care of some minister at a distance till he should show signs of reformation and be fit to take a degree. Hinman, Kellogg, Kingsbury, and Botsford were fined 2s. 6d. for being at the dance at Milford.

"Monday, 12. This day Bull, who was punished on last Friday, not liking to suffer ye penance inflicted, travelled off on foot to the westward, and it is supposed he intends to go on board of a Privateer.

"Wednesday, 14. The method in which I divide my time is as follows nearly: Go to bed at 9 o'clock; rise about — [torn off; probably 6]; prayers and recitation which last to about 7½; go to breakfast, and, if ye weather is good, commonly take a small walk. This carries it to 8 or 8¼. Commonly from this time until 11 pursue my studies, unless something special; then attend recitation, which lasts to 12; then go to dinner; after, walk or follow some other exercise till — [torn off]; then pursue my studies again till near 6, when I attend on Prayers; after prayers go to supper, and spend ye remainder of the evening commonly in conversation.

"16. This day Bull returned from his demigration, having gone no further than Milford.

"19. This morning Bull made a confession for his conduct since his punishment. Particularly going out of town and refusing to go to ye President when sent for, and so was restored to ye same standing as before his punishment, and accordingly went to live with Mr. Bellamy in Bethlem.

"21. N. B. — Got through 16th Book of Homer, where I shall stop for ye present. Afternoon. In Pope's Homer. Spent remainder of ye afternoon in drinking tea and conversation.

"Evening felt melancholy and dejected on thinking of ye difficulties my DADDE must undergo to provide for me here at college."

TIT. XI. *De Collegii Auctoritate.* 21

TITULUS XI.

De Collegii Auctoritate.

1. ✱✱✱OLLEGII hujusce Auctoritas Legiflativa penes ✱C✱ est PRÆSIDEM et SOCIOS, qui omnia ✱✱✱ Statuta, Leges, Regulas et Edicta, (Policiæ civilis Legibus non repugnantia) condendi et fanciendi, prout illis visum fuerit, Poteftate veftiuntur.

2. Hujusce Collegii Poteftas executiva præcipuè penes eft PRÆSIDEM; qui Auctoritate pollet, Collegium omniaque ad id fpectantia Negotia, necnon omnes Studentes, tam Graduatos quàm non Graduatos, imperare, gubernare et dirigere, fecundum Leges, Regulas et Statuta à Præfide et Sociis, fancita; ubi vero ea deficiant, fecundum Collegii Confuetudines antiquas et confcriptas; at illis deficientibus, pro Judicio et Arbitrio fuo. *Provifo*, quòd in Rebus difficilibus et momentofis Præfes confulet Tutores: Et in Cafibus extraordinariis, valde momentofis, citoque determinandis, Præfes cum duobus Sociis Conventum Corporationis indicet; at fi id commodè fieri non poffet, confulet quot facilè congregari poffint.

3. SINGULUS Tutor, à Præfide et Sociis conftitutus, Collegium fub Præfide procurato et moderetur: Propriamque Claffem fibi commiffam inftruat; et in quemlibet non Graduatum, propter quodvis Delictum contra Leges admiffum, Pœnam non plufquam unius Solidi, irrogandi Poteftate veftiatur. *Provifo*, quòd in Rebus dubiis et difficilibus, fine Præfidis Confulio et Directione, non progrediatur.

4. NULLUS hujusce Colegii Alumnus, nec aliquis illius Vice, quamvis Dicam aut Querelam verfus quemvis hujusce Collegii Alumnum aut Officiarium, propter Injuriam aut Defectum

738 Certificate of Candidacy for admission to Yale College, 1757, from the Emmet Collection in the New York Public Library

AN EIGHTEENTH–CENTURY MATRICULATION CERTIFICATE

THE government of an eighteenth-century college was paternal, and its rules detailed. It was ordained at Yale that "Every Student Shall diligently apply himself to his Studies in his Chamber as well as attend upon all Public Exercises appointed by the President or Tutors, and no Student Shall walk abroad, or be absent from his Chamber, Except Half an hour after breakfast, and an hour and a half after Dinner, and from prayers at Night to Nine o' the Clock, without Leave, upon Penalty of Two Pence or more to Sixpence. . . . To this End The President or Tutors Shall, by Turns, or as They conveniently can visit Student's Chambers after Nine o'Clock, to See whether they are at their Chambers, and Apply themselves to their Studies." Here is a matriculation certificate of 1757, whereby a student binds himself, in rigid Latin, to obey the rules of the college, and is then formally admitted as an "Alumnus" of Yale. Note that the term "Alumnus" is here used in its original Latin meaning of "pupil," not in the meaning to which it is now commonly restricted.

THE COLLEGE OF NEW JERSEY AT PRINCETON

THE founding of the College of New Jersey is associated with the Great Awakening of the second quarter of the eighteenth century, and helped to heal the schism between Old Side and New Side Presbyterians which had resulted from the activities of Gilbert Tennent and other men trained in the Log College (see Nos. 256, 257). Chartered in 1746, it was opened at Elizabeth, then moved to Newark, and located permanently at Princeton in 1753 on land given for the campus by Nathaniel Fitz Randolph. A *General Account* prepared for use in soliciting funds in England stated that "the two principal Objects the Trustees had in View, were Science and Religion. Their first Concern was to cultivate the Minds of the Pupils, in all those Branches of Erudition, which are generally taught in the Universities abroad; and to perfect their Design, their next Care was to rectify the Heart, by inculcating the great Precepts of Christianity, in order to make them good Men."

WHEREAS a CHARTER with full and ample Privileges, has been granted by his Majesty under the Seal of the Province of New Jersey, bearing Date the 22d October, 1746, for erecting a College within the said Province, to Jonathan Dickinson, John Pierson Ebenezer Pemberton, and Aaron Burr, Ministers of the Gospel and some other Gentlemen as Trustees of the said College; by which Charter equal Liberties and Privileges are secured to every Denomination of Christians, any different religious Sentiments notwithstanding

The said Trustees have therefore thought proper to inform the Public, that they design to open the said College the next Spring; and to notify to any Person or Persons who are qualified by preparatory Learning for Admission that some time in May next at latest, they may be there admitted to an Academic Education

739 Advertisement of the College of New Jersey, in the New York *Gazette and Weekly Post Boy*, Feb. 2, 1846–47

In the first nineteen years of its history, the college had five presidents, all men of high intellectual caliber, who died in office — Jonathan Dickinson, 1688–1747, Aaron Burr, 1716–57, Jonathan Edwards, 1703–58, Samuel Davies, 1723–61, and Samuel Finley, 1715–66. Finally, in John Witherspoon, 1722–94, called from a Scotch pulpit in 1768, the College of New Jersey found a president whose long, distinguished administration, in spite of the losses caused by the play back and forth over Princeton of the varying fortunes of the Revolutionary struggle, laid firm foundations for the Princeton University of the future. Witherspoon was succeeded by his son-in-law, Samuel Stanhope Smith, 1750–1819, who resigned in 1812.

740 Nassau Hall and President's House, from the engraving by Henry Dawkins in the possession of Princeton University

THE UNIVERSITY OF PENNSYLVANIA

THE University of Pennsylvania owes its inception to Benjamin Franklin's *Proposals relative to the Education of Youth in Pennsylvania*, published in 1749. A group of public-spirited citizens associated themselves as a Board of Trustees, with Franklin as president, and in 1751 opened an Academy in the building which had been erected as an auditorium for George Whitfield. (See p. 116.) Under charters granted in 1753 and 1755, the institution became the "College, Academy and Charitable School of Philadelphia," and Doctor William Smith, 1727–1803, was chosen provost. Under his vigorous administration the work of the

741   Library and Surgeon's Hall on Fifth Street, Philadelphia, from an engraving by Thomas Birch in the New York Public Library

institution expanded and necessary funds were secured. In 1791, after some vicissitudes due to suspicion of Doctor Smith's loyalty (he was a clergyman of the Church of England), it was combined with a new corporation under the name of the University of Pennsylvania. The pictures show the first buildings on Fourth Street, and a scene on Fifth Street in 1800 which contains in the foreground the imposing building of the Philadelphia Library Society and, farther distant, the much less substantial building occupied by the Medical School of the University. Founded in 1765, this was the first medical school in America.

742   The New Building, University of Pennsylvania, from a print in the Pennsylvania Historical Society

MORAL CONDUCT AND ORDERLY BEHAVIOR

THIS copy of the *Laws, relating to the Moral Conduct, and Orderly Behaviour, of the Students and Scholars of the University of Pennsylvania* is dated September 19, 1801. Less detailed than other and earlier sets of rules, it reflects a common-sense point of view. These rules take into account the behavior of young boys "under the age of 14 years" as well as that of college students, for a Charitable School remained a part of the University of Pennsylvania until 1877. The smallness of the college is evidenced by the requirement that each of the students in the two upper classes should deliver an oration every day.

LAWS,

RELATING TO THE

MORAL CONDUCT, AND ORDERLY BEHAVIOUR,

OF THE

STUDENTS AND SCHOLARS

OF THE

University of Pennsylvania.

1.   None of the students or scholars, belonging to this seminary, shall make use of any indecent or immoral language: whether it consist in immodest expressions; in cursing and swearing; or in exclamations which introduce the name of GOD, without reverence, and without necessity.

2.   None of them shall, without a good and sufficient reason, be absent from school, or late in his attendance; more particularly at the time of prayers, and of the reading of the Holy Scriptures.

3.   Within the walls of the building, none of them shall appear with his hat on, in presence of any of the Professors or Tutors; or, in any place, fail to treat them with all the respect which the laws of good breeding require.

4.   There shall be no playing in the yard, or in the street, during the time in which the schools are assembled; nor, within the walls of the building, at any time: nor shall any boy cut or notch the furniture of the rooms; or draw any figures or characters on the walls; or tear, deface, or in any way injure, the books, or other property, belonging either to himself or others.

5.   When the schools are dismissed, whether in the morning or afternoon, the boys shall not remain in the yard, or in the neighbourhood of the building; but shall immediately disperse without noise or tumult, and return each to his respective home, so as to be at the disposal of his parents, or of those under whose care he is placed.

6.   The students of the Philosophical classes shall, each of them in succession, deliver an oration every morning in the Hall, immediately after prayers; the succession to begin with the senior class; and, in each of the two classes, to proceed in alphabetical order.

7.   In case of the transgression of any of the above laws, the transgressor, if he belong to either of the Philosophical classes, or be above the age of 14 years, shall, for each transgression, be subject to a fine, or suspension; and, if under that age, to the same penalty, or to corporal punishment, at the discretion of the Faculty. The fine, in no case, to exceed 25 cents.

8.   And if any student of the Philosophical classes, not prevented by sickness or other unavoidable necessity, shall twice successively neglect to appear in his turn, and pronounce his oration, as above directed; he shall be considered as guilty of a wilful disobedience to the laws of the institution; and shall be suspended, until, recourse being had to his parents or guardians, some competent security can be obtained for his more orderly behaviour in future.

Extract from the Minutes of the Board of Faculty.

WILLIAM ROGERS, *Secretary.*

September 19th, 1801.

743   Laws, relating to the Moral Conduct, and Orderly Behaviour, of the Students and Scholars of the University of Pennsylvania, from the original in the New York Historical Society

BY a Law paſſed the laſt Seſſions, a publick Lottery is directed for a further Proviſion towards founding a College for the Advancement of Learning within this Colony, to conſiſt of 5000 Tickets at Thirty Shillings each, 1094 of which to be fortunate, viz.

Number of Prizes.		Value of each.		Total Value.
1	of	500 l.	is	500 l.
1	of	200	is	200
2	of	100	are	200
10	of	50	are	500
30	of	20	are	600
50	of	10	are	500
1000	of	5	are	5000

1094 Prizes,) 5000 Tickets at Thirty)
3906 Blanks,) Shillings each, makes) 7500 l.
15 per Cent to be deducted from the Prizes. As ſuch a laudable Deſign will greatly tend to the Welfare and Reputation of this Colony, it is expected the Inhabitants will readily be excited to become Adventurers. Publick Notice will be given of the preciſe Time of putting the Tickets into the Boxes, that ſuch Adventurers as ſhall be minded to ſee the ſame done, may be preſent at the doing thereof. The Drawing to commence on the firſt Tueſday in November next, or ſooner if full, at the City-Hall of New-York, under the Inſpection of the Corporation, who are impowered to appoint two or more of their Body to inſpect all and every Tranſaction of the ſaid Lottery; and two Juſtices of the Peace, or other reputable Freeholders of every County in this Colony, if they ſee Cauſe to depute the ſame at their next general Seſſion of the Peace. Public Notice will be given fourteen Days before the Drawing. The Managers are ſworn faithfully to execute the Truſt repoſed in them, and have given Security for the faithful Diſcharge of the ſame. Such as forge or counterfeit any Ticket, or alter the Number, and are thereof convicted, are by the Act to ſuffer Death, as is in Caſes of Felony. The Prizes will be publiſhed in this Paper, and the Money will be paid to the Poſſeſſors of the Benefit Tickets, as ſoon as the Drawing is finiſhed. Tickets are to be had at the Dwelling Houſes of Meſſieurs Jacobus Rooſevelt and Peter Van Brugh Livingſton, who are appointed Managers.
The Managers would acquaint the Publick, that upwards of One Thouſand Tickets are already engaged to the Hand in Hand and American Fire Companies in this City, to whom the Tickets are already delivered. The Proſperity of the Community greatly depending upon the regular Education of Youth, it is not doubted but the Lottery will ſoon fill; Thoſe therefore that Deſign to become Adventurers, are deſired ſpeedily to apply for Tickets, or they may be diſappointed.

744 Advertisement of lottery, from the New York Gazette, July 30, 1753

COLLEGE LOTTERIES

WHEN in 1746 the General Assembly of New York began to give serious consideration to the idea of founding a college in that colony, they began by authorizing the drawing of public lotteries. Here is the advertisement of one to be drawn in November, 1753. Note that forging or counterfeiting of tickets was punishable by death. The management was in the hands of men whose family names have taken high place in the annals of public service — Jacobus Roosevelt and Peter Van Brugh Livingston. But there was no thought in those days that there could be anything wrong about lotteries. At Dartmouth, in 1791, a lottery drawing was held on the preacher's desk in the college chapel. It is recorded that this action was "to the scandal of some worthy people." At the end of the eighteenth century the practice of voluntary contributions to worthy causes was not yet sufficiently fixed in American custom to make devices like lotteries for raising money unnecessary.

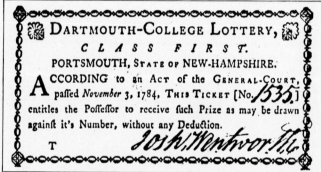

745 Dartmouth lottery ticket, from a facsimile in Frederick Chase, A History of Dartmouth College, J. Wilson Co., Cambridge, 1891–1913

INDEPENDENT REFLECTOR:

OR,

Weekly Eſſays

ON

Sundry Important SUBJECTS.

More particularly adapted to the PROVINCE of NEW-YORK.

Ne quid falſi dicere audeat, ne quid veri non audeat.
CICERO.

NEW-YORK:

Printed (until tyrannically ſuppreſſed) in MDCCLIII.

746 From the original in the New York Public Library

THE FOUNDING OF KING'S COLLEGE

A ROYAL charter was granted for King's College in 1754, and New York city was chosen for its location because Trinity Church agreed to convey to the Governors a portion of the Queen's Farm which had been given to it by Queen Anne. Because the Church made it an "express condition" of this gift that "the President of the said College forever for the time being shall be Member of and in communion with the Church of England as by law established & that the Morning and Evening Service in the said College be the Liturgy of the said Church" and because over two thirds of the Governors were members of the Church of England, there was much protest on the part of the Dutch, Lutheran, Presbyterian and other groups, who constituted the great majority of the population of the colony. It found outspoken expression in *The Independent Reflector*, published from November, 1752 to October, 1753, by William Livingston. He and others wished the college to be established by an Act of the Assembly instead of by royal charter, and they regarded the action of Trinity Church as but another example of the presumption that was seeking to make the Church of England the established church of the colony. (See p. 98.) The vestry of Trinity Church, on the other hand, is said to have feared that otherwise the college would have no religious character at all.

747 President Johnson teaching his first class at King's College, from a drawing by B. A. Mullen in *Harper's Monthly Magazine*, Oct. 1884

PRESIDENT JOHNSON

SAMUEL JOHNSON, called to be first president, met the situation with tact and good judgment, as is evidenced by the advertisement which he composed to announce the opening of the college in the vestry room of the schoolhouse of Trinity Church. Himself the entire faculty, he taught the first class there on July 17, 1754. In 1760 the college moved into its own building.

III. And that People may be the better satisfied in sending their Children for Education to this College, it is to be understood, that as to Religion, there is no Intention to impose on the Schollars, the peculiar Tenets of any particular Sect of Christians; but to inculcate upon their tender Minds, the great Principles of Christianity and Morality, in which true Christians of each Denomination are generally agreed. And as to the daily Worship in the College Morning and Evening, it is proposed that it should, ordinarily, consist of such a Collection of Lessons, Prayers and Praises of the Liturgy of the Church, as are, for the most Part, taken out of the Holy Scriptures, and such as are agreed on by the Trustees, to be in the best Manner expressive of our common Christianity; and, as to any peculiar Tenets, every one is left to judge freely for himself, and to be required only to attend constantly at such Places of Worship, on the Lord's Day, as their Parents or Guardians shall think fit to order or permit.

IV. The chief Thing that is aimed at in this College is, to teach and engage the Children to *know God in Jesus Christ*, and to love and serve him, in all *Sobriety, Godliness* and *Righteousness* of Life, with *a perfect Heart, and a willing Mind*; and to train them up in all virtuous Habits, and all such useful Knowledge as may render them creditable to their Families and Friends, Ornaments

748 From the first Advertisement of the College of New York, in *The New York Gazette or, The Weekly Post Boy*, June 3, 1754

TRIBULATIONS OF A TORY PRESIDENT

PRESIDENT JOHNSON resigned in 1763, and was succeeded by Myles Cooper, 1735–85, a young clergyman of the Church of England who had been sent to America for the purpose by the Archbishop of Canterbury.

749 Myles Cooper, from the portrait by John Singleton Copley in the Trustees Room, Columbia University, courtesy Columbia University

His administration proved that the fears of those who had protested against the close affiliation of the college with the Church of England were not altogether groundless. Warmly espousing the side of the King, he published "A Friendly Address to all Reasonable Americans on the Subject of our Political Confusions." He was accused of having given to the English authorities "assurances of the defection and submission of the Colony of New York" which were responsible for "the present hostile preparations against the American colonies." On May 10, 1775, an angry mob surged through the streets to wreak vengeance upon him. Warned by a student, whom he eulogized as

A heaven directed youth
Whom oft my lessons led to truth,

he escaped to an English war vessel, and never returned to America. There were no public commencement exercises in 1775 and 1776, and the work of King's College practically closed with the bestowal of six degrees in the latter year. Among the hundred or more students educated in the twenty-two years of its history were Alexander Hamilton, John Jay, and Robert R. Livingston.

750   William Samuel Johnson, from a portrait in
Essex Institute, Salem, Mass.

751   James Kent, from the painting by Samuel
F. B. Morse in the New York Historical Society

KING'S COLLEGE BECOMES COLUMBIA

In 1784 the Legislature of New York took action creating a body of "Regents of the University of the State of New York," whom it directed "to elect a President and Professors for the College heretofore called King's College"; and it ordained that this should be "forever hereafter called and known by the name of Columbia College." The first student to enter the revived and re-christened institution was De Witt Clinton, afterward to be one of the greatest public servants of his native state. In 1787 William Samuel Johnson, 1727–1819, son of the first President Johnson, was chosen president. He was the first layman to be elected to such an office in English-speaking lands. Graduate of Yale and of Harvard, he had been Judge of the Superior Court of Connecticut, Representative in Congress, and member of the United States Constitutional Convention. He served as United States Senator from Connecticut after his acceptance of the Columbia presidency. Under his administration, which lasted until 1800, the college made substantial progress. A notable appointment to the faculty was that of James Kent, 1763–1847, made professor of law in 1793. Subsequently Chief Justice and then Chancellor of New York, he returned to his professorship in later life, and his lectures to Columbia students became the basis of his famous *Commentaries on American Law*, which have had a lasting influence upon the national life.

JAMES MANNING, 1738–1791, FIRST PRESIDENT OF BROWN UNIVERSITY

Under the leadership of Morgan Edwards, 1722–95, the newly-arrived Welsh pastor of the First Baptist Church of Philadelphia, the Philadelphia Association of Baptists took action in 1762 looking toward the establishment of a college. They chose Rhode Island as its location because of the prevalence in that colony of the principle of religious freedom. James Manning, who had just graduated from Princeton, was selected to undertake the founding of the new institution. With the help of the Rhode Island Baptists, he secured a charter in 1764. A year later he was chosen president and opened the college at Warren with one student. In 1770, it had grown to twenty-one students, and was removed to Providence. Manning was a man of singular grace and poise of spirit. Though funds came in slowly, the college grew in public favor and the student body increased rapidly. In 1804 it was given the name Brown University, in recognition of the gifts of Nicholas Brown, one of its graduates. Its charter is liberal, guaranteeing "full, free, absolute, and uninterrupted liberty of conscience"; but it firmly ties the institution to Baptist control. The president, eight of the twelve members of the Board of Fellows, and twenty-two of the thirty-six Trustees, must be members of Baptist churches. Brown has developed into one of the leading educational institutions in the East.

752   James Manning, from a portrait by Cosmo
Alexander, in the possession of Brown University

753 Latin Broadside circulated at the first commencement of Brown University, 1769, from the original in the possession of Brown University

754 William Rogers, first student of Brown University, from a portrait in the possession of Brown University

THE FIRST STUDENT AND THE FIRST COMMENCEMENT AT BROWN UNIVERSITY

THE one student with whom President Manning began in 1765 was William Rogers, 1751–1824, who became pastor of the First Baptist Church in Philadelphia, served throughout the Revolution as a brigade chaplain, and was for twenty-three years professor of English in the University of Pennsylvania. Here is the program of the first commencement of the college in Rhode Island, 1769, when Rogers, with six others who had joined him, was graduated. It is of the same general type as the Harvard program of 1643, but the general subjects of mathematics and politics have been added, and metaphysics has been divided into ontology, pneumatology, and theology. The theses, moreover, are more adequately stated; and many of them are more nearly scientific, and less purely deductive, than in the earlier program. The program reflects, however, the classical emphasis of the eighteenth-century college education. It also suggests the function of a college as a training school for ministers. The broadside is an illustration of the use of Latin as the language of learning.

755   Samson Occom, from a mezzotint, 1768

THE MISSION OF SAMSON OCCOM

When Morgan Edwards went to England in 1767 to solicit funds for the College in Rhode Island, he found the field occupied by powerful rivals; and he wrote home in dismay about the difficulty of securing large gifts when there was so much begging going on. He got in all about nine hundred pounds; but in two years Nathaniel Whitaker and Samson Occom, 1723–92, secured more than ten times that much. It was for Moor's Indian Charity School, conducted at Lebanon, Connecticut, by Eleazar Wheelock, 1711–79, pastor of the Congregational Church. Occom was himself a Mohegan Indian, and had been Wheelock's first Indian pupil. Converted in the Great Awakening, he had been preaching to the Montauk Indians on Long Island and the Oneida Indians of the Iroquois Confederacy for twenty years. He preached over three hundred sermons in England, caught for the time the popular fancy, and raised more than ten thousand pounds for an Indian charity school. A hymn tune was named "Lebanon"; a hymn that he had written, "Awaked by Sinai's Awful Sound," was much sung; and he was even mimicked on the stage. "I little thought," he wrote, "I should ever come to that honor." Only the English bishops were indifferent. "I cannot help my thoughts," was his comment, "and I am apt to think they don't want the Indians to go to heaven with them."

757   Eleazar Wheelock, from a painting by Joseph Stewart in possession of Dartmouth College

758 Wheelock leading Chapel Service in the Open Air, from a woodcut in J. W. Barber, Historical Poetical Scenes, Boston, 1850, in the library of Dartmouth College

756   The Parting and Return of Three Indians who graduated at Dartmouth College, from a broadside in the library of Dartmouth College

THE FOUNDING OF DARTMOUTH COLLEGE

Lord Dartmouth became president of a Board of Trustees chosen to administer the English gifts. But Wheelock's plans were changing. His first thought had been to educate promising Indian boys, and to send them back as teachers and preachers to their own people. But he was disappointed in the conduct of many, and in the efficiency of others; and he decided that he must rely more upon training white young men for missionary service among the Indians. He determined to establish a college for this purpose, secured a charter from Governor Wentworth of New Hampshire in March, 1770, and chose Hanover as the site of the institution, which was named Dartmouth.

Vox Clamantis in Deserto is the motto upon the great seal of Dartmouth College — "the voice of one crying in the wilderness." When Dr. Wheelock's family, with thirty students, traveled north in September, they found only a log house with some surrounding temporary shelters. A tutor arriving from Boston with more students was compelled to construct "a tent of crotched stakes and poles covered with boughs." Till the college building could be completed, on days when the weather permitted, "Dr. Wheelock presented to God their morning and evening prayers standing at the head of his numerous family in the open air; and the surrounding forest for the first time reverberated the solemn sounds of supplication and praise."

759 Dartmouth in 1790, from an engraving by Josiah Dunham in Frederick Chase, *A History of Dartmouth College*, V. Wilson and Son, Cambridge, 1891–1913

THE GROWTH OF DARTMOUTH COLLEGE

In spite of frontier conditions, lack of money, and trouble to get proper food for the students, Dartmouth grew surprisingly. At the first commencement in 1771, four men were graduated, who had left Yale to complete their course at the new college. Fifty students were enrolled in the second year, and eighty in the third. The Revolutionary War caused a decrease; but in 1790 the number had risen to one hundred and sixty. In the last decade of the eighteenth century Dartmouth conferred almost as many degrees as Harvard, and more than either Yale or Princeton. In 1797 Daniel Webster entered Dartmouth, so awkward and dark that one of the villagers, much to his disgust, inquired whether he were a new Indian pupil. In 1801 he was graduated, refusing to speak at the commencement exercises because he had not been awarded either salutatory or valedictory.

CHARTER OF A COLLEGE

To be erected in

NEW-JERSEY,

By the Name of

QUEEN'S-COLLEGE,

For the Education of the Youth of the said Province and the Neighbouring Colonies in true Religion and useful Learning, and particularly for providing an able and learned Proteſtant Miniſtry, according to the Conſtitution of the Reformed Churches in the United Provinces, uſing the Diſcipline approved and inſtituted by the national Synod of Dort, in the Years 1618, and 1619.

NEW-YORK,

Printed by JOHN HOLT; at the EXCHANGE,

M,DCC,LXX.

760 Second Charter of Rutgers College, from the original in the Rutgers College Library

OTHER COLONIAL FOUNDATIONS

Besides Harvard, William and Mary, Yale, Princeton, Pennsylvania, Columbia, Brown, and Dartmouth, three other colleges rightfully claim a colonial origin. Upon petition of the ministers and elders of the Dutch Reformed Church, charters were granted in 1766 and 1770 for the establishment at New Brunswick, New Jersey, of Queen's College. It made little progress for fifty years; but in 1825, with a change of name to Rutgers College, in honor of a benefactor, a new era of expansion and prosperity opened.

Augusta Academy in Lexington, Virginia, was founded in 1749 and became in 1776 Liberty Hall; later, after a generous endowment by George Washington, Washington College. To the presidency of this institution Robert E. Lee, refusing all other offers, devoted the remainder of his life after the fall of the Confederacy; and after his death its name was changed to Washington and Lee University.

Hampden-Sidney College in Virginia was opened as an academy on January 1, 1776, under the care of the Presbyterians. It was chartered as a college in 1783, its name being a memorial to the English patriots, John Hampden and Algernon Sidney. It has had a continuous and honorable history of service to church and state.

761 Campus of Washington and Lee University, from a photograph, courtesy of Washington and Lee University

Harvard University in Cambridge,

Commonwealth of Massachusetts.

The Order of the Exercises of COMMENCEMENT,

July 19th, M,DCC,XCVII.

Exercises of the Candidates for the Degree of BACHELOR of ARTS.

I. A Salutatory oration in Latin.   By WILLIAM JENKS.

II. A forensic disputation upon this question—"Whether hope of reward have as much influence on human conduct as fear of punishment?"   By DANIEL BATES and ELISHA CLAP.

III. An English poem upon—"Music."   By WILLIAM ABBOT.

IV. A Greek dialogue upon—"Grecian eloquence."   By DANIEL ABBOT and NYMPHAS HATCH.

V. An English conference upon—"The comparative influence of the desire of wealth, power, fame, and knowledge on mankind." By LEONARD MELLEN, FREEMAN PARKER, ASAHEL STEARNS [and JOHN-COLLINS WARREN.

VI. A Latin oration upon—"History."   By SAMUEL FARRAR.

VII. A forensic disputation upon this question—"Whether sumptuary laws would be useful to the United States of America?"   By MOSES ADAMS and [JONATHAN WHITAKER.

VIII. A Hebrew oration.   By JEROBOAM PARKER.

IX. An English poem upon—"Invention." By WILLIAM-MERCHANT RICHARDSON.

X. A Latin conference upon—"The comparative merit of the epic poems of Homer, Virgil, Tasso, and Milton."   By SAMUEL BROWN, WILLIAM LADD, [ISSACHAR SNELL and DANIEL STONE.

XI. An English oration upon—"Enthusiasm."   By HORACE BINNEY.

XII. A French dialogue upon—"The pernicious tendency of the love of amusements."   By JOSEPH HURD and BENJAMIN WOOD.

XIII. An English conference upon—"The influence of personal figure, dress, manners, and mental accomplishments."   By DAVID GILBERT, JOHN JOY, [ROSEWELL MESSINGER and JOSEPH TILTON.

XIV. A forensic disputation upon this question—"Whether a civilized nation have a right to expel an uncivilized nation from it's territory?"   By JOHN-HUBBARD CHURCH and JABEZ KIMBALL.

XV. An English poem upon—"Patriotism."   By JAMES RICHARDSON.

XVI. An English oration upon—"The reign of prejudice." By DANIEL-APPLETON WHITE.

An Exercise in the Class of Candidates for the Degree of MASTER of ARTS.

An English oration upon—"Genius."

By Mr. JOSEPH PERKINS.

762   Harvard commencement program, 1797, from the original in the New York Historical Society

COMMENCEMENT CUSTOMS

COMMENCEMENT was a joyous occasion, and the trustees of the early colleges were much troubled by a persistent tendency to make it extravagant and riotous. Experiences at Harvard were typical. In 1693 the Corporation forbade the "commencers" to entertain their friends with "plumb-cake." In 1722 they prohibited the use of "Distilled Lyquours"; but in 1761 made an exception in favor of punch, "which as it is now usually made, is no intoxicating liquor." In 1809 a visitor's diary records his attendance at a dinner provided by one of the graduating class, where "there were five hundred persons who dined in one large tent in the fields," at an expense of "at least one thousand dollars."

The exercises were conducted in Latin, but even so it was necessary for the president to make sure that all of the parts were "orthodox and seemly," and he was enjoined by the Corporation in 1760 "to put an end to the practice of addressing the female sex." The first English oration was delivered in 1763, and soon English parts predominated. The program for 1797 is here reproduced. A "conference" was the assignment for students lowest in scholarship; an "oration" for those who stood highest. Most of the questions assigned for discussion are still unsettled — for example, the parts numbered VII, XII and XIV. Professor Andrew P. Peabody thus described the commencement in 1826, when he graduated: "The entire Common, then an unenclosed dust-plain, was completely covered on Commencement Day and the night preceding and following it, with drinking-stands, dancing booths, mountebank shows, and gambling tables; and I have never heard such a horrid din, tumult, and jargon of oath, shout, scream, fiddle, quarrelling, and drunkenness as on those two nights." Josiah Quincy, 1772–1864, when he became President in 1829, stopped all such rowdyism; and the diary of the visitor quoted above states that the commencement of 1836, which was the fifty-second Harvard commencement which he attended, was the first at which he saw not a single drunken person.

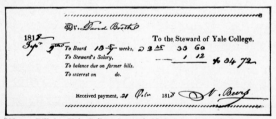

763   Bill due Yale College Steward, 1818, from the original in the New York Historical Society

764   Yale College bill for tuition, etc., 1818, from the original in the New York Historical Society

COLLEGE BILLS

WE need not wonder that the extravagantly inclined had money to spend on one-thousand-dollar dinners and other expensive commencement festivities. They spent little enough on their education itself and on necessary living expenses, if these two bills from Yale College in 1818 may be taken as typical.

THE DARTMOUTH COLLEGE CASE

IN 1816 the Legislature of New Hampshire attempted to gain control of Dartmouth College, and to make out of it a state institution. The trustees, however, held firmly to the rights granted them by charter, and resisted the action as invading these rights and "impairing the obligations of contracts." The case went to the Supreme Court of the United States, where Daniel Webster argued the cause of the college in one of the greatest speeches of his career — luminous, convincing, and with tremendous emotional power. The decision, rendered on February 2, 1819, was in favor of the college. It was of far-reaching import. According to Chancellor Kent: "The decision in that case did more than any other single act proceeding from the authority of the United States to throw an impregnable barrier around all rights and franchises derived from the grant of government; and to give solidity and inviolability to the literary, charitable, religious, and commercial institutions of our country."

REPORT

OF THE CASE OF

THE TRUSTEES OF DARTMOUTH COLLEGE

AGAINST

WILLIAM H. WOODWARD.

ARGUED AND DETERMINED IN THE SUPERIOR COURT OF JUDICATURE OF
THE STATE OF NEW-HAMPSHIRE, NOVEMBER 1817.

AND ON ERROR

IN THE SUPREME COURT OF THE UNITED STATES, FEBRUARY 1819.

BY TIMOTHY FARRAR
COUNSELLOR AT LAW

PORTSMOUTH, N. H.

PUBLISHED BY JOHN W. FOSTER,
AND
WEST, RICHARDSON, AND LORD, BOSTON.
J. J WILLIAMS, PRINTER, EXETER.

765   From the original in the New York
Public Library

Before 1780	10
1780–89	7
1790–99	7
1800–09	9
1810–19	5
1820–29	22
1830–39	38
1840–49	42
1850–59	92
1860–69	73
1870–79	61
1880–89	74
1890–99	54
Total	494

COLLEGES FOUNDED UP TO 1900

(After a table by Dexter, corrected by U.S. Comr. Educ., data. Only approximately correct.)

766   Table of colleges founded before 1900, from Cubberley, *Public Education in the United States*, Houghton, Mifflin Co., Boston, 1919

THE MULTIPLYING OF COLLEGES

ONE of the results of the decision in the Dartmouth College Case was a quickening of interest in the founding of new colleges, and confidence in the security of their endowments. The table here copied shows that twenty-one colleges had been established in the thirty years between the inauguration of Washington as first President of the United States and the publication of the Dartmouth decision; and that twenty-two colleges were founded in the next decade. Each decade witnessed the beginning of a larger number, till in the 'fifties ninety-two colleges were founded. Most of these were founded by religious denominations, or by individuals who avowed a religious purpose. "Speaking generally, higher education in the United States before 1870 was provided very largely in the tuitional colleges of the different religious denominations, rather than by the State. Of the two hundred and forty-six colleges founded by the close of the year 1860, as shown on the map, but seventeen were state institutions and but two or three others had any state connections." — E. P. CUBBERLEY, *Public Education in the United States*, p. 204, Houghton, Mifflin Co., Boston, 1919.

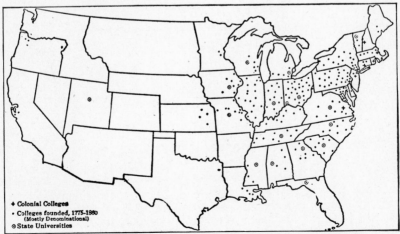

+ Colonial Colleges
• Colleges founded, 1775–1860 (Mostly Denominational)
⊙ State Universities

767   Map showing location of colleges founded before 1860, from Cubberley, *Public Education in the United States*, Houghton, Mifflin Co., Boston, 1919

768 Eliphalet Nott, from a photograph in
     the possession of Union College

ELIPHALET NOTT, 1773–1866, PRESIDENT OF UNION COLLEGE

THE first institutions on what was then the frontier of the state of New York were Union and Hamilton Colleges. Hamilton grew out of an academy organized in 1793 by Samuel Kirkland, 1741–1808, missionary for forty-four years to the Oneida Indians, and father of John T. Kirkland, fourteenth President of Harvard College. Union began as an academy in 1785 and was chartered as a college ten years later, with the proviso that no one religious denomination shall ever have a majority on its board of trustees. It had the good fortune in 1804 to secure as president Eliphalet Nott, a young minister of thirty-one, who gave to it sixty-two years of remarkable leadership. He assumed complete responsibility for the discipline of the students, which he administered paternally, but with kindness and understanding. He cut loose from the rigid classical language requirements of the traditional course, and in 1828 organized a "scientific course" designed to fit young men for practical life. He opened a course in civil engineering in 1845, forerunner of the technical training which has since developed so notably. He was personally interested in applied science, and secured patents on thirty different devices, among which was the first stove designed to burn anthracite coal.

FRANCIS WAYLAND, 1796–1865, PRESIDENT OF BROWN UNIVERSITY

PREËMINENT among the college presidents of the first half of the nineteenth century was Francis Wayland of Brown University. A pupil of President Nott at Union, and later a member of his faculty, he possessed much of Nott's spirit and made it more widely effective. Brown was at low ebb when he assumed its presidency in 1827. He recreated discipline, reorganized its work, built up a library, and provided laboratories for the study of the sciences. His *Thoughts on the Present Collegiate System in the United States* (1842) and his revolutionary *Report to the Corporation of Brown University* were prophetic of the general trends that American college education has since taken.

Wayland advocated two principles that seemed at the time visionary: "First, of carrying into practice every science which was taught in theory; and, secondly, of adapting the whole course of instruction, as far as possible, to the wants of the whole community. . . . If education is good for one class of the community, it is good for all classes. Not that the same studies are to be pursued by all, but that each one should have the same opportunity of pursuing such studies as will be of the greatest advantage to him in the course of life which he has chosen." He boldly espoused the principle of the election of studies: "The various courses should be so arranged that, in so far as it is practicable, every student may study what he chooses, all that he chooses, and nothing but what he chooses." A protagonist of popular education, he took a prominent part in the movement for free public schools, and was first president of the American Institute of Instruction. He consistently favored the inclusion in education of the practical arts. "There is talent in a cotton mill as well as in an epic."

President Wayland's textbooks on *Moral Science* (1835) and *Elements of Political Economy* (1837) were widely used for more than half a century. The first of these reached a circulation of one hundred and thirty-seven thousand copies by 1868. Its exposition of the moral wrong of slavery contributed to the formation of public opinion on that subject. A preacher of power, Wayland labored earnestly, and to good effect, in the interest of missions abroad and of prison reform at home.

769 Francis Wayland, from an engraving in *Educational Labors and Publications of Francis Wayland*

WILBUR FISK, 1792–1839, PRESIDENT OF WESLEYAN UNIVERSITY

THE Methodists of to-day like to recall the fact that "Methodism was born in a university." It was not always so. Because of lack of interest among his people, Asbury's early efforts to establish a college did not survive the ill fortune of two conflagrations. Jesse Lee, propagandist of Methodism in New England, when asked whether he and his associates were college-trained, used to answer "that he made no great pretension, yet thought he knew enough to get through the country."

A general awakening of interest in education among the Methodists began in the second quarter of the nineteenth century. It was largely due to the work of Wilbur Fisk, first president of Wesleyan University, founded by the New York and New England Conferences in 1831. His freedom from traditionalism is evidenced by the evaluation of subjects in his *Inaugural Address:* "Modern literature, the natural and exact sciences, and the application of the sciences to the useful arts, are first in importance in a useful education. Next in order I would place mental and moral philosophy, and the kindred sciences; last, and least in consequence for the great portion of students, I would place ancient literature, the graces of learning,

770 Wilbur Fisk, from an engraving after a painting, courtesy of the *Christian Advocate*, New York

and the fine arts." Fisk's early death prevented the full realization of his plans; and his new course, leading to the degree of Bachelor of Science, did not attract many students. It is for his effective leadership among the Methodists, rather than as a reformer of college education, that his name has permanent place in the history of religion and education in this country. By 1840 the Methodist Episcopal Church had sixteen colleges and twenty-six secondary schools. In 1926 it had forty-six colleges and universities, forty-one professional schools, including law, medicine and theology, and thirty secondary schools. Among these were Northwestern University, founded in 1851; Syracuse University, 1871; and Boston University, 1869.

MARK HOPKINS, 1802–1887, PRESIDENT OF WILLIAMS COLLEGE

WILLIAMS COLLEGE, founded in 1793, passed through a period of anxiety on account of the founding of Amherst College, which was opened in 1821 and chartered in 1825. It was felt that western Massachusetts could support but one such institution. The future of Williams was assured, however, by the effective administrations of Edward D. Griffin, 1770–1837, who became president in 1821, and Mark Hopkins, who succeeded him in 1836. Hopkins opposed the extreme to which he felt that the principle of election was tending. He did not believe that the immature student can wisely decide what studies he needs. "To decide this point, including the order of the studies as they are related to each other and to the opening powers of the student, requires wide information and sound judgment; and that the college should decide it seems to me due to itself and to the young men who come to it. . . . It is a mistake to suppose that by giving a wide range of option in undergraduate studies a college approximates a university. It rather approximates a high school, and may virtually become one." President Hopkins commanded the respect and devotion of his students as few men do; and he is remembered as a great teacher. President James A. Garfield expressed this strikingly when he said that a log with Mark Hopkins seated on one end and a student on the other was all that was necessary to make a college. This statement is sometimes wrongly quoted in justification of meager and inadequate material equipment for colleges. That was far from Garfield's intention.

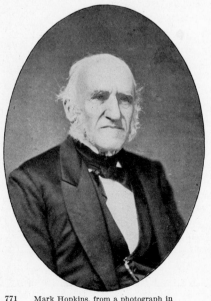

771 Mark Hopkins, from a photograph in the possession of Williams College

772 South Building, University of North Carolina, from a photograph by Forster, Chapel Hill

773   Old East Building, University of North Carolina, from
a photograph by Forster, Chapel Hill

THE UNIVERSITY OF NORTH CAROLINA

THE southern states in which no colonial colleges had been founded began movements for the promotion of higher education as soon as political independence was achieved. The University of Georgia was chartered in 1784 and opened in 1800. South Carolina College, chartered in 1801 and opened in 1805, became the University of South Carolina in 1866. Its first president was Jonathan Maxcy, 1768–1820, who had been president of Brown and of Union. The first state university to begin actual teaching was the University of North Carolina, chartered in 1789 and opened in 1795. Despite lack of legislative appropriations, the institution grew in strength and usefulness under Joseph Caldwell, 1773–1835, its first president, a Princeton graduate, and his successor, David L. Swain, 1801–69, who had been for three terms Governor of the state. Here was organized in 1823 the first state geological survey, and in 1827 was built the first college astronomical observatory. The outstanding figure on the early faculty was Elisha Mitchell, 1793–1857, a Yale graduate, who for nearly forty years taught, first mathematics and physics, then chemistry and geology. He discovered and measured the highest peak east of the Rockies, which has been named for him Mount Mitchell. He lost his life while in scientific work upon its slopes, and lies buried upon its summit.

THE UNIVERSITY OF VIRGINIA

CHARACTERISTICALLY distinctive is the University of Virginia, which has been described as "the lengthened shadow of one man" — Thomas Jefferson. After a long and sometimes bitter struggle, the act establishing the

774 Home of the President, University of North Carolina, from a photograph by Forster, Chapel Hill

University was passed on January 25, 1819. Jefferson was chosen Rector at the first meeting of the Board, and devoted the closing years of his life to the selection of its faculty and the erection of its buildings. He sought scholars of the highest type for the professorships; and organized the studies into separate "schools,"

with full freedom granted to the student to elect the schools in which he would study. The requirements for the degrees were set at a high standard; but no obligation rested upon a student to become a candidate for a degree, and a very small percentage of the matriculates in the history of the institution have ever come up for graduation. Student discipline, after a few years, was based upon an honor system. Reorganization has taken place as the University has grown and expanded; but the fundamental principles of Jefferson's philosophy of education remain. The University of Virginia was founded shortly before the decision of the Dartmouth College Case, which stimulated the establishment of both state and private institutions.

775   The approach to the Rotunda, University of Virginia.
© Detroit Publishing Co.

776 Union Academy, "The Log College," from Wilson, *A Century of Maryville College*, Maryville, Tenn., 1916

777 The Seminary and the Frame College, from Wilson, *A Century of Maryville College*, Maryville, Tenn., 1916

MARYVILLE COLLEGE, TENNESSEE

TYPICAL of scores of Christian colleges in the South is the story of devotion, sacrifice, and high idealism that constitutes the history of Maryville College in Tennessee. In 1802 Isaac Anderson, 1780–1857, pastor of a

778 A Miracle of College Re-creation, from Wilson, *A Century of Maryville College*, Maryville, Tenn., 1916

Presbyterian Church in Eastern Tennessee, opened Union Academy in a huge log building of two stories. He visited Philadelphia, New York, and Princeton, seeking men to come to the ministry of the Tennessee churches; but he had no success. "There is a feeling common to our race," he drily commented, "that the qualifications of those who live west of us can not be of the first order." Under his leadership the Synod of Tennessee founded the Southern and Western Theological Seminary in 1819, and two years later a "literary department" or college was begun and named Maryville College. This had an enrollment of over one hundred

students in 1861. Closed during the Civil War, with its buildings and equipment destroyed, it was reopened and the task of rebuilding undertaken by Thomas J. Lamar, its surviving professor, in 1866. Since then, its history has been that of steady, honest growth in service to the church and the nation. Students come to it not only from the southern mountain region within which it is located, but from many states.

779 Maryville College near the close of the Nineteenth Century, from Wilson, *A Century of Maryville College*, Maryville, Tenn., 1916

780 First page of letter written in 1834 by Mary Lyon to Miss White, from the original in the possession of Mount Holyoke College

781 Last page of letter written in 1834 by Mary Lyon to Miss White, from the original in possession of Mount Holyoke College

THE TRAINING OF THE "GENTLER SEX"

IN colonial times, and under pioneer conditions, women were usually drudges, completely occupied with domestic duties. With prosperity came emancipation from such servitude and a swing to the opposite extreme. They were treated as precious luxuries, dressed like dolls, and admired in proportion to the uselessness of their accomplishments. President Dwight, writing in the second decade of the nineteenth century, thus described the training of girls: "Miss, the darling of her father and the pride of her mother, is taught from the beginning to regard her dress as a momentous concern. She is instructed in embroidery merely that she may finish a piece of work, which from time to time is to be brought out, to be seen, admired, and praised, by visitors; or framed, and hung up in the room, to be still more frequently seen, admired and praised. She is taught music, only that she may perform a few times, to excite the same admiration, and applause, for her skill on the forte piano. She is taught to draw, merely to finish a picture, which, when richly framed and ornamented, is hung up, to become an altar for the same incense. . . . The reading of girls is regularly lighter than that of boys. When the standard of reading for boys is set too low, that for girls will be proportionally lowered."

MARY LYON, 1797–1849, FOUNDER OF MOUNT HOLYOKE COLLEGE

MARK HOPKINS described the equipment of the "female seminaries" of the period as mostly "pianos and guitars and music-books." All, even Mrs. Willard's Seminary at Troy, were private enterprises, without endowment. "Amidst all their prosperity," wrote Mary Lyon, "they have no solid foundation, and in themselves no sure principle of continued existence." She set herself resolutely to secure the establishment, and the endowment in perpetuity, of "a permanent institution consecrated to the training of young women for usefulness . . . designed to furnish every advantage which the state of education in this country will allow . . . to put within reach of students of moderate means such opportunities that none can find better."

782 Mary Lyon in 1832, from a miniature in the possession of Mount Holyoke College

MOUNT HOLYOKE COLLEGE

Miss Lyon secured a charter for Mount Holyoke Female Seminary in 1836, and opened it to students in 1837. She met ridicule and criticism; but she had the faith and poise of a great soul. In the face of epithets such as "rib-factory" and "Protestant nunnery" she appealed successfully to "common sense, intelligence, and the spirit of fair play." When told that it was unbecoming for her to go about the country addressing public meetings and soliciting subscriptions, she replied: "What do I that is wrong? . . . My heart is sick with this empty gentility, this genteel nothingness. I am doing a great work. I cannot come down."

Mary Lyon's best gift to Mount Holyoke was herself. She was its principal until her death, and she inspired the institution with her own dauntless, luminous spirit. Missionaries, she said, need "piety, a sound constitution, and a merry heart." "It is one of the nicest of mental operations to distinguish between what is very difficult and what is utterly impossible." "Faith's business is to make things real."

783 Mary Lyon in 1845, from the painting by Louise Rogers Jewett (—1914) in the possession of Mount Holyoke College

"Religion is you and I and God, nothing else." "Shall we fear what God is about to do? There is nothing in the universe that I fear, but that I shall not know all my duty or shall fail to do it." In the early nineteenth century the terms "seminary" and "college" were used with the same meaning, and Mount Holyoke did not change its name to "College" until 1893. Under Mary E. Wooley, who became its president in 1900, the College has maintained a distinctive place among American institutions for the higher education of women.

784   Original building of Mount Holyoke College, from a photograph in the possession of Mount Holyoke College

THE SPREAD OF COLLEGES FOR WOMEN

The movement to provide college education for women developed slowly until the last quarter of the nineteenth century. Georgia Female College, now the Wesleyan Female College, at Macon, Georgia, was chartered in 1837. Auburn Female University was founded in 1851, and became Elmira College four years later. In 1861 Matthew Vassar endowed Vassar College, hoping "to inaugurate a new era in the history and life of woman." It began work in 1865, the most eminent of its faculty being Maria Mitchell, 1818–89, the astronomer. Wellesley College, founded by Henry F. Durant, was chartered in 1870 and opened in 1875. In that same year was opened Smith College, founded by bequest of Sophia Smith, "to furnish young women with the means and facilities for education equal to those which are afforded in our colleges for young men." Bryn Mawr College, opened in 1885, was the first to devote special attention to graduate study. In the 'eighties five colleges for women were founded of a somewhat different type, affiliated with universities: Radcliffe College, affiliated with Harvard University; Barnard College, with Columbia University; the Women's College of Brown University; the College for Women of Western Reserve University and the H. Sophie Newcomb College, affiliated with Tulane

785 Matthew Vassar, 1792–1868, from a drawing after a photograph

University, New Orleans. Trinity College, affiliated with the Catholic University of America, was founded in 1897. A third type of provision for the higher education of women was afforded by the development, beginning in the colleges west of the Alleghenies, of a policy of co-education, admitting students of both sexes.

786 Alice Freeman Palmer, from a photograph, courtesy of Professor George Herbert Palmer, Cambridge, Mass.

ALICE FREEMAN PALMER, 1855–1902, PRESIDENT OF WELLESLEY COLLEGE

ALICE FREEMAN, twenty-two-year-old high-school principal, graduate of the University of Michigan, taught a class so well in the presence of President Angell, who was visiting her school, that he wrote to Mr. Durant "that he *must* appoint the woman whose remarkable work I had been witnessing." She became professor of history at Wellesley College in 1879, and from 1881 to 1887 was its President. She brought to the task youth, radiant personality, and a mind of the first order. In a brief administration of six years she gave lasting form to the ideals of the institution. "Her work at Wellesley," said President Eliot of Harvard, "was creation, not imitation." In 1887 she was married to George Herbert Palmer, Professor of Philosophy at Harvard; and for fifteen years succeeded in combining a happy home life with much and varied public service. One of her rules for being

787 Memorial to Alice Freeman Palmer by Daniel Chester French, in the Wellesley Chapel, from a photograph

happy was, "Do something for somebody every day."

We loved her for the loving thoughts which sped
    Straight from her heart, until they found their goal
    In some perplexed or troubled human soul,
    And broke anew the ever-living bread.
We loved the mind courageous, which no dread
    Of failure ever daunted, whose control
    Of gentleness all opposition stole;
We loved herself and all the joy she shed.
O Leader of the Leaders! Like a light
    Thy life was set, to counsel, to befriend.
Thy quick and eager insight seized the right
    And shared the prize with bounteous hand and free.
    Fed from the fountains of infinity
Thy life was service, having love to spend.

           — CAROLINE HAZARD

788   Tower Court, Wellesley College, from a photograph by the Maynard Workshop, Waban, Mass.

789   The first diploma granted to a woman by Oberlin, from the original in the possession of Oberlin College

THE COLONY AND COLLEGE AT OBERLIN

IN 1833, two home missionaries, John J. Shipherd and Philo P. Stewart, founded a Christian colony in Lorain County, Ohio, which they named after Jean Frederic Oberlin, the Alsatian pastor, educator, and community leader. In 1834 the institution which is now Oberlin College was chartered. A theological department under Charles G. Finney was begun a year later.

The manual labor plan was fashionable in educational circles at this time, and was being tried by many academies and colleges. There were other good reasons why everyone should work in the new colony; but the first circular issued by the Collegiate Institute propounded this educational philosophy: "The manual labor department is considered indispensable to a complete education. It is designed first to preserve the student's health. For this purpose, all of both sexes, rich and poor, are required to labor four hours daily. There being an intimate sympathy between soul and body, their labor promotes, as a second object, clear and strong thought, with a happy moral temperament. A third object of this system is its pecuniary advantage; for while taking that exercise necessary to health, a considerable portion of the student's expenses may be defrayed. This system, as a fourth object, aids essentially in forming habits of industry and economy; and secures, as a fifth desideratum, an acquaintance with common things. In a word, it meets the wants of man as a compound being, and prevents the common and amazing waste of money, time, health, and life."

790   Oberlin College seal, courtesy of
Oberlin College

In spite of all these advantages, the manual labor plan was soon given up here, as in other colleges. But in other respects Oberlin was a pioneer. It was the first college to undertake the co-education of men and women. In 1841 it was among the first to award the B.A. degree to women, under the same conditions as were required of men. In 1835 the trustees decided to admit students "irrespective of color." The community and the college became a powerful center of anti-slavery agitation, missionary effort, and temperance reform. James H. Fairchild, 1817–1902, a member of the first freshman class, who spent his entire subsequent life at Oberlin, as professor and President of the college, was refused license to preach by the Huron Presbytery because he would not repudiate "Oberlin ideas." The success of Oberlin under Presidents Finney, Fairchild, and Henry C. King, helped to determine the policies of denominational and missionary colleges in all the states that lay west of Ohio.

791   Newton Bateman, from a photograph,
          courtesy of Knox College

KNOX COLLEGE

TYPICAL of more than a hundred such Christian colleges are Knox College, Galesburg, Illinois, and Carleton College in Northfield, Minnesota. George W. Gale, 1789–1862, Presbyterian minister, head of Oneida Manual Labor Institute at Whitesboro, New York, conceived the plan of founding a college in the Mississippi valley to supply "an evangelical and able ministry" and to "spread the Gospel throughout the world." He led a colony of settlers to Knox County, Illinois, which he called "the Mesopotamia of the West." Here they established the town of Galesburg in 1836. Forty persons made the journey on a canal boat, traveling almost two thousand miles. When the steamers which could tow them on the Ohio and Mississippi rivers would not stop on the Sabbath, they rigged up a stern-wheel, and propelled themselves, in tread-mill fashion, by their horses. Knox Manual Labor College was chartered in 1837, and the present name adopted in 1857.

Galesburg was a "station" on the "Underground Railroad" for the escape of fugitive slaves. No advocate of slavery was admitted to the First Church of Galesburg, which voted in 1856 to expunge the word "Presbyterian" and to withdraw from the Presbytery because of dissatisfaction with its stand, or lack of stand, on the slavery question. On October 7, 1858, one of the great debates between Abraham Lincoln and Stephen Douglas was held on the campus of Knox College. Newton Bateman, 1822–97, the "Horace Mann of the West," a warm personal friend of Lincoln, had for sixteen years, as State Superintendent of Schools, organized and developed the public school system of Illinois. He became President of Knox College in 1875. It is an open secret that George Fitch, who was a student at Knox, got from it most of the local color for his diverting sketches of college life "At Good Old Siwash," home of the Eta Bita Pie and Alfalfa Delt fraternities.

CARLETON COLLEGE

NORTHFIELD COLLEGE was founded in 1866 by vote of the Minnesota Congregational Conference, then a little group of home-missionary churches. Like Congregational colleges generally, its organization provided for government by a self-perpetuating corporation, free from ecclesiastical control. In 1872 the name was changed to Carleton College, in recognition of the gift by William Carleton of Charlestown, Massachusetts, of fifty thousand dollars, the largest sum which up to that time had been given to any western institution. In 1876 the attention of the whole country was directed to Northfield because of the heroic repulse by its citizens of an attempted robbery of the bank by the James-Younger band of desperadoes. Three of the robbers were shot dead, and three captured; but Joseph L. Heywood, treasurer of the College, was killed.

James W. Strong, 1833–1913, first President, laid firm foundations in a service of thirty-two years. Goodsell Observatory, established in 1877, gave time-signals to the railroads of the Northwest; and since 1893 has published a magazine, *Popular Astronomy*. Carleton was the first college in the Northwest to abolish its preparatory academy. Since 1909 it has developed greatly in educational service and in material equipment. Carleton has not only retained the friendship and support of the Congregationalists, but has been adopted, without change of charter, by the general bodies of the Baptist and the Protestant Episcopal churches of Minnesota.

792   Airplane view of Carleton College campus, Northfield, Minn., courtesy of Carleton College

793   Law Building, University of Michigan, from a photograph. © Detroit Publishing Co., Detroit

THE UNIVERSITY OF MICHIGAN

THE first of the state universities to reach and maintain a place of leadership in the educational life of the country was the University of Michigan. After earlier schemes, adopted in 1817 and 1821, had proved abortive, the plan of John D. Pierce (see p. 283), adopted by the Legislature in 1837, laid broad and enduring foundations for a University conceived as an integral and crowning part of a state system of public schools. The grants of land which Michigan, in common with all of the Northwest Territory, received from the United States for the aid of education, were sold from time to time upon advantageous terms, and the proceeds invested in a permanent endowment. In 1851 the Board of Regents was given standing as a constituent part of the state Government, independent of legislative control.

Under Henry P. Tappan, 1805–81, who had been a pupil of President Nott at Union College, President of the University from 1852 to 1863, a scientific course was organized and the B.S. degree was first conferred in 1855; courses in engineering were established; the Law School was opened; graduate study was projected; and there began to be added to the faculty the first of the group of scholars who have maintained intellectual standards which have attracted students from all parts of the nation.

794   Alumni Memorial Hall, University of Michigan, from a photograph. © Detroit
Publishing Co., Detroit

795 James Burrill Angell, from a photograph in the
      Library of the University of Michigan

JAMES BURRILL ANGELL, 1829-1916,
PRESIDENT OF THE UNIVERSITY OF MICHIGAN

In 1871 began the forty-year-long administration of James B. Angell, who had been a pupil and associate of President Francis Wayland at Brown University, and came from five years service as President of the University of Vermont. Under him the elective system was extended, and closer relations were established between the University and the public high schools. In 1879, he established the first university chair in the country having as its field the "Science and Art of Teaching." Its objects were stated to be: "(1) To fit University students for the higher positions in the public school service; (2) to promote the study of educational science; (3) to teach the history of education and of educational systems and doctrines; (4) to secure to teaching the rights, prerogatives, and advantages of a profession; (5) to give a more perfect unity to our state educational system by bringing the secondary schools into closer relations with the University." Like departments, in most cases growing into Schools of Education, have since been established in all of the state universities.

In his first year, President Angell braved possible criticism, but anticipated future developments at most universities, by abolishing the rule which compelled students to attend daily prayers in the chapel and Sunday worship at one of the churches of Ann Arbor. "It is at least open to discussion," he said, "whether the spiritual welfare of undergraduates will be promoted by their being driven to religious service under fear of a monitor's mark."

President Angell's most notable service lay in his securing the adoption of a new principle of University support. When he came, the institution had begun to outgrow the income from the permanent University fund; and the Legislature had begun to make direct appropriations. He succeeded in convincing the lawmakers of Michigan of the wisdom of a plan of support more stable and less open to vacillation than that of annual appropriations. Accordingly they levied a tax of one twentieth of a mill, for University purposes. This has been increased from time to time, and the plan has become a settled policy of the state.

796   Pillsbury Hall, University of Minnesota, from a photograph. © Detroit Publishing Co.

THE GROWTH OF THE STATE UNIVERSITIES

THE most characteristic feature of the history of higher education in the United States since the Civil War has been the growth of the state universities. This was due in part to the development of the frontier states, untrammeled by precedent or old institutions, peopled by pioneers with vision but with little immediately available wealth, and possessing educational needs that could be met only by public resources. It was stimulated by the passage by Congress in 1862 of the Morrill Act, under which the states have received more than eleven million acres of land, to endow institutions for the teaching of agriculture and the mechanic arts. Thirty-nine of the states now have state universities; and each of the other states maintains some tax-supported agency for high education. In number, the state colleges and universities constitute one sixth of the country's institutions for higher education, but they enroll one third of the students.

THE UNIVERSITY OF WISCONSIN

THE University of Wisconsin is one of a small group of state universities which, founded in the early days of their respective states, limped along until the Morrill Act led to their reorganization and awakened them to new life. Under Presidents John Bascom, 1827–1911, Charles K. Adams, 1835–1902, and Charles R. Van Hise, 1857–1918, it has become an outstanding example of a university intimately related to the life and work of the people of the state, and deliberately undertaking to

797   Bascom Hall, University of Wisconsin, from a photograph by Photoart House, Milwaukee

be of direct practical service to them, "without regard to the preconceived notions of anybody, anywhere, concerning the scope of a university." A conspicuous example of such service was the invention by Professor

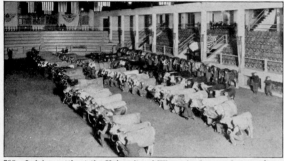

798   Judging cattle at the University of Wisconsin, from a photograph by Photoart House, Milwaukee

Stephen M. Babcock of the Babcock Milk Test for measuring the butter-fat content of milk, and his refusal, in spite of its great economic and commercial value, to permit it to be exploited under the protection of patent. In 1907 the department of University Extension was reorganized, and its aim expanded to include "the transmutation of learning into such form that it can be directly used in the ordering of affairs." The spirit of experimentation with new methods, of refusal to be trammeled by tradition, and of search for truth in the interest of life, has always characterized this institution.

THE PRINCIPLE OF ACADEMIC FREEDOM

POLITICAL domination is as fatal to education as ecclesiastical bias. It is significant that one of the clearest expressions of the principle of academic freedom has come from a state university. In 1894, when critics sought to oust Professor Richard T. Ely from the faculty of the University of Wisconsin, for alleged radical views, the Board of Regents, after a full investigation, published the following declaration of policy: "As regents of a university supported by nearly two million of people who hold a vast diversity of views regarding the great questions which at present agitate the human mind, we could not for a moment think of recommending the dismissal or even the criticism of a teacher even if some of his opinions should, in some quarters, be regarded as visionary. Such a course would be equivalent to saying that no professor should teach anything which is not accepted by everybody as true. This would cut our curriculum down to very small propor-

tions. We cannot for a moment believe that knowledge has reached its final goal, or that the present condition of society is perfect. We must therefore welcome from our teachers such discussions as shall suggest the means and prepare the way by which knowledge may be extended, present evils be removed and others prevented. . . . In all lines of academic investigation it is of the utmost importance that the investigator should be absolutely free to follow the indications of the truth wherever they may lead. Whatever may be the limitations which trammel inquiry elsewhere, we believe the great state University of Wisconsin should ever encourage that continual and fearless sifting and winnowing by which alone the truth can be found."

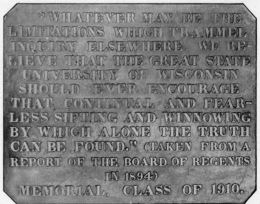

799   Inscription on University Hall, University of Wisconsin, from a photograph by Photoart House, Milwaukee

300   The Greek Theater at the University of California, from
a photograph by Gabriel Moulin, San Francisco

THE UNIVERSITY OF CALIFORNIA

THE College of California, founded in 1855 by Samuel H. Willey and his associates, gave to the state its buildings at Oakland and the beautiful new site which it had acquired at Berkeley, and became the College of Arts of the University of California, chartered in 1868. Since 1890, under the presidency of Martin Kellogg, 1828–1903, who had been one of the original faculty of the College of California, and Benjamin Ide Wheeler, 1854–1927, the University has grown rapidly. Besides the Colleges and Schools at Berkeley, various branches of the University are located at San Francisco, Los Angeles, Riverside, and La Jolla. The Lick Observatory on Mount Hamilton was founded in 1874 by the gift of James Lick, who wished to construct "a telescope superior to and more powerful than any telescope ever made." This telescope is now exceeded in size by that in the Yerkes Observatory at Williams Bay, Wisconsin, belonging to the University of Chicago. In 1896–99 an international competition of architects resulted in the adoption of a comprehensive permanent plan for the development of the buildings and grounds of the University of California. The Greek Theater, an open-air auditorium seating eight thousand persons, is a memorial to Mrs. Phoebe A. Hearst, 1842–1919, long a regent and a benefactor of the University.

CORNELL UNIVERSITY

WHEN the provisions of the Morrill Act came up for discussion in the New York Legislature, it engaged the active interest of two members of the state Senate: Ezra Cornell, 1807–74, who declared his desire to "found an Institution where any person can find instruction in any subject," and Andrew D. White, 1832–1918, who had been professor of history in the University

801   Law School of Cornell University, from a photograph by Underwood
& Underwood, New York

of Michigan. Through their efforts the "land-scrip" was devoted to the establishing of Cornell University. Cornell gave five hundred thousand dollars, and himself managed the sale of the land-scrip. White became President of the new institution, which was opened in 1868 with a freshman class of three hundred and forty-five. This was said to be the largest freshman class admitted to any American college up to that time. Cornell's success was immediate. It promptly took a place beside institutions with a long history behind them. Its charter provided that "persons of every religious denomination, or of no religious denomination, shall be equally eligible to all offices and appointments."

The founders of Cornell were convinced that the classical tradition, which dominated American education until near the close of the nineteenth century, was preventing the colleges from giving the fullest measure of service. They took advanced ground with respect to the inclusion of the practical arts in the program of the University, and did much to establish the principle that men may be "educated" in engineering or in agriculture, as well as in Latin, history, or mathematics.

Cornell is unique in one particular. It is neither a typical state university nor a wholly private institution, but a blend of both. Some departments, like that of agriculture, are supported at public expense, while the maintainance of others is derived from private funds. But this duality has not affected either the unity of the institution or the spirit of its student body. Cornell offers a remarkable example of coöperation between public and private enterprise in the field of higher education. Among the most distinguished of its alumni was David Starr Jordan. first president of Leland Stanford Junior University.

THEODORE DWIGHT WOOLSEY, 1801–1889, PRESIDENT OF YALE COLLEGE

THEODORE DWIGHT WOOLSEY, nephew of President Timothy Dwight, and great-grandson of Jonathan Edwards, for fifteen years professor of Greek in Yale College, in 1846 was elected its President, and was ordained to the Congregational ministry. Under his administration, made notable by the creative scholarship and scientific achievements of a remarkable group of teachers upon its faculty, Yale College took steps which were destined to make of it a university. Advanced work for graduate students, other than that afforded by the professional Schools of Divinity, Law and Medicine, had begun to be offered in some fields as early as 1826. Woolsey encouraged this, and in 1847 organized a Department of Philosophy and the Arts, from which developed the Sheffield

802 Statue of Theodore Dwight Woolsey, from a photograph by Pach Bros., New Haven

Scientific School and the Graduate School. Yale was the first American institution to confer the degree of Doctor of Philosophy upon the basis of resident graduate study and the presentation of a dissertation giving evidence of original research. This degree was first granted at the commencement of 1861. Yale did not assume the name of University until 1887.

803 Daniel Coit Gilman, from the portrait by Carroll Beckwith (1852–78), courtesy of Johns Hopkins University

JOHNS HOPKINS UNIVERSITY

THE "university idea" was given great impetus by the development of Johns Hopkins University, founded and endowed with three million five hundred thousand dollars by the bequest of Johns Hopkins, a wealthy merchant of Baltimore. Daniel Coit Gilman, 1831–1908, one of the Yale professors who had been instrumental in founding the Sheffield Scientific School, and had been for three years president of the University of California, was chosen as its first president. His inaugural address, in 1876, drew a clear distinction between the work of a college and that of a university, which he defined as "a place for the advanced and special education of youth who have been prepared for its freedom by the discipline of a lower school." He associated with himself a group of eminent scholars, and organized the University with especial view to the interests of graduate study and scientific and scholarly research and publication. This was the first American institution to be devoted primarily to these higher fields of education.

Mr. Hopkins gave an equal sum for the endowment of a hospital, which was opened in 1889; and in 1893 the Medical School of the University was established. These affiliated institutions have contributed to the development of medicine and surgery, and have done much to raise the standards of medical education.

804 Gilman Hall, Johns Hopkins University, from a photograph by Hughes Photo Co., Baltimore

805 Hospital, Johns Hopkins University, from a photograph by Hughes Photo Co., Baltimore

806   Frederick A. P. Barnard, courtesy of
Columbia University

THE DEVELOPMENT OF COLUMBIA UNIVERSITY

COLUMBIA COLLEGE remained a small, local institution, with about one hundred and fifty students, until a Report of a Committee of the Trustees, adopted in 1858, opened the way for expansion. Frederick A. P. Barnard, 1809–89, President from 1864 to 1889, was convinced that it was the destiny of Columbia to become a university, nation-wide in service, and he did not hesitate to lead in this direction. "Limitation of knowledge," he said, "is not like deficiency of food, attended by a craving for a larger supply. It is characteristic of ignorance to be content not to know, and of partial information, to be puffed up with the conceit that there is little more to be known. . . . The fact regarding the higher education is not that the demand creates the supply, but that the supply determines the demand." Under his administration, the curriculum of the college broke the bonds of tradition and an elective system was adopted; both study and discipline were made to depend more largely upon student initiative and student responsibility; graduate study was established upon a permanent basis, and the professional schools developed. Barnard urged that the doors of Columbia be opened "to all inquirers without distinction either of class or sex," but was met at this point by a conservatism which left to him the recourse of establishing the separate college for women which appropriately bears his name. A pioneer in the application of scientific methods to the study of education itself, and in his recognition of the need of thorough professional training for teachers, he took a prominent part in the founding (1888) of Teachers College, which has become one of the notable schools of Columbia University. Under Seth Low, 1850–1916, President from 1890 to 1901, and Nicholas Murray Butler, his successor, Columbia has grown rapidly in numbers and influence. The title University was adopted in 1896, and a year later the institution was removed to the present site upon Morningside Heights.

807   Library of Columbia University, from a photograph by A. Tennyson Beals, New York

CHARLES W. ELIOT, 1834–1926, PRESIDENT OF HARVARD UNIVERSITY

THE acknowledged leader of American university presidents was Charles W. Eliot, who became president of Harvard in 1869. In his Inaugural Address he proclaimed the principle of responsible freedom, both in conduct and in the choice of studies. In accordance with this principle, he enriched the college curriculum by the introduction of new and vital subjects, established the elective system upon a firm basis, and removed many detailed restrictions and requirements affecting the daily life of the students. He "led the way out from the narrower atmosphere of the old New England college into the large and invigorating air of the modern university." He fostered creative scholarship, and organized the Graduate School. Against strong opposition, at the outset of his administration, he insisted that the Medical School be made a real educational institution, requiring the student to pass in all departments of instruction, and affording nine months of work in each year instead of four months, as had been the practice. Later, he wrought similarly effective changes in the curriculum and methods of the Law School. In all schools of the University he stimulated better methods of teaching.

808   Charles W. Eliot, from a photograph by Underwood & Underwood, New York

President Eliot's interest extended to all stages of the educative process; and through his writings and addresses on educational reform and his service upon the Committee of Ten on the curriculum of secondary schools, he influenced the development of elementary and secondary education. He conceived the work of the educator in terms of public service. At the notable gathering in celebration of his ninetieth birthday, vigorous and keen-minded, he commended to the Harvard students Pasteur's definition of democracy: "Democracy is that form of government which leaves every citizen free to do his best for the public welfare."

809   Persis Smith Hall, a dormitory of Kirkland House, from a photograph by Underwood & Underwood, New York

X—22

810 William James, from a photograph by Keystone View Co., New
York

WILLIAM JAMES, PSYCHOLOGIST AND PHILOSOPHER

In the closing years of the nineteenth century, psychology began to develop as an empirical science. Its new methods, together with the expansion of the natural sciences under the stimulus of the evolutionary hypothesis, laid the basis for new and more vital approaches to the problems of philosophy. The students of these years learned to think for themselves in the fellowship of a remarkable group of college teachers of philosophy, among whom the most noteworthy were George T. Ladd, 1842–1921, at Yale, Borden P. Bowne, 1847–1910, at Boston University, Charles E. Garman, 1850–1907, at Amherst, George H. Howison, 1834–1917, at the University of California, and William James, 1842–1910, and Josiah Royce, 1855–1916, at Harvard.

Of these, William James will doubtless be reckoned worthy to be named beside Jonathan Edwards, as an American philosopher who both interpreted a significant stage in the life of his nation and made a permanent contribution to the thought of the world. A brother of Henry James, the novelist, he wrote in a fresh, suggestive, unconventional style that gained for him a wide reading. But his was the unconscious literary artistry of a great soul. A "radical empiricist" in method, his philosophy was "deliberately unconventional and intensely democratic," catholic in breadth of sympathy and appreciation, and free "both from ecclesiastical formality and barren free-thinking." On empirical grounds, he espoused idealistic and theistic positions in ethics and metaphysics. His doctrine of "Pragmatism" was that "both the meaning and the truth of ideas shall be tested by the empirical consequences of these ideas and by the practical results of acting them out in life." His essays on *The Will to Believe* contain a classically brilliant and penetrating exposition of the principle that man, born to creative activity, lives not by coercive knowledge alone, but rightly builds upon faith. It is the point of view of Carlyle, but, said his friend and colleague, Josiah Royce, of a "Carlyle transformed into a representative American thinker, trained as a naturalist, deeply versed in psychology, deprived of his disposition to hatred, open-minded towards the interests of all sorts and conditions of men, still a hero-worshipper, but one whose heroes could be found in the obscurest lovers of the ideal as easily as in the most renowned historical characters." — JOSIAH ROYCE, *William James and the Philosophy of Life*, pp. 26, 33, 39.

THE CATHOLIC UNIVERSITY OF AMERICA

811   The Catholic University of America, Washington, from a photograph by the
Commercial Studio, Washington

SINCE the Third Plenary Council of the Catholic Church in America held at Baltimore in 1884, great emphasis has been put upon securing a Catholic education for Catholic youth, which has resulted in the founding of new Catholic colleges, both for men and for women, and in an increase of attendance proportionally greater than the increase of attendance upon higher institutions generally. Most of the Catholic colleges are conducted by religious orders, whose members serve gratuitously upon their faculties, so that they do not need as large endowments as other colleges of the same size. Other Catholic colleges are conducted by the secular clergy, however, with salaried faculties; and in Catholic institutions generally the desirability of adequate endowments is now recognized. The Catholic University of America, projected in 1866, was founded by the Council of 1884, and was opened, with the sanction of the Pope, in 1889. It is located at Washington, where are also Georgetown University, the oldest of the Jesuit colleges in this country, and Trinity, a high-grade college for women conducted by the Sisters of Notre Dame of Namur. The Catholic University, like Johns Hopkins, was founded with graduate instruction primarily in view; but a collegiate department was added in 1905. It has under way an extensive program of scholarly research and publication.

THE UNIVERSITY OF CHICAGO

LIKE an "educational romance," says its historian, is the story of the University of Chicago. After an earlier institution of the same name had failed financially and been discontinued, the American Baptist Education Society enlisted the coöperation of John D. Rockefeller and founded a new University of Chicago in 1890. It was opened in 1892 under the presidency of William R. Harper, 1856–1906, who had been professor of Semitic Languages in Yale University. Dr. Harper's exceptional ability as a teacher, his compelling initiative, and his extraordinary gifts as an organizer and administrator stimulated and guided the institution in a rapid but sound development. Resisting all proposals to shorten or cheapen the college course, he yet sought to make the university "more democratic, in the life of its students, in relation to institutions of a lower grade, and above all in its relations to the public at large." He organized the university year by quarters, and the courses into majors and minors; and made the work in the summer quarter an integral part of the whole rather than a mere supplement. The "certificate" plan of admission from secondary schools, and well-organized systems of extension work and courses of study by correspondence, bring the university close to the life of local com-

812 William Rainey Harper, from a photograph, courtesy of the University of Chicago

munities. At the same time no American institution has been more actively interested in scholarly research and in various forms of publication. In 1910 Mr. Rockefeller announced his final gift, feeling it to be "better that the University be supported and enlarged by the gifts of many than by those of a single donor." This made the total of his gifts to the institution amount to almost thirty-five million dollars. The gifts of others have totaled about the same amount. Under President Harry P. Judson, 1849–1927, the University developed consistently, and both its assets and its attendance were nearly trebled. Ernest D. Burton, 1856–1925, who, like Judson, had been one of President Harper's associates from the beginning, initiated a comprehensive program of advance during what his colleagues love to call the "glorious two years" of his presidency, from 1923 until his death.

813 A Dormitory of the University of Chicago, from a photograph by Moffett Studios, Chicago

814 Mitchell Tower and Hutchinson Commons, University of Chicago, from a photograph by Moffett Studios, Chicago

815　　Leland Stanford Junior University, from a photograph by
Gabriel Moulin, San Francisco

LELAND STANFORD JUNIOR UNIVERSITY

LELAND STANFORD, 1824–93, trans-continental railroad builder, Governor of California, and United States Senator, with his wife, Jane Lathrop Stanford, 1825–1905, founded Leland Stanford Junior University as a memorial to their only son, who died in 1884 at the age of sixteen. They gave for its campus nine thousand acres of land near Palo Alto in the Santa Clara valley, and for its endowment securities and other lands valued at more than twenty-five million dollars. It was opened in 1891 under the presidency of David Starr Jordan, 1851–, eminent zoologist, who had been president of the University of Indiana. The founders stated the object of the University to be "to qualify students for personal success and direct usefulness in life; to promote the public welfare by exercising an influence in behalf of humanity and civilization." The elective principle is applied both to the entrance requirements and to the undergraduate curriculum, with more freedom than is commonly afforded to student election. The buildings are of stone, and are arranged in quadrangles, joined by arcades. The inner quadrangle includes twelve one-story buildings and a beautiful memorial church.

816　　Vanderbilt University, from a photograph by
Urles, Nashville

817　　Tulane University, from a photograph by Fritch,
New Orleans

ENDOWED UNIVERSITIES IN THE SOUTH

THE largest institutions in the South, outside of the state colleges and universities, are Tulane University in New Orleans, Vanderbilt University in Nashville, and Emory University in Atlanta. Tulane, replacing a former "University of Louisiana," received its present name and charter in 1884, with gifts totaling over a million dollars from Paul Tulane, 1801–87, formerly a merchant of New Orleans. Holland N. McTyeire, 1824–89, Bishop of the Methodist Episcopal Church, South, seeking to found a university, appealed to Cornelius Vanderbilt, 1794–1877, who gave a million dollars for this purpose, "to strengthen the ties between the two sections," North and South. Vanderbilt University was opened in 1875, and has prospered and grown, especially under the administration of James H. Kirkland, 1859–, Chancellor since 1893. An issue in some respects reminiscent of the Dartmouth Case was raised in 1910, when the General Conference of the Methodist Episcopal Church, South, sought to bring the institution more directly under its control. This was resisted by the Board of Trustees as an invasion of charter rights; and the Supreme Court of Tennessee decided in their favor in 1914. The Conference then voted to withdraw from all connection with the University. Encouraged by a gift of one million dollars from Asa G. Candler and a pledge of five million dollars from the citizens of Atlanta, Emory College at Oxford, Georgia, founded in 1836, was removed to Atlanta and reorganized as Emory University. An interesting evidence of changing public sentiment lies in the fact that one of the first men secured for the faculty of the new Emory University was Andrew Sledd, who had been dismissed in 1902 from his professorship in Emory College because he had contributed to the *Atlantic Monthly* an article on the negro problem which his fellow citizens did not like.

DUKE UNIVERSITY

TRINITY COLLEGE, which dates back to the founding of Union Institute in 1838, began to prosper with removal from its country site to the city of Durham, North Carolina, in 1892. Its constitution stated these to be among its pri-

818 The Women's College of Duke University, from the architect's rendering, courtesy of Duke University

mary aims: "to advance learning in all lines of truth; to defend scholarship against all false notions and ideals; to develop a Christian love of freedom and truth; to promote a sincere spirit of tolerance." In 1903 it met a severe test. One of its professors was bitterly assailed for expressing a judgment which ran counter to established opinion. When popular clamor demanded this professor's resignation, President John C. Kilgo, 1861–1922, and his faculty resolutely defended the principle of academic freedom. To the argument that the retention of this professor would hurt the college, Kilgo answered: "You cannot hurt this institution more fatally . . . than by enthroning coercion and intolerance. Bury liberty here, and with it the college is buried." The Board of Trustees voted to sustain the faculty and issued a strong statement of reasons for its actions.

Washington Duke, 1820–1905, tobacco manufacturer, gave eighty-five thousand dollars to bring Trinity College to Durham; and in succeeding years he and his sons made repeated gifts, until they helped to make of it the best-endowed college in the South Atlantic states. In 1924 one of his sons, James B. Duke, 1857–1925, established an endowment of forty million dollars for educational, religious and social purposes, over one third of which is for Trinity College, the corporate name of which is now changed to Duke University. Mr. Duke died in 1925, and left further large sums to Duke University, which now has resources which will enable it to develop into one of the major educational institutions of the nation.

819 From the painting The Graduate, by Edwin E. Blashfield (1848–), in the College of the City of New York

THE OPEN LADDER OF DEMOCRACY

IT has been the policy of America to maintain "an open ladder from the primary school to the university." Especially since the World War the number of young people who attend secondary schools and colleges has greatly increased. In 1890 there were one hundred and twenty-one thousand nine hundred and forty-two students enrolled in the colleges and universities of this country; in 1924 there were six hundred and sixty-four thousand two hundred and sixty-six. That is an increase, in thirty-four years, of four hundred and forty-five per cent. During this period, the enrollment in secondary schools increased nine hundred and fifty-one per cent, and the general population increased but seventy-eight per cent. College enrollment, therefore, has grown nearly six times as fast as the general population; and secondary school enrollment twelve times as fast.

This tremendous increase of students presents difficult problems to many colleges and universities, particularly to those state-controlled institutions which cannot adopt a policy of limiting the number of admissions. In dealing with these problems, the colleges to-day are devising more careful systems of budgeting and accounting, better ways of testing the capacities and achievements of students, and more efficient methods of teaching. They are undertaking, moreover, comprehensive studies of the curriculum itself, with a view to its revision in the interest of closer contact with life and better adaptation to individual needs and capacities. The college course, we may well hope, will never become merely vocational or utilitarian. Its aim will remain cultural. But culture is best conceived in terms of the enrichment of life. William James once said that the aim of a college education should be to make one able to recognize a good man when he sees one.

NOTES ON THE PICTURES

1. The map of the world drawn by de la Cosa is the earliest map known on which the western discoveries are shown. In 1832 the map, which had disappeared, was found and identified by Humboldt. A full size reproduction of the map is to found in Jomard, *Monumento de Geographie*.

3. For De Bry, see Notes on the Pictures, Vol. I.

4. Arnold Zocchi (1862–), was born in Florence, the son of the great sculptor, Emilio Zocchi.

7. Champlain during his years in the West Indies kept a journal of his experiences which he illustrated with drawings. The later journals of his life in Canada also contain drawings and maps.

8. This Latin translation of Las Casas has illustrations by De Bry which attempt to be realistic in showing the horrors which Las Casas witnessed.

9. Girolamo Benzoni was a Milanese who started his American travels at the age of twenty-two. His work shows an unfriendly attitude toward the Spaniards. His *Historia del Mondi Nuovo*, first published in Venice in 1565, was soon translated into French (1579), Latin (1578) and German (1579). Copies of the first Venetian edition are in the Harvard, John Carter Brown, and Cornell libraries.

14. Carl Screta was born in Prague, studied painting in Italy and became a painter of historical subjects.

24. Kino's map was published in his *Lettres Edifiantes* in 1705. Kino was convinced that Lower California, hitherto regarded as an island, was in reality a peninsula.

27. Father Serra blessed the site of the mission at San Diego on July 16, 1769. McBurney is a painter of historical pictures dealing chiefly with Southern California.

31. *Le Grand Voyage du Pays des Hurons*, Paris, 1632, is the source for the history of the first Recollet Mission. The author, Sagard, passed some time among the Hurons.

33. La Hontan was born about 1667 and came to Canada in 1683. He published his *Nouveaux Voyages* at La Haye in 1703.

34. Harry A. Ogden, well-known illustrator of American historical and military subjects.

36. De Vries, a Dutch skipper, made an effort to establish a Dutch colony in Delaware (about 1643). His published journal is illustrated with drawings of American scenes.

38. See No. 14.

44, 45. Hector A. MacNeil, American sculptor of historical subjects.

46. For Douglas Volk, see Vol. XII, p. 144.

54. Sir David Wilkie had great success as a portrait painter in London. This painting of John Knox was first exhibited in 1832.

58. Bradford's *History of Plimouth Plantation* remained in manuscript until 1856. It was found in 1855 in the Library of the Palace of the Bishop of London, and given to the Massachusetts Historical Society.

59. Albert Cuyp was a Dutch painter of landscapes, animals and marine scenes.

65. For Smibert, see Vol. XII, pp. 4, 9.

68. For Edwin A. Abbey, see Vol. XII, pp. 105, 106, 289, 295.

72. For original of Cotton portrait, see Vol. I, p. 213.

75. Cyrus Dallin was studying in Paris while Buffalo Bill and his Indians were there, and as a result of his interest in them he became a painter of Indian scenes.

78. Louis Tiffany, pupil of George Inness, is noted for his work in stained glass. His scenes are frequently oriental in character.

95. Peter Pelham was a painter of English birth, and the earliest engraver in America. He engraved in mezzotint many portraits by John Smibert, as well as many of his own painting.

125. For Saint Gaudens, see Vol. XII, pp. 180, 189, 190, 192–195.

126. For Herbert Adams, see Vol. XII, p. 200.

141. For John G. Chapman, see Vol. XII, pp. 37, 282.

143. Sir Peter Lely was born in Westphalia but lived most of his life in England where he painted many portraits of the royal family.

146. Henrietta Johnson did many portraits in pastels of men and women famous in the early days of South Carolina.

152. Tiebout was an early American engraver whose work dates back to 1789. He went to London where he learned to stipple, and returning to America engraved many portraits, of which the best is of John Jay.

159. For Charles Niehaus, see Vol. XII, p. 198.

167. For Peter Pelham, see No. 95.

169. Lawrence Kilburn came from London to New York about 1754. He painted portraits of many New York notables.

176. Hans Holbein the younger went to England in 1526 with letters to Sir Thomas More, whose portrait with those of many other important

Englishmen he painted in the years between 1526 and 1528.

180. For Emanuel Leutze, see Vol. XII, pp. 30, 35.

183. For Thomas Sulley, see Vol. XII, pp. 17, 27.

217. C. S. Reinhart, a popular illustrator of the second half of the nineteenth century whose work appears in *Harper's Weekly*, and other magazines.

227. For Benjamin West, see Vol. XII, pp. 4, 12, 29, 31, 32.

232. For J. Sartain, see Vol. XII, pp. 239, 280.

242. Anton Graff was a Swiss portrait painter who spent much of his life in Dresden. He painted many of his contemporaries, among them Lessing, Herder and Schiller.

248. Thomas Pownall, 1720–1805, was a colonial Governor of Massachusetts and of South Carolina. As a member of Parliament prior to and during the Revolutionary War he was a firm friend of the American colonies.

250. For Charles Willson Peale, see Vol. XII, pp. 5, 14.

275. Edward Valentine's most notable work is the recumbent statue of Lee in the chapel of Washington and Lee University.

277. Thomas Spence Duché went to England where he studied under Benjamin West. Two of his best known portraits are those of Bishop Provost and Bishop Seabury.

287. For Charles Willson Peale, see No. 250.

291. John Ward Dunsmore, painter of American historical subjects.

297. James E. Kelley, an illustrator for *Harper's Weekly*, *St. Nicholas*, etc., until 1881. Since then he has been interested in the sculpture of military figures and memorials.

308. Reuben Moulthrop's best known portraits are those of Ezra Stiles and Jonathan Edwards.

313. Charles Cromwell Ingham was born in Ireland and settled in New York about 1817. He became a well known portrait painter, to be remembered for his portraits of Edwin Forrest, De Witt Clinton, Lafayette, and Catherine Sedgwick.

315. For John Trumbull, see Vol. XII, pp. 16, 17, 21, 23.

321. For Chester Harding, see Vol. XII, pp. 17, 22.

326. A. T. Agate is best known as a miniature painter.

329. For Henry Augustus Lukeman, see Vol. XII, p. 213.

332. Nathaniel Hone, a versatile artist of Irish birth, did most of his work in London. He was one of the founders of the Royal Academy where he exhibited much of his work. In addition to painting in oils and water colors he did etching and mezzotinting.

350. For Gilbert Stuart, see Vol. XII, pp. 16, 18–20.

352. For Duché, see No. 277.

359. Charles B. J. F. de St. Memin was born in France. He came to Canada in 1793 and from there to New York. His method of work was unique. He first made a crayon portrait, then reduced it in size and engraved the small portrait. The Corcoran gallery has a full set of his engravings.

366. William Birch established himself in Philadelphia in 1800. He engraved many scenes of Philadelphia, marine views and landscapes and a series of the naval victories of the United States.

371. C. Y. Turner painted many historical subjects, especially those dealing with the Puritans. His best known painting is *The Grand Canal at Durdrecht*.

409. T. Doney established himself in New York about 1845. His chief work was in engraving portrait plates for periodicals.

418. For Daniel Huntington, see Vol. XII, pp. 30, 35, 65, 67.

440. For Howard Pyle, see Vol. XII, pp. 289, 293, 294.

444. Richard N. Brooks was the Vice-President of the Corcoran School of Art.

447. For Thomas Nast, see Vol. XII, pp. 289, 306, 312–313.

482. For Joseph Keppler, see Vol. XII, pp. 306, 309, 313.

545. Christian Schussele came to Philadelphia from Alsace about 1848. He became professor of drawing and painting at The Pennsylvania Academy of Fine Arts. Many of his paintings of American historical scenes and his portraits were engraved by John Sartain.

628. For F. O. C. Darley, see Vol. XII, pp. 77, 285–187.

649. For Samuel F. B. Morse, see Vol. XII, pp. 17, 25, 30, 34.

661. For Thomas Sully, see Vol. XII, pp. 17, 27.

731. For Daniel Chester French, see Vol. XII, pp. 189, 195, 196.

733. For Paul Revere, see Vol. XII, p. 227.

737. For Amos Doolittle, see Vol. XII, p. 228.

757. Joseph Stewart was born about 1750, and was graduated from Dartmouth in 1780. For a time he devoted himself to portraiture, but later became a Congregational minister. His best known portraits are of Eleazar Wheelock, John Phillips and John Kemble.

788. For Daniel Chester French, see No. 731.

803. For J. Carroll Beckwith, see Vol. XII, p. 94.

819. For Edwin Blashfield, see Vol. XII, p. 104.

INDEX

Titles of books under author are in italics; titles of illustrations under producer are in quotation marks.